THE POETICAL WORKS

OF

ROBERT BROWNING

General Editor: MICHAEL MEREDITH

THE OXFORD ENGLISH TEXTS
EDITION OF THE POETICAL WORKS
OF ROBERT BROWNING

THE POETICAL WORKS
OF
ROBERT BROWNING

Volume VIII

THE RING AND THE BOOK
Books V–VIII

EDITED BY
STEFAN HAWLIN
AND
T. A. J. BURNETT

CLARENDON PRESS · OXFORD

OXFORD
UNIVERSITY PRESS

Great Clarendon Street, Oxford OX2 6DP
Oxford University Press is a department of the University of Oxford.
It furthers the University's objective of excellence in research, scholarship,
and education by publishing worldwide in

Oxford New York
Athens Auckland Bangkok Bogotá Buenos Aires Calcutta
Cape Town Chennai Dar es Salaam Delhi Florence Hong Kong Istanbul
Karachi Kuala Lumpur Madrid Melbourne Mexico City Mumbai
Nairobi Paris São Paulo Shanghai Singapore Taipei Tokyo Toronto Warsaw
and associated companies in Berlin Ibadan

Oxford is a registered trade mark of Oxford University Press
in the UK and certain other countries

Published in the United States
by Oxford University Press Inc., New York

First published 2001

British Library Cataloguing in Publication Data
Data available.

Library of Congress Cataloging in Publication Data

Data available
ISBN–0–19–818647–9

1 3 5 7 9 10 8 6 4 2

Typeset by Kolam Information Services Pvt. Ltd, Pondicherry
Printed in Great Britain
on acid-free paper by
Biddles Ltd,
Guildford and King's Lynn

PREFACE AND
ACKNOWLEDGEMENTS

IN this volume Stefan Hawlin has been responsible for the intro-
ductions, the annotation, and Appendices A to C, and Tim Burnett
for the text, the critical apparatus, and Appendices D and E.

Our primary debt is to Michael Meredith, who has suggested
numerous improvements, and given us unflagging support and
encouragement; 'est vir tum eruditus, tum probus', as Browning's
Arcangeli might say. Philip Kelley and Scott Lewis, the editors of
The Brownings' Correspondence, helped us greatly with the previous
volume of the edition; for this volume they have again given
generously of their time and expertise. Our other main debt is to
Dr Marcella McCarthy, who has commented on the literary side of
the work at every stage.

The libraries where we have done most of our research deserve
special thanks, in particular Barry Clifton and the staff at the
Buckingham University Library, and the staffs at the Bodleian
Library and the British Library. We are also grateful to the friends
and colleagues who have contributed to our work through discus-
sion and suggestion, helped us with points of language, or patiently
borne queries on matters like Italian porcupines and the etymology
of *sclopulus*. Thanks here must go to John Drew, Robert Carver,
John Clarke, Pietro Bortoni, Samantha Schad, and Bob
Ombres OP.

We have become progressively more aware of our debt to
previous scholarship. Cook's *Commentary* (1920) has taught us
much; close students of the poem will always find it useful. It is
hard to think that the works of Hodell (1916) and Gest (1927) on
the Old Yellow Book will be bettered in their kind, and they have
been constant points of reference. The more recent work of the
Ohio editors, Roma A. King, jun., and Susan Crowl, has been an
invaluable source of comparison, inspiration, and disagreement.
Given the necessary marathon that editing the poem involves, we

are better placed than most to appreciate the fine quality of their scholarship.

The literary editor wishes to thank his own institution, the University of Buckingham, for its generous support, and the granting of additional research leave during which this volume was begun.

Our final thanks are to Dr Leofranc Holford-Strevens of Oxford University Press, who aided us so much with the previous volume of the edition, and who has again given generously of his learning and time to make this a better book.

3 August 1999   S. H., T. A. J. B.

CONTENTS

TEXTUAL NOTE TO BOOKS V–VIII

THE primary sources provide evidence of the growth of Browning's text, as follows:

1. *The Printer's copy manuscript.* The fifth book of the poem is lightly revised in manuscript. In the course of the first five pages, for instance, there are four revisions to accidentals, and eleven revisions to substantives. The revisions are predominantly in order to tighten up the sense—an example being l. 1895, where RB changes '"Guilty" is then the sentence of the Court.' to the perhaps less rhythmic but certainly more logical '"Guilty" is the decision of the Court.' Book VI is also relatively lightly revised, the first five pages yielding but one revision to the accidentals, and twenty revisions to substantives. Again, the revisions are for the most part to tighten up the sense, or to make the language more vivid—as in l. 1119, where 'No word, lest Canon Crispi break all bounds!' is changed to 'No word, lest Crispi overboil and burst!' Books VII and VIII are more heavily revised, the first five pages of the former having one revision to an accidental, but twenty-six revisions to substantives, while the first five pages of the latter have three revisions to accidentals, and thirty-five revisions to substantives. Moreover, while Book V has had fourteen lines added to the text, and Book VI eleven, Book VII has had no fewer than 110 added, and Book VIII fifty.

2. *The First Edition.* The revisions made to the text at proof stage reveal a significant difference as between Books V and VI of the poem and Books VII and VIII. In the course of four sample pages of the manuscript of Book V there are thirty-two substantive variants from the text of the first edition, and twenty-one variants in the accidentals. In the case of Book VI four sample pages of the manuscript reveal forty-three accidental variants, and twenty-one substantive variants. In the course of the whole of each book twelve lines have been added at proof stage. When we consider Book VII, however, we find that in the course of four sample pages

of the manuscript there are but six substantive variants and fourteen accidental, while four sample pages of Book VIII yield ten substantive variants and twenty-two accidental. The Yale proofs yield similar but not identical evidence. The proofs of Books V and VI are page proofs; those of VII and VIII are galleys. Very few of the changes made by RB are corrections of inaccurate typesetting or broken sorts; most are revisions. Book V is once again more heavily revised than the other books, revealing forty-one substantive changes and fifty-eight accidental, but Book VI has only fourteen substantive changes and thirty-five accidental, while Book VII has six substantive and ten accidental and Book VIII eighteen substantive and twenty-seven accidental. In all the books many of the revisions to accidentals involve the insertion of hyphens.

The principal object of the revisions was to punctuate more heavily, and to tighten up the sense. Significant revisions to substantives are, however, rare. Revisions to improve scansion, such as are found in Book IV, are met with very rarely in these four books.

3. *The Second Edition*. The textual history of the second edition of Books V–VIII differs as between the first two and the last two, the former being revised in 1883, while the latter were revised in 1872 (see the introduction to Vol. VII of this edition). This dichotomy does not, however, necessarily lead to consistency of treatment within each pair. Of the two books revised in 1883, Book V has twenty-three variants between the first and second editions, and Book VI forty-two. Of the two books revised in 1872, Book VII has thirty-one variants, while Book VIII has 257, of which 113 are accidentals and 144 substantives. Moreover, nine lines have been added to the text. Book VIII must have continued to give Browning trouble; there are eighty-seven variants between the second edition and *Poetical Works 1888–9*.

Emendations to the text

Accidentals

Book V: 308, 471, 953, 1012, 1094, 1529, 1642. Book VI: 24, 101, 136, 161, 602, 1343, 1488, 1549. Book VII: 339, 395, 527, 651, 966,

1047, 1069, 1134, 1255, 1326, 1733. Book VIII: 573, 592, 603, 640, 746, 784, 850, 1048, 1515, 1568, 1586.

Substantives

Book V: 69, 991, 1041, 1732, 2038. Book VI: 1525, 1897, 2001. Book VII: 1057, 1583. Book VIII: 7, 303, 746, 1791.

Restored paragraphs

Book V: 109, 368, 1037, 1240. Book VI: 597, 618, 1249, 1472. Book VII: 159, 220, 472, 712, 874, 947, 1044, 1190, 1707. Book VIII: 75, 139, 473, 1157, 1208, 1338, 1636.

Accidentals

Approximately half of the emendations which we have made to accidentals result from revisions made by Browning in either or both of the Dykes Campbell copy of *Poetical Works 1888–9* and the list of revisions in RB's hand to vols. iv–x of that edition, preserved at Brown University. Of these revisions, nineteen in all, sixteen were adopted in *Poetical Works 1889*, and three ignored. In the case of VI. 161, *BrU* substitutes 'come' for 'come,' (see note ad loc.). The remainder of the emendations result from editorial correction of inaccurate typesetting in the editions of 1888–9 and 1889, or from supplying missing characters caused by broken sorts found in the printing of those two editions. Of these five are of significance: VI. 136, where the line must end with an exclamation mark for the passage to make sense syntactically, VI. 602, where the contents of the letter and the instruction to the servant must be properly separated, VII. 1134, where the line must end with an exclamation mark for the passage to make sense syntactically, VIII. 640, where the line must end with a colon for the passage to make sense syntactically, and VIII. 1048, where the line must end with a comma, not a full stop, for the passage to make sense syntactically.

Substantives

We have made fourteen emendations to substantives. To deal with the simple cases first, V. 1732, 2038, VIII. 746, result from deliberate changes made by RB in both *DC* and *BrU*: V. 69, 991, 1041,

VI. 1897, VIII. 1791, are obvious typesetting errors resulting in nonsensical readings. That leaves six cases where the text found in *1888* and *1889* can be improved by critical examination of the witnesses. In one case, VI. 1525, *MS*, *1868*, and *1872* have 'a-flame', while *1888* and *1889* have 'a flame'. This seems to us to be either a typesetting error or a broken sort. In the other five cases, VI. 2001, VII. 1057, 1583, VIII. 7, 303, all the printed witnesses agree against the manuscript, but we are convinced that the latter, the latest text over which RB had immediate physical control, has the correct readings. In VI. 2001, RB has clearly written 'slinks', but the letter forms deceived the compositor, who set up 'shirks', a reading not sufficiently wrong to be picked up in any of the subsequent editions. In the same way, in VII. 1057, the manuscript clearly reads 'threat', but this was set up as 'thrust', leaving a reading which makes sense, but refers all the way back to l. 1030, whereas 'threat' refers back merely to l. 1044, making for a much more comprehensible passage. Moreover, 'this the threat and that the shame' makes a simpler and more natural phrase in this colloquial context. In the third case, VII. 1583, the manuscript clearly reads 'crashed', but in RB's hand this word is easily confused with 'crushed'. It is more likely that the 'two red plates' would be 'crashed together' than 'crushed together'; the reading found in the manuscript, moreover, avoids the close repetition of 'crushed'. In VIII. 7, the manuscript has 'me' as opposed to the printed editions' '*me*'. Browning having made the Latin word '*Qui*' into an English verb by giving it the ending 'es', the object of that verb must surely be the English 'me'. In VIII. 303, where the manuscript reads 'hounds'' and the printed editions 'hound's', the plural is required by 'their pulpy pads of paw' in l. 304, and in the paragraph as a whole Arcangeli pits his singular self, the fox, against the plural youths, who are represented by the pack of hounds.

REFERENCES AND ABBREVIATIONS

Note: the place of publication is given if it is not London or Oxford.

ABL   The Armstrong Browning Library, Baylor University, Waco, Texas.

Allingham   *William Allingham: A Diary*, ed. Helen Allingham and Dollie Radford (1907).

Altick   Richard D. Altick (ed.), *The Ring and the Book* (Harmondsworth, 1971).

Altick and Loucks   Richard D. Altick and James F. Loucks, II, *Browning's Roman Murder Story: A Reading of 'The Ring and the Book'* (University of Chicago Press, Chicago and London, 1968).

AUMLA   *Journal of the Australasian Universities Language and Literature Association*.

Aurora Leigh   *Aurora Leigh*, ed. Margaret Reynolds (University of Ohio, Athens, 1992).

Biographie universelle   *Biographie universelle, ancienne et moderne*, 52 vols. (Paris, 1811–28).

BIS   *Browning Institute Studies*, annual volumes, 1973–90.

BN   *The Browning Newsletter* (Armstrong Browning Library, Waco, Tex.).

Brady   Ann P. Brady, *Pompilia: A Feminist Reading of Robert Browning's 'The Ring and the Book'* (Ohio University Press, Athens, 1988).

Buckler   William E. Buckler, *Poetry and Truth in Robert Browning's The Ring and the Book* (New York and London, 1985).

BSN   *Browning Society Notes* (Browning Society of London).

Carlyle: *Works* (Centenary ed., 30 vols., 1896–9).

Checklist   *The Brownings' Correspondence: A Checklist*, compiled by Philip Kelley and Ronald Hudson (The Browning Institute and Wedgestone Press, Winfield, Kan., 1978; supplements in later vols. of BIS).

Cook   A. K. Cook, *A Commentary Upon Browning's 'The Ring and the Book'* (1920).

Correspondence   *The Brownings' Correspondence*, ed. Philip Kelley and Ronald Hudson to vol. viii, ed. Philip Kelley and Scott Lewis to vol. xiv (Wedgestone Press, Winfield, Kan., 1984–).

Curious Annals   Beatrice Corrigan (ed.), *Curious Annals: New Documents Relating to Browning's Roman Murder Story* (University of Toronto Press, Toronto, 1956).

Dearest Isa   *Dearest Isa: Robert Browning's Letters to Isabella Blagden*, ed. Edward C. McAleer (Austin, Tex. and Edinburgh, 1951).

EBB   Elizabeth Barrett Browning

Everyman   *The Old Yellow Book: Source of Robert Browning's The Ring and the Book*, translated and edited by Charles W. Hodell (Everyman Library series, 1911).

Gest   John Marshall Gest, *The Old Yellow Book, Source of Browning's The Ring and the Book: A New Translation with Explanatory Notes and Critical Chapters upon the Poem and Its Source* (University of Pennsylvania, Philadelphia, 1927).

Griffin and Minchin   *The Life of Robert Browning*, by William Hall Griffin, completed and edited by Harry Christopher Minchin, 3rd ed., revised and enlarged (1938; 1st ed., 1910).

Griffin Collections   William Hall Griffin, biographer of Robert Browning, 'Collections for his *Life* of Robert Browning', 7 vols., British Library, Additional MSS 45558–45564.

Hawthorne   Nathaniel Hawthorne, *The French and Italian Notebooks*, ed. Thomas Woodson (Ohio State University, Columbus, 1980), vol. xiv of the *Centenary Edition of the Works of Nathaniel Hawthorne*, 23 vols. (1964–).

Hodell   Charles W. Hodell, *The Old Yellow Book, Source of Browning's The Ring and the Book, in Complete Photo-Reproduction, with Translation, Essay, and Notes*, 2nd ed. (Carnegie Institution of Washington, 1916; 1st ed., 1908).

Honan   Park Honan, *Browning's Characters: A Study in Poetic Technique* (Yale University Press, New Haven and London, 1961).

Hudson   *Browning to his American Friends*, ed. Gertrude Reese Hudson (1965).

It.   Italian.

Jack   Ian Jack, *Browning's Major Poetry* (1973).

James   Henry James, 'The Novel in "The Ring and the Book"', in *Notes on Novelists* (1914).

Johnson   Samuel Johnson, *A Dictionary of the English Language*, Times Books facsimile of the 1755 text (1979).

Kelley and Coley   *The Browning Collections: A Reconstruction with Other Memorabilia*, compiled by Philip Kelley and Betty A. Coley (Armstrong Browning Library, Baylor University, Texas 1984).

L.   Latin.

Landis   *Letters of the Brownings to George Barrett*, ed. Paul Landis and R. E. Freeman (Urbana, Ill., 1958).

Learned Lady   *Learned Lady: Letters from Robert Browning to Mrs Thomas FitzGerald*, ed. Edward C. McAleer (Cambridge, Mass., 1966).

Letters   *Letters of Robert Browning Collected by Thomas J. Wise*, ed. Thurman L. Hood (1933).

Letters of EBB   *The Letters of Elizabeth Barrett Browning*, ed. Frederic G. Kenyon, 2 vols. (1898).

Life   *Life and Letters of Robert Browning*, by Mrs Sutherland Orr, new ed. rev. by Frederic G. Kenyon (1908; 1st ed. 1891).

Miller   Betty Miller, *Robert Browning: A Portrait* (1952).

MLR   *Modern Language Review.*

New Letters   *New Letters of Robert Browning*, ed. William Clyde DeVane and Kenneth Leslie Knickerbocker (1951).

ODEP   *Oxford Dictionary of English Proverbs*, 3rd ed., ed. F. P. Wilson (1970).

OED²   *Oxford English Dictionary*, 2nd ed., ed. J. A. Simpson and E. S. C. Weiner, 20 vols. (1989).

Ogilvy   *Elizabeth Barrett Browning's Letters to Mrs. David Ogilvy 1849–1861*, ed. Peter N. Heydon and Philip Kelley (1974).

Ohio   *The Complete Works of Robert Browning*, ed. Roma A. King, jun., *et al.* (Ohio University Press, Athens, Ohio, 1969–). *The Ring and the Book* comprises vols. vii (1985), viii (1988), and ix (1989).

OYB   Old Yellow Book. In references in the style 'OYB lxxi (78)' the roman numeral refers to Hodell's complete facsimile and translation (see Hodell), and the arabic numeral to the more widely available Everyman reprint of Hodell's translation (see Everyman). Quotations have been freshly translated, and do not necessarily correspond exactly with Hodell's translation.

Pettigrew and Collins   *Robert Browning: The Poems*, ed. John Pettigrew, supplemented and completed by Thomas J. Collins, 2 vols. (Penguin English Poets, Harmondsworth; Yale University Press, New Haven, 1981).

R&B   *The Ring and the Book.*

RB   Robert Browning

Roba di Roma   William Wetmore Story, *Roba di Roma*, 2 vols. (1863). Browning helped to edit this work: see *Story*, ii. 143–6.

Rossetti Letters   *Letters of Dante Gabriel Rossetti*, ed. Oswald Doughty and John Robert Wahl, 4 vols. (1965–7).

Rossetti Papers   *Rossetti Papers, 1862 to 1870*, compiled by William Michael Rossetti (1903).

Ruskin   *The Works of John Ruskin, Library Edition*, ed. E. T. Cook and Alexander Wedderburn, 39 vols. (London and New York, 1903–12).

SBC   *Studies in Browning and his Circle* (Armstrong Browning Library, Waco, Tex.).

SS   Secondary Source: Browning's secondary source for the poem, the Italian manuscript 'Morte dell'Uxoricida Guido Franceschini Decapitato'. References in the style 'SS 12' are to the paragraph numbers in the reprint and translation in our Vol. VII, Appendix B.

Story   Henry James, *William Wetmore Story and his Friends*, 2 vols. (1903).

Sullivan   Mary Rose Sullivan, *Browning's Voices in The Ring and the Book* (University of Toronto Press, Toronto, 1969).

Thomas   Charles Flint Thomas, *Art and Architecture in the Poetry of Robert Browning* (Troy, NY, 1991).

Tilley   M. P. Tilley, *A Dictionary of the Proverbs in England in the Sixteenth and Seventeenth Centuries* (Ann Arbor, Mich., 1950).

TLS   *Times Literary Supplement.*

Treves   Frederick Treves, *The Country of 'The Ring and the Book'* (1913).

Trumpeter   *Browning's Trumpeter: The Correspondence of Robert Browning and Frederick J. Furnivall 1872–1889*, ed. William S. Peterson (Washington, DC, 1979).

Wedgwood   *Robert Browning and Julia Wedgwood*, ed. Richard Curle (1937).

Note: references to Shakespeare are to *The Riverside Shakespeare*, ed. G. Blakemore Evans, *et al.* (Houghton Mifflin Company, Boston, 1974).

Abbreviations and signs used in the text and textual notes

*	An emendation by the editors.
....	Omission by the editors.
{ }	Comment by the editors.
>	Substitution by RB of the word or passage preceding the symbol with the word or passage following the symbol (e.g. this>that means that RB has substituted 'that' for 'this' in the MS, proof, or printed work).
^ ^	Additions within the body of the text (e.g. ^decent^ means that RB inserted 'decent' between 'as' and 'wrappage' after he had written 'as wrappage' in order to make the text read 'as decent wrappage').
⟨ ⟩	Deletion in manuscript.

[ ]   Text which is illegible in the MS. The distance between the brackets represents the length of the illegible portion of text; dubious readings are contained within square brackets and preceded by a question mark.

| Division between lines.

[—]   In the main text, a paragraph-break obscured by the pagination.

BrU   List of revisions in RB's hand to vols. iv–x of *Poetical Works*, 1888–9, preserved at Brown University Library, Providence, RI.

DC   Copy of *Poetical Works*, 1888–9, formerly belonging to James Dykes Campbell, and containing revisions by RB, preserved in the British Library.

MS   The autograph printer's copy MS for *The Ring and the Book*, 1868–9, preserved in the British Library.

Yale 1   Proofs for *The Ring and the Book*, 1868–9. Corrected page proofs of Books I–VI (with the exception of quires H and I of Book II, lines 415–1032, which are from the second edition, and carry no corrections), and corrected galley proofs of Books VII–XI, together with corrected but deleted page proofs of Book XI, pp. 193–5, and uncorrected page proofs of Book XII. Preserved in the Beinecke Library, Yale University, as 1p / B821 / 868a.

1868   *The Ring and the Book*, 1868–9.

1872   *The Ring and the Book*, 1872, [1882], [1883].

Yale 2   Sheets from the Second Edition, vols. I, III, and IV, revised by RB but mislaid so that the revisions never appeared in print. Preserved in the Beinecke Library, Yale University, as 1p / B821 / 868c.

1888   *The Poetical Works of Robert Browning*, 16 vols., 1888–9.

1889   *The Poetical Works of Robert Browning*, second impression, 16 vols., 1889.

THE RING AND THE BOOK

Books V–VIII

INTRODUCTION TO BOOK V
COUNT GUIDO FRANCESCHINI

BOOK V invites us into the central drama of the poem, and presents Count Guido Franceschini, one of the most arresting portraits of corruption in the language. Though his monologue follows the events described in the Old Yellow Book, Guido's character is a radical invention. Commentators have pointed out that the poet reads OYB against the grain, making Guido evil, and Pompilia a saint, whereas the source is patient of other readings. A more straightforward interpretation of OYB would conclude that Pompilia was a foolish girl—only twelve at marriage—who commenced an inappropriate liaison with a priest, fell pregnant by him, and then sought to escape her husband's fury and the consequences of her actions. In this scenario Guido becomes a betrayed husband, overcome with the righteousness of a seventeenth-century noble, who then murdered Pompilia and her parents in a *crime passionnel*.[1] Browning reads OYB quite differently: his Guido is not a cuckold, only a man pretending to be one.

Buckler argues that our reading of Guido will go wrong if 'despite the complex turmoil he engenders in the poem's action, [he] is perceived as simply monstrous—the dragon, an ogre, a devil, or any unequivocal incarnation of evil'.[2] Certainly there are Miltonic echoes, in a profound sense, and the idea of an 'unequivocal incarnation of evil' needs to be judged from a real moral, philosophical, or theological standpoint. Arnold Stein suggested that we need not choose between Milton's Satan being a 'tragic hero' or an 'absurd villain', that either extreme 'stamps us as a more restricted moralist than Milton the poet',[3] and this remark could be as well applied to Browning's creation of Guido Franceschini.

---

[1] Carlyle came to a similar conclusion with no first-hand knowledge of OYB. Allingham records the following remark for 2 Jan. 1872: 'C[arlyle]. praised parts of *The Ring and the Book* very highly—"showing a most intimate acquaintance with Italian life—better, I think, than anything else of Browning," he said. "But the whole is on a most absurd basis. The real story is plain enough on looking into it; the girl and the handsome young priest were lovers."': Allingham, 207. See also the view taken in the biography of Pompilia by Anna Foa: *Dizionario biografico degli italiani* (Rome, 1960–), xxvii. 678–82.

[2] Buckler, 104.

[3] Arnold Stein, *Answerable Style: Essays on Paradise Lost* (Minneapolis, 1953), 3.

When Guido starts talking, the tone is neither querulous nor hectic, but serious—despite the buoyancy of Browning's colloquial manner. The nobleman stands before the court to defend himself against the death penalty, and he eschews rhetoric in the most committed manoeuvre of all: the art that will conceal art, the deliberateness that will allow him apparently to tell 'the truth' (9–108). Altick and Loucks describe the monologue as 'a shrewd *mélange* of casuistry, nervous jokes, flattery, false humility, emotional outbursts, and appeals to class sympathy',[4] which indeed it is; but there is also, in keeping with Guido's seriousness, an overall rhetorical flow and design, which winds up the speech through a series of well-controlled climaxes.

Like Milton's Satan in *Paradise Lost*, Book I, Guido speaks in an aftermath. In 1693 he married for money the twelve-year-old Pompilia Comparini, abused her parents after they came to live with him, and tortured his wife mentally and physically, using sexual violence as a means of degradation. This course of action culminated in the brutal murders of 2 January 1698. The 'wickedness and weakness'[5] of all this is not clear to us at the start of the monologue—it is only fully apparent at the end of Book VII—but we do have some sense of Guido's life, and we may wonder how he understands his own history.

To see him as 'unequivocal evil' is to miss the profundity of what happens in the course of his apologia. Sullivan notes how he controls his audience: 'He uses the form "Sir" (or "Sirs") fourteen times in all, "my lords" (or "my sweet lords") seventeen times, and various other epithets ("you of the court", "my masters") at least a half-dozen times.' 'His defence is a brilliantly conceived and presented appeal for sympathy and clemency.'[6] With his manipulation of the judges, however, goes self-deception. He vividly paints the role he has chosen—the wounded, weary, middle-aged cuckold—but there comes a point when we know he has lost touch with himself and with any recognizable moral reality. He is full of reasons for his actions against Pompilia—too many reasons—and in the end we appropriate for him Iago's 'motiveless malignity'.[7]

The idea of evil that sustains this portrayal is a traditional one, evil apprehended not as a positive energy or force—a second principle in the universe—but rather as a parasitic distortion of good—a lack, an

    [4] Altick and Loucks, 48.
    [5] Browning's phrase, from RB to Julia Wedgwood, 19 Nov. 1868: *Wedgwood*, 159.
    [6] Sullivan, 138, 137.
    [7] Coleridge's famous phrase about Iago: see *Coleridge's Shakespearean Criticism*, ed. T. M. Raynor (2 vols., 1930), i. 49.

unreality, 'gloomy, monotonous, barren, boring'.[8] Guido may cunningly delineate his self-image for the court, but this self-image has no substance, and at some level he knows this. In this sense he is as double-minded as Milton's Satan, and like Satan ultimately confused and self-defeating.[9]

Swinburne made this point in another way when he contrasted the vigour and intensity of Shelley's Count Cenci with the weakness of Count Franceschini:

Cenci, as we see him, is the full-blown flower, the accomplished result of a life absolute in its luck, in power and success and energetic enjoyment.... What he is, good fortune has made him—"Strength, health, and pride, and lust, and length of days." What Guido Franceschini is, he has been made by ill fortune. Fed with good things from his birth, the evil nature in him might have swollen into the likeness of Cenci's; as Cenci, crossed and cramped at every turn of life, with starved energies and shrivelled lusts, might have shrunk into the shape of Guido, a pained and thwarted spirit of self-suffering evil.[10]

Pathos, of course, is the monologue's keynote, mixed with a downbeat and mundane point of view. Guido's language has an air of 'dirty realism'.[11] The flatteries that ease a bargain in the market-place are 'Flecks of oil / Flirted by chapmen where plain dealing grates' (503–4). The Comparini's covetousness is encapsulated in a low version of an Aesop's fable: it is 'purblind greed that dog-like still drops bone, / Grasps shadow, and then howls the case is hard' (565–6). Guido imagines Caponsacchi turning his 'hap' into a 'rattling ballad-rhyme.... bawled / At tavern doors' (1451–3), more popular with Christmas revellers than the jarring Abruzzi bagpipes. The culmination of this language is probably his description of what it would be like for his son to inherit 'Franceschini-hood': 'Another of the name shall keep displayed / The flag with the ordure on it, brandish still / The broken sword has served to stir a jakes' (1490–2). Early on we can identify the impact of this style, and react against it, but gradually it works to verify the pathos of the speech, and convince us that we really are dealing with a 'broken beggarly noble' (1846). Guido self-consciously sees himself as Boccaccio or Sacchetti, telling his own story as that of the cuckolded fool of the *fabliau* tradition,

[8] Simone Weil, quoted from Mary Midgley, *Wickedness: A Philosophical Essay* (1984; Ark ed., 1986; repr. 1996), 135.

[9] See *Paradise Lost*, i. 125–6, for an example of Satan's double-mindedness.

[10] Swinburne, 'Notes on the Text of Shelley', *The Fortnightly Review*, NS 5 (May 1869), 539–61, at 560–1.

[11] This phrase is usually used in connection with the short stories of Raymond Carver.

and by this self-deprecation implies the depth of the real tragedy under-
lying his ironic humour.

The trope that underlies his self-portrait surfaces explicitly on only a few
occasions but none the less controls our overall response. Guido portrays
himself as the zealous and suffering servant of God of Ps. 69, and through
that psalm implies his self-identification with the passion of Christ:

> For the zeal of thine house hath eaten me up . . . I was the song of the drun-
> kards . . . Thou hast known my reproach, and my shame, and my dishonour: mine
> adversaries are all before thee. Reproach hath broken my heart; and I am full of
> heaviness . . . They gave me also gall for my meat; and in my thirst they gave me
> vinegar to drink. (Ps. 69: 9, 12, 19–20, 21)

Guido is addressing the Law and the court, not God, but the effect is the
same. Through the monologue we need to be alert to the hints of Christ's
passion that keep this analogy in view.[12]

Unscrupulous use of religious pathos gives crucial shape to the mono-
logue. As the pathos intensifies we are drawn into the apparent reality of
Guido's world. When, near the climax, he describes how he intends to
endure his old age in Arezzo, in the broken-down palace, there is a strong
sense of ordinary things seen and felt, which, in a novelistic way, seems to
verify his whole story, even persuading us that his style, his 'realism', is a
true measure of things:

> I got such missives in the public place;
> When I sought home,—with such news, mounted stair
> And sat at last in the sombre gallery,
> ('T was Autumn, the old mother in bed betimes,
> Having to bear that cold, the finer frame
> Of her daughter-in-law had found intolerable—
> The brother, walking misery away
> O' the mountain-side with dog and gun belike)
> As I supped, ate the coarse bread, drank the wine . . .
>
> (ll. 1380–8)

So Guido matches pathos with apparently real suffering. He passes
through his Passion, his crucifixion, until at the end of the monologue
he anticipates being 'resurrected' by the court, brought through his
nightmare of marriage to a 'new life' with his son and heir.[13] As a trope,

---

[12] As well as the few crucial direct allusions to the Passion, there are also many
instances were Guido describes himself as spat at, mocked, despised and humiliated,
like Christ.

[13] See ll. 2048, 2054 nn.

the suffering, zealous servant is convincing because it matches our knowledge of reality, where evil often triumphs and good goes unrewarded. It is audacious of Guido to employ it, though ultimately it is still part of his self-deception. In the end, important questions remain unanswered. Why so much effort to convince us that Pompilia (in reality a saint) is actually a demon? What kind of negative engagement is this with a person he apparently longs to be rid of? And we can clearly see that—more even than Half-Rome—Guido's 'realism' has squeezed out of life all that makes it worthwhile: love, beauty, humour, joy.

THE RING AND THE BOOK.
1868–9.

V.

COUNT GUIDO FRANCESCHINI.

THANKS, Sir, but, should it please the reverend Court,
I feel I can stand somehow, half sit down
Without help, make shift to even speak, you see,
Fortified by the sip of . . . why, 't is wine,
Velletri,—and not vinegar and gall,   5
So changed and good the times grow! Thanks, kind Sir!
Oh, but one sip's enough! I want my head
To save my neck, there's work awaits me still.
How cautious and considerate . . . aie, aie, aie,
Nor your fault, sweet Sir! Come, you take to heart   10
An ordinary matter. Law is law.

MS {fo. 231. At the head of the page is the title '5. Guido Franceschini' in RB's
hand}   1 *MS* but should   3 *MS* ^even^   4 *MS* wine   5 *MS*
Trebbiano,>Velletri,—   *MS* not hyssop, vinegar   6 *MS* sir!   7 *MS*
enough;

---

1 *reverend Court*: the court was called the Reverend Apostolic Chamber, often
abbreviated to 'Rev. Cam. Apos.' in OYB. Here and elsewhere Browning assumes
that the judges were also priests: cf. ll. 723–4.

5 *Velletri*: a rich wine, and therefore fortifying under the circumstances. Story
describes it as one of the strongest Italian wines, 'full-bodied', 'red and roughish on
the tongue': *Roba di Roma*, i. 306, 309.

vinegar and gall: i.e. something bitter and terrible: cf. Ps. 69: 21, Matt. 27: 34, 48.
Guido is associating himself with the zealous and suffering servant of God in Ps. 69 and
with Christ in his passion, in particular Christ on the cross. For Browning the phrase
'vinegar and gall' had a weighty pathos, as can be seen in a letter about the death of his
beloved sister-in-law, Arabel Barrett: 'There has devolved on me every sort of sad
business that seems duty, and I am as full as a sponge of vinegar & gall just now': RB to
Isa Blagden, 16 June 1868: *Dearest Isa*, 297.

9 *aie, aie, aie*: little cries of pain. Someone has jogged Guido accidentally, or he has
moved awkwardly, hurting his tortured shoulder.

Noblemen were exempt, the vulgar thought,
From racking; but, since law thinks otherwise,
I have been put to the rack: all's over now,
And neither wrist—what men style, out of joint: 15
If any harm be, 't is the shoulder-blade,
The left one, that seems wrong i' the socket,—Sirs,
Much could not happen, I was quick to faint,
Being past my prime of life, and out of health.
In short, I thank you,—yes, and mean the word.   20
Needs must the Court be slow to understand
How this quite novel form of taking pain,
This getting tortured merely in the flesh,
Amounts to almost an agreeable change
In my case, me fastidious, plied too much   25
With opposite treatment, used (forgive the joke)
To the rasp-tooth toying with this brain of mine,
And, in and out my heart, the play o' the probe.
Four years have I been operated on
I' the soul, do you see—its tense or tremulous part—   30
My self-respect, my care for a good name,
Pride in an old one, love of kindred—just
A mother, brothers, sisters, and the like,
That looked up to my face when days were dim,
And fancied they found light there—no one spot,   35

13 *MS 1868 1872* racking,   14 *MS* {no comma}   15 *MS* wrist's—   17 *MS*
in   18 *MS* faint   20 *MS 1868 1872* short I   *MS* you, yes and   23 *MS*
being   26 *MS* the opposite   28 *MS* {beginning of fo. 232}   *MS*
of   30 *MS* In   32 *MS* say,   33 *MS* sisters and   34 *MS* {no
comma}   35 *MS* {no comma}

12–14 *Noblemen . . . rack*: in OYB the prosecution and the defence engaged in
elaborate legal argument as to whether Guido, as a nobleman, should be subjected
to the torture of the Vigil. The Advocate of the Fisc, Bottini, argued that nobility did
not protect against this torture, and in fact afforded no privilege whatsoever in the case
of 'most atrocious' crimes: see OYB cciv (207). The full arguments *pro* and *contra* are
laid out in Gest, 99–137.

12 *vulgar*: common or uneducated people.

15 *what . . . joint*: i.e. dislocated. The periphrasis is a slight affectation.

27 *rasp-tooth*: the tooth of a metal file.

28 *probe*: a slender surgical instrument. Guido has been 'tortured' in brain and heart,
i.e. mentally and emotionally.

Foppishly sensitive, but has paid its pang.
That, and not this you now oblige me with,
That was the Vigil-torment, if you please!
The poor old noble House that drew the rags
O' the Franceschini's once superb array   40
Close round her, hoped to slink unchallenged by,—
Pluck off these! Turn the drapery inside out
And teach the tittering town how scarlet wears!
Show men the lucklessness, the improvidence
Of the easy-natured Count before this Count,   45
The father I have some slight feeling for,
Who let the world slide, nor foresaw that friends
Then proud to cap and kiss their patron's shoe,
Would, when the purse he left held spider-webs,
Properly push his child to wall one day!   50
Mimic the tetchy humour, furtive glance,
And brow where half was furious, half fatigued,
O' the same son got to be of middle age,
Sour, saturnine,—your humble servant here,—
When things go cross and the young wife, he finds   55
Take to the window at a whistle's bid,
And yet demurs thereon, preposterous fool!—

36 *MS* {no comma}   37 *MS* what you have just obliged   40 *MS*
Of   44 *MS* Show up   48 *MS 1868 1872* the patron's   51 *MS* eye
1868 1872 glance   52 *MS 1868 1872* furious half   53 *MS* Of   *MS* to his
middle   *MS* {no comma}   55 *MS* {beginning of fo. 233}   57 *MS* And
he   *MS* fool,

38 *Vigil-torment*: in this torture the victim was raised on a bench and his bound arms
dragged upwards by a pulley; he was held in this agonizing position until he confessed.
For Browning's research into this torture see VIII. 328–44 n. and Appendix C.
43 *scarlet*: the colour signifying aristocracy (from the imperial purple).
wears: frays, wears out.
48 *to cap*: to remove one's cap, salute a superior by baring the head.
49 *when . . . spider-webs*: this way of describing an empty purse comes from the
already proverbial use in Catullus xiii. 7–8: *nam tui Catulli / plenus sacculus est aranearum*
('for the purse of your Catullus is full of cobwebs').
50 *push . . . day*: i.e. treat him with disrespect. The friends who let the father pass
honourably in the street, drawing back to clear his way, now hustle the father's son
(Guido) against the wall.
55 *cross*: wrong.
57 *demurs thereon*: i.e. hesitates to take action against this behaviour.

Whereat the worthies judge he wants advice
And beg to civilly ask what's evil here,
Perhaps remonstrate on the habit they deem   60
He's given unduly to, of beating her:
... Oh, sure he beats her—why says John so else,
Who is cousin to George who is sib to Tecla's self
Who cooks the meal and combs the lady's hair?
What! 'T is my wrist you merely dislocate   65
For the future when you mean me martyrdom?
—Let the old mother's economy alone,
How the brocade-strips saved o' the seamy side
O' the wedding-gown buy raiment for a year?
—How she can dress and dish up—lordly dish   70
Fit for a duke, lamb's head and purtenance—
With her proud hands, feast household so a week?
No word o' the wine rejoicing God and man
The less when three-parts water? Then, I say,
A trifle of torture to the flesh, like yours,   75
While soul is spared such foretaste of hell-fire,

---

59 MS ask him what's the coil,   MS coil?>coil,   61 MS 1868 1872 her   62
1868   1872 .. Oh,   63   MS Lucy's>Tecla's   64   MS That   65
MS What?   MS wrists   66 MS martyrdom,   68 MS on   69 MS
Of her   *MS 1868 1872 wedding-gown 1888 1889 wedding-grown   MS
buys   72 MS fair   73 MS of   74 MS three parts   75 MS
this,   76 MS foretastes

---

63 *sib*: relative.

65–6 *'T is ... martyrdom?*: i.e. 'In the future when you intend to martyr me, are you
only going to use *physical* torture?' Guido implies that this is nothing compared to the
mental torture that he has already endured. The opposition between physical and
mental 'torture' in this passage is also powerfully deployed by Beatrice Cenci: 'Tor-
tures! Turn / The rack henceforth into a spinning-wheel! ... My pangs are of the
mind, and of the heart, / And of the soul': Shelley, *The Cenci*, v. iii. 61–6.

68 *seamy side*: the under side of the wedding gown on which the rough edges of the
seams are visible; after Shakespeare (*Othello*, IV. ii. 146) the phrase has been used
figuratively for 'the worst, most degraded side (of life, etc.)', so that here it is both
literal and metaphorical.

71 *lamb's head and purtenance*: i.e. lamb's head and innards, intestines; cf. Exod. 12: 9:
'his [the lamb's] head with his legs, and with the purtenance thereof.' How Guido's
mother, the Signora Beatrice, used to make a sucking lamb last a whole week is
described at OYB li (52).

73 *wine ... man*: cf. Judg. 9: 13.

Is naught. But I curtail the catalogue
Through policy,—a rhetorician's trick,—
Because I would reserve some choicer points
O' the practice, more exactly parallel   80
(Having an eye to climax) with what gift,
Eventual grace the Court may have in store
I' the way of plague—what crown of punishments.
When I am hanged or headed, time enough
To prove the tenderness of only that,   85
Mere heading, hanging,—not their counterpart,
Not demonstration public and precise
That I, having married the mongrel of a drab,
Am bound to grant that mongrel-brat, my wife,
Her mother's birthright-license as is just,—   90
Let her sleep undisturbed, i' the family style,
Her sleep out in the embraces of a priest,
Nor disallow their bastard as my heir!
Your sole mistake,—dare I submit so much
To the reverend Court?—has been in all this pains   95
To make a stone roll down hill,—rack and wrench
And rend a man to pieces, all for what?

---

77 *MS* If>But   *MS* their catalogue   78 *MS* policy,>policy,—   *MS* trick,>
trick,—   80 *MS* Of   *MS* ^more exactly^   *MS* parallel, *1868* paral-
lel—   81 *MS* {no comma}   82 *MS* {beginning of fo. 234}   83 *MS*
In   *MS* plague, my *1868* my crown   86 *MS* Just>Mere   *MS* counter-
part   87 *MS* In   89 *MS* {no commas}   91 *MS* in   96 *MS*
hill, rack *Yale 1* hill,>hill,—

77–8 *curtail . . . trick*: the abrupt turning away from a subject, leaving a statement
unfinished, is known as *aposiopesis*. Guido here implies that he is open about his use of
rhetoric, that his *brevitas* here is to create a more effective employment of *climax*, the
weighty use of linked phrases of parallel construction, usually of increasing sig-
nificance. In fact, however, he does not employ the rhetorical strategy he maps out
in the following lines; his speech has a subtler overall structure: see Introduction.

88 *mongrel . . . drab*: i.e. the bastard child of a prostitute. 'Mongrel' is used here in the
sense of impure pedigree or lineage, especially the potential mixture of high and low
birth: Pompilia's mother was a prostitute, her father unknown (perhaps an aristocrat).

89 *mongrel-brat*: bastard-child; perhaps modelled on the common phrase 'beggar's
brat'.

91 *i' the family style*: a sarcastic use of a dignified phrase: Guido means 'just in the
manner of her prostitute mother'.

Why—make him ope mouth in his own defence,
Show cause for what he has done, the irregular deed,
(Since that he did it, scarce dispute can be)   100
And clear his fame a little, beside the luck
Of stopping even yet, if possible,
Discomfort to his flesh from noose or axe—
For that, out come the implements of law!
May it content my lords the gracious Court   105
To listen only half so patient-long
As I will in that sense profusely speak,
And—fie, they shall not call in screws to help!

I killed Pompilia Franceschini, Sirs;
Killed too the Comparini, husband, wife,   110
Who called themselves, by a notorious lie,
Her father and her mother to ruin me.
There's the irregular deed: you want no more
Than right interpretation of the same,
And truth so far—am I to understand?   115
To that then, with convenient speed,—because
Now I consider,—yes, despite my boast,
There is an ailing in this omoplat
May clip my speech all too abruptly short,
Whatever the good-will in me. Now for truth!   120
[—]

99 *MS* did>has   102 *MS* {no commas}   103 *MS* rope>noose   104
MS came   *MS* Law!   108 *MS* cord>screws   109 *MS* {beginning of fo.
235}   *MS* {New paragraph indicated with 'N.P.' in left-hand margin. Paragraph-
ing obscured in *1868* and *1872* by this line's being at the head of the page} *1888 1889* {no
new paragraph}   *MS* Sirs,   110 *MS* husband and wife,   112 *MS* and
mother   *MS* me and mine.   114 *MS* {no comma}   116 *MS* speed,
because   118 *MS* in>of   119 *MS* short>close, *1868* close,   120 *MS*
good will

118 *omoplat*: shoulder-blade. Perhaps this is intended to indicate the nobleman's
sprezzatura: Guido casually tosses in a technical term to show that he might have been
an expert had he bothered to study anatomy. Such casual use of technical terms is also
Browningesque: cf. the use of 'acromion' (the outer extremity of the shoulder-blade)
in 'Beatrice Signorini', 111. When young, probably in 1829, Browning had attended
lectures by Dr James Blundell at Guy's Hospital.

I' the name of the indivisible Trinity!
Will my lords, in the plenitude of their light,
Weigh well that all this trouble has come on me
Through my persistent treading in the paths
Where I was trained to go,—wearing that yoke   125
My shoulder was predestined to receive,
Born to the hereditary stoop and crease?
Noble, I recognized my nobler still,
The Church, my suzerain; no mock-mistress, she;
The secular owned the spiritual: mates of mine   130
Have thrown their careless hoofs up at her call
"Forsake the clover and come drag my wain!"
There they go cropping: I protruded nose
To halter, bent my back of docile beast,
And now am whealed, one wide wound all of me,   135
For being found at the eleventh hour o' the day
Padding the mill-track, not neck-deep in grass:
—My one fault, I am stiffened by my work,
—My one reward, I help the Court to smile!

I am representative of a great line,   140
One of the first of the old families

---

121 *MS* {New paragraph (already written thus) indicated by 'N.P.' in left-hand margin}   *MS* In   122 *1868* plenitude   123 *MS* Perpend>Weigh well   128 *MS* still   130 *MS* careless mates>mates of mine   131 *MS* Of mine>Have   *MS* call,   135 *MS* {beginning of fo. 236}   136 *MS* of   137 *MS* Inside>Padding   141 *MS* of noble families

---

121 *I' . . . Trinity*: a grand oath, and a loud one, full of Guido's pent-up indignation.

127 *hereditary . . . crease*: the bowing and kneeling that accompanies feudal ceremony, i.e. the burdens and responsibilities of nobility.

129 *suzerain*: ruler, overlord.

131 *thrown . . . call*: i.e. run off, ignoring her call.

132 *"Forsake . . . wain!"*: i.e. 'Give up pleasure and come and serve me!', compounded of the proverbial 'To live in clover' and the biblical 'Come unto me . . . Take my yoke upon you': ODEP, 129, Matt. 11: 28–30.

135 *whealed*: marked by the strokes of a stick or whip.

136 *eleventh hour o' the day*: cf. Matt. 20: 1–16. Through this, and the imagery in l. 132, Guido presents himself as someone who has heroically forsaken pleasure, heeded the Church's call for service, and now receives only punishment as his reward.

137 *mill-track*: cf. 'Like a horse in a mill': ODEP, 386.

In Arezzo, ancientest of Tuscan towns.
When my worst foe is fain to challenge this,
His worst exception runs—not first in rank
But second, noble in the next degree   145
Only; not malice' self maligns me more.
So, my lord opposite has composed, we know,
A marvel of a book, sustains the point
That Francis boasts the primacy 'mid saints;
Yet not inaptly hath his argument   150
Obtained response from yon my other lord
In thesis published with the world's applause
—Rather 't is Dominic such post befits:
Why, at the worst, Francis stays Francis still,
Second in rank to Dominic it may be,   155
Still, very saintly, very like our Lord;
And I at least descend from Guido once
Homager to the Empire, nought below—
Of which account as proof that, none o' the line
Having a single gift beyond brave blood,   160
Or able to do aught but give, give, give

---

146 *1868 1872* malice 'self   149 *MS* has   *MS* of   152 *MS* mid   153 *MS*
Saint>'tis   154 *MS* stays Francis>Francis stays   156 *MS* Lord,   157
MS 1868 1872 a Guido   159 *MS* some proof   *MS* of   161 *MS* {beginning
of fo. 237}

---

142 *Arezzo . . . towns*: for Browning's researches concerning Arezzo see our Vol.
VII, p. xxiv.

144–5 *not first in rank / But second*: the anti-Guido pamphlet in OYB makes
precisely this claim: 'It is also untrue that [Guido] and his family enjoyed the highest
rank of nobility in the city, because, from other extracts drawn from the public records
of the city, it is evident that his family is of only secondary rank': OYB ccxi (213).

149–53 *Francis . . . Dominic*: St Francis (1182–1226) and St Dominic (1170–1221)
were two of the greatest saints of the medieval Church, the first the founder of the
Franciscan order, which especially espoused poverty, the second the founder of
the Dominican order, particularly devoted to preaching. In their lifetimes the two
met and were friends, and in the *Paradiso* Dante sets them both in the fourth sphere of
heaven, in cantos that specially balance each other; none the less, there were some-
times significant rivalries and animosities between the two orders. Two of the great
churches of Florence are Santa Croce, built by the Franciscans, and Santa Maria
Novella, built by the Dominicans.

158 *Homager to the Empire*: his ancestor held a fief within the Holy Roman Empire
and his loyalty went directly to the Emperor, i.e. he was not a subject vassal.

In blood and brain, in house and land and cash,
Not get and garner as the vulgar may,
We became poor as Francis or our Lord.
Be that as it likes you, Sirs,—whenever it chanced   165
Myself grew capable anyway of remark,
(Which was soon—penury makes wit premature)
This struck me, I was poor who should be rich
Or pay that fault to the world which trifles not
When lineage lacks the flag yet lifts the pole: 170
On, therefore, I must move forthwith, transfer
My stranded self, born fish with gill and fin
Fit for the deep sea, now left flap bare-backed
In slush and sand, a show to crawlers vile
Reared of the low-tide and aright therein.   175
The enviable youth with the old name,
Wide chest, stout arms, sound brow and pricking veins,
A heartful of desire, man's natural load,
A brainful of belief, the noble's lot,—
All this life, cramped and gasping, high and dry   180
I' the wave's retreat,—the misery, good my lords,
Which made you merriment at Rome of late,—
It made me reason, rather—muse, demand
—Why our bare dropping palace, in the street
Where such-an-one whose grandfather sold tripe   185
Was adding to his purchased pile a fourth
Tall tower, could hardly show a turret sound?

---

166 MS {no comma}   167 MS Which   MS soon (168 MS must
171 MS 1868 Therefore I must make move   173 MS left to flap   175 MS
therein,—   181 MS In   182 MS made such   MS for Rome   184
MS {no comma}   185 MS suchanone   186 MS Is   MS three turretted
pile a fourth?   MS towered>turretted   187 {not found in MS}

168–70 I . . . pole: i.e. 'my poverty struck me as a particular disadvantage in a world
that is merciless to aristocrats who maintain their nobility in the face of lost wealth.'
177 pricking veins: enthusiastic spirits.
179 belief: self-belief, confidence.
184 dropping: decaying.
186–7 fourth . . . sound: i.e. a tower purely for effect, to show off wealth and status.
Guido returns to this detail at ll. 257–8: being overtaken by the nouveaux riches clearly
grates.

Why Countess Beatrice, whose son I am,
Cowered in the winter-time as she spun flax,
Blew on the earthen basket of live ash,   190
Instead of jaunting forth in coach and six
Like such-another widow who ne'er was wed?
I asked my fellows, how came this about?
"Why, Jack, the suttler's child, perhaps the camp's,
"Went to the wars, fought sturdily, took a town   195
"And got rewarded as was natural.
"She of the coach and six—excuse me there!
"Why, don't you know the story of her friend?
"A clown dressed vines on somebody's estate,
"His boy recoiled from muck, liked Latin more,   200
"Stuck to his pen and got to be a priest,
"Till one day... don't you mind that telling tract
"Against Molinos, the old Cardinal wrote?
"He penned and dropped it in the patron's desk
"Who, deep in thought and absent much of mind,   205

---

189 *MS* {beginning of fo. 238}   190 *MS* earthen-basket *Yale 1* earthen-basket
>earthen basket   191 *MS* and cape   192 *MS* such another's *Yale 1* such-
another's>such-another   194 *MS* Why, this, *Yale 1* "Why, This,>"Why,
Jack,   195–208 *MS* {no quotation marks at beginnings of lines}   197 *MS*
cape—   198 {not found in *MS*}   201 *MS* pen, soon   202 *MS 1868*
1872 day..   203 *MS* {no comma}   205 *MS* Who, much

192 *widow... wed*: i.e. a woman pretending to be a widow, in order to make the fact
she has children seem respectable. As emerges in the story at ll. 197–208, she is the
mistress of a prosperous cleric, and it is this that accounts for her wealthy lifestyle.

194 *suttler's... camp's*: a sutler is a tradesman selling provisions to an army. It is
suggested that Jack's mother, while ascribing her child's parentage to the sutler, was in
reality a 'camp-follower' or prostitute following the army, and that his parentage was
accordingly doubtful.

199 *clown*: peasant.

203 *Molinos*: Miguel de Molinos (1627–96), the Spanish mystic, arrived in Rome in
1663 and taught a version of quietism that was eventually condemned as heretical. He
was imprisoned in 1685, and his writings censured by Pope Innocent XI in 1687.
During the papacy of Alexander VIII (1689–91) some of his followers were punished
with life imprisonment. For a fuller account of the role of Molinism in the poem, see I.
307 n. Browning's allusions to Molinos are one piece of evidence of his historical
research; cf. Appendix B: 'Caponsacchi's Ancestry'. To clarify this matter, in Appendix
A we have given Bishop Burnet's contemporary account of Molinos's teaching and
influence.

"Licensed the thing, allowed it for his own;
"Quick came promotion,—*suum cuique*, Count!
"Oh, he can pay for coach and six, be sure!"
"—Well, let me go, do likewise: war's the word—
"That way the Franceschini worked at first,   210
"I'll take my turn, try soldiership."—"What, you?
"The eldest son and heir and prop o' the house,
"So do you see your duty? Here's your post,
"Hard by the hearth and altar. (Roam from roof,
"This youngster, play the gipsy out of doors,   215
"And who keeps kith and kin that fall on us?)
"Stand fast, stick tight, conserve your gods at home!"
"—Well then, the quiet course, the contrary trade!
"We had a cousin amongst us once was Pope,
"And minor glories manifold. Try the Church,   220
"The tonsure, and,—since heresy's but half-slain
"Even by the Cardinal's tract he thought he wrote,—
"Have at Molinos!"—"Have at a fool's head!
"You a priest? How were marriage possible?
"There must be Franceschini till time ends—   225
"That's your vocation. Make your brothers priests,
"Paul shall be porporate, and Girolamo step

---

208 *MS* cape, 209 *MS* "Well, 210–17 *MS* {no quotation marks at begin-
nings of lines} 211 *MS* "What, 212 *MS* of 214 *MS* {no comma}
Yale 1 roof,)>roof, 215 {not found in *MS*} *1868* gipsy 217 *MS* stick
firm, *MS* your home 218 *MS* {beginning of fo. 239} *MS* "Well *MS*
trade— 219–34 *MS* {no quotation marks at beginnings of lines} 220 *MS*
Church— 221 *MS* tonsure—and, since 222 *MS* book>tract *MS*
wrote, 225 *MS* 'till 227 *MS* {no comma}

207 *suum cuique*: to each his own (L.).

214–16 *Roam . . . us?*: this is a selfish aside by Guido's relations: 'If the young Guido
goes off to war, we shall have to look after any dependent relations he might otherwise
maintain.'

223 *Have . . . head!*: i.e. that's ridiculous! It is customary if you disagree with some-
one to interpose something nonsensical for part of what they have said, as here: 'Attack
Molinos, the heretic!' –'Attack a fool's head!' Cf. *Merry Wives*, I. iv. 126.

227 *porporate*: clad in purple, i.e. made a cardinal, from It. *porporato*, epithet of a
cardinal. OED² gives only this instance.

"Red-stockinged in the presence when you choose,
"But save one Franceschini for the age!
"Be not the vine but dig and dung its root,   230
"Be not a priest but gird up priesthood's loins,
"With one foot in Arezzo stride to Rome,
"Spend yourself there and bring the purchase back!
"Go hence to Rome, be guided!"

                           So I was.   235
I turned alike from the hill-side zig-zag thread
Of way to the table-land a soldier takes,
Alike from the low-lying pasture-place
Where churchmen graze, recline and ruminate,
—Ventured to mount no platform like my lords   240
Who judge the world, bear brain I dare not brag—
But stationed me, might thus the expression serve,
As who should fetch and carry, come and go,
Meddle and make i' the cause my lords love most—
The public weal, which hangs to the law, which holds   245
By the Church, which happens to be through God himself.
Humbly I helped the Church till here I stand,—
Or would stand but for the omoplat, you see!

228 *MS* please,   229 *MS* age.   233 *MS* back. *1872* back   235 *MS*
{no new paragraph}   240 Lords   241 *MS* want>bear   *MS* boast—>
brag—   244 *MS* in   246 *MS* {beginning of fo. 240}   *MS* church *MS*
happened   247 *MS* church   248 *MS* see.

   228 *Red-stockinged*: i.e. he will be a monsignor (an officer of the papal court or household), whose dress includes red stockings, and so entitled to be in the presence of the Pope.

   230 *dig . . . root*: cf. Luke 13: 6–9.

   231 *gird . . . loins*: i.e. assist your brothers in their careers; cf. Luke 12: 35, Eph. 6: 14, etc.

   244 *Meddle and make*: meddle and interfere. The phrase is proverbial, also occurring in the form 'mell or make'. Cf. *Much Ado*, III. iii. 48, and Charlotte Brontë, *Shirley*, ed. Herbert Rosengarten and Margaret Smith (Oxford, 1979), 418.

   245–6 *public weal . . . himself*: a social hierarchy: 'the public good, which relies upon law, which itself is sustained by the Church, which in turn is brought into being by God'.

   248 *omoplat*: cf. 118 n.

Bidden qualify for Rome, I, having a field,
Went, sold it, laid the sum at Peter's foot: 250
Which means—I settled home-accounts with speed,
Set apart just a modicum should suffice
To hold the villa's head above the waves
Of weed inundating its oil and wine,
And prop roof, stanchion wall o' the palace so   255
As to keep breath i' the body, out of heart
Amid the advance of neighbouring loftiness—
(People like building where they used to beg)—
Till succoured one day,—shared the residue
Between my mother and brothers and sisters there,   260
Black-eyed babe Donna This and Donna That,
As near to starving as might decently be,
—Left myself journey-charges, change of suit,
A purse to put i' the pocket of the Groom
O' the Chamber of the patron, and a glove   265
With a ring to it for the digits of the niece
Sure to be helpful in his household,—then
Started for Rome, and led the life prescribed.
Close to the Church, though clean of it, I assumed
Three or four orders of no consequence,   270
—They cast out evil spirits and exorcise,
For example; bind a man to nothing more,
Give clerical savour to his layman's-salt,

---

249 *MS* Bid>Bidden   *MS* I having   *MS* field   250 *MS* foot—   252
MS such modicum   253 *MS 1868 1872* keep   *MS* Villa's   255 *MS* prop
the Palace, stanchion wall of>prop roof, stanchion wall of the Palace   256 *MS*
1868 1872 It should keep   *MS* in   *MS 1868 1872* hold its own   264
MS in   *MS* groom   265 *MS* Of   *MS* chamber   267 *MS* the>
his   269 *MS* I crept>Close   272 *MS* example,   273 *MS* {beginning
of fo. 241}   *MS* layman's salt, *Yale 1* layman's salt,>layman's-salt,

---

   249–50 *I . . . foot*: cf. Acts 4: 34–7.
   255 *stanchion*: strengthen (with stanchions or props).
   265–6 *glove . . . it*: i.e. a secret gift, a bribe given subtly as though giving just a pair of
gloves.
   266 *niece*: a euphemism for 'mistress'; cf. 'Fra Lippo Lippi', 170 n.
   270 *Three or four orders*: cf. I. 263–5 n.

Facilitate his claim to loaf and fish
Should miracle leave, beyond what feeds the flock,   275
Fragments to brim the basket of a friend—
While, for the world's sake, I rode, danced and gamed,
Quitted me like a courtier, measured mine
With whatsoever blade had fame in fence,
—Ready to let the basket go its round   280
Even though my turn was come to help myself,
Should Dives count on me at dinner-time
As just the understander of a joke
And not immoderate in repartee.
Utrique sic paratus, Sirs, I said,   285
"Here," (in the fortitude of years fifteen,
So good a pedagogue is penury)
"Here wait, do service,—serving and to serve!
"And, in due time, I nowise doubt at all,
"The recognition of my service comes.   290
"Next year I'm only sixteen. I can wait."

I waited thirty years, may it please the Court:
Saw meanwhile many a denizen o' the dung
Hop, skip, jump o'er my shoulder, make him wings
And fly aloft,—succeed, in the usual phrase.   295
Everyone soon or late comes round by Rome:
Stand still here, you'll see all in turn succeed.

275 *MS* miracles>miracle   *MS* find,>leave,   279 *MS* whosoe'er>whatso-
ever   *MS* ^blade^   *MS* mastery>fame   281 {not found in *MS*}   282
MS think of   *MS* dinner-time.   283–4 {not found in *MS*}   285 *MS*
1868 1872 said   286 *MS* plenitude *Yale 1* plenitude>fortitude   287 *MS*
brisk   288 *MS* wait I service,—   *MS* serve,—   289–91 *MS* {no quota-
tion marks at beginnings of lines}   290 *MS* of service. Fifteen years!   293
MS of   296 *MS* Rome,   297 *MS* there,   *MS* in their turn

274–6 *loaf . . . friend*: alluding to the miracle of the loaves and fishes, Matt. 14: 15–21,
though here the surplus bread is the cardinal's excess wealth, some of which Guido
expects to be his.

282 *Dives*: a rich man; after the use in the parable at Luke 16: 19–31.

285 *Utrique sic paratus*: 'prepared for either event' (L.).

286–7 *fortitude . . . penury*: i.e. poverty and necessity have matured Guido and given
him courage beyond his actual age of 15 years.

Why, look you, so and so, the physician here,
My father's lacquey's son we sent to school,
Doctored and dosed this Eminence and that,   300
Salved the last Pope his certain obstinate sore,
Soon bought land as became him, names it now:
I grasp bell at his griffin-guarded gate,
Traverse the half-mile avenue,—a term,
A cypress, and a statue, three and three,—   305
Deliver message from my Monsignor,
With varletry at lounge i' the vestibule
I'm barred from, who bear mud upon my shoe.
My father's chaplain's nephew, Chamberlain,—
Nothing less, please you!—courteous all the same,   310
—He does not see me though I wait an hour
At his staircase-landing 'twixt the brace of busts,
A noseless Sylla, Marius maimed to match,
My father gave him for a hexastich
Made on my birthday,—but he sends me down,   315
To make amends, that relic I prize most—

298 *MS* here   299 *MS* he   302 *MS* {beginning of fo. 242}   *MS* And
Yale 1 So on>Soon   *MS* now;   304 *MS* avenue,   305 *MS*
three,   306 *MS* {no comma}   307 *MS* <[ ]> varletry   *MS* in   *MS*
the>that   *308 *MS 1868 1872* from, *1888 1889* from   309 *MS* Chamberlain,
312 *MS* staircase landing   *MS* {no comma}   315 *MS* birth-day,—   *MS*
down   316 *MS* {no comma}

299 *lacquey's*: footman's.

301 *certain obstinate sore*: the innuendo here is that this is the ulceration characteristic
of the first stage of syphilis.

304 *term*: a figure of Terminus, the god of boundaries, consisting of a bust ending in
a rectangular pedestal.

307 *varletry*: crowd, rabble (of attendants or menials).

309 *My . . . Chamberlain*: i.e. my father's chaplain's nephew [who has become]
Chamberlain. A chamberlain was the official in charge of the household of a noble
or high cleric. From the context here, particularly Guido's indignation at the rise from
low to high status, Browning probably means the cardinal-camerlengo ('cardinal
chamberlain'), a very high position indeed: see VIII. 1084 n. Cf. also, *The Cenci*, I.
iii. 127: 'Cardinal, thou art the Pope's chamberlain'. The abbreviated syntax in this line
is a measure of Guido's exasperation and envy.

313 *Sylla, Marius*: Lucius Cornelius Sulla (138–79 BC) and his near contemporary
Gaius Marius (157–86 BC) were two of the most powerful men in the Rome of their
day. In their maimed statues Guido sees a pathetic echo of his own fallen status.

314 *hexastich*: epigram of six lines.

The unburnt end o' the very candle, Sirs,
Purfled with paint so prettily round and round,
He carried in such state last Peter's-day,—
In token I, his gentleman and squire,   320
Had held the bridle, walked his managed mule
Without a tittup the procession through.
Nay, the official,—one you know, sweet lords!—
Who drew the warrant for my transfer late
To the New Prisons from Tordinona,—he   325
Graciously had remembrance—"Francesc . . . ha?
"His sire, now—how a thing shall come about!—
"Paid me a dozen florins above the fee,
"For drawing deftly up a deed of sale
"When troubles fell so thick on him, good heart,   330
"And I was prompt and pushing! By all means!
"At the New Prisons be it his son shall lie,—
"Anything for an old friend!" and thereat
Signed name with triple flourish underneath.

---

317 *MS* of   319 *MS* round the square   *MS* Peter's day *Yale 1* Peter's day,
—>Peter's-day,—   323 *MS* none *Yale 1* none>one   325 *MS* From
Tordinone to the Prisons New,   326 *MS 1868 1872* "Francesc.. *MS*..
what?   327–33 *MS* {no quotation marks at beginnings of lines}   327 *MS*
now.. *MS* about!   328 *MS* {no comma}   329 *MS* {beginning of fo.
243}   331 *MS* brisk

318 *Purfled*: fringed, decorated (with an elaborate pattern or border); cf. Chaucer,
Prologue, 193–4: 'I seigh his sleves purfiled at the hond / With grys'; Spenser, *Faerie
Queene*, 1. ii. st. 13: 'A goodly Lady clad in scarlot red, / Purfled with gold and pearle of
rich assay'. The word is intentionally ornate applied to a candle, and, as part of the
contemptuous alliteration 'purfled, paint, prettily', helps to enact Guido's sarcasm. Cf.
Sordello, 1. 900.

319 *Peter's-day*: 29 June, the feast of SS Peter and Paul, a major feast for the papacy.
322 *tittup*: curvet, upset.

325 *New Prisons . . . Tordinona*: the old prisons of the Tordinona were south of Ponte
S. Angelo; the New Prisons, built in the middle of the seventeenth century, were
nearby in Via Giulia. This transfer from one prison to the other is an invention, and
also a historical impossibility since the Tordinona had been destroyed in 1690. Brown-
ing clearly assumes that the Tordinona was still in use. He would have known about it
from many sources, but most obviously from the fact that members of the Cenci family
were led from there to their execution in 1599, something recorded in Shelley's MS
source to *The Cenci*: see *The Works of Percy Bysshe Shelley*, ed. by Mary Shelley
(London, 1847), pp. 163–4.

331 *prompt and pushing*: i.e. quick, eager, and ambitious.

These were my fellows, such their fortunes now,   335
While I—kept fasts and feasts innumerable,
Matins and vespers, functions to no end
I' the train of Monsignor and Eminence,
As gentleman-squire, and for my zeal's reward
Have rarely missed a place at the table-foot   340
Except when some Ambassador, or such like,
Brought his own people. Brief, one day I felt
The tick of time inside me, turning-point
And slight sense there was now enough of this:
That I was near my seventh climacteric,   345
Hard upon, if not over, the middle life,
And, although fed by the east-wind, fulsome-fine
With foretaste of the Land of Promise, still
My gorge gave symptom it might play me false;
Better not press it further,—be content   350
With living and dying only a nobleman,
Who merely had a father great and rich,
Who simply had one greater and richer yet,
And so on back and back till first and best
Began i' the night; I finish in the day.   355
"The mother must be getting old," I said;
"The sisters are well wedded away, our name

336 *MS* [ ]>And I   338 *MS* In   *MS* {no comma}   340 *MS* my place
341 *MS* the>such   343 *MS* of the time   *Yale 1* o'>of   346 *MS* over
the   347 *MS* fed although>although fed   *MS* East-wind   351 *MS* {no
comma}   355 *MS* in   356 *MS* {beginning of fo. 244}

337 *Matins and vespers*: morning and evening church services.

345 *seventh climacteric*: 49th year of age. A climacteric is a critical period in life
'containing a certain number of years, at the end of which some great change is
supposed to befall the body': Johnson. Climacteric years were believed to be the
seventh (the number of the body) and ninth (the number of the soul), and multiples of
those numbers. Cf. *Joseph Andrews*, Book IV, ch. 7: 'But when they arrive at this Period
[15 yrs.], and have now past their second Climacteric...'.

347–8 *fed...Promise*: cf. Job 15: 2: 'Should a wise man utter vain knowledge, and
fill his belly with the east wind?' and *Hamlet*, III. ii. 95: 'I eat the air, promise-
cramm'd'. To be 'fed' with wind (rather than real food) as a 'foretaste' of the Promised
Land is ironic: Guido has waited too long for nothing. 'Fulsome-fine' = richly
overfed, fed to satiety. The alliteration ('fed', 'fulsome-fine', 'foretaste') enacts Guido's
sarcasm and bitterness.

"Can manage to pass a sister off, at need,
"And do for dowry: both my brothers thrive—
"Regular priests they are, nor, bat-like, 'bide   360
" 'Twixt flesh and fowl with neither privilege.
"My spare revenue must keep me and mine.
"I am tired: Arezzo's air is good to breathe;
"Vittiano,—one limes flocks of thrushes there;
"A leathern coat costs little and lasts long: 365
"Let me bid hope good-bye, content at home!"
Thus, one day, I disbosomed me and bowed.

Whereat began the little buzz and thrill
O' the gazers round me; each face brightened up:
As when at your Casino, deep in dawn,   370
A gamester says at last, "I play no more,
"Forego gain, acquiesce in loss, withdraw

358–66 *MS* {no quotation marks at beginnings of lines}   358 *MS* always>
manage to   360 *MS* bide   362 *MS* old>spare   *MS* may>must   363
MS the fields at home give space to breathe,   *MS* air>space   364 *MS*
there,   365 *MS* leathern-coat   *MS* long,   366 *MS* give hopes up, die>
bid hope goodbye,   *MS* home."   367 *MS* So,>Thus,   ★368 *MS* {new
paragraph. Paragraphing obscured in *1868* and *1872* by this line's being at the head of
the page} *1888 1889* {no new paragraph}   *MS* shrill>thrill   369 *MS* Of   *MS*
me: *MS* up   371 *MS* last "I   372–3 *MS* {no quotation marks at begin-
nings of lines}

360–1 *bat-like . . . privilege*: the point is well illustrated by EBB's description of the
bat as 'that strange bird-mouse-creature': *Correspondence*, xi. 282. There was an original
confusion over the biological classification of bats, since they were seen as neither
animal nor bird, just as Guido, with his minor priestly orders, feels himself to be
neither a full aristocrat nor a full priest. Cf. I. 263–5, II. 296 nn.

362 *spare*: limited.

363 *Arezzo's . . . breathe*: the air was notoriously good: '[Arezzo] was the birthplace
of . . . a long list of eminent men in every branch of human knowledge—so long,
indeed, that the historian Villani attributes their number to the influence of the air, and
Michel Angelo, who was born at Caprese in the neighbourhood, good-humouredly
complimented Vasari, by attributing his talent to its climate: "Se io ho nulla di buono
nell' ingegno, egli e venuto dal nascere nella sottilità dell'aria del vostro paese di
Arezzo".': Octavian Blewitt, *A Handbook for Travellers in Central Italy, Part I* (4th ed.,
John Murray, 1857), 230–1.

364 *limes*: ensnares (by spreading the sticky substance lime on the branches of trees).
For the Italians' use of this technique, see *Roba di Roma*, ii. 78. Guido's implication
here is that he and his dependants can live cheaply.

367 *disbosomed me*: unburdened myself; cf. III. 614 n.

"Anyhow:" and the watchers of his ways,
A trifle struck compunctious at the word,
Yet sensible of relief, breathe free once more,   375
Break up the ring, venture polite advice—
"How, Sir? So scant of heart and hope indeed?
"Retire with neither cross nor pile from play?—
"So incurious, so short-casting?—give your chance
"To a younger, stronger, bolder spirit belike,   380
"Just when luck turns and the fine throw sweeps all?"
Such was the chorus: and its goodwill meant—
"See that the loser leave door handsomely!
"There's an ill look,—it's sinister, spoils sport,
"When an old bruised and battered year-by-year   385
"Fighter with fortune, not a penny in poke,
"Reels down the steps of our establishment
"And staggers on broad daylight and the world,
"In shagrag beard and doleful doublet, drops
"And breaks his heart on the outside: people prate   390
" 'Such is the profit of a trip upstairs!'
"Contrive he sidle forth, baulked of the blow
"Best dealt by way of moral, bidding down
"No curse but blessings rather on our heads
"For some poor prize he bears at tattered breast,   395

---

373 *MS* the game,>his game,   375 *MS* <dra[ ]> breathe   *MS* <better at> free
again,   378–81 *MS* {no quotation marks at beginnings of lines}   379 *MS*
Give   382 *MS* {beginning of fo. 245}   *MS* chorus   *MS* meant   384–
90 *MS* {no quotation marks at beginnings of lines}   384 *MS* stops mirth,>spoils
sport,   385 *MS* ^bruised and^   389 *MS* shabby doublet,   390 *MS*
door-sill>outside: 391 *MS* "Such   *MS* upstairs."   392–7 *MS* {no quo-
tation marks at beginnings of lines}   392 *MS* Better   393 *MS* By way of
moral, bidding bless our heads *Yale 1* ^by^   394 {not found in *MS*}

---

378 *with neither cross nor pile*: i.e. penniless, with no money. 'Cross' and 'pile' are the
obverse and reverse sides of a coin. 'Cross or pile' occurs most often in the phrase 'to
cast cross and pile', i.e. to throw a coin for heads or tails.
  379 *short-casting*: casting the dice in a short or cautious way, as opposed to the bold
'fine throw' in l. 381, the kind of throw that is supposed to change the gambler's luck.
  389 *shagrag*: shaggy, disordered.
  389–90 *drops . . . heart*: i.e. appears broken-hearted, openly dejected.
  392 *baulked*: deprived.

"Some palpable sort of kind of good to set
"Over and against the grievance: give him quick!"
Whereon protested Paul, "Go hang yourselves!
"Leave him to me. Count Guido and brother of mine,
"A word in your ear! Take courage, since faint heart   400
"Ne'er won . . . aha, fair lady, don't men say?
"There's a *sors*, there's a right Virgilian dip!
"Do you see the happiness o' the hint? At worst,
"If the Church want no more of you, the Court
"No more, and the Camp as little, the ingrates,—come,   405
"Count you are counted: still you've coat to back,
"Not cloth of gold and tissue, as we hoped,
"But cloth with sparks and spangles on its frieze
"From Camp, Court, Church, enough to make a shine,
"Entitle you to carry home a wife   410
"With the proper dowry, let the worst betide!
"Why, it was just a wife you meant to take!"

[—]

396 *MS* Some sort of palpable   397 *MS* Over against   *MS* give and   398 *MS*
{New paragraph (already written thus) indicated by 'N.P.' in left-hand margin. In *1888*
and *1889* l. 398 is at the head of p. 17, thus obscuring the paragraphing}   *MS* {no
comma}   399–412 *MS* {no quotation marks at beginnings of lines}   400 *MS*
1868 1872 {no comma}   403 *MS* of   404 *MS* wants *Yale 1* wants>
want   *MS* Camp>Court   407 *MS* guessed,   408 *MS* But saving
sparks   *MS* showing>saving   409 *MS* {beginning of fo. 246}   412 *MS*
{no quotation mark at end}   *MS* {Between 412 and 413 extra line: Deuce, ace, and
rafle! Leave the cards to me!"}

400–1 *faint . . . lady*: proverbial: 'Faint heart never won fair lady': ODEP, 238.
402 *sors . . . dip*: the *sortes Vergilianæ* (L.), 'Virgilian lots', a way of trying to tell the
future by opening Virgil's works and picking a line at random, a method widely
practised from the second century onwards. King Charles I is supposed to have used it
during the civil wars. Here Paulo has dipped, not into Virgil, but into the storehouse of
proverbs, and, as if by chance, hit on one that suggests to him the possibility of an
arranged marriage for his brother.
405 *the Camp*: i.e. the army.
406 *Count . . . counted*: a pun: i.e. 'Count, you are sized up, evaluated (in terms of
the marriage market)'.
407 *cloth of gold and tissue*: cf. *Antony and Cleopatra*, II. ii. 199.
408 *frieze*: coarse wool (backing). The contrast of materials here may be a memory
of *Aurora Leigh*, iv. 538–9: 'Half St. Giles in frieze / Was bidden to meet St. James in
cloth of gold'. This in turn echoes a sixteenth-century couplet attributed to Charles
Brandon of which EBB was fond: 'Cloth of frieze, be not too bold, / Though thou'rt
matched with cloth of gold!': see *Correspondence*, iii. 293, xi. 301.

Now, Paul's advice was weighty: priests should know:
And Paul apprised me, ere the week was out,
That Pietro and Violante, the easy pair,   415
The cits enough, with stomach to be more,
Had just the daughter and exact the sum
To truck for the quality of myself: "She's young,
"Pretty and rich: you're noble, classic, choice.
"Is it to be a match?" "A match," said I.   420
Done! He proposed all, I accepted all,
And we performed all. So I said and did
Simply. As simply followed, not at first
But with the outbreak of misfortune, still
One comment on the saying and doing—"What?   425
"No blush at the avowal you dared buy
"A girl of age beseems your granddaughter,
"Like ox or ass? Are flesh and blood a ware?
"Are heart and soul a chattel?"
                              Softly, Sirs!   430
Will the Court of its charity teach poor me
Anxious to learn, of any way i' the world,
Allowed by custom and convenience, save
This same which, taught from my youth up, I trod?
Take me along with you; where was the wrong step?   435
If what I gave in barter, style and state
And all that hangs to Franceschinihood,

---

418 *MS* "she's   *1872* {no comma}   419–20 *MS* {no quotation marks at begin-
nings of lines}   419 *MS* classed and   420 *MS* {no comma}   421
MS and>all,   *MS* {no comma} *Yale 1* all>all,   422 *MS* simply said>said and
did   423 *MS* Simply, and thence   425 *MS* This   *MS* "Beast,   426–
9 *MS* {no quotation marks at beginnings of lines}   426 *MS* avouching
>avowal   427 *MS* in>of   *MS* might be your grand-daughter>your grand-
daughter might be   431 *MS* a man   432 *MS* in   *MS* world   434
MS up I took?   435 *MS* {beginning of fo. 247}   *MS* me with   *MS* step, I
beg?

---

  416 *cits*: citizens, bourgeois (a contemptuous abbreviation); cf. IV. 341.
  418 *truck*: barter, bargain.
  quality: high status; from *qualitas* (L.), much used in OYB.
  419 *classic*: belonging to the first wealth-class of citizens, from L. *classicus*.
  436 *style*: title and family name.

Were worthless,—why, society goes to ground,
Its rules are idiot's-rambling. Honour of birth,—
If that thing has no value, cannot buy   440
Something with value of another sort,
You've no reward nor punishment to give
I' the giving or the taking honour; straight
Your social fabric, pinnacle to base,
Comes down a-clatter like a house of cards.   445
Get honour, and keep honour free from flaw,
Aim at still higher honour,—gabble o' the goose!
Go bid a second blockhead like myself
Spend fifty years in guarding bubbles of breath,
Soapsuds with air i' the belly, gilded brave,   450
Guarded and guided, all to break at touch
O' the first young girl's hand and first old fool's purse!
All my privation and endurance, all
Love, loyalty and labour dared and did,
Fiddle-de-dee!—why, doer and darer both,—   455
Count Guido Franceschini had hit the mark
Far better, spent his life with more effect,
As a dancer or a prizer, trades that pay!
On the other hand, bid this buffoonery cease,
Admit that honour is a privilege,   460
The question follows, privilege worth what?

---

438 *MS* Was   *MS* why society   439 *MS* Honor   442 *MS* to give nor
punishment   443 *MS* In   *MS* honor;   446 *MS* honor, keep that
honor   447 *MS* honor,—   450 *MS* Soap suds   *MS* in   451 *MS*
<a> touch   452 *MS* Of   *MS* and old   455 *MS* Fiddlededee!,—   457
MS {line added later}   458 *MS* singer *1868 1872 1888 1889* dancer   459 *MS*
halt this buffoonery>bid this buffoonery stop,   460 *MS* Admit nobility

439 *Honour of birth*: the prestige and intense respect accruing to ancient aristocratic
lineage. This is something long critiqued by Browning, in, for example, the irony of
the Duke's 'nine-hundred-years' old name' in 'My Last Duchess', and in the disasters
following on Lord Tresham's similar obsession with honour in *A Blot in the 'Scutcheon*:
I. ii. 1–9, 143–4, iii. 5–7, etc.
447 *gabble o' the goose!*: i.e. it becomes nonsense! (like the senseless noise of geese).
450 *gilded brave*: i.e. shining finely on the outside.
455 *Fiddle-de-dee!*: nonsense! ; cf. 'Mr Sludge', 137.
458 *prizer*: boxer, prize-fighter.

Why, worth the market-price,—now up, now down,
Just so with this as with all other ware:
Therefore essay the market, sell your name,
Style and condition to who buys them best!　　　　465
"Does my name purchase," had I dared inquire,
"Your niece, my lord?" there would have been rebuff
Though courtesy, your Lordship cannot else—
"Not altogether! Rank for rank may stand:
"But I have wealth beside, you—poverty;　　　　470
"Your scale flies up there: bid a second bid,
"Rank too and wealth too!" Reasoned like yourself!
But was it to you I went with goods to sell?
This time 't was my scale quietly kissed the ground,
Mere rank against mere wealth—some youth beside,　　　　475
Some beauty too, thrown into the bargain, just
As the buyer likes or lets alone. I thought
To deal o' the square: others find fault, it seems:
The thing is, those my offer most concerned,
Pietro, Violante, cried they fair or foul?　　　　480
What did they make o' the terms? Preposterous terms?
Why then accede so promptly, close with such
Nor take a minute to chaffer? Bargain struck,
They straight grew bilious, wished their money back,
Repented them, no doubt: why, so did I,　　　　485
So did your Lordship, if town-talk be true,
Of paying a full farm's worth for that piece

---

463 *MS* {beginning of fo. 248}　　　*MS* With this as with all other ware in the world:
464 *MS* consult>essay　　　465 *MS* conditions　　*MS* best!"　　　466 *MS* en-
quire,　　　467 *MS* be prompt　　　470–2 *MS* {no quotation marks at begin-
nings of lines}　　　470 *MS* you, *Yale 1* you,>you—　　★471 *MS 1868 1872*
second bid, *1888 1889* {no comma}　　　472 *MS* ."">!"　　*MS* reasoned>
Reasoned　　　474 *MS* {no comma}　　　478 *MS* on　　*MS* fault with me:>
fault, it seems:　　　480 *MS* foul or fair?　　　483 *MS* After a minute's chaffer-
ing?>Nor take a minute to chaffer?　　*MS* Afterward>Bargain struck,　　　486 *MS*
the town-talk's

---

465 *Style and condition*: title and social position.
478 *deal o' the square*: deal fairly.
484 *bilious*: ill-tempered, unhappy.

By Pietro of Cortona—probably
His scholar Ciro Ferri may have retouched—
You caring more for colour than design—   490
Getting a little tired of cupids too.
That's incident to all the folk who buy!
I am charged, I know, with gilding fact by fraud;
I falsified and fabricated, wrote
Myself down roughly richer than I prove,   495
Rendered a wrong revenue,—grant it all!
Mere grace, mere coquetry such fraud, I say:
A flourish round the figures of a sum
For fashion's sake, that deceives nobody.
The veritable back-bone, understood   500
Essence of this same bargain, blank and bare,
Being the exchange of quality for wealth,—
What may such fancy-flights be? Flecks of oil
Flirted by chapmen where plain dealing grates.

489 MS ^may have^   490 MS {beginning of fo. 249}   491 MS Ledas too:
Yale 1 too:>too.   492 MS [ ]>the   498 MS that deceives no one in the
world.   499 {not found in MS}   502 MS wealth,

488–91 *Pietro of Cortona . . . too*: Pietro da Cortona (1597–1669) was one of the
founders of the Roman High Baroque; his disciple and friend Ciro Ferri (1634–89)
co-operated in some of his major works and completed others, notably frescoes and
ceilings in the Pitti Palace, Florence. Here Guido implies that the judge has got tired of
the painting because of its weak colouring—Ciro Ferri was widely believed to be an
inferior colourist to Pietro da Cortona—and also 'tired of cupids too', a characteristic
feature of the baroque style. Browning's historical knowledge of Italian baroque art
came from Filippo Baldinucci's vast compendium *Notizie de' Professori del Disegno*,
which he used as early as 1847. 'Beatrice Signorini' (1889), which recent evidence
suggests was begun in the 1850s, deals with a historical anecdote about Artemisia
Gentileschi and Francesco Romanelli, the latter another relatively mediocre disciple of
Pietro da Cortona. Browning, in other words, had considered baroque art in Italy but,
like many, he thought it a lesser phase than the Renaissance: 'both in Florence and in
Rome / The elder race [of Renaissance painters] so make themselves at home / That
scarce we give a glance to ceilingfuls / Of such like as Francesco [Romanelli]':
'Beatrice Signorini', 347–50.
498 *flourish*: bold, decorative stroke of the pen, i.e. an exaggeration.
503–4 *Flecks . . . grates*: bits of oil (smooth talk or exaggeration) sprinkled onto a
negotiation by traders where more honest talk 'grates' or leads to argument. 'Flirted'
means 'flicked' or 'sprinkled' or, as Johnson defines it, 'to throw any thing with a quick
elastick motion'. This image is brusque and mundane, like most of Guido's images: see
Introduction.

I may have dripped a drop—"My name I sell;   505
"Not but that I too boast my wealth"—as they,
"—We bring you riches; still our ancestor
"Was hardly the rapscallion folk saw flogged,
"But heir to we know who, were rights of force!"
They knew and I knew where the backbone lurked   510
I' the writhings of the bargain, lords, believe!
I paid down all engaged for, to a doit,
Delivered them just that which, their life long,
They hungered in the hearts of them to gain—
Incorporation with nobility thus   515
In word and deed: for that they gave me wealth.
But when they came to try their gain, my gift,
Quit Rome and qualify for Arezzo, take
The tone o' the new sphere that absorbed the old,
Put away gossip Jack and goody Joan   520
And go become familiar with the Great,
Greatness to touch and taste and handle now,—
Why then,—they found that all was vanity,
Vexation, and what Solomon describes!
The old abundant city-fare was best,   525
The kindly warmth o' the commons, the glad clap
Of the equal on the shoulder, the frank grin
Of the underling at all so many spoons
Fire-new at neighbourly treat,—best, best and best

505 MS sell—   506 MS {no quotation mark at beginning of line}   507 MS
"We   MS riches,   508–9 MS {no quotation marks at beginnings of
lines}   508 MS 1868 1872 rapscallion, folks   509 MS force.">force!"   510
MS 1868 1872 back-bone   511 MS In   512 MS for to   517 MS gain
my   518 MS {beginning of fo. 250}   519 MS of   522 MS touch,   523
MS 1868 Why,   524 MS found first.>describes.   529 MS feast,—>treat,—

512 *to a doit*: to the last penny.
518 *qualify*: fit themselves for.
520 *goody*: female intimate (of implied lower-class status); cf. II. 513 n.
522 *Greatness . . . now*: cf. Col. 2: 20–22, 1 John 1: 1.
523–4 *all . . . describes*: cf. Eccl. 2: 11, 17, 26, etc., a book traditionally believed to
have been written by King Solomon.
526 *commons*: 'the vulgar; the lower people; those who inherit no honours': Johnson.
529 *Fire-new*: brand-new (fresh from the furnace); cf. 'Soliloquy of the Spanish
Cloister', 19. In Shakespeare, as here, this compound has a sarcastic, pejorative mean-
ing: cf. *Richard III*, 1. iii. 255, *Twelfth Night*, III. ii. 22, etc.

Beyond compare!—down to the loll itself   530
O' the pot-house settle,—better such a bench
Than the stiff crucifixion by my dais
Under the piecemeal damask canopy
With the coroneted coat of arms a-top!
Poverty and privation for pride's sake,   535
All they engaged to easily brave and bear,—
With the fit upon them and their brains a-work,—
Proved unendurable to the sobered sots.
A banished prince, now, will exude a juice
And salamander-like support the flame: 540
He dines on chestnuts, chucks the husks to help
The broil o' the brazier, pays the due baioc,
Goes off light-hearted: his grimace begins
At the funny humours of the christening-feast
Of friend the money-lender,—then he's touched   545
By the flame and frizzles at the babe to kiss!

---

530 MS ,—>!—   531 MS On   533 MS 1868 1872 piece-meal   MS
velvet>damask   MS ⟨.⟩   534 MS coronetted   536 MS bear   537
MS a-fume, 1872 a-work,   541 MS 1868 1872 chesnuts,   542 MS
of   544 MS christening feast   545 MS {beginning of fo. 251}

---

530 *loll*: tilt, unevenness.

532 *dais*: raised seat of honour (here contrasted with the 'pot-house settle', pub bench).

533 *piecemeal damask canopy*: tattered silk covering.

539–40 *banished prince . . . flame*: i.e. a real aristocrat has a grace and confidence that allows him to live in poverty as easily as the mythical lizard, the salamander, lives within fire.

541–3 *dines . . . light-hearted*: he takes his poor meal from a Roman chestnut stall. Cf. Story's description of these stalls in the Piazza Navona: 'Here, too, sacks gape with wide mouths, and show within them thousands of the great brown Roman chestnuts. All the winter long little portable furnaces smoke wherein they are roasting, to be sold at twenty for a *baiocco*, and many an old wife sits by, whose husband, perhaps, has to Aleppo gone, like her who sat "with chestnuts in her lap, / And munched, and munched, and munched" on Macbeth's heath': *Roba di Roma*, ii. 7. The way in which the aristocrat throws the chestnut husks in the brazier to help the fire parallels the way the salamander exudes juice and 'supports' the flame: in other words, the aristocrat does more than bear poverty, he reacts to it with élan and grace.

542 *baioc*: a Papal coin, of very small value. There is still the saying 'non vale un baiocco', 'it's not worth twopence'.

543–6 *grimace . . . kiss*: the aristocrat who endures poverty (the fire) without complaint only starts to 'frizzle' (burn with a sputtering sound, often used fig. of rage or shame) when he has to earn his loan from the moneylender by attending the christening of his child, and posing as his friend. For Guido's aristocrat fraternizing with and fawning upon his social inferiors is embarrassing in a way that simple poverty is not.

Here was the converse trial, opposite mind:
Here did a petty nature split on rock
Of vulgar wants predestinate for such—
One dish at supper and weak wine to boot!   550
The prince had grinned and borne: the citizen shrieked,
Summoned the neighbourhood to attest the wrong,
Made noisy protest he was murdered,—stoned
And burned and drowned and hanged,—then broke away,
He and his wife, to tell their Rome the rest.   555
And this you admire, you men o' the world, my lords?
This moves compassion, makes you doubt my faith?
Why, I appeal to . . . sun and moon? Not I!
Rather to Plautus, Terence, Boccaccio's Book,
My townsman, frank Ser Franco's merry Tales,—   560
To all who strip a vizard from a face,
A body from its padding, and a soul
From froth and ignorance it styles itself,—
If this be other than the daily hap
Of purblind greed that dog-like still drops bone,   565
Grasps shadow, and then howls the case is hard!
[—]

547 *MS* mind.   548 *MS* soul>nature   553 *MS* ^murdered,—^   *MS*
stoned,   554 *MS* Burned, drowned   555 *MS* {no comma}   556 *MS* of   557
MS Moves your>This moves   558 *MS 1868 1872* to . .   560 *MS* Franco, and
his>Franco's merry   *MS* Tales,   561 *MS* And   *MS* know>strip   563 *MS*
itself,   564 *MS* [ ]>case *Yale 1* case>hap   565 *MS* human>purblind   *MS*
^dog-like^   *MS* lets drop the bone>drops bone   566 *MS* For the shadow's, and
howls was never case so hard?>Grasps shadow, and then howls the case is hard?

559–60 *Plautus . . . Tales*: Plautus (*c.* 250–184 BC) and Terence (183–159 BC) are
famous Roman dramatists. 'Boccaccio's Book' is the *Decameron* (1353). Franco Sacchetti
(*c.*1330–1400) wrote a collection of stories in the manner of the *Decameron*, the *Trecen-
tonovelle* (*c.*1388–95). The pun 'frank Ser Franco', i.e. 'open, licentious Sir Franco' is on
account of this. Collectively, these comic writers expose greed, folly, and pretension.
The Brownings read some Sacchetti together in 1847: 'We are going through some of
old Sacchetti's novelets now: characteristic work for Florence, if somewhat dull else-
where. Boccaccios can't be expected to spring up with the vines in rows, even in this
climate': EBB & RB to Mrs Anna Jameson, Dec. [1847]: *Correspondence*, xiv. 344.

565 *purblind*: almost blind, obtuse.

565–6 *dog-like . . . hard*: an allusion to Aesop's fable 'The dog who carried the meat',
in Croxall's translation, 'The Dog and the Shadow': 'A Dog, crossing a little rivulet
with a piece of flesh in his mouth, saw his own Shadow represented in the clear mirror
of the limpid stream; and believing it to be another Dog, who was carrying another
piece of flesh, he could not forbear catching at it; but was so far from getting any thing
by his greedy design, that he dropt the piece he had in his mouth, which immediately
sunk to the bottom, and was irrecoverably lost': *Fables of Æsop, Translated into English*,
by Samuel Croxall (new ed., 1804), pp. 8–9.

So much for them so far: now for myself,
My profit or loss i' the matter: married am I:
Text whereon friendly censors burst to preach.
Ay, at Rome even, long ere I was left   570
To regulate her life for my young bride
Alone at Arezzo, friendliness outbroke
(Sifting my future to predict its fault)
"Purchase and sale being thus so plain a point,
"How of a certain soul bound up, may-be,   575
"I' the barter with the body and money-bags?
"From the bride's soul what is it you expect?"
Why, loyalty and obedience,—wish and will
To settle and suit her fresh and plastic mind
To the novel, not disadvantageous mould!   580
Father and mother shall the woman leave,
Cleave to the husband, be it for weal or woe:
There is the law: what sets this law aside
In my particular case? My friends submit
"Guide, guardian, benefactor,—fee, faw, fum,   585
"The fact is you are forty-five years old,
"Nor very comely even for that age:
"Girls must have boys." Why, let girls say so then,
Nor call the boys and men, who say the same,
Brute this and beast the other as they do!   590
Come, cards on table! When you chaunt us next
Epithalamium full to overflow

---

567 *MS* {New paragraph (already written thus) indicated by 'N.P.' in left-hand
margin}   *MS* {no comma}   568 *MS* in   569 *MS* Whereupon   571
MS {beginning of fo. 252}   574 *Yale 1* 'Purchase>"Purchase {broken sort in
proof}   575 *MS* {no quotation mark at beginning of line}   *MS* belike>may
be, *Yale 1* may be,>may-be,   576 *MS* In   *MS* beside flesh>with the
body   *MS* money-bags—   578 *MS* the wish   580 *1868* nor   581
MS {no comma}   582 *MS* woe.   586–8 *MS* {no quotation marks at
beginnings of lines}   589   *MS*   {no comma}   *MS*   as much>the
same   591 *MS* recite>chaunt

569 *censors*: gossips, officious people.
581–2 *Father...husband*: cf. Gen. 2: 24, Matt. 19: 4–6.
592 *Epithalamium*: marriage song; a poem celebrating a marriage and praying for the
prosperity of the bride and groom, originally after Spenser's 'Epithalamion' (1595).

With praise and glory of white womanhood,
The chaste and pure—troll no such lies o'er lip!
Put in their stead a crudity or two,   595
Such short and simple statement of the case
As youth chalks on our walls at spring of year!
No! I shall still think nobler of the sex,
Believe a woman still may take a man
For the short period that his soul wears flesh,   600
And, for the soul's sake, understand the fault
Of armour frayed by fighting. Tush, it tempts
One's tongue too much! I'll say—the law's the law:
With a wife I look to find all wifeliness,
As when I buy, timber and twig, a tree—   605
I buy the song o' the nightingale inside.

Such was the pact: Pompilia from the first
Broke it, refused from the beginning day
Either in body or soul to cleave to mine,
And published it forthwith to all the world.   610
No rupture,—you must join ere you can break,—
Before we had cohabited a month
She found I was a devil and no man,—
Made common cause with those who found as much,
Her parents, Pietro and Violante,—moved   615
Heaven and earth to the rescue of all three.
In four months' time, the time o' the parents' stay,
Arezzo was a-ringing, bells in a blaze,
With the unimaginable story rife

---

593 *MS* glorifyings>praise and glory   594 *MS* with lip!   595 *MS* {no comma}   598 *MS* {beginning of fo. 253}   600 *MS* this>the   603 *MS* law,—   606 *MS* of   607 *MS* {New paragraph (already written thus) indicated by 'N.P.' in left-hand margin}   613 *MS* [ ]>a   617 *MS* of   618 *MS* Arezzo rang the changes, like bells bewitched,>Arezzo was a-ringing, bells in a blaze,

---

594 *troll*: sing merrily.

602 *armour . . . fighting*: an oblique allusion to St Paul's 'whole armour of God': Eph. 6: 11–18, and also another pathetic reference to his age—he has been 'fighting' for forty-five years.

I' the mouth of man, woman and child—to-wit   620
My misdemeanour. First the lighter side,
Ludicrous face of things,—how very poor
The Franceschini had become at last,
The meanness and the misery of each shift
To save a soldo, stretch and make ends meet.   625
Next, the more hateful aspect,—how myself
With cruelty beyond Caligula's
Had stripped and beaten, robbed and murdered them,
The good old couple, I decoyed, abused,
Plundered and then cast out, and happily so,   630
Since,—in due course the abominable comes,—
Woe worth the poor young wife left lonely here!
Repugnant in my person as my mind,
I sought,—was ever heard of such revenge?
—To lure and bind her to so cursed a couch,   635
Such co-embrace with sulphur, snake and toad,
That she was fain to rush forth, call the stones
O' the common street to save her, not from hate
Of mine merely, but . . . must I burn my lips
With the blister of the lie? . . . the satyr-love   640
Of who but my own brother, the young priest,
Too long enforced to lenten fare belike,
Now tempted by the morsel tossed him full
I' the trencher where lay bread and herbs at best.

---

620 *MS* In   *MS* child,   621 *MS* misdemeanour—first   *MS* {no comma}
622 *MS* aspect,>face of things,   *MS* prodi>very   624 *MS* {beginning of fo.
254}   635 *MS* To bind   *MS* ^—and bind^   *MS* <[ ]> so   636 *MS* [ ]
>Such   639 *MS* {no comma}   640 *MS 1868 1872* lie? . .   644 *MS*
In   *MS* where the bread   *MS* herbs are

625 *soldo*: a Tuscan coin of small value.
627 *Caligula's*: the Roman emperor Caligula (AD 12–41) was infamous for murder,
cruelty, sensuality, and madness.
632 *Woe worth*: alas for, woe is; cf. OED²*woe* 4. c. 'Woe worth me' = 'Alas for me',
and Ezek. 30: 2: 'Howl ye, Woe worth the day!'
636 *sulphur . . . toad*: i.e. symbols of evil; cf. *Macbeth*, IV. i. 6–12, and R&B, II. 1377 n.
637–8 *call . . . her*: cf. Luke 19: 40.
640 *satyr-love*: bestial, lecherous love, like that of a satyr.
643–4 *morsel . . . trencher*: cf. 'I found you as a morsel, cold upon / Dead Caesar's
trencher': *Antony and Cleopatra*, III. xiii. 116–17.

Mark, this yourselves say!—this, none disallows,   645
Was charged to me by the universal voice
At the instigation of my four-months' wife!—
And then you ask "Such charges so preferred,
"(Truly or falsely, here concerns us not)
"Pricked you to punish now if not before?—   650
"Did not the harshness double itself, the hate
"Harden?" I answer "Have it your way and will!"
Say my resentment grew apace: what then?
Do you cry out on the marvel? When I find
That pure smooth egg which, laid within my nest,   655
Could not but hatch a comfort to us all,
Issues a cockatrice for me and mine,
Do you stare to see me stamp on it? Swans are soft:
Is it not clear that she you call my wife,
That any wife of any husband, caught   660
Whetting a sting like this against his breast,—
Speckled with fragments of the fresh-broke shell,
Married a month and making outcry thus,—
Proves a plague-prodigy to God and man?
She married: what was it she married for,   665
Counted upon and meant to meet thereby?
"Love" suggests some one, "love, a little word
"Whereof we have not heard one syllable."
So, the Pompilia, child, girl, wife, in one,
Wanted the beating pulse, the rolling eye,   670

649–52 MS {no quotation marks at beginnings of lines}   649 MS now con-
cerns   650 MS before,—   651 MS {beginning of fo. 255}   652 MS
answer,   Yale 1   answer,>answer   662   MS   ^Speckled^   MS   ^fresh-
broke^   668 MS {no quotation mark at beginning of line}   669 MS So
the   MS wife in

---

650 *Pricked*: provoked.

657 *cockatrice*: a monstrous creature, a serpent supposed to have been hatched from a
cock's egg, but also an abusive name for a woman: prostitute, whore. Here the senses
come together. In the following lines, Guido presents himself as trying to work out
what kind of creature has hatched from the 'pure smooth egg'. He knows that 'swans
are soft' (658), but since the creature that has hatched out tries to sting him (661) and
has 'fresh-broke shell' attached to it (662), he recognizes it as a cockatrice, a 'plague-
prodigy' (664).

The frantic gesture, the devotion due
From Thyrsis to Neæra! Guido's love—
Why not Provençal roses in his shoe,
Plume to his cap, and trio of guitars
At casement, with a bravo close beside?   675
Good things all these are, clearly claimable
When the fit price is paid the proper way.
Had it been some friend's wife, now, threw her fan
At my foot, with just this pretty scrap attached,
"Shame, death, damnation—fall these as they may,   680
"So I find you, for a minute! Come this eve!"
—Why, at such sweet self-sacrifice,—who knows?
I might have fired up, found me at my post,
Ardent from head to heel, nor feared catch cough.
Nay, had some other friend's . . . say, daughter, tripped 685
Upstairs and tumbled flat and frank on me,
Bareheaded and barefooted, with loose hair
And garments all at large,—cried "Take me thus!
"Duke So-and-So, the greatest man in Rome—
"To escape his hand and heart have I broke bounds,   690

---

672 *MS* Neæra: *Yale 1* Neæra:>Neæra!   673 *MS 1868 1872* provençal   674
MS {no comma}   678 *MS* {beginning of fo. 256}   *MS* glove>fan   679
MS {no commas}   *MS* this scrap of note   680 *MS* be these   *MS*
may   681 *MS* gain you but a   *MS* come>Come   682 *MS* for
such   684 *MS* Rosy   685 *MS 1868 1872* friend's . .   *MS* daughter
tripped   689–91 *MS* {no quotation marks at beginnings of lines}   689
MS So and So,

671–2 *devotion . . . Neæra*: i.e. a romantic, ardent love, as in pastoral poetry. The
names Thyrsis and Neæra occur originally in Theocritus, *Idyll* i and Virgil, *Eclogues* iii
and vii, and from there they were widely used in Renaissance pastoral poetry as the
names of amorous shepherds and shepherdesses. (The love-letters presented in court in
OYB used the similar pseudonyms Mirtillo and Amarilli.) Classical uses of 'Neæra'
associate it with loose morals; in particular in speech 59 of the Demosthenic corpus
Neæra is a prostitute. Guido may be implying that this is no *faithful* shepherdess. Cf.
also Milton, 'Lycidas', 69.

673 *Provençal roses*: Provence in southern France was the home of the troubadours,
the great medieval love poets. Guido, sarcastically picturing himself as a troubadour,
imagines wearing Provençal roses as appropriate emblems. The image is perhaps
influenced by the 'Provincial roses' of *Hamlet*, iii. ii. 276–7.

675 *bravo*: hired thug (needed to fight off guardians, other lovers, or a jealous
husband).

"Traversed the town and reached you!"—then, indeed,
The lady had not reached a man of ice!
I would have rummaged, ransacked at the word
Those old odd corners of an empty heart
For remnants of dim love the long disused,   695
And dusty crumblings of romance! But here,
We talk of just a marriage, if you please—
The every-day conditions and no more;
Where do these bind me to bestow one drop
Of blood shall dye my wife's true-love-knot pink?   700
Pompilia was no pigeon, Venus' pet,
That shuffled from between her pressing paps
To sit on my rough shoulder,—but a hawk,
I bought at a hawk's price and carried home
To do hawk's service—at the Rotunda, say,   705
Where, six o' the callow nestlings in a row,
You pick and choose and pay the price for such.

---

691 MS Then>then 1868 1872 Then,   698 MS every day Yale 1 every day>
every-day   703 MS [ ]>on   705 MS {beginning of fo. 257}   706 MS of

700 *true-love-knot*: an ornamental knot, usually two entwined loops, used as a symbol of reciprocal love, popular on hair decorations and rings. Pompilia's love-knot is seen as virginal white, requiring Guido's blood (passion) to turn it a suitably romantic pink.

701–3 *pigeon . . . hawk*: i.e. no soft, pretty bird kept for pleasure, as a mistress would be, but a hawk, a bird used for hunting, which must be trained to submit to its owner. The dove is traditionally sacred to Venus; the turtle-dove is emblematic of true love. Guido's prosaic use of 'pigeon' instead of 'dove' plays on the popular sense of 'pigeon' meaning 'fool' or 'dupe'. Guido's contempt for the softness and naïvety of his wife is evident in the image. Pompilia must toughen up, 'do hawk's service', if she is to be of use to him. The romantic and sexual allurements suggested by 'Venus'. . . pressing paps' are in his eyes no part of the business of marriage.

705 *To do hawk's service*; i.e. to obey.

705–7 *Rotunda . . . such*: a memory of the street market of Browning's day: 'you will find gathered around the fountain in the Piazza della Rotonda (for so the Pantheon is called by the people of Rome) a number of bird-fanciers, surrounded by cages in which are multitudes of living birds for sale. Here are Java sparrows, parrots and parroquets, grey thrushes and nightingales, redbreasts (*petti rossi*), yellow canary birds, beautiful sweet-singing little *cardellini*, and gentle ringdoves, all chattering, singing and cooing together, to the constant plashing of the fountain': *Roba di Roma*, ii. 6.

I have paid my pound, await my penny's worth,
So, hoodwink, starve and properly train my bird,
And, should she prove a haggard,—twist her neck!   710
Did I not pay my name and style, my hope
And trust, my all? Through spending these amiss
I am here! 'T is scarce the gravity of the Court
Will blame me that I never piped a tune,
Treated my falcon-gentle like my finch.   715
The obligation I incurred was just
To practise mastery, prove my mastership:—
Pompilia's duty was—submit herself,
Afford me pleasure, perhaps cure my bile.
Am I to teach my lords what marriage means,   720
What God ordains thereby and man fulfils
Who, docile to the dictate, treads the house?
My lords have chosen the happier part with Paul
And neither marry nor burn,—yet priestliness
Can find a parallel to the marriage-bond   725
In its own blessed special ordinance
Whereof indeed was marriage made the type:
The Church may show her insubordinate,

---

709 *MS* So hoodwink,   710 *MS* And should   *MS* twitch her beak>twist her neck!   712 *MS* all amiss   717 *MS* prove the>practise   *MS* of >prove my   718 *MS* duty,—to submit   720 *MS* Lords   724 *MS* priestliness,   728 *MS* My lords, too have their>The Church may show her

---

709 *hoodwink, starve*: as part of the method of training a hawk for falconry, its eyes were covered with a small hood to ensure its quiescence. If it proved difficult to handle, it might be kept awake for long periods or slightly starved till it settled to tameness and docility. Cf. Petruchio's taming of Katherina: 'My falcon now is sharp and passing empty, / And till she stoop, she must not be full-gorg'd, / For then she never looks upon her lure.... She eat no meat to-day, nor none shall eat; / Last night she slept not, nor to-night she shall not': *Taming of the Shrew*, IV. i. 190–8.

710 *prove a haggard*: i.e. prove untrainable. A haggard is a wild, untameable (female) hawk; the word is also applied fig. to a woman; cf. *Othello*, III. iii. 260–3: 'If I do prove her haggard, / Though that her jesses were my dear heart-strings, / I'ld whistle her off, and let her down the wind / To prey at fortune.'

714–15 *piped . . . finch*: finches, canaries, and other songbirds were often played music in order to encourage them to sing.

715 *falcon-gentle*: female peregrine hawk.

722 *treads the house*: i.e. keeps within the bounds of marriage.

724 *marry nor burn*: cf. 1 Cor. 7: 9.

As marriage her refractory. How of the Monk
Who finds the claustral regimen too sharp   730
After the first month's essay? What's the mode
With the Deacon who supports indifferently
The rod o' the Bishop when he tastes its smart
Full four weeks? Do you straightway slacken hold
Of the innocents, the all-unwary ones   735
Who, eager to profess, mistook their mind?—
Remit a fast-day's rigour to the Monk
Who fancied Francis' manna meant roast quails,—
Concede the Deacon sweet society,
He never thought the Levite-rule renounced,—   740
Or rather prescribe short chain and sharp scourge
Corrective of such peccant humours? This—
I take to be the Church's mode, and mine.
If I was over-harsh,—the worse i' the wife
Who did not win from harshness as she ought,   745
Wanted the patience and persuasion, lore
Of love, should cure me and console herself.
Put case that I mishandle, flurry and fright

729 *MS* wedlock>marriage   *MS* monk>friar>monk   731 *MS* fasting?>es-
say?   *MS* way>mode   732 *MS* {beginning of fo. 258}   *MS* dea-
con   733 *MS* rule>rod   *MS* of *Yale 1* of>o'   *MS* it>its   734 *MS* [ ]
>hold,   735 *MS* all unwary *Yale 1* all unwary>all-unwary   736 *MS*
made>eager to   *MS* mind,—   737 *MS* monk>Monk   738 *MS* *1868*
1872 quails,   739 *MS* {no comma} *Yale 1* society>society,   740 *MS*
^never^   *MS* levite-rule   742 *MS* ^peccant^   743 *MS* Churche's
744 *MS* ^over^ *Yale 1* over harsh>over-harsh   *MS* harsh,   *MS* in   747 *MS*
{no comma}   *MS* repay>console   *MS* herself   748 *MS* fright and fray>
flurry and fright

729 *refractory*: rebel.
730 *claustral regimen*: routine of the monastery.
733 *rod*: i.e. the authority (as represented by the Bishop's staff).
738 *Francis' . . . quails*: i.e. that a strict monastic diet meant luxury food; a play on the manna and quails of Exod. 16. Francis's manna = the diet of a monk within the Franciscan order, begging his meagre food, and accepting it as a grace from God; roast quails are synonymous with a rich, gourmet diet.
739 *sweet society*: i.e. the society of women.
740 *Levite-rule*: the rule for deacons, i.e. his vow of celibacy.
742 *peccant humours*: (fig.) sinful inclinations; the literal sense is 'corrupt or unhealthy humours' (with reference to the humoral pathology).
748 *flurry*: distress (by impatient handling or approach).

My hawk through clumsiness in sportsmanship,
Twitch out five pens where plucking one would serve—   750
What, shall she bite and claw to mend the case?
And, if you find I pluck five more for that,
Shall you weep "How he roughs the turtle there"?

Such was the starting; now of the further step.
In lieu of taking penance in good part,   755
The Monk, with hue and cry, summons a mob
To make a bonfire of the convent, say,—
And the Deacon's pretty piece of virtue (save
The ears o' the Court! I try to save my head)
Instructed by the ingenuous postulant,   760
Taxes the Bishop with adultery, (mud
Needs must pair off with mud, and filth with filth)—
Such being my next experience. Who knows not—
The couple, father and mother of my wife,
Returned to Rome, published before my lords,   765
Put into print, made circulate far and wide
That they had cheated me who cheated them?
Pompilia, I supposed their daughter, drew
Breath first 'mid Rome's worst rankness, through the deed
Of a drab and a rogue, was by-blow bastard-babe   770
Of a nameless strumpet, passed off, palmed on me

---

751 *MS* case,   753 *MS* treats>roughs   *MS 1868 1872* there?"   754 *MS*
{New paragraph (already written thus) indicated by 'N.P.' in left-hand margin}   *MS*
step: 756 *MS* monk>Monk   757 *MS* Convent, say—   758 *MS*
{beginning of fo. 259}   *MS* virtue,—save   759 *MS* of   *MS* Court, *Yale 1*
Court,>Court!   *MS* head,—   760 *MS* ingenious   761 *MS* adultery,—
mud   762 *MS* filth, *Yale 1* filth)>filth)—   763 *MS 1868 1872* experience:
who   *MS* not   764 *MS* Couple,   *MS* wife   767 *MS* them,   769
MS mid   *MS* {no comma}   770 *MS* the>was   *MS 1868 1872* bye-blow

---

750 *pens*: wing feathers.
753 *turtle*: turtle dove.
758 *pretty piece of virtue*: i.e. mistress (the use is ironic); cf. *Tempest*, I. ii. 56.
760 *ingenuous postulant*: naïve novice, i.e. the Deacon.
770 *drab*: prostitute.
  by-blow: accidental, side-stroke (adj.). Usually it is a noun, meaning 'illegitimate
child, bastard': cf. IV. 612. The alliteration of 'by-blow bastard-babe' enacts Guido's
contempt.

As the daughter with the dowry. Daughter? Dirt
O' the kennel! Dowry? Dust o' the street! Nought more,
Nought less, nought else but—oh—ah—assuredly
A Franceschini and my very wife!   775
Now take this charge as you will, for false or true,—
This charge, preferred before your very selves
Who judge me now,—I pray you, adjudge again,
Classing it with the cheats or with the lies,
By which category I suffer most!   780
But of their reckoning, theirs who dealt with me
In either fashion,—I reserve my word,
Justify that in its place; I am now to say,
Whichever point o' the charge might poison most,
Pompilia's duty was no doubtful one.   785
You put the protestation in her mouth
"Henceforward and forevermore, avaunt
"Ye fiends, who drop disguise and glare revealed
"In your own shape, no longer father mine
"Nor mother mine! Too nakedly you hate   790
"Me whom you looked as if you loved once,—me
"Whom, whether true or false, your tale now damns,
"Divulged thus to my public infamy,
"Private perdition, absolute overthrow.
"For, hate my husband to your hearts' content,   795
"I, spoil and prey of you from first to last,
"I who have done you the blind service, lured
"The lion to your pitfall,—I, thus left

---

773 *MS* Of   *MS* kennel.   *MS* Dowry, dust>Dowry? Dust   *MS* of   *MS*
street.   774 *MS* [ ]>nought   *MS* ^ay—^ *1868 1872 1888 1889* ah—   778
MS again   779 *MS* {line added later}   *MS* cheats then>the cheats   *MS* lies
now,>the lies,   780 *MS* most: 781 *MS* those who   783 *MS* urge,>
say,   784 *MS* ^point of^   786 *MS* {beginning of fo. 260}   788–807
MS {no quotation marks at beginnings of lines}   788 *MS* at me>re-
vealed   789 *MS* [ ]>your   790 *MS* [ ]>Nor   *MS* mine: how   792
MS Who, whether this ^your^ tale ⟨of yours⟩ be true or false   793 *MS* Divulge
it   797 *MS* had   798 *MS 1868 1872* pit-fall,—

   773 *kennel*: gutter, sewer.

   787–8 *avaunt / Ye fiends*: go away, you devils. 'Avaunt' is Shakespearian: cf. *Macbeth*,
III. iv. 92.

"To answer for my ignorant bleating there,
"I should have been remembered and withdrawn   800
"From the first o' the natural fury, not flung loose
"A proverb and a by-word men will mouth
"At the cross-way, in the corner, up and down
"Rome and Arezzo,—there, full in my face,
"If my lord, missing them and finding me,   805
"Content himself with casting his reproach
"To drop i' the street where such impostors die.
"Ah, but—that husband, what the wonder were!—
"If, far from casting thus away the rag
"Smeared with the plague his hand had chanced upon,   810
"Sewn to his pillow by Locusta's wile,—
"Far from abolishing, root, stem and branch,
"The misgrowth of infectious mistletoe
"Foisted into his stock for honest graft,—
"If he repudiate not, renounce nowise,   815
"But, guarding, guiding me, maintain my cause
"By making it his own, (what other way?)
"—To keep my name for me, he call it his,
"Claim it of who would take it by their lie,—

---

801 *MS* of   802 *MS 1868 1872* byeword   *MS* should>will   803 *MS*
In>At   807 *MS* in   *MS* go.>die.   808 *MS* were   809 *MS* {no
comma} *Yale 1* If far>If, far   810–31 *MS* {no quotation marks at beginnings of
lines}   810 *MS* {line added later}   *1868 1872* plague,   *MS* upon   811
MS craft,— *Yale 1* craft,—>wile,—   812 *MS* branch   814 *MS* {beginning
of fo. 261}   *MS* graft,   815 *MS* {line added later}   *MS* He, repudiated not,
renounced no wise *1868 1872* he,   816 *MS* But guarding   *MS* main-
tained   817 *MS* {no brackets}   818 *MS* To   *MS* called   819 *MS*
Claimed

---

802 *proverb . . . by-word*: cf. 'Israel shall be a proverb and a byword among all people':
1 Kings 9: 7.

806–7 *Content . . . die*: be satisfied only to accuse me and bid me die in the street.

811 *Locusta's wile*: i.e. the cunning of an expert female poisoner (here implicitly
Violante). Locusta was the notorious poisoner called in by Agrippina to help murder
Claudius, and by Nero to help murder Britannicus. Afterwards Nero is supposed to
have rewarded her with large estates and even sent her pupils: see Suetonius, *Nero* 33.
2.

813–14 *infectious mistletoe . . . graft*: a way of describing Pompilia's status as a bastard
joined to Guido's aristocratic lineage. Mistletoe is a bushy plant that grows parasitically
on many trees, and is propagated from tree to tree on birds' beaks.

"To save my wealth for me—or babe of mine   820
"Their lie was framed to beggar at the birth—
"He bid them loose grasp, give our gold again:
"If he become no partner with the pair
"Even in a game which, played adroitly, gives
"Its winner life's great wonderful new chance,—   825
"Of marrying, to-wit, a second time,—
"Ah, if he did thus, what a friend were he!
"Anger he might show,—who can stamp out flame
"Yet spread no black o' the brand?—yet, rough albeit
"In the act, as whose bare feet feel embers scorch,   830
"What grace were his, what gratitude were mine!"
Such protestation should have been my wife's.
Looking for this, do I exact too much?
Why, here's the,—word for word, so much, no more,—
Avowal she made, her pure spontaneous speech   835
To my brother the Abate at first blush,
Ere the good impulse had begun to fade:
So did she make confession for the pair,
So pour forth praises in her own behalf.
"Ay, the false letter," interpose my lords—   840
"The simulated writing,—'t was a trick:

---

820 *MS* better, take>take of mine   821 *MS* birth,   822 *MS* bade   *MS*
his   823 *MS* Refused to be a *1868* "Refuse to become   824 *MS*
gave   825 *MS* The   *MS* that great   826 {not found in *MS*}   827
MS 1868 1872 did he do   829 *MS* of   *MS* {no comma}   830 *MS*
act as   *MS* foot feels>feet feel   *MS* burn,   831 *MS* deed   834
MS 1868 1872 word so   837 *MS* fade.>fade—   *1868 1872* fade—   840 *MS*
letter" interpose you here—   841–3 *MS* {no quotation marks at beginnings of
lines}

823–6 *If he . . . time*: i.e. if Guido refuses to join with Pietro and Violante in
attempting to dissolve the marriage, even though this would give him the 'new
chance' of marrying a more congenial partner.

828–30 *who . . . scorch*: the image is of Guido harshly stamping out the burning brand
(Pompilia) he has plucked from the fire (scandal), spreading around some blackness
(anger) as he does so, and almost singeing his feet in the process; cf. Zech. 3: 2.

834–6 *word . . . Abate*: i.e. the preceding speech is Guido's interpretation of Pompi-
lia's letter to the Abate Paulo of 19 July 1694, the letter which the prosecution alleged
was forged by Guido. The actual letter, whether forged or not, is shorter, less
rhetorical, and much more matter-of-fact: see OYB lxxxviii (95).

"You traced the signs, she merely marked the same,
"The product was not hers but yours." Alack,
I want no more impulsion to tell truth
From the other trick, the torture inside there!   845
I confess all—let it be understood—
And deny nothing! If I baffle you so,
Can so fence, in the plenitude of right,
That my poor lathen dagger puts aside
Each pass o' the Bilboa, beats you all the same,—   850
What matters inefficiency of blade?
Mine and not hers the letter,—conceded, lords!
Impute to me that practice!—take as proved
I taught my wife her duty, made her see
What it behoved her see and say and do,   855
Feel in her heart and with her tongue declare,
And, whether sluggish or recalcitrant,
Forced her to take the right step, I myself
Was marching in marital rectitude!
Why who finds fault here, say the tale be true?   860
Would not my lords commend the priest whose zeal
Seized on the sick, morose or moribund,
By the palsy-smitten finger, made it cross
His brow correctly at the critical time?
—Or answered for the inarticulate babe   865

---

842 *MS* you>she   843 *MS* {beginning of fo. 262}   845 *MS* little
trick,   *MS* there—   847 *MS* nothing,—if   849 *MS* [ ]>dagger
850 *MS* of   *MS* same,   851 *MS* arm?   853 *MS* ^to me^   *MS* prac-
tice,—   856 *MS* declare.   857 *MS* {line added later}   *MS* ignorant>
sluggish   859 *MS 1868* Marching in mere   *MS* rectitude,   860 *MS 1868*
And *1872* Why,   862 *MS* Seizes   *MS* [ ]>sick,   863 *MS* makes   865
MS Or answers

---

845 *trick*: stratagem (an ironic use in relation to l. 841).

849 *lathen dagger*: wooden dagger, a phrase often used for a counterfeit weapon; cf. *I
Henry IV*, II. iv. 137.

850 *Bilboa*: a fine, hard sword. The town of Bilbao in northern Spain was famous
for the manufacture of swords, so that in English 'Bilboa' became a general name for a
good sword.

858–9 *I ... rectitude!*: a significant change from *MS, 1868*. The sense is '[the right
step that] I myself / Was marching in marital rectitude!'

862 *moribund*: dying.

At baptism, in its stead declared the faith,
And saved what else would perish unprofessed?
True, the incapable hand may rally yet,
Renounce the sign with renovated strength,—
The babe may grow up man and Molinist,—   870
And so Pompilia, set in the good path
And left to go alone there, soon might see
That too frank-forward, all too simple-straight
Her step was, and decline to tread the rough,
When here lay, tempting foot, the meadow-side,   875
And there the coppice rang with singing-birds!
Soon she discovered she was young and fair,
That many in Arezzo knew as much.
Yes, this next cup of bitterness, my lords,
Had to begin go filling, drop by drop,   880
Its measure up of full disgust for me,
Filtered into by every noisome drain—
Society's sink toward which all moisture runs.
Would not you prophesy—"She on whose brow is stamped
"The note of the imputation that we know,—   885
"Rightly or wrongly mothered with a whore,—

866 *MS* his>its   *MS* declares   867 *MS* saves   868 *MS* yet   869 *MS*
strength,   870 *MS* to a>man and   871 *MS* {beginning of fo. 263}   873
MS 1868 1872 simple-strait   876 *MS 1868* called   *MS* singing-birds.   878
MS 1868 1872 much,—   881 *MS* cavity>measure   *MS* [ ]>up   *MS* {no
comma}   882 *MS* fulsome *Yale 1* fulsome>noisome   884 *MS* prophesy
"She   885–93 *MS* {no quotation marks at beginnings of lines}   885 *MS*
shame>note   *MS* know,   886 *MS* whore,

870 *Molinist*: i.e. heretic; cf. l. 203 n.
873 *frank-forward*: straightforwardly honest.
simple-straight: naively correct.
876 *rang*: in *MS, 1868* 'called', i.e. summoned, tempted. 'Rang' improves what was
a slightly ambiguous syntax.
879 *cup of bitterness*: the cup of suffering, to drink which 'to the dregs' is proverbial
for 'experiencing completely a measure of suffering'; the image continues at ll. 903–7;
cf. Matt. 26: 42. Here the cup is slowly filled by Guido's supposed knowledge of
Pompilia's promiscuity, something he asserted to the court: 'she stands convicted as an
adulteress, not merely for this [her relationship with Caponsacchi], but for other like
excesses, which I have since heard that she committed in Arezzo with other persons':
OYB cxxvii (135).

"Such an one, to disprove the frightful charge,
"What will she but exaggerate chastity,
"Err in excess of wifehood, as it were,
"Renounce even levities permitted youth, 890
"Though not youth struck to age by a thunderbolt?
"Cry 'wolf' i' the sheepfold, where's the sheep dares bleat,
"Knowing the shepherd listens for a growl?"
So you expect. How did the devil decree?
Why, my lords, just the contrary of course! 895
It was in the house from the window, at the church
From the hassock,—where the theatre lent its lodge,
Or staging for the public show left space,—
That still Pompilia needs must find herself
Launching her looks forth, letting looks reply 900
As arrows to a challenge; on all sides
Ever new contribution to her lap,
Till one day, what is it knocks at my clenched teeth
But the cup full, curse-collected all for me?
And I must needs drink, drink this gallant's praise, 905
That minion's prayer, the other fop's reproach,
And come at the dregs to—Caponsacchi! Sirs,
I,—chin-deep in a marsh of misery,
Struggling to extricate my name and fame
And fortune from the marsh would drown them all, 910
My face the sole unstrangled part of me,—
I must have this new gad-fly in that face,

887 *MS* one— 888 *MS* Will, could>What will *MS* [ ]>What 889 *MS* wifehood as 890 *MS* youth— 891 *MS* Youth struck to age by shame the 892 *MS* "Wolf" in *MS* {no commas} *Yale 1* bleat,—>bleat, 893 *MS* {no quotation mark at end} 895 *MS* course, 898 *MS* {beginning of fo. 264} *MS* The *MS* space, 901 *MS* challenge, 903 *MS* knocks my 904 *MS* me, 905 *MS* drink up this 907 *MS* Caponsacchi: 908 *MS* I—chin deep *Yale 1* I—chin deep>I,—chin deep *1868 1872* chin deep *MS* misery— *Yale 1* misery—>misery, 912 *MS* my face,

891 *Though . . . thunderbolt*: 'though [these levities] are not appropriate for youth [like Pompilia] that has been aged by the shock of such a revelation'.
897 *hassock*: kneeling cushion.
lodge: box, from Fr. *loge*.

Must free me from the attacking lover too!
Men say I battled ungracefully enough—
Was harsh, uncouth and ludicrous beyond   915
The proper part o' the husband: have it so!
Your lordships are considerate at least—
You order me to speak in my defence
Plainly, expect no quavering tuneful trills
As when you bid a singer solace you,—   920
Nor look that I shall give it, for a grace,
Stans pede in uno:—you remember well
In the one case, 't is a plainsong too severe,
This story of my wrongs,—and that I ache
And need a chair, in the other. Ask you me   925
Why, when I felt this trouble flap my face,
Already pricked with every shame could perch,—
When, with her parents, my wife plagued me too,—
Why I enforced not exhortation mild
To leave whore's-tricks and let my brows alone,   930
With mulct of comfits, promise of perfume?

"Far from that! No, you took the opposite course,
"Breathed threatenings, rage and slaughter!" What you will!
And the end has come, the doom is verily here,

913 *MS* Defend>Must free   916 *MS* of   919 *MS* quavering,   920
MS you,   922 *MS* uno,—   923 *MS* severe   924 *MS* my limbs are>I
ache   925 *MS* {beginning of fo. 265}   926 *MS* That,   927 *MS*
perch   928 *MS* And,   929 *MS* That   *MS* some exhortation   930
MS whore's tricks   *MS* {no comma}   932 *MS* {New paragraph (already
written thus) indicated by 'N.P.' in left-hand margin}   933 *MS* {no quotation
mark at beginning of line}   *MS* rage and slaughter, threatened her" ... what   *MS*
fire>rage   934 *MS* fallen dread,>verily here

921 *grace*: gift, i.e. readily.

922 *Stans pede in uno*: standing on one foot (L.), i.e. easily, in offhand style; from
Horace, *Satires*, i. iv. 10.

930 *let my brows alone*: referring both to the 'gad-fly' image of ll. 912, 926, and also
to the old belief that a cuckold grows horns, i.e. 'stop cuckolding me'; cf. *Winter's Tale*,
i. ii. 118–19: 'O, that is entertainment / My bosom likes not, nor my brows!'

931 *mulct . . . perfume*: a fine of sweets, a promise of perfume, i.e. trivial penalties and
rewards.

933 *threatenings . . . slaughter*: cf. Acts 9: 1: 'And Saul, yet breathing out threatenings
and slaughter against the disciples of the Lord, went unto the high priest'.

Unhindered by the threatening. See fate's flare   935
Full on each face of the dead guilty three!
Look at them well, and now, lords, look at this!
Tell me: if on that day when I found first
That Caponsacchi thought the nearest way
To his church was some half-mile round by my door,   940
And that he so admired, shall I suppose,
The manner of the swallows' come-and-go
Between the props o' the window over-head,—
That window happening to be my wife's,—
As to stand gazing by the hour on high,   945
Of May-eves, while she sat and let him smile,—
If I,—instead of threatening, talking big,
Showing hair-powder, a prodigious pinch,
For poison in a bottle,—making believe
At desperate doings with a bauble-sword,   950
And other bugaboo-and-baby-work,—
Had, with the vulgarest household implement,
Calmly and quietly cut off, clean thro' bone,
But one joint of one finger of my wife,
Saying "For listening to the serenade,   955
"Here's your ring-finger shorter a full third:
"Be certain I will slice away next joint,
"Next time that anybody underneath
"Seems somehow to be sauntering as he hoped
"A flower would eddy out of your hand to his   960
"While you please fidget with the branch above
"O' the rose-tree in the terrace!"—had I done so,

936 MS Three!   937 MS Lords,   940 MS Church   941 MS concei-
ted,   MS say,   942 MS swallows making nest   943 MS of   945 MS
thereat   946 MS sate   947 MS I, instead   MS threatening,—   951
MS {beginning of fo. 266}   MS With all such bugaboo-and-baby-work,   952
MS —Had,   *953 MS 1868 1872 bone, 1888 1889 bone   954 MS {no
comma}   956–62 MS {no quotation marks at beginnings of lines}   956
MS third,   957 MS the next,   962 MS Of

936 *guilty three*: Pompilia is not actually dead yet, but as good as dead, along with
Pietro and Violante.
951 *bugaboo-and-baby-work*: i.e. pretend threats.

Why, there had followed a quick sharp scream, some pain,
Much calling for plaister, damage to the dress,
A somewhat sulky countenance next day,   965
Perhaps reproaches,—but reflections too!
I don't hear much of harm that Malchus did
After the incident of the ear, my lords!
Saint Peter took the efficacious way;
Malchus was sore but silenced for his life: 970
He did not hang himself i' the Potter's Field
Like Judas, who was trusted with the bag
And treated to sops after he proved a thief.
So, by this time, my true and obedient wife
Might have been telling beads with a gloved hand;   975
Awkward a little at pricking hearts and darts
On sampler possibly, but well otherwise:
Not where Rome shudders now to see her lie.
I give that for the course a wise man takes;
I took the other however, tried the fool's,   980
The lighter remedy, brandished rapier dread
With cork-ball at the tip, boxed Malchus' ear
Instead of severing the cartilage,
Called her a terrible nickname, and the like,

966 *MS* reflection too: 967 *MS* wrong   968 *MS* lords,   969 *MS*
way,   970 *MS* sobered   *MS* life,   971 *MS* in   *MS* field—   972
MS But Judas did,   973 *MS* thief: 974 *MS* {no commas}   975 *MS*
hand   977 *MS* otherwise,   978 *MS* {beginning of fo. 267}   979 *MS*
takes,   980 *MS* tried,>tried   *MS* fool's   984 *MS 1868 1872* like

967–8 *Malchus . . . ear*: St Peter cut off the ear of Malchus, the servant of the high
priest: see John 18:10. In this incident Guido sees implicit sanction for his would-be
cruelty to Pompilia, though in fact Christ instantly reprimanded St Peter for his action.

971–3 *Potter's Field . . . thief*: cf. Matt. 27: 3–8, John 12: 4–6, 13: 26–27. Judas looked
after the disciples' moneybag and shared the sops (dipped bread) at the Last Supper,
even though he is earlier described as thieving from the moneybag.

975 *telling beads*: counting beads, i.e. saying her rosary (as a sign of her new
obedience), and wearing gloves to hide her disfigurement.

976–7 *pricking . . . sampler*: embroidering love emblems on her sewing canvas, i.e.
being reminded of love and flirtation. Pompilia would find such embroidering 'awk-
ward' physically (with a missing finger-joint) and 'awkward' emotionally as a reminder
of her folly.

And there an end: and what was the end of that?   985
What was the good effect o' the gentle course?
Why, one night I went drowsily to bed,
Dropped asleep suddenly, not suddenly woke,
But did wake with rough rousing and loud cry,
To find noon in my face, a crowd in my room,   990
Fumes in my brain, fire in my throat, my wife
Gone God knows whither,—rifled vesture-chest,
And ransacked money-coffer. "What does it mean?"
The servants had been drugged too, stared and yawned
"It must be that our lady has eloped!"   995
—"Whither and with whom?"—"With whom but the
   Canon's self?
"One recognizes Caponsacchi there!"—
(By this time the admiring neighbourhood
Joined chorus round me while I rubbed my eyes)
" 'T is months since their intelligence began,—   1000
"A comedy the town was privy to,—
"He wrote and she wrote, she spoke, he replied,
"And going in and out your house last night
"Was easy work for one . . . to be plain with you . . .
"Accustomed to do both, at dusk and dawn   1005
"When you were absent,—at the villa, you know,
"Where husbandry required the master-mind.
"Did not you know? Why, we all knew, you see!"
And presently, bit by bit, the full and true

986 *MS* of   989 *MS* shaking   *991 *MS 1868 1872* throat *1888 1889*
thoat   994 *MS 1868* yawned,   995 *MS* Lady   996 *MS*
"Whither   *MS* whom?" With   *MS* self,   997 *MS* {no quotation mark at
beginning of line}   *MS* there,—"   1000–8 *MS* {no quotation marks at begin-
nings of lines}   1000 *MS* ago the   *MS* began,   1001 *MS* to,   1004
MS 1868 1872 one . .   1005 *MS* {beginning of fo. 268}   *MS* {no
comma}   1006 *MS* Villa,   *MS* know—

   992 *vesture-chest*: clothes-chest.
   998 *admiring*: wondering, curious.
   1000 *intelligence*: communication, close friendship (with the insinuation of some-
thing more).
   1007 *husbandry*: an ironic pun: Guido has been tending to husbandry (farmwork) at
the Villa, when he should have been exercising greater 'husbandry' (marital surveil-
lance and protection) on his wife.

Particulars of the tale were volunteered   1010
With all the breathless zeal of friendship—"Thus
"Matters were managed: at the seventh hour of night" . . .
—"Later, at daybreak" . . . "Caponsacchi came" . . .
—"While you and all your household slept like death,
"Drugged as your supper was with drowsy stuff" . . .   1015
—"And your own cousin Guillichini too—
"Either or both entered your dwelling-place,
"Plundered it at their pleasure, made prize of all,
"Including your wife . . . "—"Oh, your wife led the way,
"Out of doors, on to the gate . . . "—"But gates are shut,   1020
"In a decent town, to darkness and such deeds:

1011 *MS* With the   *MS* zealousness   1012 *MS* {no quotation mark at beginning of line}   ⋆*1868 1872 1888 1889* night" . . {the line is too long to contain the third point}   1013   *MS* . . "Later,   *MS*   daybreak"— *1868 1872*   daybreak" . .   1014–15 *MS* {lines added later}   1014 *MS* While   *MS* {no comma}   1015   *MS*   {no quotation mark at beginning of line}   *MS* stuff,"   1016 *MS* . . And   *MS* too"—   1018–23 *MS* {no quotation marks at beginnings of lines}   1018 *MS* and prize and all,   1019 *MS* wife",—   *MS* way . . .   1020 *MS* gate."   *MS* shut   1021 *MS* {no comma}

1012–13 *seventh hour . . . daybreak*: these differing statements by the excited neighbours reflect variations in the depositions. In his deposition, Caponsacchi says that 'at the seventh hour [i.e. about 1 a.m.] she came alone to the said gate [San Clemente]': OYB lxxxix (96). This is also the time given in the Sentence of the Criminal Court of Florence: OYB v (5). Pompilia, however, says 'at dawn I went downstairs, where I found Caponsacchi': OYB lxxxv (93).

1013–19 *"Caponsacchi . . . wife*: this passage follows the Sentence of the Criminal Court at Florence, which found that both Caponsacchi and Guillichini had had adulterous relations with Pompilia, and that both had aided in the robbery of Guido's goods: see next n.

1020–9 *gates . . . liberty*: the topography here is again from the Sentence of the Criminal Court of Florence, OYB v (5): 'At about one o'clock the same night, the said Canon Caponsacchi and the first Accused [Guillichini] conducted the aforesaid second Accused [Pompilia] away from the house of the husband. As the gates of the city were closed they climbed the wall of the hill of the Torrione [It. bastion, fortified tower]; and having reached the "Horse" Inn outside of the gate San Clemente, they were there awaited by the third Accused [Francesco, the driver] with a two-horse caleche.'

The Torrione, near the north-west corner of Arezzo, was part of the town walls and just east of the San Clemente gate. The Osteria del Cavallo (the 'Horse Inn') was outside the town walls, and just west of this same gate. As this passage in OYB makes clear, Pompilia climbed over the town walls in the vicinity of the Torrione because she could not go through the San Clemente gate, which was shut at night. Once she

"They climbed the wall—your lady must be lithe—
"At the gap, the broken bit . . . "—"Torrione, true!
"To escape the questioning guard at the proper gate,
"Clemente, where at the inn, hard by, 'the Horse,'   1025
"Just outside, a calash in readiness
"Took the two principals, all alone at last,
"To gate San Spirito, which o'erlooks the road,
"Leads to Perugia, Rome and liberty."
Bit by bit thus made-up mosaic-wise,   1030
Flat lay my fortune,—tesselated floor,
Imperishable tracery devils should foot
And frolic it on, around my broken gods,
Over my desecrated hearth.
                        So much   1035
For the terrible effect of threatening, Sirs!

Well, this way I was shaken wide awake,

1022 *MS* lithe . . .   1023 *MS* gap and the *Yale 1* gap the>gap, the   *MS* bit"—
"Torrione, true," . . . *1868 1872* bit . ."   1024 *MS* gate   1025–9 *MS* {no
quotation marks at beginnings of lines}   1025 *MS* Inn,   *MS* the
Horse,   1026 *MS* the Calash   1028 *MS* the Gate *Yale 1* the gate>
gate   *MS* road   1029 *MS* ;>,   1030 *MS* made up *Yale 1* made up>
made-up   1031 *MS* floor   1032 *MS* place *1868 1872 1888 1889*
tracery   1033 *MS* gods *Yale 1* gods>gods,   1034 *MS* {line added
later}   *MS* desecrate hearth, forever more.   1035–6 {not found in
MS}   1037 *MS* {beginning of fo. 269}   ⋆*MS* {New paragraph indicated by
'N.P.' in left-hand margin} *1868 1872* {new paragraph. Paragraphing obscured in *1888*
and *1889* by this line's being at the head of the page}

---

climbed over the wall she was outside the town; she then passed on the outside of the
San Clemente gate to reach the inn. Here Browning is clear about this topography, but
at VI. 1078–92 he seems to muddle it: Pompilia is expected to climb over the town
walls and then go through the gate, an impossibility. The fullest topographical and
historical reconstruction of the flight—the exact means, route, and distances—is in
Treves, 167–234.
    1026 *calash*: caleche, a light carriage, from It. *calesse*. This is the word used in the
passage from which Browning is here working: see previous n.
    1028 *gate San Spirito*: a gate on the south side of Arezzo. Pompilia and Caponsacchi
have to be driven around the outside of the town to this gate, from whence leads the
road to Perugia and Rome.
    1031 *tesselated*: i.e. made of tesserae, pieces of mosaic. His neighbours' different
pieces of information fit together to make a full, horrible picture of the adultery and
flight.

Doctored and drenched, somewhat unpoisoned so.
Then, set on horseback and bid seek the lost,
I started alone, head of me, heart of me   1040
Fire, and each limb as languid . . . ah, sweet lords,
Bethink you!—poison-torture, try persuade
The next refractory Molinist with that! . . .
Floundered thro' day and night, another day
And yet another night, and so at last,   1045
As Lucifer kept falling to find hell,
Tumbled into the court-yard of an inn
At the end, and fell on whom I thought to find,
Even Caponsacchi,—what part once was priest,
Cast to the winds now with the cassock-rags.   1050
In cape and sword a cavalier confessed,
There stood he chiding dilatory grooms,
Chafing that only horseflesh and no team
Of eagles would supply the last relay,
Whirl him along the league, the one post more   1055
Between the couple and Rome and liberty.
'T was dawn, the couple were rested in a sort,

1038 *MS* drenched and somewhat   *MS 1868 1872* so;   1039 *MS* And,   *MS*
bidden>bid   1040 *MS* Started   *1041 *MS 1868 1872* each *1888 1889*
eaeh   *MS 1868 1872* languid . .   *MS* my>sweet   1042 *MS* you,—   *Yale 1*
persuade,>persuade   1044 *MS* night and another *Yale 1* and another>
another   1047 *MS* Courtyard   *MS* Inn   1048 *MS* And   *MS* him I
found   1049 *MS* was priest of yore   1050 *MS* cassock-rags, *1868 1872*
cassock-rags: 1051 *MS* Cavalier   *MS* confessed   1055 *MS* more,
1057 *1872* T

1038 *drenched*: forcibly given medicine. The word is mainly used of animals: a horse
would be drenched by having its mouth opened and medicine poured down a funnel
or tube; cf. VIII. 350.
1042–3 *poison-torture . . . that!*: the drug Pompilia gave him is a 'poison-torture'
because his head and chest feel on fire, while his limbs feel exhausted (ll. 1040–1).
He wryly suggests to the judges that they use the drug on the next heretic they have to
torture.
1044–6 *Floundered . . . hell*: cf. Isa. 14: 12, and *Paradise Lost*, i. 50–1, vi. 871–6.
Guido's point is that at the end of the chase he discovers 'hell', the adultery of
Caponsacchi and Pompilia, but his phrasing ironically links him with the nine days
of Satan's fall from heaven.
1057 *rested in a sort*: the ironic implication is sexual intercourse, as becomes clearer
in the more overt sarcasm that follows.

And though the lady, tired,—the tenderer sex,—
Still lingered in her chamber,—to adjust
The limp hair, look for any blush astray,— 1060
She would descend in a twinkling,—"Have you out
"The horses therefore!"

           So did I find my wife.
Is the case complete? Do your eyes here see with mine?
Even the parties dared deny no one 1065
Point out of all these points.

                What follows next?
"Why, that then was the time," you interpose,
"Or then or never, while the fact was fresh,
"To take the natural vengeance: there and thus 1070
"They and you,—somebody had stuck a sword
"Beside you while he pushed you on your horse,—
" 'T was requisite to slay the couple, Count!"
Just so my friends say. "Kill!" they cry in a breath,
Who presently, when matters grow to a head 1075
And I do kill the offending ones indeed,—
When crime of theirs, only surmised before,
Is patent, proved indisputably now,—
When remedy for wrong, untried at the time,
Which law professes shall not fail a friend, 1080

1061 *MS* twinkling,—have   1062 *MS* {no quotation mark at beginning of line}   1063 *MS* {no new paragraph}   1065 *MS* {beginning of fo. 270}   1066 *MS* Point ^out^ of ^all^ these   1067 *MS* {no new paragraph}   1068 *MS* interpose   1069 *MS* fresh   1070–3 *MS* {no quotation marks at beginnings of lines}   1073 *MS* {no quotation mark at end of line}   1074 *MS 1868 1872* say—   *MS* "Kill"   1078 *MS* Are patent and proved *Yale 1* patent and>patent,   1080 *MS* Law makes profession

1069–73 *then or never . . . slay the couple*: this is a major point of legal debate in OYB. The prosecution argued that if Guido had killed the couple when he caught them in the flight, this would at least allow him to claim that he acted in the heat of passion, even if he was mistaken, and so avoid the death-penalty. The fact that he only committed the murder after a delay, some considerable time after the supposed discovery of adultery, meant both that his whole accusation was likely to be fabricated and that he did not have the excuse of passion, hence was subject to the death-penalty.

1078 *proved indisputably*: because of the birth of Gaetano, who Guido claims is the child of Pompilia and Caponsacchi.

Is thrice tried now, found threefold worse than null,—
When what might turn to transient shade, who knows?
Solidifies into a blot which breaks
Hell's black off in pale flakes for fear of mine,—
Then, when I claim and take revenge—"So rash?"   1085
They cry—"so little reverence for the law?"

Listen, my masters, and distinguish here!
At first, I called in law to act and help:
Seeing I did so, "Why, 't is clear," they cry,
"You shrank from gallant readiness and risk,   1090
"Were coward: the thing's inexplicable else."
Sweet my lords, let the thing be! I fall flat,
Play the reed, not the oak, to breath of man.
Only, inform my ignorance! Say I stand
Convicted of the having been afraid,   1095
Proved a poltroon, no lion but a lamb,—
Does that deprive me of my right of lamb
And give my fleece and flesh to the first wolf?
Are eunuchs, women, children, shieldless quite
Against attack their own timidity tempts?   1100
Cowardice were misfortune and no crime!

1081 *MS* Are   1082 *MS* knew?   1085 *MS* Now,   *MS* {no quotation mark at end of line}   1087 *MS* {no new paragraph}   1088 *MS* [ ]> I called   *MS* [ ]>and   *MS* help,   1089 *MS* And seeing   *MS* "why   *MS* you>they   1090–1 *MS* {no quotation marks at beginnings of lines}   1090 *MS* I   *MS* the gallant's *Yale 1* the gallant's>gallant   1091 *MS* Was a coward,—   1092 *MS* lords let it be so!   1093 *MS* {beginning of fo. 271} *MS* {no commas}   *MS* the breath of man: *1094 *MS* Only,—inform my ignorance, say *1868 1872* Only, *1888 1889* {no comma}   1097 *MS* the right of a   1099 *MS* women and children   1101 *MS* crime—

1081 *thrice tried now*: cf. ll. 1343, 1347–51 nn.
1082–4 *When . . . mine*: the underlying image is the stain on the aristocratic shield or escutcheon which stands symbolically for a stain or blot upon a person's honour; cf. Browning's play, *A Blot in the 'Scutcheon* (1843). Guido's shield confronts the shield of Hell; so terrible is the stain on his honour caused by Pompilia's proven infidelity that hell's black shield grows pale by comparison.
1093 *Play . . . man*: bend low (like a reed), rather than standing upright (like an oak), in response to this speech; i.e. concede a lot to it, rather than resisting it.
1096 *poltroon*: a spiritless coward.

—Take it that way, since I am fallen so low
I scarce dare brush the fly that blows my face,
And thank the man who simply spits not there,—
Unless the Court be generous, comprehend   1105
How one brought up at the very feet of law
As I, awaits the grave Gamaliel's nod
Ere he clench fist at outrage,—much less, stab!
—How, ready enough to rise at the right time,
I still could recognise no time mature   1110
Unsanctioned by a move o' the judgment-seat,
So, mute in misery, eyed my masters here
Motionless till the authoritative word
Pronounced amercement. There's the riddle solved:
This is just why I slew nor her nor him,   1115
But called in law, law's delegate in the place,
And bade arrest the guilty couple, Sirs!
We had some trouble to do so—you have heard
They braved me,—he with arrogance and scorn,
She, with a volubility of curse,   1120
A conversancy in the skill of tooth
And claw to make suspicion seem absurd,
Nay, an alacrity to put to proof

1102 *MS* Take *MS* way,>way,— 1106 *MS* Law 1107 *MS*
await   1108 *MS* I *MS* stab— 1109 *MS* How,   1110 *MS* I recog-
nized that time as immature>I still could recognize no time immature
{*sic*}   1111 *MS* on judgment-seat,   1112 *MS* And, mute my misery>
And, mute in misery>So, mute in misery *MS* knew>eyed *MS* still,>
here,   1113 *MS* Was [ ] [ ] ^Law's^ authoritative voice>[ ] till Law's authoritative
voice>[ ] Law's authoritative voice>[ ] till Law's authoritative voice>Motionless till
the authoritative word   1114 *MS* Declaring the>Pronounce *MS*
solved!   1116 *MS* Law, her delegates *Yale 1* delegates>delegate   1117 *MS*
couple there.   1120 *MS* {beginning of fo. 272} *MS* She with   1121 *MS*
with>in

1103 *blows*: infects, tries to lay its eggs on.
1107 *grave Gamaliel's nod*: i.e. the wise teacher's assent: cf. Acts 22: 3; Guido
associates himself with St Paul sitting at the feet of his teacher Gamaliel, master of
the Jewish Law.
1114 *amercement*: the appropriate penalty or fine.
1116 *law's delegate*: the district governor or Commissary responsible for Castel-
nuovo: cf. 11. 1022.

At my own throat my own sword, teach me so
To try conclusions better the next time,—　　　　1125
Which did the proper service with the mob.
They never tried to put on mask at all:
Two avowed lovers forcibly torn apart,
Upbraid the tyrant as in a playhouse scene,
Ay, and with proper clapping and applause　　　　1130
From the audience that enjoys the bold and free.
I kept still, said to myself, "There's law!" Anon
We searched the chamber where they passed the night,
Found what confirmed the worst was feared before,
However needless confirmation now—　　　　1135
The witches' circle intact, charms undisturbed
That raised the spirit and succubus,—letters, to-wit,
Love-laden, each the bag o' the bee that bore
Honey from lily and rose to Cupid's hive,—
Now, poetry in some rank blossom-burst,　　　　1140
Now, prose,—"Come here, go there, wait such a while,
"He's at the villa, now he's back again:
"We are saved, we are lost, we are lovers all the same!"
All in order, all complete,—even to a clue
To the drowsiness that happed so opportune—　　　　1145
No mystery, when I read "Of all things, find
"What wine Sir Jealousy decides to drink—

1125 *MS* time.　　1126 {not found in *MS*}　　1127 *MS* all,　　1128 *MS*
lovers,　　1129 *MS* Accusing fate>Uptraiding {*sic*} the husband　　1132 *MS*
Law!"　　1137 *MS* to-wit　　1138 *MS* of　　1139 *MS* hive,　　1140
MS blossom-burst　　1141 *MS* prose,—come　　1142-3 *MS* {no quotation
marks at beginnings of lines}　　1142 *MS* Villa,　　1143 *MS* same—　　1146 *MS*
{no commas}　　1147-9 *MS* {no quotation marks at beginnings of lines}

1125 *try conclusions*: i.e. experiment with a trial of strength.
1136-7 *witches' . . . succubus*: in this image the 'witches' circle' is the love-letters that
raised up or provoked 'the spirit and succubus', the male and female demons respect-
ively (Caponsacchi and Pompilia). Although 'raised' may not be an explicit sexual pun
here, the use of 'raised' and 'spirit' together and the connection between sexuality and
conjuring suggest a memory of *Romeo and Juliet*, II. i. 23-7.
1141-9 *"Come . . . shows."*: a fair parody of the style of the love letters, which
include covert arrangements for assignations, notes of Guido's movements, hints
about red wine—though nothing as overt as the information here—and also references
to Guido as *il Geloso*, 'the Jealous One': see OYB xcii–xcix (99–106).

"Red wine? Because a sleeping-potion, dust
"Dropped into white, discolours wine and shows."

—"Oh, but we did not write a single word!   1150
"Somebody forged the letters in our name!—"
Both in a breath protested presently.
Aha, Sacchetti again!—"Dame,"—quoth the Duke,
"What meaneth this epistle, counsel me,
"I pick from out thy placket and peruse,   1155
"Wherein my page averreth thou art white
"And warm and wonderful 'twixt pap and pap?"
"Sir," laughed the Lady, " 't is a counterfeit!
"Thy page did never stroke but Dian's breast,
"The pretty hound I nurture for thy sake: 1160
"To lie were losel,—by my fay, no more!"
And no more say I too, and spare the Court.

Ah, the Court! yes, I come to the Court's self;
Such the case, so complete in fact and proof,
I laid at the feet of law,—there sat my lords,   1165
Here sit they now, so may they ever sit

1148 *MS* {beginning of fo. 273}   1149 *MS* discolours it   1150 *MS* {no new paragraph}   1151 *MS* {no quotation mark at beginning of line}   1153 *MS* again,—"Dame,—   *MS* spouse,>Duke,   1154 *MS* {no quotation mark at beginning of line}   *MS* this epistle meaneth,   *Yale 1* this epistle meaneth,> meaneth this epistle,   1155 *MS* thus from thy>from out thy   *MS* {no comma}   1156–7 *MS* {no quotation marks at beginnings of lines}   1158 *MS* quoth>laughed   *MS* Lady " 'tis a counterfeit,   *1868* Lady " 't is   1159–60 *MS* {lines added later}   1159 *MS* {no quotation mark at beginning of line}   *MS* {no comma}   1160 *MS* {no quotation mark at beginning of line}   *MS* thou didst bestow me with:>I nurture for thy sake: 1161 *MS* {no quotation mark at beginning of line}   *MS* The lie of a>Some lie of   1162 *MS* Enough, I spare the gravity of the Court:>And no more say I too—and spare the Court: 1163 *MS* {no new paragraph}   *MS* Yes,   1164 *MS* proof   1165 *MS* Law,—   *MS* Lords,   1166 *MS* sat>sit   *MS* then, here>now, so

1152 *presently*: at once, immediately.

1153 *Sacchetti again*: cf. ll. 559–60 n. What follows is a parody of Sacchetti, not an actual quotation from his work.

1155 *placket*: a pocket in a woman's skirt or petticoat, possibly with sexual innuendo; cf. *King Lear*, III. iv. 96–7.

1161 *losel*: disreputable, worthless.
   fay: faith.

In easier attitude than suits my haunch!
In this same chamber did I bare my sores
O' the soul and not the body,—shun no shame,
Shrink from no probing of the ulcerous part,   1170
Since confident in Nature,—which is God,—
That she who, for wise ends, concocts a plague,
Curbs, at the right time, the plague's virulence too:
Law renovates even Lazarus,—cures me!
Cæsar thou seekest? To Cæsar thou shalt go!   1175
Cæsar's at Rome: to Rome accordingly!

The case was soon decided: both weights, cast
I' the balance, vibrate, neither kicks the beam,
Here away, there away, this now and now that.
To every one o' my grievances law gave   1180
Redress, could purblind eye but see the point.
The wife stood a convicted runagate
From house and husband,—driven to such a course
By what she somehow took for cruelty,
Oppression and imperilment of life—   1185
Not that such things were, but that so they seemed:
Therefore, the end conceded lawful, (since
To save life there's no risk should stay our leap)

1168 *MS* strip, bare ^my^ sores,   1170 *MS* {no comma}   1172 *MS* pla-
gue   1173 *MS* [ ],>Curbs,   *MS* curb the virulence>the plague's viru-
lence   1176 *MS 1868* Rome;   1177 *MS* {beginning of fo. 274}   *MS*
{New paragraph indicated by 'N.P.' in left-hand margin}   *MS* sides>
weights,   1178 *MS* In   *MS* balance vibrate   *Yale 1*   balance>ba-
lance,   1180 *MS* of   *MS* Law   1181 *MS* same.   *Yale 1* same.>print.
{*sic*}   1182 *MS* My>The   *MS* runaway>runagate   1184 *MS* By mine

---

1167 *haunch*: hip-joint.
1170 *Shrink . . . part*: cf. *Hamlet*, III. iv. 147–9.
1174 *renovates even Lazarus*: i.e. restores the dead to life. Browning here conflates the
Lazarus raised from the dead by Christ in John 11 with the sore-covered beggar in the
parable of Lazarus and Dives in Luke 16. In the nineteenth century 'Lazarus' was still
occasionally used as a generic name for a leper or mèndicant. In Guido's evolving image
Law has been substituted for 'Nature—which is God', since it too is powerfully restoring.
1175 *Cæsar . . . go!*: cf. Acts 25: 12; Guido again casts himself as St Paul: cf. l. 1107 n.
1181 *purblind*: cf. l. 565 n. Guido is ironic here and in the following passage at what
he takes to be Law's leniency. Justice is traditionally portrayed as blindfolded.
1182 *runagate*: runaway, deserter.

It follows that all means to the lawful end
Are lawful likewise,—poison, theft and flight.   1190
As for the priest's part, did he meddle or make,
Enough that he too thought life jeopardized;
Concede him then the colour charity
Casts on a doubtful course,—if blackish white
Or whitish black, will charity hesitate?   1195
What did he else but act the precept out,
Leave, like a provident shepherd, his safe flock
To follow the single lamb and strayaway?
Best hope so and think so,—that the ticklish time
I' the carriage, the tempting privacy, the last   1200
Somewhat ambiguous accident at the inn,
—All may bear explanation: may? then, must!
The letters,—do they so incriminate?
But what if the whole prove a prank o' the pen,
Flight of the fancy, none of theirs at all,   1205
Bred of the vapours of my brain belike,
Or at worst mere exercise of scholar's-wit
In the courtly Caponsacchi: verse, convict?
Did not Catullus write less seemly once?
Yet *doctus* and unblemished he abides.   1210
Wherefore so ready to infer the worst?
Still, I did righteously in bringing doubts
For the law to solve,—take the solution now!
"Seeing that the said associates, wife and priest,

1191 *MS* Priest's   1192 *MS* jeopardised, *1868* jeopardised;   1199 *MS*
think>hope   *MS* so, and that   1200 *MS* In   1201 *MS* [ ]>
incident   1204 *MS* {beginning of fo. 275}   *MS* of   1206 *MS*
your   1207 *MS* scholar's wit *Yale 1* scholar's wit>scholar's-wit   1208 *MS*
forsooth?   1210 *MS* doctus   1213 *MS* now.   1214–25 *MS* {no quo-
tation marks at beginnings of lines} *Yale 1* {quotation marks added at beginnings of
lines}

1191 *meddle or make*: cf. l. 244 n.
1197–8 *provident . . . strayaway*: cf. Matt. 18: 12–13; Luke 15: 3–7.
1199 *ticklish*: potentially compromising, hazardous.
1209–10 *Catullus . . . doctus*: the great Latin poet Catullus (*c*.84–*c*.54 BC) wrote
poetry which is often sensual or obscene, but he is still considered *doctus* (L. 'learned,
skilled'); cf. VI. 387–8 n.

"Bear themselves not without some touch of blame   1215
"—Else why the pother, scandal and outcry
"Which trouble our peace and require chastisement?
"We, for complicity in Pompilia's flight
"And deviation, and carnal intercourse
"With the same, do set aside and relegate   1220
"The Canon Caponsacchi for three years
"At Civita in the neighbourhood of Rome:
"And we consign Pompilia to the care
"Of a certain Sisterhood of penitents
"I' the city's self, expert to deal with such."   1225
Word for word, there's your judgment! Read it, lords,
Re-utter your deliberate penalty
For the crime yourselves establish! Your award—
Who chop a man's right-hand off at the wrist
For tracing with forefinger words in wine   1230
O' the table of a drinking-booth that bear
Interpretation as they mocked the Church!
—Who brand a woman black between the breasts
For sinning by connection with a Jew:
While for the Jew's self—pudency be dumb!   1235
You mete out punishment such and such, yet so
Punish the adultery of wife and priest!
Take note of that, before the Molinists do,

1215 *MS* without touch   1217 *MS* the peace   1224 *MS* sisterhood *Yale 1*
sisterhood>Sisterhood   1225 *MS* In   *MS* {no quotation mark at end of line}
Yale 1 {quotation mark added at end of line}   1226 *MS* Lords,   1229 *MS*
right hand   1231 *MS* {beginning of fo. 276}   *MS* On   *MS* drinking
booth   1233 *MS* Who   1234 *MS* Jew,   1235 *MS* self,—   *MS* is
dumb. *Yale 1* is dumb.>be dumb!   1237 *MS* priest.

1218–25: *"We . . . such."*: the first five lines here are a translation of the court's
'Decree of banishment of the lover', issued 24 Sept. 1697: 'Ioseph Maria Caponsac-
chius de Aretio pro complicitate in fuga, & deuiatione Franciscæ Comparinæ, &
cognitione carnali eiusdem relegatus per triennium in Ciuitate Vetula': OYB xcix
(106). 'Deviation', taken from the Latin here, means in effect 'perversion', 'leading
astray', i.e. seduction. Lines 1223–5 are Guido's addition: Pompilia was not formally
sentenced, but remanded to the convent pending further investigations.
1234 *connection*: i.e. sexual intercourse.
1235 *pudency*: modesty; the punishment implied for the Jew is castration.

And read me right the riddle, since right must be!

While I stood rapt away with wonderment,   1240
Voices broke in upon my mood and muse.
"Do you sleep?" began the friends at either ear,
"The case is settled,—you willed it should be so—
"None of our counsel, always recollect!
"With law's award, budge! Back into your place!   1245
"Your betters shall arrange the rest for you.
"We'll enter a new action, claim divorce:
"Your marriage was a cheat themselves allow:
"You erred i' the person,—might have married thus
"Your sister or your daughter unaware.   1250
"We'll gain you, that way, liberty at least,
"Sure of so much by law's own showing. Up
"And off with you and your unluckiness—
"Leave us to bury the blunder, sweep things smooth!"
I was in humble frame of mind, be sure!   1255
I bowed, betook me to my place again.
Station by station I retraced the road,
Touched at this hostel, passed this post-house by,
Where, fresh-remembered yet, the fugitives
Had risen to the heroic stature: still—   1260
"That was the bench they sat on,—there's the board

1239 MS And counsel me the cause, since cause must be!   *1240 MS {New
paragraph (already written thus) indicated by 'N.P.' in left-hand margin.
Paragraphing obscured in 1868 and 1872 by this line's being at the head of
the page} 1888 1889 {no new paragraph}   MS awhile with thoughts like
these,>away with wonderment,   1241 MS muse,   1242 MS hear?"   MS
{no comma}   1244–54 MS {no quotation marks at beginnings of lines}
1245 MS [ ]>With   MS award! Budge!>award, budge!   MS Back, Sir,
to   1249 MS in   MS so   1250 MS unaware: Yale 1 unaware:>un-
aware.   1251 MS {no commas}   1252 MS showing,—so, up Yale 1 show-
ing,—up>showing. Up   1254 MS hide>bury   MS [ ]>blunder   MS and
sweep   1255 MS mind by this—   1256 MS ⟨left⟩ betook   MS again,
Yale 1 again:>again.   1257 MS {beginning of fo. 277}   1260 MS stature,
still in mind

1245 budge!: move!

"They took the meal at,—yonder garden-ground
"They leaned across the gate of,"—ever a word
O' the Helen and the Paris, with "Ha! you're he,
"The . . . much-commiserated husband?" Step   1265
By step, across the pelting, did I reach
Arezzo, underwent the archway's grin,
Traversed the length of sarcasm in the street,
Found myself in my horrible house once more,
And after a colloquy . . . no word assists!   1270
With the mother and the brothers, stiffened me
Straight out from head to foot as dead man does,
And, thus prepared for life as he for hell,
Marched to the public Square and met the world.
Apologize for the pincers, palliate screws?   1275
Ply me with such toy-trifles, I entreat!
Trust who has tried both sulphur and sops-in-wine!

[—]

1262–3 *MS* {no quotation marks at beginnings of lines}   1262 *MS* at, yonder
Yale 1 at,>at,—   1263 *MS* off>of   *MS* {no quotation mark following
'of'}   1264 *MS* Of   *MS* "Ha,—you're he,   1265 *MS* The . .   *MS*
husband?"—step   1270 *MS* And a colloquy . . *1868 1872* colloquy . .   *MS* as-
sists . .   1271 *MS* Mother   *MS* Brothers,   1272 *MS 1868 1872*
Strait   *MS* as a dead   1273 *MS* And then   *MS* hell, . . what would you
have?   1274 *MS* square *Yale 1* square>Square   1275 *MS* Apologise   1276
MS Put away such>Ply me with your>Ply me with such *Yale 1* Play>Ply   1277 *MS*
both. Pray you, a sop of wine!>both—sulphur and sops in wine!

1264 *the Helen and the Paris*: the great lovers of Greek legend; Guido is continuing
his image of how Pompilia and Caponsacchi have 'risen to the heroic stature' (1260).
In the next line the speaker just manages not to say 'cuckold', substituting the
euphemistic 'much-commiserated husband'; cf. II. 1003 n.

1266 *pelting*: hail of insults; a slightly unusual use as a verbal noun.

1267 *underwent . . . grin*: even the shape of the archway seems to him to represent an
amused or sarcastic smile.

1270 *colloquy . . .*: conversation. By the ellipsis Guido implies how terrible it was to
have to tell his family all that had happened.

1271 *stiffened me*: a play on the rigor mortis suffered by a dead man, and the sense of
'stiffen' meaning 'to fill with resolve'.

1275 *palliate screws?*: [do you need to] excuse the torture screws? Again, Guido
implies that the physical torture he has suffered at the hands of the court is as nothing to
the mental torture caused by his stained honour: cf. ll. 65–6 n.

1277 *both . . . sops-in-wine*: i.e. extremes of pain and pleasure, symbolized by ex-
tremes of taste. Foul-tasting sulphur has been used as an ingredient in medicines since
medieval times, whereas sops-in-wine, i.e. small pieces of bread dipped in wine, is a
delicacy enjoyed by the epicurean Franklin in the *Canterbury Tales*: see 'General
Prologue', l. 332. This line gave Browning some trouble: see *MS*.

I played the man as I best might, bade friends
Put non-essentials by and face the fact.
"What need to hang myself as you advise?   1280
"The paramour is banished,—the ocean's width,
"Or the suburb's length,—to Ultima Thule, say,
"Or Proxima Civitas, what's the odds of name
"And place? He's banished, and the fact's the thing.
"Why should law banish innocence an inch?   1285
"Here's guilt then, what else do I care to know?
"The adulteress lies imprisoned,—whether in a well
"With bricks above and a snake for company,
"Or tied by a garter to a bed-post,—much
"I mind what's little,—least's enough and to spare!   1290
"The little fillip on the coward's cheek
"Serves as though crab-tree cudgel broke his pate.
"Law has pronounced there's punishment, less or more:
"And I take note o' the fact and use it thus—
"For the first flaw in the original bond,   1295
"I claim release. My contract was to wed
"The daughter of Pietro and Violante. Both
"Protest they never had a child at all.
"Then I have never made a contract: good!

1281–1306 MS {no quotation marks at beginnings of lines}   1281 MS ban-
ished,—banished   1283 MS {beginning of fo. 278}   MS the name>name
1290 MS little when least's   MS spare.   1293 MS punishment less or more,
1294 MS of   1295 MS {no comma}

1282–3 *Ultima Thule . . . Proxima Civitas*: i.e. to a far-away island or the nearest
town. 'Ultima Thule' (Virgil, *Georgics*, 1. 30) was for the ancients the proverbial
'ends of the earth', a notoriously distant place; Pliny set it six days north of Britain.
'Proxima Civitas' is also a play on 'Civitavecchia', the real location of Caponsacchi's
relegation from Rome.

1287–9 *whether . . . bed-post*: this contrast is between the sadistic and the erotic. The
first kind of imprisonment is similar to that inflicted by the sadistic Count Cenci on his
daughter: 'I thought I was that wretched Beatrice / Men speak of, whom her father
sometimes . . . pens up naked in damp cells / Where scaly reptiles crawl': Shelley, *The
Cenci*, III. i. 43–7. Cf. 'tied by a garter to a bed-post' with Guido's earlier sexual fantasy
at ll. 685–92.

1291 *fillip*: tap.

1292 *crab-tree cudgel*: a club or thick stick (used as a weapon), made of the hard wood
of the crab-apple tree.

"Cancel me quick the thing pretended one.   1300
"I shall be free. What matter if hurried over
"The harbour-boom by a great favouring tide,
"Or the last of a spent ripple that lifts and leaves?
"The Abate is about it. Laugh who wins!
"You shall not laugh me out of faith in law!   1305
"I listen, through all your noise, to Rome!"

                                                       Rome spoke.

In three months letters thence admonished me,
"Your plan for the divorce is all mistake.
"It would hold, now, had you, taking thought to wed   1310
"Rachel of the blue eye and golden hair,
"Found swarth-skinned Leah cumber couch next day:
"But Rachel, blue-eyed golden-haired aright,
"Proving to be only Laban's child, not Lot's,
"Remains yours all the same for ever more.   1315
"No whit to the purpose is your plea: you err
"I' the person and the quality—nowise
"In the individual,—that's the case in point!
"You go to the ground,—are met by a cross-suit
"For separation, of the Rachel here,   1320

1302 *MS* {no comma}   1303 *MS* lifts me   1305 *MS* Law!   1306 *MS*
{no commas}   *MS* {no quotation mark at end of line}   1308 *MS* brother
Paul>letters   thence   1309   *MS*   mistake—   *Yale*   1   mistake—>mistake.
1310–73   *MS* {no quotation marks at beginnings of lines}   1310 *MS* {beginning
of fo. 279}   1311 *MS* {no comma}   1314 *MS* Proved ^to be^   1315
MS and forever   1316 *MS* no fault>you err   1317 *MS* In   1320 *MS*
{no commas}   *MS* your injured wife>the Rachel here

   1304   *Abate*: i.e. the Abate Paolo. Abate is an honorary religious title, not literally an
abbot; cf. 1. 553 n.
   Laugh who wins!: proverbial: another version is 'He laughs best who laughs last':
ODEP, 445.
   1311–18   *Rachel . . . point*: i.e. 'you married the correct individual, even if she had a
different ancestry'. If Guido were like Jacob in Gen. 29: 16–28, married by deception
to Leah when he had intended to marry Rachel, then he would have grounds for
divorce, but he is not in this situation. Cf. the argument of the lawyer Arcangeli:
'[Guido] had put off [revenge] as long as he had any hope that he might have the
marriage annulled because of a mistake concerning the person married. For he was
ignorant of the provision of Canon Law that error as to the quality [*qualitas*] of the
person contracted does not render a marriage invalid, but only an error as to the

"From bed and board,—she is the injured one,
"You did the wrong and have to answer it.
"As for the circumstance of imprisonment
"And colour it lends to this your new attack,
"Never fear, that point is considered too!   1325
"The durance is already at an end;
"The convent-quiet preyed upon her health,
"She is transferred now to her parents' house
"—No-parents, when that cheats and plunders you,
"But parentage again confessed in full,   1330
"When such confession pricks and plagues you more—
"As now—for, this their house is not the house
"In Via Vittoria wherein neighbours' watch
"Might incommode the freedom of your wife,
"But a certain villa smothered up in vines   1335
"At the town's edge by the gate i' the Pauline Way,
"Out of eye-reach, out of ear-shot, little and lone,
"Whither a friend,—at Civita, we hope,
"A good half-dozen-hours' ride off,—might, some eve,
"Betake himself, and whence ride back, some morn,   1340
"Nobody the wiser: but be that as it may,
"Do not afflict your brains with trifles now.

1324 *MS* the colour *Yale 1* the colour>colour   1325 *MS* too.   1327 *MS*
Convent-quiet   1329 *MS* plagues>cheats   1330 *MS* parentage back again
and two times more   1332 *MS* {no comma}   1333 *MS* eye >watch   1335
MS little Villa,>Villa,   1336 *MS* Gate in   *MS* way,   1337 *MS* {begin-
ning of fo. 280}   1338 *MS* Civita we hope   1339 *MS* And a good six
hours' ride distant . . >A good half-dozen hours' ride off,— *Yale 1* half-dozen hours'
>half-dozen-hours'   1340 *MS* ^and^   *MS* [ ] away,>back,   1341 *MS*
And nobody>Nobody   *MS* the wiser:>wiser:>the wiser:

---

individual': OYB cxv (124). Laban, the father of Leah and Rachel, was Abraham's
great-nephew and a 'Syrian', i.e. an Aramaean; Lot, Abraham's nephew, was a gen-
eration higher, hence Browning can represent Guido imagining the Court implying
that he supposed Lot's daughter the better catch. But as everyone else knew, Lot's
daughters slept with their father and became the ancestresses of peoples hostile to the
Hebrews, namely the Moabites and Ammonites. Guido has not read his Bible very
well.

1326 *durance*: imprisonment.
1332–6 *their house . . . Pauline Way*: cf. II. 203 n.

"You have still three suits to manage, all and each
"Ruinous truly should the event play false.
"It is indeed the likelier so to do,   1345
"That brother Paul, your single prop and stay,
"After a vain attempt to bring the Pope
"To set aside procedures, sit himself
"And summarily use prerogative,
"Afford us the infallible finger's tact   1350
"To disentwine your tangle of affairs,
"Paul,—finding it moreover past his strength
"To stem the irruption, bear Rome's ridicule
"Of... since friends must speak ... to be round with you ...
"Of the old outwitted husband, wronged and wroth,
"Pitted against a brace of juveniles—   1356
"A brisk priest who is versed in Ovid's art
"More than his Summa, and a gamesome wife
"Able to act Corinna without book,
"Beside the waggish parents who played dupes   1360

1343 MS ^still^   1344 MS be wrong.>so prove.>play false.   1353
MS irruption of Rome's   1354 MS 1868 speak..   MS 1868 1872 you..
1355 MS husband wronged   1356 MS juveniles   1357 MS has studied >is
versed in   1358 MS A-Kempis,>his Summa,   MS spritely> gamesome

1343 three suits: Browning makes three lawsuits out of the perhaps more numerous
cases mentioned in OYB: see next n.

1347–51 vain ... affairs: cf. OYB cxlvii (150): 'And it is certain that the Abate,
seeing the cause unduly protracted, had just grounds for placing it at the feet of our
Lord [the Pope], with a memorial in which he declared that he could no longer endure
such important and such various litigation and vexation arising from that luckless
marriage, and he prayed that a special sitting [una particolare Congregazione] be appointed
for all the cases—that is the ones concerning her daughtership, her flight, her adultery,
the dowry, and others growing out of the marriage as well as the one concerning its
annulling. But he had no other reply than: "The matter rests with his Judges".'

1357 brisk: vivacious, sprightly.

Ovid's art: i.e. in Ovid's love poetry, with a partial pun on Ars Amatoria ('The Art of
Love'), the famous poem that is a mock text-book of the art of seduction.

1358 Summa: the Summa Theologica of St Thomas Aquinas (1225–74), a massive and
subtle work of philosophy and theology, was a standard text for all Roman Catholic
religious. Cf. VI. 484 n.

1359 act Corinna: i.e. play the part of a sensual mistress. Corinna is Ovid's imagined
mistress in the Amores, I. v, xi, II. vi, etc.

"To dupe the duper—(and truly divers scenes
"Of the Arezzo palace, tickle rib
"And tease eye till the tears come, so we laugh;
"Nor wants the shock at the inn its comic force,
"And then the letters and poetry—*merum sal!*)   1365
"—Paul, finally, in such a state of things,
"After a brief temptation to go jump
"And join the fishes in the Tiber, drowns
"Sorrow another and a wiser way:
"House and goods, he has sold all off, is gone,   1370
"Leaves Rome,—whether for France or Spain, who knows?
"Or Britain almost divided from our orb.
"You have lost him anyhow."
                                 Now,—I see my lords
Shift in their seat,—would I could do the same!   1375
They probably please expect my bile was moved
To purpose, nor much blame me: now, they judge,
The fiery titillation urged my flesh
Break through the bonds. By your pardon, no, sweet Sirs!
I got such missives in the public place;   1380
When I sought home,—with such news, mounted stair
And sat at last in the sombre gallery,
('T was Autumn, the old mother in bed betimes,
Having to bear that cold, the finer frame
Of her daughter-in-law had found intolerable—   1385

1362 *MS* Palace   1363 *MS* teaze the eye>teaze eye *1868 1872* teaze   *MS*
laugh— *Yale 1* laugh—>laugh;   1364 *MS* {beginning of fo. 281}   1365
MS poetry,—   1366 *MS* Paul finally,   1370 *MS* [ ]>off,   1376 *MS*
And>They   *MS* to expect   *MS* [ ]>moved   1377 *MS* purpose nor   *MS*
without reason:>much blame me   *MS* you conceive,>they judge,   1378 *MS*
The titillation   *MS* flesh break the bounds.   *MS* [ ]>flesh   1379 *MS* By your
pardon, no, lords! Nowise moved my bile.   1382 *MS* room alone   1383
MS autumn,>Autumn,   1384 *MS* {no comma}

1365 *merum sal!*: 'pure salt!' (L.), i.e. 'best joke of all!' The phrase is from Lucretius,
De Rerum Natura, IV. 1162: *parvula pumilio, chariton mia, tota merum sal*: 'if she's tiny,
she's one of the Graces, and completely brilliant'.
1372 *Britain . . . orb*: cf. Virgil, *Eclogue* i. 66: *penitus toto diuisos orbe Britannos*.
1376 *bile*: anger.
1378 *titillation*: annoyance, irritation.

The brother, walking misery away
O' the mountain-side with dog and gun belike)
As I supped, ate the coarse bread, drank the wine
Weak once, now acrid with the toad's-head-squeeze,
My wife's bestowment,—I broke silence thus: 1390
"Let me, a man, manfully meet the fact,
"Confront the worst o' the truth, end, and have peace!
"I am irremediably beaten here,—
"The gross illiterate vulgar couple,—bah!
"Why, they have measured forces, mastered mine,   1395
"Made me their spoil and prey from first to last.
"They have got my name,—'t is nailed now fast to theirs,
"The child or changeling is anyway my wife;
"Point by point as they plan they execute,
"They gain all, and I lose all—even to the lure   1400
"That led to loss,—they have the wealth again
"They hazarded awhile to hook me with,
"Have caught the fish and find the bait entire:
"They even have their child or changeling back
"To trade with, turn to account a second time.   1405
"The brother presumably might tell a tale
"Or give a warning,—he, too, flies the field,
"And with him vanish help and hope of help.
"They have caught me in the cavern where I fell,
"Covered my loudest cry for human aid   1410
"With this enormous paving-stone of shame.
"Well, are we demigods or merely clay?
"Is success still attendant on desert?
"Is this, we live on, heaven and the final state,

1387 *MS* On   1388 *MS* drank the weak wine>and drank the wine   1389
MS toad's-head-squeeze   1390 *MS* wedded wife's>wife's   *MS* I ⟨began—⟩I
broke silence thus: 1391 *MS* {beginning of fo. 282}   1392–1433 *MS* {no
quotation marks at beginnings of lines}   1393 *MS* of   1395 *MS* force
and   1397 *MS* gained>got   1398 *MS* Their>The   *MS* [ ]>change-
ling   *MS* wife,   1406 *MS* *1868* *1872* brother,   1407 *MS* too flies
1409 *MS* pitfall   *MS* lie,   1414 *MS* {no commas}   *MS* Heaven   *MS*
happy state

1389 *toad's-head-squeeze*: bitter poison (fig.); cf. II. 1377 n.

"Or earth which means probation to the end?   1415
"Why claim escape from man's predestined lot
"Of being beaten and baffled?—God's decree,
"In which I, bowing bruised head, acquiesce.
"One of us Franceschini fell long since
"I' the Holy Land, betrayed, tradition runs,   1420
"To Paynims by the feigning of a girl
"He rushed to free from ravisher, and found
"Lay safe enough with friends in ambuscade
"Who flayed him while she clapped her hands and laughed:
"Let me end, falling by a like device.   1425
"It will not be so hard. I am the last
"O' my line which will not suffer any more.
"I have attained to my full fifty years,
"(About the average of us all, 't is said,
"Though it seems longer to the unlucky man)   1430
"—Lived through my share of life; let all end here,
"Me and the house and grief and shame at once.
"Friends my informants,—I can bear your blow!"
And I believe 't was in no unmeet match
For the stoic's mood, with something like a smile,   1435
That, when morose December roused me next,
I took into my hand, broke seal to read
The new epistle from Rome. "All to no use!
"Whate'er the turn next injury take," smiled I,
"Here's one has chosen his part and knows his cue.   1440

1416 *MS* exc>escape   1418 *MS* {beginning of fo. 283}   *MS* a
bruised   1420 *MS* In   *MS* so runs the tale,   1423 *MS* Was   1425
MS {no comma} *Yale 1* end>end,   1427 *MS* Of *MS* race *Yale 1* race
>line   1429 *MS* About   *MS* said;   1430 *MS* man,   1431 *MS*
Lived   1432 *MS* my>the   *MS* the grief   1439–66 *MS* {no quotation
marks at beginnings of lines}   1439 *MS* Whatever   *MS* this injury   *MS*
{no commas}   1440 *MS* I have my>There's one has chosen his   *MS* know
my>knows his

1419–20 *long . . . Holy Land*: i.e. during the times of the crusades. The anecdote here
in invented by Browning. By it Guido intends to show how honourable his family has
been from the first, and, as a consequence of this, how vulnerable to cunning and
malevolence.

1421 *Paynims*: an archaic term for Muslims or Saracens; cf. VII. 1391.

"I am done with, dead now; strike away, good friends!
"Are the three suits decided in a trice?
"Against me,—there's no question! How does it go?
"Is the parentage of my wife demonstrated
"Infamous to her wish? Parades she now   1445
"Loosed of the cincture that so irked the loin?
"Is the last penny extracted from my purse
"To mulct me for demanding the first pound
"Was promised in return for value paid?
"Has the priest, with nobody to court beside,   1450
"Courted the Muse in exile, hitched my hap
"Into a rattling ballad-rhyme which, bawled
"At tavern-doors, wakes rapture everywhere,
"And helps cheap wine down throat this Christmas time,
"Beating the bagpipes? Any or all of these!   1455
"As well, good friends, you cursed my palace here
"To its old cold stone face,—stuck your cap for crest
"Over the shield that's extant in the Square,—

1443 *MS* question: how   1445 *MS* {beginning of fo. 284}   1448 *MS*
pay>mulct me   1450 *MS* Priest,   1451 *MS* at Civi>in exile,   1452
MS {no comma}   1453 *MS* Tavern-doors   *MS* {no comma}   *MS* every
where   1455 *MS* these,   1456 *MS* here,>here   1458 *MS*
household-coat>shield   *MS* that>that's   *MS* shown you>extant   *MS* square,—

  1446 *Loosed . . . loin*: i.e. freed of the last vestige of modesty, her lust on open display.
  1448 *mulct*: punish, fine.
  1451 *hap*: story.
  1455 *Beating the bagpipes?*: i.e more popular than the bagpipes. This is another detail
based on Browning's memory of contemporary Rome, in this case the Abruzzese
peasants who made a yearly Christmas pilgrimage to the city with their bagpipes to
worship the Madonna and Child and entertain the people: 'Their song is called a
novena, from its being sung for nine consecutive days,—first, for nine days previous to
the Festa of the Madonna, which occurs on the 8th of December, and afterwards for
the nine days preceding Christmas. . . The *pifferari* [pipers] always go in couples, one
playing on the *zampogna*, or bagpipe, the bass and treble accompaniment, and the other
on the *piffero*, or pastoral pipe, which carries the air; and for the month before
Christmas the sound of their instruments resounds through the streets of Rome,
wherever there is a shrine,—whether at the corners of the streets, in the depths of
the shops, down little lanes, in the centre of the Corso, in the interior courts of the
palaces, or on the stairways of private houses': *Roba di Roma*, i. 9. Story goes on to give
the full music and words for the novena.

"Or spat on the statue's cheek, the impatient world
"Sees cumber tomb-top in our family church: 1460
"Let him creep under covert as I shall do,
"Half below-ground already indeed. Good-bye!
"My brothers are priests, and childless so; that's well—
"And, thank God most for this, no child leave I—
"None after me to bear till his heart break   1465
"The being a Franceschini and my son!"

"Nay," said the letter, "but you have just that!
"A babe, your veritable son and heir—
"Lawful,—'t is only eight months since your wife
"Left you,—so, son and heir, your babe was born   1470
"Last Wednesday in the villa,—you see the cause
"For quitting Convent without beat of drum,
"Stealing a hurried march to this retreat
"That's not so savage as the Sisterhood
"To slips and stumbles: Pietro's heart is soft,   1475
"Violante leans to pity's side,—the pair
"Ushered you into life a bouncing boy:
"And he's already hidden away and safe
"From any claim on him you mean to make—
"They need him for themselves,—don't fear, they know
"The use o' the bantling,—the nerve thus laid bare   1481

1459 *MS* that, after age>age after age   1462 *MS* below ground   1464 *MS*
have>leave   *MS* I—">I—   1467 *MS* {no commas}   *MS* do have
1468–82 *MS* {no quotation marks at beginnings of lines}   1468 *MS* A son and
heir>A babe, your veritable   1471 *MS* {beginning of fo. 285}   *MS*
Villa,—   1472 *MS* {no comma}   1476 *MS* ;>,—   1481 *MS*
of   *MS* and>the

1459 *impatient*: i.e. disinterested, busy about other matters. In this image, the world
cares nothing about the honour and history of the Franceschini family as represented in
its tomb monuments—another image laden with pathos.

1461 *him*: i.e. the statue of l. 1459.

1469 *Lawful*: i.e. legitimate, not a bastard.

1471 *Last Wednesday*: Browning knew that Gaetano was born on 18 Dec. 1697
from OYB clxxxiv (189). From his own autograph chronology it was easy for him to
calculate that this was a Wednesday: see our Vol. VII, pp. 322–3.

1481 *bantling*: bastard, brat.

"To nip at, new and nice, with finger-nail!"

Then I rose up like fire, and fire-like roared.
What, all is only beginning not ending now?
The worm which wormed its way from skin through flesh
To the bone and there lay biting, did its best,—   1486
What, it goes on to scrape at the bone's self,
Will wind to inmost marrow and madden me?
There's to be yet my representative,
Another of the name shall keep displayed   1490
The flag with the ordure on it, brandish still
The broken sword has served to stir a jakes?
Who will he be, how will you call the man?
A Franceschini,—when who cut my purse,
Filched my name, hemmed me round, hustled me hard   1495
As rogues at a fair some fool they strip i' the midst,
When these count gains, vaunt pillage presently:—
But a Caponsacchi, oh, be very sure!
When what demands its tribute of applause
Is the cunning and impudence o' the pair of cheats,   1500
The lies and lust o' the mother, and the brave
Bold carriage of the priest, worthily crowned
By a witness to his feat i' the following age,—
And how this three-fold cord could hook and fetch

1483 MS roared—   1484 MS "What,   1485 MS snak>worm   1486 MS
1868 1872 best,   1487 MS self   1488 MS its way to the marrow>to the
inmost marrow Yale 1 the inmost>inmost   1490 MS my>the   1492 MS
bolt   1493 MS man?>man—   1494 MS Franceschini,   1495 MS fame>
name   MS and hustled>hustled   MS [ ]>me   1496 MS in   MS {no
comma}   1497 MS {beginning of fo. 286}   MS presently: 1498 MS oh
be very sure,   1500 MS the impudence> impudence   MS of   1501 MS
And >The lies and   MS of   1503 MS in Yale 1 in>i'

1492 jakes: cesspit, privy.
1500 pair of cheats: Pompilia and Caponsacchi, as explained in the next lines.
1502 carriage: bearing, mien.
1503 witness: i.e. the child Gaetano, here assumed to be Caponsacchi's son.
1504 three-fold cord: cf. Eccles. 4: 12: 'a threefold cord [i.e. comprised of three
people] is not quickly broken'. From the previous lines, the three people are Pompilia,
Caponsacchi, and Gaetano.
1504–5 could . . . pride: i.e. could do the impossible, hook up the huge leviathan

And land leviathan that king of pride!   1505
Or say, by some mad miracle of chance,
Is he indeed my flesh and blood, this babe?
Was it because fate forged a link at last
Betwixt my wife and me, and both alike
Found we had henceforth some one thing to love,   1510
Was it when she could damn my soul indeed
She unlatched door, let all the devils o' the dark
Dance in on me to cover her escape?
Why then, the surplusage of disgrace, the spilth
Over and above the measure of infamy,   1515
Failing to take effect on my coarse flesh
Seasoned with scorn now, saturate with shame,—
Is saved to instil on and corrode the brow,
The baby-softness of my first-born child—
The child I had died to see though in a dream,   1520
The child I was bid strike out for, beat the wave

1505 *MS* pride,>pride.   1508 *MS* a link was forged>fate forged a
link   1510 *MS* Found at last>Found   *MS* ^henceforth^   1511 *MS* then
when>when *Yale 1* indeed>indeed,>indeed   1512 *MS* the door,   1513
MS and>to   1514 *MS* shame,>disgrace,   1515 *MS* agony>infamy   *MS*
{no comma}   1516 *MS* slag>flesh   1517 *MS* venoms>slander>
scorn   *MS* and saturate,>saturate with shame,   1518 *MS* {no comma} 1519
MS And>The

(Guido, the rich man): cf. Job 41: 1, 34: 'Canst thou draw out leviathan with an hook?
or his tongue with a cord which thou lettest down. . . . he is a king over all the children
of pride.'

1508–13 *Was . . . escape?*: paraphrase: 'Was the reason my wife left me just at that
time because the baby really was my child? It was a link between us: she understood
how I would love it, because she loved it herself, and therefore left just then so as to
make her leaving me the more cruel ("damn my soul indeed"), covering her escape
with the "devils of the dark", matters like the drugging, the thefts, the false accusa-
tions.'

1518 *instil*: drop, infuse on.

1521–6 *child . . . aloft*: Guido presents a heroic image of himself swimming through
the 'tide of troubles' towards his child, in the way that Leander swam the Hellespont in
order to reach his love, Hero. The child is a guide to him as he struggles through the
waves, a divine 'apparition' almost like Jesus ('Mary's Babe'), and it holds up a light that
guides him through the 'night and storm' of troubles, again like Hero holding up the
light to guide Leander through the waves.

And baffle the tide of troubles where I swam,
So I might touch shore, lay down life at last
At the feet so dim and distant and divine
Of the apparition, as 't were Mary's Babe   1525
Had held, through night and storm, the torch aloft,—
Born now in very deed to bear this brand
On forehead and curse me who could not save!
Rather be the town-talk true, square's jest, street's jeer
True, my own inmost heart's confession true,   1530
And he the priest's bastard and none of mine!
Ay, there was cause for flight, swift flight and sure!
The husband gets unruly, breaks all bounds
When he encounters some familiar face,
Fashion of feature, brow and eyes and lips   1535
Where he least looked to find them,—time to fly!
This bastard then, a nest for him is made,
As the manner is of vermin, in my flesh:
Shall I let the filthy pest buzz, flap and sting,
Busy at my vitals and, nor hand nor foot   1540
Lift, but let be, lie still and rot resigned?
No, I appeal to God,—what says Himself,
How lessons Nature when I look to learn?
Why, that I am alive, am still a man
With brain and heart and tongue and right-hand too—
Nay, even with friends, in such a cause as this,   1546
To right me if I fail to take my right.
No more of law; a voice beyond the law

1524 *MS* {beginning of fo. 287}   1525 *MS 1868 1872* babe   1528 *MS* the
forehead   *1529 *MS 1868 1872* town-talk *1888 1889* town talk   *MS* the stree>
square's *1868 1872* Square's   1531 *MS* he's the priest's, bastard *1868 1872* he's   *MS*
mine,—   1532 *MS* sure,   1535 *MS* ^brow and^   *MS* lips and
ch>lips   1536 *MS* look   1538 *MS 1868 1872* flesh—   1541 *MS* Lift
but   1542 *MS* the Book>Himself,   1543 *MS* nature   1545 *MS* right
hand   1547 *MS* ^take my^   1548 *MS* the Law,   *MS* Law

1527 *brand*: i.e. brand of infamy, but also a pun on 'torch' in the previous line.
1547 *To . . . right*: to give me justice if I fail to seize it on my own account.

Enters my heart, *Quis est pro Domino?*

Myself, in my own Vittiano, told the tale   1550
To my own serving-people summoned there:
Told the first half of it, scarce heard to end
By judges who got done with judgment quick
And clamoured to go execute her 'hest—
Who cried "Not one of us that dig your soil   1555
"And dress your vineyard, prune your olive-trees,
"But would have brained the man debauched our wife,
"And staked the wife whose lust allured the man,
"And paunched the Duke, had it been possible,
"Who ruled the land yet barred us such revenge!"   1560
I fixed on the first whose eyes caught mine, some four
Resolute youngsters with the heart still fresh,
Filled my purse with the residue o' the coin
Uncaught-up by my wife whom haste made blind,
Donned the first rough and rural garb I found,   1565
Took whatsoever weapon came to hand,
And out we flung and on we ran or reeled

1549 *MS* Quis est pro Domino?   1550 *MS* {no new paragraph}   1551 *MS*
{beginning of fo. 288}   1552 *MS* was heard to the end   1554 *MS*
hest—   1555 *MS* who till>who dig   *MS* ground>soil   1556–60 *MS*
{no quotation marks at beginnings of lines}   1559 *MS* possible   1560
1868 1872 land,   *MS* and>yet   *MS* revenge."   1561 *MS* took>fixed
on   *MS 1868* four,   1563 *MS* of   *MS* ^the^   1564 *MS* Uncaught up

1549 *Quis est pro Domino?*: 'Who is for the Lord?' (L.): Exod. 32: 26. This grand
Latin declaration is one climax of pathos in this monologue. Guido casts himself as the
righteous Moses, burning with terrible anger as he sees the vile pollution of the
idolaters of the golden calf (the actions of Pompilia and her parents). He is also, of
course, the 'lord' of the assassins he is about to recruit, and this is in effect—in
blasphemous self-assertion—the question he feels inspired to ask them.

1553 *judges*: this rhetorical throw, casting his farmworkers, simple peasants, as his
'judges', is an extraordinary combination of pathos and populism: Guido sees himself as
vindicated at the court of popular opinion, and so seeks to pressure his real judges into
backing his case.

1554 *her 'hest*: i.e. judgement's behest.

1557–9 *brained . . . paunched*: cf. *Tempest*, III. ii. 88–90: 'There thou mayst brain
him, . . . or paunch him with a stake'. 'Paunch' = 'stab in the stomach, disembowel'.

1567 *flung*: hurried, rushed violently.

Romeward. I have no memory of our way,
Only that, when at intervals the cloud
Of horror about me opened to let in life,   1570
I listened to some song in the ear, some snatch
Of a legend, relic of religion, stray
Fragment of record very strong and old
Of the first conscience, the anterior right,
The God's-gift to mankind, impulse to quench   1575
The antagonistic spark of hell and tread
Satan and all his malice into dust,
Declare to the world the one law, right is right.
Then the cloud re-encompassed me, and so
I found myself, as on the wings of winds,   1580
Arrived: I was at Rome on Christmas Eve.

Festive bells—everywhere the Feast o' the Babe,
Joy upon earth, peace and good will to man!
I am baptized. I started and let drop
The dagger. "Where is it, His promised peace?"   1585
Nine days o' the Birth-Feast did I pause and pray

1568 *MS 1868 1872* Romeward,   1569 *MS* {no comma}   1570 *MS* {no
comma}   1573 *MS* Scrap>Fragment   1575 *MS* God's gift   1578 *MS*
{beginning of fo. 289}   1582 *MS* {New paragraph (already written thus) in-
dicated by 'N.P.' in left-hand margin}   *MS* Christmas Eve,—   *MS* of   *MS*
{'festive bells' interlined above undeleted 'Feast of the Babe,'}   1583 *MS* on
the   *MS* [ ]>on   1584 *MS* baptised.   1585 *MS* the>his   1586 *MS*
of

1571–3 *snatch . . . record*: in combination with 'anterior right' (1574), 'fragment of
record' perhaps suggests 'eye for eye, tooth for tooth': Exod. 21, 24, Lev. 24: 20;
'snatch / Of a legend', though, suggests a fragment of a saint's life, St George's, for
example. In either case, the resonance is pathetic, like a childhood memory suddenly
vindicating the present.

1574 *anterior*: prior, i.e. taking precedence over man-made and local laws; cf. *A
Soul's Tragedy*, II. 90: 'reverting to first principles and a justice anterior to all institu-
tions'.

1580 *wings of winds*: cf. Ps. 18: 10, 104: 3.

1583 *Joy . . . man*: cf. Luke 2: 14.

1584 *I am baptized*: i.e. 'I am a Christian, I responded to the spirit of Christmas',
perhaps in opposition to the 'anterior right' of l. 1574: see ll. 1571–3 n.

To enter into no temptation more.
I bore the hateful house, my brother's once,
Deserted,—let the ghost of social joy
Mock and make mouths at me from empty room   1590
And idle door that missed the master's step,—
Bore the frank wonder of incredulous eyes,
As my own people watched without a word,
Waited, from where they huddled round the hearth
Black like all else, that nod so slow to come.   1595
I stopped my ears even to the inner call
Of the dread duty, only heard the song
"Peace upon earth," saw nothing but the face
O' the Holy Infant and the halo there
Able to cover yet another face   1600
Behind it, Satan's which I else should see.
But, day by day, joy waned and withered off:
The Babe's face, premature with peak and pine,
Sank into wrinkled ruinous old age,
Suffering and death, then mist-like disappeared,   1605
And showed only the Cross at end of all,
Left nothing more to interpose 'twixt me
And the dread duty: for the angels' song,
"Peace upon earth," louder and louder pealed
"O Lord, how long, how long be unavenged?"   1610

1592 *MS* {no comma}   1593 *MS* {no comma}   1595 *MS 1868 1872*
come—   1597 *MS* heard only the angel's song *1868* heard only   1599
MS Of   1602 *MS* off,   1603 *MS* babe's *Yale 1* babe's>Babe's   1604
MS {beginning of fo. 290}   1605 *MS* {line added later}   1608 *MS* duty,—
louder and louder pealed *1868 1872* duty,—   1609 {not found in
MS}   1610 *MS* "Shall sin's work ever thus *Yale 1* "Shall sin's work ever
thus>"O Lord, how long, how long

1587 *enter into no temptation*: i.e. he said the 'Our Father'. Again, we can be struck by
Guido's mastery of pathos, presenting himself fervently praying in the midst of the
Christmas festival in an attempt to restrain himself from murder.

1602 *withered off*: i.e. like a flower withering off a stem.

1603 *peak and pine*: emaciation and sorrow. 'Peak and pine' is a common phrase,
originally from the witches' curse in *Macbeth*, I. iii. 23, but there and in later writers its
use is verbal; Browning's noun use is a nonce one.

1610 *O . . . unavenged*: cf. Rev. 6: 10.

On the ninth day, this grew too much for man.
I started up—"Some end must be!" At once,
Silence: then, scratching like a death-watch-tick,
Slowly within my brain was syllabled,
"One more concession, one decisive way   1615
"And but one, to determine thee the truth,—
"This way, in fine, I whisper in thy ear:
"Now doubt, anon decide, thereupon act!"

"That is a way, thou whisperest in my ear!
"I doubt, I will decide, then act," said I—   1620
Then beckoned my companions: "Time is come!"

And so, all yet uncertain save the will
To do right, and the daring aught save leave
Right undone, I did find myself at last
I' the dark before the villa with my friends,   1625
And made the experiment, the final test,
Ultimate chance that ever was to be
For the wretchedness inside. I knocked, pronounced
The name, the predetermined touch for truth,
"What welcome for the wanderer? Open straight—"   1630
To the friend, physician, friar upon his rounds,
Traveller belated, beggar lame and blind?
No, but—"to Caponsacchi!" And the door
Opened.
                    And then,—why, even then, I think,   1635

1611 *MS* day this   *MS* man, *Yale 1* man,>man.   1612 *MS* I[ ]>At once,
1613 *MS* death-watch tick,   1614 *MS* Plainly   1615–18 *MS* {no quotation
marks at beginnings of lines}   1616 *MS* one to   *MS* truth,   1617 *MS*
{no commas}   1619 *MS* {line added later}   *MS* {no new paragraph}   *MS*
ear—   1620 *MS* "I>I   1621 *MS* come." 1622 *MS* {New paragraph (al-
ready written thus) indicated by 'N.P.' in left-hand margin}   1623 *MS* {no
comma}   1625 *MS* In   *MS* Villa   1628 *MS 1868 1872* knocked—   1630
MS {no quotation mark at end of line}   1632 *MS* ,—>?— *1868 1872*
blind?—   1633 *MS* {beginning of fo. 291}   *MS* but—to Caponsacchi! And
1635 *MS* why even

1613 *death-watch-tick*: the sinister ticking sound of the death-watch beetle. It was
popularly believed to be an omen of death; perhaps here it is presaging the deaths of
Pompilia and the Comparini. Cf. 'Mesmerism', 8.

I' the minute that confirmed my worst of fears,
Surely,—I pray God that I think aright!—
Had but Pompilia's self, the tender thing
Who once was good and pure, was once my lamb
And lay in my bosom, had the well-known shape   1640
Fronted me in the door-way,—stood there faint
With the recent pang, perhaps, of giving birth
To what might, though by miracle, seem my child,—
Nay more, I will say, had even the aged fool
Pietro, the dotard, in whom folly and age   1645
Wrought, more than enmity or malevolence,
To practise and conspire against my peace,—
Had either of these but opened, I had paused.
But it was she the hag, she that brought hell
For a dowry with her to her husband's house,   1650
She the mock-mother, she that made the match
And married me to perdition, spring and source
O' the fire inside me that boiled up from heart
To brain and hailed the Fury gave it birth,—
Violante Comparini, she it was,   1655
With the old grin amid the wrinkles yet,
Opened: as if in turning from the Cross,
With trust to keep the sight and save my soul,
I had stumbled, first thing, on the serpent's head

1636 MS In   MS {no comma}   1637 MS Surely..   MS aright..
1638 MS poor>but   1639 MS [ ]>pure   MS wife   1640 MS Had lain
>And lay   *1642 MS 1868 1872 pang, perhaps, 1888 1889 pang perhaps
of   1646 MS {no commas}   1647 MS 1868 1872 practice   1652 MS
she, spring, source >spring and source   1653 MS Of   MS me,

1639–40 lamb . . . bosom: cf. 2 Sam. 12: 3: 'But the poor man [Uriah] had nothing,
save one little ewe lamb, which . . . lay in his bosom'. From this parable, Guido is
casting himself pathetically as the wronged and cuckolded Uriah the Hittite, whose
one lamb, his wife Bathsheba (Pompilia) has been taken from him by the sinful King
David (Caponsacchi). Cf. III. 1301–2 n.

1653–4 fire . . . birth: i.e. the fire of hatred within Guido rises up from his heart to his
brain and confronts the infernal spirit (Violante) that originally set the fire within him.

1659 serpent's head: i.e. Satan. Some paintings of the crucifixion show a serpent
(Satan) near the cross, his work as serpent in the Garden of Eden finally overthrown in
Christ's sacrifice on the cross.

Coiled with a leer at foot of it.   1660
                              There was the end!
Then was I rapt away by the impulse, one
Immeasurable everlasting wave of a need
To abolish that detested life. 'T was done:
You know the rest and how the folds o' the thing,   1665
Twisting for help, involved the other two
More or less serpent-like: how I was mad,
Blind, stamped on all, the earth-worms with the asp,
And ended so.
                    You came on me that night,   1670
Your officers of justice,—caught the crime
In the first natural frenzy of remorse?
Twenty miles off, sound sleeping as a child
On a cloak i' the straw which promised shelter first,
With the bloody arms beside me,—was it not so?   1675
Wherefore not? Why, how else should I be found?
I was my own self, had my sense again,
My soul safe from the serpents. I could sleep:
Indeed and, dear my lords, I shall sleep now,
Spite of my shoulder, in five minutes' space,   1680
When you dismiss me, having truth enough!
It is but a few days are passed, I find,
Since this adventure. Do you tell me, four?
Then the dead are scarce quiet where they lie,

1660 *MS* {beginning of fo. 292}   *MS* the foot   1661 *MS* {no new
paragraph}   *MS* end.   1663 *MS* fire   *MS* will   1665 *MS* of   *MS*
{no comma}   1666 *MS* {no comma}   *MS* Two   1667 *MS* serpent-like
and I   1668 *MS* those earth-worms   1670 *MS* {no new para-
graph}   1671 *Yale 1* crime,>crime   1672 *MS* remorse,—   1673 *MS*
Thirty   1674 *MS* in   1678 *MS* With my *Yale 1* With my soul>Soul>My
soul   *MS* sleep.   1679 *MS* now   1680 *MS* space   1681 *MS*
enough.   1682 *MS* days ago,   1683 *MS* From   *Yale 1* From>
Since   1684 *MS* {no comma}

   1663 *everlasting wave*: cf. II. 1433–7 n.
   1665 *folds o' the thing*: i.e. coils of the serpent (Violante); cf. *Paradise Lost*, ix. 161,
498. Guido struggling with his three snake-like adversaries is perhaps reminiscent of
the famous statue of Laocoön struggling with the serpents: cf. ll. 1958–67.
   1683 *four*: four days, i.e. Guido is speaking on 5 or 6 January.

Old Pietro, old Violante, side by side   1685
At the church Lorenzo,—oh, they know it well!
So do I. But my wife is still alive,
Has breath enough to tell her story yet,
Her way, which is not mine, no doubt at all.
And Caponsacchi, you have summoned him,—   1690
Was he so far to send for? Not at hand?
I thought some few o' the stabs were in his heart,
Or had not been so lavish: less had served.
Well, he too tells his story,—florid prose
As smooth as mine is rough. You see, my lords,   1695
There will be a lying intoxicating smoke
Born of the blood,—confusion probably,—
For lies breed lies—but all that rests with you!
The trial is no concern of mine; with me
The main of the care is over: I at least   1700
Recognize who took that huge burthen off,
Let me begin to live again. I did
God's bidding and man's duty, so, breathe free;
Look you to the rest! I heard Himself prescribe,
That great Physician, and dared lance the core   1705
Of the bad ulcer; and the rage abates,
I am myself and whole now: I prove cured
By the eyes that see, the ears that hear again,
The limbs that have relearned their youthful play,

1685 *MS* at the church>side by side   1686 *MS* Church   1689 *MS* {begin-
ning of fo. 293}   1691 *MS* ⟨He, as is right will⟩   1692 *MS* of   *MS* {no
comma}   1693 *MS 1868 1872* lavish,—   1696 *MS* fume   1698 *MS*
you. *Yale 1* you.>you!   1701 *MS 1868 1872* Recognise   1703 *MS* so
breathe *Yale 1* so>so,   1704 *MS* rest.   1706 *MS* ^bad^   *MS* ulcer,   *MS*
burning rage>rage   1707 *MS* cured>whole

1696–7 *lying . . . blood*: i.e. the bloodshed of the murders has created a choking
'smoke' of lies.

1700 *main*: majority.

1701 *who . . . off*: i.e. Christ; see next n.

1705 *great Physician*: i.e. Christ. In ll. 1705–12 Guido presents himself as following
Christ's instructions, and therefore becoming like one of the many people in the
gospels cured by the healing power of Christ's miracles.

1707–9 *I . . . play*: cf. Matt. 11: 5, etc.

The healthy taste of food and feel of clothes   1710
And taking to our common life once more,
All that now urges my defence from death.
The willingness to live, what means it else?
Before,—but let the very action speak!
Judge for yourselves, what life seemed worth to me   1715
Who, not by proxy but in person, pitched
Head-foremost into danger as a fool
That never cares if he can swim or no—
So he but find the bottom, braves the brook.
No man omits precaution, quite neglects   1720
Secresy, safety, schemes not how retreat,
Having schemed he might advance. Did I so scheme?
Why, with a warrant which 't is ask and have,
With horse thereby made mine without a word,
I had gained the frontier and slept safe that night.   1725
Then, my companions,—call them what you please,
Slave or stipendiary,—what need of one
To me whose right-hand did its owner's work?
Hire an assassin yet expose yourself?
As well buy glove and then thrust naked hand   1730
I' the thorn-bush. No, the wise man stays at home,
Sends only agents out, with pay to earn:
At home, when they come back,—he straight discards
Or else disowns. Why use such tools at all

1714 *MS* ^very^   *MS* speak—   1716 *MS* {beginning of fo. 294}   *MS* {no
commas}   1717 *MS* the danger *Yale 1* the danger>danger   1718 *MS*
thinks>cares   1719 *MS* reach>find   1720 *MS* [ ]>omits   *MS* precau-
tions,   1721 *MS* schemes he may retreat   1724 *MS* And the   1725
MS lain>slept   1726 *MS* Then my companions, *Yale 1* Then>Then,   *MS*
please,—   1727 *MS* Slaves>Slave   *MS* stipendiaries,>stipendiary,   1731
MS In   *1732 *1888* Send, *DC BrU* Send,>Sends *1889* Sends   *MS* out
with   *MS* earn,   1733 *MS* why, he

1725 *frontier*: the border of the Papal States and Tuscany, both independent states in
the seventeenth century. If Guido had managed to cross this border, he would have
escaped the legal jurisdiction in which the crime was committed, and might never
have been called to justice.
    1727 *stipendiary*: hired, paid for their labour.

When a man's foes are of his house, like mine,   1735
Sit at his board, sleep in his bed? Why noise,
When there's the *acquetta* and the silent way?
Clearly my life was valueless.

                                    But now
Health is returned, and sanity of soul   1740
Nowise indifferent to the body's harm.
I find the instinct bids me save my life;
My wits, too, rally round me; I pick up
And use the arms that strewed the ground before,
Unnoticed or spurned aside: I take my stand,   1745
Make my defence. God shall not lose a life
May do Him further service, while I speak
And you hear, you my judges and last hope!
You are the law: 't is to the law I look.
I began life by hanging to the law,   1750
To the law it is I hang till life shall end.
My brother made appeal to the Pope, 't is true,
To stay proceedings, judge my cause himself
Nor trouble law,—some fondness of conceit
That rectitude, sagacity sufficed   1755
The investigator in a case like mine,
Dispensed with the machine of law. The Pope
Knew better, set aside my brother's plea
And put me back to law,—referred the cause
Ad judices meos,—doubtlessly did well.   1760

1736 *MS* bed: why noise *Yale 1* noise>noise,   1737 *MS* acquetta   1738 *MS*
valueless: but   1739 *MS* {no new paragraph}   1742 *MS* I have *MS*
life,   1743 *MS* me: 1744 *MS* {beginning of fo. 295}   1745 *MS* aside,
1746 *MS* defence,   1748 *MS* Judges   1749 *MS* Law: 1750 *MS* Law,
1751 *MS* Law   1752 *MS* supposed>[ ]>'tis true,   1753 *MS* There [ ]
[ ]>To stay proceedings,   1760 *MS* doublessly {*sic*}

1735 *man's . . . house*: cf. Matt. 10: 36: 'And a man's foes shall be they of his own
household.'

1737 *acquetta*: (It.) poison, acqua tofana; cf. IV. 1069 n.

1760 *Ad judices meos*: 'to my judges' (L.). In the narrative of OYB this is in the third
person: *Ad Iudices Suos* ('to his judges'); for the context of the phrase see ll. 1347–51 n.

Here, then, I clutch my judges,—I claim law—
Cry, by the higher law whereof your law
O' the land is humbly representative,—
Cry, on what point is it, where either accuse,
I fail to furnish you defence? I stand   1765
Acquitted, actually or virtually,
By every intermediate kind of court
That takes account of right or wrong in man,
Each unit in the series that begins
With God's throne, ends with the tribunal here.   1770
God breathes, not speaks, his verdicts, felt not heard,
Passed on successively to each court I call
Man's conscience, custom, manners, all that make
More and more effort to promulgate, mark
God's verdict in determinable words,   1775
Till last come human jurists—solidify
Fluid result,—what's fixable lies forged,
Statute,—the residue escapes in fume,
Yet hangs aloft, a cloud, as palpable
To the finer sense as word the legist welds.   1780

1761 *MS* find>clutch   *MS* law! *Yale 1* law!>law—   1762 *MS* And by the law
of the land, and the higher law>Cry, by the higher law whereof (this) ^your^
law   1763 *MS* Wherefore it is earth's representative,>Of the land is humbly
representative,   1764 *MS* Say,>Come, *Yale 1* Come,>Cry,   *MS* what single
point where both make>what point is it, where either accuse,   1765 *MS* Fail I>I
fail   *MS* make good my>furnish you   *MS* I>who>I   1766 *MS* or actually
or *Yale 1* or actually or>actually or   1767 *MS* [ ]>By   1769 *MS* depends>
begins   1770 *MS* From>With   *MS* to your own>ends with the   *MS* here—
Yale 1 here—>here.   1771 *MS* {beginning of fo. 296}   *MS* {no com-
mas}   *MS* the [ ]>not speaks his   *MS* heard—   *Yale 1* heard—
>heard,   1772 *MS* the courts *Yale 1* the courts>each court   1773 *MS*
Conscience, and>Man's conscience,   1776 *MS* comes   *MS* law, solidifies>
jurists—solidify   1777 *MS* forged— *Yale 1* forged—>forged,   1778 *MS*
Statutes,—   1779 *MS* aloft in a *Yale 1* aloft in a>aloft, a   1780 *MS*
words> word

1762 *higher law*: i.e. the law of God.
1764 *either*: i.e. either the law of God or the law of the land.
1776 *jurists*: legal experts.
1778 *Statute*: written law.
fume: gas.
1780 *legist*: lawyer.

Justinian's Pandects only make precise
What simply sparkled in men's eyes before,
Twitched in their brow or quivered on their lip,
Waited the speech they called but would not come.
These courts then, whose decree your own confirms,—
Take my whole life, not this last act alone,   1786
Look on it by the light reflected thence!
What has Society to charge me with?
Come, unreservedly,—favour none nor fear,—
I am Guido Franceschini, am I not?   1790
You know the courses I was free to take?
I took just that which let me serve the Church,
I gave it all my labour in body and soul
Till these broke down i' the service. "Specify?"
Well, my last patron was a Cardinal.   1795
I left him unconvicted of a fault—
Was even helped, by way of gratitude,
Into the new life that I left him for,
This very misery of the marriage,—he
Made it, kind soul, so far as in him lay—   1800
Signed the deed where you yet may see his name.
He is gone to his reward,—dead, being my friend
Who could have helped here also,—that, of course!
So far, there's my acquittal, I suppose.
Then comes the marriage itself—no question, lords,   1805

1782 *MS* ^only^   *MS* a million>men's   1783 *MS* brows   1787 *MS*
thence.   1789 *MS* unreservedly, no favour, *1868* favour nor   1790 *MS*
{no comma}   1791 *MS* take,   1794 *MS* in   *MS* service—"specify?"
Yale 1 service—>service.   1795 *MS* Cardinal   1796 *MS* fault   1797
MS [But?]>And   1798 *MS* {beginning of fo. 297}   1805 *MS* Lords,

1781 *Justinian's Pandects*: the great digest or encyclopaedia of Roman Law, commis-
sioned by the Emperor Justinian, and issued in AD 533.

1797–1801 *helped . . . name*: in OYB both Guido and Paolo have patrons who are
cardinals, but it is Paolo's cardinal, not Guido's, who helps with the dowry negotia-
tions: OYB ccx (212), cf. civ (112).

1802 *dead*: an inconsistency: at II. 152–7 this cardinal is very much alive, but in the
context here this assertion is another tug of pathos: 'Even this Cardinal who could
defend me is dead—such is my bad luck!'

1803 *that, of course!*: i.e. 'that, of course, would happen!' Guido bemoans his bad
luck.

Of the entire validity of that!
In the extremity of distress, 't is true,
For after-reasons, furnished abundantly,
I wished the thing invalid, went to you
Only some months since, set you duly forth   1810
My wrong and prayed your remedy, that a cheat
Should not have force to cheat my whole life long.
"Annul a marriage? 'T is impossible!
"Though ring about your neck be brass not gold,
"Needs must it clasp, gangrene you all the same!"   1815
Well, let me have the benefit, just so far,
O' the fact announced,—my wife then is my wife,
I have allowance for a husband's right.
I am charged with passing right's due bound,—such acts
As I thought just, my wife called cruelty,   1820
Complained of in due form,—convoked no court
Of common gossipry, but took her wrongs—
And not once, but so long as patience served—
To the town's top, jurisdiction's pride of place,
To the Archbishop and the Governor.   1825
These heard her charge with my reply, and found
That futile, this sufficient: they dismissed
The hysteric querulous rebel, and confirmed
Authority in its wholesome exercise,
They, with directest access to the facts.   1830
"—Ay, for it was their friendship favoured you,
"Hereditary alliance against a breach

1808 MS {no commas}   1809 MS invalid and   1811 MS wrongs   1812
MS long, Yale 1 long,>long.   1813 MS impossible— Yale 1 impossible—>im-
possible!   1814–15 MS {no quotation marks at beginnings of lines}   1814
MS Your   MS the neck is   MS {no comma}   1815 MS Must must still
clasp,   1817 MS Of   1820 MS justice,   1823 MS {no comma}
1824 MS Town's   1825 MS {beginning of fo. 298}   1831 MS they were
your friends and>it was their friendship   MS here,>you,

1815 gangrene: i.e. poison with gangrene; cf. Shelley, The Cenci, II. i. 70–1:
'. . . when the rust / Of heavy chains has gangrened his sweet limbs'.
   1827 futile: useless, of no weight.
   1832 Hereditary alliance: i.e. the collusion of the aristocratic class.

"I' the social order: prejudice for the name
"Of Franceschini!"—So I hear it said:
But not here. You, lords, never will you say   1835
"Such is the nullity of grace and truth,
"Such the corruption of the faith, such lapse
"Of law, such warrant have the Molinists
"For daring reprehend us as they do,—
"That we pronounce it just a common case,   1840
"Two dignitaries, each in his degree
"First, foremost, this the spiritual head, and that
"The secular arm o' the body politic,
"Should, for mere wrongs' love and injustice' sake,
"Side with, aid and abet in cruelty   1845
"This broken beggarly noble,—bribed perhaps
"By his watered wine and mouldy crust of bread—
"Rather than that sweet tremulous flower-like wife
"Who kissed their hands and curled about their feet
"Looking the irresistible loveliness   1850
"In tears that takes man captive, turns" . . . enough!
Do you blast your predecessors? What forbids
Posterity to trebly blast yourselves
Who set the example and instruct their tongue?

1832–4 *MS* {no quotation marks at beginnings of lines}   1832 *MS* allies made
>alliance against   *MS* foe>breach   1833 *MS* To>In   *MS* ^social^
1834 *MS* Franceschini."—   *MS* said   1837–51 *MS* {no quotation marks at
beginnings of lines}   1839 *MS* do, *Yale 1* do,>do,—   1840 *MS* natural, a
plain>just a common   1842 *MS* beyond question,>foremost,   *MS* that>
this   *MS* ^and that^   1843 *MS* And this the spiritual of>The secular arm
of   1844 *MS* Did,   *MS* [sin's?]>wrong's   1846 *MS* broken,   1848
MS ^that^   *MS* poor>sweet   1849 *MS* That curled about their feet and kissed
their hands>That kissed their hands and curled about their feet *Yale 1* "That>
"Who   1851 *MS* turns . . .   1852 *MS* {beginning of fo. 299}   1853
MS yourselves?—   1854 *MS* You>Who   *MS* speech—>tongue

1843 *secular . . . politic*: i.e. the leading agent of government.
1851 *turns" . . .*: turns [justice from its course].
1852 *Do . . . predecessors?*: i.e. do you accuse the Governor and Archbishop of
corruption?
1854 *their*: posterity's.

You dreaded the crowd, succumbed to the popular cry,   1855
Or else, would nowise seem defer thereto
And yield to public clamour though i' the right!
You ridded your eye of my unseemliness,
The noble whose misfortune wearied you,—
Or, what's more probable, made common cause   1860
With the cleric section, punished in myself
Maladroit uncomplaisant laity,
Defective in behaviour to a priest
Who claimed the customary partnership
I' the house and the wife. Lords, any lie will serve!   1865
Look to it,—or allow me freed so far!

Then I proceed a step, come with clean hands
Thus far, re-tell the tale told eight months since.
The wife, you allow so far, I have not wronged,
Has fled my roof, plundered me and decamped   1870
In company with the priest her paramour:
And I gave chase, came up with, caught the two
At the wayside inn where both had spent the night,
Found them in flagrant fault, and found as well,
By documents with name and plan and date,   1875
The fault was furtive then that's flagrant now,

1855 MS "You   1857 MS the other way: 1858 MS rid   MS of his MS
{no comma}   1859 MS brought disgrace,   1861 MS priestly> cleric   MS
party,   1862 MS The maladroit and uncomplaisant man   1864 MS Claim-
ing   1865 MS In   1866 MS far.   1867 MS {New paragraph (already
written thus) indicated by 'N.P.' in left-hand margin}   MS come, with   1868
MS and tell you that tale eight months since—   1869 MS That the wife, you
allow I have not wronged so far, Yale 1 allow I have not wronged so far,>allow so far, I
have not wronged,   1872 MS That I,>That I pursued,>That I gave chase, 1868
1872 chace,   MS with and   MS pair Yale 1 pair>two   1874 MS
well   1875 MS {no comma}

    1855–65 You . . . wife: these lines might appropriately be in quotation marks: they
are what posterity will say about the present judges if they find Guido guilty.
    1862 Maladroit . . . laity: awkward, unobliging lay people.
    1865 any . . . serve: i.e. any lie will serve [to blast you].
    1874 in flagrant fault: in obvious crime, a partial translation of in flagrante delicto (L.)
(= in the heat of the crime), generally used of couples caught in the very act of illicit
sexual intercourse.

Their intercourse a long established crime.
I did not take the license law's self gives
To slay both criminals o' the spot at the time,
But held my hand,—preferred play prodigy   1880
Of patience which the world calls cowardice,
Rather than seem anticipate the law
And cast discredit on its organs,—you.
So, to your bar I brought both criminals,
And made my statement: heard their counter-charge,   1885
Nay,—their corroboration of my tale,
Nowise disputing its allegements, not
I' the main, not more than nature's decency
Compels men to keep silence in this kind,—
Only contending that the deeds avowed   1890
Would take another colour and bear excuse.
You were to judge between us; so you did.
You disregard the excuse, you breathe away
The colour of innocence and leave guilt black,
"Guilty" is the decision of the court,   1895
And that I stand in consequence untouched,
One white integrity from head to heel.
Not guilty? Why then did you punish them?
True, punishment has been inadequate—
'T is not I only, not my friends that joke,   1900
My foes that jeer, who echo "inadequate"—
For, by a chance that comes to help for once,
The same case simultaneously was judged
At Arezzo, in the province of the Court
Where the crime had its beginning but not end.   1905

1878 *MS* {beginning of fo. 300}   1879 *MS* on   1881 *MS* patience
that   1883 *MS* *1868 1872* you—   1884 *MS* So to   1885 *MS*
1868 {no comma}   1886 *MS* No,—   1888 *MS* In   1889 *MS* kind,
1895 *MS* then the sentence>the decision   *MS* Court.   1896 *MS* {no
comma}   1898 *MS* If innocent,>Not guilty?   *MS* ^then^   1900 *MS*
gripe,>gape,   1903 *MS* Half the case>The same case   1905 *MS* {begin-
ning of fo. 301}   *MS* *1868 1872* had beginning

1887 *allegements*: allegations.
1904 *Arezzo . . . Court*: the case of Pompilia's flight and the related robbery of
Guido's property was first judged at Arezzo before the Governor. The Arezzo verdict

They then, deciding on but half o' the crime,
The effraction, robbery,—features of the fault
I never cared to dwell upon at Rome,—
What was it they adjudged as penalty
To Pompilia,—the one criminal o' the pair   1910
Amenable to their judgment, not the priest
Who is Rome's? Why, just imprisonment for life
I' the Stinche. There was Tuscany's award
To a wife that robs her husband: you at Rome—
Having to deal with adultery in a wife   1915
And, in a priest, breach of the priestly vow—
Give gentle sequestration for a month
In a manageable Convent, then release,
You call imprisonment, in the very house
O' the very couple, which the aim and end   1920
Of the culprits' crime was—just to reach and rest
And there take solace and defy me: well,—
This difference 'twixt their penalty and yours
Is immaterial: make your penalty less—
Merely that she should henceforth wear black gloves   1925
And white fan, she who wore the opposite—

1906 *MS* of   *MS* crime   1910 *MS* of   1913 *MS* In   1914 *MS*
1868 1872 Rome   1916 *MS* {no commas after 'And' and 'priest'}   *MS* ^in
a priest^   *MS 1868 1872* vow,   1919 *MS* {no comma}   1920 *MS*
Of   *MS 1868 1872* the sole aim   1921 *MS 1868 1872* there to   1923 *MS*
twixt   1924 *MS* less   1925 *MS* wear henceforth>henceforth wear 1926
MS a white

was then passed up to the Criminal Court of Florence for final approval, Florence
being the centre of jurisdiction for Tuscany. This ratified verdict was delivered on 24
Dec. 1697.

1907 *effraction*: breaking and entering.

1913 *Stinche*: the Florence jail.

1913–14 *Tuscany's . . . husband*: the Florentine verdict does indeed focus on the
aspect of robbery, with an inventory of the jewellery and clothes taken, but it does
also assume Pompilia's adultery both with Caponsacchi and Guillichini: OYB v–viii
(5–7).

1917 *sequestration*: seclusion, removal into safe keeping; a term usually used of
property.

1918 *manageable*: i.e. not strict, amenable.

Why, all the same the fact o' the thing subsists.
Reconcile to your conscience as you may,
Be it on your own heads, you pronounced but half
O' the penalty for heinousness like hers   1930
And his, that pays a fault at Carnival
Of comfit-pelting past discretion's law,
Or accident to handkerchief in Lent
Which falls perversely as a lady kneels
Abruptly, and but half conceals her neck!   1935
I acquiesce for my part: punished, though
By a pin-point scratch, means guilty: guilty means
—What have I been but innocent hitherto?
Anyhow, here the offence, being punished, ends.

Ends?—for you deemed so, did you not, sweet lords?   1940
That was throughout the veritable aim
O' the sentence light or heavy,—to redress
Recognized wrong? You righted me, I think?
Well then,—what if I, at this last of all,
Demonstrate you, as my whole pleading proves,   1945
No particle of wrong received thereby

1927 *MS* of   *MS* subsists: *Yale 1* subsists:>subsists.   1928 *MS* {no comma}
1929 *MS* pronounce one half *Yale 1* pronounce>pronounced *1868 1872* one
half   1930 *MS* Of   1931 *MS* than for a *Yale 1* than for a>that's for a *1868*
that's for a   *MS* carnival   1932 *MS* {beginning of fo. 302}   *MS* play,   1934
MS That *Yale 1* That>Which   *MS* Lady   *MS* kneels> prays   1935 *MS* {no
comma}   *MS* only half   *MS* protects>conceals   *MS* breast:— *Yale 1* neck,—
>neck!   1936 *MS 1868 1872* part,—   1940 *MS* {New paragraph (already
written thus) indicated by 'N.P.' in left-hand margin}   *MS* Lords?   1942 *MS*
Of   *MS* heavy, *Yale 1* heavy,>heavy,—   1944 *MS* when I,   1946 *MS* the
wrong>wrong

1929–35 *you . . . neck!*: i.e. 'your punishment was too lenient, more like the kind of
punishment appropriate to trivial or accidental indiscretions'.

1932 *comfit-pelting*: throwing sweets. This aspect of the Carnival in Rome was often
noticed by nineteenth-century visitors.

1933 *handkerchief*: thin muslin scarf or fichu used to conceal the décolletage of a low
dress.

1935 *neck*; i.e. throat, bosom.

1945–6 *Demonstrate . . . wrong*: a condensed syntax, reflecting Guido's growing
anger: 'Demonstrate [to] you, as my whole pleading proves, [that] no particle of
wrong . . .'.

One atom of right?—that cure grew worse disease?
That in the process you call "justice done"
All along you have nipped away just inch
By inch the creeping climbing length of plague   1950
Breaking my tree of life from root to branch,
And left me, after all and every act
Of your interference,—lightened of what load?
At liberty wherein? Mere words and wind!
"Now I was saved, now I should feel no more   1955
"The hot breath, find a respite from fixed eye
"And vibrant tongue!" Why, scarce your back was turned,
There was the reptile, that feigned death at first,
Renewing its detested spire and spire
Around me, rising to such heights of hate   1960
That, so far from mere purpose now to crush
And coil itself on the remains of me,
Body and mind, and there flesh fang content,
Its aim is now to evoke life from death,
Make me anew, satisfy in my son   1965
The hunger I may feed but never sate,
Tormented on to perpetuity,—
My son, whom, dead, I shall know, understand,
Feel, hear, see, never more escape the sight
In heaven that's turned to hell, or hell returned   1970
(So rather say) to this same earth again,—

1947 *MS* right?   *MS* worst   1949 *MS* joint   1950 *MS* joint   *MS*
^creeping^   1954 *MS* Why, words   1957 *MS* tongue."   1958 *MS*
{beginning of fo. 303}   *MS* {no commas}   1961 *MS* {no comma}   1962
MS {no comma}   1963 *MS* mind and   *MS* feed>flesh   1970 *MS* Hea-
ven so turned to Hell, or Hell   1971 *MS* So—rather say—   *1868 1872* (So, rather,
say)   *MS* again,

1950 *creeping . . . plague*: the image here is both of ivy overwhelming and smothering
Guido's 'tree of life', and, more predominantly in the passage that follows, of a vicious,
quasi-satanic snake.

1957 *vibrant*: flickering, quivering.

1959 *spire and spire*: coil and coil; cf. *Paradise Lost*, ix. 502.

1970–1 *heaven . . . again*: if Guido goes to heaven it will be turned to 'hell' by the
sight of his suffering son; if he goes to hell it will be just like being on earth again, i.e.
he cannot escape the nightmare of seeing his son being brought up by Pompilia.

Moulded into the image and made one,
Fashioned of soul as featured like in face,
First taught to laugh and lisp and stand and go
By that thief, poisoner and adulteress   1975
I call Pompilia, he calls ... sacred name,
Be unpronounced, be unpolluted here!
And last led up to the glory and prize of hate
By his ... foster-father, Caponsacchi's self,
The perjured priest, pink of conspirators,   1980
Tricksters and knaves, yet polished, superfine,
Manhood to model adolescence by!
Lords, look on me, declare,—when, what I show,
Is nothing more nor less than what you deemed
And doled me out for justice,—what did you say?   1985
For reparation, restitution and more,—
Will you not thank, praise, bid me to your breasts
For having done the thing you thought to do,
And thoroughly trampled out sin's life at last?
I have heightened phrase to make your soft speech serve,
Doubled the blow you but essayed to strike,   1991
Carried into effect your mandate here
That else had fallen to ground: mere duty done,
Oversight of the master just supplied
By zeal i' the servant. I, being used to serve,   1995
Have simply ... what is it they charge me with?
Blackened again, made legible once more

1978 *MS* of Hell   1979 *MS 1868 1872* his .. *MS* self   1980 *MS* con-
spirators   1982 *MS 1868 1872* by...   1983 *MS* when what   *MS*
show   1984 *MS* thought,>deemed,   1985 *MS* {beginning of fo.
304}   1986 *MS* Reparation,   *MS* much more,—   1990 *MS* Words you
spoke, I respoke in heightened phrase.>I have heightened phrase to make your
half-speech serve,   1993 *MS* the ground: 1995 *MS* in   *MS 1868 1872*
servant: 1996 *Yale 1* charged>charge   1997 *MS* Rewritten and>Black-
ened again,

1976 *sacred name*: i.e. 'mother'.
1980 *pink*: best.
1981 *superfine*: extremely refined, excellent.
1995 *zeal i' the servant*: cf. Ps. 69: 9: 'For the zeal of thine house hath eaten me up':
see l. 5 n.

Your own decree, not permanently writ,
Rightly conceived but all too faintly traced.
It reads efficient, now, comminatory,   2000
A terror to the wicked, answers so
The mood o' the magistrate, the mind of law.
Absolve, then, me, law's mere executant!
Protect your own defender,—save me, Sirs!
Give me my life, give me my liberty,   2005
My good name and my civic rights again!
It would be too fond, too complacent play
Into the hands o' the devil, should we lose
The game here, I for God: a soldier-bee
That yields his life, exenterate with the stroke   2010
O' the sting that saves the hive. I need that life.
Oh, never fear! I'll find life plenty use
Though it should last five years more, aches and all!
For, first thing, there's the mother's age to help—
Let her come break her heart upon my breast,   2015
Not on the blank stone of my nameless tomb!
The fugitive brother has to be bidden back
To the old routine, repugnant to the tread,
Of daily suit and service to the Church,—

1998 *MS* tr>writ,   1999 *MS 1868 1872* traced,—   2002 *MS* of   *MS*
Law.   2003 *MS* Absolve me then, Law's   2008 *MS* of   2009 *MS*
and>for   2011 *MS* Of   *MS 1868 1872* life,   2012 *MS* {beginning of
fo. 305}   2013 *MS* {no comma}   2015 *MS* ^her^   2017 *MS*
called>bidden   2018 *MS* To the home and friends he finds too hard to bear:>To
the old routine, now bitter overmuch,>To the old routine, repugnant to the
tread,   2019 *MS* {line added later}   *MS* Of [ ]>Of daily

2000 *comminatory*: damning, denunciatory.
2007 *fond*: foolish.
2010 *exenterate*: disembowelled; the stress is on the second syllable: exénterate. After
the bee delivers its sting, it moves away and so is disembowelled. Having delivered his
'sting' (the murders) on behalf of God and the 'hive' (society), Guido argues it would
play into the hands of the devil if he lost his own life in consequence. Suggesting the
image of his mother weeping at his 'nameless tomb' is another touch of pathos by
Guido.
2016 *nameless tomb*: Browning is probably thinking of the English practice of
burying executed murderers in nameless tombs within the prison confines.
2018 *repugnant . . . tread*: i.e. hateful to his footsteps; cf. III. 572.

Thro' gibe and jest, those stones that Shimei flung! 2020
Ay, and the spirit-broken youth at home,
The awe-struck altar-ministrant, shall make
Amends for faith now palsied at the source,
Shall see truth yet triumphant, justice yet
A victor in the battle of this world! 2025
Give me—for last, best gift—my son again,
Whom law makes mine,—I take him at your word,
Mine be he, by miraculous mercy, lords!
Let me lift up his youth and innocence
To purify my palace, room by room 2030
Purged of the memories, lend from his bright brow
Light to the old proud paladin my sire
Shrunk now for shame into the darkest shade
O' the tapestry, showed him once and shrouds him now!
Then may we,—strong from that rekindled smile,— 2035
Go forward, face new times, the better day.
And when, in times made better through your brave
Decision now,—might but Eutopia be!—
Rome rife with honest women and strong men,
Manners reformed, old habits back once more, 2040
Customs that recognize the standard worth,—
The wholesome household rule in force again,
Husbands once more God's representative,

2020 *MS* {line added later}   2022 *MS* {no comma}   2026 *MS 1868 1872*
gift,   2028 *MS* Lords!   2034 *MS* Of   *MS* that showed   *MS*
now.   2035 *MS* we may,—   2036 *MS* day—   2037 *MS* days
>times   *2038 *MS* now, may but Utopia be! *1868 1872 1888* Utopia *DC BrU*
Utopia>Eutopia *1889* Utopia   2040 *MS* again,   2041 *MS* {beginning of fo.
306}

2020 *gibe . . . Shimei*: cf. 2 Sam. 16: 5–14. Guido will hurl insults and jokes at God's
anointed priest, Abate Paolo, to get him back to his work for the Church, just as
Shimei hurled stones (and insults) at God's anointed king, David. Guido intends to
suggest his own necessary temerity in goading a priest, his brother, but given Shimei's
later history the comparison does him little credit; see 1 Kgs. 2.
2021 *spirit-broken youth*: i.e. Girolamo.
2032 *paladin*: knightly hero, champion.
sire: ancestor.

Wives like the typical Spouse once more, and Priests

No longer men of Belial, with no aim   2045

At leading silly women captive, but

Of rising to such duties as yours now,—

Then will I set my son at my right-hand

And tell his father's story to this point,

Adding "The task seemed superhuman, still   2050

"I dared and did it, trusting God and law:

"And they approved of me: give praise to both!"

And if, for answer, he shall stoop to kiss

My hand, and peradventure start thereat,—

I engage to smile "That was an accident   2055

"'I' the necessary process,—just a trip

"'O' the torture-irons in their search for truth,—

"Hardly misfortune, and no fault at all."

2046 *MS* but end   2047 *MS* your own,   2048 *MS* right hand   2049
MS fathers   *MS* over again, {Ohio-Baylor prints 'once again', but the word is
unmistakably 'over'}   2051–2 *MS* {no quotation marks at beginnings of
lines}   2051 *MS* Law,   2052 *MS* me, due praise   2054 *MS*
thereat,   2055 *MS* to add   2056–8 *MS* {no quotation marks at beginnings
of lines}   2056 *MS* In   *MS* process,   *MS* slip   2057 *MS* Of   *MS*
truth,   2058 *MS* a misfortune   *Yale 1* misfortune>misfortune,   *MS* at
all.   {In right-hand margin 'L.D.I.E.' [? = 'Laus Deo, Inscriptum Est']}

2044 *typical Spouse*: in Christian typology the Church is the bride of Christ, so
providing a model for wifely obedience; cf. Eph. 5: 24: 'Therefore as the church is
subject unto Christ, so let wives be to their husbands in everything'. This typology,
however, is grounded in the idea of love (not power); Guido's use is a grotesque
misconstruction.

2045 *Belial*: Satan.

2048 *set . . . right-hand*: after his resurrection and ascension into heaven, Christ sits at
the right hand of God the Father; this language is found at Acts 2: 34, for example, but
is a matter of continuous iteration in the Christian creed: ' . . . and he [Christ] ascended
into heaven, and is seated at the right hand of the Father'. Guido echoes this language
in order to elevate the final pathetic image of his own self-righteousness.

2054 *hand . . . thereat*: an implicit parallel of himself to Christ: his hands are marked
with the torture, just as Christ's hands were marked with the nails. His son may 'start'
like the apostle St Thomas, confronted with this evidence of suffering: see John 20: 20–
9. In the previous allusion, Guido was God in heaven; now he is the resurrected
Christ. 'It is advisable for Guido now to alleviate the long-sustained emphasis upon
death [earlier in his monologue] by hopeful reference to everlasting life—his own
earthly life everlasting': Altick and Loucks, 51.

INTRODUCTION TO BOOK VI
GIUSEPPE CAPONSACCHI

THOUGH a real Giuseppe Caponsacchi lived through a series of events approximate to those depicted here, Browning's character is again (as with Guido) a radical invention; the qualities we value in Caponsacchi—his vehemence, his religious vision, his love of Pompilia—have no significant precedents in the sources. It is almost certainly unhistorical that he found himself standing before the court as *amicus curiae*, only recently informed of Pompilia's stabbing, ablaze with confusion and passion. Subsequent to the murders, the sources say nothing about him; the presumption must be that he stayed at Civitavecchia, enduring his formal penalty of relegation from Rome.

Caponsacchi is the embodiment of 'the highest in manliness and courage',[1] an ideal of a 'true' man, without any of the sexism that dominates the view of women in the poem at large.[2] He is St George rescuing the maiden (Pompilia) from the dragon (Guido). Some critics, wary of such terms, have recoiled into exaggeration of another kind. Buckler, for example, says that Caponsacchi is not the 'romantic hero' at all, that he is flawed, at various times 'exaggerated' in self-righteousness, 'self-romanticizing', even converting 'lust' for Pompilia into anger at the judges.[3] A view like this grows out of an awareness, perhaps nervousness, of the love-story at the heart of the poem—of priest and married woman, who, in different circumstances, would have made a marriage as profound as that of Browning and EBB.

Chesterton alerted readers to the implicit autobiography in the poem in 1903,[4] and we can be explicit provided we realize the limitations of this view. Browning (Caponsacchi) rescues EBB (Pompilia) from the towering anger and authority of her father (Guido Franceschini), escorting her away from London (Arezzo) where she would otherwise die, and taking carriages—sometimes night-time carriages—to freedom. EBB, like Pompilia, was in a fragile condition; Pompilia is pregnant, EBB was soon to

---

[1] Robert Langbaum, *The Poetry of Experience* (New York, 1957), 112.
[2] Brady, 108–21.
[3] Buckler, 141, 146, 135.
[4] G. K. Chesterton, *Robert Browning* (1903), 107–8.

be. In this monologue, Browning—a widower in London in the 1860s—brooded upon his decisive action of 1846.[5] The impact of the monologue comes from grief: Caponsacchi's knowledge that Pompilia is dying makes him sometimes hysterical. His last exhausted cry, 'Miserable me' (2105), is heart-broken: he will never see Pompilia alive again.

Browning's mastery is partly revealed in the extent to which the monologue transcends this autobiography. When he was imagining the character, it may be surmised, he was not sufficiently inspired by what he found in OYB and SS, and he pursued more research into the history of the Caponsacchi family. Eventually he came upon the chronicle account of Bishop Tommaso di Jacopo d'Alamanno Salviati 'originato dall'antica, e illustre Famiglia de Caponsacchi di Fiesole', appointed in 1638 to the bishopric of Arezzo, and remembered by the town's people as saint and peace-maker.[6] This appears to have been the spur to his invention of Caponsacchi. As far as is known, Browning had no grounds for formally identifying Bishop Tommaso as the great-uncle of Caponsacchi (256), though this is surely not impossible. Now, in his imagination, Caponsacchi became a worldly young man drifting into the priesthood in the wake of his renowned uncle's example.

Browning brilliantly evokes the first milieu of the aristocratic Caponsacchi, part priest, part 'fribble', 'coxcomb', 'fool' (87, 340). The world of late baroque and Counter-Reformation Italy (hinted at by references to artists, saints, and events elsewhere in the poem) comes together here as an opaque reality, believable and significant. Caponsacchi spends his time as a priest with the society ladies of Arezzo, helping them with difficult card games, acting as 'arbiter' on the size of fan mounts (348–50), and contemplating ornate, erotic verse in the manner of Giambattista Marino's *L'Adone*, the fashionable success of 1623 (333–5). Cardinals have mistresses who intrigue in the infighting of clerical society (354–5); eating ortolans with the Archbishop is *de rigueur* (463); and exchanging *risqué* jokes and discussing the more explicit of Catullus' poems with a Cardinal—all in Latin, of course—eases the way up the ladder of preferment (381–8). We also see the sexual banter of young priests, who flirt with young ladies and perhaps do more, under protection of their status in society (428–30, 447–51). For those of the right class, this is an elegant world of refined sterility, where no one really notices the sclerosis of faith.

---

[5] For a fuller discussion of the autobiographical element, see Stefan Hawlin, 'Review', BSN 25 (Dec. 1998), 94–5.

[6] For the full text of the chronicle, see Appendix B.

Caponsacchi is awakened from all this by a vision of a sixteen-year-old girl, 'tall, beautiful, strange and sad' (399). From this point the central trope is conversion in response to 'the revelation of Pompilia' (1866). The speakers of the earlier monologues, Half-Rome, Other-Half Rome, and Tertium Quid, are in different ways intent on shutting down reality, diminishing it to the limited size of their own hearts and minds. Guido's Satan-like confusions in Book V also have a negligible basis in reality. Caponsacchi moves the other way. He sets out as career-priest, aristocrat, flirt, within a society and Church that sanction this path, and then finds this life exploded by his encounter with Pompilia. In the throes of conversion, he tries to resist her appeal for help: he looks briefly to a kind of intellectualism, represented here symbolically by Aquinas (484, 953–63, 1025); and he tries for a time to cling to his status as a priest (974–1021). Nothing, though, will save him from his conscience: he has to risk 'respectability', various kinds of comfort and recognition, to do what he knows is right. In Chesterton's words, he (like Browning) has to prefer what is 'unselfish and dubious' to what is 'selfish and honourable'.[7]

Conversion is an abandonment of illusions, and an opening out to a truer, fuller life. In Caponsacchi's insistent religious imagery, Pompilia is a Madonna, and also, we might say, a Beatrice figure, mediator of divine reality and the guardian of his own salvation. During the flight in the carriage she becomes gradually more aware of the fact of her pregnancy, and for that time they become a Holy Family—Madonna, Giuseppe, and child—fleeing into Egypt away from Herod the oppressor.

The judges' thinking is essentially secular: we live, they believe, in 'undragoned days' (1772): it is only a joke when Caponsacchi evokes myths of vice and virtue. Initially, to the judges, Caponsacchi was a meddlesome priest 'personating' St George to rescue a 'mock Princess' (1771–2). Even this story must be euphemistic; fairytales are not true to the secularized mind. Now Caponsacchi turns this ridicule against them: if their vision is too comfortable and sclerous to believe in myths, perhaps they can believe in history. They cannot see a dragon: can they (like St Peter, whom they claim to follow) recognize Nero (Guido) making the gentle Christians of Rome into torches ignited for the amusement of the crowd (1788–91)?

The trope is impressive because of the way it overturns an earlier one: the Bishop telling Caponsacchi that the seventeenth century has nothing to do with the fourth century, that he can continue as an elegant fop

---

[7] Chesterton, p. 108.

within the priesthood: ' "Nobody wants you in these latter days / To prop the Church by breaking your back-bone,—/ As the necessary way was once, we know, / When Diocletian flourished and his like" ' (291–4). A universalist historical perspective should give way to a historicist one, or so it might appear: dragons are dead and gone, like true love, stuff of legend.

The essence of Caponsacchi's complaint against the judges is that they are still living in his own first world. Six months before at the trial for flight they 'tittered' at the likely indiscretions of a handsome priest caught with a pretty girl: 'I must not be unduly borne upon, / Who just romanced a little, sowed wild oats' (1725–6). Even his friends misconceive him, their banter being another of the insistent worldly voices trying to undermine the romance of the poem. When the outcome of the trial for flight seems lenient, these friends encourage him to write a mock-heroic *De Raptu Helenæ*, revenging himself on Guido by painting him as a ludicrous Menelaus (1746–9). But this is exactly the world of career, intrigue, ambition, and frivolity the ultimate sterility of which he knows he has escaped. Caponsacchi has been dragged out from a world of foppishness into a world of reality, and the different vision so startles him that he can barely convey it to the judges or to himself.

VI

GIUSEPPE CAPONSACCHI.

ANSWER you, Sirs? Do I understand aright?
Have patience! In this sudden smoke from hell,—
So things disguise themselves,—I cannot see
My own hand held thus broad before my face
And know it again. Answer you? Then that means   5
Tell over twice what I, the first time, told
Six months ago: 't was here, I do believe,
Fronting you same three in this very room,
I stood and told you: yet now no one laughs,
Who then . . . nay, dear my lords, but laugh you did,   10
As good as laugh, what in a judge we style
Laughter—no levity, nothing indecorous, lords!
Only,—I think I apprehend the mood:
There was the blameless shrug, permissible smirk,
The pen's pretence at play with the pursed mouth,   15
The titter stifled in the hollow palm
Which rubbed the eyebrow and caressed the nose,

MS {fo. 307. At the head of the page is the title '6. Giuseppe Caponsacchi' in RB's hand}   *Yale 1* V.>VI.   2 *MS* Hell,—   4 *MS* right>own   10 *MS 1868 1872* then . .   *MS* 'dear' interlined above undeleted 'good'   12 *MS* not> no   *MS* Lords,   13 *MS* recognise>apprehend   14 *MS* titter,>shrug,

---

7 *Six months ago*: the flight of Pompilia and Caponsacchi took place on 29 April–1 May 1697, i.e. eight months before. Here Browning assumes a delay before they were prosecuted; at l. 35 Caponsacchi states the correct time since the flight itself.

8 *same three*: as Browning imagines it the judges are Marco Antonio Venturini, Vice-Governor of Rome, Lord Tommati (mentioned at ll. 34, 133), and one other unnamed judge. Caponsacchi's attack on the judges for their behaviour at the earlier trial, and their reactions to him, are a crucial part of the drama of this monologue: in addition to this passage, see ll. 131–40, 1781–6, and 1884.

When I first told my tale: they meant, you know,
"The sly one, all this we are bound believe!
"Well, he can say no other than what he says.   20
"We have been young, too,—come, there's greater guilt!
"Let him but decently disembroil himself,
"Scramble from out the scrape nor move the mud,—
"We solid ones may risk a finger-stretch!"
And now you sit as grave, stare as aghast   25
As if I were a phantom: now 't is—"Friend,
"Collect yourself!"—no laughing matter more—
"Counsel the Court in this extremity,
"Tell us again!"—tell that, for telling which,
I got the jocular piece of punishment,   30
Was sent to lounge a little in the place
Whence now of a sudden here you summon me
To take the intelligence from just—your lips!
You, Judge Tommati, who then tittered most,—
That she I helped eight months since to escape   35
Her husband, was retaken by the same,
Three days ago, if I have seized your sense,—
(I being disallowed to interfere,
Meddle or make in a matter none of mine,

---

17 *MS* {no comma}   18 *MS* story: 20–4 *MS* {no quotation marks at beginnings of lines}   22 *MS* Decently let him   23 *MS* mud, *24 *MS* finger's-stretch.">finger-stretch." *1868 1872* finger-stretch! *1888 1889* finger-stretch!   27 *MS* yourself"— *Yale 1* yourself">yourself!"   28 *MS* {beginning of fo. 308}   29 *MS* {no quotation mark at beginning of line}   *MS* that for   33 *MS* just your lips *1868 1872* lips   34 *MS* most, 36 *MS* husband is *1868 1872* is   38 *MS* I   *MS* {no comma}

32 *summon me*: the dramatic situation, with Caponsacchi summoned hastily from Civitavecchia, hearing from Lord Tommati of the murderous attack on Pompilia, and then speaking to the court while still under the shock of this news, is entirely Browning's invention and has no precedent in OYB: see Introduction.

37 *Three days ago*: this places Caponsacchi as speaking on 5 Jan. 1698, the same day as Tertium Quid and Guido, and the day before Pompilia dies. At l. 1632, however, Caponsacchi says the murder was 'two days ago': either this is a mistake occasioned by passion, substituting the day he heard of the attack for the day of the attack itself, or a small inconsistency by Browning.

39 *Meddle or make*: cf. v. 244 n.

For you and law were guardians quite enough   40
O' the innocent, without a pert priest's help)—
And that he has butchered her accordingly,
As she foretold and as myself believed,—
And, so foretelling and believing so,
We were punished, both of us, the merry way: 45
Therefore, tell once again the tale! For what?
Pompilia is only dying while I speak!
Why does the mirth hang fire and miss the smile?
My masters, there's an old book, you should con
For strange adventures, applicable yet,   50
'T is stuffed with. Do you know that there was once
This thing: a multitude of worthy folk
Took recreation, watched a certain group
Of soldiery intent upon a game,—
How first they wrangled, but soon fell to play,   55
Threw dice,—the best diversion in the world.
A word in your ear,—they are now casting lots,
Ay, with that gesture quaint and cry uncouth,
For the coat of One murdered an hour ago!
I am a priest,—talk of what I have learned.   60

---

40 *MS* Law are *Yale 1* are>were   41 *MS* Of   *MS* innocent without   *MS*
help,—   42 *MS* {no comma}   43 *MS* believed   44 *MS* so,>
so   *MS* both,>it,   45 *MS* way.   48 *MS* What, shall   49 *MS*
book you   50 *MS* adventures—   *MS* yet—   52 *MS* thing—
55 *MS* {beginning of fo. 309}   *MS* and then fell   58 *MS* those gestures>that
gesture   *MS* uncouth cry,   60 *MS* priest,

---

41 *pert*: bold, forward.

49 *an old book*: i.e. the Bible. The savage irony of this reference only becomes clear
at l. 55 and after: see next n.

52–6 *multitude . . . world*: see John 19: 23–24. The parallel is passionate and sarcastic:
just as the soldiers gambled for Christ's seamless tunic or 'coat' while above them
Christ himself was dying on the cross, so the judges are engaged in idle talk while
Pompilia is 'bleeding out her life' in St Anna's hospital. Browning may be remember-
ing the treatment of the event in paintings: some show one of the soldiers throwing
dice while the others look on, with (as here) a crowd gathered round; others take an
earlier point in the action, where the soldiers are quarrelling about the garment, one
with a drawn knife about to cut it, another trying to mediate, before they agree on the
compromise of throwing dice for it.

59 *One*: i.e. Pompilia, compared directly to the crucified Christ (hence the capital-
ization).

Pompilia is bleeding out her life belike,
Gasping away the latest breath of all,
This minute, while I talk—not while you laugh?

Yet, being sobered now, what is it you ask
By way of explanation? There's the fact!   65
It seems to fill the universe with sight
And sound,—from the four corners of this earth
Tells itself over, to my sense at least.
But you may want it lower set i' the scale,—
Too vast, too close it clangs in the ear, perhaps;   70
You'd stand back just to comprehend it more.
Well then, let me, the hollow rock, condense
The voice o' the sea and wind, interpret you
The mystery of this murder. God above!
It is too paltry, such a transference   75
O' the storm's roar to the cranny of the stone!

This deed, you saw begin—why does its end
Surprise you? Why should the event enforce
The lesson, we ourselves learned, she and I,
From the first o' the fact, and taught you, all in vain?   80
This Guido from whose throat you took my grasp,
Was this man to be favoured, now, or feared,
Let do his will, or have his will restrained,
In the relation with Pompilia? Say!
Did any other man need interpose   85

---

63 *MS* tell—   *MS* laugh.   64 *MS* {no new paragraph}   65 *MS*
fact.   67 *MS* sound,   *MS* world   68 *MS* least;   69 *MS*
in   70 *MS* perhaps,   71 *MS* the more; *1868 1872* more: 73 *MS*
of   74 *MS* above,   76 *MS* Of   77 *MS* {no new paragraph}   *MS*
{no comma}   80 *MS* of   82 *MS* {beginning of fo. 310}   *MS* a
man to favor and not fear>man to be favored now, or feared,   83 *MS* will
or   84 *MS* Pompilia, say! *1868 1872* Pompilia?—say!

67 *four . . . earth*: cf. Rev. 7: 1.

72 *hollow rock*: hence with the ability to return a condensed echo of the 'voice' of
the sea and wind.

—Oh, though first comer, though as strange at the work
As fribble must be, coxcomb, fool that's near
To knave as, say, a priest who fears the world—
Was he bound brave the peril, save the doomed,
Or go on, sing his snatch and pluck his flower,   90
Keep the straight path and let the victim die?
I held so; you decided otherwise,
Saw no such peril, therefore no such need
To stop song, loosen flower, and leave path. Law,
Law was aware and watching, would suffice,   95
Wanted no priest's intrusion, palpably
Pretence, too manifest a subterfuge!
Whereupon I, priest, coxcomb, fribble and fool,
Ensconced me in my corner, thus rebuked,
A kind of culprit, over-zealous hound   100
Kicked for his pains to kennel; I gave place
To you, and let the law reign paramount:
I left Pompilia to your watch and ward,
And now you point me—there and thus she lies!

[—]

---

86 *MS* new to>strange at   87 *MS* a fribble>fribble   *MS* as>
that's   88 *MS* a knave>knave   *MS* loves   89 *MS* stop the danger,>stay
the danger,>brave the peril,   91 *MS* lie?   92 *MS* so,   94 *MS 1868
1872* path: 97 *MS* subterfuge.   98 *MS* the coxcomb, fribble and
priest,   99 *MS* Betook me to>Ensconced me in   100 *MS* over zeal-
ous   101 *MS* kennel,   *MS* and fit>I gave   *★MS 1868 1872 1888* place, *DC
BrU* place,>place *1889* place   102 *MS* You and>Let the>To you, and let
the   *MS* paramount,

---

87 *fribble*: trifler, frivolous person.

coxcomb: 'a fop; a superficial pretender to knowledge or accomplishments': Johnson.

90 *snatch*: short song.

91 *straight path*: an ironic use. This passage conflates the proverbial straight, narrow
way to Heaven and the primrose path to Hell. Had Caponsacchi ignored Pompilia's
plea for help he would have avoided scandal, and so apparently continued on the
'straight path', although living an indulgent and frivolous life. This choice is therefore
represented in terms reminiscent of the primrose path to Hell, the traveller plucking
flowers and carelessly singing bits of song.

94 *loosen flower*: i.e. let go of the flower (about to be picked). The flower is a
metaphor for pleasure and sensuousness.

103 *watch and ward*: care and protection.

Men, for the last time, what do you want with me?   105
Is it,—you acknowledge, as it were, a use,
A profit in employing me?—at length
I may conceivably help the august law?
I am free to break the blow, next hawk that swoops
On next dove, nor miss much of good repute?   110
Or what if this your summons, after all,
Be but the form of mere release, no more,
Which turns the key and lets the captive go?
I have paid enough in person at Civita,
Am free,—what more need I concern me with?   115
Thank you! I am rehabilitated then,
A very reputable priest. But she—
The glory of life, the beauty of the world,
The splendour of heaven,... well, Sirs, does no one move?
Do I speak ambiguously? The glory, I say,   120
And the beauty, I say, and splendour, still say I,
Who, priest and trained to live my whole life long
On beauty and splendour, solely at their source,
God,—have thus recognized my food in her,
You tell me, that's fast dying while we talk,   125
Pompilia! How does lenity to me,
Remit one death-bed pang to her? Come, smile!
The proper wink at the hot-headed youth
Who lets his soul show, through transparent words,
The mundane love that's sin and scandal too!   130

---

105 *MS* {no new paragraph}   *MS* what's your   106 *MS* it,   107 *MS*
me,   109 *MS* {beginning of fo. 311}   110 *MS* pay>miss   116 *MS*
you,—   117 *MS* man.   *MS* she   120 *MS* {no commas}   121 *MS*
beauty I say and   *MS* I still say,   122 *MS* I>Who   *1868* Who, a priest, trained
123 *MS* splendour solely   124 *MS* ^thus^   *Yale 1* her,>one, *1868* one,
125 *MS* {line added later}   *MS* me is *1868* is fast   126 *MS* *1868* Pompilia,—
how   *MS* me   127 *MS* *1868 1872 1888* (first impression) Come, *1888* (second
impression) *1889* Come {space for the missing comma remains}   129 *MS* {no
commas}   130 *MS* love, that's sin,

118–21 *glory...splendour*: this exalted, quasi-religious description makes clear that
for Caponsacchi Pompilia is a saint, or a Madonna or Beatrice figure, a mediator of his
salvation.

130 *mundane love*: ordinary love, i.e. sexual love of man and woman.

You are all struck acquiescent now, it seems:
It seems the oldest, gravest signor here,
Even the redoubtable Tommati, sits
Chop-fallen,—understands how law might take
Service like mine, of brain and heart and hand,   135
In good part. Better late than never, law!
You understand of a sudden, gospel too
Has a claim here, may possibly pronounce
Consistent with my priesthood, worthy Christ,
That I endeavoured to save Pompilia?   140

                                   Then,
You were wrong, you see: that's well to see, though late:
That's all we may expect of man, this side
The grave: his good is—knowing he is bad:
Thus will it be with us when the books ope   145
And we stand at the bar on judgment-day.
Well then, I have a mind to speak, see cause
To relume the quenched flax by this dreadful light,
Burn my soul out in showing you the truth.
I heard, last time I stood here to be judged,   150

---

133 *MS* {no comma}   134 *MS* Chop fallen,—   135 *MS* in   *MS*
heart and brain>brain and heart   ⋆136 *MS* Lords! *1868 1872* law! *1888*
1889 law   137 *MS* {beginning of fo. 312}   *MS* Gospel   138 *MS* Had
MS declare   139 *MS* priesthood and   *MS* {no commas}   140 *MS* help
141 *MS* {no new paragraph}   142 *MS* see though   143 *MS* {no
comma}   *MS*   man this side the grave: 144 {not found in *MS*}
145 *MS* Nay, thus   147 *MS* then I   148 *MS* flax,   *MS* light

134 *Chop-fallen*: dispirited, crest-fallen; cf. *Hamlet*, v. i. 192.
145–6 *books . . . judgment-day*: cf. Rev. 20: 12.
148–9 *relume . . . truth*: cf. Isa. 42: 1–4, *Othello*, v. ii. 7–13. Isaiah is the crucial
allusion, focused on 'quenched', 'flax', 'truth', and 'hear' at l. 153. Caponsacchi sees
himself as God's servant, making clear the true judgment of the case to the judges: 'he
[God's servant] shall bring forth judgment to the Gentiles. He shall not cry, nor lift up,
nor cause his voice to be heard in the street. A bruised reed shall he not break, and the
smoking flax shall he not quench: he shall bring forth judgment unto truth. He shall
not fail nor be discouraged, till he have set judgment in the earth': Isa. 42: 1–4.
Caponsacchi makes himself into the nearly quenched flax that will be relit to reveal
the truth.

What is priest's-duty,—labour to pluck tares
And weed the corn of Molinism; let me
Make you hear, this time, how, in such a case,
Man, be he in the priesthood or at plough,
Mindful of Christ or marching step by step   155
With . . . what's his style, the other potentate
Who bids have courage and keep honour safe,
Nor let minuter admonition tease?—
How he is bound, better or worse, to act.
Earth will not end through this misjudgment, no!   160
For you and the others like you sure to come
Fresh work is sure to follow,—wickedness
That wants withstanding. Many a man of blood,
Many a man of guile will clamour yet,
Bid you redress his grievance,—as he clutched   165
The prey, forsooth a stranger stepped between,
And there's the good gripe in pure waste! My part
Is done; i' the doing it, I pass away
Out of the world. I want no more with earth.
Let me, in heaven's name, use the very snuff   170

151 *MS* priest's duty,—   156 *MS* what may be>what's his style,   157 *MS*
be simply brave and honorable>have courage and keep honor safe, *Yale 1* safe>
safe,   158 *MS* teaze,— *1868 1872* teaze?—   *161 *MS* *1868 1872 1888 1889*
come, *BrU* come,>come {RB's note in *BrU* reads 'Page. 88. line 19.' The word
'come,' is not found in that line, but it is found in page 89, line 19, i.e. line
161}   162 *MS* as sure   *MS* will>to   164 *MS* here>yet   166 *MS*
{beginning of fo. 313}   *MS* steps between   167 *MS* waste.   168 *MS*
in   169 *MS* you.>earth.   170 *MS* God's>heaven's

151–2 *labour . . . Molinism*: i.e. labour to pluck the weeds of heresy (Molinism) out of
the cornfield of the Church. The court previously told Caponsacchi that the primary
duty of a priest was to root out heresy, to keep the Church pure, rather than go
rescuing maidens in distress. Here Caponsacchi's phrasing is ironic, since in the parable
the master advises the servants *not* to weed the tares lest they pull up the wheat also: cf.
Matt. 13: 24–30, 36–43.

156 *the other potentate*: i.e. the temporal power, representing worldliness. Capon-
sacchi is asserting that it was his duty to rescue Pompilia whether acting in a way
inspired by Christ or in a way inspired by a purely worldly ideal of courage and
honour.

167 *gripe*: i.e. the grip of the man of blood. 'Gripe' (pronounced to rhyme with
'type') is a form of 'grip'; cf. 'Soliloquy of the Spanish Cloister', 60.

170–1 *snuff / O' the taper*: the virtually extinct wick (reverting to the imagery of ll.
148–9).

O' the taper in one last spark shall show truth
For a moment, show Pompilia who was true!
Not for her sake, but yours: if she is dead,
Oh, Sirs, she can be loved by none of you
Most or least priestly! Saints, to do us good,   175
Must be in heaven, I seem to understand:
We never find them saints before, at least.
Be her first prayer then presently for you—
She has done the good to me . . .

                          What is all this?   180
There, I was born, have lived, shall die, a fool!
This is a foolish outset:—might with cause
Give colour to the very lie o' the man,
The murderer,—make as if I loved his wife,
In the way he called love. He is the fool there!   185
Why, had there been in me the touch of taint,
I had picked up so much of knaves'-policy
As hide it, keep one hand pressed on the place
Suspected of a spot would damn us both.
Or no, not her!—not even if any of you   190
Dares think that I, i' the face of death, her death
That's in my eyes and ears and brain and heart,
Lie,—if he does, let him! I mean to say,

---

171 *MS* Of   *MS* glimmer>last spark   172 *MS* true—   174 *MS* sirs,
175 *MS* priestly: saints   *MS* {no commas} *Yale 1* Saints to do us good> Saints, to
do us good,   176 *MS* understand—   177 *MS* before at least;   179 *MS*
1868 1872 me..   181 *MS* fool.   182 *MS* outset: 183 *MS* of
185 *MS* there: 186 *MS* been the touch of taint in mine   187 *MS* knaves'
policy *Yale 1* knaves' policy>knaves'-policy   191 *MS* I in   193 *MS* {be-
ginning of fo. 314}   *MS* him,

173–5 *if . . . priestly*: i.e. if Pompilia is dead she is no threat to anyone's celibacy,
neither Caponsacchi's nor the judges'.

178 *her first prayer*: i.e. her first prayer on entering heaven, when as a saint she has
the power to intercede for people on earth. It is interesting to note the sympathy with
which Browning treats Roman Catholic theology, here the doctrine of the interces-
sion of the saints. Though himself of Protestant sensibility, he enters fully into the
Catholic mind-set of his characters.

190 *Or . . . her!*: 'Or no, it would not damn her'. Caponsacchi immediately qualifies
the 'both' of the previous line, which might inadvertently imply that Pompilia was
deceptive or guilty.

So he stop there, stay thought from smirching her
The snow-white soul that angels fear to take   195
Untenderly. But, all the same, I know
I too am taintless, and I bare my breast.
You can't think, men as you are, all of you,
But that, to hear thus suddenly such an end
Of such a wonderful white soul, that comes   200
Of a man and murderer calling the white black,
Must shake me, trouble and disadvantage. Sirs,
Only seventeen!

                        Why, good and wise you are!
You might at the beginning stop my mouth: 205
So, none would be to speak for her, that knew.
I talk impertinently, and you bear,
All the same. This it is to have to do
With honest hearts: they easily may err,
But in the main they wish well to the truth.   210
You are Christians; somehow, no one ever plucked
A rag, even, from the body of the Lord,
To wear and mock with, but, despite himself,
He looked the greater and was the better. Yes,
I shall go on now. Does she need or not   215

---

195 *MS* the angels   197 *MS* tainless   *MS* {no comma}   198 *MS*
that>as   199 *MS* suddenly,   202 *MS* Shakes me, brings   204 *MS*
{no new   paragraph}   *MS* are.   205 *MS* mouth, *Yale 1* mouth,>
mouth: 206 *MS* {no commas} *Yale 1* So>So,   207 *MS* bear *Yale 1*
bear>bear,   209 *MS* {no comma}   210 *MS* truth: 211 *MS* {no
comma}   212 *MS* {no commas} *Yale 1* Lord>Lord,   213 *MS* him-
self   215 *MS* 'or not' not found

211–14 *somehow . . . better.* i.e. even the soldiers who took Christ's garments were
somehow bettered by the experience. Caponsacchi is again comparing the judges with
the soldiers of John 19: 23–24: see ll. 52–6 n. He extends the biblical account,
imagining the soldiers putting on the clothes they have taken from Christ, hence
'mocking' him. A paraphrase would be: 'even if you are not Christians in any real
sense, even the slightest contact with Christ (Pompilia) will imbue you with something
of his grace.' Caponsacchi implies that the judges, sceptical or mocking of Pompilia's
memory—like the soldiers in their treatment of Christ—may nonetheless be changed
by their contact with her. The crucifixion scene, with Pompilia as crucified Christ, is
an important image in his consciousness.

I keep calm? Calm I'll keep as monk that croons
Transcribing battle, earthquake, famine, plague,
From parchment to his cloister's chronicle.
Not one word more from the point now!

                                    I begin.   220
Yes, I am one of your body and a priest.
Also I am a younger son o' the House
Oldest now, greatest once, in my birth-town
Arezzo, I recognize no equal there—
(I want all arguments, all sorts of arms   225
That seem to serve,—use this for a reason, wait!)
Not therefore thrust into the Church, because
O' the piece of bread one gets there. We were first

---

217 *MS* plague   220 *MS* {no new paragraph}   221 *MS* {no comma}
222 *MS* {beginning of fo. 315}   *MS* of   224 *MS 1872* recognise   228 *MS*
Of   *Yale 1* there>[ ]>there

221–56 *Yes . . . brother:* the source for this family history of the Caponsacchi family
and for the account of the good Bishop Tommaso is Pietro Farulli, *Annali, overo notizie
istoriche dell'antica, nobile, e valorosa città di Arezzo in Toscana* (Foligno, 1717) or some
exact redaction of this chronicle. The passage is a clear instance of the detailed
historical research Browning undertook in addition to his study of OYB and SS: the
Caponsacchi family background is selective but basically historical.
    The chronicle makes clear the correct reading of l. 235. The date it gives, 1312, has
puzzled commentators, who take it as a mistake on Browning's part for the date at
which the Caponsacchi came down from Fiesole into Florence, an event that occurred
in the early part of the twelfth century. In fact 1312 is a year that has stuck in
Browning's mind from the chronicle as the last date at which the Caponsacchi can
be said to have 'flourished' in Florence, since in that year they were subject to a
massacre. We give the relevant lines here in translation, and a longer extract from the
original chronicle in Appendix B: 'In the year 1638 Urban VIII promoted Tommaso di
Jacopo d'Alamanno Salviati to the rank of Bishop of the city of Arezzo. [Tommaso], an
aristocrat from Florence, was a prelate of great human goodness, zeal, and erudition,
born of the ancient and famous family of Caponsacchi from Fiesole, so called after
Giovanni, known as Capo nel Sacco [Head in Sack], who had flourished in 1030. In
the year 1312 the Guelphs massacred almost the entire family because it was Ghibel-
line. The only survivor of that cruel fury was a Messer Salvi, a famous physician, from
whom the Salviati stock originates. This family of Caponsacchi came to Arezzo from
Fiesole when the latter was destroyed by the Florentines in 1010 [. . .] In the year
1303, under Puliciano di Mugello, the Florentines captured Cecco and Rodolfo
Caponsacchi, valiant captains of the White faction, and killed them. Giannuzzo
Caponsacchi was Podestà of the city of L'Aquila, in the Abruzzo region, in the year
1353. The Caponsacchi's homes, which were in the Old Market [in Florence], were
set on fire in the year 1223 and the whole neighbourhood of the piazza was burned
down. In the year 1257 the family was expelled from Florence by the enraged mob,

Of Fiesole, that rings still with the fame
Of Capo-in-Sacco our progenitor: 230
When Florence ruined Fiesole, our folk
Migrated to the victor-city, and there
Flourished,—our palace and our tower attest,
In the Old Mercato,—this was years ago,
Four hundred, full,—no, it wants fourteen just.   235
Our arms are those of Fiesole itself,
The shield quartered with white and red: a branch
Are the Salviati of us, nothing more.
That were good help to the Church? But better still—
Not simply for the advantage of my birth   240
I' the way of the world, was I proposed for priest;
But because there's an illustration, late
I' the day, that's loved and looked to as a saint
Still in Arezzo, he was bishop of,
Sixty years since: he spent to the last doit   245
His bishop's-revenue among the poor,
And used to tend the needy and the sick,
Barefoot, because of his humility.

---

230 *MS* Capo in Sacco   231 *MS* [ ]>ruined   234 *MS* Mercato;   *MS*
ago   241 *MS* In   *MS* priest,   243 *MS* In   244 *MS* {no com-
mas}   246 *MS* Bishop's revenue

---

their palaces knocked down, and the stones reused to make the city walls on the San
Giorgio side, because the Caponsacchi had united with the powerful family of Uberti
against the city government. [. . .] Let us return to the aforementioned Bishop Tom-
maso, who was prelate at Santa Vita. He used to distribute all the income of the
bishopric to the poor and to charitable foundations, and walked about the City
barefoot. He found a husband for, or made nuns of, many noble spinsters. He defended
the people of the city of Arezzo, who were accused of putting a rope around the neck
of the statue of Grand Duke Ferdinand, and he placated the wrath of Grand Duke
Ferdinand II, who wanted to raze the town to the ground and have the soil sprinkled
with salt. On this account, the people of Arezzo are deeply grateful to that family': pp.
249–50.

230 *Capo-in-Sacco*: 'Head-in-Sack' (It.); cf. II. 1249 n.

231 *Florence ruined Fiesole*: the Florentines sacked the nearby town of Fiesole in
1125, pulling down its walls and destroying many of its buildings.

234 *Old Mercato*: Old Market, the centre of the medieval town.

235 *Four. . .just*: 386 years before 1698, the year in which he is speaking, i.e. 1312.
See 221–56 n.

242 *illustration*: example, illustrious name.

He it was,—when the Granduke Ferdinand
Swore he would raze our city, plough the place   250
And sow it with salt, because we Aretines
Had tied a rope about the neck, to hale
The statue of his father from its base
For hate's sake,—he availed by prayers and tears
To pacify the Duke and save the town.   255
This was my father's father's brother. You see,
For his sake, how it was I had a right
To the self-same office, bishop in the egg,
So, grew i' the garb and prattled in the school,
Was made expect, from infancy almost,   260
The proper mood o' the priest; till time ran by
And brought the day when I must read the vows,
Declare the world renounced and undertake
To become priest and leave probation,—leap
Over the ledge into the other life,   265
Having gone trippingly hitherto up to the height
O'er the wan water. Just a vow to read!

I stopped short awe-struck. "How shall holiest flesh
"Engage to keep such vow inviolate,
"How much less mine? I know myself too weak,   270
"Unworthy! Choose a worthier stronger man!"
And the very Bishop smiled and stopped my mouth

249 *MS* {beginning of fo. 316}   *MS* was who,—>was,—   *MS* Duke>
Great-Duke   250 *MS* city to the ground   251 *MS* the place>it   *MS*
our Aretines   255 *MS* pacify the wrath   257 *MS* chance>
right   258 *MS* Of>To   *MS* was bishop>bishop   259 *MS* dressed>dra-
ped>grew   *MS* in   *MS* dress>garb   *MS* put into the path>prattled in the
school   260 *MS* deleted 'And' interlined above undeleted 'Was'   *MS* profess
>expect   *MS* {no commas}   261 *MS* of   *MS* priest,   262 *MS*
^brought^   *MS* one day   *MS* needs must I>when I must   263 *MS* obliga-
tions,>world renounced and   264 *MS* become [ ] probationer,—>become
priest and drop probationer,—>become priest and leave probation,—   265 *MS*
{no comma}   268 *MS* {no new paragraph}   269–71 *MS* {no quotation
marks at beginnings of lines}   269 *MS* [ ]>keep   *MS* keep the> keep
such   270 *MS 1868 1872* mine,—   272 *MS 1868* the mouth

261 *mood*: figure, form; the sense is from logic: see OED² *sb.*² 1.

In its mid–protestation. "Incapable?
"Qualmish of conscience? Thou ingenuous boy!
"Clear up the clouds and cast thy scruples far!   275
"I satisfy thee there's an easier sense
"Wherein to take such vow than suits the first
"Rough rigid reading. Mark what makes all smooth,
"Nay, has been even a solace to myself!
"The Jews who needs must, in their synagogue,   280
"Utter sometimes the holy name of God,
"A thing their superstition boggles at,
"Pronounce aloud the ineffable sacrosanct,—
"How does their shrewdness help them? In this wise;
"Another set of sounds they substitute,   285
"Jumble so consonants and vowels—how
"Should I know?—that there grows from out the old
"Quite a new word that means the very same—
"And o'er the hard place slide they with a smile.
"Giuseppe Maria Caponsacchi mine,   290
"Nobody wants you in these latter days
"To prop the Church by breaking your back-bone,—
"As the necessary way was once, we know,
"When Diocletian flourished and his like.
"That building of the buttress-work was done   295

274–335 *MS* {no quotation marks at beginnings of lines}   275 *MS* far.
276 *MS* {beginning of fo. 317}.   277 *MS* To take such vow:> Wherein to
take such vow   279 *MS* myself.   280 *MS* Blind > The   285 *MS*
cognate word>set of sounds   286 *MS* So jumble   288 *MS* [sound?]>
word   289 *MS* over   290 *MS* Giuseppe-Maria   292 *MS* back-bone
294 *MS* martyrs>Dioclesian *1868 1872* Dioclesian   *MS* like,— *1868 1872* like;
295 *MS* business>building

274 *Qualmish*: doubtful, full of qualms.

283 *ineffable sacrosanct*: unutterable sacredness, i.e. the name of God. 'Sacrosanct' as a
noun is rare, perhaps a neologism. The Jews, regarding the name of God as unspeak-
able through a deep sense of reverence, substitute *Adonai* for *Yahweh* in reading.
Browning also refers to the 'ineffable Name' in 'Abt Vogler' and 'Solomon and Balkis':
see Gal Manor, 'The Allure of Supernatural Language: the Ineffable Name in Robert
Browning's Poems', BSN 25 (1998), 6–17.

294 *Diocletian . . . like*: i.e. when Christians were persecuted in the first centuries of
the Church. Diocletian was the Roman Emperor whose reign (AD 284–305) was
notable for the last major persecution of the Christians.

"By martyrs and confessors: let it bide,
"Add not a brick, but, where you see a chink,
"Stick in a sprig of ivy or root a rose
"Shall make amends and beautify the pile!
"We profit as you were the painfullest   300
"O' the martyrs, and you prove yourself a match
"For the cruelest confessor ever was,
"If you march boldly up and take your stand
"Where their blood soaks, their bones yet strew the soil,
"And cry 'Take notice, I the young and free   305
"'And well-to-do i' the world, thus leave the world,
"'Cast in my lot thus with no gay young world
"'But the grand old Church: she tempts me of the two!'
"Renounce the world? Nay, keep and give it us!
"Let us have you, and boast of what you bring.   310
"We want the pick o' the earth to practise with,
"Not its offscouring, halt and deaf and blind
"In soul and body. There's a rubble-stone
"Unfit for the front o' the building, stuff to stow
"In a gap behind and keep us weather-tight;   315
"There's porphyry for the prominent place. Good lack!

---

299 *MS* ^make amends and^   300 *MS* You   301 *MS* Of the martyrs,
prove yourself a match, I say,   302 *MS 1868 1872* cruellest   303 *MS*
{beginning of fo. 318}   304 *MS* soaks and their bones strew *MS*
place,> soil,   305 *MS* "Take   306 *MS* well-to-do-in   308 *MS*
Church, *MS* two."   310 *MS* to>and   311 *MS* of *MS* practice
313 *MS* body; there's   314 *MS* of

---

296 *confessors*: those who confessed or made public avowal of their Christian faith
in the early centuries and so suffered torture or persecution at the hands of the
Roman authorities (though not death). Martyrs are those who actually died for their
faith.

302 *cruelest confessor*: i.e. a confessor who suffered the cruellest tortures: see pre-
vious n.

312 *halt*: lame; cf. 1. 320.

313 *rubble-stone*: ugly, composite rock, formed of cemented fragments, contrasted
here with porphyry, an expensive, beautifully coloured stone: see Ruskin, xxvi. 390.
In the bishop's contempt for 'rubble-stone' there is an echo of another bishop's
contempt for 'gritstone': see 'The Bishop Orders His Tomb', 115–17.

316 *Good lack!*: an exclamation.

"Saint Paul has had enough and to spare, I trow,
"Of ragged run-away Onesimus:
"He wants the right-hand with the signet-ring
"Of King Agrippa, now, to shake and use.   320
"I have a heavy scholar cloistered up,
"Close under lock and key, kept at his task
"Of letting Fénelon know the fool he is,
"In a book I promise Christendom next Spring.
"Why, if he covets so much meat, the clown,   325
"As a lark's wing next Friday, or, any day,
"Diversion beyond catching his own fleas,
"He shall be properly swinged, I promise him.
"But you, who are so quite another paste
"Of a man,—do you obey me? Cultivate   330
"Assiduous that superior gift you have
"Of making madrigals—(who told me? Ah!)

317 *MS* by this,>by now,   319 *MS* right hand   320 *MS* {no com-
mas}   321 *MS* {no comma}   323 *MS* Leibnitz>Fenelon *1868 1872*
Fenelon   *MS* {no comma}   324 *MS* spring.   325 *MS* Why if
326 *MS* larks   *MS* any>next   328 *MS* you.>him.   330 *MS* {begin-
ning of fo. 319}   331 *MS* Assiduous, *1868 1872* "Assiduous,

317–20 *Saint Paul . . . King Agrippa*: i.e. the Church wants aristocrats as priests not
lower-class people. Onesimus, the runaway slave of St Paul's Epistle to Philemon, is
used as a type of the rough, poor person, and is contrasted with King Herod Agrippa II
of Acts 25–6, a type of the gracious aristocrat. The signet-ring, however, is not from
the Bible but from the reference to Agrippa in Juvenal vi. 157–8: it signifies his wealth
and status (in contrast to ragged Onesimus) but also hints at his corruption, his
rumoured incest with his sister Berenice. Browning's sly irony suggests that the bishop
likes the idea of well-to-do priests on any terms.

321 *heavy*: dull, serious.

323 *Fénelon*: the famous French liberal ecclesiastic, François de Salignac de La
Mothe Fénelon (1651–1715). In 1695 he was made Archbishop of Cambrai,
but after the publication in 1697 of his *Explication des maximes des saints sur la vie
intérieure* he was accused by his opponents of Quietism and eventually his writings in
these areas were censured by Pope Innocent XII in 1699. If the reference here is to
the *Explication* it is anachronistic in terms of date, but long before this work
Fénelon was famous for his liberal-tending views on education, politics, Protestants,
and prayer.

329 *paste*: quality (fig.).

"Get done a Marinesque Adoniad straight
"With a pulse o' the blood a-pricking, here and there,
"That I may tell the lady 'And he's ours!'" 335

So I became a priest: those terms changed all,
I was good enough for that, nor cheated so;
I could live thus and still hold head erect.
Now you see why I may have been before
A fribble and coxcomb, yet, as priest, break word 340
Nowise, to make you disbelieve me now.
I need that you should know my truth. Well, then,
According to prescription did I live,
—Conformed myself, both read the breviary
And wrote the rhymes, was punctual to my place 345
I' the Pieve, and as diligent at my post
Where beauty and fashion rule. I throve apace,
Sub-deacon, Canon, the authority

---

334 *MS* of   *MS* if you dare,   335 *MS* "And *1868 1872* lady,   *MS*
ours!"   336 *MS* {New paragraph (already written thus) indicated by 'N.P.'
in left-hand margin}   338 *MS* my head   339 *MS* could   *MS* till
now   340 *MS* coxcomb, and yet break my word   341 *MS* {no com-
ma}   342 *MS* me true.   344 *MS* {no dash}   *MS* myself exactly, said
the mass>myself, both read the breviary   346 *MS* In   347 *MS* Beauty and
Fashion

---

333 *Marinesque Adoniad*: an epic poem about Adonis, in the manner of Marino. In
the seventeenth century Giambattista Marino (1569–1625) was a popular Italian poet.
His major work *L'Adone* ('Adonis') (1623), over 41,000 lines in length, was a version of
the story of Venus and Adonis, with many digressions and extrapolations. His style, for
which he was famous, was extremely ornate, with ingenuity of metaphor and conceit
and *double entendre*. *L'Adone* is highly sensual and erotic, with extended treatments of
Venus and Adonis's dalliance and lovemaking. Now its reputation is negligible, despite
attempts to revive it: see H. M. Priest, *Selections from L'Adone of Giambattista Marino*
(Ithaca, NY, 1967).

340 *fribble and coxcomb*: cf. l. 87 nn.

346 *Pieve*: the church of Santa Maria della Pieve, the most ancient in Arezzo, dating
from the ninth century. 'It was repaired in 1216, by *Marchione*, a native architect, with
the addition of the front and campanile.... The campanile has 5 stories of columns
with fantastic capitals. The whole building presents a singular mixture of facility of
style with irregularity of detail': Octavian Blewitt, *A Handbook for Travellers in Central
Italy, Part I* (4th ed., John Murray, 1857), p. 231. Though Caponsacchi mentions the
cathedral of Arezzo elsewhere in the monologue, this is the church with which he is
most intimately associated as a canon.

348 *Sub-deacon, Canon*: cf. l. 263–5 n.

For delicate play at tarocs, and arbiter
O' the magnitude of fan-mounts: all the while   350
Wanting no whit the advantage of a hint
Benignant to the promising pupil,—thus:
"Enough attention to the Countess now,
"The young one; 't is her mother rules the roast,
"We know where, and puts in a word: go pay   355
"Devoir to-morrow morning after mass!
"Break that rash promise to preach, Passion-week!
"Has it escaped you the Archbishop grunts
"And snuffles when one grieves to tell his Grace
"No soul dares treat the subject of the day   360
"Since his own masterly handling it (ha, ha!)
"Five years ago,—when somebody could help
"And touch up an odd phrase in time of need,
"(He, he!)—and somebody helps you, my son!
"Therefore, don't prove so indispensable   365
"At the Pieve, sit more loose i' the seat, nor grow
"A fixture by attendance morn and eve!
"Arezzo's just a haven midway Rome—

---

349 *MS* Faro,   350 *MS* Of   352 *MS* thus   353 *MS* [ ]>atten-
tion   354–92 *MS* {no quotation marks at beginnings of lines}   354 *MS*
{no comma}   356 *MS* {beginning of fo. 320}   *MS* to morrow   *MS*
mass.   357 *MS* {no comma}   *MS* Passion week;   359 *MS* Grac-
iously>And snuffles   364 *MS* son,   366 *MS* in   367 *MS* night and
day:>morn and eve: 368 *MS* midway, Rome

---

349 *delicate play at tarocs*: skilful play with tarot cards. The reference here is not to
fortune-telling, but to the original complicated game of tarot or *tarocco* (It.). Capon-
sacchi helps the society ladies to play well or to negotiate the difficult rules. The game
was played with the tarot pack, which consists of four suits roughly equivalent to those
in the modern pack, with an additional series of twenty-two picture-cards representing
various forces, characters, virtues, and vices. In the seventeenth and eighteenth
centuries the cards were often beautifully made and expensive to buy. Only at the
end of the eighteenth century, in France, did tarot cards begin to be diverted to their
present occult usage: see Michael Dummett, *The Game of Tarot* (London, 1980) and
subsequent studies by the same author.

350 *fan-mounts*: the frames upon which fans are mounted; the main sticks of the fan.
To be an 'arbiter' on the size of fan-mounts is the quintessence of frivolity.

354–5 *her . . . where*: i.e. her mother is a cardinal's mistress.

356 *Devoir*: a dutiful visit, a courtesy call.

"Rome's the eventual harbour,—make for port,
"Crowd sail, crack cordage! And your cargo be   370
"A polished presence, a genteel manner, wit
"At will, and tact at every pore of you!
"I sent our lump of learning, Brother Clout,
"And Father Slouch, our piece of piety,
"To see Rome and try suit the Cardinal.   375
"Thither they clump-clumped, beads and book in hand,
"And ever since 't is meat for man and maid
"How both flopped down, prayed blessing on bent pate
"Bald many an inch beyond the tonsure's need,
"Never once dreaming, the two moony dolts,   380
"There's nothing moves his Eminence so much
"As—far from all this awe at sanctitude—
"Heads that wag, eyes that twinkle, modified mirth
"At the closet-lectures on the Latin tongue
"A lady learns so much by, we know where.   385
"Why, body o' Bacchus, you should crave his rule

---

371 *MS* wit>presence   372 *MS* you.   374 *MS* Slouch our   375 *MS*
Cardinal   377 *MS* mirth>meat   380 *MS* fools,   382 *MS* stupid>all
this   383 *MS* {beginning of fo. 321}   384 *MS* latin   386 *MS*
would

---

370 *Crowd sail, crack cordage*: i.e. hurry on as fast as possible—by hoisting up
maximum sails, and straining the rigging to breaking point. The nautical phrase 'to
crowd sail' has parallels in 'to pack on all sail' and 'press of sail'.

373 *Brother Clout*: Brother Clod, Brother Rustic; there is a slight pun on 'lump'
earlier in the line. The word has these associations from Colin Clout, the central figure
of Spenser's *Shepheardes Calender* (1579); cf. XI. 278.

376 *clumped*: walked heavily and clumsily; the repetition is onomatopoeic and
satiric.

377 *meat . . . maid*: i.e. a good joke that everyone tells.

380 *moony dolts*: crazy, unworldly fools.

384 *closet-lectures*: private lectures (ones held as if in a small room or in the confes-
sional). There is sexual innuendo here: the worldly Cardinal enjoys a sly joke about
what a lady might learn about sex in private talks about Latin vocabulary and poetry;
cf. VIII. 1235 n.

386 *body o' Bacchus*: this is not a recondite oath, but one current in the Italy of
Browning's day: 'They [the Romans] still swear by the loveliest of the heathen deities,
the god of genial nature, Bacchus; and among their commonest exclamations are "*Per
Bacco*," "*Corpo di Bacco*," and even sometimes, in Tuscany particularly, "*Per Bacco
d'India*" or "*Per Dingi Bacco*"': *Roba di Roma*, ii. 221. Cf. 'Up at a Villa', 4.

"For pauses in the elegiac couplet, chasms
"Permissible only to Catullus! There!
"Now go to duty: brisk, break Priscian's head
"By reading the day's office—there's no help.   390
"You've Ovid in your poke to plaster that;
"Amen's at the end of all: then sup with me!"

Well, after three or four years of this life,
In prosecution of my calling, I
Found myself at the theatre one night   395
With a brother Canon, in a mood and mind
Proper enough for the place, amused or no:
When I saw enter, stand, and seat herself
A lady, young, tall, beautiful, strange and sad.
It was as when, in our cathedral once,   400
As I got yawningly through matin-song,
I saw *facchini* bear a burden up,
Base it on the high-altar, break away
A board or two, and leave the thing inside

389 *MS 1868 1872* do duty: *MS* head,   390 {not found in *MS*}
391 *MS* With   *MS* that, *Yale 1* that,>that;   392 *MS* me."   393 *MS*
{New paragraph (already written thus) indicated by 'N.P.' in left-hand
margin}   397 *MS* no,   400 *MS* Cathedral   *MS* {no commas}
402 *MS* {no comma}   403 *MS* And base

387–8 *pauses . . . Catullus*: poems lxv–cxvi by the Latin poet Catullus (*c*.84–*c*.54 BC)
are all in elegiac couplets, a metre in which the first verse is hexameter and the
second pentameter. His Eminence's rule for pauses in the elegiac couplet would be a
statement of those places where a break in sense is permitted. The Cardinal shows his
learning and sophistication by having a theory on this matter. The reference has an
undertow of sexual innuendo, for these poems by Catullus are some of his most
explicitly erotic.

389 *break Priscian's head*: i.e. 'speak bad Latin'. Priscian (*c*.AD 500) was the Latin
grammarian whose *Institutiones Grammaticae* in eighteen books became a famous work.
'To break Priscian's head', i.e. to hurt or insult him, became proverbial for 'to write or
speak bad or unclassical Latin': see ODEP, 82–3.

391 *You've . . . that*: the bishop urges Caponsacchi to read the fine Latin of Ovid to
redeem the injury done to his mind by the unclassical Latin of the church service.

401 *matin-song*: i.e. early morning prayers, or matins. One of the canonical hours of
the breviary, these prayers were often sung the previous evening rather than in the
middle of the night; cf. l. 1443 n.

402 *facchini*: porters (It.).

Lofty and lone: and lo, when next I looked,   405
There was the Rafael! I was still one stare,
When—"Nay, I'll make her give you back your gaze"—
Said Canon Conti; and at the word he tossed
A paper-twist of comfits to her lap,
And dodged and in a trice was at my back   410
Nodding from over my shoulder. Then she turned,
Looked our way, smiled the beautiful sad strange smile.
"Is not she fair? 'T is my new cousin," said he:
"The fellow lurking there i' the black o' the box
"Is Guido, the old scapegrace: she's his wife,   415
"Married three years since: how his Countship sulks!
"He has brought little back from Rome beside,
"After the bragging, bullying. A fair face,
"And—they do say—a pocketful of gold
"When he can worry both her parents dead.   420
"I don't go much there, for the chamber's cold
"And the coffee pale. I got a turn at first
"Paying my duty: I observed they crouched
"—The two old frightened family spectres—close
"In a corner, each on each like mouse on mouse   425

405 *MS* lone,   406 *MS* Rafaello.   *MS* {no comma}   407 *MS* When
"Nay,   *MS* gaze"   408 *MS* Conti,   409 *MS* paper twist   *MS*
into   410 *MS* {beginning of fo. 322}   413 *MS* lovely>fair?   *MS*
he,   414 *MS* lurking in   *MS* of   415–33 *MS* {no quotation marks at
beginnings of lines}   417 *MS* nothing>little   418 *MS* face—
419 *1868 1872* pocket-full   421 *MS* {no comma}   422 *MS* coffee's
pale: 423 *MS* devoir,— *1868* duty,—   *MS* how they   424 *MS* ^fright-
ened^   *MS 1868* spectres,

406 *Rafael*: the incident of the Raphael Madonna displayed on the high altar of the
Pieve church, referred to again at ll. 668–76 and probably at 704–7, seems to be
Browning's invention. There is no reference to it in Vasari or Baldinucci. Raphael was
EBB's favourite Italian painter and she went frequently to the Pitti Gallery to admire
his Madonnas. References to the painter occur often in her letters. She was 'giddy . . .
with the Raffaels' in 1847; both at Piazza Pitti in the winter of 1847–8, and sub-
sequently at Casa Guidi, she was glad 'to be close to the Raffaels': *Correspondence*, xiv.
210, 340. The tender humanity and purity EBB found in her favourite Madonna della
Seggiola and Madonna del Granduca is expressed in Pompilia's 'beautiful sad strange
smile'.
415 *scapegrace*: scoundrel; someone who 'escapes the grace of God'. OED[2] notes
that it is 'often used playfully'.

"I' the cat's cage: ever since, I stay at home.
"Hallo, there's Guido, the black, mean and small,
"Bends his brows on us—please to bend your own
"On the shapely nether limbs of Light-skirts there
"By way of a diversion! I was a fool   430
"To fling the sweetmeats. Prudence, for God's love!
"To-morrow I'll make my peace, e'en tell some fib,
"Try if I can't find means to take you there."

That night and next day did the gaze endure,
Burnt to my brain, as sunbeam thro' shut eyes,   435
And not once changed the beautiful sad strange smile.
At vespers Conti leaned beside my seat
I' the choir,—part said, part sung—"*In ex-cel-sis*—
"All's to no purpose; I have louted low,
"But he saw you staring—*quia sub*—don't incline   440
"To know you nearer: him we would not hold
"For Hercules,—the man would lick your shoe

---

426 *MS* In   *MS* {no comma}   427 *MS* black mean ^and^ small <man>
429 *MS* light-skirts   430 *MS* diversion.   434 *MS* {no new para-
graph}   *MS* that gaze   435 {not   found   in   *MS*}   436 *MS*
smile: 437 *MS* Vespers   438 *MS* {beginning of fo. 323}   *MS* In
439–51 *MS* {no quotation marks at beginnings of lines}   439 *MS* 1868 1872
purpose: *MS* {no comma} *Yale 1* low>low,   442 *MS* Hercules,

---

429 *Light-skirts*: a flirtatious young woman, a woman of light character. Browning is
very good here at creating the sexual banter of young men. Francis Quarles calls
Herodias 'Light-skirts' in one of his epigrammatic poems: see *Divine Fancies* (1632),
iv. 12.

437 *vespers*: formal evening prayers, one of the canonical hours; cf. l. 401 n.

438 "*In ex-cel-sis*: 'in the highest' (L.). In the following passage Conti is supposedly
singing parts of the official evening prayers at the Pieve, while actually he is whispering
to Caponsacchi about women and the possibilities of seduction. The joke is the
contrast between the high-sounding prayerfulness of the Latin, and what it disguises:
Conti's lecherous speech.

439 *louted low*: bowed low, i.e. apologized profusely (to Guido). The phrase occurs
in Spenser, Scott, and elsewhere.

440 *quia sub*: 'because under' (L.). There is interplay between this sung Latin and
Conti's actual speech. The Latin sounds like 'because under [God]' but actually Conti
implies that Guido sees Caponsacchi as 'below him' in terms of class and therefore
'don't incline [condescend, bend] / To know you nearer'.

441–2 *him . . . Hercules*: 'we don't think Guido is like Hercules', i.e. we are not
afraid of him.

"If you and certain efficacious friends
"Managed him warily,—but there's the wife:
"Spare her, because he beats her, as it is,   445
"She's breaking her heart quite fast enough—*jam tu*—
"So, be you rational and make amends
"With little Light-skirts yonder—*in secula*
"*Secu-lo-o-o-o-rum*. Ah, you rogue! Every one knows
"What great dame she makes jealous: one against one,   450
"Play, and win both!"

                Sirs, ere the week was out,
I saw and said to myself "Light-skirts hides teeth
"Would make a dog sick,—the great dame shows spite
"Should drive a cat mad: 't is but poor work this—   455
"Counting one's fingers till the sonnet's crowned.
"I doubt much if Marino really be
"A better bard than Dante after all.
"'T is more amusing to go pace at eve
"I' the Duomo,—watch the day's last gleam outside   460
"Turn, as into a skirt of God's own robe,

444 *MS* warily,   445 *MS* her as   447 *MS* {no comma}   448 *MS*
yonder *in secula*   449 *MS* Secu-loooo-rum.   450 *MS* The>What   *MS*
one.   453 *MS* "Light skirts   454–67 *MS* {no quotation marks at begin-
nings of lines}   455 *MS* To   *MS* this:>this—   460 *MS* In   *MS*
Duomo,   461 *MS* {no commas}

  443 *efficacious*: influential; cf. I. 1139 n.

  446 *jam tu*: 'now you' (L.). Conti sings these words supposedly as part of the
evening prayers, but actually they fit into his secret speech to Caponsacchi: '*now
you*—go and chase a different girl, not Pompilia'.

  448–9 *in secula* / *Secu-lo-o-o-o-rum*: 'eternally, for endless ages' (L.). This famous
liturgical phrase occurs at the end of some of the best-known hymns used at vespers.
The last word is strung out because Conti is singing it. Again there is interplay between
the Latin and Conti's secret speech: i.e. 'go and seduce Light-skirts *for ever and ever*'.

  457–8 *Marino . . . Dante*: Caponsacchi turns from the erotic love poetry of Marino
to the religious vision of Dante's *Divina Commedia*, i.e. from a smart fashionable poet to
one of enduring value: see l. 333 n.

  460 *Duomo*: cathedral. It is on the north side of Arezzo and a good example of
gothic architecture.

  461 *skirt . . . robe*: the lower part of God's robe; cf. I Sam. 24: 11, and 'Christmas
Eve', 638.

"Those lancet-windows' jewelled miracle,—
"Than go eat the Archbishop's ortolans,
"Digest his jokes. Luckily Lent is near:
"Who cares to look will find me in my stall   465
"At the Pieve, constant to this faith at least—
"Never to write a canzonet any more."

So, next week, 't was my patron spoke abrupt,
In altered guise. "Young man, can it be true
"That after all your promise of sound fruit,   470
"You have kept away from Countess young or old
"And gone play truant in church all day long?
"Are you turning Molinist?" I answered quick:
"Sir, what if I turned Christian? It might be.
"The fact is, I am troubled in my mind,   475
"Beset and pressed hard by some novel thoughts.

---

462 *MS* lancet windows   *MS* miracle,   464 *MS* near—   465 *MS* {be-
ginning of fo. 324}   466 *MS* least   467 *MS* once more."   468 *MS*
{no new paragraph}   *MS* So next   469 *MS 1868 1872* guise,   *MS* put on the
[ ]>"Young man, can it be true   470–81 *MS* {no quotation marks at beginnings
of lines}   471 *MS* the Countess   473 *MS* "I>I   *MS* him>quick *1868
1872* quick

462 *lancet-windows' jewelled miracle*: the 20 ft. stained-glass windows by Guillaume de
Marseille, a sixteenth-century French Dominican monk. 'The tall lancet windows of
the Tribune have been compared and even preferred to the "Five Sisters" of York
Minster': *Murray's Handbook: South Tuscany & Papal States*, 4th ed. (1857), 231. Brown-
ing would have remembered them from his own observation. Cf. Hawthorne's
account of the interior of the cathedral in 1858: 'We found the Cathedral very stately,
with its great arches, and darkly magnificent, with the dim, rich light coming through
its painted windows, some of which are reckoned the most beautiful that the whole
world has to show. The hues are far more brilliant than those of any painted glass I
saw in England, and a great wheel window looks like a constellation of many colored gems.
The old English glass gets so smoky, and dim with dust, that its pristine beauty cannot
any longer be even imagined; nor did I imagine it, till I saw these Italian windows':
Hawthorne, 270.

463 *ortolans*: small birds that are delicious to eat; one quotation in OED[2] aptly
describes them as 'the epicure's prime morceau' (1837). In the 'Prologue' to *Ferishtah's
Fancies* (1884) Browning describes a mouth-watering way of roasting ortolans with
bread and sage leaves, a recipe that he himself had clearly enjoyed.

467 *canzonet*: light poem or love song, from It. *canzonetta* the dim. of *canzone*. In *De
vulgari eloquentia* (II. viii) Dante says that a *canzone* has stanzas in the 'tragic style', while
the diminutive should be used for stanzas in the 'comic style'.

"This your Arezzo is a limited world;
"There's a strange Pope,—'t is said, a priest who thinks.
"Rome is the port, you say: to Rome I go.
"I will live alone, one does so in a crowd,   480
"And look into my heart a little." "Lent
"Ended,"—I told friends—"I shall go to Rome."

    One evening I was sitting in a muse
Over the opened "Summa," darkened round
By the mid–March twilight, thinking how my life   485
Had shaken under me,—broke short indeed
And showed the gap 'twixt what is, what should be,—
And into what abysm the soul may slip,
Leave aspiration here, achievement there,
Lacking omnipotence to connect extremes—   490
Thinking moreover . . . oh, thinking, if you like,
How utterly dissociated was I
A priest and celibate, from the sad strange wife
Of Guido,—just as an instance to the point,
Nought more,—how I had a whole store of strengths   495
Eating into my heart, which craved employ,
And she, perhaps, need of a finger's help,—
And yet there was no way in the wide world
To stretch out mine and so relieve myself,—

---

477 *MS* world,   478 *MS* new *Yale 1* new>strange   *MS* man ⟨that⟩ ^who^
thinks. *1872* thinks   480 *MS* alone there, as one can>alone, one does
so   481 *MS* little there.">little." "Lent   482 *MS* So I>"Ended" I   *MS*
people,>friends, *1868 1872* friends,—   483 *MS* {New paragraph (already written
thus) indicated by 'N.P.' in left-hand margin}   *MS* Next>One   *MS*
my>a   485 *MS* ^the mid-March^   *MS* looking at>thinking how
486 *MS* me,   487 *MS* be,   488 *MS* ^into^   *MS* slip—   489 *MS*
With   490 *MS* Omnipotence   491 *MS* {beginning of fo. 325}   *MS*
1868 1872 moreover . .   493 *MS* {no comma}   497 *MS* {no commas}
MS help   499 *MS 1868* myself—

---

484 *"Summa,"*: the *Summa Theologica* of St Thomas Aquinas: cf. v. 1358 n. Capon-
sacchi's study of this work suggests the new earnestness already dawning in his life in
the wake of his first view of Pompilia.

486 *broke short*: stopped suddenly (from continuing in its former course). In the
following lines, Caponsacchi sees his former life as like a bridge over a gorge, one
suddenly inadequate to its purpose.

How when the page o' the Summa preached its best,   500
Her smile kept glowing out of it, as to mock
The silence we could break by no one word,—
There came a tap without the chamber-door,
And a whisper; when I bade who tapped speak out.
And, in obedience to my summons, last   505
In glided a masked muffled mystery,
Laid lightly a letter on the opened book,
Then stood with folded arms and foot demure,
Pointing as if to mark the minutes' flight.

I took the letter, read to the effect   510
That she, I lately flung the comfits to,
Had a warm heart to give me in exchange,
And gave it,—loved me and confessed it thus,
And bade me render thanks by word of mouth,
Going that night to such a side o' the house   515
Where the small terrace overhangs a street
Blind and deserted, not the street in front:
Her husband being away, the surly patch,
At his villa of Vittiano.

                "And you?"—I asked: 520
"What may you be?" "Count Guido's kind of maid—

---

500 *MS* of   *MS* spoke>preached   *MS* {no comma}   501 *MS* speaking
louder>glowing out of it,   502 *MS* should   *MS* word—   503 *MS*
the tap   504 *MS* the whisper when *1868 1872* whisper,   *MS 1868 1872*
out,   506 *MS* masked, *Yale 1* masked,>masked   507 *MS* light
508 *MS* arms,   510 *MS* {no new paragraph}   512 *MS* just a heart
514 *MS* answer only by the>render thanks by word of   *MS* {no com-
ma}   515 *MS* to that side of his   516 *MS* the street   518 *MS* {be-
ginning of fo. 326}   519 *MS* Villa   520 *MS* {no new paragraph}
521 *MS 1868 1872* be?"—"Count

---

506 *masked . . . mystery*: Margherita, Guido's servant and mistress, through whom he
tries to provoke an affair between Pompilia and Caponsacchi: cf. III. 1097 n.
517 *blind*: unseen, not overlooked; cf. II. 358, 1365, III. 1595.
518 *patch*: fool, booby.

"Most of us have two functions in his house.
"We all hate him, the lady suffers much,
" 'T is just we show compassion, furnish help,
"Specially since her choice is fixed so well.   525
"What answer may I bring to cheer the sweet
"Pompilia?"

                Then I took a pen and wrote
"No more of this! That you are fair, I know:
"But other thoughts now occupy my mind.   530
"I should not thus have played the insensible
"Once on a time. What made you,—may one ask,—
"Marry your hideous husband? 'T was a fault,
"And now you taste the fruit of it. Farewell."

"There!" smiled I as she snatched it and was gone—   535
"There, let the jealous miscreant,—Guido's self,
"Whose mean soul grins through this transparent trick,—
"Be baulked so far, defrauded of his aim!
"What fund of satisfaction to the knave,
"Had I kicked this his messenger down stairs,   540
"Trussed to the middle of her impudence,
"And set his heart at ease so! No, indeed!
"There's the reply which he shall turn and twist
"At pleasure, snuff at till his brain grow drunk,
"As the bear does when he finds a scented glove   545

522–7 MS {no quotation marks at beginnings of lines}   524 MS 1868 1872
aid,   525 MS on you.>so well.   526 MS shall>may   528 MS {no
new paragraph}   MS 1868 1872 wrote.   530–4 MS {no quotation marks at
beginnings of lines}   535 MS {no new paragraph}   MS gone,   536–
56 MS {no quotation marks at beginnings of lines}   536 MS There— MS
miserable>jealous miscreant,   MS   self   537 MS   trick,   538 MS
aim: 539 MS Nor find the satisfaction and breathe free>What fund of satisfac-
tion to the fool,   540 MS Did I kick   MS {no comma}   541 MS {no
comma}   542 MS 1868 Setting   544 MS drunk

531 the insensible: the unfeeling one, someone unresponsive to sexual advances.
541 Trussed...impudence: i.e. tied to the middle of her impudence, as though to a
weight (so that she falls downstairs faster).
544 snuff at: sniff at.

"That puzzles him,—a hand and yet no hand,
"Of other perfume than his own foul paw!
"Last month, I had doubtless chosen to play the dupe,
"Accepted the mock-invitation, kept
"The sham appointment, cudgel beneath cloak,   550
"Prepared myself to pull the appointer's self
"Out of the window from his hiding-place
"Behind the gown of this part-messenger
"Part-mistress who would personate the wife.
"Such had seemed once a jest permissible: 555
"Now I am not i' the mood."
                                        Back next morn brought
The messenger, a second letter in hand.
"You are cruel, Thyrsis, and Myrtilla moans
"Neglected but adores you, makes request   560
"For mercy: why is it you dare not come?
"Such virtue is scarce natural to your age.
"You must love someone else; I hear you do,
"The Baron's daughter or the Advocate's wife,
"Or both,—all's one, would you make me the third—   565
"I take the crumbs from table gratefully
"Nor grudge who feasts there. 'Faith, I blush and blaze!
"Yet if I break all bounds, there's reason sure.
"Are you determinedly bent on Rome?
"I am wretched here, a monster tortures me: 570

---

546 hand—   547 *MS* {beginning of fo. 327}   *MS* paw.   548 *MS* month
I   *MS* probably>doubtless   549 *MS* mock invitation, *Yale 1* mock invita-
tion>mock-invitation   551 *MS* And been prepared   552 *MS* hiding pla-
ce   553 *MS* the messenger   554 *MS* And   mistress   555 *MS*
That   *MS* been>seemed   556 *MS 1868 1872* Now,   *MS* in   *MS* {no quo-
tation mark at end of line}   557 *MS* night>morn   *MS* came   560–
74 *MS* {no quotation marks at beginnings of lines}   562 *MS 1868 1872*
age: 566 *MS* the table   568 *MS* sure: *1868* sure,   570 *MS* miser-
able, a wretch   *MS* me—

551 *appointer's self*: i.e. Guido.

559 *Thyrsis . . . Myrtilla*: standard names for male and female lovers from *Il Pastor
Fido* by Giovambattista Guarini (1537–1612). The pseudonyms used in the actual
supposed love letters were Mirtillo and Amarilli: OYB xcii–xcviii (99–106).

567 *blush and blaze*: redden and then redden some more (with embarrassment).

"Carry me with you! Come and say you will!
"Concert this very evening! Do not write!
"I am ever at the window of my room
"Over the terrace, at the *Ave.* Come!"

I questioned—lifting half the woman's mask   575
To let her smile loose. "So, you gave my line
"To the merry lady?" "She kissed off the wax,
"And put what paper was not kissed away,
"In her bosom to go burn: but merry, no!
"She wept all night when evening brought no friend,   580
"Alone, the unkind missive at her breast;
"Thus Philomel, the thorn at her breast too,
"Sings" . . . "Writes this second letter?" "Even so!
"Then she may peep at vespers forth?"—"What risk
"Do we run o' the husband?"—"Ah,—no risk at all!   585

---

571 *MS* will—   572 *MS* with me this evening.   *MS* write.   574 *MS*
{beginning of fo. 328}   *MS* Ave.   575 *MS* {no new paragraph}   576 *MS*
free.   *MS* {no comma}   577–96 *MS* {no quotation marks at beginnings of
lines}   577 *MS* lady?"—   *MS* {no comma} 578 *MS* {no comma}   579 *MS*
burn there:>burn: 581 *MS* letter>missive   582 *MS* sharp thorn>
thorn   583 *MS* letter?"—Even   584 *MS* you will come at Vespers?"—> she
may peep at Vespers forth?"—   *MS* if?>if the>risk?>risk   585 *MS* of

---

572 *Concert*: arrange, plan for.

574 *at the Ave*: i.e. at the angelus bell, roughly 6 p.m. In Roman Catholic countries
the church bell was rung at dawn, noon, and dusk, to suggest to the faithful that they
pause for a moment and pray the angelus, a short series of prayers celebrating the
Incarnation. The prayers consist mainly of two Hail Marys, in L. *Aves*—hence the use
here—and a short concluding prayer asking God for grace and the 'glory of the
Resurrection'.

579 *go burn*: i.e. where another woman would burn an incriminating letter in the
fire to destroy it, Pompilia places it in her bosom, so heated with passion that it will
'burn' the letter.

582–3 *Philomel . . . Sings*: Philomel (the nightingale), emblem of sad lovers, is often
described as pricking her breast on a thorn and so pouring forth her song in anguish;
see for example Sidney, 'The Nightingale', where the bird 'sings out her woes, a
thorne her song-booke making' (l. 4). Here the commonplace is used to create a
pathetic image of a love-lorn Pompilia, 'pricking' herself on Caponsacchi's unkind
letter which she has tucked in her bosom, and so sobbing out her complaints and sighs.
The origin of the name Philomel is the Philomel–Tereus story in Greek mythology, as
mistold in Latin authors: in Greek sources Philomela is the swallow and Procne the
nightingale.

"He is more stupid even than jealous. Ah—
"That was the reason? Why, the man's away!
"Beside, his bugbear is that friend of yours,
"Fat little Canon Conti. He fears him,
"How should he dream of you? I told you truth: 590
"He goes to the villa at Vittiano—'t is
"The time when Spring-sap rises in the vine—
"Spends the night there. And then his wife's a child:
"Does he think a child outwits him? A mere child:
"Yet so full grown, a dish for any duke.   595
"Don't quarrel longer with such cates, but come!"

I wrote "In vain do you solicit me.
"I am a priest: and you are wedded wife,
"Whatever kind of brute your husband prove.
"I have scruples, in short. Yet should you really show   600
"Sign at the window . . . but nay, best be good!
"My thoughts are elsewhere." "Take her that!"

                                              "Again
"Let the incarnate meanness, cheat and spy,
"Mean to the marrow of him, make his heart   605
"His food, anticipate hell's worm once more!
"Let him watch shivering at the window—ay,
"And let this hybrid, this his light-of-love
"And lackey-of-lies,—a sage economy,—

587 *MS* away—   588 *MS* {no commas}   589 *MS 1868 1872* him—
590 *MS 1868 1872* truth—   591 *MS* Villa at Villiano: 592 *MS*
spring-sap   593 *MS 1868 1872* child,   594 *MS* child   595 *MS* Duke,
Yale 1 Duke>duke   *597 *MS* {no new paragraph}   *1868 1872* {new
paragraph. Paragraphing obscured in *1888 1889* by this line's being at the head of
the page} *MS* me: 598–602 *MS* {no quotation marks at beginnings
of lines}   598 *MS* {no comma}   599 *MS* be.   600 *MS* {no
comma}   601 *MS* {beginning of fo. 329}   *602 *MS 1868 1872*
elsewhere."— *1888 1889* elsewhere,"   603 *MS 1868 1872* —"Again
604–17 *MS* {no quotation marks at beginnings of lines}   604 *MS* spy
608 *MS* woman,   609 *MS* [ ]> sage

596 *cates*: delicacies.
604 *incarnate meanness*: i.e. Guido, the embodiment of unkindness.
605–6 *make . . . food*: intensifying the proverbial 'to eat one's heart out'.
606 *hell's worm*: i.e. the worm that will eat him in hell; cf. Mark 9: 43–48.
608–9 *light-of-love / And lackey-of-lies*: i.e. mistress and lying messenger.

"Paid with embracings for the rank brass coin,—   610
"Let her report and make him chuckle o'er
"The break-down of my resolution now,
"And lour at disappointment in good time!
"—So tantalize and so enrage by turns,
"Until the two fall each on the other like   615
"Two famished spiders, as the coveted fly
"That toys long, leaves their net and them at last!"

And so the missives followed thick and fast
For a month, say,—I still came at every turn
On the soft sly adder, endlong 'neath my tread.   620
I was met i' the street, made sign to in the church,
A slip was found i' the door-sill, scribbled word
'Twixt page and page o' the prayer-book in my place.
A crumpled thing dropped even before my feet,
Pushed through the blind, above the terrace-rail,   625
As I passed, by day, the very window once.
And ever from corners would be peering up
The messenger, with the self-same demand
"Obdurate still, no flesh but adamant?
"Nothing to cure the wound, assuage the throe   630
"O' the sweetest lamb that ever loved a bear?"
And ever my one answer in one tone—

---

613 *MS* take his   *MS* time—   614 *MS* So   *MS* {no comma}   616
MS {no comma}   *MS* on the   *618 *MS* {new paragraph. Paragraphing
obscured in *1868* and *1872* by this line's being at the head of the page} *1888 1889* {no
new paragraph}   620 *MS* neath   621 *MS* in   622 *MS* in the sill,
a   623 *MS* Twixt   *MS* leaf>page   *MS* of   *MS* prayer book   *MS 1868
1872* place: 624 *MS* {no comma}   625-6 *MS* {the lines are transpo-
sed}   625 *MS* terrace rail. *Yale 1* terrace-rail.>terrace-rail,   626 *MS* {no
commas}   *MS* once   627 *MS* {beginning of fo. 330}   628 *MS* self-
same soft demand   630-1 *MS* {no quotation marks at beginnings of
lines}   631 *MS* Of   632 *MS* came my   *MS* tone

---

620 *adder...tread*: a vivid image of the insinuating presence of Guido or his
messenger Margherita, the adder lining itself up with Caponsacchi's footfall so as to
avoid being seen directly.

629 *adamant*: hard stone (noun); cf. Zech. 7: 12: 'Yea, they made their hearts as an
adamant stone, lest they should hear the law'.

"Go your ways, temptress! Let a priest read, pray,
"Unplagued of vain talk, visions not for him!
"In the end, you'll have your will and ruin me!"   635

One day, a variation: thus I read:
"You have gained little by timidity.
"My husband has found out my love at length,
"Sees cousin Conti was the stalking-horse,
"And you the game he covered, poor fat soul!   640
"My husband is a formidable foe,
"Will stick at nothing to destroy you. Stand
"Prepared, or better, run till you reach Rome!
"I bade you visit me, when the last place
"My tyrant would have turned suspicious at,   645
"Or cared to seek you in, was . . . why say, where?
"But now all's changed: beside, the season's past
"At the villa,—wants the master's eye no more.
"Anyhow, I beseech you, stay away
"From the window! He might well be posted there."   650

I wrote—"You raise my courage, or call up
"My curiosity, who am but man.
"Tell him he owns the palace, not the street
"Under—that's his and yours and mine alike.

633 *MS* temptress: let   *MS* poor soul>priest read,   *MS* pray   634–5 *MS*
{no quotation marks at beginnings of lines}   634 *MS* him!">him!
635 *MS* Some day>In the end,   *MS* draw me to my>have your will and   *MS*
me."   636 *MS* read.   637 *MS* nothing>little   638–49 *MS* {no
quotation marks at beginnings of lines}   639 *MS* stalking horse   640 *MS*
You are   644 *MS* {no comma}   645 *MS* to   646 *MS* 1868 1872
was . .   *MS* {no commas}   647 *MS* he says the   648 *MS* Villa,—
650 *MS* {no quotation marks}   1872 there.'   651 *MS* {no new para-
graph}   652–8 *MS* {no quotation marks at beginnings of lines}   652 *MS*
{no comma}   653 *MS* {beginning of fo. 331}   654 *MS* mine and his and
yours>his and yours and mine

639 *stalking-horse*: a real or decoy horse, behind which a hunter could sneak up on
the prey. In this image Pompilia is the huntress, Conti the stalking-horse, and
Caponsacchi her intended prey. Cf. Webster, *The White Devil*, III. i. 34–6: 'You 'tis
said, / Were made his engine, and his stauking horse / To undo my sister.'

646 *was . . . where?*: 'was [my bedroom]': in mock modesty, the place is only implied.

"If it should please me pad the path this eve,   655
"Guido will have two troubles, first to get
"Into a rage and then get out again.
"Be cautious, though: at the *Ave!*"

                                        You of the Court!
When I stood question here and reached this point   660
O' the narrative,—search notes and see and say
If someone did not interpose with smile
And sneer, "And prithee why so confident
"That the husband must, of all needs, not the wife,
"Fabricate thus,—what if the lady loved?   665
"What if she wrote the letters?"

                                        Learned Sir,
I told you there's a picture in our church.
Well, if a low-browed verger sidled up
Bringing me, like a blotch, on his prod's point,
A transfixed scorpion, let the reptile writhe,   670
And then said "See a thing that Rafael made—
"This venom issued from Madonna's mouth!"
I should reply, "Rather, the soul of you
"Has issued from your body, like from like,
"By way of the ordure-corner!"   675

---

655 *MS* {no comma}   656 *MS* ⟨Two⟩   658 *MS* Ave!"   659 *1868*
1872 court!   661 *MS* Of   662 *MS* word *1868 1872* some one
663 *MS* {no comma}   664–6 *MS* {no quotation marks at beginnings of
lines}   664 *MS* Husband must of needs, and   *MS* wife   665 *MS*
Lady   668 *MS* Church.   670 *MS* [ ]>like   *MS* {no commas} 672
1868 1872 said,   *MS* Rafaelle   673 *MS* {no quotation mark at beginning of
line}   *MS* creature   *1868* mouth!"—   675–6 *MS* {no quotation marks
at beginnings of lines}

655 *pad*: tread, walk confidently.
658 *Ave*: cf. l. 574 n.
669 *low-browed*: i.e. stupid.
verger: an official who takes care of the interior of a church and acts as an attendant.
670 *prod*: the verger's rod or staff of office.
673 *Madonna's mouth*: i.e. the Virgin Mary's mouth in the painting by Raphael: see
ll. 406, 707 nn.
676 *ordure-corner*: dung heap. The verger is imagined first defecating the scorpion,
and then picking it up and displaying it. Buckler describes this image as 'luridly
dramatic and patently vulgar' (p. 140), but it is one of many instances of Caponsacchi's

But no less,
I tired of the same long black teasing lie
Obtruded thus at every turn; the pest
Was far too near the picture, anyhow: 680
One does Madonna service, making clowns
Remove their dung-heap from the sacristy.
"I will to the window, as he tempts," said I:
"Yes, whom the easy love has failed allure,
"This new bait of adventure tempts,—thinks he.   685
"Though the imprisoned lady keeps afar,
"There will they lie in ambush, heads alert,
"Kith, kin, and Count mustered to bite my heel.
"No mother nor brother viper of the brood
"Shall scuttle off without the instructive bruise!"   690

So I went: crossed street and street: "The next street's turn,
"I stand beneath the terrace, see, above,
"The black of the ambush-window. Then, in place
"Of hand's throw of soft prelude over lute,

677 *MS*   {no comma}   678 *MS*   *1868*   same black teazing   *1872*
teazing   680 *MS* {beginning of fo. 332}   *MS* Madonna,>the picture,   *MS*
any how: 681 *MS* {no comma}   *MS* folk   683 *MS* go to   *MS*
tempts"   684–90 *MS* {no quotation marks at beginnings of lines}
684 *MS* to lure,   685 *MS 1868* may,—he thinks.   686 {not found in
MS}   *1868* "While   687 *MS* they   be   *MS* all the brood,>heads
alert,   688 *MS* Mustering to match one man,—kith, kin and Count.>Kith,
kin and Count mustered to match my heel.   689 *MS* No viper of them>No
mother or brother viper of the brood   690 *MS* bruise."   691 *MS* {New
paragraph (already written thus) indicated by 'N.P.' in left-hand margin} *1868 1872*
So,   *MS* "the   *MS* {no comma}   692–5 *MS* {no quotation marks at begin-
nings of lines}   692 *MS* and above   693 *MS* ambush window.   *MS*
instead>in place   694 *MS* the hand's   *MS* on the lute *1868 1872* {no comma}

vehemence. How such imagery struck a typical middle-class Victorian reader is
exemplified in Julia Wedgwood's complaint: 'would not Caponsacchi have touched
more lightly on all that was foul while his soul was full of Pompilia? Might not his
speech have been free from Swift-like metaphor?': Julia Wedgwood to RB, 15 Nov.
1868: *Wedgwood*, 154–5.

681 *clowns*: peasants, bumpkins.

688–90 *bite my heal . . . bruise*: cf. Gen. 3: 15. In this image, Guido and his family are
so many serpents (Satans) intent on inflicting injury, and Caponsacchi will give them
the 'instructive bruise', a blow that will teach them a lesson.

"And cough that clears way for the ditty last,"—   695
I began to laugh already—"he will have
"'Out of the hole you hide in, on to the front,
"'Count Guido Franceschini, show yourself!
"'Hear what a man thinks of a thing like you,
"'And after, take this foulness in your face!'"   700

The words lay living on my lip, I made
The one-turn more—and there at the window stood,
Framed in its black square length, with lamp in hand,
Pompilia; the same great, grave, griefful air
As stands i' the dusk, on altar that I know,   705
Left alone with one moonbeam in her cell,
Our Lady of all the Sorrows. Ere I knelt—
Assured myself that she was flesh and blood—
She had looked one look and vanished.

                              I thought—"Just so:

698–700 *MS*   {no quotation marks at beginnings of lines}   697 *MS*
'Out   698 *MS* and show   699 *MS* Hear>Take>Hear   *MS* thinks of>
gives to>thinks of   700 *MS* face!"   701 *MS* {New paragraph (already
written thus) indicated by 'N.P.' in left-hand margin}   702 *MS 1868 1872* one
turn   704 *MS* Pompilia, with the same grave griefful air   705 *MS*
in   *MS* an altar   706 *MS* {beginning of fo. 333}   707 *MS* ^all^   *MS*
knelt . . .   710 *MS* said "Just so:

 697–700 "'*Out . . . face!*'": these are the words Caponsacchi intends to shout at the
hiding Guido. In terms of the syntax 'out of the hole . . .' connects back to 'hand's
throw' (694). The sense is that instead of a hand's 'throw' across the strings of the lute,
the chord that precedes the song, Guido will receive this first shout. Then Caponsacchi
will deliver his message—not a love song, but—'what a man thinks of a thing like you'
(699); instead of clearing his throat politely (695), he will spit in Guido's face (700).
 704 *griefful*: sorrowful, painful: see next n.
 707 *Our Lady of all the Sorrows*: the Virgin Mary, as represented in paintings as the
sorrowing mother of Jesus, the 'Mater Dolorosa'. This may be a reference to the
painting Caponsacchi has already mentioned at ll. 400–6 and 668–76. 'All the sorrows'
are the traditional seven sorrows of Mary, intensely painful moments in her life: the
prophecy of Simeon, the flight into Egypt, the loss of Jesus as a child in Jerusalem, her
meeting with Jesus on his way to crucifixion, the crucifixion itself, the taking down of
Jesus' body from the Cross, and his burial. Here Pompilia appears like the Virgin Mary
as painted in one of these scenes, poignant in suffering and sadness, 'griefful', but
somehow also—like the Virgin—pure and elevated in her humanity. The image is so
vivid that Caponsacchi almost kneels in reverence (707).

"It was herself, they have set her there to watch—   711
"Stationed to see some wedding-band go by,
"On fair pretence that she must bless the bride,
"Or wait some funeral with friends wind past,
"And crave peace for the corpse that claims its due.   715
"She never dreams they used her for a snare,
"And now withdraw the bait has served its turn.
"Well done, the husband, who shall fare the worse!"
And on my lip again was—"Out with thee,
"Guido!" When all at once she re-appeared;   720
But, this time, on the terrace overhead,
So close above me, she could almost touch
My head if she bent down; and she did bend,
While I stood still as stone, all eye, all ear.

She began—"You have sent me letters, Sir: 725
"I have read none, I can neither read nor write;
"But she you gave them to, a woman here,
"One of the people in whose power I am,
"Partly explained their sense, I think, to me
"Obliged to listen while she inculcates   730
"That you, a priest, can dare love me, a wife,
"Desire to live or die as I shall bid,
"(She makes me listen if I will or no)
"Because you saw my face a single time.
"It cannot be she says the thing you mean;   735

711–18 *MS* {no quotation marks at beginnings of lines}   712 *MS* Bid
wait some wedding-band go by, and bless>Stationed to see some wedding-band
go by   713 *MS* {line added later}   714 *MS* The bride,>
Or wait   716 *MS* {no comma}   718 *MS* worse!   719 *MS*
very lip was—   720 *MS* {no quotation mark at beginning of
line}   *MS* re-appeared   721 *MS* But this time on   725 *MS*
"She   *MS* began "You   726–828 *MS* {no quotation marks at beginnings of
lines}   734 *MS* {beginning of fo. 334}   735 *MS* mean,

---

715 *crave . . . corpse*: i.e. pray the traditional prayer for the dead as the coffin passes:
'Eternal rest grant to him, O Lord; and let perpetual light shine upon him. May he rest
in peace. Amen.'

735 *It . . . mean*: 'Her words cannot be a true reflection of what you really mean.'

"Such wickedness were deadly to us both:
"But good true love would help me now so much—
"I tell myself, you may mean good and true.
"You offer me, I seem to understand,
"Because I am in poverty and starve,   740
"Much money, where one piece would save my life.
"The silver cup upon the altar-cloth
"Is neither yours to give nor mine to take;
"But I might take one bit of bread therefrom,
"Since I am starving, and return the rest,   745
"Yet do no harm: this is my very case.
"I am in that strait, I may not dare abstain
"From so much of assistance as would bring
"The guilt of theft on neither you nor me;
"But no superfluous particle of aid.   750
"I think, if you will let me state my case,
"Even had you been so fancy-fevered here,
"Not your sound self, you must grow healthy now—
"Care only to bestow what I can take.
"That it is only you in the wide world,   755
"Knowing me nor in thought nor word nor deed,
"Who, all unprompted save by your own heart,
"Come proffering assistance now,—were strange
"But that my whole life is so strange: as strange
"It is, my husband whom I have not wronged   760
"Should hate and harm me. For his own soul's sake,
"Hinder the harm! But there is something more,
"And that the strangest: it has got to be

736 MS both   738 MS have meant it good.   740 MS {no comma}
741 MS {no comma}   MS when   743 MS take,   744 MS I might
take just one   746 MS And   747 MS strait that I may not abstain
1868 not abstain   748 MS will   750 MS Not one   751 MS think
if   752 MS been fancy-fevered   753 MS would>must   MS
sober   755 MS all the   756 MS A stranger to me in thought, word and
deed,>Knowing me not in thought, nor word nor deed,   757 MS his
>your   MS heart   758 MS now,   760 MS {no comma}   761 MS
{beginning of fo. 335}   MS me,—for   MS sake   762 MS more.

"Somehow for my sake too, and yet not mine,
"—This is a riddle—for some kind of sake   765
"Not any clearer to myself than you,
"And yet as certain as that I draw breath,—
"I would fain live, not die—oh no, not die!
"My case is, I was dwelling happily
"At Rome with those dear Comparini, called   770
"Father and mother to me; when at once
"I found I had become Count Guido's wife:
"Who then, not waiting for a moment, changed
"Into a fury of fire, if once he was
"Merely a man: his face threw fire at mine,   775
"He laid a hand on me that burned all peace,
"All joy, all hope, and last all fear away,
"Dipping the bough of life, so pleasant once,
"In fire which shrivelled leaf and bud alike,
"Burning not only present life but past,   780
"Which you might think was safe beyond his reach.
"He reached it, though, since that beloved pair,
"My father once, my mother all those years,
"That loved me so, now say I dreamed a dream
"And bid me wake, henceforth no child of theirs,   785
"Never in all the time their child at all.
"Do you understand? I cannot: yet so it is.
"Just so I say of you that proffer help:
"I cannot understand what prompts your soul,

---

764 MS too ^and^   766 MS {no comma}   767 MS breath,
770 MS two>dear   MS {no comma}   771 MS me,   772 MS
wife;   775 MS man,—fire thrilled his face and threw,>man,—his face threw
fire at mine   776 MS [Fire?]>He   MS at>on   MS {no comma}
777 MS hope and   778 MS {no commas}   780 MS {no com-
ma}   782 MS it though,   MS Comparini pair   785 MS wake become
>wake henceforth   787 MS is: 788 MS {beginning of fo. 336}   MS
help

    764–6 my sake . . . you: i.e. for the sake of her unborn child. Pompilia is roughly one
and a half months pregnant; here she is starting to have a dim sense of this, and of the
fact that she is acting not just to save her own life but also that of the baby in her
womb. When the child was eventually born, on 18 Dec. 1697, she called him Gaetano.
    774 fury: infernal spirit, devil.

"I simply needs must see that it is so,   790
"Only one strange and wonderful thing more.
"They came here with me, those two dear ones, kept
"All the old love up, till my husband, till
"His people here so tortured them, they fled.
"And now, is it because I grow in flesh   795
"And spirit one with him their torturer,
"That they, renouncing him, must cast off me?
"If I were graced by God to have a child,
"Could I one day deny God graced me so?
"Then, since my husband hates me, I shall break   800
"No law that reigns in this fell house of hate,
"By using—letting have effect so much
"Of hate as hides me from that whole of hate
"Would take my life which I want and must have—
"Just as I take from your excess of love   805
"Enough to save my life with, all I need.
"The Archbishop said to murder me were sin:
"My leaving Guido were a kind of death
"With no sin,—more death, he must answer for.
"Hear now what death to him and life to you   810
"I wish to pay and owe. Take me to Rome!
"You go to Rome, the servant makes me hear.
"Take me as you would take a dog, I think,
"Masterless left for strangers to maltreat:
"Take me home like that—leave me in the house   815
"Where the father and the mother are; and soon
"They'll come to know and call me by my name,

---

794 *MS* fled   797 *MS* me off? *Yale 1* me off? >off me?   798 *MS* {no comma}   *Yale 1* child>child,   800 *MS* Then since   801 *MS* {no comma}   802 *MS* taking—>using—   807 *MS* sin.   812 *MS* know.   815 *MS* {beginning of fo. 337}   816 *MS* are,   817 *MS* {no comma}

808–9 *My...for*: 'My leaving Guido would mean that so far as he is concerned I should be as good as dead (i.e. he would be rid of me) without any sin on his part (he would not have killed me); more death than that (i.e. my actual death by his hand) he would have to answer for': Cook, 124.

811 *pay and owe*: i.e. to pay Guido by her apparent death (see previous n.), and to owe her life to Caponsacchi.

"Their child once more, since child I am, for all
"They now forget me, which is the worst o' the dream—
"And the way to end dreams is to break them, stand,   820
"Walk, go: then help me to stand, walk and go!
"The Governor said the strong should help the weak:
"You know how weak the strongest women are.
"How could I find my way there by myself?
"I cannot even call out, make them hear—   825
"Just as in dreams: I have tried and proved the fact.
"I have told this story and more to good great men,
"The Archbishop and the Governor: they smiled.
"'Stop your mouth, fair one!'—presently they frowned,
"'Get you gone, disengage you from our feet!'   830
"I went in my despair to an old priest,
"Only a friar, no great man like these two,
"But good, the Augustinian, people name
"Romano,—he confessed me two months since:
"He fears God, why then needs he fear the world?   835
"And when he questioned how it came about
"That I was found in danger of a sin—
"Despair of any help from providence,—
"'Since, though your husband outrage you,' said he,
"'That is a case too common, the wives die   840
"'Or live, but do not sin so deep as this'—
"Then I told—what I never will tell you—
"How, worse than husband's hate, I had to bear
"The love,—soliciting to shame called love,—

818 MS for>since   819 MS of   823 MS are—   827 MS {no comma}
829 MS "Stop   MS one!"—   MS frowned   830 MS "Get   MS
feet!"   831–8 MS {no quotation marks at beginnings of lines}   832 MS
two   833 MS Augustine whom the   835 MS need   837 MS the
sin   838 MS Providence,—   839 MS "Since,   MS   you"   MS
he   841–9 MS {no quotation marks at beginnings of lines}   841 MS
this."   842 MS {beginning of fo. 338}   843 MS hate I

834 Romano: cf. III. 1017n.

"Of his brother,—the young idle priest i' the house   845
"With only the devil to meet there. 'This is grave—
" 'Yes, we must interfere: I counsel,—write
" 'To those who used to be your parents once,
" 'Of dangers here, bid them convey you hence!'
" 'But,' said I, 'when I neither read nor write?'   850
"Then he took pity and promised 'I will write.'
"If he did so,—why, they are dumb or dead:
"Either they give no credit to the tale,
"Or else, wrapped wholly up in their own joy
"Of such escape, they care not who cries, still   855
"I' the clutches. Anyhow, no word arrives.
"All such extravagance and dreadfulness
"Seems incident to dreaming, cured one way,—
"Wake me! The letter I received this morn,
"Said—if the woman spoke your very sense—   860
" 'You would die for me:' I can believe it now:
"For now the dream gets to involve yourself.
"First of all, you seemed wicked and not good,
"In writing me those letters: you came in
"Like a thief upon me. I this morning said   865
"In my extremity, entreat the thief!
"Try if he have in him no honest touch!
"A thief might save me from a murderer.
" 'T was a thief said the last kind word to Christ:
"Christ took the kindness and forgave the theft: 870

845 *MS* in   846 *MS* "This   848 *MS* {no comma}   849 *MS* and
bid>bid   *MS* hence.   850 *MS* "But,"   *MS* I "when   *MS* {no quotation
mark at end of line}   851–60 *MS* {no quotation marks at beginnings of
lines}   851 *MS* "I will write.   852 *MS* why they   *MS* dumb, the
same: *Yale 1* dumb,>dumb   855 *MS* {no commas}   856 *MS* In   *MS*
{no comma}   858 *MS* Are   *MS* way,   861 *MS* "You   *MS*
me:"   *MS* now.   863 *MS* all you   867 *MS* touch,   869 *MS* {be-
ginning of fo. 339}   870 *MS* comfort   *MS* sin:

845–6 *idle . . . meet*: a play on the proverb 'The Devil finds work for idle hands':
ODEP, 180. It is because Girolamo has nothing to do in the Franceschini household
that he 'meets the devil', who sets him to seducing Pompilia.

864–5 *you . . . me*: cf. 1 Thess. 5: 2.

869–70 *'T was . . . theft*: cf. Luke 23: 39–43.

"And so did I prepare what I now say.
"But now, that you stand and I see your face,
"Though you have never uttered word yet,—well, I know,
"Here too has been dream-work, delusion too,
"And that at no time, you with the eyes here,   875
"Ever intended to do wrong by me,
"Nor wrote such letters therefore. It is false,
"And you are true, have been true, will be true.
"To Rome then,—when is it you take me there?
"Each minute lost is mortal. When?—I ask."   880

I answered "It shall be when it can be.
"I will go hence and do your pleasure, find
"The sure and speedy means of travel, then
"Come back and take you to your friends in Rome.
"There wants a carriage, money and the rest,—   885
"A day's work by to-morrow at this time.
"How shall I see you and assure escape?"

She replied, "Pass, to-morrow at this hour.
"If I am at the open window, well:
"If I am absent, drop a handkerchief   890
"And walk by! I shall see from where I watch,
"And know that all is done. Return next eve,
"And next, and so till we can meet and speak!"
"To-morrow at this hour I pass," said I.

872 MS face   874 MS There   875 MS At   MS there,   876 MS
me:>me,   877 MS the letters   878 MS true will be,   880 MS
[ ]>Each   MS [ ]>lost   MS precious: when?>mortal: when?   881 MS
{New paragraph (already written thus) indicated by 'N.P.' in left-hand margin}
MS answered,   MS be: 882 MS will>pleasure   884 MS Return>
Come back   885–7 MS {no quotation marks at beginnings of lines}
885 MS 'other means' interlined above undeleted 'the rest,'   887 MS
concert   888 MS {New paragraph (already written thus) indicated by 'N.P.' in
left-hand margin}   MS replied "Pass,   889–93 MS {no quotation
marks at beginnings of lines}   889 MS can stand then>am   MS ^open^
891 MS And and walk by,   MS watch   892 MS done; return   893 MS
speak." 1872 speak!'   894 MS {beginning of fo. 340}   MS pass"

She was withdrawn.   895
             Here is another point
I bid you pause at. When I told thus far,
Someone said, subtly, "Here at least was found
"Your confidence in error,—you perceived
"The spirit of the letters, in a sort,   900
"Had been the lady's, if the body should be
"Supplied by Guido: say, he forged them all!
"Here was the unforged fact—she sent for you,
"Spontaneously elected you to help,
"—What men call, loved you: Guido read her mind,   905
"Gave it expression to assure the world
"The case was just as he foresaw: he wrote,
"She spoke."
             Sirs, that first simile serves still,—
That falsehood of a scorpion hatched, I say,   910
Nowhere i' the world but in Madonna's mouth.
Go on! Suppose, that falsehood foiled, next eve
Pictured Madonna raised her painted hand,
Fixed the face Rafael bent above the Babe,
On my face as I flung me at her feet: 915
Such miracle vouchsafed and manifest,
Would that prove the first lying tale was true?
Pompilia spoke, and I at once received,
Accepted my own fact, my miracle

---

897 *MS* make *Yale 1* at>at.   *MS* When last   898 *MS* {no commas}
899–908 *MS* {no quotation marks at beginnings of lines}   902 *MS* say he
MS all,   903 *MS* fact she   905 *MS* What   *MS* mind   909 *MS*
here,—   911 *MS* in   *MS* mouth: 912 *MS* Go on, suppose, *Yale 1* Go
on, suppose>Go on! Suppose   914 *MS* Rafaelle   *MS* on>above   *MS* {no
comma}   918 *MS* received

898–9 *"Here . . . error*: i.e. 'in this instance your confidence in Pompilia's truth was
mistaken'.

916–17 *Such . . . true*: Caponsacchi distinguishes between two kinds of improbabil-
ity: the idea that Pompilia could have written the crude love-letters is as grotesque and
impossible as a scorpion issuing from the mouth of the Madonna painted by Raphael.
On the other hand, the way in which she first spoke to him, recognized his good
qualities, and begged rescue, is apparently equally improbable, but in this case it is like
a religious miracle, something outside normal experience but actually genuine and
wonderful.

Self-authorized and self-explained,—she chose   920
To summon me and signify her choice.
Afterward,—oh! I gave a passing glance
To a certain ugly cloud-shape, goblin-shred
Of hell-smoke hurrying past the splendid moon
Out now to tolerate no darkness more,   925
And saw right through the thing that tried to pass
For truth and solid, not an empty lie:
"So, he not only forged the words for her
"But words for me, made letters he called mine:
"What I sent, he retained, gave these in place,   930
"All by the mistress-messenger! As I
"Recognized her, at potency of truth,
"So she, by the crystalline soul, knew me,
"Never mistook the signs. Enough of this—
"Let the wraith go to nothingness again,   935
"Here is the orb, have only thought for her!"

"Thought?" nay, Sirs, what shall follow was not thought:
I have thought sometimes, and thought long and hard.
I have stood before, gone round a serious thing,
Tasked my whole mind to touch and clasp it close,   940
As I stretch forth my arm to touch this bar.
God and man, and what duty I owe both,—
I dare to say I have confronted these
In thought: but no such faculty helped here.

920 *MS* Self-authorised   *MS* self-explained, she   921 *MS* {beginning of fo.
341}   922 *MS* oh,   923 *MS* cloud-shape-goblin shred *Yale 1* goblin
shred>goblin-shred   929–36 *MS* {no quotation marks at beginnings of
lines}   930 *MS* place   931 *MS* mistress-messenger: as   932 *MS*
{no commas}   933 *MS* chrystalline   *MS* {no commas}   934 *MS* Nor
ever took>Never mistook   *MS* [ ] [amiss?]>signs. Enough of this—   936 *MS*
her."   937 *MS* {no new paragraph}   *MS* "Thought"? Nay, sirs,   938 *MS*
{no comma}   940 *MS* {no comma}   941 *MS* grasp>touch   *MS* bar:
942 *MS* both,

920 *Self-authorized*: i.e. not authorized by the Church.
923 *goblin-shred*: fiendish, mischievous piece.
932 *at potency of truth*: i.e. in the act of speaking powerful truth.
935 *wraith*: phantom, apparition (the 'ugly cloud-shape' of l. 923).

I put forth no thought,—powerless, all that night 945
I paced the city: it was the first Spring.
By the invasion I lay passive to,
In rushed new things, the old were rapt away;
Alike abolished—the imprisonment
Of the outside air, the inside weight o' the world 950
That pulled me down. Death meant, to spurn the ground,
Soar to the sky,—die well and you do that.
The very immolation made the bliss;
Death was the heart of life, and all the harm
My folly had crouched to avoid, now proved a veil 955
Hiding all gain my wisdom strove to grasp:
As if the intense centre of the flame
Should turn a heaven to that devoted fly
Which hitherto, sophist alike and sage,
Saint Thomas with his sober grey goose-quill, 960
And sinner Plato by Cephisian reed,

---

945 *MS* {no comma}   947 *MS* In   *MS* bore passively,>was passive
to   948 *MS* {beginning of fo. 342}   *MS* away.   949 *MS* abolished
the   950 *MS* of   951 *MS* ground   952 *MS* Spring   953 *MS*
bliss,   955 *MS* mask>veil   956 *MS* grasp.   959 *MS* Whom
960 *MS* grey-goose quill *Yale 1* goose quill>goose-quill   961 *MS* {no
comma}

---

948 *In . . . away*: cf. 2 Cor. 5: 17: 'Therefore if any man be in Christ, he is a new
creature: old things are passed away; behold, all things are become new.'

954 *Death*: i.e. self-sacrifice. The passage hinges on the Christian paradox that it is
only by 'dying' to our false, selfish selves that we can uncover or awaken our living
selves, our true personalities. The most famous text is John 12: 24. The fly-candle
image in the next lines is a reworking of this paradox. Buckler describes this passage as
'one of the most lyrically impassioned and sensuously captivating in the whole poem'
(p. 144).

960–1 *Saint Thomas . . . reed*: the image is partly comic: St Thomas Aquinas (1225–
74), the major Catholic thinker, and the great pagan philosopher Plato (427–347 BC),
use their writing implements to try to prevent the fly (Caponsacchi) entering the flame
of the candle. Their writing implements, a quill and a reed-pen respectively, stand for
their philosophical writings. Caponsacchi feels that second-hand intellectual percep-
tion, truth in theory, has almost prevented him seeing the necessity of truth in action,
dangerous personal action. Cf. l. 484 n.

961 *sinner*: i.e. pagan (as opposed to the Christian Aquinas).

Cephisian reed: a pen made from a reed taken from the river Cephisus, near Athens,
Plato's home.

Would fain, pretending just the insect's good,
Whisk off, drive back, consign to shade again.
Into another state, under new rule
I knew myself was passing swift and sure;   965
Whereof the initiatory pang approached,
Felicitous annoy, as bitter-sweet
As when the virgin-band, the victors chaste,
Feel at the end the earthly garments drop,
And rise with something of a rosy shame   970
Into immortal nakedness: so I
Lay, and let come the proper throe would thrill
Into the ecstasy and outthrob pain.

I' the grey of dawn it was I found myself
Facing the pillared front o' the Pieve—mine,   975
My church: it seemed to say for the first time
"But am not I the Bride, the mystic love
"O' the Lamb, who took thy plighted troth, my priest,
"To fold thy warm heart on my heart of stone
"And freeze thee nor unfasten any more?   980
"This is a fleshly woman,—let the free

---

962 *MS*   creature's>insect's   good,   965 *MS*   sure   968 *MS*   chaste
969 *MS*   fall>drop   971 *MS*   nakedness,   972 *MS*   Helpless>Lay
and   973 *MS* extacy *1868 1872* ecstacy   *MS* repay all   974 *MS*
{no new paragraph}   *MS* In   *MS* [ ]>dawn   *MS* ^it was^   975 *MS* {be-
ginning of fo. 343}   *MS* of   978–82 *MS* {no quotation marks at beginnings of
lines}   978 *MS* Of   *MS* take thy plighted troth of priest>took, my priest, thy
plighted troth,>took thy plighted troth, my priest,   979 *MS* stony heart>heart
of stone

---

967 *Felicitous annoy*: happy annoyance.

968–71 *As ... nakedness*: as at the end of time, when the 'band' of all redeemed
people feel their earthly bodies (normally clothed) fall away from them as they rise up
in their new, naked, immortal bodies. As they enter heaven, they are almost embar-
rassed by the purity of this nakedness. The image is sensuous and mystical, perhaps
suggested by Rev. 14: 4.

977–8 *Bride ... Lamb*: the Church, the 'Bride' of the bridegroom Christ, the Lamb
of God. The Church is symbolically saying to Caponsacchi that, as a priest, he is
already 'married' to her, and so cannot rightly help Pompilia.

980 *freeze thee*: i.e. join yourself to me (by freezing). 'Freezing' here is an image of
Caponsacchi's priestly celibacy, the fact that he has forsworn sexual intercourse and
marriage.

"Bestow their life-blood, thou art pulseless now!"
See! Day by day I had risen and left this church
At the signal waved me by some foolish fan,
With half a curse and half a pitying smile   985
For the monk I stumbled over in my haste,
Prostrate and corpse-like at the altar-foot
Intent on his *corona*: then the church
Was ready with her quip, if word conduced,
To quicken my pace nor stop for prating—"There!   990
"Be thankful you are no such ninny, go
"Rather to teach a black-eyed novice cards
"Than gabble Latin and protrude that nose
"Smoothed to a sheep's through no brains and much faith!"
That sort of incentive! Now the church changed tone—   995
Now, when I found out first that life and death
Are means to an end, that passion uses both,
Indisputably mistress of the man
Whose form of worship is self-sacrifice:
Now, from the stone lungs sighed the scrannel voice   1000
"Leave that live passion, come be dead with me!"
As if, i' the fabled garden, I had gone

---

982 *MS* now."   983 *MS* day by   984 *MS* waved by any Donna's   *MS*
{no comma}   986 *MS* {no comma}   989 *MS* Threw me a cheery
word,>Was ready with her quip,   *MS* there were>there came,   990 *MS*
prating—>prater—>prating—   991–4 *MS* {no quotation marks at beginnings
of lines}   992 *MS* blackeyed   993 *MS* patter>gabble   *MS* latin
994 *MS* faith"—   996 *MS* ^first^   998 *MS* man,   999 *MS* self-
sacrifice *1868 1872* self-sacrifice—   1000 *MS* {no comma}   1002 *MS* {be-
ginning of fo. 344}   *MS* As if erewhile in the garden, once was dreamed,>As if in
the fabled garden, I had gone

---

988 *corona*: rosary, prayer beads (L.).

993 *protrude that nose*: the monk is imagined as a stupid sheep, one of the faithful
flock of the Church, sticking his nose through the edge of a grate or pen to be fed.

1000 *scrannel*: harsh, unmelodious; as in Milton's 'Lycidas' (l. 124) the word is
associated with the voice of a decadent Church; cf. 1. 1201 n.

1002–9 *fabled garden . . . watch*: see Cook, 125: 'the "hedge-fruit", the "hips and
haws", refer to the idle dalliance of 984 and 992; "the seven-fold dragon" is the
Church, which warns Caponsacchi off "the thing of perfect gold", Pompilia. "The
fabled garden" is the garden of the Hesperides, the golden apples of which were
watched by the dragon Ladon.' In this analogy Caponsacchi himself is implicitly
Hercules, a hero of action. Cf. III. 384 n.

On great adventure, plucked in ignorance
Hedge-fruit, and feasted to satiety,
Laughing at such high fame for hips and haws,   1005
And scorned the achievement: then come all at once
O' the prize o' the place, the thing of perfect gold,
The apple's self: and, scarce my eye on that,
Was 'ware as well o' the seven-fold dragon's watch.

Sirs, I obeyed. Obedience was too strange,—   1010
This new thing that had been struck into me
By the look o' the lady,—to dare disobey
The first authoritative word. 'T was God's.
I had been lifted to the level of her,
Could take such sounds into my sense. I said   1015
"We two are cognisant o' the Master now;
"She it is bids me bow the head: how true,
"I am a priest! I see the function here;
"I thought the other way self-sacrifice:
"This is the true, seals up the perfect sum.   1020
"I pay it, sit down, silently obey."

So, I went home. Dawn broke, noon broadened, I—

1003 *MS* Gone on the great adventure, I had plucked>On the great adventure,
plucked in ignorance   1004 *MS* so feasting>and feasted   1005 *MS* With
laughter>Laughing   *MS* ^high^   1006 *MS* achievent {clearly a *lapsus
calami*}   *MS* unawares>all at once   1007 *MS* On   *MS* of   1008 *MS*
apple's>wondrous apple's>apple's   1009 *MS* ware   *MS* of   *MS* watch>
guard>watch   1010 *MS* {New paragraph (already written thus) indicated
by 'N.P.' in left-hand margin}   *MS* strange,   1012 *MS* of   *MS* lady,
1013 *MS* God's: 1016–21 *MS* {no quotation marks at beginnings of
lines}   1016 *MS* cognizant of *1868 1872* cognizant   *MS* now,
1017 *MS 1868 1872* It is she   *MS* head?>head: *MS* too>how   1018 *MS*
priest: *MS* now: 1019 *MS* was self-sacrifice,   1022 *MS* {New para-
graph (already written thus) indicated by 'N.P.' in left-hand margin}   *MS* So I went
home, daw {*sic*} broke, noon somehow came,

1005 *hips and haws*: wild fruits of the rose and hawthorn.
1016 *the Master*: i.e. Christ.
1017 *She*: i.e. Pompilia.
1019: *the other way*: i.e. his previous lip-service to the priestly role. Now he
convinces himself (for a time) that true self-sacrifice involves giving up his real interest
in Pompilia: see ll. 1030–3.
1020 *seals . . . sum*: cf. Ezek. 28: 12.

I sat stone-still, let time run over me.
The sun slanted into my room, had reached
The west. I opened book,—Aquinas blazed   1025
With one black name only on the white page.
I looked up, saw the sunset: vespers rang:
"She counts the minutes till I keep my word
"And come say all is ready. I am a priest.
"Duty to God is duty to her: I think   1030
"God, who created her, will save her too
"Some new way, by one miracle the more,
"Without me. Then, prayer may avail perhaps."
I went to my own place i' the Pieve, read
The office: I was back at home again   1035
Sitting i' the dark. "Could she but know—but know
"That, were there good in this distinct from God's,
"Really good as it reached her, though procured
"By a sin of mine,—I should sin: God forgives.
"She knows it is no fear withholds me: fear?   1040
"Of what? Suspense here is the terrible thing.
"If she should, as she counts the minutes, come
"On the fantastic notion that I fear
"The world now, fear the Archbishop, fear perhaps
"Count Guido, he who, having forged the lies,   1045
"May wait the work, attend the effect,—I fear
"The sword of Guido! Let God see to that—
"Hating lies, let not her believe a lie!"

[—]

1023 *MS* stone still let   1025 *MS* West.   *MS* the book,—   1027 *MS*
{beginning of fo. 345}   1029–33 *MS* {no quotation marks at beginnings of
lines}   1031 *MS* {no commas}   1033 *MS* Then prayer   1034 *MS*
in   1036 *MS* in   1037–48 *MS* {no quotation marks at beginnings of
lines}   1037 *MS* her good   1038 *MS* she gained it though made grow>it
reached her though procured   1039 *MS* mine,   *MS* sin—   1041 *MS*
thing: 1045 *MS* who having   *MS* lies   1047 *MS* as a priest may!

1025 *Aquinas*: cf. l. 484 n.
1035 *office*: canonical hours.
1047 *sword of Guido!*: as Cook points out, the sentence breaks off with this ex-
clamation: there is no apodosis to the 'if'-clause which begins in 1042. Caponsacchi's
formal syntax strains under pressure of emotion.

Again the morning found me. "I will work,
"Tie down my foolish thoughts. Thank God so far!   1050
"I have saved her from a scandal, stopped the tongues
"Had broken else into a cackle and hiss
"Around the noble name. Duty is still
"Wisdom: I have been wise." So the day wore.

At evening—"But, achieving victory,   1055
"I must not blink the priest's peculiar part,
"Nor shrink to counsel, comfort: priest and friend—
"How do we discontinue to be friends?
"I will go minister, advise her seek
"Help at the source,—above all, not despair: 1060
"There may be other happier help at hand.
"I hope it,—wherefore then neglect to say?"

There she stood—leaned there, for the second time,
Over the terrace, looked at me, then spoke:
"Why is it you have suffered me to stay   1065
"Breaking my heart two days more than was need?
"Why delay help, your own heart yearns to give?
"You are again here, in the self-same mind,
"I see here, steadfast in the face of you,—
"You grudge to do no one thing that I ask.   1070
"Why then is nothing done? You know my need.
"Still, through God's pity on me, there is time
"And one day more: shall I be saved or no?"
I answered—"Lady, waste no thought, no word

1049 *MS* {no new paragraph}   1050–4 *MS* {no quotation marks at beginnings
of lines}   1054 *MS* {beginning of fo. 346}   *MS* Wisdom,   *MS* wise.   *MS*
^the^   1055 *MS* {no new paragraph}   *MS* "Victory is now achieved.>But
achieving victory,   1056–62 *MS* {no quotation marks at beginnings of
lines}   1057 *MS* comfort..   1063 *MS* ^leaned there,^   1066–
73 *MS* {no quotation marks at beginnings of lines}   1067 *MS* {no comma}
1068 *MS* here in   *MS* selfsame   1069 *MS* there stedfast   *MS* you.
1070 *MS* me>to do   *MS* effort>thing   *MS* ask   1073 *MS* {no quotation
mark at end of line}   1074 *MS* {New paragraph (already written thus) indicated
by 'N.P.' in left-hand margin}   *MS* "Waste>"Lady, waste   *MS* precious word on
me,>thought, no word

1056 *blink*: avoid, refuse.

"Even to forgive me! Care for what I care—   1075
"Only! Now follow me as I were fate!
"Leave this house in the dark to-morrow night,
"Just before daybreak:—there's new moon this eve—
"It sets, and then begins the solid black.
"Descend, proceed to the Torrione, step   1080
"Over the low dilapidated wall,
"Take San Clemente, there's no other gate
"Unguarded at the hour: some paces thence
"An inn stands; cross to it; I shall be there."

She answered, "If I can but find the way.   1085
"But I shall find it. Go now!"

                          I did go,
Took rapidly the route myself prescribed,
Stopped at Torrione, climbed the ruined place,
Proved that the gate was practicable, reached   1090
The inn, no eye, despite the dark, could miss,

1075–84 *MS* {no quotation marks at beginnings of lines}   1075 *MS* for par-
don.>to forgive me!   1076 *MS* {line added later}   *MS* fate.   1077 *MS*
Leave this house in the dark,>[ ] me: descend hence,>Leave this house in the
dark,   1078 *MS* daydawn: *MS* the new moon is now,>there's new crescent
moon this eve—>there's new moon this eve—   1080 *MS* {beginning of fo.
347}   1081 *MS* delapidated   1084 *MS* stands called the Steed:>stands;
cross to it;   *MS* {no quotation mark at end of line}   1085 *MS* {New para-
graph (already written thus) indicated by 'N.P.' in left-hand margin}   *MS* {no
comma}   1086 *MS* {no quotation mark at beginning of line}   1091 *MS*
inn no

1077–8 *"Leave . . . eve*: the *MS* readings in these lines and 1106–12 make clear that
Browning originally assumed that Caponsacchi was speaking here on 21 Apr. 1697 and
that the flight commenced in the early hours of the 22nd. At proof stage he made
adjustments, adding in another day of waiting, and moving the flight from 22 to 23
April, St George's Day. This strengthened the symbolic link of Caponsacchi with St
George, since Caponsacchi now rescues Pompilia from Guido (the evil dragon) on
exactly the feast of the patron saint of England. Cf. 1. 585 n.

1078 *new moon this eve*: Browning used Augustus De Morgan's *The Book of Almanacs*
(1851) to calculate this phase of the moon for 21 Apr. 1697: see our Vol. VII, pp.
320–3.

1080 *Torrione*: bastion, fortified tower (It.). In these lines Browning seems to
muddle the topography which he got exactly right at v. 1020–9: see n.

Knocked there and entered, made the host secure:
"With Caponsacchi it is ask and have;
"I know my betters. Are you bound for Rome?
"I get swift horse and trusty man," said he.   1095

Then I retraced my steps, was found once more
In my own house for the last time: there lay
The broad pale opened Summa. "Shut his book,
"There's other showing! 'T was a Thomas too
"Obtained,—more favoured than his namesake here,—
"A gift, tied faith fast, foiled the tug of doubt,—   1101
"Our Lady's girdle; down he saw it drop
"As she ascended into heaven, they say:
"He kept that safe and bade all doubt adieu.
"I too have seen a lady and hold a grace."   1105

I know not how the night passed: morning broke;
Presently came my servant. "Sir, this eve—
"Do you forget?" I started. "How forget?
"What is it you know?" "With due submission, Sir,
"This being last Monday in the month but one   1110
"And a vigil, since to-morrow is Saint George,
"And feast day, and moreover day for copes,

1092 MS Host   1094–5 MS {no quotation marks at beginnings of
lines}   1096 MS {New paragraph (already written thus) indicated by 'N.P.'
in left-hand margin}   1099–1105 MS {no quotation marks at beginnings
of lines}   1099 MS showing.   1100 MS favored MS the
namesake   1101 MS gift tied   MS doubt,   1102 MS girdle,   1103
MS Heaven,   1104 1872 'He {broken sort}   1105 MS {no quotation
mark at end of line}   1106 {not found in MS}   1868 broke: 1872 broke
1107 MS {beginning of fo. 348}   1108–16 MS {no quotation marks at begin-
nings of lines}   1108 1868 1872 started.—   1109 1868 1872 know?"—
1872 Sir   1110 MS That being the last Monday in the month   1111 {not
found in MS}   Yale 1 St.>Saint   1112 MS a Vigil,

1099–1104 Thomas . . . adieu: according to legend, the Virgin Mary loosened her
girdle during her Assumption into heaven, and it fell into the hands of the doubting
apostle, St Thomas. The story is included in the medieval collection of saints' lives The
Golden Legend, and was particularly popular with Florentine artists because of the
proximity of Prato, where the supposed girdle, the sacra cintola, was preserved in
the cathedral. Caponsacchi's use of this image is intimate and romantic, if not directly
sexual.
1106–12 I . . . copes: note MS readings and also ll. 1077–8 n.

"And Canon Conti now away a month,
"And Canon Crispi sour because, forsooth,
"You let him sulk in stall and bear the brunt   1115
"Of the octave... Well, Sir, 't is important!"

            "True!

"Hearken, I have to start for Rome this night.
"No word, lest Crispi overboil and burst!
"Provide me with a laic dress! Throw dust   1120
"I' the Canon's eye, stop his tongue's scandal so!
"See there's a sword in case of accident."
I knew the knave, the knave knew me.

          And thus
Through each familiar hindrance of the day   1125
Did I make steadily for its hour and end,—
Felt time's old barrier-growth of right and fit
Give way through all its twines, and let me go.
Use and wont recognized the excepted man,
Let speed the special service,—and I sped   1130
Till, at the dead between midnight and morn,
There was I at the goal, before the gate,
With a tune in the ears, low leading up to loud,

1114 *MS* sore   1116 *MS* ^the octave...^ *1868 1872* octave... *MS* important."   1117 *MS* "So I see.>"True." *1868* "True!" 1118–22 *MS* {no quotation marks at beginnings of lines} 1118 *MS* go to>start for *MS* to-night:>this eve. 1119 *MS* Canon Crispi break all bounds!>Crispi overboil and burst! 1120 *MS* Better provide a laic>Provide me with a laic *MS* dress—throw 1121 *MS* In *MS* {no comma} *MS* and stop a scandal so.> stop his tongue's scandal so. 1123 *MS* knave and the knave>knave, the knave 1124 *MS* {no new paragraph} 1126 *MS* at end,— 1127 *MS* barrier-gr[ ]>barrier-growth *MS* fit and wont>fit and right>fit and wont>fit and right>right and fit 1128 *MS* and let me go through twist and twine>through all its twines, and let me go; *1868* go; 1129 *MS* As recognizing>Use and wont recognized *MS* {no comma}

1115–16 *bear...octave*: i.e. carry responsibility for the more elaborate prayers in the seven days following a major feast, in this case Easter (7 April 1697).

1128 *twines*: knotted stems.

1132–7 *There...warfare*: i.e. 'there I was at the gate, with a spiritual tune in my ears, and a spiritual light in my eyes, that seemed to be growing manifestations to me of the essentially spiritual dimension of the event in which I was involved, so that even though I was alone, I was not truly alone, buoyed up as I was by this confidence of right. All these manifestations of the justice of what I was doing seemed to be coming up so as to be able to watch the outcome of the warfare of good and evil.' Brady

A light in the eyes, faint that would soon be flare,
Ever some spiritual witness new and new   1135
In faster frequence, crowding solitude
To watch the way o' the warfare,—till, at last,
When the ecstatic minute must bring birth,
Began a whiteness in the distance, waxed
Whiter and whiter, near grew and more near,   1140
Till it was she: there did Pompilia come:
The white I saw shine through her was her soul's,
Certainly, for the body was one black,
Black from head down to foot. She did not speak,
Glided into the carriage,—so a cloud   1145
Gathers the moon up. "By San Spirito,
"To Rome, as if the road burned underneath!
"Reach Rome, then hold my head in pledge, I pay
"The run and the risk to heart's content!" Just that
I said,—then, in another tick of time,   1150
Sprang, was beside her, she and I alone.

So it began, our flight thro' dusk to clear,

1134 *MS* A light>A faint light>A light   *MS* faint turned flare,>that faint would
soon be flare,   1135 *MS* the>some   1136 *MS* [ ]>crowding   *MS* the
solitude>solitude   1137 *MS* {beginning of fo. 349}   *MS* of   *MS* battle,—
>warfare,—   1139 *Yale 1* i'>in   1140 *MS* near   1141 *MS* there
was   1142 *MS* light>white   1143 *MS* body's vesture was   1147–
9 *MS* {no quotation marks at beginnings of lines}   1147 *MS* under-
neath;   1148 *MS* pledge I   1149 *Yale 1* that>that, *1868 1872* that, *1888
1889* {no comma}   1152 *MS* dark and day,>dusk to clear,

comments: 'The crescendo of sound and light will be the arrival of Pompilia whose
approach he sees in a climax of light and spiritual beauty': 109.

1146 *San Spirito*: the southern gate of Arezzo. Pompilia and Caponsacchi, at the
'Horse' Inn, are on the north side of the town; they must go around the walls to the
south side, and then on to the Perugia road for Rome.

1148 *hold ... pledge*: a strong oath. A commoner form is 'to wager one's head', i.e.
to bet one's life. Cf. 'If I stand warranter of the event, / Placing my honour and my
head in pledge, . . .': Coleridge, *The Piccolomini* (1800), 1. xii.182–3.

1152–1417 *flight ... choose*: in the following 266 lines, the incidents of the two days'
flight are exclusively Browning's invention. The real Caponsacchi is very brief on this
matter: 'Then we pursued our journey without stopping to spend the night anywhere,
and we paused only as it was necessary for refreshing ourselves and changing horses,
until we reached Castelnuovo on Tuesday evening': OYB lxxxix (97).

1152 *clear*: brightness, i.e. dawn (an elliptical use of the adj.); cf. Chapman, *Iliad*
(1611), 1. 458: 'Twilight hid the clear'.

Through day and night and day again to night
Once more, and to last dreadful dawn of all.
Sirs, how should I lie quiet in my grave   1155
Unless you suffer me wring, drop by drop,
My brain dry, make a riddance of the drench
Of minutes with a memory in each,
Recorded motion, breath or look of hers,
Which poured forth would present you one pure glass,
Mirror you plain,—as God's sea, glassed in gold,   1161
His saints,—the perfect soul Pompilia? Men,
You must know that a man gets drunk with truth
Stagnant inside him! Oh, they've killed her, Sirs!
Can I be calm?   1165

                    Calmly! Each incident
Proves, I maintain, that action of the flight
For the true thing it was. The first faint scratch
O' the stone will test its nature, teach its worth
To idiots who name Parian—coprolite.   1170
After all, I shall give no glare—at best
Only display you certain scattered lights

1153 *MS* And night>Through night>Through day and night   *MS* the night
once more>night   1154 *MS* And the>Once more, and the   *MS*
^last^   1159 *MS* speech>breath   1161 *MS* [ ]>Mirror   *MS* glassy
gold,   1164 *MS* {beginning of fo. 350}   *MS* the murder, Sirs—>they've
killed her, Sirs!   1166 *MS* Calmly—each   1169 *MS* Of   1170 *MS*
fools   *MS* the Parian coprolite. *1868 1872* Parian,   1171 *MS* glass—

   1156–62 *drop by drop . . . Pompilia?*: the 'drops' of the individual memories of the
flight would make up a 'sea' that would then 'mirror' Pompilia's saintly perfection.
Lines 1161–2 are a beautiful adaptation of Rev. 15: 2: 'And I saw as it were a sea of glass
mingled with fire: and them that had gotten the victory over the beast . . . stand on the
sea of glass, having the harps of God.' Cf. *Sordello*, 1. 364–5: 'as the sea whose fire was
mixt with glass / In John's transcendent vision'.
   1170 *Parian—coprolite*: fine white marble—dung stone. Parian marble was used by
the ancients for statuary, and it occurs in Greek and Latin poetry as an image of
whiteness and loveliness: cf. Pindar, *Nemean* iv. 81; Horace, *Odes*, 1. xix. 6. The marble
is quite often referred to in English poetry, as for example in Shelley's 'Ode to Liberty',
58 and EBB's 'Lady Geraldine's Courtship', 378. Coprolite, coined by Buckland in
1829, was the name for a piece of rock made of fossilized animal excrement.
   1171 *I shall give no glare*: see *MS* reading; i.e. 'I shall give no clear, radiant image of
the flight'. This is the image Caponsacchi promised at ll. 1160–1.
   1171–5 *at . . . wavelet*: these lines rewrite the flat, reflective image of 'God's sea' at l.
1161 into an 'abyss' full of the 'rush and roll' of waves (1173). Rather than a radiant

Lamping the rush and roll of the abyss:
Nothing but here and there a fire-point pricks
Wavelet from wavelet: well!   1175
                    For the first hour
We both were silent in the night, I know:
Sometimes I did not see nor understand.
Blackness engulphed me,—partial stupor, say—
Then I would break way, breathe through the surprise,
And be aware again, and see who sat   1181
In the dark vest with the white face and hands.
I said to myself—"I have caught it, I conceive
"The mind o' the mystery: 't is the way they wake
"And wait, two martyrs somewhere in a tomb   1185
"Each by each as their blessing was to die;
"Some signal they are promised and expect,—
"When to arise before the trumpet scares:
"So, through the whole course of the world they wait
"The last day, but so fearless and so safe!   1190
"No otherwise, in safety and not fear,
"I lie, because she lies too by my side."
You know this is not love, Sirs,—it is faith,
The feeling that there's God, he reigns and rules
Out of this low world: that is all; no harm!   1195
At times she drew a soft sigh—music seemed

1173 *MS 1868 1872* abyss—   1175 *MS* well,—   1178 *MS* under-
stand,   1181 *MS* myself>aware   1184–92 *MS* {no quotation marks
at beginnings of lines}   1184 *MS* of *Yale 1* of>o'   *MS* mystery—
1186 *MS* manner   1187 *MS* expect *1868* expect,   1188 *MS* scares
1191 *MS* other wise, *1868 1872 1888 1889* otherwise,   1192 *MS* {beginning of
fo. 351}   *MS* {no quotation mark at end of line}   1194 *MS* feeling there's
God, and He

image, Caponsacchi will only be able to shine 'scattered lights' on the rolling waves,
here and there showing a 'fire-point'; cf. *Paradise Lost*, vii. 211–12.
    1184 *mind*: meaning.
    1185–8 *two martyrs . . . scares*: this is reminiscent of the situation in Donne's 'The
Relique'.

Always to hover just above her lips,
Not settle,—break a silence music too.

In the determined morning, I first found
Her head erect, her face turned full to me,   1200
Her soul intent on mine through two wide eyes.
I answered them. "You are saved hitherto.
"We have passed Perugia,—gone round by the wood,
"Not through, I seem to think,—and opposite
"I know Assisi; this is holy ground."   1205
Then she resumed. "How long since we both left
"Arezzo?" "Years—and certain hours beside."

It was at . . . ah, but I forget the names!
'T is a mere post-house and a hovel or two;
I left the carriage and got bread and wine   1210
And brought it her. "Does it detain to eat?"
"They stay perforce, change horses,—therefore eat!
"We lose no minute: we arrive, be sure!"
This was—I know not where—there's a great hill
Close over, and the stream has lost its bridge,   1215

1197 *MS   1868   1872* {no comma}   1199 *MS* {no new paragraph}
1200 *MS* ^erect, her face^   *MS* [on?]>to   1202 *MS* hitherto: 1203–
5 *MS* {no quotation marks at beginnings of lines}   1203 *MS* Perugia,   *MS*
wall>wood   1204 *MS* think,   1205 *MS* Assisi,   1207 *MS* {no
quotation mark at beginning of line}   *MS* Arezzo?"— *1868   1872* "Are-
zzo?"—   1208 *MS* names,   1209 *MS* Tis   *MS* two, *1868   1872*
two,—   1211 *1868   1872* her.—   1212 *1868   1872* "—They   1213
MS {no quotation mark at beginning of line}   1214 *MS 1868 1872* She said—

1198 *break . . . too*: i.e. her sigh was music, but the silence it broke was music also.
1203–4 *round . . . through*: Perugia, like Assisi, was a hill town, so, unless actually
stopping there, it would be natural to follow the main road around it. This sounds like
a detail based on Browning's own recollections of travelling the Florence-Rome route
with EBB.
1205 *holy ground*: the town of Assisi and the country around it are 'holy ground'
because St Francis of Assisi lived his holy and compassionate life here. At this point
Pompilia and Caponsacchi have travelled about 58 miles from Arezzo.
1209 *post-house*: an inn or stable on main roads where horses could be changed on
long journeys. It has been calculated that in 1697 there were about fourteen of these
stations between Arezzo and Rome: see Treves, 174, 178.

One fords it. She began—"I have heard say
"Of some sick body that my mother knew,
" 'T was no good sign when in a limb diseased
"All the pain suddenly departs,—as if
"The guardian angel discontinued pain   1220
"Because the hope of cure was gone at last:
"The limb will not again exert itself,
"It needs be pained no longer: so with me,
"—My soul whence all the pain is past at once:
"All pain must be to work some good in the end.   1225
"True, this I feel now, this may be that good,
"Pain was because of,—otherwise, I fear!"

She said,—a long while later in the day,
When I had let the silence be,—abrupt—
"Have you a mother?" "She died, I was born."   1230
"A sister then?" "No sister." "Who was it—
"What woman were you used to serve this way,
"Be kind to, till I called you and you came?"
I did not like that word. Soon afterward—
"Tell me, are men unhappy, in some kind   1235
"Of mere unhappiness at being men,
"As women suffer, being womanish?
"Have you, now, some unhappiness, I mean,
"Born of what may be man's strength overmuch,
"To match the undue susceptibility,   1240

1216 *MS* She began "I   1217–27 *MS* {no quotation marks at beginnings of
lines}   1217 *MS* {no comma}   1218 *MS* part>limb   1220 *MS*
{beginning of fo. 352}   *MS* [An?]>The   *MS* ^guardian^   1224 *MS*
My   1227 *MS* fear."   1228 *MS* {no new paragraph}   *MS* day
1229 *MS* abrupt   1230 *MS 1868 1872* mother?"—   1231 *MS 1868 1872*
then?"—   *MS 1868 1872* sister."—"Whom *Yale 1* "Whom>"Who   1232–3
MS   {no quotation marks at beginnings of lines}   1234 *MS*   afterward
1235 *MS* Tell men,   1236–48 *MS* {no quotation marks at beginnings of
lines}   1237 *MS* woman   *MS* {no comma}   1238 *MS* you now
some

1234 *I . . . word*: Caponsacchi is abashed, recalling his career as society priest and
flirt: see ll. 348–50, 991–2.
1240 *undue susceptibility*: extreme sensitivity (of women).

"The sense at every pore when hate is close?
"It hurts us if a baby hides its face
"Or child strikes at us punily, calls names
"Or makes a mouth,—much more if stranger men
"Laugh or frown,—just as that were much to bear!   1245
"Yet rocks split,—and the blow-ball does no more,
"Quivers to feathery nothing at a touch;
"And strength may have its drawback weakness scapes."

Once she asked "What is it that made you smile,
"At the great gate with the eagles and the snakes,   1250
"Where the company entered, 't is a long time since?"
"—Forgive—I think you would not understand:
"Ah, but you ask me,—therefore, it was this.
"That was a certain bishop's villa-gate,
"I knew it by the eagles,—and at once   1255
"Remembered this same bishop was just he
"People of old were wont to bid me please
"If I would catch preferment: so, I smiled
"Because an impulse came to me, a whim—
"What if I prayed the prelate leave to speak,   1260
"Began upon him in his presence-hall
"—'What, still at work so grey and obsolete?
" 'Still rocheted and mitred more or less?
" 'Don't you feel all that out of fashion now?

1243 MS a child   1245 MS bear: 1246 MS Yet,   1247 MS
Flying>Quivers 1248 MS {beginning of fo. 353}   MS ^And^ 1868 1872 drawback,
*1249 1868 1872 {new paragraph. Paragraphing obscured in 1888 and 1889 by
this line's being at the head of the page}   1250–1 MS {no quotation
marks at beginnings of lines}   1251 MS entered,—   1252 MS
"Forgive—   1253–61 MS {no quotation marks at beginnings of lines}
1254 1872 'That {broken sort}   MS Bishop's   1256 MS Bishop was
the same   1258 MS {no comma}   1259 MS whim,   1262 MS
"What,   1263–5 MS {no quotation marks at beginnings of lines}   1263 MS
rochetted Yale 1 rochetted >rocheted

1246 blow-ball: the round, fluffy seed-head of the dandelion.
1250 gate . . . snakes: eagles defeating snakes are a traditional symbol of good over-
coming evil. Caponsacchi smiles because he knows the bishop's worldliness.
1263 rocheted and mitred: wearing a rochet (a special surplice) and a mitre (an arched
hat), insignia that he is a bishop; cf. l. 1878.

" 'I find out when the day of things is done!' "   1265

At eve we heard the *angelus*: she turned—
"I told you I can neither read nor write.
"My life stopped with the play-time; I will learn,
"If I begin to live again: but you—
"Who are a priest—wherefore do you not read   1270
"The service at this hour? Read Gabriel's song,
"The lesson, and then read the little prayer
"To Raphael, proper for us travellers!"
I did not like that, neither, but I read.

When we stopped at Foligno it was dark.   1275
The people of the post came out with lights:
The driver said, "This time to-morrow, may
"Saints only help, relays continue good,

1265 *MS*   done!"   1266 *MS*   {no new paragraph}   *MS*   ange-
lus: 1267 *MS* write   1268–73 *MS* {no quotation marks at beginnings
of lines}   1268 *MS* play-time: *MS* {no comma} *Yale 1* learn>learn,
1269 *MS* If life begin again:>If I begin to live again: 1272 *MS* nor>and   *MS*
[the?]>then   1273 *MS*   travellers."   1275 *MS*   {no new para-
graph}   1276 *MS* {beginning of fo. 354}   *MS* {line added later} 1277 *MS*
said "This   *MS* to-morrow night>to-morrow, may   1278–9 *MS* {no quota-
tion marks at beginnings of lines}   1278 *MS* If saints help, and relays>Saints
only help, relays

1265 *I...done*: i.e. 'I know when things have had their day, when things like
rochets and mitres are old-fashioned—but you don't!'

1266 *angelus*: the angelus bell: see l. 574 n.

1271 *Gabriel's song*: the Hail Mary. The first sentence of this prayer is the angel
Gabriel's song to the Virgin Mary in Luke 1: 28. This is not a traditional way of
referring to the prayer, but rather Browning's invention. He perhaps intends to suggest
the almost sentimental nature of Pompilia's piety.

1272 *lesson*: short extract from the Bible; the breviary contained set extracts for each
day.

1272–3 *little prayer / To Raphael*: a traditional prayer for travellers, based on Tobit's
prayer spoken in the presence of Raphael (Tobit 5:17): 'O God who didst send the
blessed Archangel Raphael to accompany thy servant on his journey, grant that we thy
servants may ever be guarded by his care and strengthened by his aid.' It was still said in
Italy in Browning's day. As a conventional, pious Catholic, Pompilia expects a priest to
say prayers appropriate to the hour and the occasion; Caponsacchi is disconcerted by
this aspect of her personality.

1275 *Foligno*: arriving at this town at the end of the first day of their flight, Pompilia
and Caponsacchi have travelled about 67 miles.

"Nor robbers hinder, we arrive at Rome."
I urged, "Why tax your strength a second night?   1280
"Trust me, alight here and take brief repose!
"We are out of harm's reach, past pursuit: go sleep
"If but an hour! I keep watch, guard the while
"Here in the doorway." But her whole face changed,
The misery grew again about her mouth,   1285
The eyes burned up from faintness, like the fawn's
Tired to death in the thicket, when she feels
The probing spear o' the huntsman. "Oh, no stay!"
She cried, in the fawn's cry, "On to Rome, on, on—
"Unless 't is you who fear,—which cannot be!"   1290

We did go on all night; but at its close
She was troubled, restless, moaned low, talked at whiles
To herself, her brow on quiver with the dream:
Once, wide awake, she menaced, at arms' length
Waved away something—"Never again with you!   1295
"My soul is mine, my body is my soul's:
"You and I are divided ever more
"In soul and body: get you gone!" Then I—
"Why, in my whole life I have never prayed!
"Oh, if the God, that only can, would help!   1300
"Am I his priest with power to cast out fiends?

1279 *MS* And robbers do not hinder, we arrive.">Nor robbers hinder, we arrive at
Rome."   1280 *1868 1872* urged,—   1281–4 *MS* {no quotation marks at
beginnings of lines}   1281 *MS* repose.   1282 *MS* and long past pursuit,>
past pursuit, go sleep   1283 *MS* hour, I   1286 *MS* [ ]>from   *MS* {no
comma}   1287 *MS* {no comma}   1288 *MS* of   *MS* {no quotation
marks}   1290 *MS* {no quotation mark at beginning of line}   1291 *MS*
{no new paragraph}   *MS* night,   1293 *MS* dream;   1296–
1300 *MS* {no quotation marks at beginnings of lines}   1299–1300 *MS* {lines
added later}

1301 *priest . . . fiends*: faced with Pompilia's nightmare of being sexually
violated afresh by Guido, Caponsacchi turns to the prayers of exorcism—the service
to rid someone of evil spirits—which his consecration as a priest allows him to
perform.

"Let God arise and all his enemies
"Be scattered!" By morn, there was peace, no sigh
Out of the deep sleep.

        When she woke at last,   1305
I answered the first look—"Scarce twelve hours more,
"Then, Rome! There probably was no pursuit,
"There cannot now be peril: bear up brave!
"Just some twelve hours to press through to the prize:
"Then, no more of the terrible journey!" "Then,   1310
"No more o' the journey: if it might but last!
"Always, my life-long, thus to journey still!
"It is the interruption that I dread,—
"With no dread, ever to be here and thus!
"Never to see a face nor hear a voice!   1315
"Yours is no voice; you speak when you are dumb;
"Nor face, I see it in the dark. I want
"No face nor voice that change and grow unkind."
That I liked, that was the best thing she said.

In the broad day, I dared entreat, "Descend!"   1320
I told a woman, at the garden-gate
By the post-house, white and pleasant in the sun,
"It is my sister,—talk with her apart!
"She is married and unhappy, you perceive;
"I take her home because her head is hurt;   1325
"Comfort her as you women understand!"

1302–3 *MS* {no quotation marks at beginnings of lines}   1303 *MS* morning
there   1304 *MS*   sleep;   1305 *MS* {no new paragraph}   *MS*
when   *MS* {no comma}   1306 *MS* "Not   1307–18 *MS* {no quotation
marks at beginnings of lines}   1308 *MS* {beginning of fo. 355}   *MS*
peril,—   *MS* brave,   1309 *MS* the>some   *MS* *1868* *1872* prize—
1310 *MS* [ ]>Then   *MS* {no commas}   1311 *MS* more journey:
1312 *MS* to be here and thus>thus to journey still!   1320 *MS* {no new para-
graph}   *MS*   "I dare entreat, descend!"   1323 *MS*   Sister,—   *MS*
apart.   1324–6 *MS* {no quotation marks at beginnings of lines}

  1302–3 *"Let . . . scattered!"*: see Ps. 68: 1.

So, there I left them by the garden-wall,
Paced the road, then bade put the horses to,
Came back, and there she sat: close to her knee,
A black-eyed child still held the bowl of milk,   1330
Wondered to see how little she could drink,
And in her arms the woman's infant lay.
She smiled at me "How much good this has done!
"This is a whole night's rest and how much more!
"I can proceed now, though I wish to stay.   1335
"How do you call that tree with the thick top
"That holds in all its leafy green and gold
"The sun now like an immense egg of fire?"
(It was a million-leaved mimosa.) "Take
"The babe away from me and let me go!"   1340
And in the carriage "Still a day, my friend!
"And perhaps half a night, the woman fears.
"I pray it finish since it cannot last:
"There may be more misfortune at the close,
"And where will you be? God suffice me then!"   1345
And presently—for there was a roadside-shrine—
"When I was taken first to my own church
"Lorenzo in Lucina, being a girl,

1327 *MS* So there   1329 *MS* sat,—   *MS* knee   1334–8 *MS* {no quota-
tion marks at beginnings of lines}   1335 *MS* {no comma}   1336 *MS*
{beginning of fo. 356}   1338 *MS* ^immense^   1340 *MS* {no quotation
mark at beginning of line}   *MS* go."   1341 *MS* friend,   1342 *MS* {no
quotation mark at beginning of line}   1343 *MS* wish it over>pray it
finish   ★*MS 1868 1872* last. *1888* last *DC BrU* last>last: *1889* last: 1344–
5 *MS* {no quotation marks at beginnings of lines}   1344 *MS* end,>close,
1345 *MS* {no quotation mark at end of line}   1346 *MS* roadside
shrine—   1348–9 *MS* {no quotation marks at beginnings of lines}

1332 *in . . . lay*: 'the Madonna image [of Pompilia] recurs, this time in real life rather
than art': Sullivan, 82.

1336–9 *tree . . . mimosa*: a beautiful, evergreen tree, with feathery bipinnated leaves.
In spring (as here) it has small, richly scented, bright yellow flowers. The 'egg of fire'
(the sun) seen within the tree is, from Pompilia, a glorious and fulfilled (if still
unconscious) image of her own pregnancy. Browning perhaps associated mimosa
with EBB, for he seems to have vividly recalled the presence of a tall mimosa outside
the window when, in Bagni di Lucca in July 1849, she first showed him *Sonnets from the
Portuguese*: see *Wedgwood*, 114.

"And bid confess my faults, I interposed
" 'But teach me what fault to confess and know!'   1350
"So, the priest said—'You should bethink yourself:
" 'Each human being needs must have done wrong!'
"Now, be you candid and no priest but friend—
"Were I surprised and killed here on the spot,
"A runaway from husband and his home,   1355
"Do you account it were in sin I died?
"My husband used to seem to harm me, not . . .
"Not on pretence he punished sin of mine,
"Nor for sin's sake and lust of cruelty,
"But as I heard him bid a farming-man   1360
"At the villa take a lamb once to the wood
"And there ill-treat it, meaning that the wolf
"Should hear its cries, and so come, quick be caught,
"Enticed to the trap: he practised thus with me
"That so, whatever were his gain thereby,   1365
"Others than I might become prey and spoil.
"Had it been only between our two selves,—
"His pleasure and my pain,—why, pleasure him
"By dying, nor such need to make a coil!
"But this was worth an effort, that my pain   1370
"Should not become a snare, prove pain threefold
"To other people—strangers—or unborn—
"How should I know? I sought release from that—
"I think, or else from,—dare I say, some cause
"Such as is put into a tree, which turns   1375
"Away from the north wind with what nest it holds,—

1349 *MS* Bid>And bid   1350 *MS* 'But   *MS* know.'   1351–79 *MS* {no
quotation marks at beginnings of lines}   1351 *MS* {no comma}   *MS* said
"You   1352 *MS* wrong!"   1353 *MS* you be   1354 *MS* to die,
be   1356 *MS* esteem>account   1357 *MS* not   1358–9 *MS* {ori-
ginally written in the order 1359, 1358, and transposed by RB}   1359 *MS*
For sin's sake and mere>Not for sin's sake and   1361 *MS* Villa   1363
MS caught   1364 *MS* {beginning of fo. 357}   1367 *MS* selves   1369 *MS*
coil.   1370 *MS*   {no comma}   1371 *MS* ^prove^   1376 *1868*
northwind   *MS* nests

1369 *coil*: fuss, bother.
1374–6 *some . . . holds*: another unconscious image of her pregnancy; her flight is
mainly to save the life of her unborn child: see ll. 764–6 n.

"The woman said that trees so turn: now, friend,
"Tell me, because I cannot trust myself!
"You are a man: what have I done amiss?"
You must conceive my answer,—I forget—   1380
Taken up wholly with the thought, perhaps,
This time she might have said,—might, did not say—
"You are a priest." She said, "my friend."

       Day wore,
We passed the places, somehow the calm went,   1385
Again the restless eyes began to rove
In new fear of the foe mine could not see.
She wandered in her mind,—addressed me once
"Gaetano!"—that is not my name: whose name?
I grew alarmed, my head seemed turning too.   1390
I quickened pace with promise now, now threat:
Bade drive and drive, nor any stopping more.
"Too deep i' the thick of the struggle, struggle through!
"Then drench her in repose though death's self pour
"The plenitude of quiet,—help us, God,   1395
"Whom the winds carry!"

     Suddenly I saw
The old tower, and the little white-walled clump
Of buildings and the cypress-tree or two,—
"Already Castelnuovo—Rome!" I cried,   1400

1377 *MS* Now, 1378 *MS* myself, 1381 *MS* {no commas} 1383 *MS*
priest"—she 1386 *MS* restlessness, the eyes that roved>restless eyes began to
rove 1387 *MS* I>mine *MS 1868 1872* see: 1389 *MS* "Gaetano!"
that 1390 *MS 1868 1872* too. 1391 *MS* threat, 1392 *MS* {begin-
ning of fo. 358} *MS* more, 1393 *MS* much>deep *MS* in *MS*
through— 1394–6 *MS* {no quotation marks at beginnings of lines}
1394 *MS* steep>drench *MS* [ ]>self 1395 *MS* help now, 1397 *MS*
{no new paragraph}

1389 *"Gaetano!"*: the name Pompilia will eventually give her baby: see previous n.
1395–6 *help . . . carry*: cf. Ps. 18: 6, 10: 'In my distress I called upon the Lord, and
cried unto my God . . . And he rode upon a cherub, and did fly: yea, he did fly upon
the wings of the wind.'
1400 *Castelnuovo*: a small hamlet, about 15½ miles from Rome. Since Browning
was not in Italy during the writing of the poem, he sometimes sought historical details
and descriptions from friends travelling or resident there; the attempt at a detailed
description in the preceding lines may have this kind of source. Treves describes

"As good as Rome,—Rome is the next stage, think!
"This is where travellers' hearts are wont to beat.
"Say you are saved, sweet lady!" Up she woke.
The sky was fierce with colour from the sun
Setting. She screamed out "No, I must not die!   1405
"Take me no farther, I should die: stay here!
"I have more life to save than mine!"
                                        She swooned.
We seemed safe: what was it foreboded so?
Out of the coach into the inn I bore   1410
The motionless and breathless pure and pale
Pompilia,—bore her through a pitying group
And laid her on a couch, still calm and cured
By deep sleep of all woes at once. The host
Was urgent "Let her stay an hour or two!   1415
"Leave her to us, all will be right by morn!"
Oh, my foreboding! But I could not choose.

I paced the passage, kept watch all night long.
I listened,—not one movement, not one sigh.
"Fear not: she sleeps so sound!" they said: but I   1420
Feared, all the same, kept fearing more and more,
Found myself throb with fear from head to foot,
Filled with a sense of such impending woe,
That, at first pause of night, pretence of gray,

1401–3 *MS* {no quotation marks at beginnings of lines}   1402 *MS* travel-
lers   1403 *MS* Lady!"   *MS* sprang>woke   1406–7 *MS* {no quotation
marks at beginnings of lines}   1407 *MS* mine."   1408 *MS* swooned:
Yale 1 swooned,>swooned.   1409 *MS* were   *MS* why was it I boded>what
was it foreboded   1411 *MS* The breathless burden—oh, the pure and pale>The
motionless and breathless, s[]>The motionless and breathless lady, pale   1412
MS crowd>group   1413 *MS* [cool?]>calm   1414 *MS* [They?]>The *MS*
Host   1415 *MS* two: 1416 *MS* {no quotation mark at beginning of
line}   1418 *MS* {no new paragraph}   1420 *MS* sound,"   *MS 1868
1872* said—   1421 *MS* {beginning of fo. 359}   1423 *MS* {no
comma}   1424 *MS* That at

Castelnuovo as it was in his day (1913), by now a larger place, but still ancient and
haphazard, a little 'pile of houses, roof above roof. . . . The town is on a headland thrust
out into the misty plain of the Campagna': see Treves, 217–18, and also the photo-
graph opp. p. 256.

I made my mind up it was morn.—"Reach Rome,   1425
"Lest hell reach her! A dozen miles to make,
"Another long breath, and we emerge!" I stood
I' the court-yard, roused the sleepy grooms. "Have out
"Carriage and horse, give haste, take gold!" said I.
While they made ready in the doubtful morn,—   1430
'T was the last minute,—needs must I ascend
And break her sleep; I turned to go.

                       And there
Faced me Count Guido, there posed the mean man
As master,—took the field, encamped his rights,   1435
Challenged the world: there leered new triumph, there
Scowled the old malice in the visage bad
And black o' the scamp. Soon triumph suppled the tongue
A little, malice glued to his dry throat,
And he part howled, part hissed... oh, how he kept   1440
Well out o' the way, at arm's length and to spare!—
"My salutation to your priestship! What?
"Matutinal, busy with book so soon
"Of an April day that's damp as tears that now
"Deluge Arezzo at its darling's flight?—   1445

1425 MS morn.   1426–7 MS {no quotation marks at beginnings of lines}
1426 MS Hell   1427 MS emerge."   1428 MS In   MS court, arou-
sed   MS grooms,   1429 MS {no quotation mark at beginning of line}   MS
Man and horse, I give gold for diligence.">Carriage and horse, give haste, take gold"
said I.   1868   1872   gold!"—   1430 MS   There they stood   MS
morn.   1432 MS summon her;>break the sleep;   1434 MS the mean
man posed>posed the mean man   1435 MS As the master,   1438
MS of   MS losel.>scamp.   MS Triumph loosed>Soon triumph suppled
1440 MS 1868 1872 hissed..   1441 MS of Yale 1 of>o'   MS spare
...   1442 MS priestship,—what?   1443–71 MS {no quotation marks at
beginnings of lines}   1443 MS soon?>soon   1445 MS flight,—

1436–8 there...scamp: i.e. 'there, in the bad and black (i.e. angry) face of the rogue
(Guido) leered a new triumph together with the old (familiar) malice.' Caponsacchi is
used to seeing malice in Guido's face, but not this new look of triumph.

1443 Matutinal: i.e. 'You are early, at your morning office'. Matutinal means 'of the
morning' from L. matutinalis. Guido's use of this ornate word is sneering. Perhaps it is
suggested to him by the heading 'Ad Matutinum' over morning prayers in the
breviary; certainly it is his way of sarcastically implying that Caponsacchi must be up
early in order to say his morning prayers ('matins') from his 'book', i.e. his breviary.

" 'T is unfair, wrongs feminity at large,
"To let a single dame monopolize
"A heart the whole sex claims, should share alike:
"Therefore I overtake you, Canon! Come!
"The lady,—could you leave her side so soon?   1450
"You have not yet experienced at her hands
"My treatment, you lay down undrugged, I see!
"Hence this alertness—hence no death-in-life
"Like what held arms fast when she stole from mine.
"To be sure, you took the solace and repose   1455
"That first night at Foligno!—news abound
"O' the road by this time,—men regaled me much,
"As past them I came halting after you,
"Vulcan pursuing Mars, as poets sing,—
"Still at the last here pant I, but arrive,   1460
"Vulcan—and not without my Cyclops too,
"The Commissary and the unpoisoned arm
"O' the Civil Force, should Mars turn mutineer.

1446 MS 'Tis on behalf of our feminity>'Tis unfair to feminity at large   1447–
8 MS {lines added later}   1448 MS claims to share   1449 MS ^There-
fore^   MS Canon: Come,   1450 MS Lady,—   1451 MS {beginning of
fo. 360}   1452 MS were undrugged last night, I see,—>you lay down un-
drugged, I see,—   1453 MS and no death in life   1454 MS me fast
1455 MS [ ]>sure,   MS had>took   1456 MS On the>The   MS
Foligno,—   1457 MS On   MS road,   MS me with   1458 MS post
by post I halted>past them I came halting   1459 MS sing—   1460 MS
I but   1462 MS an arm or so   1463 MS Of   MS in case Mars mutiny.>
should Mars turn mutineer.

1446 *feminity*: femininity; the two forms were interchangeable in the nineteenth
century. 'Feminity' would have seemed to Browning metrically superior, but—
since it is closer to the French—he may also have thought of it as the better
form.

1455–6 *you . . . Foligno*: Guido falsely implies that Pompilia and Caponsacchi slept
together.

1459 *Vulcan . . . sing*: Guido presents an ironically self-deprecating image of himself
as the hapless and lame god Vulcan trying to catch Mars (Caponsacchi) and Venus
(Pompilia) who have cuckolded him, as in *Odyssey*, VIII. 266–366; cf. III. 1450–5 n.

1461 *Cyclops*: i.e. giant or servant. Guido is extending his previous image from
Greek mythology. Traditionally the Cyclopes, great one-eyed giants, were the work-
men of Vulcan, as in Callimachus, *Hymn* iii. 46–79, for example. In *Odyssey*, IX. 345–
67 Odysseus drugs the Cyclops with wine as part of his escape plan; this giant 'arm of
the law', however, is 'unpoisoned' (1462).

"Enough of fooling: capture the culprits, friend!
"Here is the lover in the smart disguise   1465
"With the sword,—he is a priest, so mine lies still.
"There upstairs hides my wife the runaway,
"His leman: the two plotted, poisoned first,
"Plundered me after, and eloped thus far
"Where now you find them. Do your duty quick!   1470
"Arrest and hold him! That's done: now catch her!"

During this speech of that man,—well, I stood
Away, as he managed,—still, I stood as near
The throat of him,—with these two hands, my own,—
As now I stand near yours, Sir,—one quick spring,   1475
One great good satisfying gripe, and lo!
There had he lain abolished with his lie,
Creation purged o' the miscreate, man redeemed,
A spittle wiped off from the face of God!
I, in some measure, seek a poor excuse   1480
For what I left undone, in just this fact
That my first feeling at the speech I quote
Was—not of what a blasphemy was dared,
Not what a bag of venomed purulence

1464 *MS* here are   1466 *MS 1868 1872* still: 1467 *MS* in the house,
my   1468 *MS* love: *MS* were fain to poison first,   1469 *MS* Plunder
me after, last of all elope>Plunder me next and last elope thus far   1470 *MS*
now!   1471 *MS* Disarm>Arrest   *MS* him: that's well:>him: that's done:
1472 MS {New paragraph indicated by 'N.P.' in left-hand margin and the under-
lining of 1471. Paragraphing obscured in *1868* and *1872* by this line's being at the head
of the page} *1888 1889* {no new paragraph}   1473 *MS* still I   1474 *MS*
him with   *MS* hands my own   1475 *MS* to you, Sirs, you or you.   *MS*
sir,>Sirs,   1476 *MS* lo   1478 *MS* had been purged of the miscreate,
1479 *MS* {beginning of fo. 361}   *MS* God.   1480 *MS* {no commas}   *MS*
[ ] my sole>seek out some   1481 *MS* did not, in this simple fact>left undone, in
just this fact   1483 *MS* spoke,>dared,

1478 *miscreate*: the mismade one. 'Miscreate' is attested as a participial adj. in
Spenser, Shakespeare, and Swinburne, but as a noun (as here) it is rare. OED² gives
only this instance. Browning is using it because it resonates with 'miscreant', though
etymologically the latter means 'misbeliever' (from Fr. *croire*) rather than 'mismade'.
The idea here is that Guido is both an evil-doer and a mistake on the part of nature.
1484 *purulence*: pus.

Was split and noisome,—but how splendidly   1485
Mirthful, how ludicrous a lie was launched!
Would Molière's self wish more than hear such man
Call, claim such woman for his own, his wife,
Even though, in due amazement at the boast,
He had stammered, she moreover was divine?   1490
She to be his,—were hardly less absurd
Than that he took her name into his mouth,
Licked, and then let it go again, the beast,
Signed with his slaver. Oh, she poisoned him,
Plundered him, and the rest! Well, what I wished   1495
Was, that he would but go on, say once more
So to the world, and get his meed of men,
The fist's reply to the filth. And while I mused,
The minute, oh the misery, was gone!
On either idle hand of me there stood   1500
Really an officer, nor laughed i' the least:

1485 *MS* broken>split   1486 *MS* what ludicrousness>what ludicrous *1868 1872*
what ludicrous   *MS* launched.   1487 *MS* Momus   *1488 *MS* 1868
wife, *1872 1888* wife *DC BrU* wife>wife, *1889* wife,   1489 *MS* chance,
1490 *MS* {no comma}   *MS* divine: 1492 *MS* {no comma}   1493 *MS*
Licked and   1495 *MS*   Plundered and all   1496 *MS*   Was   that
1497 *MS* That   1501 *MS* in the least. *1868* least. *1872* least

1485 *noisome*: disgusting, harmful.
1487–90 *Molière's . . . divine*: 'Could Molière (1622–73), the master of comedy, have
imagined something as ludicrous as Guido implicitly claiming Pompilia as his wife—
i.e. it is as ludicrous as Molière's Don Juan, the libertine and cynic, claiming the lovely,
innocent nun Donna Elvira as *his* wife.' In Molière's *Don Juan* (1665), Don Juan first
seduces Donna Elvira out of a convent with extravagant claims of love, marries her,
and then emphatically rejects her to continue his life of pleasure-seeking. The centre of
this allusion is the incompatibility of Guido (Don Juan) and Pompilia (Donna Elvira),
the one so foul and cynical, the other so lovely and innocent. Originally here,
Browning wrote 'Momus self' rather than 'Molière's self', Momus being the ancient
Greek personification of mockery and censure. At proof stage he made Caponsacchi's
reference both more contemporary and more revealing of his character: we can believe
that, in his worldly phase, Caponsacchi might have been very much interested in the
spirit of Molière's plays. Browning used an extract from *Don Juan*, I. iii, with his own
translation, as an epigraph to *Fifine at the Fair* (1872).
1494 *slaver*: saliva. 'Slaver' is often used of animals rather than humans; cf. Pope,
'Epistle to Dr Arbuthnot', 105–6: 'Of all mad Creatures, if the Learn'd are right, / It is
the Slaver kills, and not the Bite.'

Nay, rendered justice to his reason, laid
Logic to heart, as 't were submitted them
"Twice two makes four."

              "And now, catch her!" he cried.

That sobered me. "Let myself lead the way—   1506
"Ere you arrest me, who am somebody,
"Being, as you hear, a priest and privileged,—
"To the lady's chamber! I presume you—men
"Expert, instructed how to find out truth,   1510
"Familiar with the guise of guilt. Detect
"Guilt on her face when it meets mine, then judge
"Between us and the mad dog howling there!"
Up we all went together, in they broke
O' the chamber late my chapel. There she lay,   1515
Composed as when I laid her, that last eve,
O' the couch, still breathless, motionless, sleep's self,
Wax-white, seraphic, saturate with the sun
O' the morning that now flooded from the front
And filled the window with a light like blood.   1520
"Behold the poisoner, the adulteress,
"—And feigning sleep too! Seize, bind!" Guido hissed.

She started up, stood erect, face to face
With the husband: back he fell, was buttressed there

1502 *MS 1868 1872* They rendered   1503 *MS* heart as if he   1505 *MS*
her," *1868 1872* her!"—   1506 *MS* me "Let   *MS* way   1507 *MS* {be-
ginning of fo. 362}   1507–8 *MS* {lines added later}   1508 *MS 1868 1872*
And,   *MS* priest, and privileged—   1509 *MS* Lady's chamber; *MS*
you men   1510 *MS* the truth,   1513 *MS* there."   1515 *MS* On
1517 *MS* On   *MS* breathless motionless, all sleep,   1518 *MS* seraphic>cher-
ubic   1519 *MS* Of   1520 *MS* blood: *MS* {Between 1520 and 1521
extra line: So a saint lies at dawn of judgment day.}   1521 *MS* and adulter-
ess,>the adulteress,   1522 *MS* {no quotation mark at beginning of line}   *MS*
And   *MS* bind!"—" *1868 1872* bind!"—   1523 *MS* {New paragraph (already
written thus) indicated by 'N.P.' in left-hand margin}

1524 *buttressed*: supported. This metaphorical use is only established in the nine-
teenth century. The idea here is that the morning light 'supports' Guido's case against
Pompilia and Caponsacchi, because it might seem to confirm that they have spent the
night together; yet Guido is also an 'opprobrious blur' (disgraceful stain) on the
beautiful sunrise and all it represents.

By the window all a-flame with morning-red,   1525
He the black figure, the opprobrious blur
Against all peace and joy and light and life.
"Away from between me and hell!" she cried:
"Hell for me, no embracing any more!
"I am God's, I love God, God—whose knees I clasp,   1530
"Whose utterly most just award I take,
"But bear no more love-making devils: hence!"
I may have made an effort to reach her side
From where I stood i' the door-way,—anyhow
I found the arms, I wanted, pinioned fast,   1535
Was powerless in the clutch to left and right
O' the rabble pouring in, rascality
Enlisted, rampant on the side of hearth
Home and the husband,—pay in prospect too!
They heaped themselves upon me. "Ha!—and him   1540
"Also you outrage? Him, too, my sole friend,
"Guardian and saviour? That I baulk you of,
"Since—see how God can help at last and worst!"
She sprang at the sword that hung beside him, seized,
Drew, brandished it, the sunrise burned for joy   1545
O' the blade, "Die," cried she, "devil, in God's name!"
Ah, but they all closed round her, twelve to one
—The unmanly men, no woman-mother made,

---

*1525 MS 1868 1872 a-flame 1888 1889 a flame   1526 MS and>the   MS
blot   1527 MS light and life and peace and joy>peace and joy and light and
life.   1528 MS Hell" 1868 1872 hell!"—   1529–32 MS {no quotation
marks at beginnings of lines}   1529 MS embraces   1530 MS God>
1531 MS I take His utterly most just award   1534 MS in   MS
doorway,—   1535 MS {beginning of fo. 363}   MS arms I   1537 MS
Of   1538 MS on the side of hearth and home>rampant on the side of
hearth   1539 MS And the husband, with some prospect of a fee.>Home and
the husband,—fees in prospect too.   1540 1868 1872 me.— MS "Ha—
1541–3 MS {no quotation marks at beginnings of lines}   1544 1868 1872
sprung   MS beside me,   1546 MS On   MS "Die" cried   1547 MS
one,   1548 MS men no

1538 *rampant*: violent, aggressive; also partly in the heraldic sense 'upreared' as on a
coat of arms. The crowd appears like a rampant lion on a coat of arms, on the side of
'hearth / Home and the husband'—also, as it were, figures on the shield.

Spawned somehow! Dead-white and disarmed she lay.
No matter for the sword, her word sufficed   1550
To spike the coward through and through: he shook,
Could only spit between the teeth—"You see?
"You hear? Bear witness, then! Write down .. but no—
"Carry these criminals to the prison-house,
"For first thing! I begin my search meanwhile   1555
"After the stolen effects, gold, jewels, plate,
"Money and clothes, they robbed me of and fled,
"With no few amorous pieces, verse and prose,
"I have much reason to expect to find."

When I saw that—no more than the first mad speech,   1560
Made out the speaker mad and a laughing-stock,
So neither did this next device explode
One listener's indignation,—that a scribe
Did sit down, set himself to write indeed,
While sundry knaves began to peer and pry   1565
In corner and hole,—that Guido, wiping brow
And getting him a countenance, was fast
Losing his fear, beginning to strut free
O' the stage of his exploit, snuff here, sniff there,—
Then I took truth in, guessed sufficiently   1570
The service for the moment. "What I say,

1549 *MS* somehow,—dead-white   *MS* lay,— *1868 1872* lay. *1888* lay *DC BrU*
lay>lay. *1889* lay.   1551 *MS* she>he   *MS* {no comma}   1552 *MS*
throu>between   1553–9 *MS*   {no quotation marks at beginnings of
lines}   1553 *MS* then: write   *MS* but, *1868* but, no—   1554 *MS* {no
comma}   1555 *MS*   thing: 1556 *MS* For certain   1557 *MS* {no
comma}   *MS 1868* fled: *1872* fled 1559 *MS* {no quotation mark at end of
line}   1560 *MS* {no new paragraph}   *MS* ^that,^ *1868* saw, that,—   *MS*
former>first   1561 *MS*   fool>mad   1562 *MS*   ^So^   *MS*   charge
[w?]>device   1563 *MS* {beginning of fo. 364}   *MS* man's mere
1564 *1872* down;   1565 *MS 1868 1872* And   1566 *MS* hole, as
1568 *MS* fears,   1569 *MS* On *MS* exploits,   *MS* there,   1570 *MS*
1868 I took the   *MS* saw   1571 *MS* minute "What

1567 *getting . . . countenance*: i.e. getting more confident, putting a braver face on
things.

1570–1 *guessed . . . moment*: i.e. 'I guessed sufficiently what would serve—the appro-
priate course of action—but also I guessed, as it were, the point in the religious service

"Slight at your peril! We are aliens here,
"My adversary and I, called noble both;
"I am the nobler, and a name men know.
"I could refer our cause to our own Court   1575
"In our own country, but prefer appeal
"To the nearer jurisdiction. Being a priest,
"Though in a secular garb,—for reasons good
"I shall adduce in due time to my peers,—
"I demand that the Church I serve, decide   1580
"Between us, right the slandered lady there.
"A Tuscan noble, I might claim the Duke:
"A priest, I rather choose the Church,—bid Rome
"Cover the wronged with her inviolate shield."

There was no refusing this: they bore me off,   1585
They bore her off, to separate cells o' the same
Ignoble prison, and, separate, thence to Rome.
Pompilia's face, then and thus, looked on me
The last time in this life: not one sight since,
Never another sight to be! And yet   1590
I thought I had saved her. I appealed to Rome:
It seems I simply sent her to her death.

1572–84 *MS* {no quotation marks at beginnings of lines}   1572 *MS* peril. *MS*
{no comma}   1573 *MS* and noble   1574 *MS* being>am the   *MS* a
great>and a   *MS* know: 1575 *MS* *1868* *1872* court   1576 *MS* ,—>
, but   1577 *MS* another>the nearer   *MS* jurisdiction: being   *MS* {no com-
ma}   1578 *MS* garb for   1579 *MS* peers.   1580 *MS* Rome, whose
rule>that the Church   1581 *MS* murdered   1582 *MS* {no com-
ma}   *MS* choose>claim   1583 *MS* priest I   *MS* invoke Rome,—>choose
the Church,—   1585 *MS* {New paragraph (already written thus) indicated by
'N.P.' in left-hand margin}   *MS* {no comma}   1586 *MS* of   1587 *Yale*
1 Rome.>Rome!   1588 *MS* {no commas}   1590 *MS* {beginning of fo.
365}   1591 *MS* her:

---

we had come to (and was therefore able to speak the appropriate words).' Just as Guido
has his contrived posturing and staginess as he acts out his part of outraged husband 'o'
the stage of his exploit' (1569), so, in opposition to him, Caponsacchi has his script of
the mass, of religious service, representing his faith and honour. Note the echo of
'serve' at l. 1580.

1572 *Slight at your peril !*: ignore at your own risk.
1582 *the Duke*: i.e. to be judged by the courts of the Grand Duke of Florence.

You tell me she is dying now, or dead;
I cannot bring myself to quite believe
This is a place you torture people in: 1595
What if this your intelligence were just
A subtlety, an honest wile to work
On a man at unawares? 'T were worthy you.
No, Sirs, I cannot have the lady dead!
That erect form, flashing brow, fulgurant eye,   1600
That voice immortal (oh, that voice of hers!)
That vision in the blood-red day-break—that
Leap to life of the pale electric sword
Angels go armed with,—that was not the last
O' the lady! Come, I see through it, you find—   1605
Know the manœuvre! Also herself said
I had saved her: do you dare say she spoke false?
Let me see for myself if it be so!
Though she were dying, a Priest might be of use,
The more when he's a friend too,—she called me   1610
Far beyond "friend." Come, let me see her—indeed
It is my duty, being a priest: I hope
I stand confessed, established, proved a priest?
My punishment had motive that, a priest
I, in a laic garb, a mundane mode,   1615
Did what were harmlessly done otherwise.
I never touched her with my finger-tip
Except to carry her to the couch, that eve,
Against my heart, beneath my head, bowed low,
As we priests carry the paten: that is why   1620

1593 *MS* {no comma}   *MS* dead: 1594 *MS* believe.   1598 *MS* un-
awares: 1599 *MS* dead—   1600 *MS* eye   1605 *MS* Of *MS* see—
1606 *MS* manoeuvre: also   1607 *MS* her—do   1609 *MS 1868* priest
MS being>be   1613 *MS* I am   1616 *MS* otherwise;   1618 *MS*
{beginning of fo. 366}   *MS* {no commas}

   1600 *fulgurant*: flashing, like lightning.
   1603 *electric*: shining, powerful, exciting.
   1620 *As . . . paten*: i.e. with the uttermost reverence. The paten is the small silver
plate that the priest uses in mass to carry the Eucharistic bread, which, after the
consecration, he regards as the Body of Christ.

—To get leave and go see her of your grace—
I have told you this whole story over again.
Do I deserve grace? For I might lock lips,
Laugh at your jurisdiction: what have you
To do with me in the matter? I suppose   1625
You hardly think I donned a bravo's dress
To have a hand in the new crime; on the old,
Judgment's delivered, penalty imposed,
I was chained fast at Civita hand and foot—
She had only you to trust to, you and Rome,   1630
Rome and the Church, and no pert meddling priest
Two days ago, when Guido, with the right,
Hacked her to pieces. One might well be wroth;
I have been patient, done my best to help:
I come from Civita and punishment   1635
As friend of the Court—and for pure friendship's sake
Have told my tale to the end,—nay, not the end—
For, wait—I'll end—not leave you that excuse!

When we were parted,—shall I go on there?
I was presently brought to Rome—yes, here I stood   1640
Opposite yonder very crucifix—
And there sat you and you, Sirs, quite the same.
I heard charge, and bore question, and told tale
Noted down in the book there,—turn and see
If, by one jot or tittle, I vary now!   1645

1622 *MS* again—   1623 *MS* {no comma}   1624 *MS* jurisdiction—
1627 *MS* murder>new crime;   1628 *MS* punishment's>penalty's   1631
MS medding {clearly a *lapsus calami*}   1632 *MS* for his part,   1633 *MS*
pieces: one   *MS* wroth,   1636 *1868 1872* court—   1638 *MS*
Well,   *1872* end not {broken sort}   *MS* excuse. 1639 *MS* {no new
paragraph}   1641 *MS* [ ]>Opposite   *MS* Crucifix— 1642 *MS* sate   *MS*
you, and>you and   1645 *MS* tittle I   *MS* now.

1626–7 *You . . . crime*: i.e. 'even you don't think I disguised myself as a ruffian and
had a hand in the new crime, Pompilia's murder'. Caponsacchi's point is that he has
paid for 'the old crime', his flight with Pompilia. At this moment the court has no
claim upon him; he is here voluntarily.
1631 *pert*: cf. l. 41 n.

I' the colour the tale takes, there's change perhaps;
'T is natural, since the sky is different,
Eclipse in the air now; still, the outline stays.
I showed you how it came to be my part
To save the lady. Then your clerk produced   1650
Papers, a pack of stupid and impure
Banalities called letters about love—
Love, indeed,—I could teach who styled them so,
Better, I think, though priest and loveless both!
"—How was it that a wife, young, innocent,   1655
"And stranger to your person, wrote this page?"—
"—She wrote it when the Holy Father wrote
"The bestiality that posts thro' Rome,
"Put in his mouth by Pasquin." "Nor perhaps
"Did you return these answers, verse and prose,   1660
"Signed, sealed and sent the lady? There's your hand!"
"—This precious piece of verse, I really judge,
"Is meant to copy my own character,
"A clumsy mimic; and this other prose,
"Not so much even; both rank forgery: 1665

1646 *MS* {beginning of fo. 367}   *MS* In   *MS* I now give,   *MS* perhaps—
1648 *MS* {no comma}   1651 *MS* Papers—   1652 *MS* Love—   1653
MS so   1655 *MS* "How   1656 *MS* {no quotation mark at beginning of
line}   *MS* A   1658–61 *MS* {no quotation marks at beginnings of
lines}   1658 *MS* That pasquinade that posts thro' Rome>The bestiality
that posts thro' Rome,   1659 *MS 1868 1872* Pasquin."—   1661 *MS* lady:
there's   1662 *MS* "This   *MS 1868 1872* judge   1663–7 *MS* {no quota-
tion marks at beginnings of lines}   1663 *MS* characters,   1664 *MS* {no
comma}   1666 *MS* rather Bembo's: when John wrote

1659 *Pasquin*: a battered classical torso, set up at the corner of Palazzo Braschi in
1501 and popularly called *Pasquino* after a witty tailor whose shop was supposed to have
been nearby. A custom grew up of affixing short witty poems to the statue, and hence,
in the sixteenth century, a much wider tradition of *pasquinate* or pasquinades, satiric
epigrams or lampoons, which were attributed by their anonymous authors to Pasquin,
the talking statue, the supposed mouthpiece of this wit. Story gives an account of the
tradition of coarse and scurrilous pasquinades directed at the popes in *Roba di Roma*, i.
258–69.

"Verse, quotha? Bembo's verse! When Saint John wrote
"The tract 'De Tribus,' I wrote this to match."
"—How came it, then, the documents were found
"At the inn on your departure?"—"I opine,
"Because there were no documents to find   1670
"In my presence,—you must hide before you find.
"Who forged them hardly practised in my view;
"Who found them waited till I turned my back."
"—And what of the clandestine visits paid,
"Nocturnal passage in and out the house   1675
"With its lord absent? 'T is alleged you climbed..."
"—Flew on a broomstick to the man i' the moon!
"Who witnessed or will testify this trash?"
"—The trusty servant, Margherita's self,
"Even she who brought you letters, you confess,   1680
"And, you confess, took letters in reply:

1667 *MS* "De Tribus,"   1668 *MS* "—[ ]>"—How   *MS* {no commas}
1669–73 *MS* {no quotation marks at beginnings of lines}   1669 *MS*
[ ]>At   *MS* Inn   *MS* {no comma}   1671 *MS* find: 1672 *1868 1872*
them,   *MS* view,   1673 *1868 1872* them,   1674 *MS* {beginning of fo.
368}   1675–6 *MS* {no quotation marks at beginnings of lines}   1676 *MS*
With Guido absent? *1868 1872* climbed ...'   1677 *MS* ^""—Flew^   *MS* in
1678 *MS* {no quotation mark at beginning of line}   *MS* and will   1680–2
MS {no quotation marks at beginnings of lines}   1681 *MS* confess took

1666 *quotha?*: do you say?

Bembo's verse: an ironic exclamation: 'If you are calling it poetry at all, you might as
well call it Bembo's poetry!' Pietro Bembo (1470–1547), was one of the great humanist
cardinals of the Renaissance and an arbiter of letters. He was deeply concerned with style
and correctness in Latin and in the emerging Italian language, and he helped to establish
Tuscan as the standard literary Italian. In the dedication to *Asolando* (1889) Browning
describes him as a 'thorough' purist. Caponsacchi is sharply ironic: the squalid love-
verses are the very opposite of Bembo's correct, elegant poetry. For Browning's copy of
Bembo's *Prose della volgar lingua* (1525) see Kelley and Coley, A193.

1666–7 *When ... 'De Tribus'*: i.e. when St John is proved to have written a scanda-
lous religious tract. *De Tribus Impostoribus* ('Of the three impostors') was a legendary
medieval tract attacking the founders of the monotheistic religions, Moses, Jesus, and
Muhammad. Caponsacchi's contrast here is elliptically expressed. St John is the author
of the gospel that makes one of the founding statements concerning the Trinity, the
Christian doctrine of three Persons (Father, Son, and Holy Spirit) in One God. This
sacred 'Three' is completely different from the heretical, scurrilous tract 'Of the three
impostors'. The extremity of the contrast implies how spiritual and elevated is
Caponsacchi's view of Pompilia.

1672 *practised*: worked, performed a task.

"Forget not we have knowledge of the facts!"
"—Sirs, who have knowledge of the facts, defray
"The expenditure of wit I waste in vain,
"Trying to find out just one fact of all!   1685
"She who brought letters from who could not write,
"And took back letters to who could not read,—
"Who was that messenger, of your charity?"
"—Well, so far favours you the circumstance
"That this same messenger . . . how shall we say? . . .   1690
"*Sub imputatione meretricis*
"*Laborat*,—which makes accusation null:
"We waive this woman's: nought makes void the next.
"Borsi, called Venerino, he who drove,
"O' the first night when you fled away, at length   1695
"Deposes to your kissings in the coach,
"—Frequent, frenetic . . ." "When deposed he so?"
"After some weeks of sharp imprisonment . . ."
"—Granted by friend the Governor, I engage—"
"—For his participation in your flight!   1700
"At length his obduracy melting made
"The avowal mentioned . ." "Was dismissed forthwith
"To liberty, poor knave, for recompense.
"Sirs, give what credit to the lie you can!

1682 *MS* facts."   1684–8 *MS* {no quotation marks at beginnings of lines}
1684 *MS* {no comma}   1685 *MS* all: 1686 *MS* ^letters^ 1687 *MS*
read,   1690–6 *MS* {no quotation marks at beginnings of lines}   1690 *MS*
1868 1872 messenger . .   *MS* 1868 1872 say? . .   1692 *MS* witness null and
void:>accusation null: 1693 1868 1872 woman's:—   *MS* next   1694
MS drove   1695 *MS* On   1696 *MS* {no comma} 1697 *MS* {note in
left-hand margin 'Slip 96'}   *MS* "Frequent, 1699 *MS* "Granted   1700 *MS*
"For   *MS* flight,   1701–6 *MS* {no quotation marks at beginnings of
lines}   1702 *MS* {beginning of fo. 369}   *MS* forthwith.   1703 {not
found in *MS*}

1683–5 *defray . . . all*: i.e. 'save me from wasting my wit in finding out just one fact
you already know'—the name and status of the messenger.

1691–2 *Sub . . . Laborat*: 'is under suspicion of being a prostitute' (L.): see OYB cclii
(248).

1694–1703 *Borsi . . . recompense*: this evidence of the carriage-driver and its refutation
are at OYB vi (5) and cclii f. (249) respectively.

"For me, no word in my defence I speak,   1705
"And God shall argue for the lady!"
                          So
Did I stand question, and make answer, still
With the same result of smiling disbelief,
Polite impossibility of faith   1710
In such affected virtue in a priest;
But a showing fair play, an indulgence, even,
To one no worse than others after all—
Who had not brought disgrace to the order, played
Discreetly, ruffled gown nor ripped the cloth   1715
In a bungling game at romps: I have told you, Sirs—
If I pretended simply to be pure
Honest and Christian in the case,—absurd!
As well go boast myself above the needs
O' the human nature, careless how meat smells,   1720
Wine tastes,—a saint above the smack! But once
Abate my crest, own flaws i' the flesh, agree
To go with the herd, be hog no more nor less,
Why, hogs in common herd have common rights:
I must not be unduly borne upon,   1725
Who just romanced a little, sowed wild oats,
But 'scaped without a scandal, flagrant fault.
My name helped to a mirthful circumstance:

1705 *MS*   speak: 1706 *MS* 'Tis   *MS* answer>argue   *MS*   Lady!"
1707 *MS* {no new paragraph}   1711 *MS* pretence at>affected   *MS* on our
part   *Yale 1* priest,>priest;   1712 *MS* indulgence even   1713 *MS*
me   1714 *MS* disgraced my order, ripped the cloth   1715 {not found in
MS}   1720 *MS* Of   *MS*   smells   1721 *MS*   tastes,   *MS*   but
1722 *MS* in   1724 *MS* {no comma}   *MS 1868 1872* rights—   1725
MS upon.   1726 *MS 1868* had just   *MS 1868* sown   1727 *MS* found
out in no   *MS* fault: 1728 *MS* circumstance

1721 *a saint above the smack!*: i.e. a saint above the smack (of the lips), the noise of
enjoyment made in the tasting of food or wine; cf. 'Mr Sludge', 432.

1722 *Abate my crest*: i.e. 'if I surrender my pride or reputation'.

1727 *flagrant fault*: cf. v. 1874 n.

1728 *My name*: i.e. Caponsacchi's first name, Giuseppe (It. Joseph).

"Joseph" would do well to amend his plea:
Undoubtedly—some toying with the wife,   1730
But as for ruffian violence and rape,
Potiphar pressed too much on the other side!
The intrigue, the elopement, the disguise,—well charged!
The letters and verse looked hardly like the truth.
Your apprehension was—of guilt enough   1735
To be compatible with innocence,
So, punished best a little and not too much.
Had I struck Guido Franceschini's face,
You had counselled me withdraw for my own sake,
Baulk him of bravo-hiring. Friends came round,   1740
Congratulated, "Nobody mistakes!
"The pettiness o' the forfeiture defines
"The peccadillo: Guido gets his share:
"His wife is free of husband and hook-nose,
"The mouldy viands and the mother-in-law.   1745

1729 *MS* {no quotation marks}   1732 *MS* to {evidently a *lapsus calami*}   *MS*
side.   1733 *MS* {beginning of fo. 370}   1734 *MS* verses   *MS* less
like   1735 *MS* was of   1737 *MS* {no comma}   *MS* much—
1738 *MS* spat in   *MS* {no comma}   1741 *MS* {no comma}   *MS* mistakes
the case,   1742–53 *MS* {no quotation marks at beginnings of
lines}   1742 *MS* of   1744 *MS* him and the hook nose   1745 *MS*
mother-in-law:

1729 *"Joseph"*: cf. Gen. 39, where Joseph is accused of the attempted rape of
Potiphar's wife. The judges are amused that Giuseppe (Joseph) Caponsacchi, accused
of seduction and elopement, shares his first name with the biblical Joseph, similarly
accused of rape. In the Bible story, Potiphar believes the accusations against Joseph
with regard to his wife, and has him thrown into prison—which is what Guido would
like for Caponsacchi. Caponsacchi's reference is ironic, however, for he knows that
the judges' joke rebounds on them: he, like the biblical Joseph, is innocent, and the
fact that the judges assume some flirtation on his part only shows their worldliness.

1732 *Potiphar*: i.e. the outraged husband, Guido: see previous n.

1740 *Baulk him of bravo-hiring*: i.e. frustrate Guido of the need to hire thugs to beat
you up. If Caponsacchi had been so bold as to assert his total innocence by striking
Guido in the face, the judges—believing him at least a little guilty—would have
advised him to back down; they would have felt that Guido had some right on his
side if he had arranged for Caponsacchi to be beaten up in order to satisfy his honour,
and they would want Caponsacchi to avoid an attack from Guido's thugs by apolo-
gizing.

1744 *hook-nose*: Guido's hook-nose has already been established at I. 782; see also
VII. 395–6 n.

"To Civita with you and amuse the time,
"Travesty us '*De Raptu Helenæ!*'
"A funny figure must the husband cut
"When the wife makes him skip,—too ticklish, eh?
"Do it in Latin, not the Vulgar, then!   1750
"Scazons—we'll copy and send his Eminence.
"Mind—one iambus in the final foot!
"He'll rectify it, be your friend for life!"
Oh, Sirs, depend on me for much new light
Thrown on the justice and religion here   1755
By this proceeding, much fresh food for thought!

And I was just set down to study these
In relegation, two short days ago,
Admiring how you read the rules, when, clap,
A thunder comes into my solitude—   1760
I am caught up in a whirlwind and cast here,

1746 *MS* {no comma}   1747 *MS* Translating us "de Raptu Helenæ,"
1748 *MS* doleful figure did the Husband   1750 *MS* then   1751 *MS* for
the Cardinal—>and send his Eminence— *1868 1872* Eminence!   1752 *MS*
foot—   1753 *MS* rectify and   1757 *MS* {no new paragraph} 1758 *MS*
In my   1759 *MS* when clap   1760 *MS* the solitude—   1761 *MS*
{beginning of fo. 371}   *MS* {no comma}

1747 '*De Raptu Helenæ!*': 'Of the Abduction of Helen', the only extant work of
Colluthus (*c.* AD 500). It is an elegant, slightly lubricious Greek poem describing the
Judgment of Paris, how subsequently Paris sought out Helen, and how he eloped with
her back to Troy. Caponsacchi's friends are suggesting that, as a sophisticated joke, he
write a mock-epic pastiche of the poem, drawing on his own supposed experience,
and portraying himself as the handsome Paris and Pompilia as the beautiful Helen. *De
Raptu Helenæ* was often appended to editions of the *Iliad*, particularly the Geneva
editions, and this is the most likely context in which Browning originally encountered
it. His earlier mention, in *Pippa Passes*, II. 39–42, of a fine fifteenth-century manuscript
of Colluthus perhaps suggests that he had seen such a thing during his trip to Italy in
1838.
    1749 *skip*: hurry. In the imagined mock-epic version of *De Raptu Helenæ* the
husband (the Menelaus/Guido figure) will be made to appear ridiculous as he hurries
in pursuit of the absconding lovers.
    ticklish: difficult, tricky.
    1750 *Vulgar*: the vernacular language, i.e. Italian.
    1751 *Scazons*: iambic trimeter in which a spondee or trochee takes the place of the
final iamb. Hence, in the next line, putting 'one iambus in the final foot' would be a
deliberate mistake.

Told of a sudden, in this room where so late
You dealt out law adroitly, that those scales,
I meekly bowed to, took my allotment from,
Guido has snatched at, broken in your hands,   1765
Metes to himself the murder of his wife,
Full measure, pressed down, running over now!
Can I assist to an explanation?—Yes,
I rise in your esteem, sagacious Sirs,
Stand up a renderer of reasons, not   1770
The officious priest would personate Saint George
For a mock Princess in undragoned days.
What, the blood startles you? What, after all
The priest who needs must carry sword on thigh
May find imperative use for it? Then, there was   1775
A Princess, was a dragon belching flame,
And should have been a Saint George also? Then,
There might be worse schemes than to break the bonds
At Arezzo, lead her by the little hand,
Till she reached Rome, and let her try to live?   1780
But you were law and gospel,—would one please
Stand back, allow your faculty elbow-room?

1764 *MS* bowed, and took my measure from,>bowed, took my allotment
from,   1765 *MS* burst>snatched   1766 *MS* And metes himself>Metes to
himself   1767 *MS* now: 1771 *MS* young Saint George too bold>priest
would personate Saint George   1772 *MS* the perilled>a mock   1773
MS sobers   1775 *MS* have found   *MS* {no comma} *Yale 1* Then>
Then,   1776 *MS* and>was   *MS* Dragon   *MS* flame   1777 *MS* {no
comma} *Yale 1* Then>Then,   1780 *MS* began to try and live?>and let her
try to live?   1781 *MS 1868* the law and the gospel,—

1766 *Metes*: measures, deals out. This and the next line make passionate, ironic use
of Luke 6: 38: 'Give, and it shall be given unto you; good measure, pressed down, and
shaken together, and running over, shall men give into your bosom. For with the
same measure that ye mete withal it shall be measured to you again.' Guido has
broken any give-and-take of justice and ruthlessly taken upon himself the murder of
Pompilia.
      1771 *Saint George*: cf. 1. 585 n.
      1772 *undragoned*: i.e. secularized—in the sense that good and evil, and the 'myths'
that embody them, are no longer believed in as metaphysical realities: see Introduc-
tion.

You blind guides who must needs lead eyes that see!
Fools, alike ignorant of man and God!
What was there here should have perplexed your wit   1785
For a wink of the owl-eyes of you? How miss, then,
What's now forced on you by this flare of fact—
As if Saint Peter failed to recognize
Nero as no apostle, John or James,
Till someone burned a martyr, made a torch   1790
O' the blood and fat to show his features by!
Could you fail read this cartulary aright
On head and front of Franceschini there,
Large-lettered like hell's masterpiece of print,—
That he, from the beginning pricked at heart   1795
By some lust, letch of hate against his wife,
Plotted to plague her into overt sin
And shame, would slay Pompilia body and soul,
And save his mean self—miserably caught
I' the quagmire of his own tricks, cheats and lies?   1800

1784 *MS* Man   1786 *MS* fail find>miss then   1788 *MS* Paul had>Peter   1789 *MS* {beginning of fo. 372}   *MS* not the mate of James nor John>no Apostle, John nor James   1791 *MS* Of   1793 *MS* the head   *MS* {no comma}   1794 *MS* Hell's   *MS* print,   1796 *MS* lust, and letch>some lust, letch   1798 *MS* should   1799 *MS* self miserably   1800 *MS* In

---

1783–4 *blind guides . . . Fools*: echoing Jesus' denunciation of the scribes and Pharisees, Matt. 23: 16–17, 19, 24; cf. also Matt. 15: 14.

1786: *owl-eyes*: large, solemn, but foolish eyes; cf. 11. 216 n.

1788–9 *Saint Peter . . . Nero*: ancient tradition affirms that St Peter was put to death at the hands of Nero in Rome in AD 64, during the Neronian persecution of the early Christians; this allusion overturns the implications of ll. 291–9.

1790 *made a torch*: an allusion to the way Nero had Christians made into 'torches' to burn after dark: see Tacitus, *Annals*, XV. 44. St Peter would not have needed the 'torch' of a burning fellow Christian to realize that Nero was 'no apostle, [no] John or James'.

1792 *cartulary*: large manuscript or charter. A cartulary was originally a set of monastic records, and a chartulary a collection of charters, but by the nineteenth century the words were interchangeable, and sometimes used erroneously in the sense 'charter'. The image is primarily one of size: Guido's wickedness is writ large upon his face, Caponsacchi says, and should be clear to any observer. It is possible that Browning may have been influenced in his choice of word here by the It. *carta*, paper.

1796 *letch*: craving, lechery.

—That himself wrote those papers,—from himself
To himself,—which, i' the name of me and her,
His mistress-messenger gave her and me,
Touching us with such pustules of the soul
That she and I might take the taint, be shown   1805
To the world and shuddered over, speckled so?
—That the agent put her sense into my words,
Made substitution of the thing she hoped,
For the thing she had and held, its opposite,
While the husband in the background bit his lips   1810
At each fresh failure of his precious plot?
—That when at the last we did rush each on each,
By no chance but because God willed it so—
The spark of truth was struck from out our souls—
Made all of me, descried in the first glance,   1815
Seem fair and honest and permissible love
O' the good and true—as the first glance told me
There was no duty patent in the world
Like daring try be good and true myself,
Leaving the shows of things to the Lord of Show   1820
And Prince o' the Power of the Air. Our very flight,
Even to its most ambiguous circumstance,
Irrefragably proved how futile, false . . .

1802 *MS* himself,—in the name   *MS* her and me,>me and her   1804 *MS*
Spotting both>Touching us   *MS* those pustules   1805 *Yale 1* taint>
taint,   1806 *MS* at o'er speckled   1807 *MS* That   *MS* {no com-
ma}   1808 *MS* {no comma}   1811 *MS* plot?—plot hatched>precious
plot?   1812 *MS* In that—that when we did meet at the last—>[ ]>—That
when at the last we did rush each on each,   1814 *MS* forth from our souls>from
out our souls   1815 *MS* {no commas}   *MS* through>in   1817 *MS*
{beginning of fo. 373}   *MS* Of *Yale 1* Of>O'   1818 *MS* for me>patent
MS wide world>world   1821 *MS* of   *MS* {no comma} 1822 *MS* {no
comma}

1818 *patent*: plain, obvious.
1820–1 *Lord . . . Air*: two names for Satan; cf. Eph. 2: 2.

Why, men—men and not boys—boys and not babes—
Babes and not beasts—beasts and not stocks and stones!—
Had the liar's lie been true one pin-point speck,   1826
Were I the accepted suitor, free o' the place,
Disposer of the time, to come at a call
And go at a wink as who should say me nay,—
What need of flight, what were the gain therefrom   1830
But just damnation, failure or success?
Damnation pure and simple to her the wife
And me the priest—who bartered private bliss
For public reprobation, the safe shade
For the sunshine which men see to pelt me by: 1835
What other advantage,—we who led the days
And nights alone i' the house,—was flight to find?
In our whole journey did we stop an hour,
Diverge a foot from straight road till we reached
Or would have reached—but for that fate of ours—   1840
The father and mother, in the eye of Rome,
The eye of yourselves we made aware of us
At the first fall of misfortune? And indeed

1825 *MS* stones—   1826 *MS* {no comma}   1827 *MS* And   *MS* of
1829 *MS* nay,   1830 *MS* thereby   1831 *MS* and success   1833 *MS*
barter   1834 *MS* at the best>the safe shade   1835 *MS* you *Yale 1* you>
me   1836 *MS*   advantage,   1837 *MS* in   *MS* in this>was flight
1839 *MS* the strait *1868 1872* strait   1843 *MS* misfortune: and

1824–5 *Why . . . stones!*: Caponsacchi's syntax simply breaks down under the strain
of indignation and disbelief. What he is trying to say is: 'real men (who are no longer
boys) would see the truth—in fact even boys (no longer children) would see it. Indeed
even babies (not being beasts) would see it, or beasts (who are animate) would see it'.
At the end of the catalogue lie the inanimate stocks and stones with an implicit echo of
Luke 19: 40.

1841 *in the eye of Rome*: the sense of 'eye' shifts as we read on. Initially we may read
it as 'centre, cynosure'; cf. Milton, *Paradise Regained*, iv. 240: 'Athens, the eye of
Greece'. As we pass to the next line, it becomes apparent that the main sense is 'in the
full view (and protection) [of Rome]'; cf. *Hamlet*, IV. iv. 6: 'We shall express our duty
in his eye'. We may first read the passage as 'till we reached or would have reached the
father and mother, *in the centre of Rome*'. Then, as the whole syntax becomes apparent,
we read 'till we reached or would have reached the father and mother, *in full view of all
Rome*, and in full view of you yourselves the judges . . .'. Caponsacchi's point is that he
and Pompilia were not doing anything secretive, but racing in full view towards her
parents.

You did so far give sanction to our flight,
Confirm its purpose, as lend helping hand,   1845
Deliver up Pompilia not to him
She fled, but those the flight was ventured for.
Why then could you, who stopped short, not go on
One poor step more, and justify the means,
Having allowed the end?—not see and say   1850
"Here's the exceptional conduct that should claim
"To be exceptionally judged on rules
"Which, understood, make no exception here"—
Why play instead into the devil's hands
By dealing so ambiguously as gave   1855
Guido the power to intervene like me,
Prove one exception more? I saved his wife
Against law: against law he slays her now:
Deal with him!

        I have done with being judged.   1860
I stand here guiltless in thought, word and deed,
To the point that I apprise you,—in contempt
For all misapprehending ignorance
O' the human heart, much more the mind of Christ,—
That I assuredly did bow, was blessed   1865
By the revelation of Pompilia. There!
Such is the final fact I fling you, Sirs,
To mouth and mumble and misinterpret: there!
"The priest's in love," have it the vulgar way!

1844 *MS* {no comma}   1845 *MS* {beginning of fo. 374}   *MS* {no commas}
1847 *MS* {no comma}   *MS* for: 1848 *MS* [ ]>short   1849 *MS*
means   1850 *MS* end,—   1852–3 *MS* {no quotation marks at beginnings
of lines}   1853 *MS* {no commas}   1856 *MS* as I,   1857 *MS* more:
1958 *MS* Against,>Against   1859 *MS* him.   1860 *MS* {no new para-
graph}   *MS* appeal>have done   1861 *MS* deed   1862 *MS* you,
in   1863 *MS* Of>For   1864 *MS* Of   *MS* Christ,   1869 *MS*
Priest's

1862 *apprise you*: inform you of, make known to you. After this the main sense goes
over the parenthesis to l. 1865: 'I apprise you . . . That I assuredly did bow, was blessed
/ By the revelation of Pompilia.'

Unpriest me, rend the rags o' the vestment, do—   1870
Degrade deep, disenfranchise all you dare—
Remove me from the midst, no longer priest
And fit companion for the like of you—
Your gay Abati with the well-turned leg
And rose i' the hat-rim, Canons, cross at neck   1875
And silk mask in the pocket of the gown,
Brisk Bishops with the world's musk still unbrushed
From the rochet; I'll no more of these good things:
There's a crack somewhere, something that's unsound
I' the rattle!   1880

        For Pompilia—be advised,
Build churches, go pray! You will find me there,
I know, if you come,—and you will come, I know.
Why, there's a Judge weeping! Did not I say
You were good and true at bottom? You see the truth—
I am glad I helped you: she helped me just so.   1886

But for Count Guido,—you must counsel there!
I bow my head, bend to the very dust,
Break myself up in shame of faultiness.
I had him one whole moment, as I said—   1890

1870 MS Punish that,>Unfrock me,   MS of   1871 MS disenfranchize   MS
can—   1872 MS Unfrock>Remove me   MS the>your   1874 MS
{beginning of fo. 375}   MS abbati Yale 1 Abbati>Abati   1875 MS in   MS
canons cross   1877 MS 1868 1872 bishops   1878 MS rochet: 1879 MS
wrong>crack   1880 MS In   MS rattle: 1881 MS {no new para-
graph}   MS for   1882 MS pray: you   MS there   1883 MS
know: 1884 MS in tears: did   1885 MS bottom: you   1887 MS
{no new paragraph}   MS there—   1888 MS dust   1889 MS faulti-
ness—

1874 *Abati*: (It. pl.) clerics, abbés; cf. v . 1304 n.

1876 *silk mask*: a silk eye-mask, traditionally worn at society parties and during
Carnival. The mask allows a degree of anonymity for pleasure or flirtation.

1877 *musk*: perfume (based upon the substance musk). There is an ironic contrast
between the bishops' brisk (efficient) religious manner and this heavy, sensuous
perfume which, symbolically, still hangs about them from party-going or other
worldly delights.

1878 *rochet*: white linen vestment. A rochet is a traditional piece of bishops' clothing
rather like a surplice.

As I remember, as will never out
O' the thoughts of me,—I had him in arm's reach
There,—as you stand, Sir, now you cease to sit,—
I could have killed him ere he killed his wife,
And did not: he went off alive and well   1895
And then effected this last feat—through me!
Me—not through you—dismiss that fear! 'T was you
Hindered me staying here to save her,—not
From leaving you and going back to him
And doing service in Arezzo. Come,   1900
Instruct me in procedure! I conceive—
In all due self-abasement might I speak—
How you will deal with Guido: oh, not death!
Death, if it let her life be: otherwise
Not death,—your lights will teach you clearer! I   1905
Certainly have an instinct of my own
I' the matter: bear with me and weigh its worth!
Let us go away—leave Guido all alone
Back on the world again that knows him now!
I think he will be found (indulge so far!)   1910
Not to die so much as slide out of life,
Pushed by the general horror and common hate
Low, lower,—left o' the very ledge of things,
I seem to see him catch convulsively
One by one at all honest forms of life,   1915
At reason, order, decency and use—
To cramp him and get foothold by at least;

1892 *MS* Of   1897 *MS* Me! not   ★*1888 1889* dsimiss   *MS* fear—'twas
1899 *MS* leaving her   1901 *MS* procedure—I   1903 *MS* {beginning of
fo. 376}   1904 *MS* {no comma}   1905 *MS* clearer—I   1907 *MS*
In   1908 *MS* away [now?]—>away—   1909 *MS* now.   1911 *MS*
{no comma}   1913 *MS* on   1916 *MS* use   1917 *MS* there>by *MS*
least,

1893 *stand . . . sit*: one of the judges has apparently stood up, just as at l. 1884 this
same judge, or more probably another judge, has broken down in tears. Approaching
the climax of the monologue, the judges appear agitated with emotion, profoundly
moved by what Caponsacchi has been saying.
    1917 *cramp*: fasten, hold. The sense here is Johnson, 3: 'to bind with crampirons'.

And still they disengage them from his clutch.
"What, you are he, then, had Pompilia once
"And so forwent her? Take not up with us!"   1920
And thus I see him slowly and surely edged
Off all the table-land whence life upsprings
Aspiring to be immortality,
As the snake, hatched on hill-top by mischance,
Despite his wriggling, slips, slides, slidders down   1925
Hill-side, lies low and prostrate on the smooth
Level of the outer place, lapsed in the vale:
So I lose Guido in the loneliness,
Silence and dusk, till at the doleful end,
At the horizontal line, creation's verge,   1930
From what just is to absolute nothingness—
Whom is it, straining onward still, he meets?
What other man deep further in the fate,
Who, turning at the prize of a footfall
To flatter him and promise fellowship,   1935
Discovers in the act a frightful face—
Judas, made monstrous by much solitude!

1918 *MS* clutch   1919 *MS* he then had   1920 *MS* {no quotation mark at
beginning of line}   1924 *MS* {no commas}   1925 *MS* wriggling slips,
Yale 1 wriggling>wriggling,   1926 *MS* and is low prostrate>is found low pros-
trate *Yale 1* is>lies   1927 *MS* [out?]>of the   1929 *MS* night>dusk   *MS*
{no commas}   1930 *MS* horizon's   *MS* last,>line,   *MS* {Between 1930 and
1931 extra line, which is the beginning of fo. 377: Lo, what is [that?]>this he meets
(that) strains on ^and^ still   1932 {not found in *MS*}   *1868* Lo, what is this
he meets, strains onward still?   1934 *MS* {no comma}   *Yale 1* Who>
Who,   *MS*   comfort>{*deleted* comfort}>comfort>prize   *MS*   step>footfall
1935 *MS* Close behind his and promised fellowship>To comfort his and promise
fellowship   *MS* {no comma}   1937 *1888 1889* {the 'c' of 'much' has been
damaged and appears to be an 'o'}

1925 *slidders*: 'slides with interruption': Johnson, who cites the vivid instance in
Dryden's *Aeneis*, II. 748–9: 'with that he dragg'd the trembling Sire, / Slidd'ring
through clotter'd Blood, and holy Mire'. Cf. *Sordello*, IV. 736 n.
   1927 *lapsed*: sunk down, fallen; the religious sense is also partly operative here:
'fallen into sin', 'fallen from perfection': cf. *Paradise Lost*, X. 572.
   1937 *Judas*: Judas Iscariot, who betrayed Christ with a kiss: see l. 1944 n. In these
lines Caponsacchi, overwhelmed with passion, creates a scene reminiscent of Dante's
Inferno xxxii–xxxiv, the cantos dealing with the worst abyss of Hell. Guido is like one
of 'the treacherous' of the *Inferno*, his betrayal of Pompilia's goodness an equivalent to

The two are at one now! Let them love their love
That bites and claws like hate, or hate their hate
That mops and mows and makes as it were love!   1940
There, let them each tear each in devil's-fun,
Or fondle this the other while malice aches—
Both teach, both learn detestability!
Kiss him the kiss, Iscariot! Pay that back,
That smatch o' the slaver blistering on your lip,   1945
By the better trick, the insult he spared Christ—
Lure him the lure o' the letters, Aretine!
Lick him o'er slimy-smooth with jelly-filth
O' the verse-and-prose pollution in love's guise!
The cockatrice is with the basilisk!   1950
There let them grapple, denizens o' the dark,
Foes or friends, but indissolubly bound,
In their one spot out of the ken of God
Or care of man, for ever and ever more!

[—]

1940 *MS* love;   1941 *MS* devils'-fun   1942 *MS* each>this   1943
MS Each teach, each>Both teach, both   *MS* detestability.   1945 *MS* burn>
smatch   *MS* of   *MS 1868* lip—   1946 *MS* {line added later}   1947
MS Wile him the wile of *Yale 1* Wile him the wile>Lure him the lure   1948 *MS*
shiny-smooth with the jelley-filth   1949 *MS* Of   1951 *MS* of   1954
MS the care *Yale 1* the care>care

Judas's betrayal of Christ. The way in which Guido and Judas are 'indissolubly bound'
seems a deliberate recollection of the way in which traitors in the *Inferno* are bound
together with fellow traitors in what Sinclair aptly calls 'a fierce *dis*-fellowship': see *The
Divine Comedy*, trans. with commentary by John D. Sinclair (3 vols., rev. ed. 1948), i.
414. Their locked embrace of hatred, licking, and kissing, has some of the disgusting
force of Count Ugolino chewing on Archbishop Ruggieri's skull in canto XXXII.
124–39. It is also a grotesque parody of the sexual intimacy of marriage which Guido,
as a wife-rapist, did so much to pervert: see Brady, 103.

1940 *mops and mows*: gestures and makes ugly faces; cf. I. 572 n.

1944 *Kiss . . . Iscariot*: cf. Matt. 26: 48–49.

1945 *smatch o' the slaver*: taste of the saliva; cf. l. 1494 n.

1946 *insult he spared Christ*: i.e. Judas never actually forged letters to incriminate Christ.

1947 *Aretine*: perhaps, in this context, not just 'man from Arezzo', but also 'obscene
or ribald person', after Pietro Aretino (1492–1557), the famous author of obscene
verse; cf. X. 650–6.

1950 *cockatrice . . . basilisk*: a cockatrice is a legendary and hideous monster, part
cock, part serpent, with deadly gaze and breath. 'Basilisk' is a virtual synonym,
which is the point here: Judas and Guido grappling together are virtually indistinguish-
able. Cf. I. 171–3 n.

Why, Sirs, what's this? Why, this is sorry and strange!
Futility, divagation: this from me   1956
Bound to be rational, justify an act
Of sober man!—whereas, being moved so much,
I give you cause to doubt the lady's mind:
A pretty sarcasm for the world! I fear   1960
You do her wit injustice,—all through me!
Like my fate all through,—ineffective help!
A poor rash advocate I prove myself.
You might be angry with good cause: but sure
At the advocate,—only at the undue zeal   1965
That spoils the force of his own plea, I think?
My part was just to tell you how things stand,
State facts and not be flustered at their fume.
But then 't is a priest speaks: as for love,—no!
If you let buzz a vulgar fly like that   1970
About your brains, as if I loved, forsooth,
Indeed, Sirs, you do wrong! We had no thought
Of such infatuation, she and I:
There are many points that prove it: do be just!
I told you,—at one little roadside-place   1975
I spent a good half-hour, paced to and fro
The garden; just to leave her free awhile,
I plucked a handful of Spring herb and bloom:
I might have sat beside her on the bench
Where the children were: I wish the thing had been,   1980
Indeed: the event could not be worse, you know:

1955 *MS* {New paragraph (already written thus) indicated by 'N.P.' in left-hand margin}   *MS* wrong,>poor,>strange,— *1868* strange!—   1956 *MS* and divagation:>divagation: 1957 *MS* the choice   1958 *MS* the sober man, whereas,   1959 *MS* {beginning of fo. 378}   1960 *MS* world.   1961 *MS* me   1962 *MS* And   *MS* help.   1963 *MS* myself—   1964 *MS* cause—   1966 *MS* turns   1972 *MS* wrong: we   1973 *MS* {no comma}   1974 *MS* just—   1975 *MS* roadside place   1977 *MS* garden,   1978 *MS* spring   *MS* flower: 1979 *MS* sate

1956 *divagation*: digression (from his argument).
1970 *vulgar*: ordinary, commonplace.
1981 *event*: outcome, result.

One more half-hour of her saved! She's dead now, Sirs!
While I was running on at such a rate,
Friends should have plucked me by the sleeve: I went
Too much o' the trivial outside of her face   1985
And the purity that shone there—plain to me,
Not to you, what more natural? Nor am I
Infatuated,—oh, I saw, be sure!
Her brow had not the right line, leaned too much,
Painters would say; they like the straight-up Greek: 1990
This seemed bent somewhat with an invisible crown
Of martyr and saint, not such as art approves.
And how the dark orbs dwelt deep underneath,
Looked out of such a sad sweet heaven on me!
The lips, compressed a little, came forward too,   1995
Careful for a whole world of sin and pain.
That was the face, her husband makes his plea,
He sought just to disfigure,—no offence
Beyond that! Sirs, let us be rational!
He needs must vindicate his honour,—ay,   2000
Yet slinks, the coward, in a clown's disguise,
Away from the scene, endeavours to escape.
Now, had he done so, slain and left no trace
O' the slayer,—what were vindicated, pray?
You had found his wife disfigured or a corpse,   2005
For what and by whom? It is too palpable!
Then, here's another point involving law:
I use this argument to show you meant

1982 *MS* now.   1983 {not found in *MS*}   1985 *MS* on   1986 *MS*
{no comma}   1988 *MS* {beginning of fo. 379}   *MS* sure—   1990 *MS*
say—   *MS* strait-up Greek—   1992 *MS* nor   1993 *MS* {no com-
ma}   1994 *MS 1868 1872* me—   1995 *MS* {no commas}   1996 *MS*
pain: 1997 *MS* {no commas}   1998 *MS* disfigure,   1999 *MS*
Come, >Sirs,   *MS* rational.   2001 *MS* And   *MS* slinks *1868 1872 1888*
1889 shirks   2002 *MS* escape: 2003 *MS* Could he have   *MS* killed>
slain   2004 *MS* Of   2006 *MS* [ ], and for>For   2008 *MS* Friends

---

2001 *clown's*: peasant's, countryman's.

No calumny against us by that title
O' the sentence,—liars try to twist it so: 2010
What penalty it bore, I had to pay
Till further proof should follow of innocence—
Probationis ob defectum,—proof?
How could you get proof without trying us?
You went through the preliminary form,   2015
Stopped there, contrived this sentence to amuse
The adversary. If the title ran
For more than fault imputed and not proved,
That was a simple penman's error, else
A slip i' the phrase,—as when we say of you   2020
"Charged with injustice"—which may either be
Or not be,—'t is a name that sticks meanwhile.
Another relevant matter: fool that I am!
Not what I wish true, yet a point friends urge:

2009 *MS* that act ⟨of yours⟩   2010 *MS* The>Of the   2012 {not found in
MS}   2014 *MS* get it   2017 *MS* {beginning of fo. 380}   *MS* The hate
of the adversary.   2018 *MS* more,—the thing imputed and not proved—
2020 *MS* in   2023 *MS* am—

2009–10 *that title / O' the sentence*: for this court sentence of 24 Sept. 1697 see v.
1218–25 n. Guido's defence used the sentence as a legal confirmation that Pompilia and
Caponsacchi had been lovers. The prosecution disputed this, arguing (1) that it was a
legal mistake ('a simple penman's error', l. 2019); (2) that the title of the case proved
nothing, and that only actual evidence of adultery that had emerged in the trial could
count (and there was no such evidence); and (3) that if adultery had really been proved,
the court would have imposed a harsher sentence than three years' banishment. After it
was initially promulgated on 24 Sept. 1697, the title of the sentence was emended. The
prosecution argued that this later wording removed the original implication of adultery
and that Caponsacchi's punishment was simply for his complicity in the flight; the
defence, of course, disputed this: see OYB clxvii f. (175), cxxvi f. (134). Browning,
following OYB, makes much of the legal battle over the sentence's wording: see for
example v. 1212–39, IX. 1511–41.

2013 *Probationis ob defectum*: 'Because of lack of proof [of adultery]' (L.). Caponsac-
chi quotes this phrase indignantly from the legal arguments because, in his view, he was
never tried and examined on the specific charge of adultery. The phrase occurs in the
arguments of the lawyers prosecuting Guido, who specifically affirm that it was
'because of lack of proof of adultery' that Caponsacchi received 'only banishment to
Civitavecchia': OYB lxii (66), clix (165). Caponsacchi, speaking early in Jan. 1698, is
not quoting these instances directly, since they were not spoken until Guido's trial later
in the month. Clearly Browning assumes that these arguments had been made before,
probably at the time when the wording of the sentence of 24 Sept. 1697 was in dispute:
see previous n.

It is not true,—yet, since friends think it helps,— 2025
She only tried me when some others failed—
Began with Conti, whom I told you of,
And Guillichini, Guido's kinsfolk both,
And when abandoned by them, not before,
Turned to me. That's conclusive why she turned. 2030
Much good they got by the happy cowardice!
Conti is dead, poisoned a month ago:
Does that much strike you as a sin? Not much,
After the present murder,—one mark more
On the Moor's skin,—what is black by blacker still? 2035
Conti had come here and told truth. And so
With Guillichini; he's condemned of course
To the galleys, as a friend in this affair,
Tried and condemned for no one thing i' the world,
A fortnight since by who but the Governor?— 2040
The just judge, who refused Pompilia help
At first blush, being her husband's friend, you know.
There are two tales to suit the separate courts,
Arezzo and Rome: he tells you here, we fled
Alone, unhelped,—lays stress on the main fault, 2045
The spiritual sin, Rome looks to: but elsewhere
He likes best we should break in, steal, bear off,
Be fit to brand and pillory and flog—
That's the charge goes to the heart of the Governor:

2025 {not found in MS} 2026 MS the others Yale 1 the>some 2032
MS ago, 2033 MS much— 2037 MS Guillichini, 2038 MS gal-
lies, 2039 MS in MS {no comma} 2040 MS Governor 2042
MS Husband's 2043 MS Courts, 2044 MS they tell MS {no com-
ma} 2046 MS {beginning of fo. 381} MS {no comma} 2047 MS
They like 2048 MS stuff>fit MS flog

2032 *Conti is dead*: from OYB ccxvii (219): 'it is public talk and report throughout
Arezzo that [Conti] died about a month ago under similar suspicious circumstances'.
2037–40 *Guillichini . . . Governor*: the decision of Vincenzo Marzi-Medici, Governor
of Arezzo, to sentence Guillichini (for whom see II. 934 n.) to the galleys was
authorized by the Rota of Florence, the supreme court of the city, on 24 Dec. 1697,
less than two weeks before Caponsacchi is imagined speaking: see OYB vii f. (7). In
other words, the Florentine court and the Grand Duke of Florence ratified—'signs and
seals' (2058)—the judgements of the subordinate Governor of Arezzo.

If these unpriest me, you and I may yet   2050
Converse, Vincenzo Marzi-Medici!
Oh, Sirs, there are worse men than you, I say!
More easily duped, I mean; this stupid lie,
Its liar never dared propound in Rome,
He gets Arezzo to receive,—nay more,   2055
Gets Florence and the Duke to authorize!
This is their Rota's sentence, their Granduke
Signs and seals! Rome for me henceforward—Rome,
Where better men are,—most of all, that man
The Augustinian of the Hospital,   2060
Who writes the letter,—he confessed, he says,
Many a dying person, never one
So sweet and true and pure and beautiful.
A good man! Will you make him Pope one day?
Not that he is not good too, this we have—   2065
But old,—else he would have his word to speak,
His truth to teach the world: I thirst for truth,
But shall not drink it till I reach the source.

Sirs, I am quiet again. You see, we are
So very pitiable, she and I,   2070
Who had conceivably been otherwise.
Forget distemperature and idle heat!
Apart from truth's sake, what's to move so much?
Pompilia will be presently with God;

2050 *MS* you>these   *MS* he>you   2054 *MS* The   2055 *MS* affirm,—
2056 *1868 1872* authorise!   2057 *MS* the Florence Rota's, which the Duke>
Rota's sentence, which the Duke *Yale 1* Rotas'>Rota's   2058 *MS* {no com-
ma}   2059 *MS* all that monk   2060 {not found in *MS*}   2063 *MS*
good>sweet   2066 *MS* speak   2067 *MS* And teach the world by.>His
truth to teach the world: *MS* {no comma}   2069 *MS* {New paragraph
(already written thus) indicated by 'N.P.' in left-hand margin}   *MS* again: you see
we *Yale 1* see>see,   2070 *MS* I   2071 *MS* otherwise: 2072 *MS*
heat: 2074 *MS* {beginning of fo. 382}   *MS* God,

2051 *Vincenzo Marzi-Medici*: the Governor of Arezzo: see previous n.
2060-3 *Augustinian . . . beautiful*: cf. III. 4, 18 nn.
2072 *distemperature*: i.e. anger.
idle heat: useless passion. Caponsacchi is referring to his earlier passionate tirades.

I am, on earth, as good as out of it, 2075
A relegated priest; when exile ends,
I mean to do my duty and live long.
She and I are mere strangers now: but priests
Should study passion; how else cure mankind,
Who come for help in passionate extremes? 2080
I do but play with an imagined life
Of who, unfettered by a vow, unblessed
By the higher call,—since you will have it so,—
Leads it companioned by the woman there.
To live, and see her learn, and learn by her, 2085
Out of the low obscure and petty world—
Or only see one purpose and one will
Evolve themselves i' the world, change wrong to right:
To have to do with nothing but the true,
The good, the eternal—and these, not alone 2090
In the main current of the general life,
But small experiences of every day,
Concerns of the particular hearth and home:
To learn not only by a comet's rush
But a rose's birth,—not by the grandeur, God— 2095
But the comfort, Christ. All this, how far away!
Mere delectation, meet for a minute's dream!—
Just as a drudging student trims his lamp,
Opens his Plutarch, puts him in the place

2076 *MS* {no comma}   2079 *MS* passion,   2080 *MS* call>come   2083
MS call, since   *MS* so,   2084 *MS* with what>companioned by   *MS*
[ ]>the   2085 *MS* {no commas}   2086 *MS* the miserable petty 2087 *MS*
To   2088 *MS* in   2090 *MS* [ ]>Good and   *MS* {no com-
mas}   2092 *MS* {no comma}   2093 *MS* home.   2095 *MS* rose's
apparition, not the splendor, God—   2096 *MS* mercy   2097 *MS*
dream,   2098 *MS* {no comma}

2085–96 *To live . . . Christ*: though phrased in a slightly covert way, this is Capon-
sacchi's beautifully articulated idea of what a true marriage to Pompilia would be like.
2099 *Plutarch*: the *Parallel Lives*, a series of biographies of great Roman and Greek
heroes, warriors, and statesmen, by the Greek historian and moralist Plutarch (*c.*AD
46–120). The work includes biographies of Romulus, Alexander the Great, Mark
Antony, Julius Caesar, and Coriolanus.

Of Roman, Grecian; draws the patched gown close,   2100
Dreams, "Thus should I fight, save or rule the world!"—
Then smilingly, contentedly, awakes
To the old solitary nothingness.
So I, from such communion, pass content . . .

O great, just, good God! Miserable me!   2105

2100 *MS* Grecian,   2101 *MS* {beginning of fo. 383}   *MS* Says "So should I
fight, rule or save the world"   2102 *MS* returns   2103 *MS* nothingness,
Yale 1 nothingness:>nothingness.   2104 *MS* As

2104 *communion*: intense study, imagination, i.e. his thoughts of an 'imagined life'
with Pompilia (ll. 2081–96).

INTRODUCTION TO BOOK VII
POMPILIA

THE romanticization and uplift inherent in Browning's depiction of Pompilia are underpinned by realism, a realism partly learnt from EBB's character Marian Erle in *Aurora Leigh* (1856).[1] In January 1869 Julia Wedgwood suggested to Browning that he was not always fully dramatic, that Pompilia said things too clever for a seventeen-year-old girl. As an example, she cited ll. 1495–1506. Browning replied:

What is in the *thought* about the "charter" impossible to Pompilia, if you accept the general elevation of her character? Besides, it is Italian ignorance, quite compatible with extraordinary insight and power of expression too: I have heard abundant instances of it. For the first instance that occurs,—you would not put into the mouth of an English maid, profoundly ignorant, this phrase, "She had a certain nobility of mind which, finding in itself nothing of the base and evil, could not credit their existence in others." Yet that is word for word what Annunziata said to me of my wife: "aveva una certa nobiltà d'animo", etc.[2]

Earlier in the letter he concedes some 'idealization of the characters', but his manner above is instructive: Pompilia is Italian, and 'profoundly ignorant' (i.e. wholly uneducated), just like the Brownings' maid.

Sentimentality and idealization were important factors in the depiction of women in the nineteenth century, fitting in as they did with wider perceptions and views. Because of this, for many readers Pompilia was the best character in the poem. Arthur Symons is typical:

Pompilia . . . tells the story of her life, in a simple, childlike, dreamy, wondering way, which can be compared, so far as I know, with nothing else ever written. All the 'piercing and overpowering tenderness which glorifies,' as Mr Swinburne has said, 'the poet of Pompilia' is infused into this almost faultlessly lovely poem. It is a song of serene and quiet beauty, beautiful as evening-twilight.[3]

---

[1] One discussion of how Pompilia is influenced by Marian Erle can be found in George Ridenour, 'Robert Browning and *Aurora Leigh*', *Victorian Newsletter*, 67 (1985), 26–31.

[2] RB to Julia Wedgwood, 1 Feb. 1869: *Wedgwood*, 176.

[3] Arthur Symons, *An Introduction to the Study of Browning* (1886), 140.

Twentieth-century critics, though less enthusiastic, also tend to focus on the sentimental foreground of the narrative. The 'childlike' Pompilia is marked out to some extent by her language. Park Honan points out her favourite, pathos-laden adjectives: 'good', 'poor', 'little', 'happy', 'kind'.[4] Sullivan adds two more words, 'dream' and 'strange', by which Pompilia shows 'wonderment' and 'bewilderment' at the course of her life.[5] Then, again, there is the absence of sophisticated allusion and imagery. Pompilia draws most of her examples from things seen or heard—not for her, as for Arcangeli, learned reference to the life of Aquinas. The rhythms of her speech, which Browning so carefully controls, are smooth and quiet, without the leaps, windings, and disjunctures that go to make the style of the characters who try to deceive us. On her deathbed, Pompilia speaks the truth directly, in a style mirroring her ingenuousness.

Yet we surely have something more here than 'the artless expression of powerful feelings set forth in direct, simple language with little attention to rhetorical effects'. [6] If this description were adequate, it would be hard to explain how the monologue becomes the effective first climax of the poem as a whole.

Pompilia is 12 years old when she is bartered into marriage with a sadistic aristocrat by a mother intent on advancement. She has no knowledge of the world, and has to find her way rapidly. The treatment of her sexuality is forthright, even if it is often only hinted at by the use of ellipsis.[7] On her deathbed at St Anna's hospital, surrounded by nuns as Browning imagines it, there are things she cannot bring into speech. This does not mean they are not a presence in the monologue, or that we should ignore them. 'Try and take the sense / Of what I signify, if it must be so', she pleads with the nuns, with their naive views of sexuality (739–40), and implicitly also with us.

The story she tells is of marital rape and of sex used as a weapon against her, a means to her humiliation. She defines rape within marriage (772–87), and later calls it sex 'sought for hate, not love' (806). Her otherwise meaningless assertion that her child is fatherless, is 'mine only' (897), is the obverse of this knowledge. Her loss of virginity to a husband who hated her, and who showed this through the nature of the intercourse, is disturbing and poignant (847–59). As Brady indicates, it is after this that Pompilia expresses empathy for her prostitute mother. She has now also

[4] Honan, 216.
[5] Sullivan, 89.
[6] Ibid. 95.
[7] Brady, 44, 46: see VII. 738 n.

been bought and used, and her telling language about her mother's degradation is a reflection of her own (860–94).[8]

Two other matters stand out. First, the interview with the Archbishop. Still a virgin, and faced with Guido demanding his 'rights', Pompilia flees to the spiritual overseer of Arezzo for succour and counsel. The Archbishop dismisses all that she says, and treats her as a silly adolescent. Why haven't her parents, or 'goodwives' and 'gossips', told her the facts of life (802)? When Pompilia goes further, and tells him how Guido encourages his brother to harass her sexually, the Archbishop improvises the parable of the fig, the fig-pecker, and the wasps (820–46). This is 'gruesome' because of its edge of sadism—the violence and threat implicit in the phrasing 'three hundred thousand bees and wasps' (839)—and also because it is a grotesque parody of the parable form.[9] To the complacent Archbishop rape within marriage does not exist, and the girl must be thrown back into her husband's arms.

The second matter is small, but none the less telling: the relationship between Pompilia and Margherita, the woman who is both her maid and her husband's mistress. Margherita is the pander used by Guido to try to engineer Pompilia's affair with Caponsacchi, and as one manoeuvre in this plot Margherita makes use of her own sexual relationship with Guido as a way of suggesting common ground between herself and Pompilia. As women, they both know Guido's failings. Why should Pompilia not entertain a relationship with Caponsacchi, 'the city-ladies' handsomest / Frankest and liberalest gentleman' (1084–5)? It is the worldly use of sexual innuendo here, and at ll. 1065–82, that is disturbing. One woman, the sexual toy or 'poor pastime of a minute' of a sadistic aristocrat (1080), is prepared to collude in the deception of another for her own gain.

It is from out of this tough-minded realism that the lyrical elements in the monologue escape: Pompilia's profound religious faith, her joy in her pregnancy, and her love for Caponsacchi. All three produce lyrical poetry, which clearly benefits from its interchange with the dark things outlined above.

Pompilia's religious faith produces the extraordinary and bold story at ll. 1389–1403, where she becomes the maiden at bay, apparently exposed to her enemies by a flash of lightning. She reaches out her hand into the burning 'thunderstone', and its light and heat are transformed into a

---

[8] Brady, 48: see VII. 863–77 n.
[9] 'Gruesome' is Brady's well-chosen adjective (p. 51).

sword with which she slays her enemies. The language that surrounds her pregnancy is similarly uplifting, producing, for instance, the beautiful image of the nesting sparrows at ll. 1230–5.

Her love for Caponsacchi dominates the latter half of the monologue. This is not, of course, the 'love' that Guido sought to contrive: a surreptitious affair, the love of a *cavaliere servente*, a squire of dames. Caponsacchi is the 'lover of my life', a 'soldier-saint' (1786), and her love for him is transcendent and righteous. As Julia Wedgwood coyly suggested to Browning—and he did not repudiate her conjecture— Pompilia is underpinned by EBB,[10] and the love of Pompilia for Caponsacchi is therefore a writing out of the love of EBB for Browning. That is why, at this point, we hear from Pompilia language that echoes the style and intensity of 'lyric Love', the ending of Book I.

The success of the climax of the monologue comes, it may be suggested, from what happens at ll. 1806–14. When, prior to the murders, Guido stood outside the door of the Comparini's villa, he knocked and cried 'Caponsacchi'. He did this, he claims, to give Pompilia a last chance to prove her chastity. If she shrank from the associations of the name that scandal had linked with hers, then the villa door would remain unopened: she would live. This was the 'last chance' given her by a merciful husband concerned to make no mistake in exacting revenge—so Guido would have us believe (v. 1612–33).

We do not, of course, believe him. By now we have put this version of events together with impressions gleaned from other speakers, and have concluded that the cry 'Caponsacchi' was simply a trick to gain access. Pompilia would open the door to Caponsacchi because he was unthreatening: he was the friend who had rescued her from the horror of Arezzo. But in these remarkable lines (1806–14), Pompilia affirms something more: that she started with joy at the sound of Caponsacchi's name. She radically overturns the smears. She 'sprang' up from where she sat, *not* because of an illicit affair, but because of an overwhelming, pure love, and with her declaration the web of lies falls to the ground.

The monologue ends with her aria of love for Caponsacchi. The final paragraph is literally her dying breath. Prior to this Pompilia apparently goes silent, and turns to face death: 'I withdraw from earth and man / To my own soul, compose myself for God' (1769–70). Then she rouses

---

[10] 'I can not venture to tell you all that Pompilia seems to me. I felt as if it were only half yours, but indeed I do not divide the other influence from your own': Julia Wedgwood to RB, 30 Jan. 1869: *Wedgwood*, 173.

herself for one more speech. She seems to see Caponsacchi as she is dying, and 'smells' the goodness of their brief time together. She looks forward to an angelic 'love-making' with him in heaven (1821–38), something reminiscent of the description of angelic communion in *Paradise Lost*: 'Easier than air with air, if spirits embrace, / Total they mix, union of pure with pure / Desiring; nor restrained conveyance need / As flesh to mix with flesh, or soul with soul' (viii. 626–9). Many readers may shy away from such heightened romanticism, but the ending of this section of the poem is undoubtedly a *Liebestod*, a love-death, of a very moving and English kind.

VII.

POMPILIA.

I AM just seventeen years and five months old,
And, if I lived one day more, three full weeks;
'T is writ so in the church's register,
Lorenzo in Lucina, all my names
At length, so many names for one poor child,   5
—Francesca Camilla Vittoria Angela
Pompilia Comparini,—laughable!
Also 't is writ that I was married there
Four years ago: and they will add, I hope,

MS {fo. 1. At the head of the page is the title '7. Pompilia.' in RB's hand}
2 MS three full weeks, if I lived one day more;>if I lived one day more, three full
weeks;

1–34 *I am . . . hair*: the main source for the biographical information in this passage
is a copy of Pompilia's baptismal certificate from the Church of San Lorenzo in Lucina,
one of a number of documents laid before the court in evidence and published at OYB
clv–clviii (159–62). In translation from the Latin it runs: 'I, the undersigned, certify &c.
as is found in the baptismal record, folio 152, the particulars given below, namely: "23
July 1680. I, Bartolomeo Mini, Curate, have baptized the infant daughter born on the
17th of this month to D. Pietro Comparini and D. Violante Peruzzi, who live in this
parish. To her the following name was given: Francesca Camilla Victoria Angela
Pompilia, &c. In pledge of which &c. Rome this 9th day of February 1698." Thus it
is, Pietro Ottoboni, Curate of San Lorenzo in Lucina.'
  2 *if . . . weeks*: i.e. if she lived till the next day, 7 Jan. 1698, she would be 17 years,
five months, and three weeks old. This places her monologue itself on 6 Jan. 1698,
Epiphany, the day of her death.
  6–7 *Francesca . . . Pompilia*: she is most often called Francesca or Francesca Pompilia
in OYB; Browning chose the last and most unusual of her names as his way of referring
to her.
  9 *Four years ago*: Browning follows SS, which says that the marriage of Pompilia and
Guido took place in San Lorenzo in Lucina in Dec. 1693: SS 2. In 1910 Treves
examined the marriage register at the church and found that the actual date of the
marriage was three months earlier, on 6 Sept. 1693.

When they insert my death, a word or two,—   10
Omitting all about the mode of death,—
This, in its place, this which one cares to know,
That I had been a mother of a son
Exactly two weeks. It will be through grace
O' the Curate, not through any claim I have;   15
Because the boy was born at, so baptized
Close to, the Villa, in the proper church:
A pretty church, I say no word against,
Yet stranger-like,—while this Lorenzo seems
My own particular place, I always say.   20
I used to wonder, when I stood scarce high
As the bed here, what the marble lion meant,
With half his body rushing from the wall,
Eating the figure of a prostrate man—
(To the right, it is, of entry by the door)   25
An ominous sign to one baptized like me,

---

14 *MS* weeks: it>weeks. It   15 *MS* Of   16 *MS* and>at,   17 *MS*
at>in   *MS* church,   18 *MS* {line added later}   *MS* Pretty and what I
25 *MS* To   *MS* door—

---

14 *Exactly two weeks*: Gaetano was born 18 Dec. 1697, two weeks and one day
before Guido's murderous attack on Pompilia and her parents on 2 Jan. 1698: see OYB
clxxxiv (189). In this opening paragraph, Pompilia is keen to be precise about names
and dates, almost in the manner of a will and testament.

14–15 *It . . . have*: i.e. Gaetano's name will only be added to Pompilia's entry in the
baptismal register by courtesy of the curate at San Lorenzo, since (as the following lines
explain) Gaetano himself was baptized in a different church and parish, the one
appropriate to the Comparini's villa. This is not, in fact, historical: see 11. 203 n.

17 *proper church*: i.e. the local parish church.

22–5 *marble lion . . . door*: in Dec. 1864 Browning wrote to his friend, the painter
Frederic Leighton, travelling in Rome, asking him to note details concerning the
church of San Lorenzo in Lucina: see 11. 6 n. It was presumably Leighton who supplied
him with this description of one of the pair of thirteenth-century marble lions that
stand guard on either side of the church door. One lion is benign in appearance, and it
has a small figure between its front paws, perhaps an infant, with one hand reaching up
into and caressing the underside of the lion's mane. The other lion, to which Pompilia
refers, has a more upright head and is fierce in expression. Between its paws lies what
appears a broken limb, probably (as Browning suggests) the remnants of a corpse.
There are photographs of the two lions in Thomas, 312–13, who quotes Augustus
Hare (1903) on their likely symbolism: 'the lions symbolize respectively the benignity
of the Church towards the neophyte and the docile, and her severity towards the
impenitent and heretical'. Pompilia knows nothing of this significance; to her the
fierce lion is simply a disquieting omen. She places it on the right of the entrance,

Married, and to be buried there, I hope.
And they should add, to have my life complete,
He is a boy and Gaetan by name—
Gaetano, for a reason,—if the friar   30
Don Celestine will ask this grace for me
Of Curate Ottoboni: he it was
Baptized me: he remembers my whole life
As I do his grey hair.

               All these few things   35
I know are true,—will you remember them?
Because time flies. The surgeon cared for me,
To count my wounds,—twenty-two dagger-wounds,
Five deadly, but I do not suffer much—
Or too much pain,—and am to die to-night.   40

Oh how good God is that my babe was born,
—Better than born, baptized and hid away
Before this happened, safe from being hurt!
That had been sin God could not well forgive:
He was too young to smile and save himself.   45

27 *MS* even>to be   30 *MS* {beginning of fo. 2}   *MS* monk >friar   32
MS the Curate>Curate   33 *MS* me and>me: he   *MS* all   my>my
whole   35 *MS* {new paragraph indicated by 'New P.' in right-hand mar-
gin}   40 *MS* Too>Or too   *MS* shall die to-night, they say.>am to die to-
night.   41 *MS* {New paragraph indicated by 'N.P.' in left-hand margin}   *MS*
was>is   42 *MS* sent>hid

though it is actually on the left. This mistake may stem from Leighton, from a
misunderstanding by Browning of what he had said, or Browning's own failure of
memory.

   30 *Gaetano, for a reason*: the reason emerges at ll. 101–7: see n.
   31–3 *Don Celestine . . . me*: Don Celestine was Pompilia's deathbed confessor, and the
Augustinian friar who subsequently testified to the court about her nearly saintly
demeanour during her dying: see OYB lvii f. (57–8), and III. 18–25, 45–7. Again, if
Pompilia wants not only the fact of her having a child, but also the child's name, added to
her baptismal record in San Lorenzo, she has no right to this, and would have to ask Don
Celestine to speak to the curate at San Lorenzo, Pietro Ottoboni, on her behalf. That
Ottoboni, the curate at San Lorenzo in 1698, was also the curate who baptised Pompilia
in 1680, is a small change that Browning makes to his source, a detail adding pathos: the
baptismal register shows that she was in fact baptized by Bartolomeo Mini: see ll. 1–34 n.
   38 *twenty-two dagger-wounds*: '[Pompilia] hid under a bed, but was dragged out—poor

When they took, two days after he was born,
My babe away from me to be baptized
And hidden awhile, for fear his foe should find,—
The country-woman, used to nursing babes,
Said "Why take on so? where is the great loss?   50
"These next three weeks he will but sleep and feed,
"Only begin to smile at the month's end;
"He would not know you, if you kept him here,
"Sooner than that; so, spend three merry weeks
"Snug in the Villa, getting strong and stout,   55
"And then I bring him back to be your own,
"And both of you may steal to—we know where!"
The month—there wants of it two weeks this day!
Still, I half fancied when I heard the knock
At the Villa in the dusk, it might prove she—   60
Come to say "Since he smiles before the time,
"Why should I cheat you out of one good hour?
"Back I have brought him; speak to him and judge!"
Now I shall never see him; what is worse,
When he grows up and gets to be my age,   65
He will seem hardly more than a great boy;
And if he asks "What was my mother like?"
People may answer "Like girls of seventeen"—
And how can he but think of this and that,
Lucias, Marias, Sofias, who titter or blush   70
When he regards them as such boys may do?

---

46 *MS* took,—   *MS* born,—   48 *MS* foe[?s]>foe   50 *MS* Where
51 *MS* "All>"These   55 *MS* Villa getting   56 *MS* to be yours again,>
back your own again,>back to be your own,   57 *MS* where"!   59 *MS*
{beginning of fo. 3}   62 *MS* day?>hour?   67 *MS* Pompilia>my mother
68 *MS* will say "Like girls of seventeen years—">will say "Like most girls of seven-
teen—">may answer "Like girls of seventeen—"   71 *MS* looks at>regards

unfortunate girl—murdered in the most brutal way by her own husband, with twenty-
two stab wounds': SS 11.
    57 *we know where!*: presumably another villa owned by the Comparini, out in the
Roman countryside. It is mentioned only here and at ll. 235–8, and is an addition by
Browning to his sources.

Therefore I wish someone will please to say
I looked already old though I was young;
Do I not ... say, if you are by to speak ...
Look nearer twenty? No more like, at least,   75
Girls who look arch or redden when boys laugh,
Than the poor Virgin that I used to know
At our street-corner in a lonely niche,—
The babe, that sat upon her knees, broke off,—
Thin white glazed clay, you pitied her the more: 80
She, not the gay ones, always got my rose.

How happy those are who know how to write!
Such could write what their son should read in time,
Had they a whole day to live out like me.
Also my name is not a common name,   85
"Pompilia," and may help to keep apart
A little the thing I am from what girls are.
But then how far away, how hard to find
Will anything about me have become,
Even if the boy bethink himself and ask!   90
No father that he ever knew at all,
Nor ever had—no, never had, I say!
That is the truth,—nor any mother left,
Out of the little two weeks that she lived,
Fit for such memory as might assist: 95
As good too as no family, no name,
Not even poor old Pietro's name, nor hers,
Poor kind unwise Violante, since it seems

72 *1868 1872* some one   74 *MS 1868 1872* not ..   *MS* ^by^   *MS* speak ..
78 *MS* her>a   79 *MS* sate   80 *MS* more,   82 *MS* {New paragraph
indicated by 'N.P.' in left-hand margin}   87 *MS* {beginning of fo.
4}   88 *MS* and>how   92 *MS* say—   97 *MS* name,—   98
MS Kind>Poor kind

82 *How ... write*: whether or not Pompilia could read and write was, in fact, an issue
much in contention before the court, especially in relation to the love letters.
Browning makes his heroine illiterate, hence resolving any ambiguity about her
possible authorship of the love letters to Caponsacchi, and adding another touch of
pathos to his overall portrait.

They must not be my parents any more.
That is why something put it in my head   100
To call the boy "Gaetano"—no old name
For sorrow's sake; I looked up to the sky
And took a new saint to begin anew.
One who has only been made saint—how long?
Twenty-five years: so, carefuller, perhaps,   105
To guard a namesake than those old saints grow,
Tired out by this time,—see my own five saints!

On second thoughts, I hope he will regard
The history of me as what someone dreamed,
And get to disbelieve it at the last: 110
Since to myself it dwindles fast to that,
Sheer dreaming and impossibility,—
Just in four days too! All the seventeen years,
Not once did a suspicion visit me
How very different a lot is mine   115
From any other woman's in the world.
The reason must be, 't was by step and step
It got to grow so terrible and strange.
These strange woes stole on tiptoe, as it were,
Into my neighbourhood and privacy,   120
Sat down where I sat, laid them where I lay;

---

102 *MS* but I>I   *MS* in>to   105 *MS* years—   107 *MS* four   108
MS {New paragraph indicated by 'N.P.' in left-hand margin}   110 *MS* all at
last: 115 *MS* {beginning of fo. 5}   *MS* ^very^   118 *MS* *1868*
strange: 121 *MS* Sate   *MS* sate,

101–7 *"Gaetano . . . saints!*: Browning found the name in SS 9: 'After this, Pompilia
gave birth to a son, whom she named Gaetano in honour of her favourite saint.' St
Gaetano (1480–1547) is not well known. A retiring and gentle-mannered man, he was
one of the founders, in 1524, of the Order of Theatines, along with Giampetro Carafa
(afterwards Paul IV) and two others. He was beatified by Urban VIII in 1629, and
canonized by Clement X in 1671; his feast-day is 7 August. As he worked on the
poem, Browning was curious to know why exactly Pompilia might have chosen this
name. He wrote to William Cornwallis Cartwright: 'Ask any instructed person, why a
mother in want of a name for her child would be led to call him "Gaetano"—what
virtues are there in that saint's patronage?': RB to W. C. Cartwright, 17 May 1867:
ABL. It seems probable that Cartwright did not suggest any obvious or satisfying
solution, and that either he or Browning then invented the reason given here.

And I was found familiarised with fear,
When friends broke in, held up a torch and cried
"Why, you Pompilia in the cavern thus,
"How comes that arm of yours about a wolf?   125
"And the soft length,—lies in and out your feet
"And laps you round the knee,—a snake it is!"
And so on.

                    Well, and they are right enough,
By the torch they hold up now: for first, observe,   130
I never had a father,—no, nor yet
A mother: my own boy can say at least
"I had a mother whom I kept two weeks!"
Not I, who little used to doubt . . . I doubt
Good Pietro, kind Violante, gave me birth?   135
They loved me always as I love my babe
(—Nearly so, that is—quite so could not be—)
Did for me all I meant to do for him,
Till one surprising day, three years ago,
They both declared, at Rome, before some judge   140
In some Court where the people flocked to hear,
That really I had never been their child,
Was a mere castaway, the careless crime
Of an unknown man, the crime and care too much
Of a woman known too well,—little to these,   145
Therefore, of whom I was the flesh and blood:
What then to Pietro and Violante, both
No more my relatives than you or you?

125 *MS* wolf—>wolf?   126 *MS* that soft   129 *MS* {New paragraph in-
dicated by 'N.P.' in left-hand margin}   *MS* enough   130 *MS* thus:>
now: 133 *MS* weeks"—   134 *MS* I—   *MS* ^little^   *MS* *1868*
doubt . .   137 *MS* {no brackets}   140 *MS* here, to>before
141 *MS* *1868 1872* court   144 *MS* {beginning of fo. 6}   146–8 *MS*
{lines added later}

139 *one . . . ago*: by Browning's chronology, following SS for the date of the mar-
riage, this was in April or May 1694, some time after the Comparini's return to Rome.
143 *castaway*: outcast, abandoned one: cf. III. 214, 723, perhaps with the underlying
sense of 'reprobate': see II. 1284 n. Cf. also *Aurora Leigh*, vi. 347, where the word is
used of Marian Erle, who is in many ways a prototype of Pompilia.

Nothing to them! You know what they declared.

So with my husband,—just such a surprise,   150
Such a mistake, in that relationship!
Everyone says that husbands love their wives,
Guard them and guide them, give them happiness;
'T is duty, law, pleasure, religion: well,
You see how much of this comes true in mine!   155
People indeed would fain have somehow proved
He was no husband: but he did not hear,
Or would not wait, and so has killed us all.

Then there is . . . only let me name one more!
There is the friend,—men will not ask about,   160
But tell untruths of, and give nicknames to,
And think my lover, most surprise of all!
Do only hear, it is the priest they mean,
Giuseppe Caponsacchi: a priest—love,
And love me! Well, yet people think he did.   165
I am married, he has taken priestly vows,
They know that, and yet go on, say, the same,
"Yes, how he loves you!" "That was love"—they say,
When anything is answered that they ask:
Or else "No wonder you love him"—they say.   170
Then they shake heads, pity much, scarcely blame—
As if we neither of us lacked excuse,
And anyhow are punished to the full,
And downright love atones for everything!
Nay, I heard read out in the public Court   175
Before the judge, in presence of my friends,

---

149 *MS* them,—   150 *MS* {New paragraph indicated by 'N.P.' in left-hand
margin}   153 *MS* guide and>guide them,   *MS* happiness,   154 *MS*
and law,>law,   *159 *MS* {New paragraph indicated by 'N.P.' in left-hand
margin. Paragraphing obscured in *1868* and *1872* by this line's being at the head
of the page} *1888 1889* {no new paragraph}   *MS 1868 1872* is . .   *MS*
more—   167 *MS* that and   168 *MS* say   169 *MS* ask—
170 *MS* say: *Yale 2* say.>say!   171 *MS* and scarce blame—>scarcely
blame—   174 *MS* And>[ ]>And   175 *MS* {beginning of fo. 7}   *1868*
read-out   *MS 1868 1872* court   176 *MS* the>a>the

Letters 't was said the priest had sent to me,
And other letters sent him by myself,
We being lovers!
                                Listen what this is like!   180
When I was a mere child, my mother... that's
Violante, you must let me call her so
Nor waste time, trying to unlearn the word...
She brought a neighbour's child of my own age
To play with me of rainy afternoons;   185
And, since there hung a tapestry on the wall,
We two agreed to find each other out
Among the figures. "Tisbe, that is you,
"With half-moon on your hair-knot, spear in hand,
"Flying, but no wings, only the great scarf   190
"Blown to a bluish rainbow at your back:
"Call off your hound and leave the stag alone!"
"—And there are you, Pompilia, such green leaves
"Flourishing out of your five finger-ends,
"And all the rest of you so brown and rough: 195
"Why is it you are turned a sort of tree?"
You know the figures never were ourselves
Though we nicknamed them so. Thus, all my life,—
As well what was, as what, like this, was not,—
Looks old, fantastic and impossible: 200
I touch a fairy thing that fades and fades.
—Even to my babe! I thought, when he was born,
Something began for once that would not end,

---

177 *MS* man   180 *MS* {New paragraph indicated by 'New P.' in right-hand
margin}   181 *MS 1868 1872* mother..   183 *MS 1868 1872* word,...
185 *MS* on>of 189 *MS* [?two]>spear in hand,   190 *MS* without> but
no   191 *MS* ^bluish^   197 *MS* "You   198 *MS* nick-named
199 *MS* was as   201 *MS* {line added later}   *MS* at once>and fades.
203 *MS* {no comma}

---

188 *"Tisbe*: It. version of Thisbe.

189–92 *half-moon ... alone*: an image of Diana, goddess of the moon and hunting,
pursuing Actaeon with one of his own hounds: see Ovid, *Metamorphoses*, III. 138–252.

193–6 *green leaves ... tree*: an image of Daphne turning into a bay tree as she seeks to
escape the pursuit of Apollo: see Ovid, *Metamorphoses*, I. 452–567. Even in this
children's game, Pompilia's image is that of a harried victim.

Nor change into a laugh at me, but stay
For evermore, eternally quite mine.   205
Well, so he is,—but yet they bore him off,
The third day, lest my husband should lay traps
And catch him, and by means of him catch me.
Since they have saved him so, it was well done:
Yet thence comes such confusion of what was   210
With what will be,—that late seems long ago,
And, what years should bring round, already come,
Till even he withdraws into a dream
As the rest do: I fancy him grown great,
Strong, stern, a tall young man who tutors me,   215
Frowns with the others "Poor imprudent child!
"Why did you venture out of the safe street?
"Why go so far from help to that lone house?
"Why open at the whisper and the knock?"

Six days ago when it was New Year's-day,   220
We bent above the fire and talked of him,
What he should do when he was grown and great.
Violante, Pietro, each had given the arm
I leant on, to walk by, from couch to chair
And fireside,—laughed, as I lay safe at last,   225
"Pompilia's march from bed to board is made,
"Pompilia back again and with a babe,
"Shall one day lend his arm and help her walk!"
Then we all wished each other more New Years.

---

205 *MS* {beginning of fo. 8}   209 *MS* It was well done since they have saved him
so.>Since they have saved him so, it was well done: 211 *MS* lately>that
late   212 *MS* ^bring^   214 *MS* tall,>great,   215 *MS* young man
who may tutor me,>tall young man who tutors me,   216 *MS* Chides   *MS*
one!">child!"   217–19 *MS* {lines added later}   *MS* {no quotation marks at
beginnings of lines}   219 *MS* {no quotation mark at end of line}   ★220 *MS*
{New paragraph indicated by 'N.P.' in left-hand margin}   *1868 1872* {new paragraph.
Paragraphing obscured in *1888* and *1889* by this line's being at the head of the page} *MS*
Four>Six   *MS* Year's Eve>Year's Day   *MS* {no comma}   222 *MS* great:>
great.   225 *MS* By the>And the   *MS* laughed as   *MS* last   227 *Yale 1*
Pompilia's>Pompilia   *MS* and with a babe besides!>again and with a babe,   228
MS let>help

Pietro began to scheme—"Our cause is gained;   230
"The law is stronger than a wicked man:
"Let him henceforth go his way, leave us ours!
"We will avoid the city, tempt no more
"The greedy ones by feasting and parade,—
"Live at the other villa, we know where,   235
"Still farther off, and we can watch the babe
"Grow fast in the good air; and wood is cheap
"And wine sincere outside the city gate.
"I still have two or three old friends will grope
"Their way along the mere half-mile of road,   240
"With staff and lantern on a moonless night
"When one needs talk: they'll find me, never fear,
"And I'll find them a flask of the old sort yet!"
Violante said "You chatter like a crow:
"Pompilia tires o' the tattle, and shall to bed: 245
"Do not too much the first day,—somewhat more
"To-morrow, and, the next, begin the cape
"And hood and coat! I have spun wool enough."
Oh what a happy friendly eve was that!

And, next day, about noon, out Pietro went—   250
He was so happy and would talk so much,
Until Violante pushed and laughed him forth
Sight-seeing in the cold,—"So much to see
"I' the churches! Swathe your throat three times!" she cried,

---

234 *MS* by our>ones by   235 *MS* Villa,   236 *MS* {beginning of fo.
9}   *MS* child>babe   240 {not found in *MS*}   243 *MS* yet."   245
MS of   *MS* to-bed: 248 *MS* coat;   250 *MS* {New paragraph indicated
by 'N.P.' in left-hand margin}   251 *MS* {line added later}   *MS* {no
comma}   252 *MS* Because>Until   254 *MS* times,">times"!

---

235 *other villa*: only one of two references to a third house: cf. l. 57 n.

238 *sincere*: unadulterated. In the nineteenth century the *carrettieri* who brought
wine into Rome sold off parts of it for themselves on the journey and made up the
difference with water. 'This, however, is the least danger which the wine incurs. As
soon as it enters the gates it is destined to far worse adulteration of every kind, and
lucky is he who gets a bottle of pure and sincere wine from any *osteria*, *bettola*, or *canova
di vino* within the walls': *Roba di Roma*, i. 309.

"And, above all, beware the slippery ways,   255
"And bring us all the news by supper-time!"
He came back late, laid by cloak, staff and hat,
Powdered so thick with snow it made us laugh,
Rolled a great log upon the ash o' the hearth,
And bade Violante treat us to a flask,   260
Because he had obeyed her faithfully,
Gone sight-see through the seven, and found no church
To his mind like San Giovanni—"There's the fold,
"And all the sheep together, big as cats!
"And such a shepherd, half the size of life,   265
"Starts up and hears the angel"—when, at the door,
A tap: we started up: you know the rest.

Pietro at least had done no harm, I know;
Nor even Violante, so much harm as makes
Such revenge lawful. Certainly she erred—   270
Did wrong, how shall I dare say otherwise?—
In telling that first falsehood, buying me
From my poor faulty mother at a price,
To pass off upon Pietro as his child.
If one should take my babe, give him a name,   275
Say he was not Gaetano and my own,

---

255 *MS* "And above   256 *MS* {line added later}   *MS* And   *MS* suppertime!"
258 *MS* {line added later}   260 *MS* bring him wine,>treat us to a flask
261 *MS* {line added later}   262 *MS* He had gone through the whole>Gone
sight-see through the   263 *MS* when at the door>"There's the Fold
264–6 *MS* {lines added later}   *MS* {no quotation marks at beginnings of lines}
266 *MS* door   267 *MS* started: you>started up: you   *MS* dreadful rest.>
rest.   268 *MS* {New paragraph indicated by 'N.P.' in left-hand margin}
271 *MS* wrong,—   272 *MS* {beginning of fo. 10}   274 *MS* child:

262–3 *the seven . . . San Giovanni*: Pietro has been looking at the cribs in the seven
major churches of Rome, and finds that the one at San Giovanni in Laterano is the best.
He takes childish pleasure in this Christmas-season exercise. The patriarchal basilicas of
Rome are San Giovanni in Laterano, San Paolo fuori le mura, Santa Maria Maggiore, and
San Pietro. Together with the basilicas of San Lorenzo fuori le mura, Santa Croce in
Gerusalemme, and San Sebastiano, these are the 'Seven Churches of Rome', the main
pilgrimage sites. In Browning's day the cribs were often very elaborate, with large
figures, fine costumes and jewels, and effects of perspective: see *Roba di Roma*, i. 68–9.
273 *faulty*: sinful.

But that some other woman made his mouth
And hands and feet,—how very false were that!
No good could come of that; and all harm did.
Yet if a stranger were to represent   280
"Needs must you either give your babe to me
"And let me call him mine for evermore,
"Or let your husband get him"—ah, my God,
That were a trial I refuse to face!
Well, just so here: it proved wrong but seemed right   285
To poor Violante—for there lay, she said,
My poor real dying mother in her rags,
Who put me from her with the life and all,
Poverty, pain, shame and disease at once,
To die the easier by what price I fetched—   290
Also (I hope) because I should be spared
Sorrow and sin,—why may not that have helped?
My father,—he was no one, any one,—
The worse, the likelier,—call him—he who came,
Was wicked for his pleasure, went his way,   295
And left no trace to track by; there remained
Nothing but me, the unnecessary life,
To catch up or let fall,—and yet a thing
She could make happy, be made happy with,
This poor Violante,—who would frown thereat?   300

Well, God, you see! God plants us where we grow.
It is not that because a bud is born
At a wild briar's end, full i' the wild beast's way,

---

279 *MS* thence;>of that;   *MS* came here.>did.   280 *MS* Yet did a stranger
say—"Or give him me>Yet if a stranger were to represent   281–2 *MS* {lines
added later}   286 *MS* ^poor^   287 *MS* {no comma}   291 *MS*
,>(*MS* ,>)   294 *MS* [ ]>likelier,—   *MS* *1868 1872* him,—   296
MS Leaving>And left   *MS* by: 297 *MS* The infant>Nothing but   *MS*
pitiable life>unnecessary life   301 *MS* {New paragraph indicated by 'N.P.' in
left-hand margin}   *MS* puts>plants   302 *MS* {beginning of fo. 11}   *MS*
that,—suppose,—   *1868 1872* that, *Yale 2* that,>that   303 *MS* briar's>wild
briar's   *MS* in   *MS* wild boar's>creatures'   *MS* way,—

303 *wild briar's*: wild rose's.

We ought to pluck and put it out of reach
On the oak-tree top,—say "There the bud belongs!"   305
She thought, moreover, real lies were lies told
For harm's sake; whereas this had good at heart,
Good for my mother, good for me, and good
For Pietro who was meant to love a babe,
And needed one to make his life of use,   310
Receive his house and land when he should die.
Wrong, wrong and always wrong! how plainly wrong!
For see, this fault kept pricking, as faults do,
All the same at her heart: this falsehood hatched,
She could not let it go nor keep it fast.   315
She told me so,—the first time I was found
Locked in her arms once more after the pain,
When the nuns let me leave them and go home,
And both of us cried all the cares away,—
This it was set her on to make amends,   320
This brought about the marriage—simply this!
Do let me speak for her you blame so much!
When Paul, my husband's brother, found me out,
Heard there was wealth for who should marry me,
So, came and made a speech to ask my hand   325
For Guido,—she, instead of piercing straight
Through the pretence to the ignoble truth,
Fancied she saw God's very finger point,
Designate just the time for planting me

305 *MS* oak-top, and say, there the rose shall wave.>oak-tree-top,—say, "There the rose belongs!" *1868 1872* say,   306 *MS* Moreover, she thought real>She thought moreover "real   *MS* were—lies told *1868 1872* were—   307 *MS* she had only>this had   308 *MS* to....to>for....for   309 *MS* Even to Pietro who loved babes so much>For Pietro who was meant to love a babe   311 *MS* And have his goods>Receive his house   312 *MS* wrong!—   314 *MS* heart,—the *1868 1872* heart,—   *MS* there found>hatched,   321 *MS* this—   322 *MS* {line added later}   324 *MS* money>wealth   *MS* make me wife>marry me,   325 *MS* So came   326 *MS* seeing clear>piercing straight   329 *MS* Designate the very minute>Designate just the time *MS 1868 1872* me,

313 *pricking*: i.e. like a 'prick of conscience'.
317 *the pain*: i.e. the trauma of the flight.

(The wild-briar slip she plucked to love and wear)   330
In soil where I could strike real root, and grow,
And get to be the thing I called myself:
For, wife and husband are one flesh, God says,
And I, whose parents seemed such and were none,
Should in a husband have a husband now,   335
Find nothing, this time, but was what it seemed,
—All truth and no confusion any more.
I know she meant all good to me, all pain
To herself,—since how could it be aught but pain
To give me up, so, from her very breast,   340
The wilding flower-tree-branch that, all those years,
She had got used to feel for and find fixed?
She meant well: has it been so ill i' the main?
That is but fair to ask: one cannot judge
Of what has been the ill or well of life,   345
The day that one is dying,—sorrows change
Into not altogether sorrow-like;
I do see strangeness but scarce misery,
Now it is over, and no danger more.
My child is safe; there seems not so much pain.   350
It comes, most like, that I am just absolved,
Purged of the past, the foul in me, washed fair,—
One cannot both have and not have, you know,—

---

330 *MS* wild slip she had>wild briar slip she *Yale 1* briar's slip>briar-slip *1868 1872* wild briar-slip   *MS* wear,>wear)   331 *MS* {beginning of fo. 12}   332 *Yale 2* myself:>myself.   334 *MS* seeming such>seemed such and   336 *MS* Nothing but was, this time, the thing>Find nothing, this time, but the fact   337 *MS* —Find>—All   ★339 *MS 1868 1872 1888* pain, *DC BrU* pain,>pain *1889* pain   340 *MS* Giving   341 *MS* Its   *MS* ^wilding^   345 *MS* {line added later}   352 *MS* black wiped clean,>foul in me

330 *slip*: cutting.

333 *wife . . . says*: cf. Gen. 2: 24, Mark 10: 8.

341 *wilding*: wild growing; cf. 'Oh wilding rose . . .': Scott, 'Lady of the Lake', IV, st. i.

351–2 *just absolved . . . fair*: i.e. she has just made her confession to Don Celestine, and received from him absolution for her sins.

353 *One . . . have*: i.e. one cannot both be in touch with the pain of the past and also cured of it. If you are cured of the pain of the past, you are no longer competent to judge it.

Being right now, I am happy and colour things.
Yes, everybody that leaves life sees all   355
Softened and bettered: so with other sights:
To me at least was never evening yet
But seemed far beautifuller than its day,
For past is past.

               There was a fancy came,   360
When somewhere, in the journey with my friend,
We stepped into a hovel to get food;
And there began a yelp here, a bark there,—
Misunderstanding creatures that were wroth
And vexed themselves and us till we retired.   365
The hovel is life: no matter what dogs bit
Or cats scratched in the hovel I break from,
All outside is lone field, moon and such peace—
Flowing in, filling up as with a sea
Whereon comes Someone, walks fast on the white,   370
Jesus Christ's self, Don Celestine declares,
To meet me and calm all things back again.

Beside, up to my marriage, thirteen years
Were, each day, happy as the day was long:
This may have made the change too terrible.   375
I know that when Violante told me first

---

354 *MS* set right,>right now   355 *1868* every body   360 *MS* {New para-
graph indicated by 'N.P.' in right-hand margin}   361 *MS* {beginning of fo.
13}   363 *MS* While>And   365 *MS* gave way.>retired.   368 *MS*
repose>such peace—   371 *MS* The Saviour's>Jesus Christ's   *MS* affirms,>
asserts,   373 *MS* {New paragraph indicated by 'N.P.' in right-hand margin}
MS years,>years   374 *MS* And>Were,   *MS* that>the   *MS* long—

369–72 *a sea . . . again*: Pompilia has had a 'fancy' of life as a noisy, violent 'hovel',
while outside (i.e. in eternity) all is calm. She pictures this eternity as like a sea 'flowing
in' to surround the troubled hovel, with a mysterious 'Someone' coming to greet her.
When she tells this vision to her confessor Don Celestine, he interprets it in terms of
Matt. 14: 25–32 and as an image of her death: she, like St Peter, stepping out of the
boat and walking on the waters of the Sea of Galilee, passes from storm to calm and
into the arms of Christ.

370 *white*: the moonlit water or the froth of the waves.

The cavalier—she meant to bring next morn,
Whom I must also let take, kiss my hand—
Would be at San Lorenzo the same eve
And marry me,—which over, we should go   380
Home both of us without him as before,
And, till she bade speak, I must hold my tongue,
Such being the correct way with girl-brides,
From whom one word would make a father blush,—
I know, I say, that when she told me this,   385
—Well, I no more saw sense in what she said
Than a lamb does in people clipping wool;
Only lay down and let myself be clipped.
And when next day the cavalier who came—
(Tisbe had told me that the slim young man   390
With wings at head, and wings at feet, and sword
Threatening a monster, in our tapestry,
Would eat a girl else,—was a cavalier)
When he proved Guido Franceschini,—old
And nothing like so tall as I myself,   395
Hook-nosed and yellow in a bush of beard,
Much like a thing I saw on a boy's wrist,
He called an owl and used for catching birds,—

377 *MS 1868 1872* cavalier,—   *MS* day,>morn,   378 *MS 1868 1872*
hand,—   384 *MS* And one word fit to make my>From whom one word
would make a   385 *MS* {line added later}   387 *MS* wool—   389
MS 1868 1872 came   390 *MS* {beginning of fo. 14}   *MS* tall>slim
395 *MS* {line added later}   *★MS 1868 1872* myself, *1888* myself *DC BrU* myself>
myself, *1889* myself,

377 *cavalier*: courtly gentleman, gallant.
387 *lamb . . . wool*: Pompilia is at pains to emphasize her own lack of real consent to
the marriage. A similar image is used by Other Half-Rome at III. 461–8, where her
fate as a 'lamb to the slaughter' is more explicit. The image here may be suggested by
the idea of 'fleecing', i.e. stripping someone of money, property, etc., which is what
Guido is trying to do to the Comparini through his marriage to Pompilia.
390–2 *young man . . . monster*: an image of Perseus about to slay the dragon. The
irony here is that Guido, who is supposed to be Perseus-like, is actually the dragon. For
Browning's fascination with the Perseus-St George legend, see I. 585 n.
395–6 *nothing . . . beard*: these details are adapted from SS 23: 'Franceschini was short
of stature, thin and pale ['pallido'], with a sharp nose ['naso profilato'], black hair and a
heavy beard, about 50 years of age'; cf. VI. 1744 n.

And when he took my hand and made a smile—
Why, the uncomfortableness of it all   400
Seemed hardly more important in the case
Than,—when one gives you, say, a coin to spend,—
Its newness or its oldness; if the piece
Weigh properly and buy you what you wish,
No matter whether you get grime or glare!   405
Men take the coin, return you grapes and figs.
Here, marriage was the coin, a dirty piece
Would purchase me the praise of those I loved:
About what else should I concern myself?

So, hardly knowing what a husband meant,   410
I supposed this or any man would serve,
No whit the worse for being so uncouth:
For I was ill once and a doctor came
With a great ugly hat, no plume thereto,
Black jerkin and black buckles and black sword,   415
And white sharp beard over the ruff in front,
And oh so lean, so sour-faced and austere!—
Who felt my pulse, made me put out my tongue,
Then oped a phial, dripped a drop or two
Of a black bitter something,—I was cured!   420
What mattered the fierce beard or the grim face?
It was the physic beautified the man,

---

400 *MS* ^it^   402 *MS* Than, when   *MS* spend,   403 *MS* Dirty or
shiny; if the weight aright>Dirty or shiny; if the weight be well>Its newness or its
oldness; if the piece   404 *MS* {line added later}   405 *MS* What mat-
ters>No matter   *MS* with gold:>or glare: 406 *MS* it and>the coin,
408 *MS* loved—   410 *MS* {New paragraph indicated by 'N.P.' in left-hand
margin}   *MS* meant   415 *MS* A black cloak and black habit>Black jerkin
and black buckles   417 *MS* and austere,>[ ]>and austere,   418 *MS* and
made me show>made me put out   419 *MS* a a phial, {presumably a *lapsus
calami*}   420 *MS* {beginning of fo. 15}   421 *MS* white>fierce   *MS*
sour>grim   422 *MS* physick *Yale 1* physick>physic

405 *grime or glare*: dirty or shiny (coin).
415 *jerkin*: close-fitting jacket or doublet, often of leather.
416 *sharp*: neatly trimmed, pointed.
422 *the physic*: the medicine, the medical skill.

Master Malpichi,—never met his match
In Rome, they said,—so ugly all the same!

However, I was hurried through a storm,   425
Next dark eve of December's deadest day—
How it rained!—through our street and the Lion's-mouth
And the bit of Corso,—cloaked round, covered close,
I was like something strange or contraband,—
Into blank San Lorenzo, up the aisle,   430
My mother keeping hold of me so tight,
I fancied we were come to see a corpse
Before the altar which she pulled me toward.
There we found waiting an unpleasant priest
Who proved the brother, not our parish friend,   435
But one with mischief-making mouth and eye,

---

423 *MS* yet was>met his   424 *MS* say,—>said,—   425 *MS* {New para-
graph indicated by 'N.P.' in left-hand margin}   427 *MS* Lion's-Mouth 428 *MS*
up>close   433 *MS*   towards;>toward;   434 *MS*   yesterday's>waiting
an   *MS*   man>priest   435 *MS*   Waiting,>That   proved   *MS*   priest>
friend,   436 *MS* fox-like face and ferret eye>mischief-making mouth and eye

---

423 *Master Malpichi*: Marcello Malpighi (1628–94), one of the finest physicians of his
day, was the first great practitioner of microscopic anatomy; among his various sig-
nificant areas of work were discoveries relating to the capillary systems, red blood cells,
and the microscopic subdivisions of the major organs. He spent the majority of his life at
the University of Bologna, though he also held professorships at Pisa (1656) and Messina
(1662). Parts of his work were published in the *Philosophical Transactions* of the Royal
Society in London, an indication of his European reputation. In 1691 Pope Innocent
XII honoured him by inviting him to Rome to become papal archiater or personal
physician. He would have been a grand doctor, indeed, to visit the young Pompilia. We
have been unable to trace any one likely source for Browning's knowledge of Malpighi.
It may be he discovered him in his research into the life of Innocent XII; certainly, he
has a sense of his stature as a doctor. The best known portrait, in the Rizzoli Institute,
Bologna, does not show a 'sharp beard', but it does show an austere, determined face.
426 *December's deadest day*: i.e. the solstice, the shortest day of the year. This is
Browning's addition to his source, which does not specify a day in December: see SS 2.
427–8 *our street . . . Corso*: the route to the Church of San Lorenzo in Lucina: along
Via Vittoria, then a left turn into Via della Bocca di Leone (the 'Lion's Mouth'), right
along Via dei Condotti, and then a short distance down the Corso (the main north–
south thoroughfare of Rome). Browning knew this part of Rome well; he and EBB
spent the winters of 1853–4 and 1858–9 at 43 Via della Bocca di Leone.
435 *brother*: Abate Paolo. This is Browning's addition; neither OYB nor SS specifies
the priest who performed the marriage.
436 *one . . . eye*: Pompilia originally described Paolo as 'one with fox-like face and
ferret eye': see *MS*; cf. VIII. 224–6 n.

Paul, whom I know since to my cost. And then
I heard the heavy church-door lock out help
Behind us: for the customary warmth,
Two tapers shivered on the altar. "Quick—   440
"Lose no time!" cried the priest. And straightway down
From . . . what's behind the altar where he hid—
Hawk-nose and yellowness and bush and all,
Stepped Guido, caught my hand, and there was I
O' the chancel, and the priest had opened book,   445
Read here and there, made me say that and this,
And after, told me I was now a wife,
Honoured indeed, since Christ thus weds the Church,
And therefore turned he water into wine,
To show I should obey my spouse like Christ.   450
Then the two slipped aside and talked apart,
And I, silent and scared, got down again
And joined my mother who was weeping now.
Nobody seemed to mind us any more,
And both of us on tiptoe found our way   455
To the door which was unlocked by this, and wide.
When we were in the street, the rain had stopped,
All things looked better. At our own house-door,
Violante whispered "No one syllable

---

441 *MS 1868 1872* time!"— *MS* priest—And   442 *MS* From— *1868 1872*
From . .   443 *MS* Hawknose *MS* all—   444 *MS* Guido— *MS*
hand—   445 *MS* On>O'   *MS* chancel and   448 *MS* {beginning of
fo. 16}   *MS* in this, that Christ   449 *MS* once water   453 *MS* sob-
bing>weeping *MS* now;   454 *MS* {line added later}   456 *MS* lay
wide—   457 *MS* And *MS* street: 458 *MS* better: at>better. At
MS {no comma}

442 *what's . . . hid*: Guido has been hiding behind the altar screen.
443 *Hawk-nose . . . all*: cf. l. 395–6 n.
449–50 *therefore . . . Christ*: i.e. Christ honoured marriage by performing his first
miracle at the marriage of Cana: see John 2: 1–12. Since Christ thus honoured
marriage—as a symbol of his own 'marriage' to the Church—therefore Pompilia
should obey her new husband as though he were Christ. Paolo's first assertion
is theologically sound; his own implied brutal and simplistic view of what her
'obedience' should be like is not.
451 *the two*: i.e. Guido and Paolo.

"To Pietro! Girl-brides never breathe a word!"   460
"—Well treated to a wetting, draggle-tails!"
Laughed Pietro as he opened—"Very near
"You made me brave the gutter's roaring sea
"To carry off from roost old dove and young,
"Trussed up in church, the cote, by me, the kite!   465
"What do these priests mean, praying folk to death
"On stormy afternoons, with Christmas close
"To wash our sins off nor require the rain?"
Violante gave my hand a timely squeeze,
Madonna saved me from immodest speech,   470
I kissed him and was quiet, being a bride.

When I saw nothing more, the next three weeks,
Of Guido—"Nor the Church sees Christ" thought I:
"Nothing is changed however, wine is wine
"And water only water in our house.   475
"Nor did I see that ugly doctor since
"That cure of the illness: just as I was cured,
"I am married,—neither scarecrow will return."

Three weeks, I chuckled—"How would Giulia stare,
"And Tecla smile and Tisbe laugh outright,   480
"Were it not impudent for brides to talk!"—

460 *MS* Pietro, girl-brides   462 *MS* "very   463–8 *MS* {no quotation
marks at beginnings of lines}   464 *MS* And   465 *MS* kite: 467
MS winter nights,>afternoons,   *472 *MS* {New paragraph indicated by 'New
P.' in right-hand margin} *1868 1872* {new paragraph. Paragraphing obscured in *1888*
and *1889* by this line's being at the head of the page}   *MS* {no com-
mas}   473 *MS* nor>Nor   *MS* said>thought   477–8 *MS* {no quotation
marks at beginnings of lines}   477 *MS* {beginning of fo. 17}   *MS* The *1868*
1872 "The   478 *MS* {no quotation mark at end of line}   479 *MS* {New
paragraph indicated by 'N.P.' in left-hand margin}   *MS* Three whole>Three weeks
did I chuckle—   *MS* "Gigia would>"How would Gigia   480 *MS* {no
comma}

461 *draggle-tails*: an affectionate, teasing name, indicating that Pompilia and Violante
are bedraggled by the rain, their 'tails' or skirts wet and muddy.
464–5 *To . . . kite!*: a playful image: Pietro imagines himself as a kite swooping down
on a dovecote (San Lorenzo church), in order to 'rescue' two doves (Violante and
Pompilia) from a long service.

Until one morning, as I sat and sang
At the broidery-frame alone i' the chamber,—loud
Voices, two, three together, sobbings too,
And my name, "Guido," "Paolo," flung like stones   485
From each to the other! In I ran to see.
There stood the very Guido and the priest
With sly face,—formal but nowise afraid,—
While Pietro seemed all red and angry, scarce
Able to stutter out his wrath in words;   490
And this it was that made my mother sob,
As he reproached her—"You have murdered us,
"Me and yourself and this our child beside!"
Then Guido interposed "Murdered or not,
"Be it enough your child is now my wife!   495
"I claim and come to take her." Paul put in,
"Consider—kinsman, dare I term you so?—
"What is the good of your sagacity
"Except to counsel in a strait like this?
"I guarantee the parties man and wife   500
"Whether you like or loathe it, bless or ban.
"May spilt milk be put back within the bowl—
"The done thing, undone? You, it is, we look
"For counsel to, you fitliest will advise!
"Since milk, though spilt and spoilt, does marble good,   505
"Better we down on knees and scrub the floor,
"Than sigh, 'the waste would make a syllabub!'
"Help us so turn disaster to account,

482 *MS* ^Until^   *MS* ^as^   *MS* sate   487 *MS* Priest   488 *MS*
fox-face>sly-face   497 *MS* shall I dare address?—>dare I name you so? 498
MS good>[ ]>good   *MS* sagacity>sagaciousness>sagacity   502 *MS* poured>
put   *MS* into>within   504 *MS* advise;   505 *MS* {beginning of fo.
18}   *MS* makes marble clean,>does marble good,   506 *MS* What if>Bet-
ter   507 *MS* syllabub'!   508 *MS* the matter>disaster

502 *May...bowl*: adapting the proverbial 'It is no use crying over spilt milk':
ODEP, 159.

505-7 *Since milk...syllabub!'*: Paolo contrasts a base domestic use of milk—used to
scrub and cleanse marble floors—with milk used to make a luxurious dessert.

"So predispose the groom, he needs shall grace
"The bride with favour from the very first,   510
"Not begin marriage an embittered man!"
He smiled,—the game so wholly in his hands!
While fast and faster sobbed Violante—"Ay,
"All of us murdered, past averting now!
"O my sin, O my secret!" and such like.   515

Then I began to half surmise the truth;
Something had happened, low, mean, underhand,
False, and my mother was to blame, and I
To pity, whom all spoke of, none addressed:
I was the chattel that had caused a crime.   520
I stood mute,—those who tangled must untie
The embroilment. Pietro cried "Withdraw, my child!
"She is not helpful to the sacrifice
"At this stage,—do you want the victim by
"While you discuss the value of her blood?   525
"For her sake, I consent to hear you talk:
"Go, child, and pray God help the innocent!"

I did go and was praying God, when came
Violante, with eyes swollen and red enough,
But movement on her mouth for make-believe   530

---

509 *MS* Groom he   510 *MS* Bride   512 *MS* hands!—   513 *MS*
"Ay—   514 *MS* now,—   515 *MS* secret!"—   516 *MS* {New para-
graph indicated by 'N.Par' in left-hand margin}   *MS* truth—   519 *MS*
addressed; 521 *MS* untwine>untie   522 *MS* "Retire,>"Withdraw,   523
MS party>helpful   524 *MS* when>do   *MS* well>by   525 *MS* {line
added later}   *MS* {no quotation mark at beginning of line}   *527 *1868 1872*
innocent!" *1888 1889* innocent!   528 *MS* {New paragraph indicated by 'N.P.' in
left-hand margin}   *MS* when there came>God, when came   529 *MS* {no
commas}   *MS* enough but still>enough   530 *MS* A>But   *MS* mouth
meant for a smi>mouth for make-believe

---

515 *"O . . . secret!"*: Pompilia may think the 'secret' Violante refers to is the clandes-
tine marriage, though it is in fact the secret of her own birth. Part of Violante's object
in consenting to the marriage was finally to obliterate the taint of Pompilia's origins
and her own guilt concerning the deception of Pompilia's birth: Pompilia would be
established high in the social scale, legitimized by her husband.

520 *chattel*: possession, property; cf. *Taming of the Shrew*, III. ii. 230.

Matters were somehow getting right again.
She bade me sit down by her side and hear.
"You are too young and cannot understand,
"Nor did your father understand at first.
"I wished to benefit all three of us,   535
"And when he failed to take my meaning,—why,
"I tried to have my way at unaware—
"Obtained him the advantage he refused.
"As if I put before him wholesome food
"Instead of broken victual,—he finds change   540
"I' the viands, never cares to reason why,
"But falls to blaming me, would fling the plate
"From window, scandalize the neighbourhood,
"Even while he smacks his lips,—men's way, my child!
"But either you have prayed him unperverse   545
"Or I have talked him back into his wits:
"And Paolo was a help in time of need,—
"Guido, not much—my child, the way of men!
"A priest is more a woman than a man,
"And Paul did wonders to persuade. In short,   550
"Yes, he was wrong, your father sees and says;
"My scheme was worth attempting: and bears fruit,
"Gives you a husband and a noble name,
"A palace and no end of pleasant things.
"What do you care about a handsome youth?   555
"They are so volatile, and tease their wives!
"This is the kind of man to keep the house.

---

531 *MS* again:>again.   532 *MS* And told me to sit by>She bade me sit down
by   533 *MS* understand—   534 *MS* {beginning of fo. 19}   *MS*
Father   538 {not found in *MS*}   540 *MS* smells>finds   541 *MS*
{line added later}   543 *MS* {line added later}   546 *MS* reasoned>talked
him   *MS* [?sense]>back   *MS* wits,   551 *MS* says—   552 *MS*
attempting—   555–7 *MS* {lines added later}   556 *MS 1868 1872* teaze

537 *at unaware*: i.e. surreptitiously.
540 *broken victual*: i.e. leftovers.
545 *unperverse*: perhaps a coinage: OED² gives only this example.
556 *tease*: irritate, vex.
557 *to keep the house*: to stay at home, i.e. be loyal, sexually and otherwise.

"We lose no daughter,—gain a son, that's all:
"For 't is arranged we never separate,
"Nor miss, in our grey time of life, the tints   560
"Of you that colour eve to match with morn.
"In good or ill, we share and share alike,
"And cast our lots into a common lap,
"And all three die together as we lived!
"Only, at Arezzo,—that's a Tuscan town,   565
"Not so large as this noisy Rome, no doubt,
"But older far and finer much, say folk,—
"In a great palace where you will be queen,
"Know the Archbishop and the Governor,
"And we see homage done you ere we die.   570
"Therefore, be good and pardon!"—"Pardon what?
"You know things, I am very ignorant:
"All is right if you only will not cry!"

And so an end! Because a blank begins
From when, at the word, she kissed me hard and hot,   575
And took me back to where my father leaned
Opposite Guido—who stood eyeing him,
As eyes the butcher the cast panting ox
That feels his fate is come, nor struggles more,—

559 MS do not>never   MS {no comma}   560 MS {no commas}   561
MS like rosy>to match with   563 MS Cast all three>And cast our   564 MS
^all three^   MS lived before—>lived—   565 MS that famed>that's a   MS
town—   567 MS ^far^   MS ^much^   MS 1868 1872 folks,—   568 MS
{beginning of fo. 20}   MS fine>great   MS Queen MS {no com-
ma}   569 MS {line added later}   MS {no quotation mark at beginning of
line}   572 MS ignorant,   573 MS cry."   574 MS {New paragraph
indicated by 'N.P.' in left-hand margin}   MS end—because   575 MS
hot   576 MS sat   577 MS Guido,—   MS was eying him,>stood o'er
him,—eyed,   578 MS some cast panting ox>the cast prostrate ox>the cast
panting ox   579 MS fallen,>come,

560–1 *tints . . . morn*: i.e. Pompilia will continue to light up, give joy, to the 'eve' of
Violante and Pietro's lives.

564 *die . . . lived*: this, and other elements of this speech, are highly ironic in the light
of the future.

578 *cast*: thrown on its side. The ox would have had its legs tied together and then
been pulled over, prior to its slaughter.

While Paul looked archly on, pricked brow at whiles   580
With the pen-point as to punish triumph there,—
And said "Count Guido, take your lawful wife
"Until death part you!"

                              All since is one blank,
Over and ended; a terrific dream.   585
It is the good of dreams—so soon they go!
Wake in a horror of heart-beats, you may—
Cry "The dread thing will never from my thoughts!"
Still, a few daylight doses of plain life,
Cock-crow and sparrow-chirp, or bleat and bell   590
Of goats that trot by, tinkling, to be milked;
And when you rub your eyes awake and wide,
Where is the harm o' the horror? Gone! So here.
I know I wake,—but from what? Blank, I say!
This is the note of evil: for good lasts.   595
Even when Don Celestine bade "Search and find!
"For your soul's sake, remember what is past,
"The better to forgive it,"—all in vain!
What was fast getting indistinct before,
Vanished outright. By special grace perhaps,   600
Between that first calm and this last, four years
Vanish,—one quarter of my life, you know.
I am held up, amid the nothingness,

---

582 *MS* {no comma}   *MS* wife again>lawful wife   584 *MS* {New paragraph indicated by 'N.P.' in right-hand margin}   585 *MS* ended,—   *MS* dream— 586 *MS* that thus>—so soon   588 *MS 1868 1872* Cry,   591 *MS* milked,   593 *MS* Why, where's   *MS* ^harm of>o' the^   594 *MS* say. 595 *MS* evil—it lasts not>evil—for good lasts.   598 *MS* {beginning of fo. 21}   603 *MS* {no commas}   *MS* that>the

580–1 *pricked . . . there*: an odd but vivid image. Paolo's habit of touching his pen to his brow is seen as an act of priestly mortification, an attempt to avoid openly showing his triumph at having contrived the marriage. Cf. 'One Word More', 35–41.

596–8 *Don Celestine . . . it*: the Augustinian friar who heard Pompilia's death-bed confession: cf. ll. 31–3 n. Here, in relation to that confession, he urges Pompilia to a close examination of her conscience, which necessarily involves recalling as much as possible of the events in which she has played a part.

By one or two truths only—thence I hang,
And there I live,—the rest is death or dream,   605
All but those points of my support. I think
Of what I saw at Rome once in the Square
O' the Spaniards, opposite the Spanish House:
There was a foreigner had trained a goat,
A shuddering white woman of a beast,   610
To climb up, stand straight on a pile of sticks
Put close, which gave the creature room enough:
When she was settled there he, one by one,
Took away all the sticks, left just the four
Whereon the little hoofs did really rest,   615
There she kept firm, all underneath was air.
So, what I hold by, are my prayer to God,
My hope, that came in answer to the prayer,
Some hand would interpose and save me—hand
Which proved to be my friend's hand: and,—blest bliss,—   620
That fancy which began so faint at first,
That thrill of dawn's suffusion through my dark,
Which I perceive was promise of my child,
The light his unborn face sent long before,—
God's way of breaking the good news to flesh.   625
That is all left now of those four bad years.

---

605 *MS* and>or   *MS* dream—   608 *MS* {no comma}   *MS* Spanish>
the Spanish   610 *MS* thing [ ]>beast,   611 *MS* and stand>stand straight
617 *MS* the>my   618 *MS* The hope, that came in>My [ ] hope, which [ ]   [ ]
>My hope, that came in   619 *MS* That>Some   *MS* save, one day,>save
me—that>save me—hand   620 *MS* and, the>and,—blest   621 *MS*
Even in that fancy that began so faint,>That fancy all began so faint at first,>That
fancy which began so faint at first,   622 *MS* The thrill of that star's daw-
ning>That thrill of dawn's beginning>That thrill of dawn's suffusion   623 *MS*
I now>Which I   625 *MS* {line added later}

607–8 *Square . . . House*: the long and irregular Piazza di Spagna took its name from
the Palazzo di Spagna, the residence of the Spanish ambassador.
   609–16 *There . . . air*: this extraordinary trick may be something Browning himself
had witnessed. We have been unable to trace any other reference to it.
   625 *God's . . . flesh*: the hints God gave Pompilia of the child growing in her womb
are implicitly paralleled with the gospel ('good news'), i.e. Christ growing slowly in
the Virgin Mary's womb.

Don Celestine urged "But remember more!
"Other men's faults may help me find your own.
"I need the cruelty exposed, explained,
"Or how can I advise you to forgive?"   630
He thought I could not properly forgive
Unless I ceased forgetting,—which is true:
For, bringing back reluctantly to mind
My husband's treatment of me,—by a light
That's later than my life-time, I review   635
And comprehend much and imagine more,
And have but little to forgive at last.
For now,—be fair and say,—is it not true
He was ill-used and cheated of his hope
To get enriched by marriage? Marriage gave   640
Me and no money, broke the compact so:
He had a right to ask me on those terms,
As Pietro and Violante to declare
They would not give me: so the bargain stood:
They broke it, and he felt himself aggrieved,   645
Became unkind with me to punish them.
They said 't was he began deception first,
Nor, in one point whereto he pledged himself,
Kept promise: what of that, suppose it were?
Echoes die off, scarcely reverberate   650
For ever,—why should ill keep echoing ill

627 *MS* {beginning of fo. 22}   *MS* [ ]>urged   *MS* more—   628 *MS* point
us to>help me find   *MS* own—   629 *MS* cruelties explained [ ]>cruelties
exposed, explained,   630 *MS* forgive them all?">you to forgive?"   632
MS he was right>which is true: 634 *MS* ^of me^   636 *MS* forgive
the>imagine   637 *MS* {line added later}   640 *MS* marriage, marriage>
marriage? Marriage   642 *MS* {no comma}   643 *MS* And>As   *MS* re-
fuse>declare   644 *MS* {line added later}   *MS* [ ]>me: so,   645 *MS*
They did not:>They broke it: 646 *MS* to>with   648 *MS* And, in all
things>Nor, in one point   649 *MS* Broke promise—>Kept promise—
650 *MS* do not>scarcely   651 *MS* waking>echoing   ★*MS 1868 1872 1888* ill,
DC BrU ill,>ill *1889* ill

632 *ceased forgetting*: i.e. ceased to blank out the years of her marriage.
634–5 *by . . . life-time*: in her dying moments, it is as though Pompilia sees her own
history with God's eyes, from outside time.

And never let our ears have done with noise?
Then my poor parents took the violent way
To thwart him,—he must needs retaliate,—wrong,
Wrong, and all wrong,—better say, all blind!   655
As I myself was, that is sure, who else
Had understood the mystery: for his wife
Was bound in some sort to help somehow there.
It seems as if I might have interposed,
Blunted the edge of their resentment so,   660
Since he vexed me because they first vexed him;
"I will entreat them to desist, submit,
"Give him the money and be poor in peace,—
"Certainly not go tell the world: perhaps
"He will grow quiet with his gains."   665

                                        Yes, say
Something to this effect and you do well!
But then you have to see first: I was blind.
That is the fruit of all such wormy ways,
The indirect, the unapproved of God: 670
You cannot find their author's end and aim,
Not even to substitute your good for bad,
Your straight for the irregular; you stand
Stupefied, profitless, as cow or sheep
That miss a man's mind, anger him just twice   675

---

655 *MS* ^and^   *MS* blind!—   657 *MS* {beginning of fo. 23}   *MS* mys-
tery,—   *MS* ^for^   659 *MS* {line added later}   660 *MS* And turn the
drift of all their rage on me:>Blunted the edge of their resentment so,   661 *MS*
Say,>Since   *MS* me he vexed   *MS* since>because   664 *MS*
world,—   666 *MS* {New paragraph indicated by 'New Par.' in right-hand
margin}   *MS* say—>say   667 *MS* {line added later}   *MS* well—
668 *MS*   see, and>see first: 669 *MS*   hidden>wormy   670 *MS*
God,—   671 *MS* You>[?We]>You   672 *MS* Even to substitute>Not
even substitute>Not even to substitute   *MS* your>our>your   *MS* {no comma}
673 *MS* Your>Our>Your   *MS* *1868 1872* open   *MS* you>we>you   675
MS ^man's^

669 *fruit . . . ways*: i.e. the outcome of all such devious, unseen manoeuvres; the
implicit image is of a worm- or maggot-eaten apple.

By trial at repairing the first fault.

Thus, when he blamed me, "You are a coquette,

"A lure-owl posturing to attract birds,

"You look love-lures at theatre and church,

"In walk, at window!"—that, I knew, was false: 680

But why he charged me falsely, whither sought

To drive me by such charge,—how could I know?

So, unaware, I only made things worse.

I tried to soothe him by abjuring walk,

Window, church, theatre, for good and all,   685

As if he had been in earnest: that, you know,

Was nothing like the object of his charge.

Yes, when I got my maid to supplicate

The priest, whose name she read when she would read

Those feigned false letters I was forced to hear   690

Though I could read no word of,—he should cease

Writing,—nay, if he minded prayer of mine,

Cease from so much as even pass the street

Whereon our house looked,—in my ignorance

I was just thwarting Guido's true intent;   695

Which was, to bring about a wicked change

Of sport to earnest, tempt a thoughtless man

To write indeed, and pass the house, and more,

Till both of us were taken in a crime.

He ought not to have wished me thus act lies,   700

---

680 *MS* window"—   *MS* false—   682 *MS* so, unaware,>how could I
know?   683 *MS* worse—   686 *MS* earnest—   *MS* know>[ ]>
know   688 *MS* pray for me>supplicate   689 *MS* {beginning of fo.
24}   *MS* That he,>The priest,   690 *MS* Those letters to me I was for-
ced>Those letters I was therefore forced>Those feigned, false letters I was forced
693 *MS* ^from^   *MS* even as>as even   *MS* pass down the>pass the
695 *MS* intent   696–7 *MS* {lines added later}   696 *MS* {no com-
ma}   *MS* wickedness—>wicked change   698 *MS* My friend should write,
>My priest should write,>To write indeed,   699 *MS* trap.>crime.

676 *By trial*: i.e. by the attempt.
678 *lure-owl*: an owl, usually placed on a pole with a mirror beneath, used by the
Italians to attract birds so that they can then be shot by the huntsman: see III. 338 n.
679 *love-lures*: entrapping, seductive looks.

Simulate folly: but,—wrong or right, the wish,—
I failed to apprehend its drift. How plain
It follows,—if I fell into such fault,
He also may have overreached the mark,
Made mistake, by perversity of brain,   705
I' the whole sad strange plot, the grotesque intrigue
To make me and my friend unself ourselves,
Be other man and woman than we were!
Think it out, you who have the time! for me,—
I cannot say less; more I will not say.   710
Leave it to God to cover and undo!

Only, my dulness should not prove too much!
—Not prove that in a certain other point
Wherein my husband blamed me,—and you blame,
If I interpret smiles and shakes of head,—   715
I was dull too. Oh, if I dared but speak!
Must I speak? I am blamed that I forwent
A way to make my husband's favour come.
That is true: I was firm, withstood, refused . . .

701 MS guilt,—>folly, 1868 1872 folly,—   MS but, wrong   MS of him,>the
wish,   702 MS take the>apprehend the wish.>apprehend its drift.   MS
Why then>How plain   704 MS Why may not he have>He also may
have   MS himself,>the mark,   705 MS Mistaken,>Made mistake,   706
MS In the whole plot, from first to last,>In the whole sad strange plot, from first to
last,>In the whole sad strange plot, this same intrigue 1868 In 1868 this same intri-
gue   709 MS for me   710 MS I cannot well say less, will not say more;>I
cannot say less, I will not say more;>I cannot say less, more I will not
say;   711 MS forgive!>undo!   ★712 MS {New paragraph indicated by
'N.P.' in left-hand margin.   Paragraphing obscured in 1868 and 1872 by this line's
being at the head of the page} 1888 1889 {no new paragraph} MS does not prove at
all>should not prove too much,   713 MS That in a certain single point—
wherein>Not prove that in a certain other point   714 MS My husband blamed
^me,^ and you also blame,> Wherein my husband blamed me, and you
blame,   715 MS shakes of head aright,—>smiles and shakes of
head,   716 MS {line added later}   MS I did so very wrong, if I dared speak!>I
was dull too,—oh, if I dared but speak!   718 MS had made>to make

707 unself: OED² cites this instance of the verb, but has examples going back to 1654.
711 cover: hide (the crime).
718 A way . . . come: i.e. by being eager to have sexual intercourse with him.

—Women as you are, how can I find the words?   720

I felt there was just one thing Guido claimed
I had no right to give nor he to take;
We being in estrangement, soul from soul:
Till, when I sought help, the Archbishop smiled,
Inquiring into privacies of life,   725
—Said I was blameable—(he stands for God)
Nowise entitled to exemption there.
Then I obeyed,—as surely had obeyed
Were the injunction "Since your husband bids,
"Swallow the burning coal he proffers you!"   730
But I did wrong, and he gave wrong advice
Though he were thrice Archbishop,—that, I know!—
Now I have got to die and see things clear.
Remember I was barely twelve years old—
A child at marriage: I was let alone   735
For weeks, I told you, lived my child-life still
Even at Arezzo, when I woke and found
First . . . but I need not think of that again—
Over and ended! Try and take the sense
Of what I signify, if it must be so.   740

---

720 *MS* {beginning of fo. 25}   *MS* I cannot>how can I   721 *MS* {New paragraph indicated by 'N.P.' in left-hand margin}   *MS* that there was one>there was just one   722 *MS* take—   723 *MS* Being in such>We being in   *MS* soul,—   724 *MS* Till the Archbishop said>smiled, when I sought help,   725 *MS* [?Enquiring]>Inquiring   726 *MS* That   *MS* wholly wrong—>blameable—   *MS* God—)   727 *MS* there,—   729 *MS* bids,—   730 *MS* gives his wife!">proffers you!"   731 *MS* for he   732 *MS* say,>know   733 *MS* plain.>clear.   737 *MS* When I woke at Arezzo, and found first>Even at Arezzo, when I woke and found   738 *MS* [?There] . . >First . .   *1868 1872* First . .   *MS* [ ]>again—

720 *Women as you are*: cf. 1. 1087, where Browning notes a doctor and a lawyer at the death-bed. Here he seems to assume an audience of nuns.

738 *First . . .*: see Brady, 44, 46: 'In Pompilia's account of her sexual relations with Guido, one finds only a recording of forced intercourse which she will not name and finds it difficult to relate. As she lies dying from multiple stab wounds, she seems to ignore these, yet suffers anew to recount the progress of her brutal sexual initiation at the hands of Guido. . . . The ellipsis here [l. 738] is her own, and accompanies every explicit reference to sexual intercourse with Guido.'

After the first, my husband, for hate's sake,
Said one eve, when the simpler cruelty
Seemed somewhat dull at edge and fit to bear,
"We have been man and wife six months almost:
"How long is this your comedy to last?   745
"Go this night to my chamber, not your own!"
At which word, I did rush—most true the charge—
And gain the Archbishop's house—he stands for God—
And fall upon my knees and clasp his feet,
Praying him hinder what my estranged soul   750
Refused to bear, though patient of the rest:
"Place me within a convent," I implored—
"Let me henceforward lead the virgin life
"You praise in Her you bid me imitate!"
What did he answer? "Folly of ignorance!   755
"Know, daughter, circumstances make or mar
"Virginity,—'t is virtue or 't is vice.
"That which was glory in the Mother of God
"Had been, for instance, damnable in Eve
"Created to be mother of mankind.   760
"Had Eve, in answer to her Maker's speech
" 'Be fruitful, multiply, replenish earth'—
"Pouted 'But I choose rather to remain
" 'Single'—why, she had spared herself forthwith
"Further probation by the apple and snake,   765
"Been pushed straight out of Paradise! For see—

---

741 *MS* Know then that when>After the first   743 *MS* dulled>dull   *MS*
bearable,>fit to bear,   744 *MS* almost a year.>six months almost.   748
MS {beginning of fo. 26}   750 *MS* spare me>hinder   754 *MS* imita-
te"!   755 *MS* answer?—"Folly   758 *MS* a glory>glory   759 *MS*
been—for instance—   760 *MS* Mother   *MS* Man: had Eve>Mankind.
761 *MS* In>Had Eve, in   *MS* first command>speech   764 *MS* "A virgin'—
she>"Single'—Why, she

---

741 *After the first*: i.e. after the first months of marriage.
751 *patient of*: enduring.
754 *Her*: i.e. the Virgin Mary.
762 *'Be . . . earth'*: cf. Gen. 1: 28.
765 *probation*: testing.

"If motherhood be qualified impure,
"I catch you making God command Eve sin!
"—A blasphemy so like these Molinists',
"I must suspect you dip into their books."
Then he pursued " 'T was in your covenant!"   770

No! There my husband never used deceit.
He never did by speech nor act imply
"Because of our souls' yearning that we meet
"And mix in soul through flesh, which yours and mine
"Wear and impress, and make their visible selves,   776
"—All which means, for the love of you and me,
"Let us become one flesh, being one soul!"
He only stipulated for the wealth;
Honest so far. But when he spoke as plain—
Dreadfully honest also—"Since our souls   780
"Stand each from each, a whole world's width between,
"Give me the fleshly vesture I can reach
"And rend and leave just fit for hell to burn!"—
Why, in God's name, for Guido's soul's own sake   785
Imperilled by polluting mine,—I say,
I did resist; would I had overcome!

My heart died out at the Archbishop's smile;
—It seemed so stale and worn a way o' the world,

---

767 *MS* Motherhood   768 *MS* a sin—>Eve sin—   769 *MS* "A   *MS* {no comma}   772 *MS* {New paragraph indicated by 'N.P.' in left-hand margin}   773 *MS* word or deed>speech or act   774 *MS* "Pompilia, for the> Because of our souls'   *MS* ^we^   775 *MS* "And mix through flesh, your soul and mine>"And mix in soul through flesh, which yours and mine   776 *MS* {beginning of fo. 27}   *MS* make [ ] [?at] themselves,>and make their visible selves,   777 *MS* absolute love>love   780 *MS* far: but>far. But 782 *MS* the>a   783 *1868 1872* fleshy   785 *MS* and>for   786 *MS* say   787 *MS* resist,—   788 *MS* {New paragraph indicated by 'N.P.' in left-hand margin}   789 *MS* worn and stale>stale and worn   *MS* of>o'

771 *covenant*: i.e. marriage vows.

775-6 *which . . . impress*: i.e. the flesh that our souls clothe themselves in, moulding them to the shape of their own being.

As though 't were nature frowning—"Here is Spring,   790
"The sun shines as he shone at Adam's fall,
"The earth requires that warmth reach everywhere:
"What, must your patch of snow be saved forsooth
"Because you rather fancy snow than flowers?"
Something in this style he began with me.   795
Last he said, savagely for a good man,
"This explains why you call your husband harsh,
"Harsh to you, harsh to whom you love. God's Bread!
"The poor Count has to manage a mere child
"Whose parents leave untaught the simplest things   800
"Their duty was and privilege to teach,—
"Goodwives' instruction, gossips' lore: they laugh
"And leave the Count the task,—or leave it me!"
Then I resolved to tell a frightful thing.
"I am not ignorant,—know what I say,   805
"Declaring this is sought for hate, not love.
"Sir, you may hear things like almighty God.
"I tell you that my housemate, yes—the priest
"My husband's brother, Canon Girolamo—
"Has taught me what depraved and misnamed love   810
"Means, and what outward signs denote the sin,
"For he solicits me and says he loves,
"The idle young priest with nought else to do.
"My husband sees this, knows this, and lets be.
"Is it your counsel I bear this beside?"   815
"—More scandal, and against a priest this time!
"What, 't is the Canon now?"—less snappishly—

---

790 *MS* 'twas>'twere   *MS* Nature   791 *MS* birth,>fall,   792 *MS* be>
reach   *MS* everywhere,—   795 *MS* {line added later}   *MS* me—   802 *MS*
gossip's   805 *MS* {beginning of fo. 28}   *MS* say   808 *MS* the young>
yes—the   811 *MS* Means and   814 *MS* and>this,   *MS* this and   816 *MS*
—"More scandal and

---

798 *God's Bread!*: i.e. By the holy Eucharist! (an oath). This indignant oath is
intended to suggest the Archbishop's harsh tone.

802 *Goodwives' instruction*: the (sexual) instruction appropriately given by virtuous
wives (to young girls).

gossips' lore: knowledge gleaned from close friends.

"Rise up, my child, for such a child you are,
"The rod were too advanced a punishment!
"Let's try the honeyed cake. A parable!   820
" 'Without a parable spake He not to them.'
"There was a ripe round long black toothsome fruit,
"Even a flower-fig, the prime boast of May:
"And, to the tree, said . . . either the spirit o' the fig,
"Or, if we bring in men, the gardener,   825
"Archbishop of the orchard—had I time
"To try o' the two which fits in best: indeed
"It might be the Creator's self, but then
"The tree should bear an apple, I suppose,—
"Well, anyhow, one with authority said   830
" 'Ripe fig, burst skin, regale the fig-pecker—
" 'The bird whereof thou art a perquisite!'
" 'Nay,' with a flounce, replied the restif fig,
" 'I much prefer to keep my pulp myself:
" 'He may go breakfastless and dinnerless,   835
" 'Supperless of one crimson seed, for me!'

---

821 *MS 1868* them.' "   824 *MS 1868 1872* said . .   *MS* Spirit   *MS* of>o'
MS Fig,   825 *MS* gardener   827 *MS* of>o'   832 *MS* "That   *MS*
you are>thou art   833 *MS* {beginning of fo. 29}   *MS* 'Nay' with   *MS*
flounce replied   834 *MS* seeds my own,>pulp myself,   835 *MS* go din>
go   836 *MS* a single>one crimson   *MS* me.'

819 *rod*: cane, birch. The Archbishop refers obliquely to the proverb 'Spare the rod
and spoil the child': ODEP, 759. He implies that Pompilia is too childish to warrant
harsh correction.

821 *'Without . . . them.'*: cf. Matt. 13: 34. By this quotation from scripture the
Archbishop pompously associates himself with Christ.

823 *flower-fig*: a fig of the first crop. 'There are two crops of figs on each tree. The
first, which ripen in July, and are called *fichi-fiori*, or flower figs, are little esteemed [for
human consumption] and have not much flavour; but the second figs which ripen
later, though smaller, are far richer and better': *Roba di Roma*, ii. 9.

831 *regale*: feast, yield goodness to.

fig-pecker: a literal rendering of It. *beccafico*, 'a name given in Italy to small migratory
birds of the genus Sylvia, much esteemed as dainties in the autumn, when they have
fattened on figs and grapes': OED[2]; cf. 'flower-pecker', a bird of the family Dicæidæ.

832 *perquisite*: property, reward.

833 *restif*: rebellious, resisting.

834 *pulp*: soft flesh (of the fig).

"So, back she flopped into her bunch of leaves.
"He flew off, left her,—did the natural lord,—
"And lo, three hundred thousand bees and wasps
"Found her out, feasted on her to the shuck: 840
"Such gain the fig's that gave its bird no bite!
"The moral,—fools elude their proper lot,
"Tempt other fools, get ruined all alike.
"Therefore go home, embrace your husband quick!
"Which if his Canon brother chance to see,   845
"He will the sooner back to book again."

So, home I did go; so, the worst befell:
So, I had proof the Archbishop was just man,
And hardly that, and certainly no more.
For, miserable consequence to me,   850
My husband's hatred waxed nor waned at all,
His brother's boldness grew effrontery soon,
And my last stay and comfort in myself
Was forced from me: henceforth I looked to God
Only, nor cared my desecrated soul   855

---

837 *MS* So back   *MS* leaves,   838 *MS* ^flew off,^   *MS* [ ] natural>natural   840 *MS* shuck,—   843 *MS* alike,   844 *MS* and kiss your husband's hand>embrace your husband quick,   845 *MS* The better if his brother>Which if his Canon brother   *MS* {no comma}   846 *MS* Who sooner will back to breviary again.">He the sooner will back to book again.">He will the sooner back to book again."   847 *MS* {New paragraph indicated by 'N.P.' in left-hand margin}   *MS* {no commas after 'So . . . . so'}   *MS* go,—   *MS* befell—   848 *MS* So I   *MS* mere>just   849 *MS* more—   850 *MS* As the utter>For, miserable   854 *MS* cared for>looked to   855 *MS* not for the>nor cared my

838 *natural lord*: i.e. the fig-pecker; in the context of the parable, the husband, Guido.
840 *to the shuck*: to the husk, to the last bit; cf. 'Fra Lippo Lippi', 84.
843 *ruined*: this has partly its sense of 'sexually dishonoured'.
848–9 *I . . . more*: see Brady, 52: 'Pompilia's narration of this interview shows an increasingly critical distancing of herself from [the Archbishop] to whom she had had recourse for spiritual direction. Her reproduction of his tone, his cynicism, his worldliness and complete complicity in the sexual debasement of her marriage manifests a definite moral judgment of him.'
851 *waxed nor waned*: i.e. did not change.
853–4 *my . . . me*: i.e. she lost her virginity.

Should have fair walls, gay windows for the world.
God's glimmer, that came through the ruin-top,
Was witness why all lights were quenched inside:
Henceforth I asked God counsel, not mankind.

So, when I made the effort, freed myself,   860
They said—"No care to save appearance here!
"How cynic,—when, how wanton, were enough!"
—Adding, it all came of my mother's life—
My own real mother, whom I never knew,
Who did wrong (if she needs must have done wrong)   865
Through being all her life, not my four years,
At mercy of the hateful: every beast
O' the field was wont to break that fountain-fence,
Trample the silver into mud so murk
Heaven could not find itself reflected there.   870
Now they cry "Out on her, who, plashy pool,
"Bequeathed turbidity and bitterness
"To the daughter-stream where Guido dipt and drank!"

[—]

856 *MS* So much as wonder how the world—>Should have fair walls, a window for the world—>Should have fair walls, gay windows for the world—   858 *MS* wherefore all was black inside.>why all lights were quenched inside.   859 *MS* mankind: 860 *MS* {New paragraph indicated by 'N.Par.' in left-hand margin}   *MS 1868 1872* saved   861 *MS* {beginning of fo. 30}   *MS* Then   865 *MS* wrong—   *MS* wrong—   866 *MS* lying>being   867 *MS 1868 1872* hateful,—   868 *MS* Of>O'   869 *MS* Tread>Trample   870 *MS 1868 1872* there,—   871 *MS* the>who,   *MS* pool,   872 *MS* That lends> Bequeathed   873 *MS* dips and drinks!">dipt and drank!"

856–8 *fair . . . inside*: Pompilia compares her 'desecrated' soul and body to a dark, ruined castle, with only a glimmer of God's sunlight entering from the top.
861–2 *"No . . . enough!"*: i.e. 'She is worse than wanton, she is cynical: she cares nothing about the world's view of her.'
863–77 *mother's life . . . hate*: see Brady, 48: '[Pompilia] sees her life with Guido as a shorter version of, but essentially the same as her mother's life of prostitution. Pompilia claims affinity and understanding in mutual degradation'.
869 *murk*: dark, dirty.
871 *plashy*: swampy, boggy.
872 *turbidity*: cloudiness, dirtiness.

Well, since she had to bear this brand—let me!
The rather do I understand her now,   875
From my experience of what hate calls love,—
Much love might be in what their love called hate.
If she sold . . . what they call, sold . . . me her child—
I shall believe she hoped in her poor heart
That I at least might try be good and pure,   880
Begin to live untempted, not go doomed
And done with ere once found in fault, as she.
Oh and, my mother, it all came to this?
Why should I trust those that speak ill of you,
When I mistrust who speaks even well of them?   885
Why, since all bound to do me good, did harm,
May not you, seeming as you harmed me most,
Have meant to do most good—and feed your child
From bramble-bush, whom not one orchard-tree
But drew bough back from, nor let one fruit fall?   890
This it was for you sacrificed your babe?
Gained just this, giving your heart's hope away
As I might give mine, loving it as you,
If . . . but that never could be asked of me!

There, enough! I have my support again,   895
Again the knowledge that my babe was, is,
Will be mine only. Him, by death, I give
Outright to God, without a further care,—

---

*874 MS {New paragraph indicated by 'New Par.' in left-hand margin}   1868 1872
{new paragraph. Paragraphing obscured in 1888 and 1889 by this line's being at the
head of the page} MS this, why not I?>this brand—let me!   875 MS 1868 1872
now,—   877 MS {line   added   later}   MS   hate—   878 MS
Why>If   MS 1868 1872 sold . .   MS 1868 1872 sold . .   879 MS {line added
later}   884 MS {no comma}   885 MS ^even^   889 MS bramble-
bushes, whom each>bramble-bush, whom not one   890 MS Drew back its
bough>But drew back bough 1868 1872 drew-back bough   891 MS {beginning
of fo. 31}   MS even me,>your babe,   894 MS 1868 1872 If . .   895 MS
{New paragraph indicated by 'New Par.' in left-hand margin}   MS enough—
896 MS The>Again the

881–2 not . . . she: i.e. not, like her mother, be condemned and dismissed as a
prostitute even before she entered the trade. Pompilia imagines her mother living in
circumstances of poverty that foredoomed her to prostitution.

But not to any parent in the world,—
So to be safe: why is it we repine?   900
What guardianship were safer could we choose?
All human plans and projects come to nought:
My life, and what I know of other lives,
Prove that: no plan nor project! God shall care!

And now you are not tired? How patient then   905
All of you,—Oh yes, patient this long while
Listening, and understanding, I am sure!
Four days ago, when I was sound and well
And like to live, no one would understand.
People were kind, but smiled "And what of him,   910
"Your friend, whose tonsure the rich dark-brown hides?
"There, there!—your lover, do we dream he was?
"A priest too—never were such naughtiness!
"Still, he thinks many a long think, never fear,
"After the shy pale lady,—lay so light   915
"For a moment in his arms, the lucky one!"
And so on: wherefore should I blame you much?
So we are made, such difference in minds,
Such difference too in eyes that see the minds!
That man, you misinterpret and misprise—   920
The glory of his nature, I had thought,
Shot itself out in white light, blazed the truth
Through every atom of his act with me:
Yet where I point you, through the crystal shrine,
Purity in quintessence, one dew-drop,   925

902 *MS 1868 1872* nought,   903 *MS* life and   904 *MS* that,—   *MS*
project,—   905 *MS* {New paragraph (already written thus) indicated by 'N.P.'
in left-hand margin}   *MS* now,   908 *MS* {no comma}   911 *MS 1868*
1872 tonsure,   *MS* dark brown   912 *MS* there,—   914 *MS* Still
he   916 *MS* man!">one!"   918 *MS* {beginning of fo. 32}   *MS* So
men   920 *MS* {no comma}   *MS* you need to jest with   921 *MS*
[?glance]>glory   924 *MS* {no commas}   *MS 1868 1872* chrystal *Yale 2* chrys-
tal>crystal

---

914 *think*: OED[2] records this noun as colloquial, the earliest example being 1834.
920 *misprise*: fail to appreciate, undervalue.
924 *crystal shrine*: shrine holding crystals = a shimmering, dew-covered spider web.

You all descry a spider in the midst.
One says "The head of it is plain to see,"
And one, "They are the feet by which I judge,"
All say, "Those films were spun by nothing else."

Then, I must lay my babe away with God,   930
Nor think of him again, for gratitude.
Yes, my last breath shall wholly spend itself
In one attempt more to disperse the stain,
The mist from other breath fond mouths have made,
About a lustrous and pellucid soul: 935
So that, when I am gone but sorrow stays,
And people need assurance in their doubt
If God yet have a servant, man a friend,
The weak a saviour and the vile a foe,—
Let him be present, by the name invoked,   940
Giuseppe-Maria Caponsacchi!

                                    There,
Strength comes already with the utterance!
I will remember once more for his sake
The sorrow: for he lives and is belied.   945

---

926 *MS* would find   927 *MS* says,— *1868 1872* says,   *MS* "[ ], the head>"The
head of it   928 *MS* "It is>"They are   929 *MS* "those   930 *MS*
{New paragraph indicated by 'New Par.' in left-hand margin}   *MS* {no com-
mas}   *MS* will>must   931 *MS* in>for   *MS* gratitude—   932 *MS*
breath>[ ]>breath   934 *MS* foul breath foolish>other breath fond   *MS* {no
comma}   935 *MS* soul,   937 *MS* someone needs>[ ] needs>people
need   *MS* his>their   938 *MS* servant in the world>servant, man a friend,
939 *MS* world a [ ],—>vile a foe,—   940 *MS* invoked by the name>by the
name invoked   942 *MS* {New paragraph indicated by 'New Par' in right-hand
margin}   945 *MS* old woe,—>sorrow,—

---

934 *fond*: foolish, stupid.

935 *pellucid soul*: transparent, clear soul. Rossetti read this line in Feb. 1869 and felt
compelled to change the identical image in the MS of his 'Love's Nocturn' before its
publication in *Poems* (1870): 'There is a similar case [of apparent plagiarism] in the
Nocturn (page 8)—"Lamps of an *auspicious* soul" stood in my last correction (made long
ago) "pellucid" which is much finer. But lately in the *Ring and Book* I came on *pellucid
soul*, applied to Caponsacchi, and the inevitable charge of plagiarism struck me at once
as impending whenever my poem should be printed': D. G. Rossetti to W. M.
Rossetti, 27 Aug. 1869: *Rossetti Letters*, ii. 726.

Could he be here, how he would speak for me!

I had been miserable three drear years
In that dread palace and lay passive now,
When I first learned there could be such a man.
Thus it fell: I was at a public play,   950
In the last days of Carnival last March,
Brought there I knew not why, but now know well.
My husband put me where I sat, in front;
Then crouched down, breathed cold through me from behind,
Stationed i' the shadow,—none in front could see,—   955
I, it was, faced the stranger-throng beneath,
The crowd with upturned faces, eyes one stare,
Voices one buzz. I looked but to the stage,
Whereon two lovers sang and interchanged
"True life is only love, love only bliss: 960
"I love thee—thee I love!" then they embraced.
I looked thence to the ceiling and the walls,—
Over the crowd, those voices and those eyes,—
My thoughts went through the roof and out, to Rome
On wings of music, waft of measured words,—   965
Set me down there, a happy child again,
Sure that to-morrow would be festa-day,
Hearing my parents praise past festas more,
And seeing they were old if I was young,

---

946 *MS* Had he been>Could he be   *MS* {no comma}   947 *MS* {beginning
of fo. 33}   *MS* {New paragraph indicated by 'N.P.' in left-hand margin} *1868 1872*
{new paragraph. Paragraphing obscured in *1888* and *1889* by this line's being at the
head of the page} 948 *MS* [?was] [?patient]>lay passive   949 *MS* was such man
alive.>could be such a man.   950 *MS* the theatre,—>a public
play,   951 *MS* {line added later}   *MS* first>last   952 *MS* know well:>
know>know well: 953 *MS* front—   955 *MS* in>i'   956 *MS* {line
added later}   *MS* I it was faced the strangers poured   957 *MS* Of
the>The   *MS* stare   959 *MS* sang and>sang: they   960 *MS* and love
is bliss.>love only bliss.   961 *MS* love:"   963 *MS* {line added
later}   964 *MS* soared to Rome>out, reached Rome>out, to Rome   965
MS and>waft   *966 *MS* again, a happy child, *1868 1872* again, *1888 1889*
again   967 *MS* was some>would be

---

950 *fell*: happened, occurred.
967 *festa-day*: feast day, festival.

Yet wondering why they still would end discourse   970
With "We must soon go, you abide your time,
"And,—might we haply see the proper friend
"Throw his arm over you and make you safe!"

Sudden I saw him; into my lap there fell
A foolish twist of comfits, broke my dream   975
And brought me from the air and laid me low,
As ruined as the soaring bee that's reached
(So Pietro told me at the Villa once)
By the dust-handful. There the comfits lay:
I looked to see who flung them, and I faced   980
This Caponsacchi, looking up in turn.
Ere I could reason out why, I felt sure,
Whoever flung them, his was not the hand,—
Up rose the round face and good-natured grin
Of one who, in effect, had played the prank,   985
From covert close beside the earnest face,—
Fat waggish Conti, friend of all the world.
He was my husband's cousin, privileged
To throw the thing: the other, silent, grave,
Solemn almost, saw me, as I saw him.   990

There is a psalm Don Celestine recites,

971 *MS* must abide>abide   974 *MS* {New paragraph indicated by 'New Par.'
in left-hand margin}   *MS* came>fell   976 *MS* ^me^   979 *MS* {begin-
ning of fo. 34}   980 *MS* then>and   984 *MS* goodnatured   985 *MS*
1868 him who,   986 *MS* [ ]>face,—   987 *MS* world— 991 *MS* {New
paragraph indicated by 'New P.' in left-hand margin}

971 *"We . . . time*: i.e. 'You will naturally outlive us'.

975 *twist of comfits*: a small package of sweets in a roll of paper, secured with a twist at
either end.

977–9 *ruined . . . dust-handful*: the source is the bathetic image that brings to an end
the battle of the bees in Virgil, *Georgics*, IV. 86–7: 'hi motus animorum atque haec
certamina tanta / pulveris exigui iactu compressa quiescunt' ('These storms of passion,
these conflicts so fierce, by the toss of a little dust are checked and quieted').

986 *covert*: hiding place, concealment.

988 *cousin*: relative (the wider sense of the word). Conti's brother had married
Guido's sister.

"Had I a dove's wings, how I fain would flee!"
The psalm runs not "I hope, I pray for wings,"—
Not "If wings fall from heaven, I fix them fast,"—
Simply "How good it were to fly and rest,   995
"Have hope now, and one day expect content!
"How well to do what I shall never do!"
So I said "Had there been a man like that,
"To lift me with his strength out of all strife
"Into the calm, how I could fly and rest!   1000
"I have a keeper in the garden here
"Whose sole employment is to strike me low
"If ever I, for solace, seek the sun.
"Life means with me successful feigning death,
"Lying stone-like, eluding notice so,   1005
"Forgoing here the turf and there the sky.
"Suppose that man had been instead of this!"

Presently Conti laughed into my ear,
—Had tripped up to the raised place where I sat—
"Cousin, I flung them brutishly and hard!   1010
"Because you must be hurt, to look austere

---

992 *MS* fly!">flee!"   994 *MS* they>wings   *MS* fast>here,"—   995
MS a thing>it were   996 *MS* {line added later}   *MS* content—   997
MS be>do   *MS* be!">do!"   1000 *MS* would   1003 *MS* "If I look up,
for solace, to sun or star.>If ever I, for solace, seek the sun.   1006 *MS* "Fore-
going   *MS* garden,>turf and   1007 *MS* this man   *MS* that!"   1008 *MS*
{beginning of fo. 35}   *MS* {New paragraph indicated by 'N.P.' in left-hand mar-
gin}   *MS* {no comma}   1010 *MS* hit you> flung them   *MS* hard—
1011 *MS* {no comma}   *MS* so grave,>austere,

---

992 *"Had . . . flee!"*: Ps. 55: 6: 'And I said, Oh that I had wings like a dove! for then
would I fly away, and be at rest'. Verses 1–5 of this psalm make it one that might
naturally occur to Pompilia, since they speak of intense suffering, 'the oppression of the
wicked', and 'the terrors of death'.

1001 *keeper in the garden*: i.e. Guido, as a kind of Adam figure. Perhaps this image is
suggested by the Archbishop's image at l. 825.

1006 *turf . . . sky*: as a bird, Pompilia can neither live in the garden that is Guido's
world, nor escape it.

"As Caponsacchi yonder, my tall friend
"A-gazing now. Ah, Guido, you so close?
"Keep on your knees, do! Beg her to forgive!
"My cornet battered like a cannon-ball.   1015
"Good-bye, I'm gone!"—nor waited the reply.

That night at supper, out my husband broke,
"Why was that throwing, that buffoonery?
"Do you think I am your dupe? What man would dare
"Throw comfits in a stranger lady's lap?   1020
" 'T was knowledge of you bred such insolence
"In Caponsacchi; he dared shoot the bolt,
"Using that Conti for his stalking-horse.
"How could you see him this once and no more,
"When he is always haunting hereabout   1025
"At the street-corner or the palace-side,
"Publishing my shame and your impudence?
"You are a wanton,—I a dupe, you think?
"O Christ, what hinders that I kill her quick?"
Whereat he drew his sword and feigned a thrust.   1030

[—]

1012 MS "Grave as the Caponsacchi, yon tall friend,>"Grave as the Caponsacchi,
yonder friend,>As Caponsacchi, yonder, my tall friend,   1013 MS there
too?>so close?   1014–15 MS {lines added later}   1016 MS we left the
theatre>nor waited the reply.   1017 MS {New paragraph indicated by 'N.P.' in
left-hand margin}   MS broke—   1018 MS comfit-throwing buffoonery?>
throwing, that buffoonery?   1021 MS "Knowledge of you has bred this inso-
lence>" 'Twas knowledge of you bred such insolence   1022 MS Caponsac-
chi,—   MS play the fool,>shoot the bolt,   1023 MS "That creature
Conti>"Using that Conti   1024 MS did>could   MS {no com-
ma}   1025 MS hereabouts   1027 MS "Telling [ ] the town my shame,
your>"Publishing my shame and your   1030 MS {line added later}

1012 *tall friend*: Caponsacchi is tall, like Pompilia, as opposed to Guido who is
repeatedly referred to as squat.

1015 *cornet*: a piece of paper, rolled in a conical form and used to wrap things; here
the 'twist of comfits': see l. 975 n.

1022 *bolt*: arrow.

1023 *stalking-horse*: here Caponsacchi uses Conti as his stalking-horse as he 'hunts'
Pompilia: see VI. 639 n.

1029–30 *O . . . thrust*: cf. Pompilia's own deposition, OYB lxxxiv (92): 'At the time
of the affair of the play told above, as soon as we had returned home, he pointed a
pistol at my breast saying: "Oh Christ! What hinders me from laying you out here?" '

All this, now,—being not so strange to me,
Used to such misconception day by day
And broken-in to bear,—I bore, this time,
More quietly than woman should perhaps;
Repeated the mere truth and held my tongue.   1035

Then he said, "Since you play the ignorant,
"I shall instruct you. This amour,—commenced
"Or finished or midway in act, all's one,—
" 'T is the town-talk; so my revenge shall be.
"Does he presume because he is a priest?   1040
"I warn him that the sword I wear shall pink
"His lily-scented cassock through and through,
"Next time I catch him underneath your eaves!"

But he had threatened with the sword so oft
And, after all, not kept his promise. All   1045
I said was "Let God save the innocent!
"Moreover, death is far from a bad fate.
"I shall go pray for you and me, not him;
"And then I look to sleep, come death or, worse,

1031 *MS* {New paragraph indicated by 'New Par.' in left-hand margin}
1032 *MS* with>to   1033 *MS* broken in   1034 *MS* a wife> wo-
man   *MS* perhaps—   1035 *MS* peace.>tongue.   1036 *MS* {New para-
graph indicated by 'New Par.' in left-hand margin}   *MS* said—   1037 *MS*
begun>commenced   1038 *MS* ended>finished   1039 *MS* {beginning of
fo. 36}   *MS* Is>" 'Tis   1040 *MS* {line added later}   *MS* {no quotation
mark at beginning of line}   *1044 *MS* {New paragraph indicated by 'New
Par.' in left-hand margin} *1868 1872* {new paragraph. Paragraphing obscured in *1888*
and *1889* by this line's being at the head of the page}   *MS* me with swords>with the
swords   1046 *MS* was— *1868 1872* was,   *1047 *MS 1868 1872* "Moreover,
1888 1889 "Moreover   1049 *MS* death or worse.>death or, worse,

---

1037 *amour*: love affair (usually illicit); cf. Dryden, *Marriage A-la-Mode* (1673), II. i.
14–15: 'Intrigue, *Philotis*! that's an old phrase; I have laid that word by; *Amour* sounds
better.'

1041 *pink*: stab, pierce.

1042 *lily-scented*: sweet smelling, effeminate, with the implication of cowardice: see
OED² *lily* adj. 1. b. The lily flower was traditionally associated with Mary and Joseph,
the patron saints of Giuseppe Maria Caponsacchi.

1046 *"Let . . . innocent*: repeating the prayer urged on her by Pietro at l. 527.

"Life." So, I slept.

               There may have elapsed a week,
When Margherita,—called my waiting-maid,
Whom it is said my husband found too fair—
Who stood and heard the charge and the reply,
Who never once would let the matter rest   1055
From that night forward, but rang changes still
On this the threat and that the shame, and how
Good cause for jealousy cures jealous fools,
And what a paragon was this same priest
She talked about until I stopped my ears,—   1060
She said, "A week is gone; you comb your hair,
"Then go mope in a corner, cheek on palm,
"Till night comes round again,—so, waste a week
"As if your husband menaced you in sport.
"Have not I some acquaintance with his tricks?   1065
"Oh no, he did not stab the serving-man
"Who made and sang the rhymes about me once!
"For why? They sent him to the wars next day.
"Nor poisoned he the foreigner, my friend,
"Who wagered on the whiteness of my breast,—   1070
"The swarth skins of our city in dispute:

1050 *MS* So I did.>"Life." So I slept.   1051 *MS* {New paragraph indicated by
'N.P.' in right-hand margin}   *MS* {no comma}   1054 *MS* {line added la-
ter}   1056 *MS* forward, rang the *Yale 1* forward>forward,   ★1057 *MS*
threat *1868 1872 1888 1889* thrust   *MS* charge,>shame,   1058 *MS* A cau-
se *MS* men>fools,   1059 *MS* poor>young>same   1061 *MS* said "A
1063 *MS* so waste   1064 *MS* for a>you in   1065 *MS* [ ]>Have
1067 *MS* ^made and^ *MS* once,—   ★1069 *MS 1868 1872* friend, *1888 1889*
friend   1070 *MS* {beginning of fo. 37}   *MS* {no quotation mark at beginning
of line}   1071 *MS* brown>swarth *MS* the>our *MS* dispute,—

    1057 *threat . . . shame*: the 'threat' refers back to 'threatened with the sword' in l.
1044, and is Guido's threat to kill Caponsacchi in ll. 1041–3. The 'shame' is the
opprobrium Pompilia has to bear as an accused but innocent wife. Notice the textual
emendation here: see variants.
    1069 *foreigner*: i.e. a person from another town, from outside Arezzo.
    1071 *swarth*: dark, swarthy. The foreigner, in an argument about the dark-skinned
nature of the people of Arezzo, bets on the whiteness of Margherita's body—a
pointedly intimate reference.

"For, though he paid me proper compliment,
"The Count well knew he was besotted with
"Somebody else, a skin as black as ink,
"(As all the town knew save my foreigner)   1075
"He found and wedded presently,—'Why need
" 'Better revenge?'—the Count asked. But what's here?
"A priest that does not fight, and cannot wed,
"Yet must be dealt with! If the Count took fire
"For the poor pastime of a minute,—me—   1080
"What were the conflagration for yourself,
"Countess and lady-wife and all the rest?
"The priest will perish; you will grieve too late:
"So shall the city-ladies' handsomest
"Frankest and liberalest gentleman   1085
"Die for you, to appease a scurvy dog
"Hanging's too good for. Is there no escape?
"Were it not simple Christian charity
"To warn the priest be on his guard,—save him
"Assured death, save yourself from causing it?   1090
"I meet him in the street. Give me a glove,
"A ring to show for token! Mum's the word!"

I answered "If you were, as styled, my maid,

1072 *MS* {line added later}   *MS* {no quotation mark at beginning of line}
1073 *MS* For he was then besotted with the fool>The Count well knew, he was
besotted with   1074 *MS* {line added later}   *MS* with a soul as>else, a soul
as   1075 {not found in *MS* }   1076 *MS* "Why>'Why   1077 *MS*
"Better revenge?"—>'Better revenge?'—   1078 *MS* priest— *1868 1872*
priest,   *MS* fight,>[ ]>fight,   1081 *MS* yourself?>yourself   1082 *MS*
{line added later}   *MS* "—Countess   1083 *MS* Priest   1091 *MS* street:
give>street. Give   1092 *MS* token: mum's>token! Mum's   1093 *MS*
{New paragraph indicated by 'N.P.' in left-hand margin}   *MS* answered— *1868*
1872 answered,   *MS* maid—

1075 *(As . . . foreigner)*: i.e. the local people know about the dark skin of the woman
the outsider is in love with. Presumably she uses cosmetics to disguise this on the face,
and the outsider will only discover her swarthiness on marriage.
1079 *took fire*: was kindled, set alight (with rage).
1085 *Frankest*: freest, with an overtone of licentiousness: cf. v. 686.
1086 *scurvy dog*: contemptible wretch.
1092 *Mum's the word*: i.e. 'I can keep your secret'.

"I would command you: as you are, you say,
"My husband's intimate,—assist his wife   1095
"Who can do nothing but entreat 'Be still!'
"Even if you speak truth and a crime is planned,
"Leave help to God as I am forced to do!
"There is no other help, or we should craze,
"Seeing such evil with no human cure.   1100
"Reflect that God, who makes the storm desist,
"Can make an angry violent heart subside.
"Why should we venture teach Him governance?
"Never address me on this subject more!"

Next night she said "But I went, all the same,   1105
"—Ay, saw your Caponsacchi in his house,
"And come back stuffed with news I must outpour.
"I told him 'Sir, my mistress is a stone:
"'Why should you harm her for no good you get?
"'For you do harm her—prowl about our place   1110
"'With the Count never distant half the street,
"'Lurking at every corner, would you look!
"''T is certain she has witched you with a spell.
"'Are there not other beauties at your beck?
"'We all know, Donna This and Monna That   1115
"'Die for a glance of yours, yet here you gaze!
"'Go make them grateful, leave the stone its cold!'

1094 *MS* you,—   1096 *MS* 'be   1099 *MS* no other>no>no other *MS*
1868 course, *1872* cause,   1101 *MS* arise>desist,   1102 *MS* {beginning of
fo. 38}   1105 *MS* {New paragraph indicated by 'N.P.' in left-hand mar-
gin}   *MS* said—   *1868 1872* said,   1106 *MS* the>your   1108 *1868 1872*
him,   *MS* "Sir,   1109 *MS* "Why   *MS* do>should   1110 *MS*
"For   *MS* harm—why>harm her—   *MS* the>our   1111 *MS* "With
1112 *MS* "Lurking   1113 *MS* "'Tis   *MS* you have witched him>she has
witched you   1114 *MS* "Are   1115 *MS* "We   1116 *MS* "Die
1117 *MS* "Go

1099 *craze*: go mad.
1101 *God . . . desist*: cf. Ps. 107: 29, Mark. 4: 35–41, etc.
1113 *witched*: bewitched, enchanted.
1115 *Donna . . . That*: Mistress This and Lady That. 'Donna' and 'Monna' are both
Italian titles of respect, roughly equivalent to English 'Lady'.

"And he—oh, he turned first white and then red,
"And then—'To her behest I bow myself,
"'Whom I love with my body and my soul: 1120
"'Only a word i' the bowing! See, I write
"'One little word, no harm to see or hear!
"'Then, fear no further!' This is what he wrote.
"I know you cannot read,—therefore, let me!
"'*My idol!*'"...   1125

        But I took it from her hand
And tore it into shreds. "Why, join the rest
"Who harm me? Have I ever done you wrong?
"People have told me 't is you wrong myself:
"Let it suffice I either feel no wrong   1130
"Or else forgive it,—yet you turn my foe!
"The others hunt me and you throw a noose!"

She muttered "Have your wilful way!" I slept.

Whereupon...no, I leave my husband out!
It is not to do him more hurt, I speak.   1135
Let it suffice, when misery was most,

1118 MS {line added later}   1119 MS myself—   1120 MS {line added
later}   MS "Whom   MS soul—   1121 MS "Only, 1868 "'Only,   MS
in>i'   MS bowing.   1122 MS "One   MS only>little   MS hear,—
1123 MS "Then,   1125 MS idol'!'... Yale 1 "'My idol!'">"'My idol!'" 1868
1872 "'My idol!'"....   1126 MS {New paragraph indicated by 'New Par.' in
right-hand margin}   1127 MS shreds—   MS 1868 {no comma} 1128 MS
hurt?>wrong?   1129 MS myself,—   1130 MS [?never] feel the>either
feel no   1131 MS here are you,   the same,>yet you turn my
foe!   1133 MS {beginning of fo. 39}   MS {New paragraph indicated by
'New P.' in left-hand margin}   1868 1872 muttered,   1134 MS {New para-
graph (already written thus) indicated by 'N.P.' in left-hand margin}   MS 1868
1872 Whereupon..   ★MS 1868 1872 out! 1888 1889 out   1135 MS {line added
later}   MS harm,>hurt,

1125 '*My idol!*': one of the love letters deposited in court begins 'Amato Idolo mio',
though in fact it is signed 'Amarillis' (therefore supposed to be by Pompilia): OYB
xcvii (104).

1134 *Whereupon...no*: the implication is that Pompilia suffers some physical or
sexual abuse at Guido's hands, which she is not now going to mention: cf. l. 738 n.

One day, I swooned and got a respite so.
She stooped as I was slowly coming to,
This Margherita, ever on my trace,
And whispered—"Caponsacchi!"   1140
                    If I drowned,
But woke afloat i' the wave with upturned eyes,
And found their first sight was a star! I turned—
For the first time, I let her have her will,
Heard passively,—"The imposthume at such head,   1145
"One touch, one lancet-puncture would relieve,—
"And still no glance the good physician's way
"Who rids you of the torment in a trice!
"Still he writes letters you refuse to hear.
"He may prevent your husband, kill himself,   1150
"So desperate and all fordone is he!
"Just hear the pretty verse he made to-day!
"A sonnet from Mirtillo. 'Peerless fair...'
"All poetry is difficult to read,
"—The sense of it is, anyhow, he seeks   1155
"Leave to contrive you an escape from hell,
"And for that purpose asks an interview.

1137 *MS* One day, and>Once, and>One day,   *MS* ^a^   *MS* thus.   1138
MS stooped,   1139 *MS* {line added later}   1140 *MS* "Caponsac-
chi"!   1141 *MS* {New paragraph indicated by 'New Par.' in right-hand
margin}   1142 *MS* in>i'   *MS* {no comma}   1146 *MS* little>touch,
one 1148 *MS* "Would rid>"Who rids   1149 *MS* that you hate>you refu-
se   1150 *MS* will>may   *MS* himself—   1151 *MS* he.   1152 *MS*
{line added later}   *MS* to-day—   1153 *MS fair,'...*   1154 *MS* {line
added later}   1155 *MS* that he   1156 *MS* direct you how to escape
this>contrive you an escape from

1139 *trace*: track.
1145 *imposthume...head*: abscess so fully developed, i.e. your suffering so intense;
cf. III. 403, 404 nn.
1150 *prevent*: anticipate, act before.
1151 *fordone*: exhausted, despairing.
1153 *sonnet from Mirtillo*: the name that occurs in the love letters, OYB xcii, xcviii
(100, 105). There is no actual poetry in the love letters, but there is a reference by
Amarillis to 'your very gallant verses, which are so far different from what I merit':
OYB xcv (102).

"I can write, I can grant it in your name,
"Or, what is better, lead you to his house.
"Your husband dashes you against the stones;   1160
"This man would place each fragment in a shrine:
"You hate him, love your husband!"

                                    I returned
"It is not true I love my husband,—no,
"Nor hate this man. I listen while you speak,   1165
"—Assured that what you say is false, the same:
"Much as when once, to me a little child,
"A rough gaunt man in rags, with eyes on fire,
"A crowd of boys and idlers at his heels,
"Rushed as I crossed the Square, and held my head   1170
"In his two hands, 'Here's she will let me speak!
"'You little girl, whose eyes do good to mine,
"'I am the Pope, am Sextus, now the Sixth;
"'And that Twelfth Innocent, proclaimed to-day,
"'Is Lucifer disguised in human flesh!   1175
"'The angels, met in conclave, crowned me!'—thus
"He gibbered and I listened; but I knew
"All was delusion, ere folk interposed

1158–9 *MS* {lines added later}   *MS* {no quotation marks at beginnings of lines}
1162 *MS* "Yet you hate him, and love>"You hate him, love   1163 *MS* {New
paragraph indicated by 'N. Par.' in right-hand margin}   *MS 1868 1872* return-
ned,   1164 *MS* untrue>not true   1165 *MS* love>hate   1168 *MS*
{beginning of fo. 40}   *MS* rags with   1170 *MS* square>Square   1171
MS With>In   1173 *MS* [ ]>now the   1175 *MS* as>in   1176 *MS*
The angels told me!",—thus he gibbered on—>The angels met in conclave, crowned
me!"—thus   1177 *MS* fast: I>and I   1178 *MS 1868 1872* folks

---

1160–1 *"Your...shrine*: the image is of a statue, Pompilia, smashed by Guido her
husband. The pieces are then rescued, set up in a shrine and worshipped by Capon-
sacchi.
   1173 *Sextus ... Sixth*: a wild pun appropriate to a madman: since *sextus* (L.) = sixth,
the man is calling himself 'the Sixth Sixth'. There has never been a Pope Sextus; the
madman's confusion arises from the name Sixtus, borne by five popes, the last being
Sixtus V, Felice Peretti (ruled 1585–90). This name has nothing to do with the number
six, but is a corruption of Xystus, itself a Latinization of Ξυστος.
   1174 *proclaimed to-day*: Browning sets this imaginary incident on 12 July 1691, the
day Innocent XII was proclaimed pope, five days before Pompilia's eleventh birthday.

"'Unfasten him, the maniac!' Thus I know
"All your report of Caponsacchi false,   1180
"Folly or dreaming; I have seen so much
"By that adventure at the spectacle,
"The face I fronted that one first, last time:
"He would belie it by such words and thoughts.
"Therefore while you profess to show him me,   1185
"I ever see his own face. Get you gone!"

"—That will I, nor once open mouth again,—
"No, by Saint Joseph and the Holy Ghost!
"On your head be the damage, so adieu!"

And so more days, more deeds I must forget,   1190
Till . . . what a strange thing now is to declare!
Since I say anything, say all if true!
And how my life seems lengthened as to serve!
It may be idle or inopportune,
But, true?—why, what was all I said but truth,   1195
Even when I found that such as are untrue
Could only take the truth in through a lie?
Now—I am speaking truth to the Truth's self:
God will lend credit to my words this time.

[—]

1179 *MS* maniac',—thus   1180 *MS* this   1181 *MS* dreaming: 1183
MS time;   1184 *MS* thoughts: 1187 *MS* {New paragraph indicated by
'New Par' in left-hand margin}   1189 *MS* be the damage,>the damage be,>be
the damage,   *MS* and adieu!">and so adieu!"   *1190 *MS* {New paragraph
(already written thus) indicated by 'N.P.' in left-hand margin. Paragraphing obscured
in *1868 1872 1888 1889* by this line's being at the head of the page}   *MS* and>
more   1191 *MS 1868 1872* Till . .   *MS* I am to declare!   1192 *MS*
all,—is best.>all, if true:—   1193 *MS* [ ]>And   *MS* is *Yale 1* serve>
serve!   1195 *MS* {beginning of fo. 41}   *MS* Why,   *MS* is it I say>was all I
said   1196 *MS* though>when   1197 *MS* Can>Could   1198 *MS*
Him the Truth.>the Truth's self—

1182 *adventure . . . spectacle*: i.e. the incident at the play, described at ll. 950–90.
1188 *Saint . . . Ghost!*: St Joseph and the Holy Ghost are the two guardians of the
Virgin Mary, the first as her husband, the second as the agent of her pregnancy. By this
oath, Margherita may be suggesting that Pompilia is putting her chastity on something
of a pedestal.
1198 *Truth's self*: i.e. God; cf. John 14: 6.

It had got half through April. I arose   1200
One vivid daybreak,—who had gone to bed
In the old way my wont those last three years,
Careless until, the cup drained, I should die.
The last sound in my ear, the over-night,
Had been a something let drop on the sly   1205
In prattle by Margherita, "Soon enough
"Gaieties end, now Easter's past: a week,
"And the Archbishop gets him back to Rome,—
"Everyone leaves the town for Rome, this Spring,—
"Even Caponsacchi, out of heart and hope,   1210
"Resigns himself and follows with the flock."
I heard this drop and drop like rain outside
Fast-falling through the darkness while she spoke:
So had I heard with like indifference,
"And Michael's pair of wings will arrive first   1215
"At Rome, to introduce the company,
"And bear him from our picture where he fights

1200 *MS* {New paragraph indicated by 'N.P.' in left-hand margin}   *MS* Then it
had got thro'>It had got half thro'   1202 *MS* years—   1206 *MS* the
prattle of>prattle by   *MS* {no comma}   1207 *MS* The gaieties>Gaieties
1209 *MS* City   *MS* spring,—   1212 *MS* outside>that fell—>outside
1213 *MS* {line added later}   *MS* Outsi>Fast-falling   1214 *MS* {no com-
ma}   1216 *MS* {line added later}   *MS 1868* Rome to   1217 *MS* "Bear-
ing   *1868* "Will

1203 *cup drained*: cf. v. 879 n.

1204 *over-night*: preceding evening (adj.), applying to 'sound in my ear', with the
implication that it continues to affect her through the night till the next day.

1208 *Archbishop . . . Rome*: this draws on information given in one of the love letters
of 'Mirtillo': 'I wish to know whether you can leave Sunday evening, that is,
tomorrow evening, for if you do not go away tomorrow evening, God knows when
you will be able to do so, because of the scarcity of carriages, owing to the fact that on
Wednesday the Bishop departs with three carriages': OYB xcviii (105).

1210 *Even Caponsacchi*: in his examination for the trial for flight Caponsacchi
affirmed that he had decided to go to Rome 'on business' and had told his intention
to Canon Conti *before* he was approached by Pompilia: OYB lxxxviii (95).

1215–19 *Michael's . . . defender*: the painting Pompilia refers to as 'our picture' is the
fresco 'Triumph of St Michael' by Spinello Aretino (1346–1410) in the Church of San
Francesco, Arezzo. It depicts the archangel St Michael, with golden wings, slaying the
dragon, Satan. In Pompilia's image St Michael is Caponsacchi (her protecting angel)
who is departing for Rome, and Guido is the dragon, Satan, left free to wreak terror.
The fresco is reproduced in Thomas: 317.

"Satan,—expect to have that dragon loose
"And never a defender!"—my sole thought
Being still, as night came, "Done, another day!   1220
"How good to sleep and so get nearer death!"—
When, what, first thing at daybreak, pierced the sleep
With a summons to me? Up I sprang alive,
Light in me, light without me, everywhere
Change! A broad yellow sunbeam was let fall   1225
From heaven to earth,—a sudden drawbridge lay,
Along which marched a myriad merry motes,
Mocking the flies that crossed them and recrossed
In rival dance, companions new-born too.
On the house-eaves, a dripping shag of weed   1230
Shook diamonds on each dull grey lattice-square,
As first one, then another bird leapt by,
And light was off, and lo was back again,
Always with one voice,—where are two such joys?—
The blessed building-sparrow! I stepped forth,   1235
Stood on the terrace,—o'er the roofs, such sky!
My heart sang, "I too am to go away,
"I too have something I must care about,
"Carry away with me to Rome, to Rome!
"The bird brings hither sticks and hairs and wool,   1240
"And nowhere else i' the world; what fly breaks rank,
"Falls out of the procession that befits,
"From window here to window there, with all
"The world to choose,—so well he knows his course?

1219 *MS* only>sole   *MS* thought was still>thought   1220 *MS* {line added later}   *MS* {no quotation mark at beginning of line}   1222 *MS* woke>pierced   1224 *MS* me,—   1225 *MS* ^yellow^   *MS* 1868 1872 sun-beam   1226 *MS* {beginning of fo. 42}   1229 *MS* newborn   *MS* 1868 1872 1888 1889 too. BrU too>too. {point printed badly in 1888}   1230 *MS* eaves outside,>house-eaves,   1231 *MS* my>each   1232 *MS* [?lit there]>leapt by, 1237 *MS* sang "I   1238 *Yale 2* I>"I   1241 *MS* in>i'

1230–5 *house-eaves . . . building-sparrow*: the image is of a joyful pair of sparrows building a nest in the palace's eaves, each sparrow shaking glittering rainwater from a clump of weed on the eaves as it goes to and fro at its work. This nest-building image is a beautiful affirmation of Pompilia's pregnancy.

1233 *light . . . again*: lightly and quickly flew away and then returned.

"I have my purpose and my motive too,   1245
"My march to Rome, like any bird or fly!
"Had I been dead! How right to be alive!
"Last night I almost prayed for leave to die,
"Wished Guido all his pleasure with the sword
"Or the poison,—poison, sword, was but a trick,   1250
"Harmless, may God forgive him the poor jest!
"My life is charmed, will last till I reach Rome!
"Yesterday, but for the sin,—ah, nameless be
"The deed I could have dared against myself!
"Now—see if I will touch an unripe fruit   1255
"And risk the health I want to have and use!
"Not to live, now, would be the wickedness,—
"For life means to make haste and go to Rome
"And leave Arezzo, leave all woes at once!"

Now, understand here, by no means mistake!   1260
Long ago had I tried to leave that house
When it seemed such procedure would stop sin;
And still failed more the more I tried—at first
The Archbishop, as I told you,—next, our lord
The Governor,—indeed I found my way,   1265
I went to the great palace where he rules,

1245 MS "I have my purpose in my march to Rome>"I have my motive for my
march to Rome>"I have my purpose and my motive too   1246 MS {line added
later}   MS For my   1248 MS die—   1249 MS Let Guido have>
Wished Guido all   1250 MS it was all a harmless trick!>poison, sword, was
but a trick—   1251 MS {line added later}   MS Harmless—   1252 MS
was   1255 MS "Now,—   *MS 1868 1872 1888 fruit, DC BrU fruit,>fruit 1889
fruit   1256 MS {beginning of fo. 43}   1258 MS Rome,   1259 MS
"Leave this Arezzo and>"And leave Arezzo leave   1260 MS {New paragraph
indicated by 'N.P.' in left-hand margin}   MS Now understand   MS and>by
no   MS mistake,—>mistake!—   1263 MS tried;   1264 MS I have
told   1266 MS dwells>lives>rules,

1253–4 nameless . . . myself: i.e. she contemplated suicide.
1255 unripe fruit: Pompilia is so protective of her unborn child that she will avoid
unripe fruit, superstitiously believed to bring on labour; cf. The Duchess of Malfi, II. i,
where unripe apricots have this effect.

Though I knew well 't was he who,—when I gave
A jewel or two, themselves had given me,
Back to my parents,—since they wanted bread,
They who had never let me want a nosegay,—he   1270
Spoke of the jail for felons, if they kept
What was first theirs, then mine, so doubly theirs,
Though all the while my husband's most of all!
I knew well who had spoke the word wrought this:
Yet, being in extremity, I fled   1275
To the Governor, as I say,—scarce opened lip
When—the cold cruel snicker close behind—
Guido was on my trace, already there,
Exchanging nod and wink for shrug and smile,
And I—pushed back to him and, for my pains   1280
Paid with . . . but why remember what is past?
I sought out a poor friar the people call
The Roman, and confessed my sin which came
Of their sin,—that fact could not be repressed,—
The frightfulness of my despair in God: 1285

1269 *MS* parents when>parents,—since   1271 *MS* who should keep>if they
kept   1272 *MS* their's, doubly so:>so doubly their's,   1273 *MS* {line
added later}   *MS* Yet   1274 *MS* who[ ]>who   *MS* this—   1275 *MS*
sought>fled   1276 *MS* The>To the   1279 *MS* {line added later}
1280 *MS* I,   *MS* and for   *1868 1872* pains,   1281 *MS 1868 1872*
with . .   1282 *MS* I went at last to a friar, a [?man] they call>I sought out a
poor friar the people call   1283 *MS* sin—   1284 *MS* that much   *MS*
repressed:>repressed,—   1285 *MS* {line added later}   *MS* God:—

1267–73 *he who . . . all*: this is based on a detail in the letter of the Governor of
Arezzo to Abate Paolo, 2 Aug. 1694: 'Finally, these same Comparini had taken away all
her jewellery from the Signora [Pompilia], which I forced them to restore to her':
OYB lxxxi (90). The way Browning uses this detail is an interesting instance of his
awareness of issues of patriarchy and property: he transforms the apparently just
decision of OYB into one that emphasizes Pompilia's powerlessness and her lack of
rights, showing the aristocrats of Arezzo ganging up against her and her parents.
   1274 *who . . . this*: i.e. Guido, who had informed the Governor.
   1281 *Paid with . . .*: 'Guido, it seems clear, punishes her by rape': Brady, 53.
   1283 *The Roman*: Pompilia's deposition mentions him briefly as 'an Augustinian
father, whom they call the Roman': OYB lxxxiv (92). He is also mentioned at SS 7.
For another account of Pompilia's beseeching of 'the Roman' see III. 1015–38.
   1285 *frightfulness . . . God*: i.e. her thoughts of suicide: see ll. 1253–4 n. It is this that
accounts for the priest's 'horror' in the next line.

And, feeling, through the grate, his horror shake,
Implored him, "Write for me who cannot write,
"Apprise my parents, make them rescue me!
"You bid me be courageous and trust God:
"Do you in turn dare somewhat, trust and write   1290
"'Dear friends, who used to be my parents once,
"'And now declare you have no part in me,
"'This is some riddle I want wit to solve,
"'Since you must love me with no difference.
"'Even suppose you altered,—there's your hate,   1295
"'To ask for: hate of you two dearest ones
"'I shall find liker love than love found here,
"'If husbands love their wives. Take me away
"'And hate me as you do the gnats and fleas,
"'Even the scorpions! How I shall rejoice!'   1300
"Write that and save me!" And he promised—wrote
Or did not write; things never changed at all:
He was not like the Augustinian here!
Last, in a desperation I appealed
To friends, whoever wished me better days,   1305
To Guillichini, that's of kin,—"What, I—
"Travel to Rome with you? A flying gout
"Bids me deny my heart and mind my leg!"
Then I tried Conti, used to brave—laugh back
The louring thunder when his cousin scowled   1310

1287 *MS* {beginning of fo. 44}   *MS* Entreated>Implored him   1288 *MS*
Inform>"Apprise   1290 *MS* send just this>trust and write   1293 *MS*
"'Th[ ]>This   1294 *MS* difference,—   1296 *MS* {line added later}
1298 *MS* wives: take>wives. Take   1299 *MS* fleas—   1300 *MS* scor-
pions—   1302 *MS* I>things   *MS* all.   1303 {not found in *MS*}
1304 *MS* {no comma}   *MS* cried>appealed   1306 *MS* The   1307
MS you, [ ] [ ] []>you? A   1309 *MS* Then Conti,>Then [ ] Conti,>Then I
tried Conti,   *MS* that's to try>used to brave—

1303 *the Augustinian*: i.e. Don Celestine: see ll. 31–3 n.

1306 *Guillichini . . . kin*: Signor Gregorio Guillichini, relative and friend of Guido,
was charged by the prosecution with complicity in the elopement and adultery with
Pompilia; here, as elsewhere, Browning sees this as false; cf. II. 934 n.

1307 *flying gout*: an attack of gout, an inflammatory disease, which manifests itself in
different joints.

At me protected by his presence: "You—
"Who well know what you cannot save me from,—
"Carry me off! What frightens you, a priest?"
He shook his head, looked grave—"Above my strength!
"Guido has claws that scratch, shows feline teeth;   1315
"A formidabler foe than I dare fret:
"Give me a dog to deal with, twice the size!
"Of course I am a priest and Canon too,
"But.. by the bye.. though both, not quite so bold
"As he, my fellow-Canon, brother-priest,   1320
"The personage in such ill odour here
"Because of the reports—pure birth o' the brain!
"Our Caponsacchi, he's your true Saint George
"To slay the monster, set the Princess free,
"And have the whole High-Altar to himself: 1325
"I always think so when I see that piece
"I' the Pieve, that's his church and mine, you know:
"Though you drop eyes at mention of his name!"

That name had got to take a half-grotesque
Half-ominous, wholly enigmatic sense,   1330
Like any by-word, broken bit of song

1311 *MS* presence—   1312 *MS* {line added later}   *MS* [ ]>best 1313
MS off,—what   1315 *MS* a long [?scratch], pulls many wires,—   1316
MS man>foe   *MS* [ ]>fret—   1318 *MS* {beginning of fo. 45}   *MS* {no
comma}   1319 *MS* not quite so bold, though both,>though both, not quite so
bold, *1868* bold,   1320 *MS* the one [ ]>he, my fellow-Canon,   1322 *MS*
calumny>[ ] o' the brain—>birth o' the brain— *1868* brain—   1323 *MS*
[?On]>Our   *MS* your>our   1325-7 *MS* {lines added later}   *MS* {no quo-
tation marks at beginnings of lines}   *1326 *MS* *1868* *1872* "I *1888* *1889*
'I {broken sort}   1329 *MS* {New paragraph indicated by 'N.P.' in left-hand
margin}   1331 *MS* *1868* *1872* bye-word,

1316 *fret*: annoy.

1323 *Saint George*: cf. I. 585, VI. 1077–8 nn.

1325-7 *High-Altar... Pieve*: the painting on the high altar of the Church of the
Pieve is Giorgio Vasari's 'St George and the Dragon'. It shows a swashbuckling St
George on a large white horse, already having speared the upreared dragon in the
mouth, about to slash off its head with a sword. In 1865 the painting was moved to the
Church of the Abbey of Santa Flora and Lucina, also in Arezzo. There is a good
reproduction in Thomas, 318.

1331 *by-word*: proverb, common saying.

Born with a meaning, changed by mouth and mouth
That mix it in a sneer or smile, as chance
Bids, till it now means nought but ugliness
And perhaps shame.

1335

               —All this intends to say,
That, over-night, the notion of escape
Had seemed distemper, dreaming; and the name,—
Not the man, but the name of him, thus made
Into a mockery and disgrace,—why, she
Who uttered it persistently, had laughed,
"I name his name, and there you start and wince
"As criminal from the red tongs' touch!"—yet now,
Now, as I stood letting morn bathe me bright,
Choosing which butterfly should bear my news,—
The white, the brown one, or that tinier blue,—
The Margherita, I detested so,
In she came—"The fine day, the good Spring time!
"What, up and out at window? That is best.
"No thought of Caponsacchi?—who stood there
"All night on one leg, like the sentry crane,
"Under the pelting of your water-spout—
"Looked last look at your lattice ere he leave

1340

1345

1350

1332 *MS* Bor[?ne]>Born   *MS* {no comma}   1333 *MS* mix[?t]>mix
1334 *MS* Lends,   1336 *MS* {New paragraph indicated by 'N.P.' in right-hand
margin}   1338 *MS* seemed>been   1339 *MS* that name of his, rema-
de   1341 *MS* Who uttered it cried "There you start and wince>Who uttered
it persistently, would laugh.   1342 *MS* {line added later}   *MS* "I name his
name, and there you start and wince   1346 *MS* one or   1347 *MS* {line
added later}   1348 *MS* time of Spring!>Spring time!   1349 *MS*
[?at]>out   *MS* [ ]>at   *MS* good too.> best.   1352 *MS* {beginning of fo.
46}   1353 *MS* His>Looked

1336 *this intends to say*: as Cook notes, an Italian idiom: 'ciò vuol dire'.

1351 *one leg . . . crane*: see Aelian, *De Natura Animalium* (*c*.AD 200), III. 13, 'Cranes
and their migrations': '. . . three or four mount guard for all the others; and in order to
avoid falling asleep during their watch they stand on one leg, but with the other held
up they clutch a stone firmly and securely in their claws. Their object is that, if they
should inadvertently drop off to sleep, the stone should fall and wake them with the
sound'; cf. I. 232 n. This provides a comic image of Caponsacchi as the besotted lover.

"Our city, bury his dead hope at Rome.
"Ay, go to looking-glass and make you fine,   1355
"While he may die ere touch one least loose hair
"You drag at with the comb in such a rage!"

I turned—"Tell Caponsacchi he may come!"

"Tell him to come? Ah, but, for charity,
"A truce to fooling! Come? What,—come this eve?   1360
"Peter and Paul! But I see through the trick!
"Yes, come, and take a flower-pot on his head,
"Flung from your terrace! No joke, sincere truth?"

How plainly I perceived hell flash and fade
O' the face of her,—the doubt that first paled joy,   1365
Then, final reassurance I indeed
Was caught now, never to be free again!
What did I care?—who felt myself of force
To play with silk, and spurn the horsehair-springe.

"But—do you know that I have bade him come,   1370
"And in your own name? I presumed so much,
"Knowing the thing you needed in your heart.
"But somehow—what had I to show in proof?

1354 *MS* hopes   *MS 1868* Rome?   1358 *MS* {New paragraph indicated by
'N.P.' in left-hand margin}   1359 *MS* {New paragraph indicated by 'N.P.' in
left-hand margin}   *MS* [ ]>but,   1360 *MS* Come and>Come? What,—
1361 *MS 1868* trick—   1362 *MS 1868* head   1363 *MS* all sincere?">
sincere truth?"   1364 *MS* {New paragraph indicated by 'N.P.' in left-hand
margin}   *MS* such>hell   1365 *MS* On   *MS* dashed the>first dashed
1366 *MS* The final *Yale 1* Then[ ]>Then,   1367 *MS* springed, caught>caught
now,   1369 *MS* the fetter,>the silk, and   *MS* horsehair springe.   1370–6
MS {lines added later}   1370 *MS* {New paragraph indicated by 'New Par.' in
left-hand margin}   *MS* come—   1371 *MS* name?—   *MS* {no comma}

1361 *Peter and Paul!*: by St Peter and St Paul (an oath).

1368–9 *of force . . . horsehair-springe*: capable of playing with the bait or decoy, while
avoiding the trap itself. Birds were attracted by bright-coloured silk into a tougher
snare. Cf. *Hamlet*, I. iii. 115: 'springes to catch woodcocks'.

"He would not come: half-promised, that was all,
"And wrote the letters you refused to read.   1375
"What is the message that shall move him now?"

"After the Ave Maria, at first dark,
"I will be standing on the terrace, say!"

"I would I had a good long lock of hair
"Should prove I was not lying! Never mind!"   1380

Off she went—"May he not refuse, that's all—
"Fearing a trick!"

                    I answered, "He will come."
And, all day, I sent prayer like incense up
To God the strong, God the beneficent,   1385
God ever mindful in all strife and strait,
Who, for our own good, makes the need extreme,
Till at the last He puts forth might and saves.
An old rhyme came into my head and rang

1375 {not found in *MS*}   1376 *1868* {no quotation mark at end of line}
1377 *MS* {New paragraph indicated by 'N.P.' in left-hand margin}   *MS*—
"After   1378 *MS* {no quotation mark at end of line}   1379 *MS* {no new
paragraph}   1381 *MS* {New paragraph indicated by 'N.P.' in left-hand mar-
gin}   1382 *MS* {no quotation mark at beginning of line}   1383 *MS* {no
new paragraph}   *MS* answered—   1384 *MS* {New paragraph indicated by
'N.P.' in left-hand margin}   *MS* All that>And all   *MS* {no commas}   1385 *MS*
[ ]>strong,   *MS* strong and merciful,>beneficent,   1386 *MS* present>mind-
ful   *MS* all kind of straits,>strife and strait,>all strife and strait,   1387 *MS*
good makes us need Him much,>good makes the need extreme,   1388 *MS*
Then>Till   *MS* ^He^   *MS* His might>might   1389 *MS* sang

---

1377 *After the Ave Maria*: i.e. after the angelus bell, about 6 p.m.: see VI. 574 n.

1379 *lock of hair*: a traditional love token. Margherita is asking for such a love token
to show Caponsacchi; Pompilia, of course, silently refuses it.

1384 *prayer like incense*: cf. Ps. 141: 2: 'Let my prayer be set forth before thee as
incense; and the lifting up of my hands as the evening sacrifice.'

1389 *old rhyme*: the story that follows is intended to be like an incident in a medieval
saint's life, set at the time of the crusades. We have not traced this 'old rhyme' or ballad,
and suspect it is Browning's invention, especially given the way it contrasts with
Guido's crusader tale at V. 1419–25.

Of how a virgin, for the faith of God,   1390
Hid herself, from the Paynims that pursued,
In a cave's heart; until a thunderstone,
Wrapped in a flame, revealed the couch and prey
And they laughed—"Thanks to lightning, ours at last!"
And she cried "Wrath of God, assert His love!   1395
"Servant of God, thou fire, befriend His child!"
And lo, the fire she grasped at, fixed its flash,
Lay in her hand a calm cold dreadful sword
She brandished till pursuers strewed the ground,
So did the souls within them die away,   1400
As o'er the prostrate bodies, sworded, safe,
She walked forth to the solitudes and Christ:
So should I grasp the lightning and be saved!

And still, as the day wore, the trouble grew
Whereby I guessed there would be born a star,   1405
Until at an intense throe of the dusk,
I started up, was pushed, I dare to say,

1390 *MS* {beginning of fo. 47}   *MS* Virgin,   1391 *MS* paynims   1392
MS ca[ ]>cave's   *MS* heart until   *MS* thunderbolt>thunderstone   1393 *MS*
flame—   *MS* prey; *1868 1872* prey: 1394 *MS* "Thank the>"Thanks
to   1395 *MS* Fire>Wrath   *MS* befriend His child!"   1396 {not found
in *MS*}   1398 *MS* dread great>dreadful   1399 *MS* earth,> ground,
1400 *MS* hearts>souls   *MS* at once,   1401 *MS* [?And]>As   *MS* safe
1402 *MS* and>of   1404 *MS* {New paragraph indicated by 'N.P.' in left-hand
margin}   1405 *MS* [ ]>Whereby   *MS* you know>you knew>I guessed *MS*
will>would   1406 *MS* one last>an   *MS* ^the^

1391 *Paynims*: see v. 1421 n.
1392 *thunderstone*: meteorite. Browning originally wrote 'thunderbolt', suggesting
the old idea of lightning as a solid bolt or dart that is the destructive force within the
lightning flash.
1393 *couch*: hiding place; cf. the use of the verb at l. 1480.
1397 *fixed its flash*: i.e. solidified.
1404–5 *trouble . . . star*: cf. l. 1387: Pompilia feels that, since her difficulty is intensi-
fying, therefore God will rescue her by means of the star (Caponsacchi), just as, in the
tale she has just told, the virgin at the point of her deepest need was rescued by the
shooting star, the meteorite. Like the meteorite, Caponsacchi initially seems a source
of danger, but is then transformed by God into an agent of rescue.
1406 *throe*: convulsion, birth-pang: an unusual image.
1407 *pushed . . . say*: cf. i. 40–1, where the poet himself is 'pushed' by the 'Hand' of
God.

Out on the terrace, leaned and looked at last
Where the deliverer waited me: the same
Silent and solemn face, I first descried   1410
At the spectacle, confronted mine once more.

So was that minute twice vouchsafed me, so
The manhood, wasted then, was still at watch
To save me yet a second time: no change
Here, though all else changed in the changing world!   1415

I spoke on the instant, as my duty bade,
In some such sense as this, whatever the phrase.

"Friend, foolish words were borne from you to me;
"Your soul behind them is the pure strong wind,
"Not dust and feathers which its breath may bear: 1420
"These to the witless seem the wind itself,
"Since proving thus the first of it they feel.
"If by mischance you blew offence my way,
"The straws are dropt, the wind desists no whit,
"And how such strays were caught up in the street   1425
"And took a motion from you, why inquire?
"I speak to the strong soul, no weak disguise.
"If it be truth,—why should I doubt it truth?—
"You serve God specially, as priests are bound,
"And care about me, stranger as I am,   1430
"So far as wish my good,—that miracle

1409 *MS* me—   1410 *MS* Silent, grave, [ ]>Silent and   *MS* before revealed
>I first descried   1412 *MS* {New paragraph indicated by 'N.P.' in left-hand
margin}   *MS* ^that^   1413 *MS* {no commas}   1414 *MS* time,
1415 *MS* and>though   1416 *MS* {New paragraph indicated by 'N.P.' in left-
hand margin}   *MS* bade—   1418 *MS* {no new paragraph} *MS*—"Friend,
1419 *MS* {beginning of fo. 48}   *MS* wind—   1420 *MS* bear,—   1421
MS Seem itself since the first of it they feel.>These to the witless seem the
wind itself   1422 *MS* {line added later}   1427 *MS* such>weak
1431 *MS* me [ ],—>my good,— *Yale 2* good,—>good:

    1431 *that miracle*: this miracle (from the preceding line) is the thought that, as a
stranger, Caponsacchi nonetheless wishes her good. All Pompilia's experience has told
against the possibility of such generosity.

"I take to intimate He wills you serve
"By saving me,—what else can He direct?
"Here is the service. Since a long while now,
"I am in course of being put to death: 1435
"While death concerned nothing but me, I bowed
"The head and bade, in heart, my husband strike.
"Now I imperil something more, it seems,
"Something that's truelier me than this myself,
"Something I trust in God and you to save.   1440
"You go to Rome, they tell me: take me there,
"Put me back with my people!"

                                    He replied—
The first word I heard ever from his lips,
All himself in it,—an eternity   1445
Of speech, to match the immeasurable depth
O' the soul that then broke silence—"I am yours."

So did the star rise, soon to lead my step,
Lead on, nor pause before it should stand still
Above the House o' the Babe,—my babe to be,   1450
That knew me first and thus made me know him,
That had his right of life and claim on mine,
And would not let me die till he was born,
But pricked me at the heart to save us both,

1433 *MS* it>he   1440 *MS* Which I [?relie up]>Something I trust
in   1443 *MS* {New paragraph indicated by 'N P.' in right-hand mar-
gin}   1444 *MS* back from him,>from his lips,   1446 *MS* immeasurable
depths of soul>to span the unfathomed depths [ ]>to span the unfathomed depths of
soul>to match the immeasurable depths *1868* depths   1447 *MS* Of that soul
that>Of that soul>O' the soul that   1448 *MS* {New paragraph indicated by
'N.P.' in left-hand margin}   *MS* step—   1449 *MS* {beginning of fo.
49}   *MS* ^should^   1450 *MS* house   *MS* of>o'   *MS* babe,—
>Babe,—   *MS* be—   1451 *MS* {line added later}   *MS* first:>first
1452 *MS* rights>right   *MS* {no comma}   1453 *MS* {no comma}

1450 *House o' the Babe*: Caponsacchi is the star that will guide Pompilia to the
Comparini's villa, the house where her child will be born, just as the star in Matt. 2:
9–11 led the Magi to the house of the Christ-child at Bethlehem.

Saying "Have you the will? Leave God the way!"   1455
And the way was Caponsacchi—"mine," thank God!
He was mine, he is mine, he will be mine.

No pause i' the leading and the light! I know,
Next night there was a cloud came, and not he:
But I prayed through the darkness till it broke   1460
And let him shine. The second night, he came.

"The plan is rash; the project desperate:
"In such a flight needs must I risk your life,
"Give food for falsehood, folly or mistake,
"Ground for your husband's rancour and revenge"—
So he began again, with the same face.   1466
I felt that, the same loyalty—one star
Turning now red that was so white before—
One service apprehended newly: just
A word of mine and there the white was back!   1470

"No, friend, for you will take me! 'T is yourself
"Risk all, not I,—who let you, for I trust
"In the compensating great God: enough!
"I know you: when is it that you will come?"
                         [—]

1455 *MS* will,—leave>will?—Leave   1457 *MS* {line added later}
1458 *MS* {New paragraph indicated by 'N.P.' in left-hand margin}   *MS*
in   1459 *MS* ^cloud^   *MS* he—   1461 *MS* He said—"The plan is
rash;>The second night, he came.   1462 *MS* {line added later}   *MS* {New
paragraph indicated by 'N. P.' (deleted) in right-hand margin and 'New Par.' above
line}   1463 *MS* must needs be risk of life,>needs must I risk your life,
1464 *MS* Food for men's lying,>"Give food for lying,   1466 *MS* {line added
later}   *MS* {no comma}   1467 *MS* that—   *MS* loyalty,—   1468 *MS* be-
fore,—   1470 *MS* was! "No,>was back!   1471 *MS* {New paragraph in-
dicated by 'New P.' in left-hand margin}   *MS* me: 'tis>me! 'Tis   1472 *MS*
"That risks,>"Risk all,   1473 *MS* enough—   1474 *MS* "We understand
each other. You>"I know you: when is it that you

1456 *"mine,"*: a reference to Caponsacchi's "I am yours", l. 1447.
1467–8 *one star. . . before*: Caponsacchi (the star) turns 'red' with embarrassment as
he explains to Pompilia how compromising her flight with him might appear. His
'service' or commitment to her (l. 1469) is never in doubt.

"To-morrow at the day's dawn." Then I heard 1475
What I should do: how to prepare for flight
And where to fly.

        That night my husband bade
"—You, whom I loathe, beware you break my sleep
"This whole night! Couch beside me like the corpse 1480
"I would you were!" The rest you know, I think—
How I found Caponsacchi and escaped.

And this man, men call sinner? Jesus Christ!
Of whom men said, with mouths Thyself mad'st once,
"He hath a devil"—say he was Thy saint, 1485
My Caponsacchi! Shield and show—unshroud
In Thine own time the glory of the soul
If aught obscure,—if ink-spot, from vile pens
Scribbling a charge against him—(I was glad
Then, for the first time, that I could not write)— 1490
Flirted his way, have flecked the blaze!

                For me,

1475 *MS* {New paragraph indicated by 'New P.' in left-hand margin}   *MS* day break.">day's dawn."   1476 *MS* What I should do. That night my husband bade>What I should do: how to prepare for flight   1477 *MS* {line added later}   1478 *MS* {New paragraph indicated by 'N.Par.' in right-hand margin}   1479 *MS* let me not lose one wink>beware you break my sleep 1480 *MS* Of>"This   *MS* night, lie>night, couch *Yale 1* Couched> Couch   1481 *MS* {'The rest you know, I think—' changed to new paragraph and then changed back again}   1483 *MS* {beginning of fo. 50}   *MS* {New paragraph indicated by 'N.P.' in left-hand margin}   *MS* they>men   *MS* Christ,   1484 *MS* thyself made>Thyself mad'st   1487 *MS* One day thine>In Thine   *MS* splendor>glory   1488 *MS* if>some>if   1489 *MS* against—I>against him—(I   1490 *MS* write—>write)—   1491 *MS* has *Yale 1* has>have   *MS* white!>blaze!   1492 *MS* {New paragraph indicated by 'N.P.' in right-hand margin}

    1480 *Couch*: lie (often used of animals).

    1485 *"He hath a devil"*: cf. John 7: 20, 8: 48, etc., words spoken against Christ. Just as people misunderstood and persecuted Christ, so they misunderstand and persecute Caponsacchi. Pompilia appeals to Christ to proclaim Caponsacchi a saint.

    1486 *Shield and show*: protect and reveal.

    1491 *Flirted his way*: splashed, flicked in his direction—referring to the ink-spot of l. 1488.

    flecked the blaze: spotted or dimmed the lustre (of the revealed soul of Caponsacchi). The alliterative pairing of 'flirted' and 'flecked' also occurs at v. 503–4.

'T is otherwise: let men take, sift my thoughts
—Thoughts I throw like the flax for sun to bleach!
I did pray, do pray, in the prayer shall die,   1495
"Oh, to have Caponsacchi for my guide!"
Ever the face upturned to mine, the hand
Holding my hand across the world,—a sense
That reads, as only such can read, the mark
God sets on woman, signifying so   1500
She should—shall peradventure—be divine;
Yet 'ware, the while, how weakness mars the print
And makes confusion, leaves the thing men see,
—Not this man sees,—who from his soul, re-writes
The obliterated charter,—love and strength   1505
Mending what's marred. "So kneels a votarist,
"Weeds some poor waste traditionary plot
"Where shrine once was, where temple yet may be,
"Purging the place but worshipping the while,
"By faith and not by sight, sight clearest so,—   1510

1493 *MS* otherwise,—   *MS* take and sift>take, sift   *MS* thoughts!   1494 *MS*
grain, the sun shall bleach:>flax for sun to bleach: 1495 *MS 1868* think, do
think,   *MS 1868* thought   *MS* now>shall   *MS* die—   1496 *MS 1868* That
to   *MS* friend—>guide, *1868* guide,   1498 *MS* man>sense   1499 *MS*
To see, as such men only see,>To see, as only such men see,>That reads, as only such
can read,   1500 *MS* [ ]>God   1501 *MS* They should be, shall hereafter
be, divine>She should, shall peradventure be, divine—   1504 *MS* man,—
who from his own   1505 *MS* [?glory],—>[ ],—>charter,—   1506 *MS*
marred,—so *1868* marred: 1507–11 *MS* {no quotation marks at beginnings of
lines}   1507 *MS* spot>plot   1508 *MS* [ ]>shrine once   *MS* shall>
may   1509 *MS* ^but^   *MS* while.   1510 *MS* {line added later}   *MS*
so, *Yale 1* so,>so,—

1499–1501 *mark . . . divine*: i.e. the pains of childbirth in Gen. 3: 16, the mark of
woman's fallen nature, but also a promise of her redemption, since it is through the
birth of Christ that humanity is redeemed.
1504 *this man*: i.e. Caponsacchi.
1506 *votarist*: devotee, religious worshipper.
1507 *traditionary*: hallowed by tradition, ancient.
1510 *By faith . . . sight*: cf. 2 Cor. 5: 7: 'For we walk by faith, not by sight', John 20:
29: 'blessed are they that have not seen, and yet have believed', etc.

"Such way the saints work,"—says Don Celestine.
But I, not privileged to see a saint
Of old when such walked earth with crown and palm,
If I call "saint" what saints call something else—
The saints must bear with me, impute the fault   1515
To a soul i' the bud, so starved by ignorance,
Stinted of warmth, it will not blow this year
Nor recognize the orb which Spring-flowers know.
But if meanwhile some insect with a heart
Worth floods of lazy music, spendthrift joy—   1520
Some fire-fly renounced Spring for my dwarfed cup,
Crept close to me, brought lustre for the dark,
Comfort against the cold,—what though excess
Of comfort should miscall the creature—sun?
What did the sun to hinder while harsh hands   1525
Petal by petal, crude and colourless,
Tore me? This one heart gave me all the Spring!

Is all told? There's the journey: and where's time

1511 *Yale 1* Such>"Such   *MS* work,—   *MS* Celestine—   1513 *MS* {beginning of fo. 51}   1515 *MS* [ ], [?you must]>Saintship must bear with me—   1516 *MS* in>i'   *MS* dwarfed>starved   1517 *MS* sun>warmth   1518 *MS* understand>justify>recognize   *MS* spring-flowers   *MS* bless:>know: 1519 *MS* an>some   *MS* heart—   1521 *MS* [?A]>Some *MS* starved>dwarfed   1522 *MS* {no commas}   *MS* *1868* me with lustre   1526 *MS* crude, blank, odourless,>crude and colourless, 1527 *MS* *1868* brought   1528–31 *MS* {lines added later}   *1528 *MS* {New paragraph indicated by 'N.P.' in right-hand margin} *1868* *1872* {new paragraph. Paragraphing obscured in *1888* and *1889* by this line's being at the head of the page}

---

   sight clearest so: i.e. sight being clearest when you worship by faith and not by physical sight. Cook (p. 155) notes this as an absolute construction typical of Browning.

   1513 *crown and palm*: the traditional iconographic attributes of a martyr, after texts like Rev. 4: 4, 7: 9.

   1518 *the orb*: i.e. the sun.

   1519–20 *some insect . . . joy*: i.e. some insect (Caponsacchi) so vital that it is worth all the delights of spring. The insect renounces these delights in order to warm the starved bud (Pompilia).

   1522 *lustre . . . dark*: i.e. brightness to illuminate my darkness.

To tell you how that heart burst out in shine?
Yet certain points do press on me too hard.   1530
Each place must have a name, though I forget:
How strange it was—there where the plain begins
And the small river mitigates its flow—
When eve was fading fast, and my soul sank,
And he divined what surge of bitterness,   1535
In overtaking me, would float me back
Whence I was carried by the striding day—
So,—"This grey place was famous once," said he—
And he began that legend of the place
As if in answer to the unspoken fear,   1540
And told me all about a brave man dead,
Which lifted me and let my soul go on!
How did he know too,—at that town's approach
By the rock-side,—that in coming near the signs
Of life, the house-roofs and the church and tower,   1545
I saw the old boundary and wall o' the world
Rise plain as ever round me, hard and cold,
As if the broken circlet joined again,
Tightened itself about me with no break,—
As if the town would turn Arezzo's self,—   1550

1529 *MS* To tell that point where that heart burst in shine?   1530 *MS* hard—
1531 *MS* forget—   1532 *MS* the>[ ]>the   1533 *MS* [ ]>small
1534 *MS* {line added later}   *MS* it>eve   *MS* [ ]ing>fading 1535 *MS* the>
what   *MS* {no comma}   1536 *MS* Was overtaking fast,>In overtaking
me,   1537 *MS* till the day broke down—>by the striding day—
1538 *MS* {line added later}   *MS* And—>So,—   *MS* once", 1540 *MS*
fear—   1541 *MS* {line added later}   1542 *MS* Which>{*deleted*
Which}>Which   1543 *MS* could>did   *MS* know—at that old>know
too,—at that   1544 *MS* rock-side,   *MS* world>signs *1868*
signs,   1545 *MS* {line added later}   1546 *MS* walls of life>wall o' the
world   1548 *MS* {no comma}   1549 *MS* {beginning of fo. 52}   *Yale 1*
Frightened>Tightened   1550 *MS* {line added later}   *MS* self;

1532–8 *the plain . . . grey place*: commentators have tried to identify this and other
locations of the flight, but suggested places do not convincingly fit both the timings of
the journey and the details of the topography.
1548–9 *As . . . break*: cf. IV. 791–6.

The husband there,—the friends my enemies,
All ranged against me, not an avenue
To try, but would be blocked and drive me back
On him,—this other, ... oh the heart in that!
Did not he find, bring, put into my arms   1555
A new-born babe?—and I saw faces beam
Of the young mother proud to teach me joy,
And gossips round expecting my surprise
At the sudden hole through earth that lets in heaven.
I could believe himself by his strong will   1560
Had woven around me what I thought the world
We went along in, every circumstance,
Towns, flowers and faces, all things helped so well!
For, through the journey, was it natural
Such comfort should arise from first to last?   1565
As I look back, all is one milky way;
Still bettered more, the more remembered, so
Do new stars bud while I but search for old,

1551 *MS* Husband   *MS* even the Parents too>the friends my enemies,
1552 *MS* Ranged, all>All ranged   1553 *MS* I try *1868* I try,   *MS* {no comma}   1554 *MS* he brought and put into my arms>this other, .. oh the heart in that!   *1868 1872* other, ..   1555 *MS* {line added later}   *MS* How did   1556 *MS* new born babe—   *MS* found>saw   *MS* round>beam   1557 *MS* Of the mother and gossips enjoying my surprise>Of the young mother proud to teach me joy—   1558 *MS* {line added later}   *MS* ^round^   *MS* enjoying>expecting   1559 *MS* burst through that let>through earth that lets   1561 *MS* worn>woven   *MS* [ ]>me   1562 *MS* circumstance—   1563 *MS* went so well.   1564 *MS* For through the journey,—   1566 *MS* galaxy>milky way>Milky way   1567 *MS* still>so   1568 *MS* New stars bud out>Do new stars bud   *MS* search for the>but search for

---

1555–6 *put ... babe*: like the other events of the flight, and the conversation between Pompilia and Caponsacchi on the journey, this incident is Browning's invention, with no precedent whatsoever in the sources; see Caponsacchi's version of this moment at VI. 1321–40. See also VI. 1152–1417 n.

1558 *expecting*: looking for.

1559 *sudden ... heaven*: the paradox is that something ordinary and earthy, like a hole in the ground (i.e. motherhood), suddenly lets in a touch of the divine joy.

1566 *milky way*: both the band of stars in the sky (implying the magical quality of the ride with Caponsacchi), but also with the connotations of 'milky' as 'comforting, soothing, easy'.

And fill all gaps i' the glory, and grow him—
Him I now see make the shine everywhere.   1570
Even at the last when the bewildered flesh,
The cloud of weariness about my soul
Clogging too heavily, sucked down all sense,—
Still its last voice was, "He will watch and care;
"Let the strength go, I am content: he stays!"   1575
I doubt not he did stay and care for all—
From that sick minute when the head swam round,
And the eyes looked their last and died on him,
As in his arms he caught me, and, you say,
Carried me in, that tragical red eve,   1580
And laid me where I next returned to life
In the other red of morning, two red plates
That crashed together, crushed the time between,
And are since then a solid fire to me,—
When in, my dreadful husband and the world   1585

1569 *MS* in   *MS* all grow>grow   1570 *MS* He   *MS* at the last>I now
see   *MS* makes   1571 *MS* {New paragraph indicated by 'New Par.' in left-
hand margin}   1573 *MS* all too>too   1574 *MS* was—   *MS* care,
1575 *MS* {no quotation mark at beginning of line}   *MS* and be>I am 1576
MS {New paragraph indicated by 'New Par.' in left-hand margin}   1577 *MS*
^the^   1578 *MS* my>the   *MS* him.>him,   1579 *MS* he caught me ^in
his^ arms,>in his arms he caught me, *1868* me and   *MS* as you>you   1580 *MS*
{beginning of fo. 53}   *1583 *MS* That crashed *1868 1872 1888 1889* That
crashed   *MS* and crushed the>and crushed>crushed the time   1584 *MS* me,
1585 *MS* {no comma}

1580–4 *tragical red eve . . . me*: Cook's note cannot be bettered: 'Pompilia deposed in
the Process of Flight, a bare fortnight after the flight itself, that she arrived at
Castelnuovo with Caponsacchi on the Wednesday morning "at dawn", and when
cross-examined she stuck to her assertion: "I did in truth arrive at Castelnuovo at the
reddening of dawn": OYB lxxxv, lxxxvi (94). It is certain, however, that this was not
the case; Pompilia's statement . . . was unsupported by other evidence and was contra-
dicted by three witnesses for the prosecution as well as by Caponsacchi himself: OYB
cxi (120), lxxxix (97). The time of the arrival was about half-past seven (*sub hora prima
noctis cum dimidio*) on the Tuesday evening.

'Either then Pompilia made a mistake or she was guilty of what Guido's lawyers, in
their print of her deposition, called a *mendacium*. If she made a mistake, it was a very
strange one; the incident which she misrepresented was very recent and was of capital
importance, it would (so it seemed) have been accurately fixed in her memory. If on
the other hand she lied, the lie had obviously a strong motive. These considerations
impressed the friendly lawyers; they might perhaps have argued that Pompilia would

Broke,—and I saw him, master, by hell's right,
And saw my angel helplessly held back
By guards that helped the malice—the lamb prone,
The serpent towering and triumphant—then
Came all the strength back in a sudden swell,   1590
I did for once see right, do right, give tongue
The adequate protest: for a worm must turn
If it would have its wrong observed by God.
I did spring up, attempt to thrust aside
That ice-block 'twixt the sun and me, lay low   1595
The neutralizer of all good and truth.
If I sinned so,—never obey voice more
O' the Just and Terrible, who bids us—"Bear!"
Not—"Stand by, bear to see my angels bear!"
I am clear it was on impulse to serve God   1600

1586 MS him stand triumphant there,>him, master, by hell's right,   1587 MS
And my   MS ^good angel^   1588 MS did his bidding—>helped his mal-
ice—   MS Lamb   1589 Yale 2 triumphant—>triumphant: 1591 MS
act>do   MS and make>give   1592 MS protest,—   1595 MS twixt
1597 MS did wrong,—>sinned so,—   1598 MS Of   1599 MS [ ] un-
moved, my>see, unmoved, [ ]>see, unmoved, my   1600 MS true impulse>
impulse

---

scarcely have lied where detection of a lie was certain, but they did not so argue; they
admitted the *mendacium*, while protesting that it did not prove her guilty of the graver
misconduct alleged. Thus Bottini: "Though Francesca Pompilia in her examination
aimed at concealing a longer stay at the said inn by asserting that she came there in the
dawn, yet no proof of the alleged adultery can be argued from the said lie, because she
told it, perhaps, with a view to averting more thoroughly the suspicion of violated
modesty, which might have been conceived from a longer delay and a better oppor-
tunity": OYB clxxxi (187). And Lamparelli, who was specially concerned to maintain
the good name of Pompilia, says precisely the same: OYB ccliv (250).

'Browning was of course dissatisfied with any halting vindication of his heroine, and
some words above-quoted from her disposition ("at the reddening of dawn", *al
rosseggiar dell'alba*) suggested to his resourceful mind a means of clearing her memory
from the imputation of falsehood. Worn out, he conceived, by her distresses and her
fatigue, she mistook "the reddening white" of sunset for "the whitening red" of
sunrise': Cook, 156–7.

1592 *worm must turn*: proverbial: 'Tread on a worm and it will turn': ODEP, 837.
1597–9 *If . . . bear*: 'If that was sinful, no one need again obey or trust the voice of
God ("the Just and Terrible"); it was clearly, however, not sinful, since God tells us to
bear ill treatment for ourselves, but not to stand by while others are mistreated.'
Pompilia here refers to her fiery, physical defence of Caponsacchi.

Not save myself,—no—nor my child unborn!
Had I else waited patiently till now?—
Who saw my old kind parents, silly-sooth
And too much trustful, for their worst of faults,
Cheated, brow-beaten, stripped and starved, cast out   1605
Into the kennel: I remonstrated,
Then sank to silence, for,—their woes at end,
Themselves gone,—only I was left to plague.
If only I was threatened and belied,
What matter? I could bear it and did bear;   1610
It was a comfort, still one lot for all:
They were not persecuted for my sake
And I, estranged, the single happy one.
But when at last, all by myself I stood
Obeying the clear voice which bade me rise,   1615
Not for my own sake but my babe unborn,
And take the angel's hand was sent to help—
And found the old adversary athwart the path—
Not my hand simply struck from the angel's, but
The very angel's self made foul i' the face   1620

1601 *MS* me,—had I waited else till now?>myself—no—nor my child unborn!
1602 *MS* {line added later}   *MS* now?   1603 *MS* I who had seen>I had
seen   1604 *MS* all too>too much   1606 *MS* kennel,—   1607 *MS*
silence; for,   1608 *MS* They were gone,>Themselves gone,   1609 *MS*
{beginning of fo. 54}   *MS* So I was beaten and cursed,>So I was beaten, cursed,>So
only I was   1610 *MS* Myself>I   *MS* bear—   1611 *MS* one lot for us
all,>still one lot for all,   1612 *MS* {line added later} 1613 *MS* Not me the
single and happy. But when at last,—>And I estranged, the single happy
one.   1614 *MS* {line added later}   1615 *MS* voice of God
1617 *MS* Taking   1618 *MS* I found   *MS* in>athwart 1619 *MS* [?only]>
simply   1620 *MS* in>i'

1603 *silly-sooth*: naïve; cf. III. 805–6 n.
1606 *kennel*: gutter.
1611 *still . . . all*: i.e. we were all treated in the same way.
1612–13 *They . . . one*: i.e. Guido persecuted Violante and Pietro, but, when they
were driven away, he persecuted Pompilia in the same manner. Pompilia takes some
comfort in the fact that she is not exempt from persecution: she intimates that it is
harder to bear the persecution of those you love than to bear it yourself.
1618 *athwart*: across.
1619–21 *Not . . . there*: i.e. not just myself separated from Caponsacchi, but Capon-
sacchi himself made to appear less like an angel by Guido's slanderous attack on him.

By the fiend who struck there,—that I would not bear,
That only I resisted! So, my first
And last resistance was invincible.
Prayers move God; threats, and nothing else, move men!
I must have prayed a man as he were God   1625
When I implored the Governor to right
My parents' wrongs: the answer was a smile.
The Archbishop,—did I clasp his feet enough,
Hide my face hotly on them, while I told
More than I dared make my own mother know?   1630
The profit was—compassion and a jest.
This time, the foolish prayers were done with, right
Used might, and solemnized the sport at once.
All was against the combat: vantage, mine?
The runaway avowed, the accomplice-wife,   1635
In company with the plan-contriving priest?
Yet, shame thus rank and patent, I struck, bare,
At foe from head to foot in magic mail,
And off it withered, cobweb-armoury

1621 *MS* spat   *MS* bear—   1622 *MS* That I resisted; and so my first and
last>That only I resisted; and so my first *Yale 1* So>So,   1623 *MS* Resistance
was invincible, it would seem.>And last resistance was invincible.   1624 *MS*
God,   *MS* threats move men, and nothing else—>threats and nothing else move
men—   1625 *MS* such prayer as God deserves>a man as he were
God   1629 *MS* on them, hotly>hotly on them,   1630 *MS* to make my
mother know,—>make my own mother know?—   1631 *MS* Weep my brain
dry. As well have prayed the winds.>The profit was—compassion and a jo-
ke.   1632 *MS* the prayers were done with, right used might>the foolish prayers
were done with, right   1633 *MS* {line added later}   1634 *MS* trial, no
vantage mine,>combat—vantage, mine?   1635 *MS* avowed runaway,   *MS*
accomplice caught>accomplice-wife   1637 *MS* The shame was patent, in full
show—? Cobwebs>My shame thus rank and patent, as the>My shame thus rank and
patent, as in proof>My shame thus rank and patent, I fought, bare,>My shame thus
rank and patent, I struck, bare,   1638 *MS* {line added later}   *MS* The foe I
fight with? Cobweb armoury>With a foe from head to foot in magic mail—>At a foe
from head to foot in magic mail—   1639 *MS* {line added later}   *MS* with-
ered—

1629 *hotly*: i.e. blushing.
1631 *compassion and a jest*: the Archbishop's so-called compassion is shown at ll.
755–71, 788–803, 817–20; his 'jest' is his distasteful parable, ll. 820–46.
1633 *sport*: i.e. the jest of l. 1631.
1638 *magic mail*: enchanted armour.

Against the lightning! 'T was truth singed the lies   1640
And saved me, not the vain sword nor weak speech!

You see, I will not have the service fail!
I say, the angel saved me: I am safe!
Others may want and wish, I wish nor want
One point o' the circle plainer, where I stand   1645
Traced round about with white to front the world.
What of the calumny I came across,
What o' the way to the end?—the end crowns all.
The judges judged aright i' the main, gave me
The uttermost of my heart's desire, a truce   1650
From torture and Arezzo, balm for hurt,
With the quiet nuns,—God recompense the good!
Who said and sang away the ugly past.
And, when my final fortune was revealed,
What safety while, amid my parents' arms,   1655
My babe was given me! Yes, he saved my babe:
It would not have peeped forth, the bird-like thing,
Through that Arezzo noise and trouble: back
Had it returned nor ever let me see!
But the sweet peace cured all, and let me live   1660
And give my bird the life among the leaves
God meant him! Weeks and months of quietude,

1640 *MS* lightning, God's>lightning! 'Twas   1641 *MS* and weak   1642
MS {beginning of fo. 55}   *MS* {no new paragraph}   *MS* fail—   1643 *MS*
me and>me: 1645 *MS* of>o'   1647 *MS* {line added later}   1648
MS of *Yale 1* end,>end   *MS* all: 1649 *MS* in>i'   *MS* end,>main,
1650 *MS* desire,—   1651 *MS* Arezzo and the torture,   *MS 1868* hurt
1653 *MS* sang and said   *MS* past—   1656 *MS* me,—yes,   *MS* babe—
1657 *MS* thing *Yale 1* thing>thing,   1658 *MS* [ ]>Through   *MS*
the>that   *MS* trouble,—   1661 *MS* [ ]>bird   *MS* God meant him! Months
>among the leaves   1662 *MS* {line added later}   *MS* quietude—

1642 *service*: Caponsacchi's service to her.
1644 *I wish nor want*: i.e. I neither wish nor want; once a fairly common idiom,
though now archaic.
1645 *point*: part.
1646 *front*: confront. The image here seems to be of an enchanted white circle.
1651 *balm for hurt*: cf. *Macbeth*, II. ii. 36.

I could lie in such peace and learn so much—
Begin the task, I see how needful now,
Of understanding somewhat of my past,—   1665
Know life a little, I should leave so soon.
Therefore, because this man restored my soul,
All has been right; I have gained my gain, enjoyed
As well as suffered,—nay, got foretaste too
Of better life beginning where this ends—   1670
All through the breathing-while allowed me thus,
Which let good premonitions reach my soul
Unthwarted, and benignant influence flow
And interpenetrate and change my heart,
Uncrossed by what was wicked,—nay, unkind.   1675
For, as the weakness of my time drew nigh,
Nobody did me one disservice more,
Spoke coldly or looked strangely, broke the love
I lay in the arms of, till my boy was born,
Born all in love, with nought to spoil the bliss   1680
A whole long fortnight: in a life like mine
A fortnight filled with bliss is long and much.
All women are not mothers of a boy,
Though they live twice the length of my whole life,
And, as they fancy, happily all the same.   1685
There I lay, then, all my great fortnight long,
As if it would continue, broaden out
Happily more and more, and lead to heaven:
Christmas before me,—was not that a chance?

1663 *MS* Of quietude—I could lie and learn so much—>I could lie in such peace and
learn so much—   1665 *MS* all my difficult>somewhat of my   1667 *MS*
{line added later}   1670 *MS* a better   1671 *MS* {no comma}   1673
MS {beginning of fo. 56}   *MS* all benignant   1675 *MS* unkind—   1677
MS one disservice to me more>me one disservice more   1680 *MS* the joy
1682 *MS* joy   1684 *MS* {no comma}   1686 *MS* lay then, *Yale 2* There
I lay, then,>There, then, I lay,   *MS* long   1688 *MS* all the way>more and
more,   *MS* Heaven: 1689 *MS* good chance?

1671 *breathing-while*: breathing space.
1676 *my time*: i.e. her labour.

I never realized God's birth before—   1690
How He grew likest God in being born.
This time I felt like Mary, had my babe
Lying a little on my breast like hers.
So all went on till, just four days ago—
The night and the tap.   1695

               Oh it shall be success
To the whole of our poor family! My friends
. . . Nay, father and mother,—give me back my word!
They have been rudely stripped of life, disgraced
Like children who must needs go clothed too fine,   1700
Carry the garb of Carnival in Lent.
If they too much affected frippery,
They have been punished and submit themselves,
Say no word: all is over, they see God
Who will not be extreme to mark their fault   1705
Or He had granted respite: they are safe.

For that most woeful man my husband once,
Who, needing respite, still draws vital breath,
I—pardon him? So far as lies in me,
I give him for his good the life he takes,   1710

1690 *MS* realised   1691 *MS 1868* he   1696 *MS* {New paragraph indi-
cated by 'N.P.' in right-hand margin}   *1868 1872* O   *MS* success!   1697 *MS*
friends—   1698 *MS 1868 1872* .. Nay,   *MS* mother, let me say this once—
>mother,—give me my own word—>mother,—give me back my word—   1700
MS garbed>clothed   1701 *MS* Lent,   *1868 1872* Lent: *Yale 2* Lent:>
Lent.   1702 *MS* {beginning of fo. 57}   1704 *MS* with>see   1706 *MS*
he   *1707 *MS 1868 1872* {new paragraph. Paragraphing obscured in *1888* and
1889 by this line's being at the head of the page}   *MS* {no comma}

1695 *the tap*: cf. l. 267.
1696–7 *Oh . . . family*: i.e. the murders have been a 'success' to Pompilia and her
parents, a paradox showing her deep religious faith. At ll. 1667–93 she has explained
how the fortnight of love before her murder gave her a 'foretaste' of heaven, to which,
in faith, she looks forward. Now—as she goes on to explain—Pietro and Violante will
see God in heaven, their murders a penance cleansing them of their small amount of
affectation and bluster.
1706 *Or . . . respite*: i.e. God would have given them time to confess their sins.

Praying the world will therefore acquiesce.
Let him make God amends,—none, none to me
Who thank him rather that, whereas strange fate
Mockingly styled him husband and me wife,
Himself this way at least pronounced divorce,   1715
Blotted the marriage-bond: this blood of mine
Flies forth exultingly at any door,
Washes the parchment white, and thanks the blow.
We shall not meet in this world nor the next,
But where will God be absent? In His face   1720
Is light, but in His shadow healing too:
Let Guido touch the shadow and be healed!
And as my presence was importunate,—
My earthly good, temptation and a snare,—
Nothing about me but drew somehow down   1725
His hate upon me,—somewhat so excused
Therefore, since hate was thus the truth of him,—
May my evanishment for evermore
Help further to relieve the heart that cast
Such object of its natural loathing forth!   1730
So he was made; he nowise made himself:
I could not love him, but his mother did.
His soul has never lain beside my soul:
But for the unresisting body,—thanks!
He burned that garment spotted by the flesh.   1735

1712 *MS* none—none   1717 *MS* door—   1721 *MS* light,—   1723
MS importunate,   1724 *MS* snare,   1729 *MS* {beginning of fo.
58}   1730 *MS* forth: *1733 *MS* soul, *1868 1872* soul; *1888* soul *DC BrU*
soul>soul: *1889* soul: 1734 *MS* thanks—   1735 *MS* *1868 1872* flesh!

1717 *Flies . . . door*: i.e. is happy to take any means of escaping the marriage.
1718 *parchment*: i.e. the marriage contract.
1722 *Let . . . healed*: cf. Luke 8: 43–8, Acts 5: 15. Guido will be like the woman with
a haemorrhage, cured by even a touch of Christ's garment, or like the sick people
cured by having Peter's shadow pass over them.
1723 *importunate*: troublesome, burdensome (to Guido).
1728 *evanishment*: disappearance.
1734 *But . . . body*: except for the passive body (in sexual intercourse). In this sense
Pompilia has lain next to Guido, but never in a fuller sense, soul to soul.
thanks!: this exclamation leads immediately into the next line; the *MS* 'thanks—'
perhaps made this clearer.

Whatever he touched is rightly ruined: plague
It caught, and disinfection it had craved
Still but for Guido; I am saved through him
So as by fire; to him—thanks and farewell!

Even for my babe, my boy, there's safety thence—   1740
From the sudden death of me, I mean: we poor
Weak souls, how we endeavour to be strong!
I was already using up my life,—
This portion, now, should do him such a good,
This other go to keep off such an ill!   1745
The great life; see, a breath and it is gone!
So is detached, so left all by itself
The little life, the fact which means so much.
Shall not God stoop the kindlier to His work,
His marvel of creation, foot would crush,   1750
Now that the hand He trusted to receive
And hold it, lets the treasure fall perforce?
The better; He shall have in orphanage
His own way all the clearlier: if my babe
Outlived the hour—and he has lived two weeks—   1755
It is through God who knows I am not by.
Who is it makes the soft gold hair turn black,
And sets the tongue, might lie so long at rest,
Trying to talk? Let us leave God alone!
Why should I doubt He will explain in time   1760

1736 *MS* ruined—   1737 *MS* {no comma}   1739 *MS* fire: 1742
MS strong—   1743 *MS* life,   1745 *MS* ill,   1746 *MS* life,—
1748 *MS* much,   1749 *MS* his>His   1750 *MS* creation foot   1751
MS he>He   1753 *MS* better, He have   1755 *MS* Lives out   1756
MS {beginning of fo. 59}

1738–9 *I . . . fire*: cf. 1 Cor. 3: 15: 'If any man's work shall be burned, he shall suffer
loss: but he himself shall be saved; yet so as by fire.'

1748 *little life*: i.e. the life of her baby (as opposed to her own life, 'the great life', in
l. 1746).

1752 *perforce*: of necessity.

1753 *in orphanage*: i.e. with the baby as an orphan.

1757 *Who . . . black*: who is it makes a baby's fair hair darken? i.e. God.

What I feel now, but fail to find the words?
My babe nor was, nor is, nor yet shall be
Count Guido Franceschini's child at all—
Only his mother's, born of love not hate!
So shall I have my rights in after-time.   1765
It seems absurd, impossible to-day;
So seems so much else, not explained but known!

Ah! Friends, I thank and bless you every one!
No more now: I withdraw from earth and man
To my own soul, compose myself for God.   1770

Well, and there is more! Yes, my end of breath
Shall bear away my soul in being true!
He is still here, not outside with the world,
Here, here, I have him in his rightful place!
'T is now, when I am most upon the move,   1775
I feel for what I verily find—again
The face, again the eyes, again, through all,
The heart and its immeasurable love
Of my one friend, my only, all my own,
Who put his breast between the spears and me.   1780
Ever with Caponsacchi! Otherwise
Here alone would be failure, loss to me—
How much more loss to him, with life debarred
From giving life, love locked from love's display,

1761 *MS* {no comma}   *MS* words—   1763 *MS* Count Franceschini's
1764 *MS* hate?—   1765 *MS* aftertime   1767 *MS 1868* {no comma}
1868 known.   1782 *MS* {beginning of fo. 60}

1771 *my end of breath*: Pompilia's 'last breath' is from here to the end of the
monologue, when, on the words 'I rise', she dies.

1773 *He*: i.e. Caponsacchi.

1774 *Here, here*: with her, in imagination, at the bedside, or perhaps, more empha-
tically, 'in my heart', to which she points.

1775 *most . . . move*: i.e. about to leave the world.

1783–4 *debarred . . . display*: i.e. debarred from fathering a child, or (as a celibate)
forbidden from displaying his love for a woman.

The day-star stopped its task that makes night morn!   1785
O lover of my life, O soldier-saint,
No work begun shall ever pause for death!
Love will be helpful to me more and more
I' the coming course, the new path I must tread—
My weak hand in thy strong hand, strong for that!   1790
Tell him that if I seem without him now,
That's the world's insight! Oh, he understands!
He is at Civita—do I once doubt
The world again is holding us apart?
He had been here, displayed in my behalf   1795
The broad brow that reverberates the truth,
And flashed the word God gave him, back to man!
I know where the free soul is flown! My fate
Will have been hard for even him to bear:
Let it confirm him in the trust of God,   1800
Showing how holily he dared the deed!
And, for the rest,—say, from the deed, no touch
Of harm came, but all good, all happiness,
Not one faint fleck of failure! Why explain?
What I see, oh, he sees and how much more!   1805
Tell him,—I know not wherefore the true word
Should fade and fall unuttered at the last—
It was the name of him I sprang to meet
When came the knock, the summons and the end.
"My great heart, my strong hand are back again!"   1810

1785 *MS* morn.   1789 *MS* 1868 1872 tread,   1795 *MS* unfurled   1796
MS {no comma}   1799 *MS* bear—   1801 *MS* deed: 1807 *MS*
last,—   1810 *MS* {beginning of fo. 61}

1793 *He is at Civita*: a dramatic irony; Pompilia does not know that Caponsacchi is
in Rome.

1798 *I . . . flown*: i.e. Caponsacchi may be restrained physically at Civitavecchia, but
Pompilia is sure that his soul has already flown to be with her.

1804 *fleck*: spot, stain.

1806–10 *Tell . . . again*: this is an extraordinary and moving moment in *The Ring and
the Book* as a whole, because it is the culmination of various patterns within the
dramatic irony. Guido and others have fixed on this incident—the use of Caponsacchi's
name outside the villa door—as crucial proof of Pompilia's adultery and her delinquent
nature. Here their smears are radically overturned. Pompilia *did* start with joy at the

I would have sprung to these, beckoning across
Murder and hell gigantic and distinct
O' the threshold, posted to exclude me heaven:
He is ordained to call and I to come!
Do not the dead wear flowers when dressed for God?   1815
Say,—I am all in flowers from head to foot!
Say,—not one flower of all he said and did,
Might seem to flit unnoticed, fade unknown,
But dropped a seed, has grown a balsam-tree
Whereof the blossoming perfumes the place   1820
At this supreme of moments! He is a priest;
He cannot marry therefore, which is right:
I think he would not marry if he could.
Marriage on earth seems such a counterfeit,
Mere imitation of the inimitable: 1825
In heaven we have the real and true and sure.
'T is there they neither marry nor are given
In marriage but are as the angels: right,
Oh how right that is, how like Jesus Christ
To say that! Marriage-making for the earth,   1830
With gold so much,—birth, power, repute so much,
Or beauty, youth so much, in lack of these!
Be as the angels rather, who, apart,
Know themselves into one, are found at length

1813 *MS* heaven—   1819 *MS 1868* {no comma}   1827 *MS* "In hea-
ven>Tis there   1830 *MS* {no comma}   1832 *MS* much in   *MS* these:

sound of Caponsacchi's name, not because of an illicit affair, but because of an
overwhelming, pure, and sudden-found love.

1811 *beckoning*: gesturing (to me).

1819 *balsam-tree*: a large, aromatic tree, the resin of which was supposed to have
healing properties. It is sometimes called just 'balm'; cf. Jer. 8: 22.

1827–8 *neither . . . angels*: cf. Matt. 22: 29–30: 'Jesus answered and said unto them, Ye
do err, not knowing the scriptures, nor the power of God. For in the resurrection they
neither marry, nor are given in marriage, but are as the angels of God in heaven.'

1833–4 *who . . . one*: 'who, though separate, unite (spiritually) through mutual and
perfect knowledge of each other'. Pompilia looks forward to an angelic union with
Caponsacchi in heaven, boldly punning on the biblical sense of 'know' = to have
sexual intercourse. Cf. Raphael's description of angelic sexuality in *Paradise Lost*, viii.
626–9: 'Easier than air with air, if spirits embrace, / Total they mix, union of pure with
pure / Desiring; nor restrained conveyance need / As flesh to mix with flesh, or soul
with soul.'

Married, but marry never, no, nor give   1835
In marriage; they are man and wife at once
When the true time is: here we have to wait
Not so long neither! Could we by a wish
Have what we will and get the future now,
Would we wish aught done undone in the past?   1840
So, let him wait God's instant men call years;
Meantime hold hard by truth and his great soul,
Do out the duty! Through such souls alone
God stooping shows sufficient of His light
For us i' the dark to rise by. And I rise.   1845

1835 *MS* Married but   1836 *MS* marriage, then   1837 *MS* wait—
1838 *MS* {beginning of fo. 62}   1841 *MS* So let   *MS* years,   1843 *MS*
duty: through *Yale 1* duty: through>duty! Through

1841 *God's instant . . . years*: cf. Ps. 90: 4.

1845 *And I rise*: Pompilia speaks these words at the moment of her death, as she
'rises' towards God and heaven.

INTRODUCTION TO BOOK VIII

DOMINUS HYACINTHUS DE ARCHANGELIS

AFTER the tragedy of Book VII, Book VIII transports us into a bumptious comedy, full of verve and exhilaration. The lawyers, Books VIII and IX, are *terra incognita* for many critics, variously apologized for or defended as supposed longueurs.[1] Really, they are among the most vital of Browning's creations, their linguistic playfulness with Latin giving them a more 'modern' than 'Victorian' feel. The first lawyer, Arcangeli, *Pauperum Procurator* ('Advocate of the Poor'), is a Falstaff of domesticity, whose good humour and wit are a complex foil to the poem's heroic aspect.

Browning's remarks in the correspondence with Julia Wedgwood are less helpful here than with Pompilia. He refers to the 'buffoon lawyers'; and then, in a later letter:

I hate the lawyers: and confess to tasting something of the satisfaction, as I emphasize their buffoonery, which was visible (they told me at Balliol, the other day) on the sour face of one Dr Jenkins, whilehome [*sic*] Master of the College, when, having to read prayers, he would of a sudden turn and apostrophize the obnoxious Fellows, all out of the discreet words of the Psalmist, "As for liars, I hate and abhor them!"—then go on quietly with his crooning.[2]

He is warning Wedgwood, shocked or disappointed at the darkness of the poem she had read so far, that there was more she would find distasteful. The remark should be seen in this light, though critics have sometimes followed its lead. Thus, Hodell:

. . . of the law Browning had ample opportunity to judge in the pages [of OYB] before him. He uses this material with strong, satiric scorn. He was evidently moved to indignation by the shrewd sophistries of the arguments in the case. Ideally the law stands for justice between man and man, but here it had become a cunning machine devised for defeating real equity and justice. His contempt and irony are poured full upon the 'patent, truth-extracting process.' His indignation

---

[1] There are only a small number of good studies focused on these monologues; see in particular Simon Petch, 'Browning's Roman Lawyers', in *Browning Centenary Essays*, a special issue of *AUMLA*: 71 (1989), 109–38.

[2] RB to Julia Wedgwood, 19 Nov. 1868, and 1 Feb. 1869: *Wedgwood*, 160, 177.

was stirred against a class of men who had been in close contact with the tragedy without feeling the slightest sympathy for the sufferers.[3]

This takes the description of the law in i. 1105–16, and extends it too much into Book VIII. In fact 'satiric scorn' and 'indignation' are in the background. If we interpret Book VIII in the way suggested here, we shall see just satire and miss out on the more complex effects of comedy.

Source study can be elucidating. As Hodell has shown, and as seen in the commentary below, over 95 per cent of the Latin comes almost verbatim from OYB.[4] To say this without qualification can be misleading. The main legal arguments that Arcangeli advances, and most citations of precedent and example—Dolabella, Cassiodorus, St Ambrose, etc.—are from OYB, so that Browning seems to be literally reproducing the manner of the original pleadings. As the commentary makes clear, however, he moves about rapidly within the source. He takes a passage, a sentence, a phrase from the speech of one lawyer, and marries it with a quotation from somewhere else in the source, welding fragments into a complex whole. (From the way he skips around, it can be surmised he knew OYB virtually by heart.) Having made these gleanings, he exaggerates the legal argument by the nature and mood of Arcangeli's translations of the Latin, and by other changes and additions to the material and its context.

A real lawyer's argument, only verging on the ludicrous, is taken from OYB (though we may suppose otherwise); an argument immediately following is Browning's invention, and tips the scale into high comedy. A reader unfamiliar with the source may conjecture gross parody, not wry adaptation. A simple example may serve. At one point Arcangeli, building his case that Guido murdered to avenge injured honour, quotes Christ as saying: '"*Honorem meum nemini dabo!*" "No, / My honour I to nobody will give!"' (666–7). Since Christ obviously said no such thing, we may assume an extravagant irony on Browning's part, when really this bungling error is straight from OYB. The legal speeches of OYB are in the main efficient and well executed in the tradition of Roman law. Browning selects this particular error—actually from the anonymous pamphlet 10, and not from an official pleading—and gives it prominence in Arcangeli's speech.

What changes the appearance of all the strictly legal argument is the invented character that Browning sets around it, which (aside from the name) has no precedent in OYB. Arcangeli is obsessed with good food,

[3] Hodell, 271.   [4] Ibid. 330–4.

good Latin, with his son Giacinto, his extended family, with the satisfac-
tions of bourgeois wealth and married sexuality, and with the ingenuity of
his own wit. He has something of that fullness of self-satisfaction that goes
with the greatest comic creations. Like Falstaff, who 'lards the lean earth
as he walks along', he is a puffing and blowing fat man, 'Cheek and jowl
all in laps with fat and law, / Mirthful as mighty' who 'Wheezes out law-
phrase, whiffles Latin forth' (1. 1132–3, 1151). Much of Hazlitt's descrip-
tion of Falstaff could be aptly applied to Arcangeli:

> [His] wit is an emanation of a fine constitution; an exuberance of good-humour
> and good-nature; an overflowing of his love of laughter and good-fellowship; a
> giving vent to his heart's ease, and over-contentment with himself and others. He
> would not be in character, if he were not so fat as he is; for there is the greatest
> keeping in the boundless luxury of his imagination and the pampered self-
> indulgence of his physical appetites.[5]

Arcangeli's monologue is smattered with his thoughts about fried liver
with fennel and parsley, Orvieto, and the splendid Est wine, as he
anticipates the family banquet for his son's birthday. The few additions
that Browning makes to the Latin of the source establish him as a poet
manqué : references to Horace, Ovid, and the scholia of Persius all act in
this way. Arcangeli's wit is less full than Falstaff's, but, as Browning
emphasizes, more learned. When, at ll. 680–4, Arcangeli 'can't quite
recollect' a saying of St Ambrose, he simply forgets a passage cited in
OYB; but elsewhere Browning adds to his array of learning citations of
Aristotle, the Septuagint, and the *Scaligeriana* (489, 492, 498–501). On one
occasion, indeed, he proves more learned than Browning's critics: his
allusion to the story of St Thomas Aquinas and the King of France has
gone unappreciated until the present edition (1313).

   Of course, there is also a negative side to his character: he is concerned
that older relations in his family should leave their wealth to himself or his
son; he is avaricious in this way, even (ruthlessly we might think)
celebrating the way he bought up the necklace that Pietro Comparini
pawned after his flight from Arezzo (1801–5). His doting love for his son,
Giacinto, is a reflex of egotism. Most troubling of all is his professional
detachment from the humanity of the case, a detachment so complete
that he will actually alter a fact in his pleading in order to display more
excellently his Latin style and the deficiencies of his opponent's (212–17).

---

[5] William Hazlitt, *Characters of Shakespear's Plays* (1817); quoted here from *The Romantics on Shakespeare*, ed. by Jonathan Bate (1992), 356.

But none of these qualities—the side of him that would imply a satirical reading—is able to diminish the Falstaffian aspect of his being.

In the approach to the climax of the monologue, Browning extends the humour to the widest possible range. At l. 1385 Arcangeli is in the throes of rebutting the accusation that the homicide was a wound against the 'Majesty of the Sovereign'; suddenly he breaks off with an anxious thought about the incompetence of Gigia, the cook, who is to prepare the food for the evening feast:

> (There is a porcupine to barbacue;
> Gigia can jug a rabbit well enough,
> With sour-sweet sauce and pine-pips; but, good Lord,
> Suppose the devil instigate the wench
> To stew, not roast him? Stew my porcupine?
> If she does, I know where his quills shall stick!
> Come, I must go myself and see to things:
> I cannot stay much longer stewing here.) (ll. 1385–92)

Of course, this aside establishes ludicrously that the chasm between Arcangeli as a professional and a family man is complete to the point of amorality. But this, like moralizings about Falstaff ('glutton', 'braggart', 'corrupter'), misses the point of the wider comedy. Why choose porcupine as the particular object of Arcangeli's gastronomic concern? Browning knew that porcupine was a normal roast in Rome in the nineteenth century, and he transposed the detail back to the seventeenth century—though not, surely, innocently. He is playing with readers' responses. A reader who knows this fact experiences a frisson of realism that grounds the humour in an unusual way. A reader who does not may assume a deliberate extravagance. In either case, the ambiguity itself is an extension of the farce.

Harold Bloom contrasts the 'immanent' Falstaff and the 'transcendent' Hamlet: 'We cannot know whether Shakespeare was more Falstaff or Hamlet'.[6] Perhaps a similar perception helps here. Arcangeli worries minutely about Giacinto's advancement in Latin, just as Browning, in the 1860s, worried about Pen's.[7] Arcangeli struggles with the rhetorical shape of his speech, and later, we are assured, as a would-be Ciceronian, will polish every word into the best possible Latin style: he is a poet

---

[6] Harold Bloom, *Shakespeare: The Invention of the Human* (1999), 287.
[7] See VIII. 5–6n. below.

manqué. He is also what Browning had been till 1861, a joyous family man. One could extend comparisons further, not to establish the monologue as autobiographical, but to show—if it needs demonstrating—the extent to which Browning is as committed to this farce as to the high pathos of Pompilia's death.

A Note on the Latin in Book VIII

As emphasized above, most of the Latin in Book VIII comes verbatim from OYB. Where it does not, this is clearly indicated in our notes. Arcangeli is imagined thinking his Latin out aloud, and translating it immediately in a loose, vivid way. Because of this, further translation in the commentary seems redundant. We have, however, given guidance where the reader without Latin might have difficulty co-ordinating Latin and translation, or where there are special points of interest. We have also given more extended references to OYB in the form OYB cxiv (122), Arcangeli, pam. 8, so that how Browning takes the legal Latin from different lawyers' speeches can be seen at a glance. By supplying translation within the text, Browning clearly intended this Book and Book IX to be available to the non-Latinist. For those with Latin, he never lets Arcangeli translate baldly, but always in a manner or tone that continues to reveal his character, and adds to our enjoyment.

DOMINUS HYACINTHUS DE ARCHANGELIS,

PAUPERUM PROCURATOR.

AH, my Giacinto, he's no ruddy rogue,
Is not Cinone? What, to-day we're eight?
Seven and one's eight, I hope, old curly-pate!
—Branches me out his verb-tree on the slate,
Amo -as -avi -atum -are -ans,
Up to *-aturus*, person, tense, and mood,

5

MS {fo. 63. At the head of the page is the title '8. *Dominus Hyacinthus de Archangelis, Pauperum Procurator.*' in RB's hand}   5 MS atum, are,>atum—are—   6 MS tense and

---

1 *Giacinto*: the name of Arcangeli's much-beloved son, here given in Italian, later in its Anglo-Latin form Hyacinth (see ll. 1464, 1756, 1761). This son, who is entirely Browning's invention, is named after his father.

no ruddy rogue: no sunburnt brat, i.e. he's not a street urchin.

2 *Cinone*: this is the first of many diminutives of endearment that Arcangeli has for his son, showing how much he dotes on him, and also his mastery of language, his resourceful variety as taught by the rhetoricians. These pet names litter the monologue: Cinone, Cinozzo, Cinoncello, Cinuolo, Cinicello, Cinino, Ciniccino, Cinucciatolo, Cinoncino, Cinarello, Cinotto, Giacintino, Cinuccino, Cinuzzo, Cintino, Cineruggiolo, Cinuccio.

2–4 *eight . . . slate*: Honan notes the internal and end rhyme in these lines, and suggests that they help create Arcangeli's mood as he contemplates the coming family banquet, and also underline 'his basic lightheartedness'. He notes other rhymes in the monologue: 'ermine-vermin', 'soar and pour', 'name and fame', 'round and sound', 'landed and stranded': 'Although the device is not employed extensively in his portrait, it has the effect of emphasizing his obtuse and carefree nature as he conjures up a defence for Guido': Honan, 263–4. In fact, there is a range of other instances: see ll. 18, 33, 152–3, 965–71, 1812 nn.

5–6 *Amo . . . —aturus*: the paradigm of the first-conjugation Latin verb, the first verb learnt by beginners in Latin. It is apt as another expression of Arcangeli's doting love for his son. In the years he was writing *The Ring and the Book* Browning himself was an

Quies me *cum subjunctivo* (I could cry)
And chews Corderius with his morning crust!
Look eight years onward, and he's perched, he's perched
Dapper and deft on stool beside this chair,   10
Cinozzo, Cinoncello, who but he?
—Trying his milk-teeth on some crusty case
Like this, papa shall triturate full soon
To smooth Papinianian pulp!
                              It trots   15
Already through my head, though noon be now,
Does supper-time and what belongs to eve.

---

*7 MS me *1868 1872 1888 1889* me   9 MS *1868* perched,   12 MS
milkteeth   14 MS Papinian *Yale 1* Papinian>Papinianian   15 MS In
truth, it trots *Yale 1* In truth, it>It   17 MS suppertime

---

anxious father helping to teach his son Latin. Sometimes, in his letters, he sounds like
Arcangeli: 'Pen is thoroughly good & honest—and after all, he reads without previous
preparation, a hundred lines of Virgil in an hour: does so every day here [at Ste Marie,
near Pornic]—we have thus read together the 6th 7th 8th 9th & nearly the 10th book of
the Aeneid: and then he spends half an hour or more in producing a very fair Greek
translation, which I correct: and he has two years more—oh, I am sure he'll *do!*': RB to
Isa Blagden, 19 Sept. 1865: *Dearest Isa*, 224.

   7 *Quies* . . . SUBJUNCTIVO: 'uses *qui* for me with the subjunctive mood' (where
appropriate in Latin)—hence showing his skill in the language. Browning has taken the
Latin relative pronoun *qui* (in italics) and added the English ending '-es' (in roman), so
making up a third-person singular English verb 'Qui-es', i.e. uses *qui* correctly. The
subjunctive is used after *qui* in final and consecutive clauses, in both of which it is
compulsory, but also—and this is a mark of the best Ciceronian style—when the
relative clause has the flavour of 'because' or 'although'. Hence if young Giacinto is a
sound Latinist, he knows the final and consecutive usages of *qui* with the subjunctive; if
a really promising Latinist, he knows the causal and concessive.

   8 *Corderius*: the elementary Latin textbook written by Mathurin Cordier (*c.*1480–
1564), Calvin's schoolmaster, which was still being used well into the nineteenth
century.

   13 *triturate*: grind down, masticate (from L. *triturare*, to thresh).

   14 *Papinianian pulp*: i.e. a well-digested, well-explained legal case, but with also a
play on 'pap' = soft food for infants. This *jeu d'esprit* and the tongue-twisting ending
'-inianian' are again indicative of Arcangeli's high spirits. Aemilius Papinianus (d. AD
212) was a leading lawyer at the end of the second century and a close associate of the
emperor Severus. His *Quaestiones* ('Problems') and *Digesta responsa* ('Ordered Opin-
ions') were long regarded as definitive within the tradition of Roman law. He is
mentioned prominently in the first speech of the real Arcangeli at OYB xiii (15): 'And
Papinianus clearly recognized [the anger of cuckolds] in *l. si Adulterium cum incæstu* . . .
where we read, "Since it is most difficult to restrain just resentment".'

Dispose, O Don, o' the day, first work then play!
—The proverb bids. And "then" means, won't we hold
Our little yearly lovesome frolic feast,   20
Cinuolo's birth-night, Cinicello's own,
That makes gruff January grin perforce!
For too contagious grows the mirth, the warmth
Escaping from so many hearts at once—
When the good wife, buxom and bonny yet,   25
Jokes the hale grandsire,—such are just the sort
To go off suddenly,—he who hides the key
O' the box beneath his pillow every night,—
Which box may hold a parchment (someone thinks)
Will show a scribbled something like a name   30
"Cinino, Ciniccino," near the end,
"To whom I give and I bequeath my lands,
"Estates, tenements, hereditaments,
"When I decease as honest grandsire ought."
Wherefore—yet this one time again perhaps—   35
Shan't my Orvieto fuddle his old nose!
Then, uncles, one or the other, well i' the world,
May—drop in, merely?—trudge through rain and wind,

---

20 *MS* {no comma}   21 *MS* Cinozzo's>Cinuolo's   *MS* birthnight,   27
MS As   28 *MS* night—   29 *MS* {beginning of fo. 64}   *1868 1872* some
one *Yale 2* some one>someone   30 *MS* That shows>May shows {*sic*}   34
MS should:">ought:" *1868* ought:"   35 *MS* perchance—>perhaps—   36
MS 1868 1872 Sha'n't

  18 *Dispose . . . play*: with 'day' and 'play', Arcangeli makes a sing-song rhyme out of
the proverb 'first work then play', something he does again even more emphatically
with 'away' and 'play' at l. 1812.
  Don: master, adept (a humorous reference to himself).
  27 *go off*: i.e. die.
  33 *tenements, hereditaments*: land or property held by tenure or lease, and any kind of
property that can be inherited (corporeal or incorporeal). Though these terms do
sometimes occur together in English law, Arcangeli is again enjoying the rhyme.
  36 *Orvieto*: 'a pale faint-coloured wine, of a sweetish flavour, half way between the
purest cider and champagne': *Roba di Roma*, i. 306.
  fuddle . . . nose: i.e. make him drunk.
  37–9 *Then . . . Rather!*: i.e. the uncles do not come casually, but avidly to the feast.

Rather! The smell-feasts rouse them at the hint
There's cookery in a certain dwelling-place!   40
Gossips, too, each with keepsake in his poke,
Will pick the way, thrid lane by lantern-light,
And so find door, put galligaskin off
At entry of a decent domicile
Cornered in snug Condotti,—all for love,   45
All to crush cup with Cinucciatolo!

                                   Well,
Let others climb the heights o' the court, the camp!
How vain are chambering and wantonness,
Revel and rout and pleasures that make mad!   50
Commend me to home-joy, the family board,
Altar and hearth! These, with a brisk career,
A source of honest profit and good fame,
Just so much work as keeps the brain from rust,
Just so much play as lets the heart expand,   55
Honouring God and serving man,—I say,
These are reality, and all else,—fluff,

39 *MS* smellfeasts rouze   40 *MS* domicile—>dwelling-place: 42 *MS*
their>the   43 *MS* reach door,>reach [ ],>find door,   44 *MS* comfortable
house>decent domicile   46 *MS* To crush a>All to crush   54 *MS* heart>
brain   57 *MS* {beginning of fo. 65}   *MS* reality—

39 *smell-feasts*: parasites, spongers: the uncles referred to in the previous lines. Cf.
Thomas Heyrick, *The New Atlantis* (1687), III. 552–4: 'I'l call them *Smell feasts* that
attend for fare; / I, that like Flies, to' every Board repair / And vex the weary
Thresholds, find them there'.

41 *keepsake*: present.

43 *galligaskin*: outer leggings or trousers, worn as protection against rain; cf.
'He wears a huge pair . . of galligaskins . . made of thick stiff leather, but so as to
fit the leg exactly': Anthony Trollope, *The West Indies and the Spanish Main* (1859),
p. 150.

45 *Condotti*: the Via Condotti goes from the Spanish Steps to the Corso. It is not
far from Via Vittoria, where the Comparini lived, but it is even nearer to the Church
of San Lorenzo in Lucina, where the bodies of the Comparini were laid out after the
murder. Arcangeli and his son had only to go to the end of the road and then across the
Corso to view the bodies: see ll. 1351–2. This is presumably one of the reasons why
Browning chose Via Condotti for Arcangeli's home.

46 *crush cup*: i.e. to clink cups together in a toast.

48 *climb . . . camp*: i.e. aspire ambitiously to high position in the court or army.

49 *chambering and wantonness*: cf. Rom. 13: 13.

52 *brisk*: busy, successful.

Nutshell and naught,—thank Flaccus for the phrase!
Suppose I had been Fisc, yet bachelor!

Why, work with a will, then! Wherefore lazy now?　60
Turn up the hour-glass, whence no sand-grain slips
But should have done its duty to the saint
O' the day, the son and heir that's eight years old!
Let law come dimple Cinoncino's cheek,
And Latin dumple Cinarello's chin,　65
The while we spread him fine and toss him flat
This pulp that makes the pancake, trim our mass
Of matter into Argument the First,
Prime Pleading in defence of our accused,
Which, once a-waft on paper wing, shall soar,　70
Shall signalize before applausive Rome
What study, and mayhap some mother-wit,
Can do toward making Master fop and Fisc
Old bachelor Bottinius bite his thumb.

[—]

---

59 *MS* were the Fisc, and>had been Fisc, yet　60 *MS* {New paragraph indicated
by 'New Par' in left-hand margin}　61 *MS* hourglass whence no
sandgrain　65 *MS* latin>Latin　71 *1868 1872* signalise　73 *MS*
towards　*MS* [ ]>fop　74 *MS* Bottinius bite his thumb nail to the blood.>Old
bachelor Bottinius bite his thumb.

---

58 *Nutshell . . . Flaccus*: an empty nut is proverbially worthless; cf. 'Not worth a
nutshell': ODEP, 584. Arcangeli takes his 'nutshell' from Horace (in L., Quintus
Horatius Flaccus), *Satires*, II. v. 35–6: 'eripiet quivis oculos citius mihi quam te /
contemptum cassa nuce pauperet': 'Sooner will someone pluck out my eyes than hold
you in contempt or make you the poorer by a nutshell'.

59 *Suppose . . . bachelor*: Arcangeli, a married man, and Bottini the Fisc, his oppon-
ent, a bachelor, are a parallel in this respect to Half-Rome and Other Half-Rome,
though all four characters show very different attitudes towards women.

64–5 *Let . . . chin*: i.e. let law dimple (indent) the boy's cheek as he is amused and
smiles, and let Latin dumple his chin (make his chin stick out) as he concentrates to
understand it. 'Dumple' is a nonce-formation, used for its assonance with 'dimple', and
as such it is typical of Arcangeli's high-spirited playfulness with language.

67 *pulp . . . pancake*: i.e. the well-digested legal argument out of which the finished
defence speech will be made; cf. l. 14 n.

74 *bite his thumb*: i.e. become frustrated and impotent with rage, so that all he can do
in response is make a futile rude gesture. For the insulting connotations of biting one's
thumb see *Romeo and Juliet*, I. i. 42–51.

Now, how good God is! How falls plumb to point   75
This murder, gives me Guido to defend
Now, of all days i' the year, just when the boy
Verges on Virgil, reaches the right age
For some such illustration from his sire,
Stimulus to himself! One might wait years   80
And never find the chance which now finds me!
The fact is, there's a blessing on the hearth,
A special providence for fatherhood!
Here's a man, and what's more, a noble, kills
—Not sneakingly but almost with parade—   85
Wife's father and wife's mother and wife's self
That's mother's self of son and heir (like mine!)
—And here stand I, the favoured advocate,
Who pluck this flower o' the field, no Solomon
Was ever clothed in glorious gold to match,   90
And set the same in Cinoncino's cap!
I defend Guido and his comrades—I!
Pray God, I keep me humble: not to me—
Non nobis, Domine, sed tibi laus!
How the fop chuckled when they made him Fisc!   95
We'll beat you, my Bottinius, all for love,
All for our tribute to Cinotto's day.
Why, 'sbuddikins, old Innocent himself
May rub his eyes at the bustle,—ask "What's this
"Rolling from out the rostrum, as a gust   100

---

*75 *MS* {New paragraph indicated by 'N.P.' in left-hand margin. Paragraphing obscured in *1868* and *1872* by this line's being at the head of the page}   77 *MS* Now— *MS* year—   78 *MS* Virgil—   82 *MS* hearth—   86 *MS* {beginning of fo. 66}   89 *MS* plucks   91 *MS* Cinarello's>Cinoncino's   93 *MS* {line added later}   *MS* I hope>Pray God   95 *MS* {line added later}   97 *MS 1868 1872* day!   100 *MS* [] [ ]>a gust

---

78 *Verges on Virgil*: i.e. has Latin good enough to begin reading Virgil; cf. ll. 5–6 n. 89–90 *flower . . . match*: cf. Matt. 6: 28–9.

94 *Non . . . laus*: 'not to us, O Lord, but to thee the praise' (L.). This is Browning's version of Ps. 115: 1, not the phrasing of the Vulgate: 'Non nobis, Domine, non nobis; sed nomini tuo da gloriam' (Ps. 113: 9).

98 *'sbuddikins*: an abbreviation of the oath 'God's bodikins', i.e. 'God's dear body'.

"O' the *Pro Milone* had been prisoned there,
"And rattled Rome awake?" Awaken Rome,
How can the Pope doze on in decency?
He needs must wake up also, speak his word,
Have his opinion like the rest of Rome,   105
About this huge, this hurly-burly case:
He wants who can excogitate the truth,
Give the result in speech, plain black and white,
To mumble in the mouth and make his own
—A little changed, good man, a little changed!   110
No matter, so his gratitude be moved,
By when my Giacintino gets of age,
Mindful of who thus helped him at a pinch,
Archangelus *Procurator Pauperum*—
And proved Hortensius *Redivivus!*   115

                              Whew!

---

102 *MS* If Rome's awake,>Awaken Rome,   104 *MS* say his say,>speak his
word,   105 *MS* Give>Have   *MS* {no comma}   106 *MS* huge and
>huge, [ ]>huge, [ ]>huge and>huge, this   *MS* hurlyburly case—   108 *MS*
in plain words>in speech, plain   *MS* white   110 *MS* changed!—   111
MS {line added later}   *MS* moved,—>moved,   112 *MS* {line added later}
114 *MS* {line added later}   *MS* Arcangelus   116 *MS* Come>Whew!

101 *Pro Milone*: 'For Milo' (52 BC), one of the most brilliant legal speeches ever
written, Cicero's defence of Titus Annius Milo on the charge of the murder of
Clodius. 'As a literary effort the speech owes its celebrity to the skilful blending of all
three elements, proof, paradox, and pathos. . . . If the whole is made up of exquisitely
proportioned parts, the details are hardly less perfect': *Pro Milone*, ed. by A. B. Poynton
(Oxford, 1892), p. 16. It is notorious, however, that Cicero never actually delivered it,
being intimidated at the trial into stammering a few sentences and sitting down.
(Pompey, governing Rome without a colleague, was determined to throw Milo to
the masses before appeasing the respectable.) Hence *Pro Milone* is the archetype of the
advocate's speech for its own sake, rather than in its context. Arcangeli, the true
professional, cares more for advancing his own career than saving Guido and the
peasants from Mannaia.
   106 *hurly-burly*: tumultuous, confusing.
   107 *excogitate*: think through, work out.
   108 *plain black and white*: i.e. 'clear', but also 'printed'.
   109 *mumble in the mouth*: (a pun) 'to speak indistinctly', but also 'to chew in a
childish way'.
   115 *Hortensius Redivivus*: Hortensius 'Come back to life'. Quintus Hortensius (114–
49 BC), the friend and rival of Cicero, was one of the great Roman orators of his day.
Like Cicero, he was renowned for his abundant and ornate style. There is, however, an

To earn the *Est-est*, merit the minced herb
That mollifies the liver's leathery slice,
With here a goose-foot, there a cock's-comb stuck,
Cemented in an element of cheese!   120
I doubt if dainties do the grandsire good:
Last June he had a sort of strangling... bah!
He's his own master, and his will is made.
So, liver fizz, law flit and Latin fly
As we rub hands o'er dish by way of grace!   125
May I lose cause if I vent one word more
Except,—with fresh-cut quill we ink the white,—
P-r-o-pro Guidone et Sociis. There!

[—]

---

120 *MS* {beginning of fo. 67}   *MS* cheese—   121–3 *MS* {lines added
later}   122 *MS* strangling seizure...>a sort of strangling...   *MS*
[ ]>bah!   124 *MS* How shall the Law>So, liver fizz, Law   *MS* the Latin>
Latin   126 *MS* say>vent   127 *MS* {line added later}   *MS* This then,—
>Except,—

---

element of irony here. Hortensius' most famous case is the defence of Verres, in which
he was completely overwhelmed by Cicero's unexpected tactics and reduced to silence
in face of the damning facts. In later life he withdrew from politics and was famous for
his love of gourmet cuisine—something that makes another ironic comparison with
Arcangeli.

117 *Est-est*: a particularly fine wine from Montefiascone, about 50 miles NNW
from Rome. 'In the northern portions of the Roman States the richest and most
esteemed wine is the famous *Est*, grown in the vicinity of Montefiascone. It owes its
name to the Bishop Johann Fugger, who, being fond of good living, was in the habit of
sending his servant before him, whenever he travelled, to ascertain where the best
wines were to be found, so that the worthy bishop might take his night's repose at
towns where he could best satisfy his palate. The servant, wherever he found a good
wine, wrote on the walls the Latin word *est* (*it is*); and when he came to Montefias-
cone, so impressed was he with the excellence of its wine that he wrote *est, est, est*, to
signify that it was trebly good; and so indeed the excellent bishop found it to his cost,
for here he died, as the story goes, from partaking of it too freely. In the Cathedral, any
one who doubts the fact may see his monument, with this inscription, written by his
valet: "*Est—est—est. Propter nimium est, Joannes de Foucris, dominus meus, mortuus est.*"':
Roba di Roma, i. 307. Hawthorne sampled what the waiter assured him was 'the
genuine Est-wine' during his 1858 tour of Italy: 'It was of golden colour, and very
delicate, somewhat resembling still champagne, but finer, and requiring a calmer pause
to appreciate its subtle delight': Hawthorne, 484.

119 *goose-foot...cock's-comb*: kinds of herbs.

128 *pro Guidone et Sociis*: 'In defence of Guido and his companions', the title of
Arcangeli's defence speech. At the beginning of the line he spells out the letters of *pro*.

Count Guido married—or, in Latin due,
What? *Duxit in uxorem?*—commonplace!   130
Tædas jugales iniit, subiit,—ha!
He underwent the matrimonial torch?
Connubio stabili sibi junxit,—hum!
In stable bond of marriage bound his own?
That's clear of any modern taint: and yet . . .   135

Virgil is little help to who writes prose.
He shall attack me Terence with the dawn,
Shall Cinuccino! Mum, mind business, Sir!

Thus circumstantially evolve we facts,
Ita se habet ideo series facti: 140
He wedded,—ah, with owls for augury!
Nupserat, heu sinistris avibus,
One of the blood Arezzo boasts her best,
Dominus Guido, nobili genere ortus,
Pompiliæ . . .
       But the version afterward!   145

129 *MS* {New paragraph indicated by 'New Par.' in left-hand margin}   *MS* Latin, say>Latin due   130 *MS Duxit in uxorem*—which sounds>What? *Duxit in uxorem?*—   131 *MS iniit*—   134 *MS* he him>his own—   136 *MS* {line added later}   *MS* {New paragraph indicated by 'New Par.' in left-hand margin}   *MS* prose—   *139 *MS* {New paragraph indicated by 'New Par.' in left-hand margin. Paragraphing obscured in *1868* and *1872* by this line's being at the head of the page}   141 *MS* the owl was>with owls for   145 *MS* {New paragraph indicated by 'New Par' in right-hand margin}   *MS* Latin>version

130–5 *Duxit . . . yet*: Arcangeli sneers at 'duxit in uxorem' ('He led for wife') as commonplace, and toys with phrasings that are more resonant and literary: 'He entered upon, underwent, the marriage torch . . . He joined himself by stable marriage'. The first option echoes Catullus lxiv. 302: 'taedas . . celebrare iugalis', and the second Virgil, *Aeneid*, I. 73, IV. 126: 'conubio iungam stabili'. The ability to show variety in phrasing the same idea was a quality much prized in Renaissance Latin; as someone concerned with artistic Latin style, Arcangeli prides himself on his ingenuity in this respect: cf. ll. 200–17. The ultimate textbook on this aspect of stylistics is the *De copia* of Erasmus.

137 *Terence*: the comedies of Terence (190–159 BC) were often thought good for schoolboys learning Latin. In the nineteenth century, for example, Newman produced expurgated school editions of *Phormio, Eunuchus*, and *Andria*.

142–5 *Nupserat . . . Pompiliæ*: with the exception of *heu* ('alas'), which Browning adds, these are the actual opening words of the first argument of the real Arcangeli: 'Count Guido, born of noble race, had married, alas with bad birds for omen, Pompilia . . .' : OYB ix (11), pam. 1.

Curb we this ardour! Notes alone, to-day,
The speech to-morrow and the Latin last:
Such was the rule in Farinacci's time.
Indeed I hitched it into verse and good.
Unluckily, law quite absorbs a man,   150
Or else I think I too had poetized.
"Law is the pork substratum of the fry,
"Goose-foot and cock's-comb are Latinity,"—
And in this case, if circumstance assist,
We'll garnish law with idiom, never fear!   155
Out-of-the-way events extend our scope:
For instance, when Bottini brings his charge,
"That letter which you say Pompilia wrote,—
"To criminate her parents and herself
"And disengage her husband from the coil,—   160
"That, Guido Franceschini wrote, say we:
"Because Pompilia could nor read nor write,
"Therefore he pencilled her such letter first,
"Then made her trace in ink the same again."
—Ha, my Bottini, have I thee on hip?   165

147 *MS* version>Latin   *MS* last—   149–51 *MS* {lines added later}   149
MS good: 150 *MS* man   151 *MS* poetized: 152 *MS* dish,>
fry,   153 *MS* cockscomb *1868* cocks-comb   155 *MS* all>law   156
MS the>our   157 *MS* {beginning of fo. 68}   *MS* charge   158 *MS* —
"That   *MS 1868 1872* wrote,   161 *MS* we say—>say we—   163 *MS*
the>such   164 *MS* the same again in ink.">in ink the same again."

148 *Farinacci's time*: the works of Prospero Farinacci (1544–1616), the leading Italian
jurist of his day, are cited over a hundred times in OYB. Browning knew him from
here but also from his interest in the Cenci: Farinacci was famous as the lawyer who
had defended Beatrice Cenci in an attempt to avoid the death penalty. Browning
consulted Sir George Bowyer during his research for his poem (see our Vol. VII, p.
xix), and he knew Bowyer's *A Dissertation on the Statutes of the Cities of Italy, and a
Translation of the Pleading of Prospero Farinacio in Defence of Beatrice Cenci* (1838). Bowyer
reproduced the whole of Farinacci's speech in a careful translation with notes (pp. 73–
101), and in addition to OYB this would have given Browning another insight into the
methods and manner of Roman law as practised in the seventeenth century. See ll.
328–44 n., and Appendix C.

152–3 *fry . . . Latinity*: here Arcangeli does 'poetize': 'Latinity' is pronounced so as to
make another of his sing-song rhymes with 'fry'.

165 *have . . . hip*: have I got the advantage of you? (a metaphor from wrestling); cf.
Merchant of Venice, I. iii. 46–7: 'If I can catch him once upon the hip, / I will feed fat the
ancient grudge I bear him'.

How will he turn this and break Tully's pate?
"*Existimandum*" (don't I hear the dog!)
"*Quod Guido designaverit elementa*
"*Dictæ epistolæ, quæ fuerint*
"*(Superinducto ab ea calamo)*   170
"*Notata atramento*"—there's a style!—
"*Quia ipsa scribere nesciebat.*" Boh!
Now, my turn! Either, *Insulse!* (I outburst)
Stupidly put! Inane is the response,
Inanis est responsio, or the like—   175
To-wit, that each of all those characters,
Quod singula elementa epistolæ,
Had first of all been traced for her by him,
Fuerant per eum prius designata,
And then, the ink applied a-top of that,   180
Et deinde, superinducto calamo,
The piece, she says, became her handiwork,
Per eam, efformata, ut ipsa asserit.
Inane were such response! (a second time:)
Her husband outlined her the whole, forsooth?   185
Vir ejus lineabat epistolam?
What, she confesses that she wrote the thing,

166 MS *1868* nor break   167 MS dog?)   173 MS "*Insulse!*—" I outburst,>*Insulse!*—I outburst, *1868 Insulse!*—I outburst,   174 MS were>is   180 *Yale 2* ink>pen   182 MS handywork,   186 MS {beginning of fo. 69}   187 MS So,   MS thing—

166 *How . . . pate?*: 'how will he counter my wrestling move / translate this statement, and how will he offend against Ciceronian Latin?' 'Turn this' has the two senses indicated. 'Break Tully's pate' is on the model of 'break Priscian's head': cf. VI. 389 n.

167–72 "*Existimandum . . . nesciebat.*": 'It is to be supposed that Guido marked out the characters of the aforesaid letter, which she afterwards inked (by tracing them over with a pen), because she herself did not know how to write' (L.). This is how Arcangeli imagines Bottini will translate into Latin the charge at ll. 161–4. The real Bottini uses similar phrasing at OYB clxxii (179–80), Bottini, pam. 13. Here the Latin is good legalese, but there are many aspects of the phrasing that are un-Ciceronian, and for this Arcangeli mocks it: see l. 1753 n.

173 *Insulse!*: 'Stupidly' (L.).

175–83 *Inanis . . . asserit*: OYB civ (112), Arcangeli, pam. 8.

186 *Vir . . . epistolam?*: these words are from one of the formal annotations (in type) in the margin of Pompilia's printed cross-examination, one of a number of documents and letters presented to the court: OYB lxxxvi (94), pam. 7.

Fatetur eam scripsisse, (scorn that scathes!)
That she might pay obedience to her lord?
Ut viro obtemperaret, apices   190
(Here repeat charge with proper varied phrase)
Eo designante, ipsaque calamum
Super inducente? By such argument,
Ita pariter, she seeks to show the same,
(Ay, by Saint Joseph and what saints you please)   195
Epistolam ostendit, medius fidius,
No voluntary deed but fruit of force!
Non voluntarie sed coacte scriptam!
That's the way to write Latin, friend my Fisc!
Bottini is a beast, one barbarous: 200
Look out for him when he attempts to say
"Armed with a pistol, Guido followed her!"
Will not I be beforehand with my Fisc,
Cut away phrase by phrase from underfoot!
Guido Pompiliam—Guido thus his wife   205
Following with igneous engine, shall I have?
Armis munitus igneis persequens—
Arma sulphurea gestans, sulphury arms,
Or, might one style a pistol—popping-piece?
Armatus breviori sclopulo?   210

---

188 *MS scripsisse* (in scorn>*scripsisse* (scorn   189 *MS* lord,   194 *MS pari-*
ter—   *MS* [?She]>she   *MS* same   195 *MS* Ay,   *MS* please,   197 *MS*
force,   202 *MS* her"!   206 *MS* say?>have?   208 *MS gestans*—   *MS*
sulphureous>sulphury   *MS* arms—   209 *MS* Or—   *MS* popping-piece

---

188–93 *Fatetur . . . inducente*: OYB lxxi (77), Bottini, pam. 6.

194–8 *Ita . . . scriptam*: OYB ccxlviii (245), Lamparelli, pam. 17. Browning adds to
the original the phrase *medius fidius*, an elliptical version of *ita me Dius Fidius iuvet* = 'So
help me God!' Arcangeli translates it in the next line 'Ay, by Saint Joseph and what
saints you please'. The phrase enacts his scorn at Pompilia's claim.

199 *That's . . . Latin*: actually Arcangeli is not writing strict Ciceronian: *voluntarie* is
not found till Hyginus, *coacte* first in Gellius, and there with the sense 'tersely' or
'precisely'. Better would have been *non sponte sed cogente marito*.

207–10 *Armis . . . sclopulo?*: at ll. 202–4 Arcangeli says he intends to use all the possible
Latin translations of 'Armed with a pistol, Guido followed her', so that when Bottini
makes his speech he will have no way of being original. Here he tries out three terms
for firearms: 'following with fiery arms . . . carrying sulphurous arms . . . armed with a
short pistol'. All of these occur in OYB, the last, *breviori sclopulo*, at OYB ccxlvi (244):

We'll let him have been armed so, though it make
Somewhat against us: I had thought to own—
Provided with a simple travelling-sword,
Ense solummodo viatorio
Instructus: but we'll grant the pistol here: 215
Better we lost the cause than lacked the gird
At the Fisc's Latin, lost the Judge's laugh!
It's Venturini that decides for style.
Tommati rather goes upon the law.
So, as to law,—   220

                         Ah, but with law ne'er hope
To level the fellow,—don't I know his trick!
How he draws up, ducks under, twists aside!
He's a lean-gutted hectic rascal, fine
As pale-haired red-eyed ferret which pretends   225
'T is ermine, pure soft snow from tail to snout.
He eludes law by piteous looks aloft,

---

213 *MS* {quotation marks at beginning and end>no quotation marks at beginning and end}   *MS* {no comma}   215 *MS* {beginning of fo. 70}   217 *MS* latin, >Latin,   *MS* with>lost   218 *MS* observes on>decides for   219 *MS* {line added later}   220 *MS* Then>So,   221 *MS* {no new paragraph}   *MS* {no comma}   225 *MS* the pale-haired>pale-haired

Lamparelli, pam. 17. *Sclopulus*, obviously not in classical Latin, stands for *schioppo*, the standard Italian word for a flintlock or musket. It is related to *scoppio* (explosion, bang) as a noun and *scoppiare* (to explode) as a verb. Browning himself was very much up to the game of translating modern terms into Latin: see his 'On Being Defied to Express in a Hexameter: "You Ought to Sit on the Safety-Valve"', a *jeu d'esprit* of 22 Feb. 1866: Pettigrew and Collins, ii. 954.

214–15 *Ense . . . Instructus:* OYB cxiv (122), Arcangeli, pam. 8. The real Arcangeli claimed Guido was armed with a light, traveller's sword, and makes no mention of a pistol. Bottini refuted the implications of this claim at OYB clxxxiii (188), pam. 13.

216 *gird:* gibe, 'dig'. The real Arcangeli made no such gibe; the obsession with Latin style is all Browning's invention.

224–6 *fine . . . snout:* fine as a nasty creature (a ferret, a variety of common polecat) cunningly pretending to be a lovely white creature (the ermine, the European stoat). The fur of ermine is used on the gowns of judges, so that figuratively 'ermine' can mean judge: the implication is that Bottini insinuates for himself a judge-like status. The eyes of ferrets were proverbially red. Cf. the whole of this image with *Julius Caesar*, I. ii. 185–8: 'Cicero / Looks with such ferret and such fiery eyes / As we have seen him in the Capitol, / Being cross'd in conference by some senators'. Cf. also VII. 436 n.

Lets Latin glance off as he makes appeal
To saint that's somewhere in the ceiling-top:
Do you suppose I don't conceive the beast?   230
Plague of the ermine-vermin! For it takes,
It takes, and here's the fellow Fisc, you see,
And Judge, you'll not be long in seeing next!
Confound the fop—he's now at work like me:
Enter his study, as I seem to do,   235
Hear him read out his writing to himself!
I know he writes as if he spoke: I hear
The hoarse shrill throat, see shut eyes, neck shot-forth,
—I see him strain on tiptoe, soar and pour
Eloquence out, nor stay nor stint at all—   240
Perorate in the air, then quick to press
With the product! What abuse of type and sheet!
He'll keep clear of my cast, my logic-throw,
Let argument slide, and then deliver swift
Some bowl from quite an unguessed point of stand—   245
Having the luck o' the last word, the reply!
A plaguy cast, a mortifying stroke:
You face a fellow—cries "So, there you stand?
"But I discourteous jump clean o'er your head!

228 *MS* latin>Latin   229 *MS* —To the saint *1868* the saint   *MS 1868 1872*
ceiling-top,—   230 *MS* {line added later}   *MS 1868* that I don't see   231
MS ermine-vermin, for it takes—   232 *MS* The trick,>It takes—   234 *MS*
Follow the fellow—>Confound the fop—   *MS* ^now^   236 *MS* himself
—   239 *MS* —They say he strains>I see he strain {*sic*}   *MS* soars and
pours>soar and pour   240 *MS* stays nor stints>stay nor stint   241 *MS*
Perorates>Perorate   *MS* and all in print!>and so, to press! *1868* and so, to
242 *MS* {line added later}   *MS* product: what   *MS 1868* type is here!   243
MS   logic's throw,>logic-throw,   244   *MS*   roll,>slide,   245   *MS*
an[ ]>an   *MS* stand,—   247 *MS* stroke,   248 *MS* {beginning of fo. 71}

238–9 *hoarse . . . tiptoe*: cf. the same allusion as at I. 1203–4. Bottini is like Chaucer's
ludicrous cock Chauntecleer: see *The Nun's Priest's Tale*, ll. 4521–3.

248–9 *"So . . . head!*: Dr Johnson said of Foote the comedian: 'One species of wit he
has to an eminent degree, that of escape. You drive him into a corner with both hands;
but he's gone, Sir, when you think you have got him—like an animal that jumps over
your head': *Boswell's Life of Johnson*, ed. by G. B. Hill, rev. L. F. Powell (6 vols.,
Oxford, 1934–50), iii. 69. We are indebted to Cook for this parallel.

"You take ship-carpentry for pilotage,   250
"Stop rat-holes, while a sea sweeps through the breach,—
"Hammer and fortify at puny points?
"Do, clamp and tenon, make all tight and safe!
" 'T is here and here and here you ship a sea,
"No good of your stopped leaks and littleness!"   255

Yet what do I name "little and a leak"?
The main defence o' the murder's used to death,
By this time, dry bare bones, no scrap we pick:
Safer I worked the new, the unforeseen,
The nice by-stroke, the fine and improvised   260
Point that can titillate the brain o' the Bench
Torpid with over-teaching, long ago!
As if Tommati (that has heard, reheard
And heard again, first this side and then that—
Guido and Pietro, Pietro and Guido, din   265
And deafen, full three years, at each long ear)
Don't want amusement for instruction now,
Won't rather feel a flea run o'er his ribs,
Than a daw settle heavily on his head!
Oh I was young and had the trick of fence,   270

250–5 *MS* {no quotation marks at beginnings of lines}   250 *MS* act
ship-carpenter, not pilot now,— *1868* play ship-carpenter, not pilot so,—   251 *MS*
breach—   252 *MS 1868 1872* points!   253 *MS* safe,   254 *MS* ^and
here^   255 *MS* {no quotation mark at end of line} *Yale 2* littleness!">little
taps!"   256 *MS* {no new paragraph}   *MS 1868 1872* leak?"   257 *MS*
known by now,>used to death,   258 *MS* {line added later}   *MS* bones
no   *MS* to pick— *1868* to pick: 259 *MS* at the novel>at the new, the *1868*
at the new,   260 *MS 1868 1872* bye-stroke,   *MS 1868* improvised, *Yale 2* The
nice bye-stroke, the fine and improvised>Played the nice bye-stroke, fine and im-
provised   261 *MS* Points *Yale 2* Point>Pass   262 *MS* by this time,— *1868*
by this time!   263 *MS 1868* Tommati, that   264 *MS* now>first   *MS*
now>then   *MS 1868* that,—   265 *MS 1868* Guido din   266 *MS* these
full three years, with the case,>full three years, at each long ear, *1868* ear,—   267
MS now—   268 *MS* skip>run   269 *MS* an owl>a daw   *MS* pate!>
head!   270 *MS 1868 1872* Oh,

253 *clamp and tenon*: i.e. employ joinery skills to tighten the ship's structure.
266 *long ear*: i.e. ass's ear: the implication is that Tommati is stupid.
269 *daw*: in *MS*, Browning sharpens the irony and comedy of this image, substitut-
ing the chattering jackdaw for the solemn owl.

Knew subtle pass and push with careless right—
My left arm ever quiet behind back,
With dagger ready: not both hands to blade!
Puff and blow, put the strength out, Blunderbore!
There's my subordinate, young Spreti, now,   275
Pedant and prig,—he'll pant away at proof,
That's his way!

          Now for mine—to rub some life
Into one's choppy fingers this cold day!
I trust Cinuzzo ties on tippet, guards   280
The precious throat on which so much depends!
Guido must be all goose-flesh in his hole,
Despite the prison-straw: bad Carnival
For captives! no sliced fry for him, poor Count!

Carnival-time,—another providence!   285
The town a-swarm with strangers to amuse,
To edify, to give one's name and fame
In charge of, till they find, some future day,
Cintino come and claim it, his name too,

---

272 *MS 1868* The   *MS 1868* quietly   *MS 1868* {no comma}   273 *MS 1868* the dagger in't: *MS* the blade!   275 *MS 1868* That's   *MS* Spreti now,   278 *MS* {New paragraph indicated by 'New P.' in left-hand margin} 279 *MS* {beginning of fo. 72}   280 *MS* puts>ties   *MS* cloak and cape.>tippet, guards   281 *MS* {line added later}   282 *MS* show>be *MS* {no comma}   283 *MS* carnival   284 *MS* No *MS* dog!   285 *MS* {New paragraph indicated by 'New Par.' in left-hand margin} *MS* providence!—   287 [?to]>and   288 *MS* charge until>charge of, till *MS* find some *MS* day   289 *MS* comes>come *MS* claims>claim

271 *with careless right*: untroubled, deft right hand.

274 *Puff . . . Blunderbore!*: i.e. 'try as hard as you like, you great lumbering giant'. The allusion is to the nursery tale in which Jack the Giant-killer outwits the giant Blunderbore and in the end tricks him into stabbing himself to death. Arcangeli paints himself as the nimble, quick-witted folk-hero. In the following lines he gives his subordinate Spreti as a type of the earnest but stupid giant.

279 *choppy fingers*: chapped fingers: cf. *Macbeth*, I. iii. 44.

280 *tippet*: fur scarf.

283 *Carnival*: in his chronology of events, Browning carefully calculated the real ending of Carnival in 1698 as 12 Feb.: see our Vol. VII, p. 323.

Pledge of the pleasantness they owe papa— 290
Who else was it cured Rome of her great qualms,
When she must needs have her own judgment?—ay,
When all her topping wits had set to work,
Pronounced already on the case: mere boys,
Twice Cineruggiolo's age with half his sense, 295
As good as tell me, when I cross the court,
"Master Arcangeli!" (plucking at my gown)
"We can predict, we comprehend your play,
"We'll help you save your client." Tra-la-la!
I've travelled ground, from childhood to this hour, 300
To have the town anticipate my track?
The old fox takes the plain and velvet path,
The young hounds' predilection,—prints the dew,
Don't he, to suit their pulpy pads of paw?
No! Burying nose deep down i' the briery bush, 305
Thus I defend Count Guido.

                    Where are we weak?
First, which is foremost in advantage too,
Our murder,—we call, killing,—is a fact
Confessed, defended, made a boast of: good! 310
To think the Fisc claimed use of torture here,

---

290 *MS* gratitude>pleasantness   *MS* Papa!—   291 *MS* [ ] who it was cured>
Who else was it, cured *1868* it,   *MS* qualms?   292 *MS* judgment,—   *MS*
1868 {no comma}   293 *MS 1868* Since   294 *MS* boys—   295 *MS*
1868 and half   *MS* sense—   296 *MS* [?when]>me,   297 *MS* Arcan-
geli!"—plucking   *MS* gown—   298 *MS* understand>comprehend   300
MS 1868 till   *MS* hour   301 *MS 1868 1872* track!   302 *MS* [ ]>and   *MS*
{no comma}   *303 *MS* hounds' *1868 1872 1888 1889* hound's   305 *MS* {no
comma}   306 *MS* I>we   308 *MS* {beginning of fo. 73}   *Yale 2* First,>
First,—   *Yale 2* too,>too,—   309 *MS* This>Our   *Yale 2* murder,>
murder,—   311 *MS* {no comma}

---

290 *pleasantness*: i.e. favour.

291 *qualms*: anxieties, difficulties with the rights and wrongs of the legal case.

293 *topping*: finest.

304 *pulpy*: soft, flabby.

305 *Burying . . . bush*: i.e. going a difficult route, where the hounds cannot follow
him = using tangled, prickly arguments that young lawyers do not expect. Arcangeli
paints himself as the crafty old fox outwitting the hounds.

And got thereby avowal plump and plain
That gives me just the chance I wanted,—scope
Not for brute-force but ingenuity,
Explaining matters, not denying them!   315
One may dispute,—as I am bound to do,
And shall,—validity of process here:
Inasmuch as a noble is exempt
From torture which plebeians undergo
In such a case: for law is lenient, lax,   320
Remits the torture to a nobleman
Unless suspicion be of twice the strength
Attaches to a man born vulgarly:
We don't card silk with comb that dresses wool.
Moreover 't was severity undue   325
In this case, even had the lord been lout.
What utters, on this head, our oracle,
Our Farinacci, my Gamaliel erst,
In those immortal "Questions"? This I quote:
"Of all the tools at Law's disposal, sure   330
"That named *Vigiliarum* is the best—
"That is, the worst—to whoso needs must bear:
"Lasting, as it may do, from some seven hours
"To ten; (beyond ten, we've no precedent;
"Certain have touched their ten, but, bah, they died!)   335

---

315 *MS* them.   316 *MS* do,—   317 *MS* the process>process   320
MS very clear,>lenient, lax   324 *MS* flax.   325 *MS* 1868 1872 More-
over,   *MS* undue severity>severity undue   328 *MS* My>Our   329 *MS*
[ ] [ ]>What I 1868 What I   330 *MS* disposal—   332 *MS* 1868 has
to   334 *MS* ten,—beyond 1868 ten, (beyond   *MS* there's>we've   *MS* pre-
cedent,—   335 *MS* {line added later}   *MS* {no quotation mark at beginning
of line}   *MS* ten but, bah—they died— 1868 1872 ten but,

328–44 *Farinacci . . . we!"*: see l. 148 n. Browning consulted the works of Farinacci in
the British Museum. Here he is paraphrasing a passage that had particularly struck him
in the *Quaestiones*, more properly the *Praxis et Theorica Criminalis*, at Qu. 38, nos. 70–1.
Spreti, Arcangeli's subordinate, cites this reference in the form '*Farinacc. qu. 38. num.*
71': OYB xxxv (not in Everyman). Browning seems to have followed it up from here.
The real Farinacci is very serious about this form of torture, describing it as 'cruel and
severe'. Browning makes Arcangeli adapt his quotation of Farinacci to his own
sanguine, buoyant style. See our Vol. VII, p. xix, and Appendix C at the end of the
present volume.

"It does so efficaciously convince,
"That,—speaking by much observation here,—
"Out of each hundred cases, by my count,
"Never I knew of patients beyond four
"Withstand its taste, or less than ninety-six   340
"End by succumbing: only martyrs four,
"Of obstinate silence, guilty or no,—against
"Ninety-six full confessors, innocent
"Or otherwise,—so shrewd a tool have we!"
No marvel either: in unwary hands,   345
Death on the spot is no rare consequence:
As indeed all but happened in this case
To one of ourselves, our young tough peasant-friend
The accomplice called Baldeschi: they were rough,
Dosed him with torture as you drench a horse,   350
Not modify your treatment to a man:
So, two successive days he fainted dead,
And only on the third essay, gave up,
Confessed like flesh and blood. We could reclaim,—
Blockhead Bottini giving cause enough!   355
But no,—we'll take it as spontaneously
Confessed: we'll have the murder beyond doubt.
Ah, fortunate (the poet's word reversed)
Inasmuch as we know our happiness!

---

336 *MS 1868* {no comma}   338 *MS* {beginning of fo. 74}   339 *MS* have I
known>I knew   340 *MS* That could withstand—>Withstand its taste—
341 *MS* That ended>End   *MS* ^only^   345 *MS* "No   346 *MS* con-
sequence.   349 *MS* Baldeschi,—   350 *MS* {no comma}   351 *MS*
man,   352 *MS* So two   353 *MS* up   355 *MS* The blockhead giving
cause enough! But no!>Blockhead Bottini giving cause enough!   356 *MS* We'll
take it as confessed>But no,—we'll take it as   357   *MS*   {line   added
later}   358 *MS* {no comma}

349–54 *Baldeschi . . . blood*: the two faintings of Baldeschi are from SS 18.
350 *drench*: cf. v. 1038 n.
354 *reclaim*: appeal, protest (against the use of torture and the confessions).
358–9 *fortunate . . . happiness*: cf. Virgil, *Georgics*, II. 458–9: 'O fortunatos nimium,
sua si bona norint, / agricolas!': 'O too fortunate, the countrymen, *if* they but knew
their happiness'.

Had the antagonist left dubiety,   360
Here were we proving murder a mere myth,
And Guido innocent, ignorant, absent,—ay,
Absent! He was—why, where should Christian be?—
Engaged in visiting his proper church,
The duty of us all at Christmas-time,   365
When Caponsacchi, the seducer, stung
To madness by his relegation, cast
About him and contrived a remedy
In murder: since opprobrium broke afresh,
By birth o' the babe, on him the imputed sire,   370
He it was quietly sought to smother up
His shame and theirs together,—killed the three,
And fled—(go seek him where you please to search)—
Just at the time when Guido, touched by grace,
Devotions ended, hastened to the spot,   375
Meaning to pardon his convicted wife,
"Neither do I condemn thee, go in peace!"—
And thus arrived i' the nick of time to catch
The charge o' the killing, though great-heartedly
He came but to forgive and bring to life.   380
Doubt ye the force of Christmas on the soul?
"Is thine eye evil because mine is good?"

So, doubtless, had I needed argue here
But for the full confession round and sound!

360 MS a shade of doubt>a dubiety   362 MS absent, ay   364 MS
Church,   365 1868 Christmas-time;   367 MS {beginning of fo.
75}   368 MS 1868 remedy: 369 MS To stave off the 1868 To stave off
what   370 MS 1868 the birth   371 MS 1868 He came and   372 MS
three   374 MS 1868 moment, Guido,   376 MS wife—   378 MS And
yet>Who thus 1868 Who   MS be>catch   379 MS Charged with>The charge
o'   MS who greatheartedly>though greatheartedly   380 MS Came rather>He
came but   MS life: 383 MS {no new paragraph}   MS we>I

364 *proper church*: cf. VII. 17 n.
377 "*Neither . . . peace!*": see John 8: 11.
382 "*Is . . . good?*": see Matt. 20: 15.

Thus might you wrong some kingly alchemist,— 385
Whose concern should not be with showing brass
Transmuted into gold, but triumphing,
Rather, about his gold changed out of brass,
Not vulgarly to the mere sight and touch,
But in the idea, the spiritual display, 390
The apparition buoyed by winged words
Hovering above its birth-place in the brain,—
Thus would you wrong this excellent personage
Forced, by the gross need, to gird apron round,
Plant forge, light fire, ply bellows,—in a word, 395
Demonstrate: when a faulty pipkin's crack
May disconcert you his presumptive truth!
Here were I hanging to the testimony
Of one of these poor rustics—four, ye gods!
Whom the first taste of friend the Fiscal's cord 400
May drive into undoing my whole speech,
Undoing, on his birthday,—what is worse,—

---

385 *MS* Thus would you have the>So would you have some *1868* would you have *MS* alchemist— 386 *MS* business>concern *MS* proving clay>proving brass *1868* proving 387 *MS* *1868* Transmutable to *MS* triumphing 388 *MS* *1868* above *MS* clay,>brass, 389 *MS* gross>mere *MS* {no comma} 391 *MS* *1868* Proud 392 *MS* brain— 393 *MS* *1868* Here *MS* *1868* have 394 *MS* {no commas} *MS* vulgar>gross need *MS* tie>gird 395 *MS* {beginning of fo. 76} *MS* coal,>fire, 396 *MS* *1868* Demonstrate— *1872* Demonstrate: 397 *MS* his [ ]>you his 398 *MS* might I hang on>were I hanging 399 *MS* animals—there are five—>rustics— four, ye gods! *1868* Gods! 401 *MS* *1868* Might *MS* twist>drive *MS* unsaying>undoing *MS* speech,— 402 {not found in *MS* *1868*}

385–401 *Thus . . . speech*: Arcangeli thinks he can prove any case by 'spiritual display' (390)—like a proud and charismatic alchemist he can claim (without actually demonstrating) that he has turned brass to gold. In this instance, if he had lowered himself and actually set about turning Guido from a murderer into a merciful husband before the eyes of the court, his case could have been destroyed by the confessions of the accomplices—he would be like the alchemist, forced physically to demonstrate his powers, who had his work wrecked by a broken piece of equipment. The contrast is between the level at which Arcangeli likes to work—imagination and oratory—and the mundane level of facts and truth which he sees as both problematic and beneath his dignity.

396 *pipkin*: a small earthenware pot (part of the alchemist's equipment).
398 *hanging to*: depending on.

My son and heir!

               I wonder, all the same,
Not so much at those peasants' lack of heart;   405
But—Guido Franceschini, nobleman,
Bear pain no better! Everybody knows
It used once, when my father was a boy,
To form a proper, nay, important point
I' the education of our well-born youth,   410
That they took torture handsomely at need,
Without confessing in this clownish guise.
Each noble had his rack for private use,
And would, for the diversion of a guest,
Bid it be set up in the yard of arms,   415
And take thereon his hour of exercise,—
Command the varletry stretch, strain their best,
While friends looked on, admired my lord could smile
'Mid tugging which had caused an ox to roar.
Men are no longer men!   420

               —And advocates
No longer Farinacci, let us add,
If I one more time fly from point proposed!
So, *Vindicatio,*—here begins the speech!—
Honoris causa; thus we make our stand: 425

---

403 *MS 1868* Shaming truth so!   405 *MS* ^so much^   *MS* wretched animals
>peasants' lack of heart,   406 *MS* to confess, a>Franceschini,   409 *MS*
[?an]>nay,   410 *MS* noble>well-born   *MS* {no comma}   411 *MS* To
^take^   the   *1868*   To take the   *MS*   decently>handsomely   412   *MS*
guise: 413 *MS* had a rack built for his>noble had a rack for   414 *MS*
guest   416 *MS* And>To *1868* To   *MS* exercise,   417 *MS* varlets stretch
and>varletry stretch,   *MS* best   419 *MS* lout>ox   420 *MS* men—
421   *MS* {New paragraph indicated by 'New P' in right-hand margin}   *MS*
nay,>And,   422 *MS* one might>let men *1868* men   424 *MS* So—   *MS*
same!,— *1868* same!—   425 *1868* so

---

412 *clownish guise*: peasant-like way.

415 *yard of arms*: the enclosure or courtyard where the nobleman's men-at-arms
would normally practise.

417 *varletry*: servants, common folk.

424–5 *Vindicatio . . . Honoris causa*: 'A Righting . . . of the Cause of Honour' (L.). See
Cook, 168: 'Even apart from their confessions the evidence against Guido and his

Honour in us had injury, we prove.
Or if we fail to prove such injury
More than misprision of the fact,—what then?
It is enough, authorities declare,
If the result, the deed in question now,   430
Be caused by confidence that injury
Is veritable and no figment: since,
What, though proved fancy afterward, seemed fact
At the time, they argue shall excuse result.
That which we do, persuaded of good cause   435
For what we do, hold justifiable!—
So casuists bid: man, bound to do his best,
They would not have him leave that best undone
And mean to do his worst,—though fuller light
Show best was worst and worst would have been best.   440
Act by the present light!—they ask of man.
Ultra quod hic non agitur, besides
It is not anyway our business here,
De probatione adulterii,
To prove what we thought crime was crime indeed,   445
Ad irrogandam pœnam, and require

---

426 *MS* {beginning of fo. 77}   *MS* Honor   *MS 1868* we shall prove. *MS* prove
[?:]>prove.   431 *MS* Were>Be   *MS* such injury   432 *MS* Was>
Were   *MS* figment,—why,   433 *MS* This,>What,   434 *MS* and>I trow
{interlined above undeleted 'and'}   *MS* whate'er ensue.> result.   435 *MS*
there is>of good   436 *MS* is>hold   437 *MS 1868 1872* The   438
MS You>They   439 *MS* [?For] meaning to do>And mean to do
the   440 *MS* was best. Let man   441 *MS* light, they ask no more. *1868*
light,   *MS* [ ]>they   442 *MS* agitur—beside *Yale 1* beside>beside,   443
MS {no comma}   446 *MS* to [ ]>and require

---

associates was abundant and conclusive. Their lawyers therefore admitted the kill-
ing . . . but contended that their clients should be absolved from guilt, or at least could
claim some relaxation of the murder-penalty, on the ground that their motive had
been the vindication of Guido's honour. Whether vindication of honour, even if long
postponed, was a good defence in law, whether Guido's honour had in fact "had
injury", whether, if so, its vindication was the motive of the killing, are the principal
questions in dispute.'

428 *misprision of the fact*: a mistaken belief that such injury was a fact.
437 *casuists*: moral experts, thinkers on complex moral points.
442–55 *Ultra . . . claim*: OYB xi (13), Arcangeli, pam. 1.

Its punishment: such nowise do we seek:
Sed ad effectum, but 't is our concern,
Excusandi, here to simply find excuse,
Occisorem, for who did the killing-work,   450
Et ad illius defensionem, (mark
The difference) and defend the man, just that!
Quo casu levior probatio
Exuberaret, to which end far lighter proof
Suffices than the prior case would claim: 455
It should be always harder to convict,
In short, than to establish innocence.
Therefore we shall demonstrate first of all
That Honour is a gift of God to man
Precious beyond compare: which natural sense   460
Of human rectitude and purity,—
Which white, man's soul is born with,—brooks no touch:
Therefore, the sensitivest spot of all,
Wounded by any wafture breathed from black,
Is,—honour within honour, like the eye   465
Centred i' the ball,—the honour of our wife.
Touch us o' the pupil of our honour, then,

---

447 *MS* [ ] punishment:>Its punishment: which>such no-wise do we seek: 448
MS effectum—   *MS* {no commas}   449 *MS Excusandi*—   *MS* {no commas}
MS ^here^   450 *MS* ^the^   *MS* killing-[ ]>killing-work   451 *MS defen-*
sionem,—mark   452 *MS* difference!,— 1868 difference!)   *MS* I>we   *MS*
[ ]>ourselves: just that 1868 that.   454 *MS Exuberaret*,—   455 *MS* {begin-
ning of fo. 78}   456–7 *MS* {lines added later}   457 *MS* establish>demons
>establish   458   *MS* establish>demonstrate   459   *MS* Honor   *MS*
the>a   460 *MS 1868* compare,—   *MS* the>which   461 *MS* {line added
later}   462 *MS* The>Which   *MS* with, bears 1868 with,   *MS* speck:>
touch: 463 *MS* And that>Therefore   *MS* [ ]>spot   464 *MS* Woundable
by a   *MS* wafture,—[?word], do I say?>wafture breathed from black, 1868 a waf-
ture   465 *MS* That's gross: a [ ]>Is,—honour within honour, like the
eye   466 *MS* honor   *MS* his>our   *MS* wife: 467 *MS* him>us   *MS*
his>our

---

464 *wafture*: i.e. the faintest hint (wafted through the air). According to OED²,
'wafture' was coined by Nicholas Rowe in his 1709 emendation to *Julius Caesar*, II. i.
246–7, and gained literary currency thereafter: 'But with an angry wafture [originally
'wafter': Folio] of your hand / Gave sign for me to leave you'. Browning's use is highly
metaphorical and very much his own.

Not actually,—since so you slay outright,—
But by a gesture simulating touch,
Presumable mere menace of such taint,—   470
This were our warrant for eruptive ire
"To whose dominion I impose no end."

(Virgil, now, should not be too difficult
To Cinoncino,—say, the early books.
Pen, truce to further gambols! *Poscimur!*)   475

Nor can revenge of injury done here
To the honour proved the life and soul of us,
Be too excessive, too extravagant:
Such wrong seeks and must have complete revenge.
Show we this, first, on the mere natural ground: 480
Begin at the beginning, and proceed

---

468 *MS* actually—   *MS* ^so^   *MS* him [ ]>outright,—   470 *MS* Presumably
the   471 *MS* This—this is>This were our   472 *MS* end—"   ★473
1868 1872 {new paragraph. Paragraphing obscured in *1888* and *1889* by this line's being
at the head of the page}   474 *MS* [?not]>—say   *MS* books.... *1868* say the
books....   475 *MS* gambols, *poscimur!*)>gambols! *Poscimur!*)   476 *MS* {no
new paragraph}   477 *MS* {line added later}   478 *MS* extravagant,
479 *MS* It needs and needs>Such wrong seeks and   480 *MS* ground.   481
MS [?to]>and

---

472 *"To...end".*: see Virgil, *Aeneid*, 1. 278–9: 'his ego nec metas rerum nec
tempora pono: / imperium sine fine dedi': 'On them [the Romans] I fix no limits
of fortune or time: I have given them an empire that will know no end'. This is
Jupiter's majestic pronouncement on the future of Rome.

475 *Poscimur!*: 'We are summoned!' (L.), the opening word of Horace, *Odes*, 1.
xxxii. Horace, talking to his lyre, responds to a call for poetry; Arcangeli, talking to his
pen, goads himself back to his legal argument. Here, and at other points, Arcangeli is
very much a poet *manqué*: cf. ll. 973, 1182–4.

476–846 *Nor...it!*: see Cook, 169: 'That injured honour requires vindication is
argued at length (1) "on the mere natural ground" that such vindication is claimed by
"bird and beast" and "the very insects" (480–542); (2) "on Heathen grounds"—it is
claimed by pagan jurisprudence (550–79); (3) on the authority of "Apostle and
Evangelist and Saint", and even "our Lord Himself, made all of mansuetude" (580–
683); (4) on that "of Papal doctrine in our blaze of day" (684–727); and finally (5) on
that of "Civility", "the acknowledged use and wont" (731–846).'

Incontrovertibly. Theodoric,
In an apt sentence Cassiodorus cites,
Propounds for basis of all household law—
I hardly recollect it, but it ends,   485
"Bird mates with bird, beast genders with his like,
"And brooks no interference." Bird and beast?
The very insects . . . if they wive or no,
How dare I say when Aristotle doubts?
But the presumption is they likewise wive,   490
At least the nobler sorts; for take the bee
As instance,—copying King Solomon,—
Why that displeasure of the bee to aught

---

484 *MS* this for the>for   *MS* ^all^   *MS* household-law: *Yale 2* law—>law . . .
485 *MS* {line added later}   *MS* ends—   487 *MS* {no quotation mark at
beginning of line}   *MS* interference:" bird and beast, say I?>interference:" bird
and beast? *1868* interference:" bird   489 *MS* {beginning of fo. 79}   *Yale 2*
say when>say, when   490 *MS* marry too>likewise wive,   491 *MS*
sorts,   *MS* Bee   493 *Yale 2* Why that>Why, that

482–7 *Theodoric . . . interference."*: Arcangeli only recalls this sentence in the vaguest
terms; it is quoted correctly by the real lawyer Spreti at OYB xxvii f. (28–9), pam. 2:
'Bulls defend their cows with their horns, rams fight with their heads for their ewes,
horses vindicate their mares with kicks and bites . . . How then can man endure to leave
adultery unavenged?' Theodoric the Ostrogoth became king of Italy (AD 493–526)
and established one of the most powerful of the post-Roman states. Many of his
sayings were recorded by his minister Cassiodorus in his *Variae* (*c.*537), which Spreti
duly gives as his source. Cf. I. 231 n.

489 *when Aristotle doubts*: Aristotle's detailed discussion of this matter is in *De
Generatione Animalium*, Bk. III. He believes that some insects reproduce by copulation,
others by spontaneous generation. In the case of bees, in particular, he was puzzled,
and, after rehearsing various theories, still unsure. He ended his discussion with the
well-known dictum: 'the facts have not yet been sufficiently ascertained; and if at any
future time they are ascertained, then credence must be given to the direct evidence of
the senses rather than to theories,—and to theories too provided that the results which
they show agree with what is observed': III. x.

492 *copying King Solomon*: the text that best fits this allusion is Proverbs 6: 8, not in
the standard Hebrew, Latin, or English texts, but only in the Septuagint, where the bee
is extolled for its conscientiousness and industry: 'Or go thou to the bee and learn how
diligent she is, and how noble is the work that she doeth; whose labours kings and
private men use for health, and she is desired and honourable in the eyes of all: though
she be weak in strength, by honouring wisdom she is advanced'. This seems an erudite
allusion, and is perhaps intended to appear so: the man who quotes the 'Sayings of
Scaliger' and the words of St Thomas Aquinas, may be allowed this off-hand allusion
to the Septuagint.

Which savours of incontinency, makes
The unchaste a very horror to the hive?   495
Whence comes it bees obtain their epithet
Of *castæ apes*, notably "the chaste"?
Because, ingeniously saith Scaliger,
(The young sage,—see his book of Table-talk)
"Such is their hatred of immodest act,   500
"They fall upon the offender, sting to death."
I mind a passage much confirmative
I' the Idyllist (though I read him Latinized)
"Why" asks a shepherd, "is this bank unfit
"For celebration of our vernal loves?"   505
"Oh swain," returns the instructed shepherdess,
"Bees swarm here, and would quick resent our warmth!"

494 *MS 1868* That   495 *MS* man the horror of>a very horror to *Yale 2* hive?>
hive!   496 *MS* they obtain their>bees obtain the   *MS* epithet, *1868* the
epithet   497 *MS* Are>[ ]>Are   *MS 1868* apes?   *MS* styled>notably *1868*
1872 chaste?"   498 *MS* {no commas}   *MS* Scaliger—   499 *MS* {line
added later}   *MS* The   *MS* one— *1868* one—   *MS* Table-talk—   500
MS {no comma}   501 *MS* {no quotation marks}   503 *MS* Idyllist—though
Yale 1 idyllist>Idyllist   *MS* Latinized—   504 *MS* {no comma} 505 *MS*
spring-time>vernal   506 *MS 1868* wiser

---

497 *castæ apes*: chaste bees (L.): see next n.

498–501 *Scaliger...death.*": Joseph Justus Scaliger (1540–1609), son of the also
distinguished Julius Caesar Scaliger, was known as the most erudite scholar of his
age. This is his explanation of the phrase *castæ apes*, taken from the *Scaligeriana* ('Sayings
of Scaliger'): 'Les Abeilles sentent, si un homme a couché avec sa femme, indubitable-
ment le lendemain s'il approche il est picqué': 'If a man has slept with his wife, the bees
can tell, and if he approaches them the following day they will invariably sting him':
Scaligeriana, ed. F.F.P.P. (The Hague, 1666), p. 6. This allusion is not from OYB, but
from Browning's own reading in Scaliger, though we do not know which edition he
used.

503–7 *Idyllist...warmth!*": the 'Idyllist' is Theocritus (*c.*310–*c.*250 BC), the Helle-
nistic Greek poet whose idylls are the origin of pastoral poetry. This passage is not a
direct translation of anything in Theocritus, but is probably suggested by *Idyll* i. 105–7.
From Meineke's edition of Theocritus onwards, these lines have come to be under-
stood via a passage in Plutarch's *Natural Questions*, xxxvi (a passage surviving only from
the Latin version of Gybertus Longolius) discussing bees' hatred of the smell of illicit
sex. Before quoting the lines in Theocritus, Plutarch comments: 'Unde apud Theo-
critum iocose Venus ad Anchisen a pastore ablegatur, uti apum aculeis propter
adulterium commissum pungatur': 'Hence the jest in Theocritus when Aphrodite is
dispatched by the herdsman to Anchises, with the intention that he shall be stung by
bees because of their adultery.' This allusion to Theocritus is not in OYB, but is
another learned flourish that Browning gives Arcangeli.

Only cold-blooded fish lack instinct here,
Nor gain nor guard connubiality:
But beasts, quadrupedal, mammiferous,   510
Do credit to their beasthood: witness him
That Ælian cites, the noble elephant,
(Or if not Ælian, somebody as sage)
Who seeing, much offence beneath his nose,
His master's friend exceed in courtesy   515
The due allowance to his master's wife,
Taught them good manners and killed both at once,
Making his master and the world admire.
Indubitably, then, that master's self,
Favoured by circumstance, had done the same   520
Or else stood clear rebuked by his own beast.
Adeo, ut qui honorem spernit, thus,
Who values his own honour not a straw,—
Et non recuperare curat, nor
Labours by might and main to salve its wound,   525
Se ulciscendo, by revenging him,
Nil differat a belluis, is a brute,
Quinimo irrationabilior
Ipsismet belluis, nay, contrariwise,
Much more irrational than brutes themselves,   530
Should be considered, *reputetur!* How?
If a poor animal feel honour smart,
Taught by blind instinct nature plants in him,

---

510 *MS* the quadrupedal,>quadrupedal,   511 *MS 1868* him,   512 *1872*
That Ælian cities,   514 *MS 1868* seeing much *Yale 2* seeing,>seeing   516
MS [?his]>that *1868* that   517 *MS* manners, killing>manners and killed   *MS*
{no comma}   518 *MS 1868* all men   519 *MS* {beginning of fo. 80}   *MS*
{no commas}   *MS* Master's   *1868* self   522 *MS* spernit,—thus   524
MS {Latin not underlined}   *MS* curat recuperare>recuperare curat   525 *MS*
cure *Yale 1* cure>salve   526 *MS* ulciscendo,—   527 *MS* belluis,—   *MS*
brute,—   529 *MS* belluis,—but contrariwise *Yale 1* contrariwise>contrari-
wise,   530 *MS* As>Much   *MS* beasts>brutes

---

510 *mammiferous*: i.e. mammalian, of the class of creatures that suckle their young.
512–21 *Ælian . . . beast*: OYB cxlv f. (149), anon., pam. 10. The story is from
Aelian's *De Natura Animalium* (*c*.AD 200), XI. 15. Cf. I. 232 n.
522–31 *Adeo . . . reputetur*: OYB cxxxvii (142), Spreti, pam. 9.

Shall man,—confessed creation's master-stroke,
Nay, intellectual glory, nay, a god, 535
Nay, of the nature of my Judges here,—
Shall man prove the insensible, the block,
The blot o' the earth he crawls on to disgrace?
(Come, that's both solid and poetic!) Man
Derogate, live for the low tastes alone, 540
Mean creeping cares about the animal life?
Absit such homage to vile flesh and blood!

    (May Gigia have remembered, nothing stings
Fried liver out of its monotony
Of richness, like a root of fennel, chopped 545
Fine with the parsley: parsley-sprigs, I said—
Was there need I should say "and fennel too"?
But no, she cannot have been so obtuse!
To our argument! The fennel will be chopped.)

From beast to man next mount we—ay, but, mind, 550
Still mere man, not yet Christian,—that, in time!
Not too fast, mark you! 'T is on Heathen grounds
We next defend our act: then, fairly urge—
If this were done of old, in a green tree,
Allowed in the Spring rawness of our kind, 555

---

534 *MS* masterpiece,>master-stroke,   539 *MS* {brackets added later}   *MS*
Shall man *1868* poetic)—man   540 *MS* alone?—   541–2 {not found in
MS}   542 {not found in *1868*}   *1872* Absit,   543 *MS* {New paragraph
indicated by 'New Par.' in left-hand margin}   *MS 1868* May   544 *MS* The>
Fried   545 *MS 1868* richness like   546 *MS* {no comma}   547 *MS*
{line added later}   *MS* "And   *MS 1868 1872* too?"   549 *MS* found. *1868*
chopped.   550 *MS* {beginning of fo. 81}   *MS* {New paragraph indicated by
'New Par.' in left-hand margin}   551 *MS* Mere man, the>Shall mere
man,   552 *MS* meanwhile: 'tis>mark you!: 'tis   553 *MS* add—
>urge   554 *MS* tree

---

540 *Derogate*: degenerate, act in a way unworthy of his true nature; cf. *Aurora Leigh*,
III. 439–40: 'I'm well aware I do not derogate / In loving Romney Leigh'.

542 *Absit*: away with (L.).

543 *Gigia*: Arcangeli's cook; he worries again about her competence at ll. 1385–92.

554–7 *If ... man?*: i.e. if such revenge was practised even under paganism, how
much more is it permissible in the maturity of the Christian era? Cf. Luke 23: 31.

What may be licensed in the Autumn dry
And ripe, the latter harvest-tide of man?
If, with his poor and primitive half-lights,
The Pagan, whom our devils served for gods,
Could stigmatise the breach of marriage-vow   560
As that which blood, blood only might efface,—
Absolve the husband, outraged, whose revenge
Anticipated law, plied sword himself,—
How with the Christian in full blaze of noon?
Shall not he rather double penalty,   565
Multiply vengeance, than, degenerate,
Let privilege be minished, droop, decay?
Therefore set forth at large the ancient law!
Superabundant the examples be
To pick and choose from. The Athenian Code,   570
Solon's, the name is serviceable,—then,
The Laws of the Twelve Tables, that fifteenth,—
"Romulus" likewise rolls out round and large;
The Julian; the Cornelian; Gracchus' Law:

<hr>

556 *1868* dry,   557 *MS* harvest-[ ]>harvest-tide   558 *MS* If—   *MS*
half-lights—   559 *MS* natural   Pagan,   devils   561 *MS* could
efface—   564 *MS 1868* day?   566 *MS* degenerate   569 *MS* are the
instances>the examples be   572 *MS* Fifteenth,—   573 *MS* {no quotation
marks}   *MS* well>round   *MS* [ ]>and   *MS 1868 1872* large. *1888* large *DC BrU*
large>large; *1889* large;   574 *MS* The Julian Law,>The Julian,   *MS* the Cor-
nelian,> Cornelian,>the Cornelian,   *MS* Gracchus' [ ]>Gracchus' Law:

<hr>

559 *our . . . gods*: traditionally the angels who fell to Hell with Satan became the gods
of the pagan world: cf. *Paradise Lost*, i. 356–521.

567 *minished*: lessened, cut back.

570–4 *Athenian Code . . . Law*: all these ancient laws are mentioned at OYB x (12),
Arcangeli, pam. 1, though Browning has conflated two groups of citations and re-
arranged the order in which they appear: 'Great indeed is his crime, but one very
greatly to be pitied, and most worthy of excuse, to which the severest laws are
indulgent . . . l. *Si Adulterium cum incæstu* 38 §. *Imperatores ff. ad leg. Iul[iam] de Adulter[-
iis] . . . leg. Gracchus C. cod. leg.* 1 §. *Fin. ff. ad leg. Cornel[iam] de Sycar[iis] . . .* This same
thing was sanctioned in the laws of the Athenians and of Solon (wisest of legislators),
and what is more, even in the rude age of Romulus, law 15, where we read: "A man
and his relatives may kill as they wish a wife convicted of adultery".' Browning made a
slip in the *MS* which he never subsequently corrected: the punctuation at the end of l.
572 associates 'that fifteenth' with 'the Laws of the Twelve Tables', when, to be
accurate, it should read 'that fifteenth "Romulus" '. Cf. 1. 222–3, 226–8.

So old a chime, the bells ring of themselves! 575
Spreti can set that going if he please,
I point you, for my part, the belfry plain,
Intent to rise from dusk, *diluculum*,
Into the Christian day shall broaden next.

First, the fit compliment to His Holiness 580
Happily reigning: then sustain the point—
All that was long ago declared as law
By the natural revelation, stands confirmed
By Apostle and Evangelist and Saint,—
To-wit—that Honour is man's supreme good. 585
Why should I baulk Saint Jerome of his phrase?
Ubi honor non est, where no honour is,
Ibi contemptus est; and where contempt,
Ibi injuria frequens; and where that,
The frequent injury, *ibi et indignatio;* 590
And where the indignation, *ibi quies*
Nulla: and where there is no quietude,
Why, *ibi*, there, the mind is often cast
Down from the heights where it proposed to dwell,
Mens a proposito sæpe dejicitur. 595
And naturally the mind is so cast down,

---

575 *MS* themselves—!   577 *MS* I point out the belfry, for my part,>I point you,
for my part, the belfry out. *1868* out, *Yale 2* plain,>plain,—   578 *MS* {beginning
of fo. 82}   579 *MS* and broaden round.>shall broaden next. *Yale 2* shall broaden
>that broadens   580 *MS* {New paragraph indicated by 'New Par.' in right-hand
margin}   581 *MS* reigning,—   *MS* point,   582 *MS* That which>
All that   583 *MS 1868* early Revelation,   *MS* is>stands *Yale 2* the natural>
natural   585 *MS* Honor   *MS* the supreme good: *1868* the supreme   587
MS est—   *MS* is—   588 *MS est*—   589 *MS frequens*—   590 *MS*
indignatio,   592 *MS Nulla, 1868 Nulla;*   ★*MS 1868 1872* quietude, *1888* quietude
DC BrU quietude>quietude, *1889* quietude,   596 *MS* And naturally so cast
down, since harder 'tis,>And naturally is the mind cast down,>And naturally the
mind is so cast down,

578 *diluculum*: half light (L.).
586–95 *Saint Jerome . . . dejicitur.* OYB cl (153), anon., pam. 10. St Jerome (*c.*345–
420), the greatest biblical scholar of the early church, wrote many letters; this quota-
tion, wrenched from its context, is from letter xiv, 'To Heliodorus', § 7.

Since harder 't is, *quum difficilius sit*,
Iram cohibere, to coerce one's wrath,
Quam miracula facere, than work miracles,—
So Gregory smiles in his First Dialogue.   600
Whence we infer, the ingenuous soul, the man
Who makes esteem of honour and repute,
Whenever honour and repute are touched
Arrives at term of fury and despair,
Loses all guidance from the reason-check: 605
As in delirium or a frenzy-fit,
Nor fury nor despair he satiates,—no,
Not even if he attain the impossible,
O'erturn the hinges of the universe
To annihilate—not whoso caused the smart   610
Solely, the author simply of his pain,
But the place, the memory, *vituperii*,
O' the shame and scorn: *quia*,—says Solomon,

597 *MS* {line added later}   598 *MS* Coerce one's anger than work miracles,—
>Iram cohibere—to coerce one's wrath   599 *MS* {line added later}   *MS*
facere—   600 *MS 1868 1872* Saint *Yale 2* Saint>So   *MS* saith>smiles   *MS*
1868 Dialogue: 601 *MS* We formulate then,>Whence we draw inference—
>Whence we infer—   602 *MS* Which>Who   *603 *MS* Whenever in
such honor [ ]>Whenever in such honor is offence,>Whenever honor and repute
are touched, *1868 1872 1888* touched, *DC BrU* touched,>touched *1889*
touched   604 *MS* Arrived at the>Arrives at   605 *MS* Losing>Loses   *MS*
his reason light,>the reason-check,   606 *MS* Like a delirious man, one frenetic,
>As in delirium or a frenzy-fit, *1868* delirium,   607 *MS* Fury and despair he
cannot satiate>Nor fury nor despair he satiates,—no—   608 *MS* attained>at-
tain   609 *MS* {beginning of fo. 83}   *MS* O'er-turned>O'erturn   610
MS the authors of his [?woe]>whoso caused the smart   611 *MS* {line added
later}   *MS* authors>author   *MS* pain   612 *MS* memory of his shame and
scorn>memory *vituperii*   613 *MS* And vituperii—>O' the shame & scorn:

597–600 *Since . . . First Dialogue*: OYB cxxxvii (142), Spreti, pam. 9. St Gregory the
Great (*c.*540–604), one of the greatest popes, wrote several works that came to have
wide currency in the Church; this quotation is from the first of his 'Dialogues' (*c.*593).

601–73 *ingenuous soul . . . world*: with the exception of the interjections (625, 636–
43, 658–9, 665), this 70-line passage loosely translates a whole page (in Italian) of OYB:
cli (154–5), anon., pam. 10.

609 *hinges of the universe*: translating OYB's 'i Cardini dell'Universo': see previous n.

613 *quia*: because (L.).

613–15 *Solomon . . . end*: cf. Prov. 6: 34–5. The phrasing here, which may look so
Browningesque, is a literal rendering of OYB cli (154): 'come parla in questo proposito
lo Spirito santo per bocca di Salomone nei Proverbi al 6. in fine': see ll. 601–73 n.

(The Holy Spirit speaking by his mouth
In Proverbs, the sixth chapter near the end)   615
—Because, the zeal and fury of a man,
Zelus et furor viri, will not spare,
Non parcet, in the day of his revenge,
In die vindictæ, nor will acquiesce,
Nec acquiescet, through a person's prayers,   620
Cujusdam precibus,—nec suscipiet,
Nor yet take, *pro redemptione*, for
Redemption, *dona plurium*, gifts of friends,
Mere money-payment to compound for ache.
Who recognizes not my client's case?   625
Whereto, as strangely consentaneous here,
Adduce Saint Bernard in the Epistle writ
To Robertulus, his nephew: "Too much grief,
"*Dolor quippe nimius non deliberat*,
"Does not excogitate propriety,   630
"*Non verecundatur*, nor knows shame at all,
"*Non consulit rationem*, nor consults
"Reason, *non dignitatis metuit*
"*Damnum*, nor dreads the loss of dignity;
"*Modum et ordinem*, order and the mode,   635
"*Ignorat*, it ignores:" why, trait for trait,
Was ever portrait limned so like the life?

---

614 *MS* {bracket added later}   615 *MS* sixt {*sic*}   *MS* end,>end)   616
MS man   619 *MS* acquiesce   620 *MS* prayers   621 *MS* susci-
piet   622 *MS* will>yet   623 *MS* friends—   624 *MS* {line added
later}   *MS 1868* Nor   *Yale 1* ache>ache.   625 *MS 1868 1872* recogni-
ses   *MS* our client here?>our client's case?   626 *MS* [ ],>here,   627 *MS*
That of>Con[?fer]>Conduce   628 *MS* Robert, nephew: since excessive>Ro-
bertulus, his nephew: too much   629–36 *MS* {no quotation marks at beginnings
of lines}   630 *MS* consult>excogitate propriety,   634 *MS* dignity, *Yale 1*
dignity,>dignity;   635 *MS ordinem—   MS* {no commas}   *MS* ^the^ 636 *MS*
1868 ignores: why,

627–8 *Saint Bernard . . . Robertulus*: St Bernard of Clairvaux (1090–1153), the great
abbot and mystic. The quotation is from the beginning of Letter I (*c*.1119), 'To his
cousin Robert, who had withdrawn from the Cistercian Order to the Cluniac'.
          630 *excogitate*: consider, think about.
          637 *limned*: painted.

(By Cavalier Maratta, shall I say?
I hear he's first in reputation now.)
Yes, that of Samson in the Sacred Text: 640
That's not so much the portrait as the man!
Samson in Gaza was the antetype
Of Guido at Rome: observe the Nazarite!
Blinded he was,—an easy thing to bear:
Intrepidly he took imprisonment,   645
Gyves, stripes and daily labour at the mill:
But when he found himself, i' the public place,
Destined to make the common people sport,
Disdain burned up with such an impetus
I' the breast of him that, all the man one fire,   650
Moriatur, roared he, let my soul's self die,
Anima mea, with the Philistines!
So, pulled down pillar, roof, and death and all,
Multosque plures interfecit, ay,
And many more he killed thus, *moriens*,   655
Dying, *quam vivus*, than in his whole life,
Occiderat, he ever killed before.
Are these things writ for no example, Sirs?
One instance more, and let me see who doubts!
Our Lord Himself, made all of mansuetude,   660

638–9 *MS* {lines added later}   638 *MS* Frederic Barroccio,   640 *MS*
Sampson   *MS* Text! *1868 1872* Text: *1888 1889* Text   641 {not found in
MS}   642 *MS* {beginning of fo. 84}   *MS* Sampson   643 *MS* in the
Villa: mark the Nazarite—>at Rome: for, note the Nazarite—   *1868*   for
note   644 *MS 1868* bear,   645 *MS* [?bore]>took   646 *MS* Stripes
and the>Gyves, stripes and   650 *MS* all of him one>all of him was *1868* all of
him on   653 *MS* So pulled   *MS* thereby—>and all   656 *MS* In
dying,   657 *MS* before?   659 *MS* more—   660 *MS* ^made up^
1868 made up

---

638 *Cavalier Maratta*: Carlo Maratta (1625–1713), the Roman painter; cf. III.
58–9 n.

640–57 *Samson . . . before*: cf. Judg. 16: 21–30.

642 *antetype*: forerunner.

643 *Nazarite*: cf. Judg. 13: 5. Samson was vowed from birth to be a Nazarite; for the
significance of this practice see Num. 6.

660 *mansuetude*: gentleness; again the phrasing is from OYB cli (154): 'ancorche
fosse mansuetissimo'.

Sealing the sum of sufferance up, received
Opprobrium, contumely and buffeting
Without complaint: but when He found Himself
Touched in His honour never so little for once,
Then outbroke indignation pent before—   665
"*Honorem meum nemini dabo!*" "No,
"My honour I to nobody will give!"
And certainly the example so hath wrought,
That whosoever, at the proper worth,
Apprises worldly honour and repute,   670
Esteems it nobler to die honoured man
Beneath Mannaia, than live centuries
Disgraced in the eye o' the world. We find Saint Paul
No recreant to this faith delivered once:
"Far worthier were it that I died," cries he,   675
Expedit mihi magis mori, "than
"That anyone should make my glory void,"
Quam ut gloriam meam quis evacuet!
See, *ad Corinthienses:* whereupon
Saint Ambrose makes a comment with much fruit,   680
Doubtless my Judges long since laid to heart,

---

662 *MS* contumely,>contumely   *MS* [ ]>buffeting   663 *MS* ^he^   *MS*
himself>Himself *Yale 1* he>He   664 *MS* once—   666 *MS dabo*" cried,>
dabo." "No,   667 *MS* give"!   668 *MS* {no comma} *Yale 1* wrought>
wrought,   670 *MS* honour and a good>worldly honour and   671 *MS*
{beginning of fo. 85}   *MS* far better die an>it nobler to die   675 *MS* bet-
ter>worthier   676 *MS* than   677 *MS* {no quotation mark at beginning of
line}   *MS* any man>anyone   *MS* glory>glorying   *MS* void—   679 *MS*
Corinthienses—   680 *MS* the>a   *MS* which, with fruit,>with much fruit,
681 *MS* studied long ago,>long since laid to heart,

666–7 "*Honorem . . . give!*": since Christ obviously said no such thing, this may
appear an extravagant irony on Browning's part. Again, however, like the rest of this
passage, it comes directly from OYB cli (154–5), and is simply transferred to Arcangeli:
see ll. 601–73 n.

672 *Mannaia*: guillotine.

673–83 *Saint Paul . . . it*: see 1 Cor. 9: 15. These citations are from OYB cxxxvii
(142): Spreti, pam. 9. The quotation Arcangeli 'can't quite recollect' from St Ambrose
is given in full by Spreti: 'For who does not consider an injury to the body or the loss
of property rights as less than an injury to the spirit or the loss of reputation?'

So I desist from bringing forward here.
(I can't quite recollect it.)

                              Have I proved
Satis superque, both enough and to spare,   685
That Revelation old and new admits
The natural man may effervesce in ire,
O'erflood earth, o'erfroth heaven with foamy rage,
At the first puncture to his self-respect?
Then, Sirs, this Christian dogma, this law-bud   690
Full-blown now, soon to bask the absolute flower
Of Papal doctrine in our blaze of day,—
Bethink you, shall we miss one promise-streak,
One doubtful birth of dawn crepuscular,
One dew-drop comfort to humanity,   695
Now that the chalice teems with noonday wine?
Yea, argue Molinists who bar revenge—
Referring just to what makes out our case!
Under old dispensation, argue they,
The doom of the adulterous wife was death,   700
Stoning by Moses' law. "Nay, stone her not,
"Put her away!" next legislates our Lord;

---

682 *MS* So I desist here—have I proved my point>So I desist from bringing forward
here— *1868* here—   683 *MS* {line added later}   *MS* Simply demanding have I
proved my point>(I can't quite recollect it)—have I proved   684 *MS* {no new
paragraph}   685 *MS* amply>[ ]>both enough   687 *MS* effervese   *MS*
rage,>ire,   690 *MS* [ ]>Then,   *MS* budding law>this law-bud   691 *MS*
and now>now and   693 *MS* you,—   695 *MS* One comfort to humanity,
in the bud,—>One budding comfort to humanity,—   696 *MS* rosy chalice>
chalice   *MS* ^noonday^   698 *MS* case—   701 *MS* {beginning of fo.
86}   *MS* Moses law: nay,>Moses law. "Nay,   702 *MS* {no quotation mark
at beginning of line}   *MS* Divorce>Put her away,"

---

694 *crepuscular*: dim, just commencing.

699–727 *Under . . . behind*: this is an exaggerated version of an argument that the real
Arcangeli advances at OYB xiii (14), pam. 1. Browning has made the argument
extreme by adding references to the Mosaic law of stoning, and by making the
whole a *tour de force* of biblical allusion: see following nn.

701–2 *stone her not . . . Lord*: cf. John 8: 3–11.

And last of all, "Nor yet divorce a wife!"
Ordains the Church, "she typifies ourself,
The Bride no fault shall cause to fall from Christ."   705
Then, as no jot nor tittle of the Law
Has passed away—which who presumes to doubt?
As not one word of Christ is rendered vain—
Which, could it be though heaven and earth should pass?
—Where do I find my proper punishment   710
For my adulterous wife, I humbly ask
Of my infallible Pope,—who now remits
Even the divorce allowed by Christ in lieu
Of lapidation Moses licensed me?
The Gospel checks the Law which throws the stone,   715
The Church tears the divorce-bill Gospel grants:
Shall wives sin and enjoy impunity?
What profits me the fulness of the days,
The final dispensation, I demand,
Unless Law, Gospel and the Church subjoin   720
"But who hath barred thee primitive revenge,
"Which, like fire damped and dammed up, burns more fierce?
"Use thou thy natural privilege of man,
"Else wert thou found like those old ingrate Jews,

703 *MS* wife,   *MS* {no quotation mark at end of line}   704 *MS* Pope—
>Church—   *MS* the Church,>ourself,   705 *MS* Christ's>The   *MS* away>
from Christ   706 *MS* law>Law   707 *MS* doubt?—   708 *MS* [ ]>ren-
dered   *MS* vain,—   709 *MS* Which could not   *MS* Heaven   *MS* were
blank,—   710 *MS* And as the Pope>—Where do I find   711 *MS* ask,
Yale 1 ask,>ask   712 *MS* Pope who *Yale 1* Pope who>Pope—who   714 *MS* the
lapidation>lapidation   *MS* [ ]?>me?   715 *MS* would throw   716 *MS*
denies divorce the>tears the divorce-bill   *MS* grants,— *1868* grants,   717 *MS*
{line added later}   *MS* There stands my wife, enjoys impunity! *1868* The wife sins
and enjoys impunity!   721 *MS* thy natural>the primitive   722 *MS*
"Should,   *MS* a fire restricted, burn>fire damped and dammed up, burn   *MS*
[ ]>more   723 *MS* {line added later}   *MS* the natural   724 *MS* ^old^
MS {no comma}

706–7 *no jot . . . away*: cf. Matt. 5: 18.
708–9 *As . . . pass*: cf. Matt. 24: 35.
713 *divorce . . . Christ*: cf. Matt. 5: 31–2.
714 *lapidation*: stoning to death; from L. *lapidare*.
718–19 *fulness . . . dispensation*: cf. Eph. 1: 10.
724–7 *ingrate Jews . . . behind*: cf. Num. 11: 4–6.

"Despite the manna-banquet on the board,   725
"A-longing after melons, cucumbers,
"And such like trash of Egypt left behind!"

(There was one melon had improved our soup:
But did not Cinoncino need the rind
To make a boat with? So I seem to think.)   730

Law, Gospel and the Church—from these we leap
To the very last revealment, easy rule
Befitting the well-born and thorough-bred
O' the happy day we live in, not the dark
O' the early rude and acorn-eating race.   735
"Behold," quoth James, "we bridle in a horse
"And turn his body as we would thereby!"
Yea, but we change the bit to suit the growth,
And rasp our colt's jaw with a rugged spike
We hasten to remit our managed steed   740
Who wheels round at persuasion of a touch.
Civilization bows to decency,
The acknowledged use and wont: 't is manners,—mild
But yet imperative law,—which make the man.
Thus do we pay the proper compliment   745
To rank, and what society of Rome
Hath so obliged us by its interest,
Taken our client's part instinctively,

725 MS Christian banquet>manna-banquet   726 MS 1868 cucumbers   727
MS the good fare   MS behind."   728 MS 1868 {no new paragraph}   MS
1868 melon,   MS the>our   MS 1868 soup,   731 MS {beginning of fo.
87}   MS {New paragraph indicated by 'New Par' in left-hand margin}   732
MS ^very^   MS light and easy>easy   733 MS thoroughly bred   734 MS
the—better day—, not our sires,>the—happy day we live in,—not our sires, 1868
in,—   735   MS The   737   MS   thereby;"   739   MS   the
colt's   740 MS the managed   743 MS 1868 wont, the   744 MS
man—   *746 MS rank, the good society>rank, that choice society 1868 1872
1888 that DC BrU that>what 1889 that   *MS 1868 1872 1888 Rome, DC BrU
Rome,>Rome 1889 Rome,   747 MS That hath>Hath so   748 Yale 1
clients'>client's   MS {no comma}

736-7 "Behold . . . thereby!": cf. Jas. 3: 2-3.

As unaware defending its own cause.
What *dictum* doth Society lay down 750
I' the case of one who hath a faithless wife?
Wherewithal should the husband cleanse his way?
Be patient and forgive? Oh, language fails,—
Shrinks from depicturing his turpitude!
For if wronged husband raise not hue and cry, 755
Quod si maritus de adulterio non
Conquereretur, he's presumed a—foh!
Presumitur leno: so, complain he must.
But how complain? At your tribunal, lords?
Far weightier challenge suits your sense, I wot! 760
You sit not to have gentlemen propose
Questions gentility can itself discuss.
Did not you prove that to our brother Paul?
The Abate, *quum judicialiter*
Prosequeretur, when he tried the law, 765
Guidonis causam, in Count Guido's case,
Accidit ipsi, this befell himself,
Quod risum moverit et cachinnos, that
He moved to mirth and cachinnation, all
Or nearly all, *fere in omnibus* 770
Etiam sensatis et cordatis, men
Strong-sensed, sound-hearted, nay, the very Court,

---

751 *MS* him>one   752 *MS* Husband   753 *MS 1868* fails—   754 {not
found in *MS*}   *1868* punishment!   755 *MS* {line added later}   *MS* cry—
757 *MS Conquereretur*—   758 *MS* {no comma}   *MS* must—   759 *MS*
Lords?   760 *MS* [ ]>challenge   761 *MS* {beginning of fo. 88}   *MS* not
here that   762 *MS* discuss: 765 *MS* law   767 *MS Ipsi accidit,>Accidit
ipsi,*   770 *MS* all—   772 *MS* ^very^   *MS* Court

752 *Wherewithal . . . way?*: cf. Ps. 119: 9: 'Wherewithal shall a young man cleanse his
way?'
754 *depicturing his turpitude*: depicting, painting in words, his shame, disgrace. Cf.
EBB, *The Seraphim*, 193–5: 'I have beheld the ruined things / Only in depicturings /
Of angels from an earthly mission'.
755–8 *For . . . leno*: OYB xxxi (32), Spreti, pam. 2. The word Arcangeli leaves
untranslated, substituting 'foh!', is *leno*: pander, pimp.
764–74 *quum . . . dicam*: OYB xxxii (32), Spreti, pam. 2.
769 *cachinnation*: loud or immoderate laughter.

Ipsismet in judicibus, I might add,
Non tamen dicam. In a cause like this,
So multiplied were reasons *pro* and *con*,   775
Delicate, intertwisted and obscure,
That Law refused loan of a finger-tip
To unravel, re-adjust the hopeless twine,
Since, half-a-dozen steps outside Law's seat,
There stood a foolish trifler with a tool   780
A-dangle to no purpose by his side,
Had clearly cut the embroilment in a trice.
Asserunt enim unanimiter
Doctores, for the Doctors all assert
That husbands, *quod mariti*, must be held   785
Viles, cornuti reputantur, vile,
Fronts branching forth a florid infamy,
Si propriis manibus, if with their own hands,
Non sumunt, they fail straight to take revenge,
Vindictam, but expect the deed be done   790
By the Court—*expectant illam fieri*
Per judices, qui summopere rident, which
Gives an enormous guffaw for reply,
Et cachinnantur. For he ran away,
Deliquit enim, just that he might 'scape   795
The censure of both counsellors and crowd,

773 *MS* Non tamen dicam>*Ipsismet   MS* judicibus,—   *MS* say,—>add,—   774
MS Ipsismet>*Non tamen*   775 *MS* {Latin not underlined}   777 *MS 1868*
law were shamed to lend a   778 *MS* readjust   779 *MS* While, half a dozen
1868 1872 While,   *MS* the Court, *1868* the court,   781 *MS* At dangle   *MS*
{no comma}   782 *MS* fitly>cleanly   *MS* tangle   *784 *MS 1868* assert,
1872 assert *1888* assert, *DC BrU* assert,>assert *1889* assert,   786 *MS 1868*
vile   787 *MS 1868* And   788 *MS* hands   789 *MS 1868* they take not
straightway *1872* they fail straightway take   790 *MS* {beginning of fo. 89}   *MS*
Vindictam—   *MS* [ ]>deed   792 *MS* judices—   *MS* rident,—   793 *MS*
in>for   *MS* {no comma}   795 *MS* scape   796 *MS* Counsellors   *MS*
{no comma}

780 *foolish trifler*: i.e. Guido himself.

783–801 *Asserunt . . . superadderet*: OYB cxxxiii (139), Spreti, pam. 9.

795 *Deliquit*: Gest and Hodell translate this as 'he [Guido] sinned', 'he committed a
crime'. Browning renders it as 'he ran away', perhaps thinking of the etymology of the
word (<*linquere*, to leave), as well as its connection with English 'delinquent'.

Ut vulgi et doctorum evitaret
Censuram, and lest so he superadd
To loss of honour ignominy too,
Et sic ne istam quoque ignominiam   800
Amisso honori superadderet.
My lords, my lords, the inconsiderate step
Was—we referred ourselves to Law at all!
Twit me not with "Law else had punished you!"
Each punishment of the extra-legal step,   805
To which the high-born preferably revert,
Is ever for some oversight, some slip
I' the taking vengeance, not for vengeance' self.
A good thing, done unhandsomely, turns ill;
And never yet lacked ill the law's rebuke.   810
For pregnant instance, let us contemplate
The luck of Leonardus,—see at large
Of Sicily's Decisions sixty-first.
This Leonard finds his wife is false: what then?
He makes her own son snare her, and entice   815
Out of the town walls to a private walk
Wherein he slays her with commodity.
They find her body half-devoured by dogs:
Leonard is tried, convicted, punished, sent
To labour in the galleys seven years long: 820
Why? For the murder? Nay, but for the mode!

---

797 *1868 1872 Doctorum*   799 *MS* honour, ignominy>honour [ ] ignominy>hon-
our ignominy   800 *MS* Still worse>*Et sic* {etc.}   803 *MS* Was that
we>Was—we *1868 1872* law   804 *MS* with,— *1868 1872* with,   *MS* "law>
"Law   *MS* you,"—   805 *MS* for>of   *MS* {no comma}   806 *MS* gen-
tle>high-born   *MS* {no comma}   807 *MS* fault>slip   808 *MS* In>I'
MS not the vengeance' self: 809 *MS 1868* {no commas}   *MS* ill,   810
MS Law's   811 *MS* ^pregnant^   *MS* {no comma}   813 *MS* sixty-
first: 816 *MS 1868* town-walls   *MS* place>walk: *1868 1872* walk,   817
MS commodity;   818 *MS* dogs.   819 *MS* {beginning of fo. 90}   *MS*
condemned and>convicted,   820 *MS* gallies   821 *MS* Why,—for>Why?
For

812–35 *Leonardus . . . exile*: these two cases occur together at OYB cxxxiv (140),
Spreti, pam. 9.
817 *commodity*: ease, convenience; cf. 1. 690.

Malus modus occidendi, ruled the Court,
An ugly mode of killing, nothing more!
Another fructuous sample,—see "*De Re*
"*Criminali*," in Matthæus' divine piece.   825
Another husband, in no better plight,
Simulates absence, thereby tempts his wife;
On whom he falls, out of sly ambuscade,
Backed by a brother of his, and both of them
Armed to the teeth with arms that law had blamed.   830
Nimis dolose, overwilily,
Fuisse operatum, did they work,
Pronounced the law: had all been fairly done
Law had not found him worthy, as she did,
Of four years' exile. Why cite more? Enough   835
Is good as a feast—(unless a birthday-feast
For one's Cinuccio) so, we finish here.
My lords, we rather need defend ourselves
Inasmuch as, for a twinkling of an eye,
We hesitatingly appealed to law,—   840
Than need deny that, on mature advice,
We blushingly bethought us, bade revenge
Back to its simple proper private way
Of decent self-dealt gentlemanly death.
Judges, here is the law, and here beside,   845
The testimony! Look to it!

                                 Pause and breathe!

---

824 *MS* sample,   *MS* "*de*>"*De*   825   *MS*   masterpiece:>divine
piece: 826 *MS* {no commas}   827 *MS* the wife, *1868* the wife;   828
MS an>sly   830 *MS* the>that   *MS* forbade.   832 *MS* was his work *1868*
was it worked,   833 *MS* Law: 834 *MS* She>Law   835 *MS* Four
whole>Of four   836 *MS* birthday feast   837 *MS* Cinuccio)>Cinuccio:
1868 Cinuccio: *MS* {no comma}   *MS 1868* we'll   *MS 1868* here)   838
MS In fine—   839 *MS* Inasmuch for one>Inasmuch as, for a   *1868* {no
commas}   *MS* eye   840 *MS* hesitated and>hesitatingly   841 *MS* Rather
than deny, on more *1868* Rather than   *MS* that>deny   *MS* advice   842 *MS*
took ourselves   843 *MS 1868* the simple   845 *MS 1868* there   *MS*
law—   *MS* what beside? *1868* this beside   846 *MS* testimony.   847 *MS*
{beginning of fo. 91}

---

  824 *fructuous*: fruitful, apposite.
  845–6 *Judges . . . testimony*: cf. Isa. 8: 20: 'To the law and to the testimony: if they
speak not according to this word, it is because there is no light in them'.

So far is only too plain; we must watch:
Bottini will scarce hazard an attack
Here: best anticipate the fellow's play   850
And guard the weaker places—warily ask,
What if considerations of a sort,
Reasons of a kind, arise from out the strange
Peculiar unforeseen new circumstance
Of this our (candour owns) abnormal act,   855
To bar the right of us revenging so?
"Impunity were otherwise your meed:
"Go slay your wife and welcome,"—may be urged,—
"But why the innocent old couple slay,
"Pietro, Violante? You may do enough,   860
"Not too much, not exceed the golden mean:
"Neither brute-beast nor Pagan, Gentile, Jew,
"Nor Christian, no nor votarist of the mode,
"Is justified to push revenge so far."

No, indeed? Why, thou very sciolist!   865
The actual wrong, Pompilia seemed to do,
Was virtual wrong done by the parents here—
Imposing her upon us as their child—
Themselves allow: then, her fault was their fault,
Her punishment be theirs accordingly!   870
But wait a little, sneak not off so soon!
Was this cheat solely harm to Guido, pray?
The precious couple you call innocent,—

---

848 *MS 1868* watch,   850 *MS 1868 1872* let's   *★MS 1868 1872 1888* play, *DC BrU*
play,>play *1889* play   853 *MS* kind arise   *MS* strange,   854 *MS* Peculiar,
unforseen,   855 *MS* our—   *MS* owns—   856 *MS* May   *MS* so[ ]>
so,   857–64 *MS* {no quotation marks at beginnings of lines}   857 *MS*
The impunity   *MS* our meed?   858 *MS* welcome,—   862 *MS* pagan,
863 *MS* mode   864 *MS* Were free at all *1868* "Were free at all *1872* "Was
justified   *MS* far! *1868 1872* far!"   865 *MS* {no new paragraph}   866
MS {no commas}   867 *MS* here

    863 *votarist of the mode*: worshipper of custom, 'the acknowledged use and wont' of
l. 743.
    865 *sciolist*: pretender to knowledge, novice.

Why, they were felons that Law failed to clutch,
Qui ut fraudarent, who that they might rob,   875
Legitime vocatos, folk law called,
Ad fidei commissum, true heirs to the Trust,
Partum supposuerunt, feigned this birth,
Immemores reos factos esse, blind
To the fact that, guilty, they incurred thereby,   880
Ultimi supplicii, hanging or what's worse.
Do you blame us that we turn Law's instruments,
Not mere self-seekers,—mind the public weal,
Nor make the private good our sole concern?
That having—shall I say—secured a thief,   885
Not simply we recover from his pouch
The stolen article our property,
But also pounce upon our neighbour's purse
We opportunely find reposing there,
And do him justice while we right ourselves?   890
He owes us, for our part, a drubbing say,
But owes our neighbour just a dance i' the air
Under the gallows: so, we throttle him.
That neighbour's Law, that couple are the Thief,
We are the over ready to help Law—   895
Zeal of her house hath eaten us up: for which,
Can it be, Law intends to eat up us,

---

874 *MS* are *Yale 1* are>were *1868 1872* law   875 *MS* {beginning of fo. 92}   *MS*
fraudarent—   *MS* {no commas}   876 *MS vocatos*—folks *1868 1872* folks   *MS*
{no commas}   877 *MS fideicommissum*—   878 *MS supposuerunt*—   *MS*
{no commas}   879 *MS esse*—   880 *MS* thereby   881 *MS suppli-*
cii—   *MS 1868* aught worse.   882 *MS 1868 1872* law's   *MS 1868* {no
comma}   889 *MS* [ ]>there   891 *MS* say,—   892 *MS* He   893
MS gallows-tree: we throttle   *MS* strangle>throttle   *1868* {no comma}   894
MS 1868 The   *1868* the couple   895 *MS 1868* over-ready   897 *MS* {no
commas}   *MS* us—

875–81 *Qui . . . worse*: OYB xix f. (20), Arcangeli, pam. I.
891 *drubbing*: beating, thrashing.
892–3 *dance . . . gallows*: i.e. a hanging. To 'dance in air', 'to dance on nothing', 'to
dance the Tyburn jig', were all phrases describing the convulsions of a hanged man.
896 *Zeal . . . up*: cf. Ps. 69: 9, John 2: 17.

Crudum Priamum, devour poor Priam raw,
('T was Jupiter's own joke) with babes to boot,
Priamique pisinnos, in Homeric phrase?   900
Shame!—and so ends my period prettily.

But even,—prove the pair not culpable,
Free as unborn babe from connivance at,
Participation in, their daughter's fault:
Ours the mistake. Is that a rare event?   905
Non semel, it is anything but rare,
In contingentia facti, that by chance,
Impunes evaserunt, go scot-free,
Qui, such well-meaning people as ourselves,
Justo dolore moti, who aggrieved   910
With cause, *apposuerunt manus*, lay
Rough hands, *in innocentes*, on wrong heads.
Cite we an illustrative case in point:
Mulier Smirnea quædam, good my lords,
A gentlewoman lived in Smyrna once,   915

---

898 *MS* raw   899 *MS* 'Twas   *MS* joke,   *MS* his babes>babes   900 *MS*
pisinnos—   901 *MS* end the   902 *MS* {New paragraph indicated by 'New
Par.' in left-hand margin}   *MS* inculpable,   903 *MS* {beginning of fo.
93}   904 *MS* {no comma}   908 *MS* scot-free   909 *MS* Qui—
MS {no commas}   911 *MS* justice>cause,   912 *MS* {no commas}
914 *MS* {Latin not underlined}   *MS* quædam—   915 *MS* {no comma}

898–900 *Crudum . . . pisinnos*: a Latin version of *Iliad*, IV. 35; the full line is: 'Cru-
dum manduces Priamum Priamque pisinnos': '(if you were to) chew Priam raw and
Priam's little ones'. This is part of a speech by Zeus against Hera; Arcangeli is invoking
both Zeus' anger and his sarcasm. In this Latin version, the line is the only surviving
fragment of a translation of the *Iliad* by Attius Labeo, and is preserved in the scholia to
Persius, *Satire* i. 5, 50, where Attius' translation is mocked. It is often quoted in
commentaries on the *Iliad*.

906–61 *Non . . . convent*: the whole passage, including citations, is from OYB xxii
(22), Arcangeli, pam. 1. The story of the Areopagus' verdict 'come back after a
hundred years' was a popular one; as well as occurring in Valerius Maximus (see l.
948 n.) from whom Arcangeli quotes it, it is repeated in Aulus Gellius, XII. 7, in
Rabelais, III. 44, and in various other authorities: see Gest, 412. Arcangeli (in OYB as
well as Browning) perverts the facts to suit his case. Whereas in every writer from
Valerius to Thomas Grammaticus, both the woman's second husband and their son
had taken part in the murder, Arcangeli lays it to the husband's charge alone, in order
to make the son an innocent victim. Cf. l. 230.

Virum et filium ex eo conceptum, who
Both husband and her son begot by him
Killed, *interfecerat, ex quo*, because,
Vir filium suum perdiderat, her spouse
Had been beforehand with her, killed her son,   920
Matrimonii primi, of a previous bed.
Deinde accusata, then accused,
Apud Dolabellam, before him that sat
Proconsul, *nec duabus cædibus*
Contaminatam liberare, nor   925
To liberate a woman doubly-dyed
With murder, *voluit*, made he up his mind,
Nec condemnare, nor to doom to death,
Justo dolore impulsam, one impelled
By just grief; *sed remisit*, but sent her up   930
Ad Areopagum, to the Hill of Mars,
Sapientissimorum judicum
Cœtum, to that assembly of the sage
Paralleled only by my judges here;
Ubi, cognito de causa, where, the cause   935
Well weighed, *responsum est*, they gave reply,
Ut ipsa et accusator, that both sides
O' the suit, *redirent*, should come back again,
Post centum annos, after a hundred years,
For judgment; *et sic*, by which sage decree,   940

---

916 *MS* {Latin not underlined}   917 *MS* son that he begot   *1868 1872*
him,   918 *MS ex quo* because,   919 *MS* {Latin not underlined}   920
MS son   922 *MS accusata,—*   *MS* accused   923 *MS* [ ]>him   925
MS liberare,—   926 *MS* one tw>a woman {etc.}   927 *MS* murder—
voluit—   *MS* {no commas}   928 *MS* {Latin not underlined}   *MS* condem-
nare—   *MS* {no commas}   *MS* condemn>to doom   929 *MS* {Latin not
underlined}   *MS* {no comma}   930 *MS 1868 1872* grief,   *MS* sent up
932 *MS* {beginning of fo. 94}   933 *MS Cœtum,—*   *MS* assemblage>assem-
bly   934 *MS* Only to be paralleled>Paralleled only   935 *MS* {Latin not
underlined}   *MS* where the   936 *MS* {Latin not underlined} *MS* est,—
MS reply   938 *MS redirent* should   *MS* again   939 *MS annos* after   *MS*
in>after   940 *MS* judgment, *Yale 1* judgment,>judgment;

---

931 *Areopagum . . . Mars*: the Areopagus ('Hill of Ares'), an ancient court of Athens,
named after the hill on which it held its meetings.

Duplici parricidio rea, one
Convicted of a double parricide,
Quamvis etiam innocentem, though in truth
Out of the pair, one innocent at least
She, *occidisset*, plainly had put to death,   945
Undequaque, yet she altogether 'scaped,
Evasit impunis. See the case at length
In Valerius, fittingly styled *Maximus*,
That eighth book of his Memorable Facts.
Nor Cyriacus cites beside the mark: 950
Similiter uxor quæ mandaverat,
Just so, a lady who had taken care,
Homicidium viri, that her lord be killed,
Ex denegatione debiti,
For denegation of a certain debt,   955
Matrimonialis, he was loth to pay,
Fuit pecuniaria mulcta, was
Amerced in a pecuniary mulct,
Punita, et ad pœnam, and to pains,
Temporalem, for a certain space of time,   960

---

941 *MS* {Latin not underlined}   *MS* rea—   942 *MS* {no comma}   943
MS {Latin not underlined}   944 *MS* One innocent at least out of the
pair   945 *MS* She *occidisset*,   946 *MS* {Latin not underlined}   *MS*
scaped   948 *MS* Valerius—   *MS Maximus*—   950 *MS* D[ ] >Nor
MS mark—   951 *MS* {no comma}   952 *MS* {no commas}   953
MS {no commas}   954 *MS* {no comma}   955 *MS* {no comma}   956
MS Matrimonialis he   957 *MS* {Latin not underlined}   *MS* mulcta—   958
MS {no comma}   959 *MS* {Latin not underlined}   *MS* pains   960 *MS*
{Latin not underlined}

948 *Valerius . . . Maximus*: the Latin writer Valerius Maximus made, *c.*AD 29, a
collection of historical anecdotes entitled *Factorum et dictorum memorabilium* ('Memorable Deeds and Sayings'). Presumably Arcangeli says he is 'fittingly styled *Maximus*
[Great]' because of its sheer length. Though little valued in Browning's day, its earlier
popularity is attested by at least sixty editions before the end of the seventeenth
century.

950 *Cyriacus*: Franciscus Niger Cyriacus, in his *Controversiarum Forensium Liber
Primus* (Venice, 1644), 420^b (105. 39).

954–6 *Ex . . . Matrimonialis*: 'for denial of the debt of marriage' (L.), i.e. denial of
sexual intercourse.

958 *Amerced . . . mulct*: punished with a financial penalty.

In monasterio, in a convent.

                               (Ay,

In monasterio! He mismanages

In with the ablative, the accusative!

I had hoped to have hitched the villain into verse   965

For a gift, this very day, a complete list

O' the prepositions each with proper case,

Telling a story, long was in my head.

"What prepositions take the accusative?

Ad to or at—*who saw the cat?*—down to   970

Ob, for, because of, *keep her claws off!*" Tush!

Law in a man takes the whole liberty:

The muse is fettered: just as Ovid found!)

And now, sea widens and the coast is clear.

What of the dubious act you bade excuse?   975

---

961 *MS* {beginning of fo. 95}   *MS* convent: 962 *MS* {no new paragraph}   *MS* ay, *1868* Ay,   963 *MS* {Latin not underlined}   *MS* monasterio—how he manages *1868* How he manages *1872* How he manages,   965 *MS* hitched him into   966 *MS* {no commas}   968 *MS* {no comma} *MS* head—   969 *MS 1868 1872* {no quotation mark at beginning of line} 970 *MS* who saw the cat?—   971 *MS* {Latin not underlined}   *MS* keep her claws off! *1868 1872 off* !   *MS 1868 1872* {no quotation mark}   *MS 1868 1872* Ah,   972 {not found in *MS*}   *1868 1872* liberty!   973 *MS 1868* fettered,—   *MS 1868* found!   974 *MS* skies brighten>sky brightens>sea widens   *MS* clear—   975 *MS* murky>dubious   *MS* we cleanse?>be plain?

963 *He*: i.e. Giacinto, Arcangeli's son, who is learning Latin.

964 *In . . . accusative*: in Latin the preposition *in* takes either the ablative or accusative case.

965–71 *I . . . off!*": Arcangeli had hoped to make his son a poem whose sing-song rhymes would help him remember the correct use of Latin prepositions. In the small extract here, 'at' rhymes with '*cat*' (970), and 'because of' (in its nineteenth-century pronunciation) rhymes comically with '*claws off*' (971). Cook points out the biographical echo here. Browning's father 'had also an extraordinary power of versifying, and taught his son from babyhood the words he wished him to remember, by joining them to a grotesque rhyme; the child learned all his Latin declensions in this way': *Life*, 12. We may conjecture that Browning himself used a similar method with Pen: see ll. 5–6 n.

973 *as Ovid found*: the famous Roman poet Ovid (43 BC–AD 17) started to train in forensic oratory, but found it impossible to stop his prose drifting into poetry: '. . . I tried to write words freed from rhythm, yet all unbidden song would come upon befitting numbers and whatever I tried to write was verse': *Tristia*, IV. x. 24–6. Later, after half-heartedly beginning a public career in Rome, he turned full time to poetry. Cf. l. 475 n.

Surely things broaden, brighten, till at length
Remains—so far from act that needs defence—
Apology to make for act delayed
One minute, let alone eight mortal months
Of hesitation! "Why procrastinate?"   980
(Out with it my Bottinius, ease thyself!)
"Right, promptly done, is twice right: right delayed
"Turns wrong. We grant you should have killed your wife,
"But killed o' the moment, at the meeting her
"In company with the priest: then did the tongue   985
"O' the Brazen Head give license, 'Time is now!'
"Wait to make mind up? 'Time is past' it peals.
"Friend, you are competent to mastery
"O' the passions that confessedly explain
"An outbreak: you allow an interval,   990
"And then break out as if time's clock still clanged.
"You have forfeited your chance, and flat you fall
"Into the commonplace category
"Of men bound to go softly all their days,

---

976 {not found in MS}   1868 1872 brighten, brighten,   980 MS hesitation?>
hesitation.   MS {no quotation mark at end of line}   981 {not found in
MS}   983 MS might>should   984 MS But on   MS moment,— 1868
"But on the moment,   984–91 MS {no quotation marks at beginnings of
lines}   985 MS ^the^   MS priest,—   986 MS "time>"Time   MS
now"!   987 MS You make your mind up: 1868 "You make your mind
up: MS "Time   MS past"   MS clangs.>peals.   989 MS excuse   990
MS out-break,—yet   1868 outbreak,—yet   991 MS Break>And then
break   992 MS {beginning of fo. 96}   994 MS {no comma}

986–7 *Brazen Head . . . past'*: Roger Bacon (1214–94) was believed to have made a
brazen head capable of speech and capable of answering any question proposed to it.
There were different versions of the legend; according to that followed by Browning
here and by Byron in *Don Juan*, 1, st. 217—'Now, like Friar Bacon's brazen head, I've
spoken, / "Time is, Time was, Time's past" '—the head, after uttering the words
quoted, the time for consulting it having been neglected, tumbled from its stand and
was shattered: Cook, 172.

991–4 *clock . . . days*: cf. Isa. 38: 8, 15. As Hezekiah lay dying, God moved the sun
'ten degrees' backwards, so turning back the clock (sundial), as a sign to Hezekiah that
he would save Israel from the Assyrians, and give him fifteen more years of life. On
realizing he would live, Hezekiah promised 'I shall go softly all my years in the
bitterness of my soul'.

"Obeying Law."   995
              Now, which way make response?
What was the answer Guido gave, himself?
—That so to argue came of ignorance
How honour bears a wound. "For, wound," said he,
"My body, and the smart soon mends and ends: 1000
"While, wound my soul where honour sits and rules,
"Longer the sufferance, stronger grows the pain,
"Being *ex incontinenti*, fresh as first."
But try another tack, urge common sense
By way of contrast: say—Too true, my lords!   1005
We did demur, awhile did hesitate:
Since husband sure should let a scruple speak
Ere he slay wife,—for his own safety, lords!
Carpers abound in this misjudging world:
Moreover, there's a nicety in law   1010
That seems to justify them should they carp.
Suppose the source of injury a son,—
Father may slay such son yet run no risk:
Why graced with such a privilege? Because
A father so incensed with his own child,   1015
Or must have reason, or believe he has:
Quia semper, seeing that in such event,

---

995 *MS 1868 1872* law."   996 *MS* {no new paragraph}   *MS* rispost?   998
MS That   *MS* comes>came   999 *MS 1868 1872* wound: for wound,
1000–2 *MS* {no quotation marks at beginnings of lines}   1000 *MS* is worst at
first— *1868* is worst at first: 1001 *MS* Wound>While, wound   *MS* my
honour>honour   1002 *MS* pain,—   1003 *MS* 'Tis *1868* "'Tis   *MS* in-
continenti—   *MS* first.   1004 *MS* Best   *MS* tack—calm commonsense *1868*
calm common   1005 *MS* contrast—as—too   *MS* as—">as— *1868* as—   *MS*
lords—   1006 *MS* did hesitate awhile:>awhile did hesitate: 1007 *MS 1868*
Yet   *MS* each scruple   1009 *MS* world, *1868* world.   1011 *MS 1868*
carp: 1012 *MS* son,   1017 *MS* semper—

    1003 *ex incontinenti*: from incontinence, passion (L.). The expression *incontinenti* (not
ex incontinenti) is often used in the pleadings, e.g. at OYB xiv, xv, in relation to killing a
wife 'incontinently', at the moment when discovered in misconduct. It is contrasted
with *ex intervallo* ('after an interval'). Browning's addition of 'ex' is redundant.
    1012–26 *Suppose . . . husband*: this 'nicety in law' is given at OYB cxcvii (200–1),
Bottini, pam. 14.

Presumitur, the law is bound suppose,
Quod capiat pater, that the sire must take,
Bonum consilium pro filio,   1020
The best course as to what befits his boy,
Through instinct, *ex instinctu,* of mere love,
Amoris, and, *paterni,* fatherhood;
Quam confidentiam, which confidence,
Non habet, law declines to entertain,   1025
De viro, of the husband: where finds he
An instinct that compels him love his wife?
Rather is he presumably her foe.
So, let him ponder long in this bad world
Ere do the simplest act of justice.   1030
                              But
Again—and here we brush Bottini's breast—
Object you, "See the danger of delay!
"Suppose a man murdered my friend last month:
"Had I come up and killed him for his pains   1035
"In rage, I had done right, allows the law:
"I meet him now and kill him in cold blood,
"I do wrong, equally allows the law:
"Wherein do actions differ, yours and mine?"
In plenitudine intellectus es?   1040

1018 *MS Presumitur—*   *MS* {no commas}   1019 *MS pater—*   *MS* {no commas}   1020 *MS* {no comma}   1021 *MS* boy.   1022 *MS* {beginning of fo. 97}   *MS* {Latin not underlined}   *MS* instinct—ex instinctu—   *MS* {no commas}   1023 *MS* And fatherhood—*amoris* paterni>*Amoris* paterni>*Amoris,* and, *paterni,* fatherhood.   1024 *MS confidentiam—*   *MS* {no commas}   1025 *MS* {Latin not underlined}   *MS* habet—   *MS* {no commas}   1026 *MS* {no comma}   *MS* husband—where has *1868* has   1028 *MS 1868* foe: 1029 *MS* {no comma}   1030 *MS* Ere he the simplest act of justice do.   1031 {not found in *MS*}   *MS* {no new paragraph}   1033 *MS* you.   *MS* delay: 1034 *MS* has killed   1036 *MS* rage—   *MS* right—   1038 *MS* "And   *MS* wrong—   1040 *MS* {line added later}

1032 *brush Bottini's breast*: i.e. come to close quarters with him, as in a sword fight.
1040 *In . . . es?*: Are you in your full mind? (L.). Browning has made this sneering question out of a phrase that is used in a non-interrogatory, matter-of-fact way by Spreti to describe Guido's mental state: OYB cxxxvi (142), pam. 9, ccxxix (232), pam. 16.

Hast thy wits, Fisc? To take such slayer's life,
Returns it life to thy slain friend at all?
Had he stolen ring instead of stabbing friend,—
To-day, to-morrow or next century,
Meeting the thief, thy ring upon his thumb,   1045
Thou justifiably hadst wrung it thence:
So, couldst thou wrench thy friend's life back again,
Though prisoned in the bosom of his foe,
Why, law would look complacent on thy wrath.
Our case is, that the thing we lost, we found: 1050
The honour, we were robbed of eight months since,
Being recoverable at any day
By death of the delinquent. Go thy ways!
Ere thou hast learned law, will be much to do,
As said the gaby while he shod the goose.   1055
Nay, if you urge me, interval was none!
From the inn to the villa—blank or else a bar
Of adverse and contrarious incident
Solid between us and our just revenge!
What with the priest who flourishes his blade,   1060
The wife who like a fury flings at us,
The crowd—and then the capture, the appeal
To Rome, the journey there, the jaunting thence
To shelter at the House of Convertites,
The visits to the Villa, and so forth,   1065
Where was one minute left us all this while

1043 *MS* friend   1044 *MS* century   1047 *MS* {no commas}   1048
MS my>his   *MS* foe *1868 1872* foe, *1888 1889* foe.   1049 *1868* rush.   1050
MS is that   1052 *MS* {beginning of fo. 98}   1053 *MS* delinquent: go>
delinquent. Go   *MS* ways,   1054 *MS* though>thou   1055 *Yale 2* As>—
As   *MS 1868* rustic   *MS* goose!   1056 *MS* But,   *Yale 2* me,>yet,   1059
MS revenge.   1063 *MS 1868 1872* journey thence,   1064 *MS 1868 1872*
The   1065 *MS* visit

1055 *gaby*: simpleton, fool; originally 'rustic': see *MS, 1868*.
    shod the goose: proverbial for 'did something useless': ODEP, 725. Even an idiot can
see that Bottini will never make a good lawyer.
    1056–68 *interval . . . instant*: this argument is made by the real Arcangeli at OYB xvii
(17–18), pam. 1.

To put in execution that revenge
We planned o' the instant?—as it were, plumped down
O' the spot, some eight months since, which round sound
      egg,
Rome, more propitious than our nest, should hatch!   1070
Object not, "You reached Rome on Christmas-eve,
"And, despite liberty to act at once,
"Waited a whole and indecorous week!"
Hath so the Molinism, the canker, lords,
Eaten to our bone? Is no religion left?   1075
No care for aught held holy by the Church?
What, would you have us skip and miss those Feasts
O' the Natal Time, must we go prosecute
Secular business on a sacred day?
Should not the merest charity expect,   1080
Setting our poor concerns aside for once,
We hurried to the song matutinal
I' the Sistine, and pressed forward for the Mass
The Cardinal that's Camerlengo chaunts,

1067 MS revenge,—   1068 MS Believe, dear Lords,—we planned o' the instant,
plumped   1069 MS Down, a sound egg, o' the spot, some eight months hence,
1868 A round sound egg, o' the spot, some eight months since, Yale 2 since,>
since: 1070 MS hatch?   1071 MS S>Remark   MS not—you   MS
arrive>reach Rome   MS Christmas-night,>Christmas-eve,   1072–3 MS {no
quotation marks at beginnings of lines}   1073 MS Wait a full week—indecorous
delay! Yale 1 Wait a full>Waited a 1868 "Waited a week—indecorous delay!"   MS
{no quotation mark at end of line}   1074 MS Molinism canker, 1868
Molinism-canker,   1075 MS 1868 1872 the bone?   1080 MS {beginning
of fo. 99}   1083 MS to>for

1068–70 plumped . . . hatch: i.e. the murder in Rome was just the 'hatching out' of
the murder originally intended eight months earlier.
1074 canker: cancer (of heresy); for Molinism, see V. 203 n.
1078 Natal Time: i.e. Christmas, imitating Natale, the Italian for Christmas.
1082 song matutinal: matins; cf. VI. 401 n.
1084 Cardinal that's Camerlengo: prior to Pius VII's reorganization of the Papal
Government in the early nineteenth century, the cardinal-camerlengo ('chamberlain')
was a powerful office. It included 'not only the supervision of the immediate proper-
ties of the Holy See, but also the fiscal administration of the Pontifical States. . . . Briefly
the Camerlengo of the Holy Roman Church was, for the Papal States, Minister of
Finance, Public Works, and Commerce': The Catholic Encyclopedia (16 vols., New
York, 1907–14), iii. 217.

Then rushed on to the blessing of the Hat   1085
And Rapier, which the Pope sends to what prince
Has done most detriment to the Infidel—
And thereby whetted courage if 't were blunt?
Meantime, allow we kept the house a week,
Suppose not we were idle in our mew!   1090
Picture us raging here and raving there—
" 'Money?' I need none. 'Friends?' The word is null.
"Restore the white was on that shield of mine
"Borne at" . . . wherever might be shield to bear.
"I see my grandsire, he who fought so well   1095
"At" . . . here find out and put in time and place,
Or else invent the fight his grandsire fought:
"I see this! I see that!"

                    (See nothing else,
Or I shall scarce see lamb's fry in an hour!   1100

1086 *MS* ^to^   *MS* Prince *Yale 1* Prince>prince   1088 *MS 1868* whet
our   1089 *MS* suppose   1090 *MS* cage: *1868* mew: 1091 *MS 1868*
Picture Count Guido raging here and there—   1092 *MS* "Money?"   *MS 1868*
none—"Friends? The   1093–6 *MS* {no quotation marks}   1093 *MS*
Match me *1868* "Match me   1094 *MS* Born at.. *1868 1872* at".. *Yale 1*
bear,>bear; *1868* bear;   1096 *MS* At.. *1868 1872* "At"..   *MS* out, put in
the   *MS 1868* place   1097 *MS 1868* Of what might be a   *MS* found, *Yale 1*
fought,>fought;   1098 *MS* I see this—I see that—see to it all, *1868* this— *1868*
that—"   1099 {not found in *MS*}   *MS* {no new paragraph}   *1868* See to it
all,   1100 *Yale 1* shall I>I shall   *MS* hour:

1085–7 *blessing . . . Infidel*: this detail is not from OYB. The ceremony referred to,
normally conducted in connection with one of the three Christmas masses, was
instituted by the Avignon popes (it is first attested in 1357), and given its definitive
form under Julius II by Paride de' Grassi, the master of ceremonies. The blessed hat
and sword were symbols of the defence of Christianity and the victory of Good over
Evil. After their papal blessing, they were sent with great ceremony to the ruler or
noble who was honoured to receive them. An excellent recent account is that given by
Flynn Warmington in Paula Higgins (ed.), *Antoine Busnoys: Method, Meaning, and
Context in Late Medieval Music* (Oxford, 1999), 109–17. The Brownings were at
St Peter's on Christmas Day 1858; we have been unable to determine if they actually
saw the ceremony.

1090 *mew*: cage, prison; cf. 'Fra Lippo Lippi', 47.

1093–4 *"Restore . . . at"*: i.e. 'restore my honour to its ancient state, as it was at [some
battle in which a member of the Franceschini family distinguished himself]'.

What to the uncle, as I bid advance
The smoking dish? "Fry suits a tender tooth!
"Behoves we care a little for our kin—
"You, Sir,—who care so much for cousinship
"As come to your poor loving nephew's feast!"   1105
He has the reversion of a long lease yet—
Land to bequeath! He loves lamb's fry, I know!)

Here fall to be considered those same six
Qualities; what Bottini needs must call
So many aggravations of our crime,   1110
Parasite-growth upon mere murder's back.
We summarily might dispose of such
By some off-hand and jaunty fling, some skit—
"So, since there's proved no crime to aggravate,
"A fico for your aggravations, Fisc!"   1115
No,—handle mischief rather,—play with spells
Were meant to raise a spirit, and laugh the while

1101 *MS* I'll nod to the Uncle, *MS* say>nod *1868*—Nod 1102 *MS* dish—
"Sir, for your tender teeth! *1868* dish, "This, for your tender teeth! 1103–5 *MS*
{no quotation marks at beginnings of lines} 1103 *MS 1868* us *MS* kin 1104
MS Sir, who 1105 *MS* for *MS* {no quotation mark at end of line} 1107
MS He may *MS 1868* know! 1108 *MS* {beginning of fo. 100} 1109
MS Qualities, 1111 *MS* back: 1113 *MS* fling—

1101 *uncle*: given the indication of age in the speech that follows, this is Arcangeli's own uncle, Giacinto's great uncle, and Arcangeli himself is the 'loving nephew' of l. 1105.

1106 *reversion . . . lease*: i.e. Arcangeli's uncle owns the freehold rights on an estate; when the lease ends, the estate returns to him. Arcangeli clearly hopes to flatter his uncle into bequeathing him the estate.

1108–9 *six /Qualities*: the question of the presence or absence of aggravating circumstances (*circumstantiæ aggravantes, circumstantiæ præ se ferentes rigorosam pœnam*, sometimes called *qualitates*) in Guido's crimes is introduced in Arcangeli's first pleading and much discussed throughout the trial. The 'qualities' are somewhat variously stated in different places (hence Browning speaks of 'five qualities of bad' in l. 169, but of six here). Arcangeli here deals with (1) the gathering of armed men (1119–56); (2) the alleged use of prohibited arms (1157–1249); (3) the place chosen for the murders (1250–1313); (4) the alleged use of disguise (1314–38); (5) the contention that Pompilia was under the control of the judge (1339–71); (6) the treason (*læsa majestas*) alleged to be involved in the crime (1371–1455): Cook, 173.

1115 *fico*: fig (It.); cf. *Merry Wives of Windsor*, I. iii. 29: ' "Convey", the wise it call. "Steal"? foh! a *fico* for the phrase!'

We show that did he rise we stand his match!
Therefore, first aggravation: we made up—
Over and above our simple murderous selves—　　　　　1120
A regular assemblage of armed men,
Coadunatio armatorum,—ay,
Unluckily it was the very judge
That sits in judgment on our cause to-day
Who passed the law as Governor of Rome:　　　　　1125
"Four men armed,"—though for lawful purpose, mark!
Much more for an acknowledged crime,—"shall die."
We five were armed to the teeth, meant murder too?
Why, that's the very point that saves us, Fisc!
Let me instruct you. Crime nor done nor meant,—　　　1130
You punish still who arm and congregate:
For wherefore use bad means to a good end?
Crime being meant not done,—you punish still
The means to crime, whereon you haply pounce,
Though accident have baulked them of effect.　　　　　1135
But crime not only compassed but complete,
Meant and done too? Why, since you have the end,
Be that your sole concern, nor mind those means

1118 *MS* had he risen we are *1868 1872* we are　　1119 *MS* Therefore—First
Aggravation:　　1120 *MS 1868* murdering　　1121 *MS* {no comma}　　1123
MS Judge　　1124 *MS 1868 1872* Who　　*MS* judment {*sic*}　　1125 *MS 1868
1872* That　　1126 *MS* armed— *Yale 1* armed,—>armed,"—　　*MS* mark— *1868*
Four {broken sort}　　1127 *MS* "Much　　*MS* crime—shall die." *Yale 1* shall>
"shall　　1131 *MS* We>You　　*MS* [ ]>still　　*MS* congregate　　1132 *MS*
1868 why have used　　1133 *MS* ^being^　　*MS* done,　　1134 *MS* Those
MS {no commas}　　*MS* you haply pounce upon　　*1868* you haply pounce upon,
1135 *MS 1868* circumstance　　*MS 1868* you of their end:　　1136 *MS* com-
plete?　　1137 *MS* {beginning of fo. 101}　　*MS* end　　1138 *MS* {no
comma}

1122 *Coadunatio armatorum*: assemblage of armed men (L.).

1123–7 *very judge . . . die*: OYB lxiv (68), Gambi, pam. 5: 'The first of these [ag-
gravating circumstances] is the assembling of armed men, for which according to the
Banns of the Governor of this City there is imposed the penalty of death and
confiscation of goods upon him who is the head of the assembly, even if those
assembled are only four in number, as we read in chapter 82 of the said Banns.'
Browning takes dramatic licence in assuming that one of the judges was previously
Governor and hence responsible for this particular law.

No longer to the purpose! Murdered we?
(—Which, that our luck was in the present case,   1140
Quod contigisse in præsenti casu,
Is palpable, *manibus palpatum est*—)
Make murder out against us, nothing else!
Of many crimes committed with a view
To one main crime, Law overlooks the less,   1145
Intent upon the large. Suppose a man
Having in view commission of a theft,
Climbs the town-wall: 't is for the theft he hangs,
In case he stands convicted of such theft:
Law remits whipping, due to who clomb wall   1150
Through bravery or wantonness alone,
Just to dislodge a daw's nest, plant a flag.
So I interpret you the manly mind
Of him about to judge both you and me,—
Our Governor, who, being no Fisc, my Fisc,   1155
Cannot have blundered on ineptitude!

Next aggravation,—that the arms themselves
Were specially of such forbidden sort
Through shape or length or breadth, as, prompt, Law plucks

1139 *MS* purpose: murdered we?   1140 *MS* —Which,   1141 *MS* {no comma}   1142 *MS* palpable—   *MS est*—   1143 *MS* more! *1868 1872* less!   1144 *MS* Are   1145 *MS* you overlook the less *1868* you over-look   1148 *1868* Climb   *MS* you>'tis {etc.}   1149 {not found in *MS*}   *Yale 1* {line 'Suppose you can convict him of such theft,' added} *1868* Suppose you can convict him of such theft,   1150 *MS* Remit the whipping due to who climbs wall *1868* Remitted whipping due *1868* climbs   1151 *MS 1868* For   1152 *MS 1868* nest and no more. *1872* nest or plant flag. *Yale 2* plant flag.>pluck flower. {there may be a '?' above 'flower'}   1868 1872* him the Judge shall judge   1155 *MS 1868* O' the   *MS* my Fisc, who, being no babe,>who, being no babe, my Fisc, *1868* no babe,   1156 *MS* ineptitude.   ★1157 *1868 1872* {new paragraph. Paragraphing obscured in *1888* and *1889* by this line's being at the head of the page}   1159 *1868* law

1141–2 *Quod . . . est*: from OYB xxxii (32), Spreti, pam. 2; the words occur in a different context from the present argument.

1144–52 *Of . . . flag*: this principle and its illustration are from OYB cxx (128), Arcangeli, pam. 8, though without the detail of the nest and the flag.

From single hand of solitary man,   1160
Making him pay the carriage with his life:
Delatio armorum, arms against the rule,
Contra formam constitutionis, of
Pope Alexander's blessed memory.
Such are the poignards with the double prong,   1165
Horn-like, when tines make bold the antlered buck,
Each prong of brittle glass—wherewith to stab
And break off short and so let fragment stick
Fast in the flesh to baffle surgery:
Such being the Genoese blade with hooked edge   1170
That did us service at the villa here.
Sed parcat mihi tam eximius vir,
But,—let so rare a personage forgive,—
Fisc, thy objection is a foppery!
Thy charge runs that we killed three innocents: 1175
Killed, dost see? Then, if killed, what matter how?
By stick or stone, by sword or dagger, tool

1161 *MS 1868* And makes   1162 *MS armorum*—   *MS* {no commas}   1163
MS {no comma}   1165 *1872* is   *MS* poniard *1868 1872* poignard   *MS* of>
with   1167 *MS 1868* And all *1872* And made   *MS* ^brittle^   *MS* for man to
stab *1868* for man   1168 *MS* {beginning of fo. 102}   1170 *MS 1868* And
such   *MS 1868* hooks at   1171 *MS 1868* Villa   1172–3 *MS* {lines added
later}   1172 *MS Sed*—   *MS eximious vir*— {*sic*}   1173 *MS 1868*
But,   *MS* choice>rare   *MS 1868* forgive,   1174 *MS* foppery.   1175
MS is— *1868* runs,   1176 *MS* do you see: if killed— *1868 1872*
how?—   1177 *MS* and stone,   *MS* and dagger, tools

1162–4 *Delatio . . . memory*: OYB lxv (69), Gambi, pam. 5. Pope Alexander VIII
(1689–91) was Innocent XII's immediate predecessor.

1165–70 *poignards . . . edge*: this is elaborated from SS 14: 'Franceschini's knife was in
the Genoese style, triangular, with barbed hooks on the back of the blade that made
fatal any wound from which it was withdrawn'. The poignard described here has a
single blade, with pairs of hooks on each side, like the 'tines' or prongs on a buck's
antlers. The Ohio editor suggests that 'glass' is figurative, meaning 'of a brittle,
breakable composition', but Venice and other cities had experimented with literal
glass blades and hooks that broke off to devastating effect, and it may well be
that Browning is thinking of these, even though the source gives him no obvious
warrant.

1172 *Sed . . . vir.* 'But may that very distinguished man pardon me'. The real
Arcangeli uses this grand formula twice, at OYB xliii (42), pam. 3, and cii (110),
pam. 8.

Long or tool short, round or triangular—
Poor slain folk find small comfort in the choice!
Means to an end, means to an end, my Fisc!   1180
Nature cries out, "Take the first arms you find!"
Furor ministrat arma: where's a stone?
Unde mî lapidem, where darts for me?
Unde sagittas? But subdue the bard
And rationalize a little. Eight months since,   1185
Had we, or had we not, incurred your blame
For letting 'scape unpunished this bad pair?
I think I proved that in last paragraph!
Why did we so? Because our courage failed.
Wherefore? Through lack of arms to fight the foe: 1190
We had no arms or merely lawful ones,
An unimportant sword and blunderbuss,
Against a foe, pollent in potency,
The *amasius*, and our vixen of a wife.
Well then, how culpably do we gird loin   1195
And once more undertake the high emprise,
Unless we load ourselves this second time
With handsome superfluity of arms,
Since better is "too much" than "not enough,"

1178 *MS* tools   1179 *MS* Poor folks, they find no comfort in a choice! *1868* Poor folks, they *1872* Poor slain folks   1181 *MS 1868 1872* {no comma}   *MS* find"!   1183 *MS lapidem,—   MS* or where my darts?>where darts for me?   1184 *MS* Intermit>But subdue   1185 *MS 1868* little: eight *Yale 2* little.>little!   1186 *MS* {no commas}   1187 *MS* [ ]>letting   *MS* scape 1188 {not found in *MS*}   *Yale 2* that in>that, in   1190 *MS* means   *MS* foe,   1193 *MS* that foe,   1195 *MS* culpably we gird our loins   1196 *MS* again attempt   1199 *MS 1868* better say   *MS* {no quotation mark at end of line}

1182 *Furor . . . arma:* 'Wild passion finds weapons for men's hands': *Aeneid*, I. 150. This is quoted by the anonymous pamphleteer at OYB cl (154), pam. 10; Browning has transferred it to Arcangeli.

1183–4 *Unde . . . sagittas?:* 'where can I get a stone? . . . Where are my arrows?': part of the witty ending of Horace, *Satires*, II. vii (l. 116). This is not from OYB, and is a literary flourish giving us another touch of Arcangeli as poet *manqué*. After this, he has to 'subdue the bard' (1184), i.e. tame his literary bent, and get back to the legal case.

1192 *blunderbuss:* 'a short gun with a large bore, firing many balls or slugs, and capable of doing execution within a limited range without exact aim': OED^2. This is in effect another translation of *sclopulus:* cf. ll. 207–10 n.

And "*plus non vitiat*," too much does no harm,   1200
Except in mathematics, sages say.
Gather instruction from the parable!
At first we are advised—"A lad hath here
"Seven barley loaves and two small fishes: what
"Is that among so many?" Aptly asked: 1205
But put that question twice and, quite as apt,
The answer is "Fragments, twelve baskets full!"

And, while we speak of superabundance, fling
We word by the way to fools who cast their flout
On Guido—"Punishment were pardoned him,   1210
"But here the punishment exceeds offence:
"He might be just, but he was cruel too!"
Why, grant there seems a kind of cruelty
In downright stabbing people he could maim,
(If so you stigmatize the stern and strict)   1215
Still, Guido meant no cruelty—may plead
Transgression of his mandate, over-zeal
O' the part of his companions: all he craved
Was, they should fray the faces of the folk,

1200 *MS* {beginning of fo. 103}   *MS* {Latin not underlined}   *MS* vitiat"—
1201 *MS* people   1203 *MS* hear—>are advised—   *MS* among us hath>hath
here   1204–5 *MS* {no quotation marks at beginnings of lines}   1204 *MS*
^barley^   *MS* fishes—what is that>fishes—what   1205 *MS* Among>Is that
among   *MS* many?—   1206 *MS 1868 1872* apt   1207 *MS* were "Frag-
ments—   *MS* basketsful!"   *1208 *1868 1872* {new paragraph. Paragraphing
obscured in *1888* and *1889* by this line's being at the head of the page}   *MS* hers,
1868 1872 1888 1888 fling   1209 *MS 1868* A   *MS 1868* that   1210 *MS*
exceeds offence, *1868* exceeds offence: 1211 *MS 1868* {not found}   1212
MS 1868 "You   *MS 1868* {no comma}   *MS* you were   *MS* here."   1213–
14 *MS 1868* {not found}   1215 *MS 1868* If   *MS* stigmatise   *MS 1868*
strict,   1216 *MS* he is not without excuse—   *1868* he is not without ex-
cuse—   1217 *MS* [ ]>his mandate,   1218 *MS* On   *MS* [ ]>his   1219
MS Was—   *MS* three *1868* three:

1200 *plus non vitiat*: 'More does not spoil it' (L.). This is described as 'a medieval
philosophic term' by Hodell (p. 334), but we have been unable to trace it.
1203–7 *At . . . full*: cf. John 6: 8–13.
1209 *flout*: 'a mock, an insult, a word or act of contempt': Johnson.
1219 *fray*: abrade, slightly damage.

Merely disfigure, nowise make them die.   1220
Solummodo fassus est, he owns no more,
Dedisse mandatum, than that he desired,
Ad sfrisiandum, dicam, that they hack
And hew, i' the customary phrase, his wife,
Uxorem tantum, and no harm beside.   1225
If his instructions then be misconceived,
Nay, disobeyed, impute you blame to him?
Cite me no Panicollus to the point,
As adverse! Oh, I quite expect his case—
How certain noble youths of Sicily   1230
Having good reason to mistrust their wives,
Killed them and were absolved in consequence:
While others who had gone beyond the need
By mutilation of each paramour—
As Galba in the Horatian satire grieved   1235

1220 *MS 1868* {not found}   1221 *MS est*—   *MS* {no commas}   1222
MS desired   1223 *MS* {Latin text not underlined}   1224 *MS* his
wife   1225 *MS* {Latin text not underlined}   *MS* tantum—   1226 *MS*
our   1227 *MS* Disobeyed,>Nay, disobeyed,   *MS* us?   1228 *MS* {no
comma}   1232 *MS* consequence.   1233 *MS* {beginning of fo. 104}
1234 *MS* the *1868* the paramour   1235 *MS* (As *1868* (So   *MS* ^Hora-
tian^   *MS* had to grieve>grieved) *1868* grieved)

1221–5 *Solummodo . . . beside*: OYB xxxv (34), Spreti, pam. 2. Browning, probably
inadvertently, changes the original 'ad sfrisiandum dictam suam Uxorem tantum' to 'ad
sfrisiandum, dicam, uxorem tantum', converting the participle 'dictam', '(his) said
(wife)', into the finite verb 'dicam', 'shall I say', apologizing for the vernacularism
'sfrisiandum'.

1228 *Panicollus*: there are two small slips by Browning here: firstly, the correct name
of the jurist is Caesar de Panimolla; secondly, OYB in fact cites the following case from
Sanfelicius, not Panimolla. After the case, the following reference occurs: 'Panimoll.
dec. 86 in n. 20, and many sections following, discusses this matter very fully': OYB
xxix (29). Browning wrongly assumes that Panimolla refers to the same case, when in
fact—as Gest shows—he refers to a related but different one. See Gest, 325, and also ll.
1240–3 n.

1235 *Galba . . . grieved*: Galba grieved at the fate of a man whose testes and penis
were cut off in revenge for adultery: cf. Horace, *Satires*, 1. ii. 44–6. Browning follows
the reading of the scholia, that Galba was a legal expert made queasy at such mutilation
because of his own sexual adventures. The more obvious reading of Horace's lines is
that Galba himself was the victim of this punishment. By this allusion (not in OYB)
Browning makes clear the meaning here without having to quote the explicit Latin of
his source: see next n. He also gives Arcangeli another literary flourish. It is interesting
that both here, and at ll. 1805–7, Arcangeli alludes to parts of Horace that were

—These were condemned to the galleys, cast for guilt
Exceeding simple murder of a wife.
But why? Because of ugliness, and not
Cruelty, in the said revenge, I trow!
Ex causa abscissionis partium;   1240
Qui nempe id facientes reputantur
Naturæ inimici, man revolts
Against them as the natural enemy.
Pray, grant to one who meant to slit the nose
And slash the cheek and slur the mouth, at most,   1245
A somewhat more humane award than these
Obtained, these natural enemies of man!
Objectum funditus corruit, flat you fall,
My Fisc! I waste no kick on you, but pass.

Third aggravation: that our act was done—   1250
Not in the public street, where safety lies,
Not in the bye-place, caution may avoid,
Wood, cavern, desert, spots contrived for crime,—

1236 *MS* These   *MS* gallies, as for *1868* as for   1238 *MS* {no comma}   1239
MS Cruelty in   1240 *MS partium*—   1241 *MS 1868 Quia*   1242 *MS*
inimici,—   1243 *MS 1868* Against such   *MS* enemy—   1244 *MS* Is this
mere slitting nose and slashing cheek?>Allow our slitting nose and slashing
cheek   1245 *MS* {not found}   1246 *MS 1868* these!   1247 *MS 1868*
{not found}   1248 *MS corruit*:   1249 *MS 1868* {no comma}   1250
MS {new paragraph indicated by 'New Par.' in left-hand margin}   *MS*
done   1251 *MS* {no commas}   1253 *MS* crime,

sidelined in Browning's lifetime. One nineteenth-century translator, Corpus Professor
of Latin at Oxford, says simply: 'I have omitted two entire satires [I. ii, viii] and several
passages from others. Some of them no one would wish to see translated: some, though
capable of being rendered without offence a hundred or even fifty years ago, could
hardly be so rendered now': John Conington, *The Satires, Epistles, and Art of Poetry of
Horace* (London, 1870), p. xxi.

1240–2 *Ex . . . inimici*: OYB xxix (29), Spreti, pam. 2. Browning censors the ori-
ginal Latin: 'ex causa abscissionis genitalium de facto secutæ quia nempe id facientes
reputantur inimici naturæ': '[this punishment was imposed] because of the mutilation
of the genitals which followed, because those who do such things are considered
enemies of nature'.

1248 *Objectum . . . corruit*: 'this objection falls to the ground completely' (L.): OYB
xviii (19), Arcangeli, pam. 1.

But in the very house, home, nook and nest,
O' the victims, murdered in their dwelling-place,   1255
In domo ac habitatione propria,
Where all presumably is peace and joy.
The spider, crime, pronounce we twice a pest
When, creeping from congenial cottage, she
Taketh hold with her hands, to horrify   1260
His household more, i' the palace of the king.
All three were housed and safe and confident.
Moreover, the permission that our wife
Should have at length *domum pro carcere,*
Her own abode in place of prison—why,   1265
We ourselves granted, by our other self
And proxy Paolo: did we make such grant,
Meaning a lure?—elude the vigilance
O' the jailor, lead her to commodious death,
While we ostensibly relented?   1270

                            Ay,
Just so did we, nor otherwise, my Fisc!
Is vengeance lawful? We demand our right,
But find it will be questioned or refused
By jailer, turnkey, hangdog,—what know we?   1275
Pray, how is it we should conduct ourselves?
To gain our private right—break public peace,
Do you bid us?—trouble order with our broils?

1254 *MS* our victim's very home and nest,   1255 *MS* {not found}   1256
MS {no comma}   1257 *MS* confidence.>peace and joy.   1258 *MS* spider,
crime,>spider crime>spider, crime,   *MS* seems twice a noxious>pronounce we
twice a   1259 *MS* having>creeping   1260 *MS* hands and houseth so>
hands and horrifies   1261 *MS* I'>His household so, i'   1264 *MS* {no
comma}   1265   *MS*   {beginning of fo. 105}   1266   *MS*   {no
comma}   1267 *MS* the grant,   1268 *MS* lure,—   *MS* vigilance of>vigi-
lance   1271 *MS* —Ay,   1274 *MS* And   *MS* and   1276 {not found
in *MS*}

1256 *In . . . propria*: 'in their home and proper dwelling-place' (L.): OYB lxvi (70),
Gambi, pam. 5.

1260 *Taketh . . . hands*: i.e. sets up a web.

1269 *commodious*: convenient, easy (to Guido); cf. l. 1327 where *commodius* = with
more ease.

1275 *hangdog*: a despicable gaoler or executioner (someone only fit to 'hang a dog').

Endanger . . shall I shrink to own . . ourselves?—

Who want no broken head nor bloody nose   1280

(While busied slitting noses, breaking heads)

From the first tipstaff that may interfere!

Nam quicquid sit, for howsoever it be,

An de consensu nostro, if with leave

Or not, *a monasterio*, from the nuns,   1285

Educta esset, she had been led forth,

Potuimus id dissimulare, we

May well have granted leave in pure pretence,

Ut aditum habere, that thereby

An entry we might compass, a free move   1290

Potuissemus, to her easy death,

Ad eam occidendam. Privacy

O' the hearth, and sanctitude of home, say you?

Shall we give man's abode more privilege

Than God's?—for in the churches where He dwells,   1295

In quibus assistit Regum Rex, by means

Of His essence, *per essentiam*, all the same,

Et nihilominus, therein, *in eis*,

Ex justa via delinquens, whose dares

To take a liberty on ground enough,   1300

Is pardoned, *excusatur*: that's our case—

1279 *MS* Endanger . . >Endanger   1280 *MS* [ ]>want   1281 {not found in
MS}   1282 *MS 1868* shall please   1283 *MS sit*—   *MS* {no com-
mas}   *MS* howsover   1284 *MS nostro*—   1285 *MS* not—   *MS* {no
commas}   1286 *MS esset*—   *MS* {no commas}   1289 *MS* {Latin not
underlined}   *MS* that to have   1290 *MS* entry, potuissemus, gain we might>
entry, we might compass by the   1291 *MS Potuissemus*—   *MS* {no com-
mas}   1294 *MS* Then you *1868* Would you   1295 *MS* {no comma}
1296 *MS* {beginning of fo. 106}   *MS Rex*—   1297 *MS* {no commas}   *MS*
essentiam—yet no less   1298 *MS* {Latin not underlined}   *MS* nihilomi-
nus—   1299 *MS delinquens*—who makes bold   1300 *MS* fitting cause
MS {no comma}   1301 *MS* {Latin not underlined}   *MS* {no comma}

1282 *tipstaff*: constable, law officer.

1283–92 *Nam . . . occidendam*: this apparently extreme argument was made by the
real Arcangeli at OYB xviii (19), pam. 1.

1295–1301 *for . . . excusatur*: OYB xxxiv (33–4), Spreti, pam. 2. As at ll. 1221–5,
Browning makes a small slip in the transcription of the Latin. In the second half of the

Delinquent through befitting cause. You hold,
To punish a false wife in her own house
Is graver than, what happens every day,
To hale a debtor from his hiding-place   1305
In church protected by the Sacrament?
To this conclusion have I brought my Fisc?
Foxes have holes, and fowls o' the air their nests;
Praise you the impiety that follows, Fisc?
Shall false wife yet have where to lay her head?   1310
"Contra Fiscum definitum est!" He's done!
"Surge et scribe," make a note of it!
—If I may dally with Aquinas' word.

[—]

1302 *MS* a fitting   *MS* say   *MS* {no comma}   1305 *MS* hiding place
1307 *MS* Fisc!   1308 *MS* "Foxes>Foxes   *MS* holes">holes—   *MS* ^o'
the air^   *MS* nests—   1309 *MS* What follows—I shall let the Fisc de-
clare—   *MS* T>What   *MS* [?have]>let   1310 {not found in
MS}   1311 *MS* {Latin not underlined}   *MS* fiscum   *MS* 1868 done,
1312–13 *MS* {lines added later}   1312 *MS* {Latin not underlined}   *MS*
scribe!"—Make   1313 *MS* word:

sentence here, the original has '& nihilominus delinquens in eis ex iusta Ira . . . excu-
satur': 'and yet one who commits crime in [churches] from just anger . . is excused'.
Browning has substituted 'via' for 'ira', and so produced a slightly different sense.

1308–10 *Foxes . . . head?*: cf. Matt. 8: 20.

1311 *"Contra . . . est!"*: 'this is conclusive against the Fisc' (L.).

1312 *Surge et scribe*: 'Arise and write' (L.): see next n.

1313 *Aquinas' word*: implicitly, at l. 1311, Arcangeli is congratulating himself on
producing an argument as well constructed as one in Aquinas' *Summa Theologica*—a
self-aggrandizing claim indeed, since Aquinas is one of the masters of rational philo-
sophical discourse: cf. v. 1358 n. At l. 1312, *'Surge et scribe'* ('Arise and write') was the
command of Aquinas to his secretary when he was inspired with a theological
argument. In a witty, if egotistical way, Arcangeli presents himself as similarly inspired
with legal argument. The main instance of this phrase occurs in the story of Aquinas at
a banquet with Louis IX in 1269: 'And sitting there at table, suddenly the truth about
[the Manichaean heresy] flashed into his mind, and he struck the table, exclaiming:
"That settles the Manichees!" Then, calling his *socius* by name, as though he were still
at study in his cell, he cried, "Reginald, get up and write!" But the prior touched his
hand, saying, "Master, master, you are at dinner with the king of France, not in your
cell!" Then Thomas, coming to himself, blushed and, bowing to the king, said: "Pray
excuse me, your majesty; I thought I was at my desk. . . . I have begun a work against
the Manichees." But the holy king, marvelling at such detachment from the senses and
much edified, had the presence of mind to call at once for a secretary to write down
there and then the thoughts with which the master had been inspired': *The Life of St
Thomas Aquinas: Biographical Documents*, ed. by Kenelm Foster (London, 1959), pp.

Or in the death-throe does he mutter still,
Fourth aggravation, that we changed our garb,   1315
And rusticized ourselves with uncouth hat,
Rough vest and goatskin wrappage; murdered thus
Mutatione vestium, in disguise,
Whereby mere murder got complexed with wile,
Turned *homicidium ex insidiis?* Fisc,   1320
How often must I round thee in the ears—
All means are lawful to a lawful end?
Concede he had the right to kill his wife:
The Count indulged in a travesty; why?
De illa ut vindictam sumeret,   1325
That on her he might lawful vengeance take,
Commodius, with more ease, *et tutius,*
And safelier: wants he warrant for the step?
Read to thy profit how the Apostle once

1314 *MS* {no new paragraph}   *MS* still?— *1868* still?   1316 *MS* cloak>
weed,>hat,   1317 *MS* hat>vest   1318 *MS* vestium— *Yale 1* vestisum,>
vestium,   1319 *MS* {no comma}   1320 *MS* Turns   *MS 1868* insidiis.
1323 *MS* wife,—   1324 *MS* travesty. So   1325 *MS* {Latin not under-
lined}   *MS* {no comma}   1326 *MS* That he on her might vengeance take
thereby   1327 *MS* Commodius et tutus, with more ease   1328 *MS* {begin-
ning of fo. 107}   *MS* safety: 1329 *MS* Apostle Paul>the Apostle once

---

44–5. The medieval original is the *Vita S. Thomae Aquinatis* (*c.*1323) by Bernard Gui,
OP, which is published in *Fontes Vitae Sancti Thomae Aquinatis*, ed. Dominicus
Prümmer (Toulouse, 1912), pp. 168–222. The story above appears at p. 191. Browning
probably knew the story from a painting of the incident seen in Italy, but we have been
unable to trace an exact source.

1315–20 *Fourth . . . insidiis*: this aggravation is only put forward at OYB lxvi (70),
Gambi, pam. 5.

1316–17 *uncouth . . . wrappage*: adapting SS 23. Browning draws on this detail on
several occasions, clearly much struck that a noble should disguise himself in this way
and eventually be executed in such clothes.

1319 *complexed*: mixed up, combined in a complex manner. OED² gives this as a
rare word, citing only one instance before Browning, from *Burton's Diary* (1658): 'The
question is complexed of matter-of-fact and matter-of-right'.

1320 *homicidium ex insidiis*: murder by stratagem, by ambush (L.).

1321 *round . . . ears*: emphasize, din into your ears; cf. IV. 600 n.

1324 *travesty*: disguise.

1325–8 *De . . . safelier*: OYB xxxii (32), Spreti, pam. 2.

1329–36 *Apostle . . . Troas*: cf. Acts 9: 25, 2 Cor. 11: 32–3, 2 Tim. 4: 13. Just as St
Paul escaped arrest by the Governor and the mob at Damascus by covert means, so

For ease and safety, when Damascus raged,   1330
Was let down in a basket by the wall
To 'scape the malice of the governor
(Another sort of Governor boasts Rome!)
—Many are of opinion,—covered close,
Concealed with—what except that very cloak   1335
He left behind at Troas afterward?
I shall not add a syllable: Molinists may!

Well, have we more to manage? Ay, indeed!
Fifth aggravation, that our wife reposed
Sub potestate judicis, beneath   1340
Protection of the judge,—her house was styled
A prison, and his power became its guard
In lieu of wall and gate and bolt and bar.
This is a tough point, shrewd, redoubtable:
Because we have to supplicate that judge   1345
Shall overlook wrong done the judgment-seat.
Now, I might suffer my own nose be pulled,
As man: but then as father... if the Fisc
Touched one hair of my boy who held my hand
In confidence he could not come to harm   1350

1330 *MS* ease, for   *MS* in Damascus caged,>when Damascus raged,   1331 *MS*
1868 1872 wall,   1333 {not found in *MS*}   1334 *MS* too,   1335 *MS*
with what   *1338 1868 {new paragraph. Paragraphing obscured in *1872* by this
line's being at the head of the page}   *MS* indeed.   1341 *MS* [ ]>styled
1344 *MS 1868* This a   *MS* redoubtable.   1345 *MS* call upon>supplicate   *MS*
1868 1872 the *Yale 2* the>that   1346 *MS* To overlook wrong>Overlook insult
Yale 2 Shall overlook>Overlook *Yale 2* the>his own   *MS* judgment-seat;   1347
MS pulled *Yale 2* my own nose be pulled,>you to pull my nose,   1348 *MS 1868*
1872 man—   *MS 1868 1872* father..

Guido should be allowed his disguise to execute his righteous murder. This argument
is not in OYB.

1333 *Another...Rome!*: a complimentary aside to the ex-Governor of Rome, who
is one of the judges. Whereas the Governor of Damascus persecuted Paul the Apostle,
the Governor of Rome will not make the same mistake by persecuting the righteous
Guido.

1340 *Sub potestate judicis*: OYB lxvi (70), Gambi, pam. 5. The lawyers discuss this
point at five other places.

Crossing the Corso, at my own desire,
Going to see those bodies in the church—
What would you say to that, Don Hyacinth?
This is the sole and single knotty point:
For, bid Tommati blink his interest,   1355
You laud his magnanimity the while:
But baulk Tommati's office,—he talks big!
"My predecessors in the place,—those sons
"O' the prophets that may hope succeed me here,—
"Shall I diminish their prerogative?   1360
"Count Guido Franceschini's honour!—well,
"Has the Governor of Rome none?"

                                        You perceive,
The cards are all against us. Make a push,
Kick over table, as shrewd gamesters do!   1365
We, do you say, encroach upon the rights,
Deny the omnipotence o' the Judge forsooth?
We, who have only been from first to last
Intending that his purpose should prevail,
Nay more, at times, anticipating it   1370
At risk of his rebuke?

                                        But wait awhile!
Cannot we lump this with the sixth and last
Of the aggravations—that the Majesty

1351 *MS* {no commas}   *MS* desire—   1352 {not found in *MS*}   1353
MS —What   1355 *MS* interest—   1357 *MS* big—   1358 *MS* {no
quotation mark at beginning of line}   *MS* Predecessors *Yale 1* Predecessors>prede-
cessors   *MS* place—   1359 *MS* {beginning of fo. 108}   *MS* "Of   *MS*
there,—   1360 *MS* prerogative?"   1363 *MS* {no new paragraph}   *MS*
Brief,   1364 *MS* us: make   1365 *MS* our gamesters do: *1868* our game-
sters   1368 *MS* {no comma}   1369 *MS* Intent his mind and *1868* Intent
on   1370 *MS* Even, though, *1868 1872* Nay,   *MS 1868* both   1371 *MS* a
rebuke... *1868* a rebuke?   1372 *MS* {no new paragraph}   *MS* but wait
awhile..   1373 *MS* Sixth   1374 *MS* Aggravations—

1351–2 *Crossing...church*: cf. l. 45 n.
1355 *blink*: shut his eyes to, ignore.
1358–9 *sons /O' the prophets*: cf. Acts 2: 17.

O' the Sovereign here received a wound? to-wit,   1375
Læsa Majestas, since our violence
Was out of envy to the course of law,
In odium litis? We cut short thereby
Three pending suits, promoted by ourselves
I' the main,—which worsens crime, *accedit ad*   1380
Exasperationem criminis!

Yes, here the eruptive wrath with full effect!
How, did not indignation chain my tongue,
Could I repel this last, worst charge of all!
(There is a porcupine to barbacue;   1385
Gigia can jug a rabbit well enough,
With sour-sweet sauce and pine-pips; but, good Lord,
Suppose the devil instigate the wench
To stew, not roast him? Stew my porcupine?
If she does, I know where his quills shall stick!   1390
Come, I must go myself and see to things:
I cannot stay much longer stewing here.)
Our stomach . . . I mean, our soul is stirred within,

1375 *MS* an impious wound, *1868* wound,   1376 *MS* for   1377 *MS* {no comma}   1378 *MS litis:* we   1382 *MS* {no new paragraph}   *MS* Yes,—   1383 *MS* How—   *1868* How—   *MS* {no commas}   *1868* tongue—   1384 *MS* {no comma}   1385 *MS* barbacue—   1386–91 {not found in *MS*}   1392 *MS 1868* here)   1393 *MS 1868 1872* stomach . .   *MS* soul—is *1868* soul—

1376–81 *Læsa . . . criminis:* 'Injurious to Majesty . . . because of anger over a law-suit . . . added for increasing the crime' (L.): OYB lxxviii (85), Bottini, pam. 6.

1379 *Three pending suits:* see v. 1343, 1347–51 nn.

1385 *porcupine to barbacue:* a seemingly exotic but actually mundane detail, hence raising interesting questions about reader response. Porcupine was a common roast for the Romans in the nineteenth century and Browning has simply transferred this fact back to the seventeenth; cf. *Roba di Roma*, ii. 4: 'The Roman market is rich in game of all kinds. Here may be seen the brown rough hide and snarling snout of the wild boar, the smooth "leathern coats" of slender deer, and the black and white quills of the "fretful porcupine".' Porcupines used to be fairly widespread in Italy but have declined in number in recent years. Even a standard modern work still points out that their flesh is edible: see *Dizionario della lingua e della civiltà italiana contemporanea*, ed. by E. De Felice and A. Duro (Palermo, 1974), p. 1053. Although commonly called *porcospino*, the more formal term in Italian is *istrice*.

1386 *jug:* stew.

And we want words. We wounded Majesty?
Fall under such a censure, we?—who yearned   1395
So much that Majesty dispel the cloud
And shine on us with healing on her wings,
That we prayed Pope *Majestas'* very self
To anticipate a little the tardy pack,
Bell us forth deep the authoritative bay   1400
Should start the beagles into sudden yelp
Unisonous,—and, Gospel leading Law,
Grant there assemble in our own behoof
A Congregation, a particular Court,
A few picked friends of quality and place,   1405
To hear the several matters in dispute,—
Causes big, little and indifferent,
Bred of our marriage like a mushroom-growth,—
All at once (can one brush off such too soon?)
And so with laudable despatch decide   1410
Whether we, in the main (to sink detail)
Were one the Pope should hold fast or let go.
"What, take the credit from the Law?" you ask?
Indeed, we did! Law ducks to Gospel here:

1395 *MS* we,—who *1868* we,—   1396 *MS* {beginning of fo. 109}   1397
MS in its *1868* on its   1398 *MS* We prayed the Pope—   *MS* self— *1868* We
prayed the Pope, *Majestas'* very self,   1399 *MS* [ ]>pack,   1401 *MS*
[ ]>yelp   1406 *MS* Should   *MS 1868 1872* dispute,   1408 *MS 1868 1872*
mushroom-growth,   1409 *MS* once—can   *MS* soon?—   1410 *MS*
decide with laudable dispatch>with laudable dispatch decide *1868 1872* dis-
patch   1411 *MS* main—to   *MS* detail—   1412 *MS 1868* Church   *MS*
up or cast down,—   1413 *MS* And—"take   1414 {not found in *MS*}
Yale 1 {line 'Indeed, we did! Law ducks to Gospel here:' added}

1396–7 *dispel . . . wings*: cf. Mal. 4: 2: 'But unto you that fear my name shall the Sun
of righteousness arise with healing in his wings; and ye shall go forth, and grow up as
calves of the stall.'

1402 *Unisonous*: of the same pitch. Cook gives this as a coinage, but OED² gives the
earliest use as 1781.

1403 *behoof*: benefit, advantage.

1404 *Congregation . . . Court*: 'una particolare Congregazione' (It.); for this passage of
OYB see v. 1347–51 n.

1414 *ducks*: makes a perfunctory bow, yields.

Why should Law gain the glory and pronounce   1415
A judgment shall immortalize the Pope?
Yes: our self-abnegating policy
Was Joab's—we would rouse our David's sloth,
Bid him encamp against a city, sack
A place whereto ourselves had long laid siege,   1420
Lest, taking it at last, it take our name
Nor be styled *Innocentinopolis.*
But no! The modesty was in alarm,
The temperance refused to interfere,
Returned us our petition with the word   1425
"*Ad judices suos,*" "Leave him to his Judge!"
As who should say "Why trouble my repose?
"Why consult Peter in a simple case,
"Peter's wife's sister in her fever-fit
"Might solve as readily as the Apostle's self?   1430
"Are my Tribunals posed by aught so plain?
"Hath not my Court a conscience? It is of age,
"Ask it!"

We do ask,—but, inspire reply

1415–16 *MS* {lines added later}   1416 *MS* The   1418 *MS* rouze   1422
MS 1868 And be not   1423 *MS* But—the   1424 *MS* holiness   1426
MS {Latin not underlined}   *MS* suos"—   1427 *MS* say—   *1868* say—
1428–33 *MS* {no quotation marks at beginnings of lines}   1428 *MS* {beginning
of fo. 110}   *MS* case might solve *Yale 1* case>case,   1429 *MS* fever-fit?   1430
{not found in *MS*}   1431 *MS* so incompetent,>posed by aught so
plain?   1432 *MS* conscience,—   1434 *MS* {no new paragraph}   *MS*
[?did]>do   *MS* [ ]>but,   *MS* reply,

1418–22 *Joab's . . . Innocentinopolis*: Joab, commander of David's army, had defeated
the Ammonite city of Rabbah. Rather than enter it himself and claim the glory, he
sent a message to David to 'gather the rest of the people together, and encamp against
the city, and take it: lest I take the city, and it be called after my name': 2 Sam. 12: 28.
Innocentinopolis = Innocent's city.

1426 *"Ad judices suos,"*: 'to his judges' (L.); cf. v. 1760.

1429–30 *Peter's . . . self*: cf. Matt. 8: 14–15. Arcangeli treats the biblical text jovially,
altering mother-in-law to sister-in-law.

1431 *posed*: troubled, given difficulty.

1432–3 *It . . . /Ask it!"*: i.e. 'it is a mature institution, ask it.' The words are those of
the parents of the young blind man cured by Christ: 'Therefore said his parents, He is
of age; ask him': John 9: 23.

1434–5 *We . . . asked*: although obeying the Pope's order to refer the case back to
the original court, Arcangeli asks that, in return for this obedience, the Pope should

To the Court thou bidst me ask, as I have asked—   1435
Oh thou, who vigilantly dost attend
To even the few, the ineffectual words
Which rise from this our low and mundane sphere
Up to thy region out of smoke and noise,
Seeking corroboration from thy nod   1440
Who art all justice—which means mercy too,
In a low noisy smoky world like ours
Where Adam's sin made peccable his seed!
We venerate the father of the flock,
Whose last faint sands of life, the frittered gold,   1445
Fall noiselessly, yet all too fast, o' the cone
And tapering heap of those collected years:
Never have these been hurried in their flow,
Though justice fain would jog reluctant arm,
In eagerness to take the forfeiture   1450
Of guilty life: much less shall mercy sue
In vain that thou let innocence survive,

1435 {not found in MS}   Yale 1 court>Court   1436 MS lendest ear>dost
attend   1437 MS these>even   MS my few, my   1439 MS To thy pure
1441 MS {no comma}   Yale 1 too>too,   1443 MS seed.   1444 MS Oh,
venerated>We, venerable the   1446 MS noiselessy {sic} yet   MS fast,
the   1447 MS O' the heap>O' the tapering Yale 1 The>And   MS years,—
1868 1872 years,—   1448 MS {no comma}   1449 MS {line added
later}   MS When   MS had jogged   1450 MS By

'inspire' the reply that the court will give. This plea for influence is then elaborated by
the subsequent prayer.

1436 *thou*: i.e. the Pope.

1443 *peccable*: capable of sinning.

1444 *father of the flock*: i.e. the Pope, as shepherd of the people of God.

1445 *frittered gold*: i.e. the last, worn fragments of gold (sand) in the hour-glass of life.
The image is full of pathos: 'frittered' = broken into tiny particles, suggests the
exhaustion of the Pope's old age: cf. *Sordello*, IV. 776, R&B, IV. 143. 'Gold' suggests
the preciousness of these last moments of life. Ohio rightly suggests that this hour-glass
image is probably called to mind by the real hour-glass of l. 61, now running out:
Ohio, viii. 376.

1452 *innocence*: a pun: the innocent person, i.e. Guido, but also Innocent XII.
Arcangeli ingeniously links together Guido and the Pope, as he suggests that if the
Pope hurries Guido towards execution he may also hasten the end of his own fast-
ebbing life.

Precipitate no minim of the mass
O' the all-so precious moments of thy life,
By pushing Guido into death and doom!   1455

(Our Cardinal engages to go read
The Pope my speech, and point its beauties out.
They say, the Pope has one half-hour, in twelve,
Of something like a moderate return
Of the intellectuals,—never much to lose!   1460
If I adroitly plant this passage there,
The Fisc will find himself forestalled, I think,
Though he stand, beat till the old ear-drum break!
—Ah, boy of my own bowels, Hyacinth,
Wilt ever catch the knack, requite the pains   1465
Of poor papa, become proficient too
I' the how and why and when, the time to laugh,
The time to weep, the time, again, to pray,
And all the times prescribed by Holy Writ?
Well, well, we fathers can but care, but cast   1470
Our bread upon the waters!)
                                    In a word,
These secondary charges go to ground,
Since secondary, and superfluous,—motes

1454 {not found in *MS*}   *Yale 1* life.>life,   1456 *MS* {no new para-
graph}   *MS* read my speech—   *1868* read my speech: 1457 {not found in
MS 1868}   1458 *MS* he>the Pope   *MS* half-hour in the twelve>half-hour in
twelve *Yale 1* half-hour in twelve>half-hour, in twelve,   1460 *MS 1868 1872*
lose!—   1461 *MS* he   *MS* plants   1463 *MS* {beginning of fo.
111}   *MS* knock>beat   1465 *MS* knack,—   *1868* knack,—   1467 *MS*
when—   *1868* when—   1469 *MS* described>prescribed   *MS* in   1470
MS a>we   *MS* trust,>hope,>care,   1471 *MS* His>Our   *MS* waters—)
1472 *MS* {no comma}   1473 *MS* {no comma}   1474 *MS* and superfluous,
so>[?since] superfluous, so>so superfluous,—motes

1453 *minim*: smallest particle (of sand in the hour-glass).
1460 *the intellectuals*: i.e. the mental powers.
1467–9 *time . . . Writ*: cf. Eccles. 3: 1–8.
1470–1 *cast . . . waters*: i.e. do our best (and then hope for the best): proverbial, from
Eccles. 11: 1.
1473 *go to ground*: vanish (like a fox in a hunt).

Quite from the main point: we did all and some,   1475
Little and much, adjunct and principal,
Causa honoris. Is there such a cause
As the sake of honour? By that sole test try
Our action, nor demand if more or less,
Because of the action's mode, we merit blame   1480
Or may-be deserve praise! The Court decides.
Is the end lawful? It allows the means:
What we may do, we may with safety do,
And what means "safety" we ourselves must judge.
Put case a person wrongs me past dispute: 1485
If my legitimate vengeance be a blow,
Mistrusting my bare arm can deal that blow,
I claim co-operation of a stick;
Doubtful if stick be tough, I crave a sword;
Diffident of ability in fence,   1490
I fee a friend, a swordsman to assist:
Take one—he may be coward, fool or knave:
Why not take fifty?—and if these exceed
I' the due degree of drubbing, whom accuse
But the first author of the aforesaid wrong   1495
Who put poor me to such a world of pains?
Surgery would have just excised a wart;
The patient made such pother, struggled so
That the sharp instrument sliced nose and all.

1475 *MS* point,—   1476 *MS* adjuncts>adjunct   *MS* principal   1477 *MS*
honoris: is   *MS* thing>cause   1478 *MS* Try by that sole test>By that sole test
try   1479 *MS* The action here:>Our action,   *MS* less   1480 *MS* {no
comma}   1481 *MS* praise:—the *1868* praise.   *MS* decides—   1482 *MS*
means.   1483 *MS 1868* do we   *MS* must>may   1485 *MS* {line added
later}   *MS* man has wronged   1486 *MS* is   1487 *MS* fitly strike,>deal
the same, *1868* the same,   1488 *MS* club,>stick   1489 *MS* Doubtful the
stick   *MS* sword,   1490 *MS* [ ]>ability   *MS* to fence,   1491 *MS* I take
a swordsman shall assist me—take>I take a friend, a swordsman may assist: 1492
MS One—who may turn out>Take one—who may be *1868* who may   *MS*
knave—   1493 *MS* {beginning of fo. 112}   1494 *MS* whose the fault>
whom accuse   1495 *MS* ^aforesaid^   1496 *MS* Has   1497 *MS* A
surgeon wants to just excise>Surgery would have just excised   1498 *MS* makes
a>made such   1499 *MS* cuts>sl>sliced

Taunt us not that our friends performed for pay!   1500
Ourselves had toiled for simple honour's sake:
But country clowns want dirt they comprehend,
The piece of gold! Our reasons, which suffice
Ourselves, be ours alone; our piece of gold
Be, to the rustic, reason he approves!   1505
We must translate our motives like our speech,
Into the lower phrase that suits the sense
O' the limitedly apprehensive. Let
Each level have its language! Heaven speaks first
To the angel, then the angel tames the word   1510
Down to the ear of Tobit: he, in turn,
Diminishes the message to his dog,
And finally that dog finds how the flea
(Which else, importunate, might check his speed)
Shall learn its hunger must have holiday   1515
By application of his tongue or paw:
So many varied sorts of language here,

1501 *MS* For us—enough the *1868* For us, enough were   *MS* sake— *1872* Ourselves,
the simple honour's sake sufficed: 1502 *MS* For country clowns—the dirt *1868*
Give *1868* the dirt   1503 *MS* {no comma}   *MS* gold: our   1504 *MS* {no
comma}   1505 *MS* {no commas}   *MS* and to spare: *1868* reason and to
spare!   1506 *MS 1868* {no comma}   1507 *MS* may suit   1508 *MS*
Of   *MS* limited   intelle>limitedly-apprehensive,   let   1509   *MS* lan-
guage: 1511 *MS* Tobit,—   1513 *MS* to>that   *MS* to the first>finds
how the   1514 *MS* Which   *MS* speed,   1515 *MS* his   *MS 1868 1872*
holiday,— *1888* holiday, *DC BrU* holiday,>holiday *1889* holiday *Yale 2* {ll. 1515 and
1516 transposed}   1516–17 {not found in *MS*}   1516 {not found in
1868}   1517 *1868* How

1500–19 *Taunt . . . æquis*: this argument is Browning's, not from OYB.
1502 *clowns*: peasants.
1508 *apprehensive*: intelligent.
1510–16 *angel . . . paw*: see Tobit 5: 16. In the apocryphal book of Tobit the arch-
angel Raphael descends from heaven in order to protect Tobit's son, Tobias. After
speaking with the old and blind Tobit, Raphael accompanies the young Tobias on a
journey, together with Tobit's dog. The theme of the angel and the boy on the road,
dressed as travellers, with the dog at their feet, was popular with Florentine artists of
the Renaissance because of the confraternities in the city devoted to the archangel
Raphael. Probably Browning is remembering one such painting. The 'Tobias and the
Angel', attributed to Andrea del Verrocchio, now in the National Gallery, London,
but still in Florence until 1867, is a particularly beautiful treatment of the theme.

Each following each with pace to match the step,
Haud passibus æquis!

                    Talking of which flea,   1520
Reminds me I must put in special word
For the poor humble following,—the four friends,
Sicarii, our assassins caught and caged.
Ourselves are safe in your approval now:
Yet must we care for our companions, plead   1525
The cause o' the poor, the friends (of old-world faith)
Who lie in tribulation for our sake.
Pauperum Procurator is my style:
I stand forth as the poor man's advocate:
And when we treat of what concerns the poor,   1530
Et cum agatur de pauperibus,
In bondage, *carceratis*, for their sake,
In eorum causis, natural piety,
Pietas, ever ought to win the day,
Triumphare debet, quia ipsi sunt,   1535
Because those very paupers constitute,
Thesaurus Christi, all the wealth of Christ.
Nevertheless I shall not hold you long
With multiplicity of proofs, nor burn
Candle at noon-tide, clarify the clear.   1540
There beams a case refulgent from our books—

1519 *MS æquis.*   1520 *MS* {no new paragraph}   *1868* {no comma}   1523
MS in your charge: *1868* in your charge   1524 *MS* now,—   1525 *MS*
{beginning of fo. 113}   1526 *MS* poor,—   *MS* {no brackets}   1527
MS 1868 are   1528 {not found in *MS*}   1529 *MS* advocate,   1530
MS {no comma}   1531 *MS Cum>Et cum*   *MS* {no comma}   1532 *MS*
{no commas}   *MS carceratis*—   1533 *MS* piety   1534 *MS* {no com-
mas}   1535 *MS* Triumphare debet, {not underlined}   *MS sunt*   1536
MS poor do   *MS* {no comma}   1537 *MS Christi*:   1541 *MS* is>
beams   *MS* in>from

1519 *Haud passibus æquis!*: 'not with equal steps' (L.), i.e. with shorter strides
according to height; cf. *Aeneid*, II. 724.

1523 *Sicarii*: assassins (L.).

1530–7 *And . . . Christ*: OYB cxxxix (144), Spreti, pam. 9: these are the final words
of this speech.

1541 *refulgent*: shining, resplendent.

Castrensis, Butringarius, everywhere
I find it burn to dissipate the dark.
'T is this: a husband had a friend, which friend
Seemed to him over-friendly with his wife   1545
In thought and purpose,—I pretend no more.
To justify suspicion or dispel,
He bids his wife make show of giving heed,
Semblance of sympathy—propose, in fine,
A secret meeting in a private place.   1550
The friend, enticed thus, finds an ambuscade,
To-wit, the husband posted with a pack
Of other friends, who fall upon the first
And beat his love and life out both at once.
These friends were brought to question for their help;   1555
Law ruled "The husband being in the right,
"Who helped him in the right can scarce be wrong"—
Opinio, an opinion every way,
Multum tenenda cordi, heart should hold!
When the inferiors follow as befits   1560
The lead o' the principal, they change their name,
And, *non dicuntur*, are no longer called
His mandatories, *mandatorii*,
But helpmates, *sed auxiliatores;* since
To that degree does honour' sake lend aid,   1565
Adeo honoris causa est efficax,

1543 *MS* dark;   1545 *MS* more than friendly>over-friendly   1546 *MS*
we   1551 *MS* friend enticed thus finds   1555 *1868* help.   1556 *MS*
{beginning of fo. 114}   1557 *MS* {no quotation mark at beginning of
line}   1558 *MS Opinio*—   *MS* everyway   1559 *MS* {no comma}   *MS*
hold.   1561 *MS* the styl>the name,   1562 *MS* {no commas}   1563
MS {no commas}   1564 *MS* {no comma}   1566 *MS Honoris*   *MS* {no
comma}

1542–59 *Castrensis . . . hold!*: loosely adapting OYB xxxvi f. (35), Spreti, pam. 2.
Paulus Castrensis (1360–1447) and Jacobus Butrigarius (1274–1348) were both great
legal experts of their day.

1560–74 *When . . . self*: OYB xli (41) and xliv (43), Arcangeli, pam. 3.

1565 *honour' sake*: Ohio emends to 'honour's sake', but since the elided apostrophe *s*
is common practice for Browning, in accord with his concern for the effect of living
speech, we leave it unchanged, as in all editions.

That not alone, *non solum*, does it pour
Itself out, *se diffundat*, on mere friends
We bring to do our bidding of this sort,
In mandatorios simplices, but sucks   1570
Along with it in wide and generous whirl,
Sed etiam assassinii qualitate
Qualificatos, people qualified
By the quality of assassination's self,
Dare I make use of such neologism,   1575
Ut utar verbo.

Haste we to conclude.
Of the other points that favour, leave some few
For Spreti; such as the delinquents' youth.
One of them falls short, by some months, of age   1580
Fit to be managed by the gallows; two
May plead exemption from our law's award,
Being foreigners, subjects of the Granduke—
I spare that bone to Spreti, and reserve
Myself the juicier breast of argument—   1585
Flinging the breast-blade i' the face o' the Fisc
Who furnished me the tid-bit: he must needs

1567 *MS* {no commas}   1568 *MS* {no commas}   *MS* knaves>friends   *★MS*
friends *1868 1872 1888* friends, *DC BrU* friends,>friends *1889* friends   1569 *MS*
pay>bring   *MS* {no comma}   1571 *MS* {no comma}   1572 *MS* assassi-
ni[ ]>assassinii   1573 *MS* *Qualificatos*—   1575 *MS* a barbarous word,>neo-
logism—   1577 *MS* {no new paragraph}   *MS* conclude— *1868 1872*
conclude: 1579 *MS* Spreti—   *MS* youth— *1868 1872* youth: 1582
MS effect>award *Yale 1* award>award,   1584 *MS* toss>spare   *MS 1868* {no
comma}   *MS* pick bare   1585 *1872* jucier *Yale 2* jucier>juicier   1586 *MS*
{beginning of fo. 115}   *MS* And fling the breast-bone in   *★MS 1868 1872 1888*
Fisc, *DC BrU* Fisc,>Fisc *1889* Fisc   1587 *MS* would

1575–6 *Dare . . . verbo*: *assassinium*, of medieval coinage like *sclopulus* and *sfrisiare*, is
the neologism apologized for by *ut utar verbo*.

1586 *breast-blade*: i.e. breast-bone (see *MS*). Arcangeli keeps the best part of the
argument for himself (the chicken breast), and, having worked it out (eaten it), he
takes the essence of it (the breast-bone) and throws it in the face of the Fisc, who
first suggested to him this line of attack.

1587 *tid-bit*: titbit, fig. an interesting piece of information.

Play off his privilege and rack the clowns,—
And they, at instance of the rack, confess
All four unanimously made resolve,—   1590
The night o' the murder, in brief minute snatched
Behind the back of Guido as he fled,—
That, since he had not kept his promise, paid
The money for the murder on the spot,
So, reaching home again, might please ignore   1595
The pact or pay them in improper coin,—
They one and all resolved, these hopeful friends,
'T were best inaugurate the morrow's light,
Nature recruited with her due repose,
By killing Guido as he lay asleep   1600
Pillowed on wallet which contained their fee.

I thank the Fisc for knowledge of this fact:
What fact could hope to make more manifest
Their rectitude, Guido's integrity?
For who fails recognize the touching truth   1605
That these poor rustics bore no envy, hate,

1588 MS 1868 armoury   1589 1868 confessed   1590 MS 1868
did   1591 MS 1868 That   MS 1868 minutes   1593 MS kept his promise,
paid>promptly paid their zeal,>kept his promise, paid   1594 MS {line added
later}   1595 MS Thus reaching home, might even ignore the pact>And, reach-
ing home again, might even ignore   1595 1868 And,   1868 even   1596
1868 past   MS 1868 pay it   MS 1868 coin,   1597 {not found in
MS}   1598 MS 1868 They would   1599 MS Taking the necessary rest
meanwhile,>Having recruited strength with needful rest, 1868 Having recruited
strength with needful rest,   1601 MS 1868 by   Yale 1 fee>fee.   1602
{not found in MS}   1603 MS {no new paragraph}   MS act   1604 MS
rectitude and his   1605 MS recognise apparent here. 1868 recognise apparent
here, 1872 recognise   1606 MS The harmless silly rustics bore no hate,>The silly
rustics bore no envy, hate,

1588 Play off: demonstrate, show off; cf. II. 75 n.
1589–1601 And . . . fee: based on SS, not on any detail in OYB: '[The accomplices]
also confessed their intention to choose their moment and rob Franceschini, because
he had reneged on his promise to pay them as soon as they left Rome': SS 18.
1602 I . . . fact: this fact is not mentioned by the Fisc or any other lawyer in OYB; it
derives from SS: see previous n.
1603–31 What . . . pay: this farcical, ingenious argument is not from OYB, but is
one Browning has invented to help Arcangeli's speech towards its climax.

Malice nor yet uncharitableness
Against the people they had put to death?
In them, did such an act reward itself?
All done was to deserve the simple pay,   1610
Obtain the bread clowns earn by sweat of brow,
And missing which, they missed of everything—
Hence claimed pay, even at expense of life
To their own lord, so little warped (admire!)
By prepossession, such the absolute   1615
Instinct of equity in rustic souls!
Whereas our Count, the cultivated mind,
He, wholly rapt in his serene regard
Of honour, he contemplating the sun
Who hardly marks if taper blink below,—   1620
He, dreaming of no argument for death
Except a vengeance worthy noble hearts,—
Dared not so desecrate the deed, forsooth,
Vulgarize vengeance, as defray its cost
By money dug from out the dirty earth,   1625
Irritant mere, in Ovid's phrase, to ill.

1608 MS death: 1609 MS the deed reward itself? No, Sirs—   1610 MS
1868 their   1611 MS And eat the bread they gained 1868 they earned   MS 1868
brow: 1612 MS Missing of this, 1868 Missing this pay,   1613 MS 1868
it,   MS expence   1614 MS 1868 warped were they   1615 MS prepos-
sion,   1616 MS souls.   1617 MS 1868 While he the   1618 MS
{beginning of fo. 116}   1619 MS Of honor, as who contemplates the morn
Yale 1 morn>sun 1868 as who contemplates 1872 sun,   1620 MS And little minds
what tapers blink beneath, 1868 And hardly minds what tapers blink below, 1872
below,   1622 MS 1868 the   MS 1868 hearts,   1623 MS 1868 Would
he   MS {no commas} 1868 deed forsooth,   1624 MS 1868 1872 Vulgarise
MS {no comma}   MS by>as   1625 MS 1868 out of   MS {no
comma}   1626 MS And irritants, in Maro's phrase, to ill? 1868 Mere irritant,
in Maro's phrase, to ill?

1615 prepossession: feeling in favour of, preconceived opinion.
   1626 Irritant . . . ill: i.e. only a spur to wickedness, echoing Ovid's 'inritamenta
malorum' in Metamorphoses, I. 138–40: 'sed itum est in viscera terrae,/quasque recon-
diderat Stygiisque admoverat umbris,/effodiuntur opes, inritamenta malorum': 'but
men explored the bowels of the earth, and what the earth had hidden away near the
Stygian shades, they exposed to view, spurs to sin and wickedness'. The original
reading here was 'Maro's [i.e. Virgil's] phrase': see MS, 1868.

What though he lured base hinds by lucre's hope,—
The only motive they could masticate,
Milk for babes, not strong meat which men require?
The deed done, those coarse hands were soiled enough,
He spared them the pollution of the pay.   1631
So much for the allegement, thine, my Fisc,
Quo nil absurdius, than which nought more mad,
Excogitari potest, may be squeezed
From out the cogitative brain of thee!   1635

And now, thou excellent the Governor!
(Push to the peroration) *cæterum*
Enixe supplico, I strive in prayer,
Ut dominis meis, that unto the Court,
Benigna fronte, with a gracious brow,   1640
Et oculis serenis, and mild eyes,
Perpendere placeat, it may please them weigh,
Quod dominus Guido, that our noble Count,
Occidit, did the killing in dispute,
Ut ejus honor tumulatus, that   1645

1627 *MS* hope of pay,—>lucre's hope,—   1631 *MS* the>them   1633 *MS*
absurdius—   *MS* mad—   1634 *MS potest* may squeezed   1635 *MS*
brain.   *MS*   {Between 1635 and 1636 extra line and new paragraph: 'And
now,'}   ★1636 *1868* {new paragraph. Paragraphing obscured in *1872* by this line's
being at the head of the page}   *MS* now,—most>now,—thou   *MS* Gov-
ernor!—   1637 *MS* (Stay Tully, to thy laurels)>(Look, Tully, to thy laurels)>
(Push to the peroration)   1638 *MS supplico*—   *MS* {no commas}   1639 *MS*
{no commas}   1640 *MS* {no commas}   1641 *MS* {no commas}   1642
MS placeat—   *MS* {no commas}   *MS* they   1643 *MS* {Latin not under-
lined}   *MS*   {no   commas}   1644   *MS*   *Occidit*—   *MS*   {no com-
mas}   1645 *MS* {no comma}

1627 *hinds*: rustics.
1629 *Milk . . . require*: cf. 1 Cor. 3: 1–2, Heb. 5: 13–14.
1633–5 *Quo . . . thee!*: OYB clxxxii (187–8), Bottini, pam. 13. A more literal trans-
lation would be: 'than which nothing more absurd can be thought of'.
1637 *peroration*: the rhetorical conclusion or summing-up.
1637–1736 *cæterum . . . fall*: with only minor changes and elisions, the Latin in this
hundred-line climax is taken verbatim from the climax of the real Arcangeli's speech at
OYB cxxii f. (130), pam. 8. Browning's translation, with the exception of a few
flourishes, is faithful rhetorically and emotionally to the original.

The honour of him buried fathom-deep
In infamy, *in infamia*, might arise,
Resurgeret, as ghost breaks sepulchre!
Occidit, for he killed, *uxorem*, wife,
Quia illi fuit, since she was to him,   1650
Opprobrio, a disgrace and nothing more!
Et genitores, killed her parents too,
Qui, who, *postposita verecundia*,
Having thrown off all sort of decency,
Filiam repudiarunt, had renounced   1655
Their daughter, *atque declarare non*
Erubuerunt, nor felt blush tinge cheek,
Declaring, *meretricis genitam*
Esse, she was the offspring of a drab,
Ut ipse dehonestaretur, just   1660
That so himself might lose his social rank!
Cujus mentem, and which daughter's heart and soul,
They, *perverterunt*, turned from the right course,
Et ad illicitos amores non
Dumtaxat pellexerunt, and to love   1665
Not simply did alluringly incite,
Sed vi obedientiæ, but by force
O' the duty, *filialis*, daughters owe,
Coegerunt, forced and drove her to the deed:

\

1646 *MS* {beginning of fo. 117}   *MS* fathom deep   1647 *MS* {no commas}
1648 *MS* {no comma}   *MS 1868* ghosts break   1649 *MS Occidit* killed, I say,
uxorem wife   1650 *MS* {no commas}   1651 *MS* {no comma}   *MS*
more!—   1652 *MS genitores*—   *MS* {no commas}   1653 *MS* {no commas}
1654 *MS* {no comma}   1655 *MS* {Latin not underlined}   *MS* repudiar-
unt—   1656 *MS* {no comma}   1657 *MS* {no commas}   1658 *MS*
{Latin not underlined}   *MS* {no comma}   1659 *MS* {Latin not under-
lined}   *MS* Esse—   *MS* {no commas}   1660 *MS* {Latin not underlined}
MS {no comma}   1662 *MS* {Latin not underlined}   *MS* mentem—   *MS* of
which daughter mind and soul>which daughter's heart and soul>of which daughter
heart and soul   1663 *MS* They *perverterunt*—   1664 *MS* {Latin not under-
lined}   1665 *MS* {Latin not underlined}   *MS* lawless love *Yale 1* lawless
love>love   1666 *MS* ^alluringly^   *MS* {no comma}   1668 *MS* ^the^
MS {no commas}   1669 *MS Cogerunt   Yale 1 Cogerunt,>Coegerunt,   MS* deed

---

1659 *drab*: prostitute.

Occidit, I repeat he killed the clan,   1670
Ne scilicet amplius in dedecore,
Lest peradventure longer life might trail,
Viveret, link by link his turpitude,
Invisus consanguineis, hateful so
To kith and kindred, *a nobilibus*   1675
Notatus, shunned by men of quality,
Relictus ab amicis, left i' the lurch
By friends, *ab omnibus derisus*, turned
A common hack-block to try edge of jokes.
Occidit, and he killed them here in Rome,   1680
In Urbe, the Eternal City, Sirs,
Nempe quæ alias spectata est,
The appropriate theatre which witnessed once,
Matronam nobilem, Lucretia's self,
Abluere pudicitiæ maculas,   1685
Wash off the spots of her pudicity,
Sanguine proprio, with her own pure blood;
Quæ vidit, and which city also saw,
Patrem, Virginius, *undequaque*, quite,

1670 *MS* clan   1671 *MS* {no comma}   1672 *MS* drag>trail   1673
MS Viveret link   *MS* hog-like trail>link by link   1674 *MS* {Latin not under-
lined}   *MS* consanguineis—   1675 *MS* {beginning of fo. 118}   1676
MS Notatus shunned   *MS* his own>quality,   1680 *MS* {Latin not under-
lined}   *MS* Occidit—   *MS* {no commas}   *MS* these   1682 *MS* {Latin
not underlined}   *MS* {no comma}   1683 *MS* As the appropriate theatre
witnessed once   *MS* witness>witnessed   1684 *MS* {no commas}   1685
MS {no comma}   1686 *MS* {no comma}   1687 *MS proprio—   MS*
blood:—   1688 *MS* {no commas}   *MS* City   *MS* {Between 1688 and
1689 extra line later deleted: 'Now find it in Valerius Maximus'}   1689 *MS*
Patrem—   *MS* {no commas}

1684 *Lucretia*: Lucretia was a famous type of heroic virtue, preferring death to
dishonour. After she had been raped by the son of the king of Rome, she summoned
her father and husband, told them of the rape, swore them to vengeance, and then
committed suicide by stabbing herself in the heart. Subsequently Brutus proclaimed
the rape in the centre of Rome and so commenced the rebellion that led to the
expulsion of the Tarquinii as kings of Rome. The ultimate source of the story is Livy's
History, 1. 57–60; the most famous literary treatment is Shakespeare's *Rape of Lucrece*
(1594).

1686 *pudicity*: modesty, chastity.

1689 *Virginius*: in about 450 BC, Appius Claudius, a lecherous judge, tried a legal
ruse to get his hands on a young girl, the 14-year-old Verginia, daughter of the

Impunem, with no sort of punishment,   1690
Nor, *et non illaudatum*, lacking praise,
Sed polluentem parricidio,
Imbrue his hands with butchery, *filiæ*,
Of chaste Virginia, to avoid a rape,
Ne raperetur ad stupra; so to heart,   1695
Tanti illi cordi fuit, did he take,
Suspicio, the mere fancy men might have,
Honoris amittendi, of fame's loss,
Ut potius voluerit filia
Orbari, he preferred to lose his child,   1700
Quam illa incederet, rather than she walk
The ways an, *inhonesta*, child disgraced,
Licet non sponte, though against her will.
Occidit—killed them, I reiterate—
In propria domo, in their own abode,   1705
Ut adultera et parentes, that each wretch,
Conscii agnoscerent, might both see and say,
Nullum locum, there's no place, *nullumque esse*
Asylum, nor yet refuge of escape,
Impenetrabilem, shall serve as bar,   1710

1690 MS {no commas}   1691 MS [ ], *et*>Nor *et*   1692 MS *Se*   MS
polluens>*polluentem Yale 1 pollutum*>*polluentem*   MS {no comma}   1693 MS
Pollute him>Imbrue his   MS slaughter>butchery   MS {no commas}   1694
MS lest she suffer>to avoid a   MS {no commas}   1695 MS *stupra*, *Yale 1*
stupra,>*stupra*;   MS heart   1696 MS He took it, *tanti illi cordi fuit*>*Tanti illi*
cordi fuit, did he take   1697 MS {no commas}   1698 MS *ammittendi*   MS
{no commas}   MS honour's   MS loss>flight   1699 MS {Latin not under-
lined}   MS Ut potius filia voluerit>Voluerit ut potius filia *or* Ut potius voluerit
filia   1700 MS {Latin not underlined}   MS *1868* that he chose   MS [ ]>
lose   MS child   1701 MS {no comma}   MS see walk   1702 MS {no
commas}   MS that *inhonesta*   1704 MS {beginning of fo. 119}   1705
MS {no commas}   1706 MS {no commas}   MS the three>this guilt   1707
MS {no commas}   1708 MS {Latin not underlined}   MS {no com-
mas}   1709 MS {no commas}   1710 MS {Latin not underlined}   MS
{no commas}

---

centurion Verginius. Verginius, when he saw that Appius' trick was going to succeed,
and that his daughter would probably be raped, killed his daughter rather than lose his
honour by such means. The ultimate source of the story is Livy's *History*, III. 44–8;
subsequent literary treatments occur in Petrarch, the *Roman de la Rose* (5589 ff.), and in
Chaucer, 'The Physician's Tale'.

Honori læso, to the wounded one
In honour; *neve ibi opprobria*
Continuarentur, killed them on the spot,
Moreover, dreading lest within those walls
The opprobrium peradventure be prolonged,   1715
Et domus quæ testis fuit turpium,
And that the domicile which witnessed crime,
Esset et pœnæ, might watch punishment:
Occidit, killed, I round you in the ears,
Quia alio modo, since by other mode,   1720
Non poterat ejus existimatio,
There was no possibility his fame,
Læsa, gashed griesly, *tam enormiter*,
Ducere cicatrices, might be healed:
Occidit ut exemplum præberet   1725
Uxoribus, killed her, so to lesson wives
Jura conjugii, that the marriage-oath,
Esse servanda, must be kept henceforth:
Occidit denique, killed her, in a word,
Ut pro posse honestus viveret,   1730
That he, please God, might creditably live,
Sin minus, but if fate willed otherwise,
Proprii honoris, of his outraged fame,
Offensi, by Mannaia, if you please,

1711 *MS* {Latin not underlined}   *MS* {no comma}   1712 *MS* honour as were
we;>honour as we;   *MS* {Latin not underlined}   1713 *MS* {Latin not under-
lined}   *MS* lest within those walls   *1868 1872* spot   1714 {not found in
MS}   1715 *MS* to that honour   *Yale 1* were>be   *MS* {no comma}
1716 *MS* {Latin not underlined}   *MS* {no comma}   1717 *MS* {no
comma}   1718 *MS* {Latin not underlined}   *MS* witness punishment.   1719
MS {Latin not underlined}   *MS* I>killed,   1720 *MS* mode   1721 *MS*
{no comma}   1722 *MS* {no comma}   1723 *MS* *Læsa* gashed griesly
tam   1724 *MS* {no comma}   *MS* get to heal.   1726 *MS 1868* her
so   1727 *MS* {no commas}   *MS* marriage oath   1728 *MS* {no
comma}   *MS* henceforth.   1729 *MS* {Latin not underlined}   *MS* deni-
que—   1731 *MS* if, it might be, he   *MS* ^creditably^   *MS* live— *Yale 1*
live>live,   1732 *MS minus* but   *MS* will   1733 *MS* {beginning of fo.
120}   *MS offensi* of his own   *MS* {no commas}   1734 {not found in
MS}   *1868 1872* Mannaja

1719 *round . . . ears*: cf. l. 1321 n.
1734 *Mannaia*: guillotine.

Commiseranda victima caderet,   1735
The pitiable victim he should fall!

Done! I' the rough, i' the rough! But done! And, lo,
Landed and stranded lies my very speech,
My miracle, my monster of defence—
Leviathan into the nose whereof   1740
I have put fish-hook, pierced his jaw with thorn,
And given him to my maidens for a play!
I' the rough: to-morrow I review my piece,
Tame here and there undue floridity.
It's hard: you have to plead before these priests   1745
And poke at them with Scripture, or you pass
For heathen and, what's worse, for ignorant
O' the quality o' the Court and what it likes
By way of illustration of the law.
To-morrow stick in this, and throw out that,   1750
And, having first ecclesiasticized,
Regularize the whole, next emphasize,
Then latinize, and lastly Cicero-ize,
Giving my Fisc his finish. There's my speech!
And where's my fry, and family and friends?   1755

1735 *MS* {no comma}   1736 *MS* ^pitiable^   *MS* fall.   1737 *MS* done
and,   1738 *MS 1868* own,   1739 *MS* nay, monster of defence—>my
monster, my defence— *Yale 1* nay,>my   1741 *MS* thorn   1742 *MS* for>
to   *MS* play.   1743 *MS* rough,— *1868* rough,—   1744–51 {not found in
MS}   1744 *1868* floridity,—   1749 *1868* law: 1753 *MS 1868 1872*
latinize and   *MS* Ciceroize,   1754 *MS* finish—   *MS* speech—   *1868*
speech—   1755 *MS* fry, my>fry and

1738–42 *Landed . . . play!*: 'I've completed (landed) this huge speech (like the vast
creature Leviathan)!', i.e. 'I've done the impossible!': cf. Job 41: 1, 2, 5: 'Canst thou
draw out leviathan with an hook? . . . or bore his jaw through with a thorn? . . . or wilt
thou bind him for thy maidens?' Cf. v. 1504–5 n.

1751 *ecclesiasticized*: i.e. added more allusions to Scripture, to please the judges who
are also priests.

1753 *Cicero-ize*: i.e. convert into the best possible Latin style; a playful neologism.
For the Renaissance, Cicero was the supreme Latin stylist, and 'the great father of all
eloquence'. Some went to ridiculous lengths to imitate his style exactly: see Erasmus'
satire on this in the *Ciceronianus* (1528). Cicero was still the model in the schools of
Browning's day and later.

Where's that huge Hyacinth I mean to hug
Till he cries out, "*Jam satis! Let me breathe!*"
Now, what an evening have I earned to-day!
Hail, ye true pleasures, all the rest are false!
Oh the old mother, oh the fattish wife!   1760
Rogue Hyacinth shall put on paper toque,
And wrap himself around with mamma's veil
Done up to imitate papa's black robe,
(I'm in the secret of the comedy,—
Part of the program leaked out long ago!)   1765
And call himself the Advocate o' the Poor,
Mimic Don father that defends the Count:
And for reward shall have a small full glass
Of manly red rosolio to himself,
—Always provided that he conjugate   1770
Bibo, I drink, correctly—nor be found
Make the *perfectum, bipsi,* as last year!
How the ambitious do so harden heart
As lightly hold by these home-sanctitudes,
To me is matter of bewilderment—   1775
Bewilderment! Because ambition's range
Is nowise tethered by domestic tie.
Am I refused an outlet from my home

1756 *MS* ^that old^ *1868* old   *MS* hug to death?>hug   1757 *MS* {Latin not underlined}   1758 *MS 1868* Oh,   1760 *MS 1868 1872* Oh, *1868 1872* oh,   1761 *MS* {no comma}   1762 *MS* mama's   1766 *MS* {no comma}   1767 *MS* the father   *MS 1868* Count,   1769 *MS* {no comma}   1770 *MS* {beginning of fo. 121}   1772 *MS* {no commas} 1773 *MS* can>do   1774 *MS* ^by^   *MS* home sanctitudes *Yale 1* sanctitudes> sanctitudes,   1776 *MS* Bewilderment.   1777 *MS* tie— *1868 1872* tie:

1757 "*Jam satis!*: 'That's enough!' (L.).

1761 *toque*: cap, from It. *tocca*; presumably in imitation of his father's lawyer's hat.

1769 *rosolio*: a sweet cordial made in Italy from spirits, raisins, and sugar.

1772 *perfectum, bipsi*: 'the perfect tense, *bipsi*'. The correct perfect of *bibo* (I drink) is *bibi*. Giacinto got this wrong, though for someone who does not know or has forgotten the correct form of the perfect *bipsi* is a plausible guess. The essential point here is the endearing picture of family life and Arcangeli's love of it: the 7-year-old Giacinto dresses up as his father, does his party trick of conjugating a Latin verb, and is rewarded with the grown-up drink of rosolio.

To the world's stage?—whereon a man should play
The man in public, vigilant for law,   1780
Zealous for truth, a credit to his kind,
Nay,—since, employing talent so, I yield
The Lord His own again with usury,—
A satisfaction, yea, to God Himself!
Well, I have modelled me by Agur's wish,   1785
"Remove far from me vanity and lies,
"Feed me with food convenient for me!" What
I' the world should a wise man require beyond?
Can I but coax the good fat little wife
To tell her fool of a father the mad prank   1790
His scapegrace nephew played this time last year
At Carnival! He could not choose, I think,
But modify that inconsiderate gift
O' the cup and cover (somewhere in the will
Under the pillow, someone seems to guess)   1795
—Correct that clause in favour of a boy

1779 *MS* stage,   1782 *MS* through the talent so employed it yields *1868* through
the talent so employed as yield   1783 *MS 1868* his   1784 *MS* {no commas}
1785 *MS* made my own wise>modeled me by   *MS* Agar's>Agur's   *MS*
wish   1786 *MS* {line added later}   1790 *MS 1868* of the prank   *1791
MS 1868 1872 scapegrace *1888 1889* scapegrace   1792 *MS* the Carnival,—he>
Carnival,—he *1868* Carnival,—he   1794 *MS* cover—somewhere   1795
MS guess—   1796 *MS* Correct *Yale 1* Correct>—Correct   *MS* my boy

1782–3 *employing . . . usury*: i.e. 'employing my talent for law in this way, I give God
back his gifts to me with interest'. Arcangeli is referring to the parable of the talents
(Matt. 25: 14–30) and implicitly contrasting himself with the 'wicked and slothful
servant' who simply buried his talent in the ground.

1785 *Agur's wish*: i.e. the wise man's wish. Agur is the name of the sage responsible
for Proverbs, ch. 30, from which Arcangeli goes on to quote: 'The words of Agur the
son of Jakeh . . . Remove far from me vanity and lies: give me neither poverty nor
riches; feed me with food convenient for me: Lest I be full, and deny thee, and say,
Who is the Lord? or lest I be poor, and steal, and take the name of my God in vain':
Prov. 30: 1, 8–9. Arcangeli twists this plea for wisdom and humility into self-
congratulation on his bourgeois lifestyle.

1791 *scapegrace nephew*: mischievous nephew. This would be Giacinto's first cousin
once removed, clearly a boy older than Giacinto and able to get into trouble at
Carnival: see variants.

1793 *inconsiderate*: ill-advised, extravagant.

1794 *cup and cover*: cup and lid; clearly some ornate goblet.

The trifle ought to grace, with name engraved,
Would look so well, produced in future years
To pledge a memory, when poor papa
Latin and law are long since laid at rest—   1800
Hyacintho dono dedit avus! Why,
The wife should get a necklace for her pains,
The very pearls that made Violante proud,
And Pietro pawned for half their value once,—
Redeemable by somebody, *ne sit*   1805
Marita quæ rotundioribus
Onusta mammis . . . baccis ambulet:
Her bosom shall display the big round balls,
No braver proudly borne by wedded wife!
With which Horatian promise I conclude.   1810

    Into the pigeon-hole with thee, my speech!
Off and away, first work then play, play, play!

1797 *MS* ^to^   *MS 1868* {no commas}   1798–1800 *MS* {lines added
later}   1798 *MS 1868* (Would   *MS 1868* {no comma}   *MS* feasts to
come—>years to come   *1868* years to come   1799 *MS 1868* {no comma}   *MS*
Papa   1800 *MS 1868* rest)   1801 *MS avus,—why,*   1802 *MS*
shall   1803 *MS* {beginning of fo.   122}   1804 *MS* Which
>And   1805 *MS* And still redeemable by somebody—>Redeemable by some-
body—ne sit *1868* somebody—   1806 *MS* Her bosom shall those big round balls
adorn>Her bosom shall display those brave round balls>*Marita quae rotundiori-
bus*   1807 *MS* No bigger borne by wedded wife *ne sit*>Onusta mammis . . . baccis
ambulet *1868* ambulet,   1808 *MS* {no comma}   1809 *MS 1868* should
be   *MS* wife,—   1810 *MS* to>I   *MS* conclude;>conclude.   1811
MS 1868 {no new paragraph. Paragraphing obscured in *1872* by this line's being at
the head of the page}

1801 *Hyacintho . . . avus*: 'Hyacinth's grandfather gave it to him as a gift' (L.).

1805–7 *ne . . . ambulet*: 'and may no other wife strut loaded with rounder breasts
. . . pearls'. Arcangeli makes a Freudian slip in quoting Horace, *Epode* viii. 13–14,
momentarily substituting *mammis* (breasts) for the original's *bacis* (pearls). This botched
quotation is a wonderful close to his monologue, drawing together as it does his solid
satisfaction in the comforts of married sexuality and his pride and complacency in his
middle-class wealth. The lines here from Horace are moderate and playful, but the rest
of *Epode* viii was not quoted in the nineteenth century on account of its lubricity: see l.
1235 n.

1812 *Off . . . play*: cf. l. 18 n.

Bottini, burn thy books, thou blazing ass!
Sing "Tra-la-la, for, lambkins, we must live!"

1813 *MS 1868* your   *MS 1868* you

1814 *lambkins . . . live*: i.e. my dears, we must live, i.e. enjoy ourselves. Cf. *Henry V*,
II. i. 127–8, the words of Pistol: 'Let us condole the knight, for, lambkins, we will
live'. This final flourish appropriately associates Arcangeli, with his love of food and
drink, and a fat man himself, with the world of Falstaff: see Introduction.

APPENDIX A

MOLINISM

THE first three appendices in this volume are concerned with Browning's historical research into the 1680s and 1690s. As our introductions to individual books of the poem make clear, Browning was in no way hamstrung by his sources: in creating characters and situations he gave his imagination free rein, and did not feel bound by a minute fidelity to historical fact. On the other hand, he went out of his way to investigate some historical details in a scholarly way. This apparent opposition is very characteristic of Browning. It is as though his imagination needed to be grounded in a sense of reality in order to be free to create beyond it.

'Molinism', as found in Roman Catholic reference books, refers to the body of doctrine taught by Luis de Molina (1535–1600). Browning uses it to refer to the teachings of the Spanish mystic Miguel de Molinos (1627–96), who came to Rome in 1663 and subsequently fell foul of the authorities as his teachings were judged heretical. Molinism is referred to thirty-one times in the poem as a whole, and our commentary suggests some of its significance. Here we wish to consider other aspects of this pattern of allusions.

Molinism is a self-consciously unusual reference: Browning could not expect his readers to know about this obscure heresy. His characters usually refer to Molinism in an off-hand way, as an obvious contemporary point of reference, and this is an important aspect of Browning's use of it. The historical past is 'another country', and Browning uses Molinism as a constant reminder to the reader of the otherness of the past. Many other details in the poem function in this way: references to artists, for example, who are now obscure, or the occasional use of Italian words, like 'Mannaia', that give the reader pause, but whose meaning is apparent from the context. These references all serve to establish a distance, a disjunction, between the present and the past. They take us out of ourselves, out of our own time, into the imaginative realm of the poem: 'thus by step and step / I [lead] you from the level of to-day / Up to the summit of so long ago' (I. 1330–1).

There is, as far as we are aware, no obvious single source for Browning's knowledge of Miguel de Molinos and his teachings. Most probably he came on various references in the lives of the popes which he read as background for his creation of Innocent XII, and then, on the back of these, did some more detailed research. In seizing on this matter, he shows a Carlyle-like instinct for how to bring the past alive, and in fact, as we hope the following extract shows, the references have a real air of *vraisemblance*. Though Molinos died in prison in 1696, two years before the main action of the poem, it is reasonable of Browning to assume that he and his teachings were still a topical point of conversation and that he still had professed followers. Gilbert Burnet's description of the movement was written on 8 December 1685, some months after Molinos' initial arrest and imprisonment. Overtly biased as it is, and with limited theological nuance, it none the less gives a sense of how much Molinos was a 'subject of the day'.

Gilbert Burnet, *Some Letters, Containing, An account of what seemed most remarkable in Switzerland, Italy, &c.* (Rotterdam, Abraham Acher, 1686), pp. 197–200.

The new method of Molinos doth so much prevail in Naples, that it is beleeved he hath above twenty thousand followers in this City; And since this hath made some noise in the World, and yet is generally but little understood, I will give you some account of him: He is a Spanish Priest that seems to be but an ordinary Divine, and is certainly a very ill reasoner when he undertakes to prove his opinions: He hath writ a Book, which is intituled *il Guida Spirituale*, which is a short abstract of the Mystical Divinity; the substance of the whole, is reduced to this, that in our prayers and other devotions, the best methods are to retire the mind from all gross Images, and so to form an act of Faith, and thereby to present our selves before God; and then to sink into a silence and cessation of new acts, and to let God act upon us, and so to follow his conduct: This way he prefers to the multiplication of many new acts, and different forms of devotion, and he makes small account of corporal austerities, and reduces all the exercizes of Religion to this simplicity of mind: He thinks this is not only to be proposed to such as live in Religious Houses, but even to Secular persons, and by this he hath proposed a great reformation of men's minds and manners: He hath many Priests in Italy, but chiefly in Naples, that dispose those who confess themselves to them, to follow his methods: The Jesuits have set themselves much against this conduct, as foreseeing that it may much weaken the Empire that Superstition hath over the minds of people, that it may make Religion become a more plain and simple thing, and may also open a door to Enthusiasms: they also pretend that his conduct is factious and seditious, that this may breed a Schism in the Church. And because he saith, in some places of his Book, that the mind may rise up to such a simplicity in its acts, that it may rise in some of its devotions to God immediately, without contemplating the Humanity of Christ, they have accused him, as intending to lay aside the Doctrine of Christ's Humanity; tho it is plain that he speaks only of the purity of some single acts: Upon all those heads they have set themselves much against Molinos; and they have also pretended that some of his Disciples, have infused it into their Penitents, that they may go and communicate as they find themselves disposed without going first to Confession, which they thought weakned much the yoke, by which the Priests subdue the Consciences of the people to their Conduct: Yet he was much supported both in the Kingdom of Naples and in Sicily; he hath also many friends and followers at Rome. So the Jesuits, as a Provincial of the Order assured me, finding they could not ruin him by their own force, got a great King that is now extreamly in the Interests of their Order to interpose, and to represent to the Pope the danger of such Innovations. It is certain the Pope understands the matter very little, and that he is possessed with a great opinion of Molino's sanctity, yet upon the complaints of some Cardinals, that seconded the zeal of that King, he and some of his followers were clapt in the Inquisition, where they have been now for some months, but still they are well used, which is beleeved to flow from the good opinion that the Pope hath on him, who saith still, that tho he may erre, yet he is certainly a good man: Upon this imprisonment Pasquin said a pleasant thing: in one week, one man had been condemned to the Gallies for some what he had said, another had been hanged for some what he had writ, and Molinos was clapt in Prison, whose Doctrine consisted chiefly in this, that men ought to bring their minds to a State of inward quietness, from which the name of Quietists was given to all his followers: The Pasquinade upon all this, was *si parliamo, in Galere, si scrivemmo Impiccati, si stiamo in quiete all Sant' Officio, e che bisogna fare: If we speak we are sent to the Gallies, if we write we are hanged: if we stand quiet we are clapt up in the Inquisition: what must we do then?* Yet his Followers at Naples are not daunted, but they beleeve he will come out of this trial victorious.

APPENDIX B

CAPONSACCHI'S ANCESTRY

As well as his intense study of OYB and SS, Browning undertook another series of studies in order to understand the historical basis of his story. In the case of Caponsacchi's ancestry (VI. 221–56) we have been able to identify a source in Pietro Farulli's *Annali . . . di Arezzo* (Foligno, 1717). It may be that Browning knew this part of the annals in another redaction, but if this is the case it must have been substantively similar to Farulli given the extent of the correspondence.

Browning leaves out the darker aspects of the Caponsacchi family history—their sufferings in the internal politics of Florence—and concentrates on their antiquity and on the saintly Bishop Tommaso, whose example may have inspired the Caponsacchi of the poem to enter the priesthood. Many points in our commentary show that Browning was not minutely careful in the way he handled the historical material of OYB and SS, but—as this instance makes clear—he was keen to enter into the fabric of history, even if he also insisted upon the role of the imagination in penetrating its meanings. The following extract from the *Annali* begins just before the relevant passage and ends just after it, in order to give some sense of the nature of the work as a whole.

Pietro Farulli, *Annali, overo notizie istoriche dell'antica, nobile, e valorosa Città di Arezzo in Toscana dal suo Principio fino al presente Anno 1717* (Foligno, 1717), pp. 249–50.

L'anno 1632. alcuni Nobili Aretini di Casa Bacci, e Albergotti si portarono in Germania à militare contro il Rè di Svezia che fece gran strage, il quale di colpo di Terzetta restò morto nella famosa Battaglia di Luzen vicino à Lipsia. Se s'impadroniva dell'Imperio fù concetto che si sarebbe portato à Roma. Fiorì in questo tempo nella Città di Arezzo un' Valoroso Capitano detto Gio. che servì gran tempo i Venisi, e Gustavo Adolfo Rè di Svezia. L'anno 1635. si vidde nel Cielo una Cometa, che diede molto da discorrere. L'anno 1638. fù promosso all' Vescovado della Città di Arezzo Tommaso di Jacopo d'Alamanno Salviati Patrizio Fiorentino da Urbano Ottavo Prelato di gran bontà, zelo, e dottrina, originato dall' anticha, e illustre Famiglia de Caponsacchi di Fiesole, così detta da Gio. detto Capo nel Sacco, fiorì nel 1030. [C]ome Ghibellina, l'anno 1312. fù quasi tutta trucidata da Guelfi restando solo Meser Salvi famoso Medico, salvato da quella furia crudele, da cui originarono i Salviati. Questa Famiglia Caponsacchi è in

Arezzo venuta da Fiesole quando fù abbattuta da Fiorentini nel 1010. e da essa è uscito Gio. Caponsacchi celebre Filosofo che fiorì l'anno 1320. come nota lo Spinelli nel suo Diario. In Firenze poi da Caponsacchi uscirono Donato, e Caponsaccho Caponsacchi Consoli il primo l'anno 1183, il secondo l'anno 1187. Gio. di Lione l'anno 1276. del 6. del Duomo si ritrovò alla Pace del Card. Latin. Orsini frà Guelfi, e Ghibellini. L'anno 1303. i Fiorentini sotto Puliciano di Mugello fecero prigioni Cecco, e Ridolfo Caponsacchi valorosi Capitani della Fazzione de Bianchi, e li fecero morire. Giannozzo Caponsacchi l'anno 1353. fù Podestà della Città dell'Aquila in Abruzzo. Le loro Case erano in Mercato Vecchio, alle quali si appicciò in fuoco l'anno 1223. arse tutto il Borgo di Piazza. L'anno 1257. fù cacciata di Firenze à furia di Popolo, e i loro Palagi abbattuti , e delle Pietre si servirono per far le Mura della Città dalla parte di San Giorgio, perche si erano uniti con la potente Famiglia degli Uberti che erano contro il Governo. Fondarono il nobile Monastero di San Domenico, e dal Monastero di San Jacopo di Ripoli ove erano l'anno 1292. 60. Monache 36. ne andarono nel nuovo Monastero di San Domenico di Cafaggiolo, frà le quali Suora Lucia Caponsacchi, come si prova dalla Cronica del Padre Fontana Domenicano à carte 248. e da Scipione Ammirati nelle sue Istorie Fiorentine. Ritornando al predetto Vescovo Tommaso fù Prelato di Santa Vita. Dispensava tutta la sua entrata del Vescovato à Poveri, e Luoghi Pii; andava per la Città a piedi nudi. Maritò, e monacò molte nobile Zitelle. Difese i Cittadini incolpati di aver messo al Collo della Statua del Gran Duca Ferdinando una Fune, e metigò lo sdegno di Ferdinando Secondo Gran Duca che voleva atterrare la Città, e farci seminare il Sale; Onde gli Aretini molto sono tenuti à questa Casa, e al Conte Ferdinando Bardi, che dissuase il Gran Duca da si fatta esecuzione, come suo Consigliere di Stato, e Segretario di Guerra con dirli, che averebbe auto nel suo Stato una Città di meno, parole così sagge, che rimossero il Sovrano da atterrare una sì nobile, e antica Città. Gli Aretini si portarono molti à militare sotto il Principe Mattias Fratello di Ferdinando contro il Pontefice Urbano Ottavo per sostenere le ragioni dei Duca di Parma Odoardo l'anno 1640. e si dimostrarono molto valorosi nella conquista di Castiglione del Lago Castello forte, & altre Terre del Perugino, ove fecero gran danno. Il Generale Pesero, poi Marco Giustiniano suo Successore fecero gran danno nel Ferrarese. Il Duca di Modena, e di Parma nel Bolognese.

In the year 1632 some aristocrats from Arezzo, of the Bacci and the Albergotti family, went to Germany to wage war against the King of Sweden, who created great slaughter, but who was himself shot dead at the famous battle of Lützen near Leipzig. It was supposed that, had he become master of the Empire, he would have gone on to Rome. Around this time, a valiant captain named Giovanni flourished in Arezzo. He was for a long time at the service of the Venetians and of Gustavus Adolphus the King of Sweden. Then, in the year 1635, a comet appeared in the sky, and this caused quite a stir.

In the year 1638 Pope Urban VIII promoted Tommaso di Jacopo d'Alamanno Salviati to the rank of Bishop of the city of Arezzo. [Tommaso], an aristocrat from

Florence, was a prelate of great human goodness, zeal, and erudition, born of the ancient and famous family of Caponsacchi from Fiesole, so called after Giovanni, known as Capo nel Sacco [Head in the Sack], who had flourished in 1030.

In the year 1312 the Guelphs massacred almost the entire family because it was Ghibelline. The only survivor of that cruel fury was a Messer Salvi, a famous physician, from whom the Salviati stock originates. This family of Caponsacchi came to Arezzo from Fiesole when the latter was destroyed by the Florentines in 1010; from that family came Giovanni Caponsacchi, a renowned philosopher, who flourished in the year 1320, as Spinelli records in his Diary. In Florence from the Caponsacchi came Donato and Caponsaccho Caponsacchi; these became consuls in 1183 and 1187 respectively. In the year 1276, Giovanni di Lione, one of the Six Canons of the Duomo, took part in the peace negotiations that Cardinal Latino Orsini arranged between the Guelphs and the Ghibellines.

In the year 1303, under Puliciano di Mugello, the Florentines captured Cecco and Rodolfo Caponsacchi, valiant captains of the White faction, and killed them. Giannuzzo Caponsacchi was Podestà of the city of L'Aquila, in the Abruzzo region, in the year 1353. The Caponsacchi's homes, which were in the Old Market [in Florence], were set on fire in the year 1223 and the whole neighbourhood of the piazza was burned down. In the year 1257 the Caponsacchi family was expelled from Florence by the enraged mob, their palaces knocked down, and the stones reused to make the city walls on the San Giorgio side, because the Caponsacchi had united with the powerful family of Uberti against the city government.

The Caponsacchi founded the noble monastery of St Dominic: from the monastery of St James of Ripoli, where in 1292 there were sixty nuns, thirty-six went to the new monastery of St Dominic of Cafaggiolo. Amongst these was Sister Lucia Caponsacchi, as is attested by the Dominican Fontana in his *Chronicle* at page 248, and by Scipione Ammirati in his *History of the Florentines*.

Let us return to the aforementioned Bishop Tommaso, who was prelate at Santa Vita. He used to distribute all the income of the bishopric to the poor and to charitable foundations, and walked about the City barefoot. He found a husband for, or made nuns of, many noble spinsters. He defended the people of the city of Arezzo, who were accused of putting a rope around the neck of the statue of Grand Duke Ferdinand, and he placated the wrath of Grand Duke Ferdinand II, who wanted to raze the town to the ground and have the soil sprinkled with salt. On this account, the people of Arezzo are deeply grateful to that family, and to Count Ferdinando Bardi, who, in his capacity as State Councillor and Secretary of War, talked the Grand Duke out of his plan by pointing out that he would have one less town in his territory—words so wise that they dissuaded the sovereign from razing to the ground this noble and ancient city.

In the year 1640 the people of Arezzo went to fight in large numbers under Prince Matthias, Ferdinand's brother, siding with Odoardo, Duke of Parma, against Pope Urban VIII; they proved themselves very brave in the conquest of the fortified castle at Castiglione del Lago, and of other territories in the territory of Perugia, where they caused considerable damage. General Pesero and later his successor, Marco Giustiniano, inflicted great destruction in the Ferrara region. The Duke of Modena and Parma did the same in the area of Bologna.

APPENDIX C

THE TORTURE OF THE VIGIL

BROWNING'S investigation into the torture of the vigil seems typical of the man and his character, but it is also further evidence of the extent to which he wanted to enter into the spirit of a particular historical epoch. It seems clear that he took his cue from OYB xxxv (34), one of the pleadings of Spreti, the second defence lawyer:

Yet since the Fisc alleges the right to torture the defendant [Guido] in order to prove some further alleged truth, in such case the torture shall be simple; for there can be no question as to the torture of the Vigil, because the Constitution promulgated by Paul V, of sacred memory, for the reformation of the courts of this city, stands in the way. This is contained among other Constitutions of the said Pope as the 71st in order, Tit. de Judic. Criminalib., which is § 10, n. 30; vol. 3 Bullar. page 108; by which it was decreed that this kind of torture cannot be inflicted unless these two requisites jointly concur, namely: that the crime be 'most atrocious' and that the defendant be burdened with the most cogent suspicions of guilt. So affirm Spad. cons. 114, n. 4, lib. 1; Farinac. qu. 38, n. 71; Locatel. Quaestiones Judiciariae crimin. inspect. 1, n. 44; Guazzin. def. 30, cap. 21, vers. Et hic; Eusebius, my predecessor in office, of most distinguished memory, in his Allegatio printed with Passerin. cap. 1, sub. n. 70 in the beginning de homicidio in 6.

Browning followed up the second reference here, 'Farinac. qu. 38, n. 71', probably because the great Italian jurist Prospero Farinacci had already featured in his researches (see our Vol. VII, p. xix). The complete works of Farinacci that he consulted in the British Museum (now the British Library) are in nine huge volumes, bound in plain vellum (711. g. 5–13). It is a made-up set from different editions, but all printed at Nuremberg between approximately 1670 and 1723. Given their size, he might have been expected to have trouble finding the reference, but it is in fact in the first volume, and easy to locate because of the clear, chapter-like divisions into 'Quæstiones'. Browning refers to the work simply as the '*Quæstiones*' or 'Questions', one of the subtitles, but it is properly the *Praxis et Theorica Criminalis*. The relevant passage is at Lib. I (in some editions II), Tit. v 'de Indiciis & Torturis', Quæst. XXXVIII, nos. 70–1, p. 610. Below we give the full Latin and then a translation.

Quintum & ultimum est apud nos in usu tormentum vigilæ, de quo tormento meminit Marsil. *in d. l. I. in prin. ff. de quæst. n. 76. vers. nam ponitur reus*, & tempore Marsilii, qui, ut ipse testatur, videtur fuisse inventor hujus tormenti, ponebatur reus super uno scamno ad sedendum, & ibi aderant duo ad ejus custodiam ne dormiat, & si dormire voluerit illum expergiscunt, & nec dormire, nec quiescere sinunt per horas quadraginta: in tantum quod promissa sibi quiete infra tale tempus fateri cogitur, & huic tormento inquit Marsil. liceat videatur res ridiculosa, nemo tamen tamferox invenitur, ut illi possit resistere, & ita alias se fuisse expertum testatur: sed hodie malæ nostræ tempestatis fato nescio, an ob judicum severitatem, an vero ob sceleratorum delinquentium obstinationem detur hoc tormenti genus acriori. & crudeliori modo. Nam scamnum hujusmodi, quod aliqui Capram & aliqui Equum nuncupant, est altum à terra quantum est statura unius hominis, & illius summitas est non plana, sed in medio aliquantulum altior, & ex altitudine quatuor pendent latera unius palmi cum dimidio in circa pro quolibet latere. Ponitur in hac scamni seu equi summitate reus denudatus, & undique ligatus, ne forsan caderet, cum manibus retro vinctis, & funi supra scamnum existenti applicatis, non aliter ac si torquendus esset, & quod pejus est cum brachiis ab eodem fune extensis, vel in totum, vel pro parte, prout judici videbitur, & ibidem infelix reus sic nudus ligatis retro manib. funi applicatis, & cum brachiis quandoq; extensis detinetur per quinq;,aut per decem horas, & quandoque etiam paulo plus judicis arbitrio: ita quod eodem tempore, & funis, & vigiliæ tormentum patitur: quod miserandum est, & ex centum hominib. qui hoc tormentum passi sunt non credo quatuor, aut quinq; fuerint martyres, reliqui vero confessores: est nempe tormentum insupportabile tum ratione temporis, tum ratione immensi cruciatus & doloris. Bene verum est, quod illud solum in atrocissimis consuetum video, ut in crimine læsæ majestatis, assissinio stratarum, latrociniis, disrobatoribus famosis, bannitis & his similibus: iccirco in infligendo tale tormentum vadant judices multum temperati, & super omnia advertant non facere multum extendere brachia rei, quia talis extensio longo temporis intervallo de se periculosa est, & plures ob id mortui fuerunt in ipso tormento, & quam plurimi defecerunt, &, ut dixi eo non utantur nisi in atrocissimis, & nisi in casu, in quo indicia sint nedum urgentia, sed urgentissima contra reum & ita apud nos servatur. Et dum hæc jam scripseram, pervenit ad manus meas practica interrogan. reo. Flam. Carta. *qui in 4. lib. c. 2. n. 7 & 8.* bene etiam ponit formulam constituendi reos in hoc vigiliæ tormento.

The fifth and last torture in use with us is the torture of the Vigil of which Marsilius makes mention in *dict.* l, 1 *in princ. ff. de quaest. n.* 76, ver. 'nam ponitur reus.' In the time of Marsilius, who as he himself asserts, seems to have been the inventor of this torture, the defendant was placed upon a bench in a sitting posture, and two men were present to watch him lest he should sleep, and if he wanted sleep they aroused him, and did not permit him to sleep or be quiet for forty hours, insomuch that when rest was promised him he was forced to confess within that time. And as to this form of torture, Marsilius says that although the thing seems ridiculous, yet no one is found so hardy as to be able to resist it, and so in another place he asserts that he himself made trial of it. But today, by the fate of our evil times, I do not know whether it be on account of the severity of the Judges, or in truth the obstinacy of our abandoned criminals, this kind of torture is administered in a manner that is more cruel and severe. For a bench of the kind that some call the 'she-goat' and others 'the horse' is raised above the ground as much as a man's height, its top is not level but a little higher in the middle, and from its highest point its four sides slope away about a hand's breadth and a half on each side. The defendant is placed upon the top of this bench, stripped naked and tied on every side so that he should not by chance fall off, with his hands bound behind him and fastened to a rope that is placed above the bench, just as if he were to be tortured (with the Cord), and what is worse, with his arms stretched by the said rope either to their full length or partially, as it pleases the judge. And there the unlucky defendant, thus naked and with his hands bound behind him and fastened to the rope, and with his arms stretched out, is kept for five or ten hours and sometimes even a little longer at the discretion of the Judge, so that he suffers at the same time the torture of both the Cord and the Vigil which is a pitiable thing. And out of a hundred men who have suffered this torture, I do not believe four or five have been martyrs, the rest were confessors. The torture is indeed insupportable by reason not only of the time but also of the terrible pain and anguish. It is very true that I have observed this as customary only in the cases of most atrocious crimes, as treason, murder in the open streets, highway robbery, notorious robbers, persons under ban and the like; therefore in inflicting such torment let the judges proceed with great restraint, and above all things take care not to stretch the arms of the defendant very much, because such stretching for a long time is dangerous of itself, and many have died because of it during the torture itself, and very many have fainted. And as I have said let them not use this torture except in the most atrocious crimes, and in a case where the evidences are not only urgent, but most urgent against the defendant, and so it is practised with us. And just as I had written this there has come to hand the *Practice of Interrogation of Defendants* by Flaminius Chartarius, who in book 4, ch. 2, n. 7 and 8, well lays down the formula for the examination of defendants in the torment of the Vigil.

APPENDIX D

YALE VARIANTS

THE majority of the revisions unique to *Yale 2* made in Books VII and VIII are to accidentals. The effect is to strengthen the punctuation. In four cases comma becomes comma and dash, in one case it becomes colon, and in another case comma and dash become colon. In one case dash becomes colon, in another case three full stops. Colon itself becomes full stop in one instance, and in two others full stop becomes exclamation mark. In three cases (VIII. 489, 493, and 1188) a comma is inserted. In ll. 489 and 1188 this has the effect of a caesura, and improves the rhythm of the line, while the addition of the comma in 493 combined with the change from query to exclamation mark in 495 improves both the sense and the syntax of the passage.

The substantive revisions are either designed to improve the rhythm (VII. 1686 There I lay, then,>There, then, I lay, VIII. 260 The nice bye-stroke, the fine and improvised>Played the nice bye-stroke, fine and improvised, and VIII. 1346, Shall overlook wrong done the judgment-seat.>Overlook wrong done his own judgment-seat), or to render the sense more vivid and specific (VIII. 255 littleness!">little taps!", VIII. 261 Point>Pass, a term more particular to the game in question). In VIII. 1152 RB may have made a tentative revision, since there seems to be a query above 'nest or plant flag.>nest or pluck flower.'. The revised version would perhaps have been more logical, since dislodging a daw's nest and plucking a flower are similar kinds of action. In VIII. 1347 RB has simplified the line by substituting 'you to pull my nose,' for 'my own nose be pulled,'. Lastly, he transposes VIII 1515 and 1516, which not only improves the rhythm of the couplet but also renders the sense easier to follow.

Revisions in *Yale 2* and *1888* compared

Line	In *Yale 2* only	In *Yale 2* and *1888* (* = corrected literal)	In *1888* conflicting with *Yale 2*
Book VII			
170	say.>say!	that,>that	
302	myself>myself.		
332		chrystal>crystal	
924	I>"I		
1238	good,—>good:		
1431	triumphant—>triumphant:		
1589	There I lay, then,>		
1686	There, then, I lay,		
1701		Lent:>Lent.	
Book VIII			
29		some one>someone	
180	ink>pen		
255	litleness!"> little taps!"		
260	The nice bye-stroke, the fine and improvised>Played the nice bye-stroke, fine and improvised		
261	Point>Pass		
308	First,>First,—		
309	too,>too,— murder,>murder,—		

484	law—>law ...
489	say when>say, when
493	Why that>Why, that
495	hive?>hive!
514	seeing,>seeing
577	plain,>plain,—
579	shall broaden>that broadens
583	the natural>natural
600	Saint>So
1055	As>—As
1056	me,>yet,
1069	since,>since:
1152	nest or plant flag,> nest, plant a flag.
	nest or pluck flower.
	{there may be a '?'
	above 'flower'}
1185	little.>little!
1188	that in>that, in
1345	Shall overlook the>that
1346	wrong done the
	judgment-seat.>
	Overlook wrong
	done his own
	judgment-seat.
1347	my own nose be pulled,>
	you to pull my nose,
1515, 1516	*transposed.*
1585	jucier>juicier★

APPENDIX E

COMPOSITORS

V.

1–160	B. Suth[erland]
161–328	Jarvis
329–489	Aylward
490–650	Ker
651–813	Plumb
814–977	Broadhead
978–1034	B. Suth[erland]
1035–1147	Malcolm
1148–1256	B. Suth[erland]
1257–1363	Malcolm
1364–1470	Jarvis
1471–1577	Grace
1578–1688	B. Suth[erland]
1689–1797	Plumb
1798–1851	Jarvis
1852–1957	Aylward
1958–end	Broadhead

VI.

1–108	Jenkins
109–221	Chace
222–329	Parsons
330–437	Robinson
438–546	Barsham
547–652	Jarvis
653–760	Plumb
761–868	Broadhead
869–974	Malcolm
975–1079	Broadhead
1080–1191	<Robinson> Ker
1192–1219	Jarvis
1220–1307	Broadhead
1308–1420	Ker

1421–1534	Malcolm
1535–1645	Aylward
1646–1760	Plumb
1761–1873	Broadhead
1874–1987	Ker
1988–2045	Aylward
2046–end	Jarvis

VII.

1–58	[Jarvis?]
59–114	Ker
115–74	Barsham
175–301	Plumb
302–60	Chace
361–419	Ker
420–76	Hales
477–533	Parsons
534–97	[Plumb?]
598–656	Ker
657–719	[ ]
720–832	Ker
833–90	Barsham
891–1069	Ker
1070–1132	Plumb
1133–94	[Parsons?]
1195–1255	Plumb
1256–1317	Ker
1318–89	Barsham
1390–1448	Ker
1449–1512	Hales
1513–79	Plumb
1580–1641	Ker
1642–end	Barsham

VIII.

1–119	[Barsham?]
120–247	Ker
248–366	Hales
367–488	Plumb
489–608	Barsham
609–730	B. Sutherland
731–846	[B. Sutherland]
847–960	Hales
961–1079	Ker
1080–1199	Plumb
1200–1327	[B. Sutherland?]
1328–1462	Ker
1463–1585	[Chace?]
1586–1703	Ker
1704–end	B. Sutherland